Lecture Notes in Computer Science 16697

The series Lecture Notes in Computer Science (LNCS), including its subseries Lecture Notes in Artificial Intelligence (LNAI) and Lecture Notes in Bioinformatics (LNBI), has established itself as a medium for the publication of new developments in computer science and information technology research, teaching, and education.

LNCS enjoys close cooperation with the computer science R & D community, the series counts many renowned academics among its volume editors and paper authors, and collaborates with prestigious societies. Its mission is to serve this international community by providing an invaluable service, mainly focused on the publication of conference and workshop proceedings and postproceedings. LNCS commenced publication in 1973.

Giuseppe De Giacomo · Jianwen Li · Lili Xiao
Editors

Theoretical Aspects of Software Engineering

20th International Symposium, TASE 2026
Shanghai, China, July 4–6, 2026
Proceedings

Springer

Editors
Giuseppe De Giacomo
University of Oxford
Oxford, UK

Jianwen Li
East China Normal University
Shanghai, China

Lili Xiao
Donghua University
Shanghai, China

ISSN 0302-9743 ISSN 1611-3349 (electronic)
Lecture Notes in Computer Science
ISBN 978-3-032-30692-0 ISBN 978-3-032-30693-7 (eBook)
https://doi.org/10.1007/978-3-032-30693-7

This Springer imprint is published by the registered company Springer Nature Switzerland AG
The registered company address is: Gewerbestrasse 11, 6330 Cham, Switzerland

Preface

The International Symposium on Theoretical Aspects of Software Engineering (TASE) brings together researchers and practitioners interested in new results and innovative advances in software engineering. It records the latest developments in formal and theoretical software engineering methods and techniques.

TASE 2026 was the 20th International Symposium on Theoretical Aspects of Software Engineering, a series of symposia started in 2007 with the aim to bring together researchers and developers from academia and industry with interest in the theoretical aspects of software engineering. In past years, TASE took place in Shanghai (2007), Nanjing (2008), Tianjing (2009), Taipei (2010), Xi'an (2011), Beijing (2012), Birmingham (2013), Changsha (2014), Nanjing (2015), Shanghai (2016), Sophia Antipolis (2017), Guangzhou (2018), Guilin (2019), Hangzhou (2020), Shanghai (2021), Cluj-Napoca (2022), Bristol (2023), Guiyang (2024) and Limassol (2025).

TASE 2026 was held in Shanghai, China during July 4–6, 2026. This year we received 64 effective submissions covering different areas of theoretical software engineering. Each paper was single-blindly reviewed by at least three reviewers and the Program Committee accepted 23 regular long papers and 5 short papers, leading to an attractive scientific program. This edition of TASE was enhanced by the presence of 3 keynote speakers, Alessandro Cimatti (FBK), Alessandro Abate (University of Oxford), and Jun Sun (Singapore Management University).

TASE 2026 would not have succeeded without the deep investment and involvement of the Program Committee members and the external reviewers who evaluated and selected the best contributions. This event would not exist without the authors and contributors who submitted their papers. We address our thanks to everyone–reviewers, authors, Program Committee members, and organization committee members–involved in the success of TASE 2026.

The EasyChair system was set up for the management of TASE 2026, supporting submission, review, and volume preparation processes. It proved to be a powerful framework. We thank Springer for the smooth cooperation in the production of this proceedings volume.

TASE 2026 was hosted by East China Normal University, Shanghai, China, and sponsored by the government of Lingang New Area, Pudong District, Shanghai. The local organization committee offered all the facilities to run the event in a lovely and friendly atmosphere. Many thanks to all the local organizers, in particular, the general and local organization chairs.

Lastly, we wish to express our special thanks to the steering committee members, in particular Shengchao Qin and Huibiao Zhu, for their valuable support.

May 2026

Giuseppe De Giacomo
Jianwen Li

Organization

Steering Committee

Keijiro Araki	Kumamoto College, Japan
Jifeng He	East China Normal University, China
Michael Hinchey	Lero, Ireland
Shengchao Qin	Xidian University, China
Huibiao Zhu	East China Normal University, China

General Chair

Geguang Pu	East China Normal University, China

Program Co-chairs

Giuseppe De Giacomo	University of Oxford, England
Jianwen Li	East China Normal University, China

Publicity Co-chairs

Jonathan P. Bowen	London South Bank University, UK
Lili Xiao	Donghua University, China

Local Organization Chair

Qin Li	East China Normal University, China

Program Committee

Yamine Ait Ameur	IRIT/INPT-ENSEEIHT, France
Dongdong An	Shanghai Normal University, China
Jie An	Chinese Academy of Sciences, China
Jonathan Bowen	London South Bank University, UK

Ningning Chen	University of Shanghai for Science and Technology, China
Giuseppe De Giacomo	University of Oxford, UK
Hongfei Fu	Shanghai Jiao Tong University, China
Alberto Griggio	Fondazione Bruno Kessler, Italy
Zhe Hou	Griffith University, Australia
Daisuke Kimura	Toho University, Japan
Guoqiang Li	Shanghai Jiao Tong University, China
Jianwen Li	East China Normal University, China
Qin Li	East China Normal University, China
Ximeng Li	Capital Normal University, China
Yeting Li	Chinese Academy of Sciences, China
Wanwei Liu	National University of Defense Technology, China
Yepang Liu	Southern University of Science and Technology, China
Teng Long	China University of Geosciences, China
Zhi Ma	Xidian University, China
Frédéric Mallet	Université Côte d'Azur, France
Dominique Mery	Université de Lorraine, France
Bertrand Meyer	ETH Zurich, Switzerland
Yu Pei	Hong Kong Polytechnic University, China
Shengchao Qin	Teesside University, UK
Kristin Yvonne Rozier	Iowa State University, USA
Xiaomu Shi	Shenzhen University, China
Meng Sun	Peking University, China
Stefano Tonetta	Fondazione Bruno Kessler, Italy
Cheng Wen	Xidian University, China
Lili Xiao	Donghua University, China
Hui Xu	Fudan University, China
Jiaqi Yin	Northwestern Polytechnical University, China
Yedi Zhang	National University of Singapore, Singapore
Hengjun Zhao	Southwest University, China
Lixiao Zheng	Huaqiao University, China
Chenyang Zhu	University of Southampton, UK
Shufang Zhu	University of Liverpool, UK

Additional Reviewers

Bergeron, Ghilain
Chang, Xi
Chen, Minyu
Dreier, Jannik
Faisal Al Ameen, Mahmudul
Gamboa Guzman, Laura P.
Gan, Ting
Geatti, Luca
Huang, Yihao
Ke, Jingyu
Li, Jingyang
Li, Zhuohua
Liu, Jiaxiang
Merz, Stephan
Micheletti, Christian
Nakazawa, Koji
Nicoli, Matteo
Redondi, Gianluca
Wang, Keyin
Wang, Sinan
Wang, Zili
Wei, Zeming
Wu, Ling-I
Xiao, Shengping
Zhang, Manqing
Zhu, Hengcheng

Invited Talks

The OPERA Framework: Formal Design of Railways Interlocking Systems

Alessandro Cimatti

Fondazione Bruno Kessler, Italy

Abstract. Many railways interlocking systems are still based on electromechanical solutions. They are hard to understand and costly to modify, and can be considered legacy systems. In this talk I will present the research underlying a novel process for the development of interlocking applications. The proposed methodology is able on one side to analyze and reverse-engineer legacy relay-based interlocking systems, and on the other to support the specification and verification of interlocking procedures by means of a model-based approach. Research challenges include modeling and verification of continuous-time, real-valued transition systems, automated abstraction for reverse engineering and specification mining, automated test generation, and parameterized verification.

Neural Proofs for Sound Verification of Complex Programs and Systems

Alessandro Abate

University of Oxford, UK

Abstract. I discuss the construction of sound proofs for the formal verification and control of complex models, encompassing broad classes of (probabilistic) reactive programs and (stochastic) dynamical systems.

Neural proofs comprise two parts. Firstly, proof rules encode formal requirements ensuring the verification of general temporal specifications over the models of interest. Then, certificates can be constructed from said proof rules: we leverage an inductive approach, which accesses samples generated from the model's dynamics to train neural nets, whilst generalising them via SAT-modulo-theory queries, based on full knowledge of the models.

In the context of sequential decision-making problems, I also discuss how to additionally generate policies/strategies/controllers in order to formally attain general temporal specifications.

Building Trustworthy AI Agents: Challenges and Attempts

Jun Sun

Singapore Management University, Singapore

Abstract. Large language models and AI agents are advancing at an extraordinary pace, exhibiting increasingly sophisticated capabilities in reasoning, planning, and autonomous decision-making. Yet, these advances are accompanied by growing safety and security concerns, particularly as such systems move toward deployment in high-stakes and safety-critical settings. Ensuring their reliability is therefore no longer optional—it is a fundamental requirement. In this talk, I will examine the challenge of developing systematic approaches to AI safety, and present three complementary families of techniques for improving the safety and trustworthiness of large-scale AI systems. For each, I will highlight key open theoretical problems and discuss emerging research efforts that begin to address them.

Contents

Automated Trace Link Recovery Between Natural Language Requirements and Formal Specifications via LLMs

Jiandong Li[1] and Shaoying Liu[2](✉)

[1] Peking University, Beijing 100871, China
jiandong.li@pku.edu.cn
[2] East China Normal University, Shanghai 200062, China
syliu@sei.ecnu.edu.cn

Abstract. Formal methods have widespread use in high-assurance software development. In practice, the formal specification is derived from the informal user requirements, but traceability links between them are often not explicitly established by formal specification developers. These links are essential and desirable for validating the formal specification and maintaining the formal specification as requirements evolve. Manually creating trace links is not recommended due to its time-consuming nature. Additionally, we have applied some existing automated trace links recovery techniques based on textual similarity and found them suffer from low precision and F1-score. To address these problems, this paper proposes an improved method for automatic establishment of trace links from the informal requirements to the formal specification by leveraging the remarkable capability of LLMs. Our approach consists of three key activities: identifying desired functions from a structured natural language requirements document, deriving process (operation) specifications along with their associated type declarations from the formal specification, and establishing the trace links between them using LLMs. A tool is developed to support the proposed method. We evaluate the proposed method across four projects such as the ATM system and the Sun Search System in avionics. The experiment results demonstrate that the proposed method performs significantly better in precision, recall and F1-score than the existing text-based similarity techniques, including Latent Semantic Indexing, Vector Space Model, Word2Vec embeddings, and LLM-based embeddings. Specifically, our evaluation involving GPT-4o, Gemini 3.1 Pro, and DeepSeek V3 shows that while all three LLMs achieve consistent precision, recall, and F1-score, GPT-4o is the most time-efficient for trace link recovery.

Keywords: Requirements traceability · Trace links recovery · Formal specification

1 Introduction

Formal methods, such as Z, B, VDM-SL and SOFL offer rigorous techniques for specifying and verifying systems, especially in safety-critical domains [4]. A

G. De Giacomo et al. (Eds.): TASE 2026, LNCS 16697, pp. 1–16, 2027.
https://doi.org/10.1007/978-3-032-30693-7_1

formal specification is typically derived from user requirements [8] and incrementally refined into code, with its correctness ensured through model checking or formal proofs [29].

Requirements are often captured in natural language or structured formats such as UML, Problem Frames, or KAOS diagrams [3,15,16,25]. In this work, we focus on natural language functional requirements, as natural language is the most intuitive way for users to express their needs and facilitates effective communication among stakeholders. By contrast, non-functional requirements are challenging to specify formally by model-based formal languages and are not considered here.

Traceability between user requirements and formal specifications is essential for validating the formal specification against original intents and for maintaining it as requirements evolve [2,17]. However, in practice, such trace links are often omitted or left implicit [12,15]. This work addresses the problem of "after-the-fact" requirements tracing, recovering trace links between user requirements and their formalized counterparts.

Manual approaches dominate current practice [10,17]. Li and Liu proposed an inspection method to validate SOFL specifications against natural langauge requirements, where trace links are manually established by inspectors [17]. Hallerstede et al. introduced a tool to trace Program Frames requirements to Event-B specification, yet still rely on manual efforts [10]. Manual tracing is time-consuming and error-prone. Other works explore conceptual mappings, such as from UML or KAOS concepts to B specification concepts [14,16,25], but they primarily define relationships rather than providing practical methods to trace links establishment, leaving the workload unchanged.

Automating trace links recovery is thus highly desirable, but little work has addressed traceability specifically between user requirements and formal specifications. Existing automatic techniques [6,9,18,26], mainly developed for requirements-to-code trace links recovery,fall into three categories: (1) information retrieval (IR)-based approaches, (2) machine learning (ML) or deep learning-based techniques, and (3) generative AI models-based methods. The ML-based methods are unsuitable due to the lack of large, comprehensive training datasets required for achieving viable, high-precision results. The IR-based approaches were applied, but yielded low precision, recall, and F1-scores. The low performance is primarily attributed to the knowledge gap (or the term mismatch) between different artifacts and the refinement nature during the transformation from informal requirements to a formal specification.

To address this, we propose a method that leverages large language models (LLMs), such as ChatGPT, for recovering trace links between natural language requirements and formal specifications. LLMs have recently shown strong performance in software engineering tasks [7,13,22], including specification synthesis, formal verification, and repairing specification. Recent efforts also explore LLMs for traceability, such as linking requirements to goals descirbed in GRL models [11] or to code elements [24]. However, no prior work has specifically addressed LLM-based trace link recovery between requirements and formal specifications, which is a gap that this work aims to fill.

Our method consists of three steps: (1) extracting desired functions from structured natural language requirements, (2) generating process specifications and their associated type declarations from the formal specification using syntactic and dependency analysis, and (3) using an LLM to automatically link the desired functions to their corresponding process specifications. We implement a tool integrating GPT-4o, Gemini 3.1 Pro and DeepSeek V3 to support this workflow.

We conduct four experiments to evaluate the performance of the proposed trace links recovery approach, using the following datasets: natural language requirements documents and formal specifications of *an ATM system, a lab research award management system, a library borrowing management system, and a sun search system* in avionic and embedded system. We also compare our approach against four commonly used automatic methods. They are latent semantic indexing (LSI), vector space model (VSM-cosine), Word2Vec embeddings, and LLM-based embeddings. The experiment results demonstrate that our approach achieves much higher precision, recall and F1-score than automatic LSI, VSM-cosine, Word2Vec embeddings, and LLM-based embeddings methods. Furthermore, we conducted a comparative evaluation using three LLMs: GPT-4o, Gemini 3.1 Pro, and DeepSeek V3. The findings reveal that all three models achieve consistent and comparable performance in terms of precision, recall, and F1-score in our datasets. However, GPT-4o emerges as the most efficient model, requiring less time to recover the trace links.The dataset, the implementation of the tool and the experiment results are provided in[1].

2 The Trace Links Recovery Problem

2.1 Structured Natural Language Requirements

We adopt *a structured natural language requirements* for documenting user requirements [20]. Prior studies [19,28] confirm that a structured requirements improve formal specification development. It documents a set of desired functions or services to be provided by the potential software system. Some high-level function can be further decomposed into lower-level sub-functions, creating a hierarchical description of system functionalities. Each desired function is briefly described in natural language, along with its required data and constraints.

Figure 1 illustrates the natural language requirements of an *electronic mail address book*. It is required to (1) *check whether a given email address already exists in the email address book*, (2) *to add a new email address to the email book*, and (3) *to remove a given mail address from the email address book*. Additionally, a constraint is imposed on the function of adding a new email address to the email book. The constraint is that duplicate email addresses are not allowed.

Formally, a *structured natural language requirements* is represented as a (directed acyclic graph) DAG $RSG = (V, E)$. Here, V is the set of vertices, where each vertex $v \in V$ represents a desired function in the system, either a

[1] https://app.box.com/s/v72gsota48fo7qqf53ruw672160acl47.

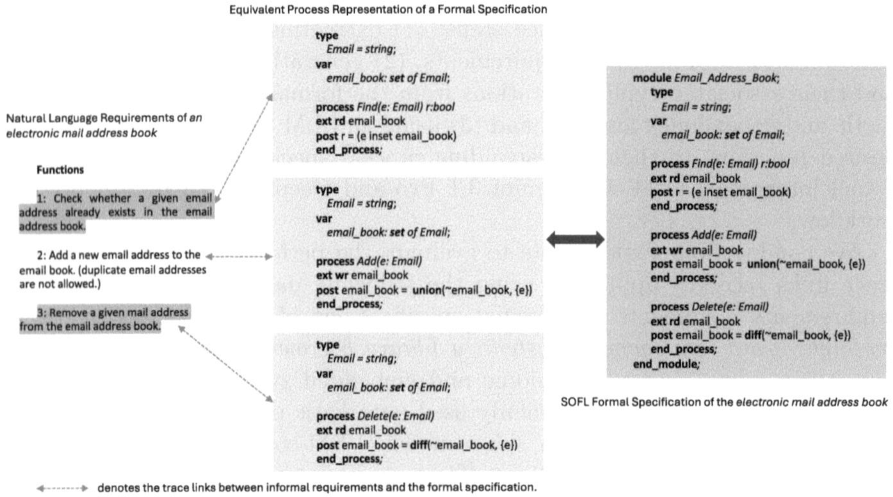

Fig. 1. An example of the trace links between the informal requirements and the formal specification.

high-level functions or a decomposed low-level function. $E \subseteq V \times V$ is a set of directed edges that capture the decomposition relationships among desired functions. An edge $(v_i, v_j) \in E$ indicates that the function v_j (child function) is a sub-function of the function v_i (parent function). A vertex with no incoming edges is called the root vertex, which represents the overall system or top-level function. A vertex with no outcoming edges is called a sink vertex, which represents a fully decomposed desired function that requires no further breakdown. The RSG has exactly one root vertex and one or multiple sink vertexes. We denote the set of sink vertexes as $sink(RSG)$, which corresponds to the set of fully decomposed desired functions that do not require further subdivision.

2.2 Model-Based Formal Specification

The formal specification specifies user requirements precisely. In this paper, we focus on the formal specification written in any model-based formal notations, such as VDM-SL, Z, B, and SOFL. A model-based formal specification typically consists of a collection of processes (equivalent to operations in general term) along with necessary type declarations. The type declarations define the data types that operations or processes can interact with or manipulate. The data types generally include constant declarations, basic data types such as integers, Booleans, and characters, as well as composite types like records or unions, and collection types like sets or sequences. Each operation (or process) is defined using pre- and post-conditions expressed in predicate logic, specifying the functional requirements of the system.

The transformation from requirements to the formal specification is a process of refinement and extension. Refinement means that the formal speciation improves the requirements specification by resolving non-determinism or removing ambiguities, leading to a more concrete and precise specification. Extension means the addition of new components to the specification, such as a data type declaration. Modification means the change in syntax of the specification. Figure 1 also demonstrates these features of refinement and extension.

Each process specification in the formal specification specifies a fully decomposed desired function that do not require further subdivision and depends on some type declarations and variable declarations within the same formal specification. For example, in Fig. 1, the *Find()* process depends on the type declaration *Email* and the variable declaration *email_book*. Together, the *Find()* process specification, the *Email* type declaration and the *email_book* variable formally specify the desired function of checking whether a given email address already exists in the email address book in Fig. 1.

Consider a process specification P depends on a declaration D (e.g., a type declaration or a variable declaration or a function definition in SOFL) in a formal specification. Dependence means that the identifier of the declaration D is appeared in the text (or content) of process specification P. Based on these dependences, a dependence graph PDG can be constructed for each process specification P in a formal specification, representing the process P and its associated (multiple) declarations $D_1, \ldots, D_M$. We represent a formal specification FS as a collection of process dependence graphs, representing its process specifications along with their associate declarations:

$$FS = \{PDG_1, \ldots, PDG_N\} \tag{1}$$

where N is the total number of process specifications in FS. We refer to this representation as the equivalent *process specification form* of the formal specification. Figure 1 also shows the equivalent process specification form of the *electronic mail address book* formal specification.

2.3 Trace Links Recovery Problem Statement

The goal to automatically recover the trace links between the desired functions in the requirements and their formalized counterparts in the formal specification. Figure 1 illustrates these trace links. Formally, let RSG denote *a structured natural language requirements* and $sink(RSG)$ denote a set of fully decomposed desired functions that do not require further subdivision. Let FS denote the corresponding formal specification of RSG written in model-based formal language. Let $PSF = \{PDG_1, \ldots, PDG_N\}$ represent the process specification form of FS, which is a collection of the constituent process specifications of FS along with their associate declarations. We are interested in working out a new trace links recovery method that can automatically discover whether a trace link *Link* exists for all possible pairs of desired functions from $sink(RSG)$ and process specification forms from $\{PDG_1, \ldots, PDG_N\}$ of FS. That is,

$$Links = \{(f, \leftrightarrow, p) | f \in sink(RSG), p \in PSF, f \leftrightarrow p\} \tag{2}$$

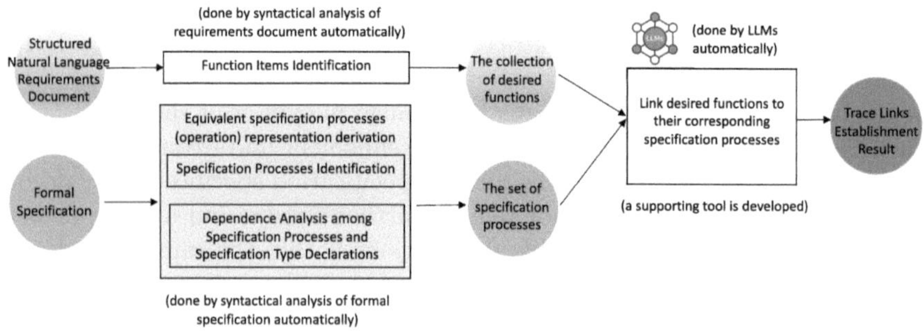

Fig. 2. The proposed trace links recovery process.

, where $(f, \leftrightarrow, p)$ is called the tranformative link and indicates that the desired function f in RSG is formally described by p in the formal specification FS.

3 The Trace Links Recovery Approach

We propose to advance trace links recovery by leveraging the remarkable capabilities of LLMs, such as ChatGPT or Gemini. Figure 2 illustrates the proposed trace links recovery process. It consists of the following activities:

1. Identifying fully decomposed desired functions that do not require further subdivision from the *structured natural language requirements document* automatically.
2. Deriving the equivalent process specification form of the formal specification automatically through syntactical analysis and dependence analysis.
3. Establishing the trace links between the identified fully decomposed desired functions and the derived process specifications along with their associated declarations automatically by LLMs.

In *activity (1)*, a directed graph can be easily constructed from the *structured natural language requirements document* through dependence parsing based on its structure. The nodes of the constructed directed graph represent functions and edges indicate decomposition. The fully decomposed desired functions can be easily and automatically identified as leaf nodes using graph traversal techniques like Depth-First Search (DFS).

The *activity (2)* takes the formal specification as input and derives its equivalent process specification form representation. This derivation is achieved by following steps. First, various types of constituent components within the formal specification should be identified and this can be easily and automatically done through rules based on the syntactical analysis. For example, in a SOFL formal specification, any segment starting from modifier '*process*' and ending with '*end_process*' is recognized as a process specification component, as illustrated in Fig. 1. Second, a dependence analysis is conducted to determine the associated declarations, such as type declarations and variable declarations, for each

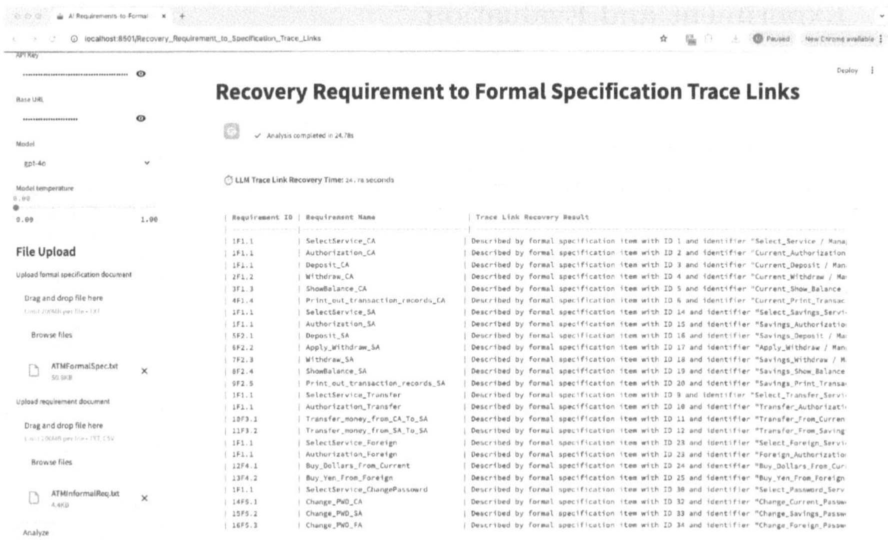

Fig. 3. A snapshot of the developed tool supporting trace links recovery task.

identified process specification component. As a result, a dependence graph is constructed for each identified process specification, associating it to its related type declarations or variable declarations. Here, dependence is defined as the occurrence of the identifier of a declaration within the text (or content) of a process specification. The dependence analysis can also be automatically performed. Based on the identified constituent components within the formal specification in step 1 and the constructed dependence graph for each process specification component in step 2, each process specification can be reorganized along with its associated declaration to generate a modular and self-contained specification for each process specification. Finally, an equivalent process specification representation of the formal specification is formed.

In *activity (3)*, the LLM takes both a set of the fully decomposed desired functions identified in activity (1) and a set of process specifications along with their associated declarations derived in *activity (2)* as input, analyzes them automatically by appropriate prompts to recover and establish the trace links between them, and presents the established trace links result. We also develop a tool to support it, leveraging LLM GPT-4o, Gemini 3.1 Pro and DeepSeek V3 to automate trace links establishment. As shown in Fig. 3, the software tool is developed as a Streamlit web app using Python3. The source code of the developed tool and the used prompt, which integrates expert role-playing, Chain-of-Thought reasoning, and Few-Shot learning, are available[2]. To run the tool locally, users can execute the command '*streamlit run app.py*' in the console and can access it through their local browsers at *https://localhost:8501/*.

[2] https://app.box.com/s/v72gsota48fo7qqf53ruw672160acl47.

4 Experiment and Evaluation

4.1 Experiment Data

Table 1 summarizes the four datasets used in our experiments and can be accessible from [2]. The first one involves an ATM system, with natural language requirements and a formal specification written in SOFL. It includes 25 distinct desired functions such as *deposit, withdraw, show balance, transfer, foreign currency exchange, change password* and 36 process specifications derived from the formal specification. The ATM project totally contains 25 trace links. The second project covers a library borrowing management system. It is required to provide 6 desired functions: *borrow books, return books, search for books, renew books, manage overdue books, and process fine payment.* From its SOFL formal specification, 6 processes specifications along with their associated declarations are also derived, yielding 6 trace links. The third project comes from a laboratory research award management system for students with 5 desired functions, such as *update budget, register student, and award money. Form the formal specification,* and 5 process specifications together their related declarations are also derived. It has 5 trace links in total. The fourth project involves a sun search system in avionics and embedded systems, which is developed by a team from Institute of Software, Chinese Academy of Sciences. The software controller of the sun search system is required to provide 12 desired functions across three aspects: sensor device data collection (e.g., *collecting data from gyros, sun sensors, and thrusters*), computation (e.g., *calculating the gyroscope correlation matrix*), and actuator control (e.g., *sending control output to the thrusters*). The software controller's 12 desired functions are formally specified by 12 processes specification in a pre- and post-condition style based on predicate logic along with necessary type declaration such as matrix. There are totally 12 trace links in the fourth project. The user requirements and formal specifications of the software controller of the sun search system cannot be made open source due to data privacy restrictions, but the readers can access the data of other three projects.

4.2 Comparison Methods

We integrate three well-known LLMs, GPT-4o, Gemini 3.1 Pro, and DeepSeek-V3, in our proposed method for comparative analysis. Furthermore, we select four existing automatic text-based similarity techniques as baselines. They are latent semantic indexing (LSI) technique and vector space model (VSM) technique, Word2Vec embeddings technique (*word2vec-google-news-300*), and LLM-based embeddings technique (*text-embedding-ada-002*). These techniques are chosen for their widespread use, and their good effectiveness and high feasibility in establishing trace links between software artifacts. Additionally, machine learning-based techniques to establish trace links are excluded, as their applicability is limited in our situation by the lack of large and high-quality training datasets about the informal requirements and their corresponding formal specifications.

Table 1. Experiment data statistics.

Project	Num. of Functions	Num. of Process Specifications	Num. of Trace Links
ATM	25	36	25
Library Borrowing Management	6	6	6
Research Award Management	5	5	5
Sun Search System	12	12	12

4.3 Research Questions and Evaluation Metrics

To evaluate our work, we focus on the following research questions:

- How effective is our proposed method in recovering informal-requirements-to-formal specification trace links? (RQ1)?
- Does the proposed method outperform existing automatic approaches, including VSM, LSI, Word2Vec embeddings, and LLM-based embeddings methods? (RQ2)

We evaluate the performance of these trace links recovery methods using three metrics: *precision*, *recall*, and *F1-score*. The reasonableness of our definitions to these metrics are also supported by [11]. Additionally, for RQ1, we report the time efficiency of different LLMs in recovering the trace links to assess their practical efficiency.

4.4 RQ1 and Its Experiment Results

Table 2 presents the performance of the proposed method, which integrates the GPT-4o, Gemini 3.1 Pro and DeepSeek-V3 model. From Table 2, we can see that the proposed method achieves high precision, recall, and F1-score across all four projects. Notably, all three models exhibit identical precision, recall and F1-score metrics for each specific project. For the ATM project, both the precision and the recall are 96%, resulting in an F1-score of 0.96. For the Library Borrowing Management, Research Award Management, and Sun Search System, the method attains 100% precision and recall, yielding a perfect F1-score of 1.0. While the accuracy remains consistent across the models, their execution times vary, with GPT-4o consistently requiring the least amount of time to complete the recovery tasks. Overall, these results confirm that integrating LLMs-based techniques offers an effective and reliable solution for automatic trace links recovery.

4.5 RQ2 and Its Experiment Results

Each selected trace links recovery technique utilizes a specific threshold to determine the traceability links, optimizing performance based on precision,

Table 2. The performance of the proposed method integrating LLMs.

Project	LLM	Precision	Recall	F1-Score	Execution Time
ATM	GPT-4o	96% (24/25)	96% (24/25)	0.96	24.78 s
	Gemini 3.1 Pro	96% (24/25)	96% (24/25)	0.96	39.87 s
	DeepSeek V3	96% (24/25)	96% (24/25)	0.96	47.07 s
Library Borrowing Management	GPT-4o	100% (6/6)	100% (6/6)	1	6.43 s
	Gemini 3.1 Pro	100% (6/6)	100% (6/6)	1	13.35 s
	DeepSeek V3	100% (6/6)	100% (6/6)	1	11.63 s
Research Award Management	GPT-4o	100% (5/5)	100% (5/5)	1	3.60 s
	Gemini 3.1 Pro	100% (5/5)	100% (5/5)	1	45.75 s
	DeepSeek V3	100% (5/5)	100% (5/5)	1	9.19 s
Sun Search System	GPT-4o	100% (12/12)	100% (12/12)	1	6.79 s
	Gemini 3.1 Pro	100% (12/12)	100% (12/12)	1	18.83 s
	DeepSeek V3	100% (12/12)	100% (12/12)	1	20.24 s

Table 3. Various techniques, their score range, and the used threshold for comparison.

Technique	Score Range	Used Threshold
LLMs-Based Embeddings	[0, 1]	0.76
Word2Vec Embedding	[0, 1]	0.27
VSM	[0, 1]	0.02
LSI	[-1, 1]	0.0000001

recall, and F1-score. Table 3 presents the chosen threshold values used for different traceability techniques to predict trace links, along with their corresponding score range.

Table 4 presents a comparison of the performance between the proposed method and selected four traceability recovery techniques, as applied to the four projects using the thresholds selected in Table 3. Based on the experiment result in Table 4, we calculate *the average precision, the average recall, and the average F1-score* of each trace links establishment method across the across the *ATM, Library Borrowing Management System, Research Award Management System,* and *Sun Search System* projects. The details are reflected in Table 5.

Based on Tables 4 and 5, we can see a clear difference in the performance of various trace links recovery techniques. The proposed method, which integrates LLM, achieves the highest average F1-score of 0.99. It stands out as the best-performing technique, surpassing both traditional methods and embedding-based approaches by a significant margin. The modern LLM-based embeddings method, with an average F1-score of 0.605, also performs well across the four projects but noticeably lags behind the proposed method. Despite its strong performance in the research award management project, it falls short of maintaining consistent high performance across the other three projects, a level of reliability demonstrated by the proposed method. The Word2Vec embed-

Table 4. Performance comparison of various methods.

Project	Technique	Precision	Recall	F1-Score
ATM	VSM	8% (2/25)	8% (2/25)	0.08
	LSI	0% (0/25)	0% (0/25)	0
	Word2Vec Embeddings	4% (1/25)	4% (1/25)	0.04
	LLM-based Embeddings	64% (16/25)	64% (16/25)	0.64
	Proposed Method	96% (24/25)	96% (24/25)	0.96
Library Borrowing Management	VSM	20% (1/5)	17% (1/6)	0.18
	LSI	40% (2/5)	33% (2/6)	0.36
	Word2Vec Embeddings	33% (2/6)	33% (2/6)	0.33
	LLM-based Embeddings	33% (2/6)	33% (2/6)	0.33
	Proposed Method	100% (6/6)	100% (6/6)	1
Research Award Management	VSM	20% (1/5)	20% (1/5)	0.20
	LSI	60% (3/5)	60% (3/5)	0.60
	Word2Vec Embeddings	25% (1/4)	20% (1/5)	0.22
	LLM-based Embeddings	100% (5/5)	100% (5/5)	1
	Proposed Method	100% (5/5)	100% (5/5)	1
Sun Search System	VSM	40% (2/5)	17% (2/12)	0.24
	LSI	22% (2/9)	17% (2/12)	0.19
	Word2Vec Embeddings	25% (3/12)	25% (3/12)	0.25
	LLM-based Embeddings	50% (5/10)	42% (5/12)	0.45
	Proposed Method	100% (12/12)	100% (12/12)	1

Table 5. Average performance comparison of various methods across four projects.

Technique	Avg Precision	Avg Recall	Avg F1-Score
VSM	22%	15.5%	0.175
LSI	30%	29.25%	0.295
Word2Vec Embeddings	21.75%	20.5%	0.21
LLM-based Embeddings	61.75%	59.75%	0.605
Proposed Method	99%	99%	0.99

dings achieves an average F1-score of 0.21, which is much lower compared to LLM-based embeddings and the proposed method. Despite the popularity of Word2Vec, this pre-trained model struggles to accurately establish trace links, suggesting it may not be well-suited for tasks involving informal-requirements-formal-specification relationships. VSM achieves an average F1-score of 0.175, performing considerably lower than the top-performing techniques. LSI achieves a slightly higher average F1-score of 0.295, performing better than VSM, but it still lacks the precision, the recall and the F1-score seen in the top-performing techniques. Traditional methods like LSI and VSM are largely outclassed by the more advanced techniques. Overall, the proposed method stands out as the clear leader in the automatic informal-requirements-to-formal-specification trace links recovery tasks.

4.6 Threats to Validity

The main threats to the validity of our experiment come from the following aspects. One threat is the design of the prompts used in our tool to guide the LLMs' analysis and generation of response. Well-crafted prompts can lead to more accurate, relevant, and useful responses. To achieve optimal model performance, we craft our prompts following established best practices. The developed tool can effectively recover the trace links.

Additionally, the LLMs can produce varied responses to the same prompts and the same input due to inherent randomness. To mitigate this threat, we set the parameter of model temperature to a lower value (0) for the reliable and consistent results.

Another threat is the dataset scale. While the four projects used in our experiments may not represent the complexity of large-scale industrial systems, they are of reasonable size for academic evaluation. For example, the number of the desired functions to be provided by the ATM system is 25 and the original SOFL formal specification of the ATM system spans approximately 22 pages and is still a reasonable size for the purposes of this study. The sun search system from the industry includes 12 functions. These scales are sufficient to demonstrate the method's effectiveness. Moreover, three of the four datasets are publicly available, supporting reproducibility by other researchers.

Finally, one threat could be data leakage or data contamination. Three projects, including *the ATM system, the Library Borrowing Management System, and the Research Award Management System*, may overlap the data used for training LLMs, as GPT-4o's or Gemini's training corpus is are proprietary and undisclosed. To mitigate this, we included the *Sun Search System*, an industrial avionics project. Its industrial nature significantly reduces the likelihood of public exposure. On this *Sun Search System* project, our method achieves 100% precision, recall and F1-score, confirming its robustness in unseen scenarios.

5 Related Work

Requirements traceability [9,26] establishes clear and meaningful links between the requirements and various artifacts throughout the software development life cycle. It is generally divided into two categories: the pre-requirements traceability and the post-requirements traceability. Pre-requirements specification traceability focuses on linking requirements to their origins, such as interviews with stakeholder, meeting protocols, or legacy systems. Mucha et al. conducted a systematic literature review on this aspect [23]. The post-requirements traceability is a big family of traceability and encompasses multiple types of traceability, including the requirements-to-formal-specification traceability [10,17], the requirements-to-code traceability [9,26], the requirements-to-design traceability, etc. Actively supporting requirements traceability benefits a broad set of software engineering activities, such as the validation and the maintenance of the formal specification [16,17], and the verification and maintenance of the code [21]. Driven by the product certification standard, customer request or the benefits of traceability, some companies implemented and integrated the traceability into their development process [5,27]. Our work in this paper focus on the informal-requirements-to-formal-specification traceability, which is essential for the validation and maintenance of the formal specification.

The formal specifications are usually divided into three categories: model-based formal specification such as such as Z, VDM-SL, B and SOFL., property-based formal specification such as LTL and STL, and process algebra-based formal specification such as CSP. Informal requirements may be expressed in natural language, UML, KAOS, or Problem Frames. Among these, our work use natural language requirements and formal specification written in model-based formal notations.

Existing approaches to recovering trace links between informal user requirements and model-based formal specifications are predominantly manual [10,17]. This reliance on human effort makes the process labor-intensive, time-consuming, and prone to errors. Additionally, some studies have explored the conceptual mapping between user requirements and formal specifications, such as aligning UML concepts with B specifications [16,25] or mapping the KAOS requirements model to B specifications [3,15]. While these efforts enhance traceability conceptually, they primarily focus on defining relationships rather than providing practical, automated methods for establishing trace links.

Given that both natural language requirements and model-based formal specifications are expressed as text, existing automated traceability approaches [6,9,18,26] for text-based software artifacts primarily fall into three categories: information retrieval (IR)-based, machine learning (ML)-based, and large language model (LLM)-based methods. These techniques operate on the principle that related artifacts exhibit higher textual similarity compared to unrelated artifacts. IR-based methods [26] employ classical text similarity techniques such as the Vector Space Model (VSM), Latent Semantic Indexing (LSI), Latent Dirichlet Allocation (LDA), Jensen-Shannon Models (JSMs), and voter-based approaches. More recent advancements incorporate LLM-based embeddings to enhance textual representation. However, traditional IR methods often struggle with term mismatch problems and polysemy, limiting their effectiveness in capturing deeper semantic relationships. To overcome these limitations, deep learning-based approaches [6,18] have been introduced, leveraging neural network architectures to better understand contextual and semantic similarities between artifacts. These methods improve upon IR-based approaches by addressing synonymy, polysemy, and domain-specific linguistic variations, leading to more accurate trace link recovery. Given the success of these automated techniques in other domains, we investigate their applicability to establishing trace links between natural language requirements and formal specifications, aiming to bridge the gap in automated traceability within model-based development.

More recently, large language models (LLMs) have been employed to automatically establish trace links by leveraging prompt-based techniques [9,24]. Our work falls within this category of LLM-based approaches. Large Language Models (LLMs) have demonstrated remarkable capabilities across various software engineering tasks, with growing interest in their application to trace link recovery [9,11,24]. Recent studies have explored LLM-driven approaches for enhancing traceability across different artifacts in software development. Hassine [11] introduced an LLM-based method for generating security-related traceability links between natural language requirements and goals represented in GRL models. Ali et al. [1] proposed a retrieval-augmented generation (RAG) approach leveraging LLMs to improve traceability from natural language use-case requirements to code repositories. Rodriguez et al. [24] utilized the Claude LLM to establish traceability links between natural language requirements and Java classes, demonstrating its effectiveness in connecting high-level requirements with implementation artifacts.

6 Conclusion

In this paper, we propose a method for automatically recovering trace links between textual user requirements and formal specifications written in any model-based formal notation. Our approach is distinguished by two key innovations: (1) deriving an equivalent process specification representation of the formal specification and (2) leveraging LLMs to automatically link functional descriptions in the user requirements document to their formalized counterparts in the specification. The trace link establishment process follows a structured, step-by-step methodology comprising three core activities: (1) identifying desired functions from the textual user requirements document, (2) deriving process specifications from the formal specification, which transforms a formal specification into its process specification representation, including associated type and variable declarations, to ensure completeness and self-containment, (3) establishing trace links between them using LLMs. For each of these activities, we discuss specific techniques and optimizations to enhance accuracy and robustness. To support our method, we have also developed an automated tool that streamlines the trace link recovery process and provides practical usability for users. Furthermore, we conducted a comprehensive comparative evaluation of our approach against existing IR-based traceability techniques, including VSM, LSI, Word2Vec embeddings, and LLM-based embeddings. Our findings demonstrate that our method significantly outperforms these techniques in terms of accuracy and effectiveness in recovering trace links. By improving traceability between user requirements and formal specifications, our approach strengthens formal specification validation processes and facilitates long-term specification maintenance.

Acknowledgment. We appreciate Assistant Prof. Xiong Xu from Institute of Software, Chinese Academy of Sciences and Beijing Institute of Control Engineering, for offering us the natural language user requirements and the formal specifications of the Sun Search System in avionics.

References

1. Ali, S.J., Naganathan, V., Bork, D.: Establishing traceability between natural language requirements and software artifacts by combining rag and LLMs. In: International Conference on Conceptual Modeling, pp. 295–314. Springer, Heidelberg (2024). https://doi.org/10.1007/978-3-031-75872-0_16
2. Alkhammash, E., Butler, M., Fathabadi, A.S., Cîrstea, C.: Building traceable event-b models from requirements. Sci. Comput. Program. **111**, 318–338 (2015)
3. Aziz, B., Arenas, A.E., Bicarregui, J., Ponsard, C., Massonet, P.: From goal-oriented requirements to event-b specifications. In: Proceedings of the First NASA Formal Methods Symposium (2009)
4. ter Beek, M.H., et al.: Formal methods in industry. Formal Aspects Comput. **37**(1), 1–38 (2024)
5. Cleland-Huang, J., Gotel, O.C., Huffman Hayes, J., Mäder, P., Zisman, A.: Software traceability: trends and future directions. In: Future of Software Engineering Proceedings, pp. 55–69 (2014)
6. Dai, P., Yang, L., Wang, Y., Jin, D., Gong, Y.: Constructing traceability links between software requirements and source code based on neural networks. Mathematics **11**(2), 315 (2023)
7. De Lucia, A., Fasano, F., Oliveto, R., Tortora, G.: Enhancing an artefact management system with traceability recovery features. In: 20th IEEE International Conference on Software Maintenance, 2004. Proceedings, pp. 306–315. IEEE (2004)
8. Feng, J., et al.: Frepa: an automated and formal approach to requirement modeling and analysis in aircraft control domain. In: Proceedings of the 28th ACM Joint Meeting on European Software Engineering Conference and Symposium on the Foundations of Software Engineering, pp. 1376–1386 (2020)
9. Guo, J.L., Steghöfer, J.P., Vogelsang, A., Cleland-Huang, J.: Natural language processing for requirements traceability. In: Handbook on Natural Language Processing for Requirements Engineering, pp. 89–116. Springer, Heidelberg (2025). https://doi.org/10.1007/978-3-031-73143-3_4
10. Hallerstede, S., Jastram, M., Ladenberger, L.: A method and tool for tracing requirements into specifications. Sci. Comput. Program. **82**, 2–21 (2014)
11. Hassine, J.: An LLM-based approach to recover traceability links between security requirements and goal models. In: Proceedings of the 28th International Conference on Evaluation and Assessment in Software Engineering, pp. 643–651 (2024)
12. Hayes, J.H., Dekhtyar, A., Sundaram, S.K.: Advancing candidate link generation for requirements tracing: the study of methods. IEEE Trans. Softw. Eng. **32**(1), 4–19 (2006)
13. Hou, X., et al.: Large language models for software engineering: a systematic literature review. ACM Trans. Softw. Eng. Methodol. **33**(8), 1–79 (2024)
14. Idani, A., Ledru, Y.: Object oriented concepts identification from formal b specifications. Electron. Notes Theor. Comput. Sci. **133**, 159–174 (2005)
15. Jastram, M., Leuschel, M., Bendisposto, J., Russo Jr, A.: Mapping requirements to b models. DEPLOY Deliverable (2009)

16. Laleau, R., Polack, F.: Coming and going from UML to B: a proposal to support traceability in rigorous IS development. In: Bert, D., Bowen, J.P., Henson, M.C., Robinson, K. (eds.) ZB 2002. LNCS, vol. 2272, pp. 517–534. Springer, Heidelberg (2002). https://doi.org/10.1007/3-540-45648-1_27
17. Li, M., Liu, S.: Integrating animation-based inspection into formal design specification construction for reliable software systems. IEEE Trans. Reliab. **65**(1), 88–106 (2015)
18. Lin, J., Liu, Y., Zeng, Q., Jiang, M., Cleland-Huang, J.: Traceability transformed: generating more accurate links with pre-trained bert models. In: 2021 IEEE/ACM 43rd International Conference on Software Engineering (ICSE), pp. 324–335. IEEE (2021)
19. Liu, S.: A three-step hybrid specification approach to error prevention. J. Syst. Softw. **178**, 110975 (2021)
20. Liu, S.: Agile-SOFL. Springer, Heidelberg (2024)
21. Mäder, P., Egyed, A.: Do developers benefit from requirements traceability when evolving and maintaining a software system? Empir. Softw. Eng. **20**, 413–441 (2015)
22. Moran, K., et al.: Improving the effectiveness of traceability link recovery using hierarchical bayesian networks. In: Proceedings of the ACM/IEEE 42nd International Conference on Software Engineering, pp. 873–885 (2020)
23. Mucha, J., Kaufmann, A., Riehle, D.: A systematic literature review of pre-requirements specification traceability. Requirements Eng. **29**(2), 119–141 (2024)
24. Rodriguez, A.D., Dearstyne, K.R., Cleland-Huang, J.: Prompts matter: insights and strategies for prompt engineering in automated software traceability. In: 2023 IEEE 31st International Requirements Engineering Conference Workshops (REW), pp. 455–464. IEEE (2023)
25. Snook, C., Butler, M.: Uml-b: formal modeling and design aided by uml. ACM Trans. Softw. Eng. Methodol. (TOSEM) **15**(1), 92–122 (2006)
26. Wang, B., Zou, Z., Wan, H., Li, Y., Deng, Y., Li, X.: An empirical study on the state-of-the-art methods for requirement-to-code traceability link recovery. J. King Saud Univ.-Comput. Inf. Sci. **36**(6), 102118 (2024)
27. Winkler, S., von Pilgrim, J.: A survey of traceability in requirements engineering and model-driven development. Softw. Syst. Model. **9**(4), 529–565 (2010)
28. Yeganefard, S., Butler, M.: Control systems: phenomena and structuring functional requirement documents. In: IEEE 17th International Conference on Engineering of Complex Computer Systems, pp. 39–48. IEEE (2012)
29. Zhou, L., Qin, J., Wang, Q., Appel, A.W., Cao, Q.: VST-A: a foundationally sound annotation verifier. Proc. ACM Program. Lang. **8**(POPL), 2069–2098 (2024)

The Robustness Profile: A Metamorphic Testing Framework for Multi-dimensional Evaluation of DRL Agents

Kaicheng Shao[1], Yuteng Lu[2], and Meng Sun[1](✉)

[1] Peking University, Beijing, China
kevinskc@pku.edu.cn , sunm@pku.edu.cn
[2] China Ship Research and Development Academy, Beijing, China

Abstract. The reliability of Deep Reinforcement Learning (DRL) agents is a major obstacle to their deployment in safety-critical domains. Traditional evaluations, focused on maximizing cumulative rewards, often mask critical vulnerabilities and fail to capture the nuances of agent behavior. To address this gap, we introduce the **DRL Metamorphic Testing Framework (DRL-MTF)**, a systematic approach for evaluating agent robustness through a novel taxonomy of 11 parameterized Metamorphic Relations (MRs). We evaluated prominent Proximal Policy Optimization (PPO) and Deep Q-Network (DQN) agents on the Atari benchmark, revealing a stark divergence between reward-based (outcome) and action-based (behavioral) robustness. For instance, a DQN agent passed 70% of reward-based tests for `Horizontal Flip` but failed all corresponding behavioral checks, indicating it maintained its score through entirely different actions. Similarly, a PPO agent achieved a 100% reward pass rate for `Noise Injection` but only a 4% behavioral pass rate, exposing severe policy instability. These findings show that agents often learn brittle, non-generalizable strategies. Our framework synthesizes these multi-faceted results into a **Robustness Profile**, an actionable diagnostic tool that uncovers hidden fragilities missed by traditional metrics, paving the way for more reliable DRL agents.

Keywords: Deep Reinforcement Learning · Metamorphic Testing · Robustness · Autonomous Agents

1 Introduction

RL is a machine learning method that allows an intelligent agent to learn a decision policy for a task through repeated interactions. The agent is designed to maximize the cumulative reward. RL has demonstrated remarkable capabilities from complex game mastery [13,19,20] to robotic control [11,15,16]. However, reliability of RL systems has always been an urgent concern, especially in safety-critical applications such as autonomous driving [5,24] and medical diagnosis [8].

The challenge of ensuring RL reliability stems from intrinsic properties that make testing notoriously difficult, most notably the absence of a test oracle [23]—

G. De Giacomo et al. (Eds.): TASE 2026, LNCS 16697, pp. 17–35, 2027.
https://doi.org/10.1007/978-3-032-30693-7_2

for a given state, there is often no single verifiable "correct" action. This, combined with environmental stochasticity and vast state-action spaces, has led to a reliance on aggregate reward metrics or subjective human judgment for validation. Such methods are insufficient, however, as they are prone to inconsistencies, can be misled by reward hacking [4,17,21], and often fail to reveal underlying policy flaws. A more systematic and automated approach is desperately needed.

Metamorphic Testing (MT) [3], a fault-based validation methodology, offers a powerful solution to these challenges. It circumvents the oracle problem by verifying relational properties between multiple test executions. Instead of checking the absolute correctness of a single output, MT verifies that a specific transformation of the input leads to a predictable variation in the output. This enables automated validation without human judgment or a predefined oracle.

Ensuring the reliability of RL systems is a critical challenge, especially as they are deployed in high-stakes domains. This has spurred research into diverse testing strategies, from efforts aimed at making "black-box" policies more interpretable and trustworthy [14], to search-based methods that systematically hunt for failures [25]. Building on this landscape, we advocate for the emerging application of MT to RL, a practice we term MT4RL. This approach not only bypasses the notorious "oracle problem" but also provides a principled way to express domain knowledge, which can be used to evaluate and even actively improve RL policies [22]. By providing a practical means for verification, MT offers a powerful and complementary path toward more reliable RL systems.

This paper leverages MT to investigate a critical, underexplored question: *Do high-performing Deep Reinforcement Learning (DRL) agents learn robust, generalizable concepts, or do they rely on brittle, superficial features of their training environment?*

We probe the robustness of two DRL models, Deep Q-Network (DQN) and Proximal Policy Optimization (PPO), by designing and implementing metamorphic relations that test their invariance to temporal and visual perturbations. Our experiments are conducted in the classic Atari game MsPacmanNoFrameskip-v4 [1,2], a standard benchmark for DRL research. Our contributions are:

1. We propose the DRL-MTF, a systematic approach for evaluating DRL robustness built on a novel, multi-dimensional taxonomy of MRs that probe agent resilience across state perturbations, semantic invariances, action space disruptions, and temporal dynamics.
2. Through a large-scale empirical study on PPO and DQN agents, we uncover critical, previously undocumented failure modes. Crucially, we introduce a dual-oracle approach that distinguishes between **outcome robustness** (task success) and **behavioral robustness** (policy consistency), revealing that apparent performance can mask catastrophic shifts in agent strategy.
3. We introduce the **Robustness Profile**, a novel analysis artifact that synthesizes complex test results into a concise, visual summary of an agent's strengths and weaknesses, enabling direct comparison and clear identification of high-risk vulnerabilities.

4. We demonstrate that the Robustness Profile is an **actionable diagnostic tool** that pinpoints specific weaknesses (e.g., PPO's fragility to symmetry transformations) and provides a clear roadmap for targeted remediation, bridging the gap between failure detection and building safer DRL systems.

2 Preliminaries

2.1 Reinforcement Learning

Reinforcement Learning (RL) is a machine learning paradigm where an agent learns to make optimal decisions through trial-and-error interactions with an environment. The standard RL framework is formalized as a Markov Decision Process (MDP), a tuple $\mathcal{M} = (\mathcal{S}, \mathcal{A}, P, R, \gamma)$, where:

- $\mathcal{S}$ is the set of all possible states, including an initial state distribution.
- $\mathcal{A}$ is the set of actions the agent can take.
- $P(s'|s,a)$ is the transition probability function, defining the probability of transitioning to state s' given the current state s and action a.
- $R(s,a)$ is the reward function, providing immediate feedback for taking action a in state s.
- $\gamma \in [0,1]$ is the discount factor, determining the weight of future rewards.

The agent's behavior is governed by a policy $\pi(a|s)$, which specifies the probability of taking action a in state s. The goal of the agent is to learn an optimal policy π^* that maximizes the expected cumulative discounted reward, or return, defined as $G_t = \sum_{k=0}^{\infty} \gamma^k R_{t+k}$.

To find such a policy, modern RL algorithms can be broadly categorized into:

- **Value-based methods** (e.g., DQN), which learn a value function (like $Q(s,a)$) and derive a policy from it.
- **Policy gradient methods** (e.g., PPO), directly optimizing the policy $\pi(a|s)$.
- **Actor-critic methods**, which combines both value estimation and direct policy optimization.

2.2 Metamorphic Testing

MT [3] is a software testing technique designed to alleviate the *oracle problem*, which arises when a definitive test oracle for verifying a single output is unavailable or impractical. Whereas traditional testing validates an output $P(x)$ directly, MT checks for the satisfaction of MRs. An MR specifies an expected relationship between the outputs of a program P given a source input x and a follow-up input $x' = T(x)$, which is generated via a transformation T.

A violation of this relation indicates a likely defect. Key MR patterns include:

- *Equivalence Relations*: $P(x) \equiv P(x')$ (e.g., invariance to input permutation).
- *Inequality Relations*: $P(x) \leq P(x')$ (e.g., performance gain with resources).
- *Statistical Properties*: $\text{dist}(P(x), P(x')) \leq \epsilon$ (e.g., robustness to input noise).

MT is thus particularly effective for testing systems like machine learning models, where defining the "correct" output for a single input is often impossible, but expected behavioral properties can be readily specified and verified.

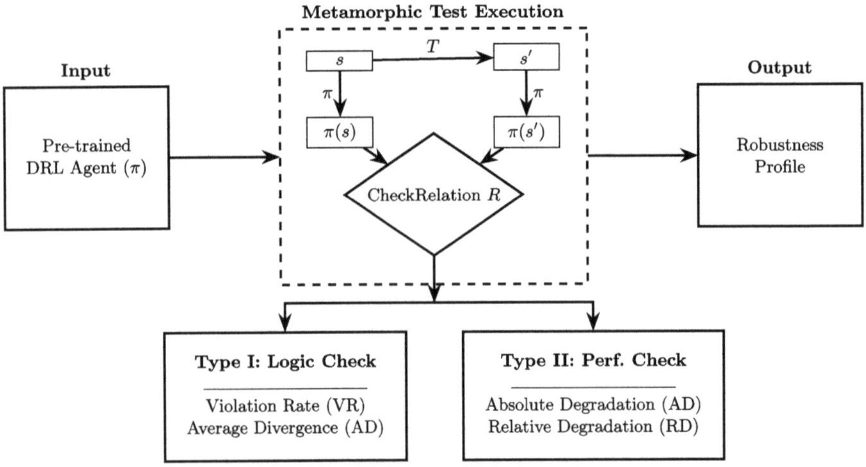

Fig. 1. The overall architecture of our proposed DRL-MTF (Deep Reinforcement Learning Metamorphic Testing Framework), illustrating the end-to-end process from a pre-trained agent (Input), through a three-stage pipeline consisting of **Test Generation**, **Behavior Execution**, and **Oracle Verification**, to a final **Robustness Profile** (Output).

3 A Taxonomy of Metamorphic Relations for DRL

To systematically evaluate DRL agent robustness, we introduce a new taxonomy of MRs, detailed in Subsects. 3.1 through 3.4. This taxonomy synthesizes a mutation testing framework on DNN testing [10] to cover key failure points, from perception to action execution.

At the heart of our method is a **dual-oracle evaluation protocol**, illustrated in Fig. 1. It assesses each MR from two distinct dimensions: **Policy Output Consistency (Type I)** and **Performance Degradation (Type II)**. As the diagram shows, Type I relations perform a static, state-wise check of logical consistency, while Type II relations conduct a dynamic, trajectory-wise evaluation of performance. Before detailing the MR categories, we first define these two general relation types, which underpin all concrete MRs.

General Relation Type I: Policy Output Consistency

This relation is defined over a pair of states: a **source state** s and a **follow-up state** s'. It asserts that the policy's outputs for this pair, $\pi(\cdot|s)$ and $\pi(\cdot|s')$, should exhibit a specified consistency, without considering their future consequences or cumulative rewards. The core of a specific Type I MR lies in how this (s, s') pair is generated and what consistency is expected.

The follow-up state s' can be generated in several ways, providing a flexible framework for different tests:

- *Synthetic Transformation:* The follow-up state is generated by applying a transformation to the source state, $s' = T_S(s)$. This is used to test properties like equivariance, invariance, and robustness to perturbation.

– *Natural Evolution:* The source and follow-up states are consecutive states from a trajectory, $(s, s') = (s_t, s_{t+1})$. This is used to test properties like temporal smoothness.

Regardless of how the (s, s') pair is obtained, the expected consistency is formalized as follows, using a unified action-space tolerance $\epsilon_a \geq 0$:

For a deterministic policy, the distance between the policy's output at s' and the transformed output from s should be bounded. This is represented using an action transformation $T_A : A \to A$ and a distance metric d_A on A.

$$d_A(\pi(s'), T_A(\pi(s))) \leq \epsilon_a$$

The strict equivariance/invariance case corresponds to $\epsilon_a = 0$. For simple invariance or smoothness, T_A is the identity function.

For a probabilistic policy, the divergence between the output distribution at s' and the (transformed) output distribution from s should be bounded. This is formalized using a divergence metric D_A (e.g., KL-divergence or Jensen-Shannon divergence) on the space of action probability distributions, and a distributional transformation $\mathcal{T}_A$ induced by T_A.

$$D_A\big(\pi(\cdot|s') \,||\, \mathcal{T}_A[\pi(\cdot|s)]\big) \leq \epsilon_a$$

Here, $\mathcal{T}_A[\pi(\cdot|s)]$ represents the transformed distribution resulting from applying the transformation logic to the original probability distribution. The theoretical ideal of strict consistency is captured by the case where $\epsilon_a = 0$.

General Relation Type II: Performance Degradation

This relation type assesses the policy's ability to maintain performance under perturbation. It performs a **trajectory-wise** evaluation. The policy π is executed in both the original environment M and the perturbed environment M', generating cumulative rewards C and C', respectively. The core idea is that the policy must handle the cascading effects of the transformation, where the entire trajectory can diverge from the original path. This relation posits that the performance should not catastrophically degrade. This degradation is specified using one of the following two metrics:

Absolute Degradation. The performance degradation is bounded by an absolute tolerance $\epsilon \geq 0$.

$$C - C' \leq \epsilon$$

Relative Degradation. Alternatively, the degradation can be measured relative to the original performance, bounded by a relative tolerance $\delta \in [0, 1]$.

$$\frac{C - C'}{|C|} \leq \delta \quad (\text{for } C \neq 0)$$

In practice, for stochastic environments or policies, these relations are checked by comparing the average cumulative rewards obtained over multiple episodes.

These two relation types measure distinct and complementary aspects of robustness. Type I focuses on logical consistency in isolation, while Type II measures performance resilience in a dynamically evolving, perturbed world. They serve as the fundamental templates from which specific MRs are instantiated. Based on these general types, we now proceed to define four categories of MRs.

3.1 State Transformation MRs

This category transforms the state space S via $T_S : S \to S$ to alter observations while preserving underlying environmental properties. This assesses the policy's generalization and robustness to input variations.

1. Spatial and Structural Symmetry. This MR leverages inherent environmental symmetries (e.g., reflection, rotation), expecting the policy to exhibit corresponding behavioral symmetry [12].

State Transformation T_S: We focus on reflection, implemented as a `Horizontal Flip` of the input frame in Ms. Pac-Man. The flip is applied only to symmetric components, leaving fixed elements like UI unchanged.

Action Transformation T_A: The corresponding action transformation T_A is formally constrained by the environment's dynamics to ensure equivariance. For a deterministic environment with transition function $f(s, a)$, this relationship is captured by the following commutative diagram:

$$\begin{array}{ccc} s & \xrightarrow{\quad a \quad} & f(s,a) \\ {\scriptstyle T_S}\downarrow & & {\scriptstyle T_S}\downarrow \\ T_S(s) & \xrightarrow{T_A(a)} & f(T_S(s), T_A(a)) \end{array}$$

This diagram dictates that $T_S(f(s, a)) = f(T_S(s), T_A(a))$. In other words, taking the transformed action in the transformed state must yield the transformed version of the original next state (Fig. 2).

Example 1. For a `Horizontal Flip` T_S in Ms. Pac-Man, the action "left" is mapped to "right" precisely because moving right in a flipped world is dynamically equivalent to moving left in the original world.

Metamorphic Relation R:

Type I (Equivariance). The policy π must be equivariant with the symmetry, such that $\pi(T_S(s)) = T_A(\pi(s))$, where T_A is constrained by the dynamics as shown in the diagram.

Type II (Performance Degradation). Specified directly by the general definitions for performance degradation.

2. Semantic Invariance. This MR posits that a policy should be invariant to state transformations that alter an observation's raw representation but preserve the semantic information crucial for decision-making. Since the underlying strategic situation is unchanged, the optimal action should remain the same.

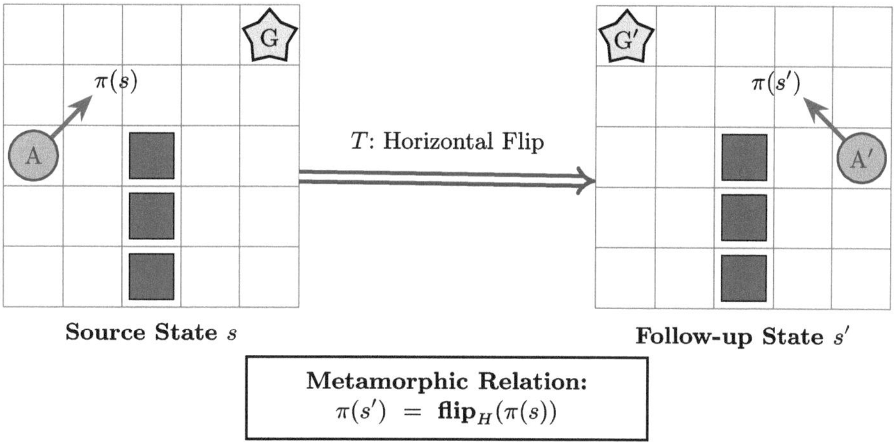

Fig. 2. An illustration of the `Horizontal Flip` MR, which expects the policy to produce a spatially corresponding action for the transformed state.

State Transformation T_S**:** A semantic-preserving transformation on the state space, $s' = T_S(s)$.

Action Transformation T_A**:** The identity function, $T_A(a) = a$, as the optimal action should not change. Unless otherwise specified, we assume that T_A is the identity function.

Example 2. For Ms. Pac-Man, we can apply a `Score Blackout`, which masks the score display area. Since the score is typically not a direct input for the agent's decision-making process, a robust policy should produce the same action regardless of this occlusion. Another example is `Color Inversion`, which changes the game's color palette without altering the identity or function of game entities.

Metamorphic Relation R**:** This relation verifies that the policy's behavior mirrors the environment's symmetry. For this transformation, both Type I and Type II relations, as defined in the general framework, can be specified.

Type I (Invariance) The policy output must remain unchanged: $\pi(s') = \pi(s)$.
Type II (Performance Degradation) Specified by the general definitions.

3. Robustness to Perturbation. This MR evaluates policy stability against simple, parameterized transformations that represent low-complexity changes to the state [9].

State Transformation T_S**:** A parameterized perturbation $T_\delta(s)$, where δ controls the intensity. Examples include global visual adjustments (e.g., `Brightness`), noise injection (e.g., `Noise Injection`), and localized occlusion (e.g., `Random Occlusion`).

Metamorphic Relation R**:** For small perturbations, the optimal action is assumed to be unchanged.

Type I (Invariance). The policy's output should remain invariant, as T_A is the identity function.

Type II (Performance Degradation). Specified by the general definitions, this checks that minor perturbations do not cause catastrophic failure.

3.2 Action Execution Robustness

This class of MRs evaluates resilience to imperfections in action execution by transforming the agent's chosen action before it affects the environment.

Action Execution Failure. This MR posits that a policy's performance should degrade gracefully in the face of intermittent action execution failures.

Action Execution Transformation T_{AE}: This transformation intercepts the policy's intended action a_t and maps it to an actually executed action a'_t.

Example 3. This can be implemented as a probabilistic `Action Drop/Noise`, where the intended action a_t is replaced by a "no-operation" (NOOP) or a random action with a certain probability p. Alternatively, one could implement periodic failures where the action is interrupted every k steps.

Metamorphic Relation R: Metamorphic Relation R: As the transformation is post-decision, only a Type II (performance-based) relation is applicable.

Type II (Performance Degradation). This relation evaluates how gracefully the cumulative reward handles imperfect action execution.

3.3 Temporal Dynamics

This class of MRs focuses on the relationships between policy outputs across consecutive time steps.

1. Action Smoothness and Stability. This MR posits that a well-behaved policy's actions should exhibit smoothness and not oscillate erratically in the absence of abrupt state changes.

Metamorphic Relation R: The source and follow-up states are two consecutive states, s_t and s_{t+1}, from a single trajectory. The relation tests the local consistency of the policy's behavior, assuming the state change is small.

Type I (Temporal Smoothness) If the state change is small ($d_S(s_t, s_{t+1}) \leq \epsilon_s$), the policy's output should also be close. For deterministic policies, $d_A(\pi(s_t), \pi(s_{t+1})) \leq \epsilon_a$; for probabilistic policies, the divergence between output distributions should be bounded.

Type II (Performance Degradation) Not specified, as the goal is to analyze micro-behavioral characteristics.

2. Robustness to Action Repetition. This MR tests if a policy has learned a stable strategy or if its success relies on high frequent micro-corrections.

Metamorphic Relation R: The source trajectory is generated with the policy acting at every step ($k = 1$). The follow-up trajectory is generated with the policy acting only every k steps ($k > 1$), holding the action constant in between.

Type I (Policy Output Consistency). Not applicable, as the test is about the consequence of the altered protocol on performance.

Type II (Performance Degradation). Asserts that robust performance should degrade gracefully as the decision frequency decreases (i.e., as k increases).

3.4 Model Property and Logic MRs

This advanced class of MRs does not necessarily transform the state input, but instead verifies the internal logical consistency of the learned model (i.e., the value function or Q-function).

1. Action Optimality via Empirical Rollout. This MR provides a powerful sanity check by confronting the policy's internal beliefs with empirical evidence. It verifies whether the action deemed optimal by the value function, $a^* = \arg\max_a Q(s, a)$, actually leads to the highest expected return in practice.

Metamorphic Relation R: This relation empirically validates the policy's chosen optimal action by comparing its rollout return against returns from other actions.

- The **source trajectory** τ is generated by first executing the policy's chosen optimal action, a^*, and then following the policy π for a given horizon.
- A set of **follow-up trajectories** $\{\tau'\}$ is generated by first executing a supposedly suboptimal action $a' \neq a^*$, and then following the policy π.

This comparison directly tests the core assumption of a value-based policy.

Type I (Policy Output Consistency). A Type I relation is not applicable here, as the test is fundamentally about the long-term consequences (cumulative reward) of an initial action choice, not about the policy's logical consistency between different states.

Type II (Performance Degradation). This relation asserts that the empirical return from the source trajectory must be greater than or equal to the return from any follow-up trajectory. Let C be the cumulative reward from the source trajectory (starting with a^*) and C' be the reward from a follow-up trajectory (starting with a'). We expect:

$$C \geq C'$$

A violation, where $C < C'$ for some alternative action a', is a critical failure. It demonstrates a state where the agent's belief about action optimality is empirically false, revealing a significant flaw in the learned value function.

2. Domain Knowledge and Causality. This powerful class of MRs leverages expert knowledge or known causal rules to verify if a policy can adapt its behavior when a small state change introduces a critical safety constraint. It moves beyond static checks by creating test cases dynamically from existing states.

Metamorphic Relation R: This relation checks if the policy can adapt to synthetically-created critical scenarios. This relation is defined by applying a carefully constructed transformation to a non-critical source state to generate a critical follow-up state.

- The **source state** s is taken from a standard trajectory. Let the policy's original action be $a = \pi(s)$.
- A **synthetic transformation** T_S is applied to create a **follow-up state** $s' = T_S(s)$. T_S is designed to introduce a specific condition where a known rule applies, and crucially, where the original action a is now considered unsafe or forbidden.

For example, if s is a state representing a clear road, T_S could add an obstacle, making the original action $a =$ "accelerate" forbidden in the new state s'.

Type I (Adaptive Rule Compliance). This relation asserts that the policy must adapt its output in response to the critical change introduced in s'. Let $A_{\text{forbidden}}(s')$ be the set of forbidden actions at state s', which by construction now includes the original action a. The policy must select a different action:

$$\pi(s') \notin A_{\text{forbidden}}(s')$$

A violation indicates the policy has failed to recognize a critical causal change, revealing a significant safety flaw.

Type II (Performance Degradation). A Type II relation is generally not specified for this MR. The primary goal is to verify a critical, often binary, behavioral change (the Type I relation), not to measure a spectrum of performance degradation. A failure in the Type I check is assumed to lead to a catastrophic outcome, making a quantitative performance comparison less meaningful than the logical check itself.

3. Value Function Self-Consistency. Beyond metamorphic testing, we can also perform internal self-consistency checks on the agent's learned components. These are not MRs in our framework but are valuable for debugging. The most fundamental check is for Bellman consistency.

Check Definition: For any batch of transitions (s, a, r, s') from the environment or a replay buffer, compute the one-step Bellman error for the Q-function:

$$\Delta = \left(r + \gamma \max_{a'} Q(s', a')\right) - Q(s, a)$$

Expectation: For a well-converged agent, the average Bellman error $\mathbb{E}[\Delta]$ across a large sample of transitions should be close to zero. A persistently large or biased error may indicate implementation bugs (e.g., in gradient calculations, target network updates), learning instability, or a value function that has failed to capture the environment's dynamics.

4 Experiments and Results

To demonstrate the utility of our proposed taxonomy and to conduct a broad investigation into the robustness of modern DRL agents, we present a large-scale case study. This study applies a comprehensive suite of metamorphic tests to two canonical DRL models within the popular MsPacmanNoFrameskip-v4 environment [1,2].

Our study is guided by two primary research questions:

RQ1: Effectiveness. How effectively does our MR taxonomy identify diverse failure modes in DRL agents that are missed by standard metrics?

RQ2: Actionability. How can the results be translated into an actionable "robustness profile" to compare agents and guide improvements?

4.1 Methodology

Experimental Setup. Our experiments use the Ms. Pac-Man environment from the Arcade Learning Environment (ALE) [1]. We evaluate two widely-used agents, a value-based Deep Q-Network (DQN) and a policy-gradient Proximal Policy Optimization (PPO) agent, using pre-trained models from the Stable-Baselines3 library [18] to ensure we test competent policies. Standard preprocessing is applied: grayscale conversion, 84×84 resizing, and stacking 4 frames (Table 1).

Evaluation Metrics. For each metamorphic test, we compare a source run (original) with a follow-up run (mutated). We use two oracle types:

1. *Reward-based* (_rew): Passes if the reward drop is within a 15% threshold.
2. *Action-based* (_act): A stricter, state-wise oracle that compares the agent's policy between an original state s and its transformed counterpart $s' = T(s)$. It fails if the policies $\pi(\cdot|s)$ and $\pi(\cdot|s')$ deviate in over 15% of states. This method directly tests policy consistency, avoiding trajectory divergence by not generating a follow-up trajectory.

Table 1. Robustness Evaluation of Two Agents Across Metamorphic Tests

Metamorphic Relation	PPO		DQN	
	Pass Rate	Drop/Div.	Pass Rate	Drop/Div.
Reward-Based Evaluation (_rew)				
State Transformation				
Brightness (+30)	100%	-1.36%	0%	-81.67%
Brightness (-30)	0%	-40.82%	0%	-69.49%
Color Inversion	0%	-87.97%	0%	-96.07%
Horizontal Flip	20%	-22.90%	70%	-18.79%
Noise Injection (SD = 20.0)	100%	-3.43%	0%	-54.90%
Noise Injection (SD = 40.0)	30%	-22.36%	Not Tested	
Random Occlusion (20 × 20)	94%	-3.88%	0%	-58.74%
Random Occlusion (40 × 40)	0%	-41.67%	Not Tested	
Score Blackout (10 rows)	100%	-1.29%	74%	-8.02%
Score Blackout (15 rows)	30%	-20.26%	0%	-63.56%
Action Space Robustness				
Action Drop (Prob = 0.1)	60%	-15.00%	82%	-9.00%
Action Drop (Interval = 10)	66%	-23.20%	76%	-10.13%
Action Noise (Prob = 0.1)	24%	-26.44%	52%	-17.37%
Action Noise (Interval = 10)	28%	-26.95%	54%	-15.63%
Temporal Dynamics				
Frame Drop (Prob = 0.5)	100%	-1.10%	36%	-25.05%
Frame Drop (Interval = 2)	100%	-2.26%	46%	-20.64%
Frame Stutter (Prob = 0.5)	78%	-12.36%	4%	-43.49%
Frame Stutter (Interval = 2)	100%	-2.19%	14%	-35.82%
Frame Lag (2 steps)	80%	-9.59%	0%	-45.67%
Action-Based Evaluation (_act)				
State Transformation				
Brightness (+10)	100%	6.85%	0%	57.18%
Brightness (–10)	74%	13.61%	0%	42.65%
Brightness (+30)	0%	20.43%	0%	83.31%
Brightness (-30)	0%	40.01%	0%	70.19%
Horizontal Flip	0%	81.09%	0%	80.96%
Noise Injection (SD = 20.0)	4%	16.98%	0%	71.34%
Noise Injection (SD = 40.0)	0%	32.89%	Not Tested	
Random Occlusion (20 × 20)	8%	17.00%	0%	61.22%
Random Occlusion (40 × 40)	0%	37.46%	Not Tested	
Score Blackout (10 rows)	100%	2.49%	0%	28.76%
Score Blackout (15 rows)	0%	27.86%	0%	59.17%

through data augmentation with flipped states during training. For DQN, the priority would be to improve its generalization to visual perturbations, for which techniques like randomized smoothing or adversarial training could be employed. This demonstrates how the profiles translate diagnostic results into a concrete and actionable roadmap for targeted agent improvement. The framework thus bridges the gap between merely testing for failures and actively enabling the development of more reliable and trustworthy agents.

Future work could extend this taxonomy to more complex domains, such as multi-agent or partially observable environments. Another promising direction is to integrate these metamorphic tests directly into the training loop ("Metamorphic Robustness Training"), using the violation of these relations as a signal to guide the agent towards learning more generalizable and robust policies.

Sensitivity Analysis of Evaluation Oracles. A critical aspect of our framework is the definition of the oracles used to determine a pass or fail. The thresholds chosen (e.g., 15% for reward drop or action divergence) are pragmatic but can be seen as subjective. To investigate the impact of this choice, we conducted a sensitivity analysis for the `Horizontal Flip` MR, which revealed some of the most interesting discrepancies between the agents. We executed 1000 test runs for each agent and varied the reward-based "pass/fail" threshold from 0% to 100%. The results are shown in Fig. 4.

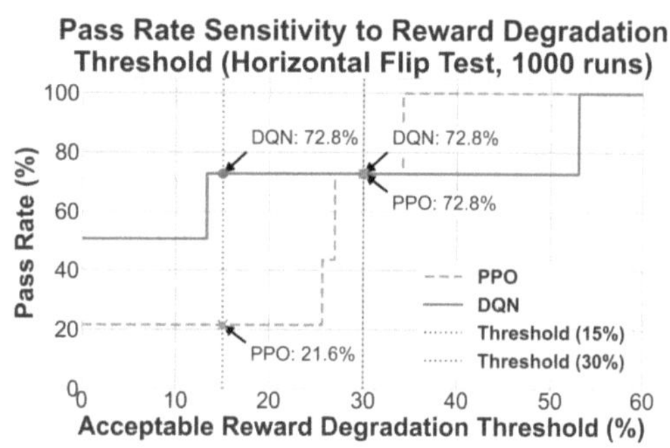

Fig. 4. Sensitivity analysis of the reward-based oracle for the `Horizontal Flip` MR. The plot shows the pass rate versus the performance degradation threshold for PPO and DQN over 1000 runs, highlighting that the interpretation of "robustness" is sensitive to the strictness of the evaluation criteria.

The plot reveals several key insights. With a 15% degradation threshold, DQN's pass rate is already 72.8%, indicating a high level of performance consistency. This suggests that while it may not be perfectly equivariant, its performance degradation is often minor. In stark contrast, PPO's pass rate is only 21.6% at the same threshold. However, its pass rate climbs steeply as the oracle becomes more permissive, matching DQN's 72.8% pass rate at a 30% threshold. This indicates that PPO's policy is more sensitive to minor performance deviations for this transformation, failing the test with small degradations but passing once a higher tolerance is allowed. This analysis demonstrates that the binary "pass/fail" metric, while useful for high-level summaries like the Robustness Profile, can be complemented by a more nuanced view of the **magnitude** of failure. It also validates our choice of a 15% threshold as a reasonable middle ground that is strict enough to detect meaningful deviations while still allowing for minor stochastic variations.

5 Discussion

While our framework provides a significant step towards structured robustness evaluation, our findings also illuminate deeper challenges and trade-offs inherent in developing reliable DRL agents. We discuss these implications and acknowledge limitations that open avenues for future work.

The Performance-Robustness Trade-off and Shortcut Learning. Our work implicitly advocates for satisfying MRs as a path to more robust agents. However, this exposes a fundamental trade-off between robustness and peak performance. Our results suggest that high scores can be achieved by exploiting spurious correlations—a phenomenon widely known as **shortcut learning** [7]. For instance, an agent might learn to associate a specific, non-generalizable background artifact with high rewards. Enforcing an MR, such as `Noise Injection`, would disrupt this shortcut, potentially lowering the score but compelling the agent to learn more generalizable features, like the actual shape of game objects.

This trade-off has profound implications for AI safety: is a seemingly "smarter" but brittle agent preferable to a slightly lower-performing but more predictable and reliable one? Our framework does not eliminate this dilemma but rather makes it explicit and quantifiable. The Robustness Profile allows practitioners to see where a policy's high performance might come at the cost of fragility. Future work could explore this trade-off more deeply, investigating multi-objective optimization techniques that aim to maximize both performance and robustness, allowing developers to select a policy that best fits the specific safety and performance requirements of their application.

From Diagnosis to Remediation. A key long-term goal is to close the loop from testing to development. While our framework provides a clear roadmap for *what* to fix, the question of *how* to fix it remains non-trivial. Techniques like data augmentation (for symmetry) and adversarial training (for perturbations) are promising, but they are not silver bullets. A critical challenge is **catastrophic forgetting** [6]: fine-tuning an agent to improve its robustness against one class of MRs might inadvertently degrade its performance on others. This suggests that a holistic **"Metamorphic Robustness Training"** regime, where a diverse set of MR violations are used as a training signal from the outset, may be more effective than post-hoc repairs. For instance, this could involve a curriculum that progressively hardens transformations, or a dynamic strategy that focuses training on the MRs revealing the most critical failures.

Scope and Generalizability. Our study is necessarily focused, using a specific environment (Ms. Pac-Man) and two agents to establish the framework's principles. While the taxonomy is not exhaustive and oracle thresholds are pragmatic choices, the core methodology provides a strong foundation. Future work should naturally extend this approach to more complex, stochastic environments and a broader spectrum of agent architectures.

6 Conclusion

The evaluation of DRL agents has long been dominated by performance metrics that can obscure critical vulnerabilities. This paper challenges that paradigm by introducing the DRL-MTF, a systematic approach to move beyond aggregate scores and toward a holistic understanding of agent robustness. Our core contribution is the "Robustness Profile," a novel, data-driven artifact that provides a multi-dimensional, actionable visualization of agent strengths and weaknesses.

Our application of this framework to PPO and DQN agents yielded crucial insights. We confirmed that robustness is not a monolithic attribute but a landscape of trade-offs. The agents exhibited starkly divergent profiles: PPO excelled in temporal dynamics but failed at spatial symmetry, whereas DQN showed the opposite pattern. Critically, our dual-oracle approach revealed that apparent performance robustness can mask deep behavioral fragility, underscoring the need for multi-faceted evaluation over dangerously misleading single-score metrics.

Furthermore, we demonstrated that these Robustness Profiles are not merely diagnostic but also prescriptive. They provide an actionable roadmap for targeted improvements, guiding developers toward the most effective strategies for enhancing agent reliability—be it addressing PPO's symmetry flaws through data augmentation or tackling DQN's extreme vulnerability to perturbations.

Ultimately, the shift from a single-score evaluation to a multi-faceted Robustness Profile is more than a methodological refinement; it is a necessary step towards engineering trustworthy autonomous systems. As DRL agents move from simulated games to real-world applications in robotics, finance, and healthcare, the ability to systematically diagnose and understand their failure modes becomes a prerequisite for safe deployment. By providing a practical and extensible foundation for this crucial endeavor, and by charting a path from root cause analysis to automated remediation, this work aims to foster a new standard of rigor in DRL evaluation, paving the way for agents that are not only high-performing but also demonstrably reliable. We argue that for advanced AI, reliability is not a feature, but the foundation.

Acknowledgments. This work was supported by the National Natural Science Foundation of China under Grant No. 92582102, 62572013 and 62172019.

Data and Code Availability. The source code, experimental data, and analysis scripts used in this study are publicly available on GitHub at https://github.com/kevinshao-pku/Metamorphic-Testing-for-DRL.

References

1. Bellemare, M.G., Naddaf, Y., Veness, J., Bowling, M.: The arcade learning environment: an evaluation platform for general agents (extended abstract). In: Proceedings of the 24th International Joint Conference on Artificial Intelligence, IJCAI 2015, pp. 4148–4152 (2015)
2. Brockman, G., et al.: Openai gym. CoRR arxiv:1606.01540 (2016)

3. Chen, T.Y., et al.: Metamorphic testing: a review of challenges and opportunities. ACM Comput. Surv. **51**(1), 4:1–4:27 (2018)
4. Chen, T.Y., Poon, P., Xie, X.: METRIC: metamorphic relation identification based on the category-choice framework. J. Syst. Softw. **116**, 177–190 (2016)
5. Coelho, D., Oliveira, M., Santos, V.: Rlfold: reinforcement learning from online demonstrations in urban autonomous driving. In: 38th AAAI Conference on Artificial Intelligence, AAAI, 36th Conference on Innovative Applications of Artificial Intelligence, IAAI, 14th Symposium on Educational Advances in Artificial Intelligence, EAAI, pp. 11660–11668 (2024)
6. French, R.M.: Catastrophic interference in connectionist networks: can it be predicted, can it be prevented? In: Advances in Neural Information Processing Systems, 7th NIPS Conference, vol. 6, pp. 1176–1177 (1993)
7. Geirhos, R., et al.: Shortcut learning in deep neural networks. Nat. Mach. Intell. **2**(11), 665–673 (2020)
8. Huang, K., Nogueira, R.: EpiRL: a reinforcement learning agent to facilitate epistasis detection. In: Shaban-Nejad, A., Michalowski, M. (eds.) W3PHAI 2019. SCI, vol. 843, pp. 187–191. Springer, Cham (2020). https://doi.org/10.1007/978-3-030-24409-5_19
9. Huang, S.H., Papernot, N., Goodfellow, I.J., Duan, Y., Abbeel, P.: Adversarial attacks on neural network policies. In: 5th International Conference on Learning Representations, ICLR 2017, Workshop Track Proceedings (2017)
10. Humbatova, N., Jahangirova, G., Tonella, P.: Deepcrime: mutation testing of deep learning systems based on real faults. In: ISSTA '21: 30th ACM SIGSOFT International Symposium on Software Testing and Analysis, pp. 67–78 (2021)
11. Kaelbling, L.P.: The foundation of efficient robot learning. Science **369** (2020)
12. Laskin, M., Lee, K., Stooke, A., Pinto, L., Abbeel, P., Srinivas, A.: Reinforcement learning with augmented data. In: Advances in Neural Information Processing Systems 33: Annual Conference on Neural Information Processing Systems 2020, NeurIPS 2020 (2020)
13. Li, J., et al.: Suphx: mastering mahjong with deep reinforcement learning. CoRR arxiv:2003.13590 (2020)
14. Milani, S., et al.: MAVIPER: learning decision tree policies for interpretable multi-agent reinforcement learning. In: Machine Learning and Knowledge Discovery in Databases - European Conference, ECML PKDD 2022, Grenoble, France, 19–23 September 2022, Proceedings, Part IV. Lecture Notes in Computer Science, vol. 13716, pp. 251–266. Springer, Heidelberg (2022). https://doi.org/10.1007/978-3-031-26412-2_16
15. OpenAI, et al.: Learning dexterous in-hand manipulation. CoRR arxiv:1808.00177 (2018)
16. Peng, X.B., Abbeel, P., Levine, S., van de Panne, M.: Deepmimic: example-guided deep reinforcement learning of physics-based character skills. ACM Trans. Graph. **37**(4), 143 (2018)
17. Qiu, K., Zheng, Z., Chen, T.Y., Poon, P.: Theoretical and empirical analyses of the effectiveness of metamorphic relation composition. IEEE Trans. Softw. Eng. **48**(3), 1001–1017 (2022)
18. Raffin, A., Hill, A., Gleave, A., Kanervisto, A., Ernestus, M., Dormann, N.: Stable-baselines3: reliable reinforcement learning implementations. J. Mach. Learn. Res. **22**, 268:1–268:8 (2021)
19. Schrittwieser, J., et al.: Mastering atari, go, chess and shogi by planning with a learned model. Nat. **588**(7839), 604–609 (2020)

20. Silver, D., et al.: Mastering the game of go with deep neural networks and tree search. Nature **529**(7587), 484–489 (2016)
21. Sun, C., Jin, H., Wu, S., Fu, A., Wang, Z., Chan, W.K.: Identifying metamorphic relations: a data mutation directed approach. Softw. Pract. Exp. **54**(3), 394–418 (2024)
22. Tappler, M., Lopez-Miguel, I.D., Tschiatschek, S., Bartocci, E.: Rule-guided reinforcement learning policy evaluation and improvement. CoRR arxiv:2503.09270 (2025)
23. Weyuker, E.J.: On testing non-testable programs. Comput. J. **25**(4), 465–470 (1982)
24. Zhao, Y., et al.: CADRE: a cascade deep reinforcement learning framework for vision-based autonomous urban driving. In: 36th AAAI Conference on Artificial Intelligence, AAAI, 34th Conference on Innovative Applications of Artificial Intelligence, IAAI, The 12th Symposium on Educational Advances in Artificial Intelligence, EAAI, pp. 3481–3489 (2022)
25. Zolfagharian, A., Abdellatif, M., Briand, L.C., Bagherzadeh, M., S., R.: A search-based testing approach for deep reinforcement learning agents. IEEE Trans. Softw. Eng. **49**(7), 3715–3735 (2023)

Generation of Non-matching Strings for Testing Regular Expressions via Complement Automaton Coverage

Minghuang Lin, Weihao Lan, Lixiao Zheng(✉), and Haibo Li

College of Computer Science and Technology, Huaqiao University, Xiamen, China
zhenglx@hqu.edu.cn

Abstract. Regular expressions (regexes) are widely used but error-prone, making effective testing critical. A common testing approach involves generating a set of strings from a given regex and checking whether they are accepted or rejected as intended. However, existing string generation methods focus mainly on matching strings, overlooking non-matching strings that are crucial for detecting *overly restrictive* errors, a type of fault that accounts for a majority of real-world regex bugs. In this paper, we propose a method for systematically generating non-matching strings to test regexes. We adapt graph-based edge-pair coverage to the complement automaton of the regex and perform a depth-first traversal to generate a set of non-matching strings satisfying this criterion. To keep test suites compact, we incorporate a three-level reduction strategy including alphabet-level reduction, path-level reduction, and semantic-level filtering. Experimental results on a dataset containing 1,738 faulty regexes detectable by non-matching strings show that our method achieves 68.53% detection rate, a nearly 1.2× improvement over the nearest competitor. Furthermore, it yields compact test suites with an average of 24 strings per regex, where 90% of the strings have a length ≤ 10.

Keywords: Regular expression · Finite automata · String generation · Coverage criteria · Test reduction

1 Introduction

Regular expressions (regexes) are widely used across computer science for critical tasks such as input sanitization [9], network protocol analysis [28], and text classification [18]. Studies indicate that regexes appear in 30–50% of software projects, with roughly half of developers employing them weekly [11,14]. Despite their usefulness and prevalence, developers often find regexes challenging to work with due to their complex syntax and semantics [8,15,21]. While recent advances in large language models (LLMs) can automatically generate regexes from natural language descriptions, studies show that the generated regexes frequently contain mistakes, often deviating from the intended language specification [23].

G. De Giacomo et al. (Eds.): TASE 2026, LNCS 16697, pp. 36–54, 2027.
https://doi.org/10.1007/978-3-032-30693-7_3

Such incorrect regex semantics can introduce critical vulnerabilities: according to the Common Weakness Enumeration (CWE) taxonomy, regex flaws in input validation can lead to **CWE-20: Improper Input Validation** [1]. If the pattern is too permissive, malicious strings may bypass security checks; if too restrictive, legitimate user input can be blocked. These consequences underscore the persistent need for effective testing techniques to uncover regex defects before deployment.

Existing approaches to testing regexes suffer from several shortcomings. A common practice is to rely on developers to manually supply test strings to check whether a regex behaves as expected [3]. This approach is highly dependent on developer expertise and provides no guarantee of test adequacy. Indeed, regex testing has been comparatively neglected in practice: an empirical study on open-source Java projects show that only 17% regexes have dedicated human-provided test strings. Even when tests exist, they are typically insufficient: about a half use just a single test string, leading to extremely low coverage of regex automaton-level behavior [27].

To reduce dependence on manual effort, several methods generate test strings directly from the regex, enabling users to validate them against expected matching behavior [2,4,7,17,25,29,31]. If a generated positive (matching) string should be rejected, or a generated negative (non-matching) string should be accepted by the intended specification, this indicates a semantic error in the regex. However, existing generation tools focus primarily on producing matching strings. Relying only on matching strings is inadequate for uncovering "too restrictive" errors–cases where the language L defined by the regex under test is a proper subset of the intended language L_I (i.e., $L \subsetneq L_I$). Such errors can only be detected by non-matching strings, because every matching string w belongs to L and thus also to L_I. Empirical studies show that among bugs in real-world open-source projects, about two-thirds are of this type [26]. Therefore, generating effective non-matching strings is crucial for detecting regex faults in real-world scenarios.

Two practical tools capable of generating non-matching test strings for regex are EGRET [17] and MutRex [7]. However, both have limitations. EGRET employs a relatively simple generation strategy: it produces non-matching strings primarily by altering the iteration counts of repetition operators. For complex regexes, it often fails to expose subtle semantic errors, and in some cases, may generate no non-matching strings at all for a given regex. MutRex adopts a mutation testing approach: it construct mutants for the regex and selects strings distinguishing them from the original. However, its effectiveness is inherently constrained by the scope of the predefined mutation operators, which may not capture a comprehensive range of semantic error types. RgxGen [4] also supports non-matching strings but uses random generation, which fails to ensure adequate coverage of key regex structures. In fact, the problem of generating effective non-matching strings is quite challenging: **(1) How to select meaningful, fault-revealing non-matching strings from an often infinite complement language? (2) How to control the size of the generated test suite to keep it manageable for manual inspection?**

To address these issues, we propose a novel method for systematically generating non-matching strings for testing regexes. Our method is guided by three core ideas. First, we generate non-matching strings from the complement automaton of the regex, a natural and complete source of negative test strings. Automata offer a more foundational modeling of regex semantics, enabling systematic exploration of the exact set of strings that a regex rejects rather than relying on random or mutation-based strategies. Second, we apply well-established graph coverage criteria to guide string generation. Specifically, we adopt edge-pair coverage, the strongest among the commonly used criteria, to ensure thorough exploration of the automaton's structure and thereby maximize fault detection capability. Third, we introduce a three-level reduction strategy including alphabet-level reduction, path-level reduction, and semantic-level filtering, to compact the generated test suites while preserving their fault-detecting power.

We evaluate our method on a large benchmark of faulty regexes produced by LLMs when solving real-world regex composition tasks. Experimental results show that our method detects 68.53% of the 1,738 faulty regexes that are theoretically detectable by non-matching strings, significantly outperforming the existing tools EGRET (24.91%), MutRex (58.17%) and RgxGen (5.12%). Furthermore, when our method is combined with these tools, the overall detection rate rises to 84.87%. Beyond its high effectiveness, our method also generates compact test suites that remain practical for manual inspection.

In summary, this paper makes the following contributions:

- **A non-matching string generation method.** We propose a method that systematically generates non-matching strings for regexes by constructing the complement automaton and using edge-pair coverage to guide path exploration. To our knowledge, this is the first approach to leverage graph coverage criteria on the complement automaton for regex test generation.
- **A multi-stage reduction strategy.** We introduce a three-level test reduction strategy: alphabet-level reduction, path-level reduction, and semantic-level filtering, that together produce compact test suites without decreasing fault detection capability. This addresses the practical challenge of test suite explosion inherent in strong coverage criteria and large alphabets.
- **Comprehensive empirical evaluation[1].** We construct a large benchmark of 1,738 faulty regexes derived from real-world tasks and evaluate our approach against state-of-the-art tools. Experimental results show that our method achieves a 68.53% fault detection rate, outperforming the nearest competitor (58.17%) by a factor of nearly 1.2, while generating only 24 strings per regex on average where 90% of the strings have a length ≤ 10, demonstrating both effectiveness and practicality.

The remainder of this paper is organized as follows. Section 2 provides necessary background on regexes, finite automata, and graph coverage criteria.

[1] Source code and datasets are available at https://github.com/lmh1024-dev/CEPRex.

Section 3 details our non-matching string generation method. Section 4 describes experimental evaluation. Section 5 discusses related work, and Sect. 6 concludes the paper.

2 Preliminaries

2.1 Regex and Automaton

Regex: Let Σ be an alphabet (a finite set of characters). A regex is a string formed by combining characters from Σ with regular operators, including concatenation, alternation |", Kleene star∗", and parentheses for grouping. A regex defines a language $L(r)$, i.e., the set of all strings that match the pattern described by r. A string $w \in L(r)$ is called accepted (matching) by r, otherwise called rejected (non-matching) by r. Two regexes r_1 and r_2 are equivalent if and only if $L(r_1) = L(r_2)$. Apart from the above standard regular operators, some applications may allow to use additional operators such as positive closure +, optional ?, character class [] and so on. These operators can be equivalently expressed by standard operators and thus are still regular. Some modern regex engines even support non-regular operators, such as backreferences or lookaround assertions [13]. In this paper we only consider regular operators.

Deterministic Finite Automaton (DFA): A deterministic finite automaton (DFA) is a 5-tuple $A = (Q, \Sigma, \delta, q_0, F)$ where: Q is a finite set of states; Σ is a finite input alphabet; $\delta : Q \times \Sigma \rightarrow Q$ is a transition function; $q_0 \in Q$ is the initial state; $F \subseteq Q$ is the set of accepting (final) states. The language accepted by A, denoted $L(A)$, consists of all strings $w \in \Sigma^*$ such that the path starting from q_0 and following the transitions dictated by w ends in a state belonging to F. For every regex r, there exists an equivalent DFA A with $L(A) = L(r)$. Given a DFA $A = (Q, \Sigma, \delta, q_0, F)$, its complement automaton $A^{\mathbb{C}}$ is obtained by swapping the accepting and non-accepting states: $A^{\mathbb{C}} = (Q, \Sigma, \delta, q_0, Q \setminus F)$. (If A is not complete, it is first made complete by adding a sink state.) $A^{\mathbb{C}}$ accepts the complement of the language accepted by A, i.e., $L(A^{\mathbb{C}}) = \Sigma^* \setminus L(A)$.

Brics Automaton The *Brics*[2] Automaton library is a lightweight and efficient Java utility providing efficient support for regexes and automata operations over the full Unicode alphabet. Brics employs an *interval merging and compression* strategy to handle the full Unicode alphabet: consecutive characters with identical transition behavior are merged into character intervals (e.g., `[a-z]` or `[0-9]`), and a single transition edge represents the entire interval. This compact representation drastically reduces the number of transitions stored per state and enables scalable automaton operations even for large character set regexes. In this paper, we use this library to construct the complement DFA from an input regex and to perform subsequent automaton operations.

[2] https://www.brics.dk/automaton/.

2.2 Coverage Criteria

Graph-Based Coverage Criteria: In software testing, coverage criteria are used to measure the adequacy of a test suite and to guide the generation of test inputs. When the system under test can be modeled as a graph (i.e., a control flow graph or a finite automaton), graph coverage criteria require that certain structural elements of the graph be exercised by the test paths. Three commonly used coverage criteria on graphs are proposed [6], including node coverage (NC), edge coverage (EC), and edge-pair coverage (EPC). Node coverage requires that every reachable node be visited by at least one test path; edge coverage extends this to every edge; edge-pair coverage further requires that every pair of consecutive edges be traversed, making it the strongest among the three.

Coverage Criteria on Automaton When applying graph coverage criteria to a DFA, we treat the automaton as a directed graph where states correspond to nodes and transitions correspond to edges. A *test path* is a sequence of transitions that starts at the initial state and ends at an accepting state, corresponding to a concrete string accepted by the automaton. In this paper, we use edge-pair coverage to guide string generation. For a DFA, an *edge-pair* is a sequence of two consecutive transitions $q_1 \xrightarrow{c_1} q_2$ and $q_2 \xrightarrow{c_2} q_3$, which corresponds to a path of length two in the automaton graph where the two transitions are labeled by c_1 and c_2 respectively. For our complement automaton, satisfying edge-pair coverage means that for every sequence of two consecutive transitions, we generate at least one non-matching string whose test path traverses that exact sequence. This provides a systematic exploration of the automaton's structure, thereby enhancing the fault detection capability of the generated strings.

3 Generation of Non-matching Strings

3.1 Overview

The complete workflow of our approach is illustrated in Fig. 1. It begins with complement automaton construction: the input regex is converted into its canonical minimal DFA, from which the complement automaton is derived. We utilize the library Brics to implement the above operations. Subsequently, EPC guided generation traverses the complement automaton while simultaneously applying three reduction strategies: alphabet-level reduction, path-level reduction, and semantic-level filtering, to produce a compact test suite of non-matching strings for the input regex. The whole process consists of four main steps:

1. **Alphabet-level reduction.** The complement automaton constructed by the Brics library spans the entire Unicode range, introducing numerous irrelevant transitions. We exclude characters that do not appear in the original regex to reduce the transition space while preserving all structural properties needed for the subsequent coverage-guided string generation.

2. **EPC-guided traversal.** On the reduced complement automaton, we perform a depth-first search (DFS) traversal to obtain test paths satisfying the edge-pair coverage criterion, ensuring that every pair of consecutive transitions of the complement automaton is exercised.
3. **Path-level reduction.** The raw set of paths produced by the traversal often contains redundant sequences due to overlapping coverage of edge-pairs. We therefore apply a greedy reduction algorithm that iteratively selects a subset of paths while preserving full edge-pair coverage. This eliminates redundancy and retain only a compact set of representative paths.
4. **Semantic-level filtering.** The remaining paths are concretized into strings. Using a golden matching string as a reference, we filter out strings that exhibit "homogeneous" errors: among those with similar pattern structure, only the one with the smallest edit distance to the golden string is kept. This yields a final test suite that is both compact and effective at detecting faults.

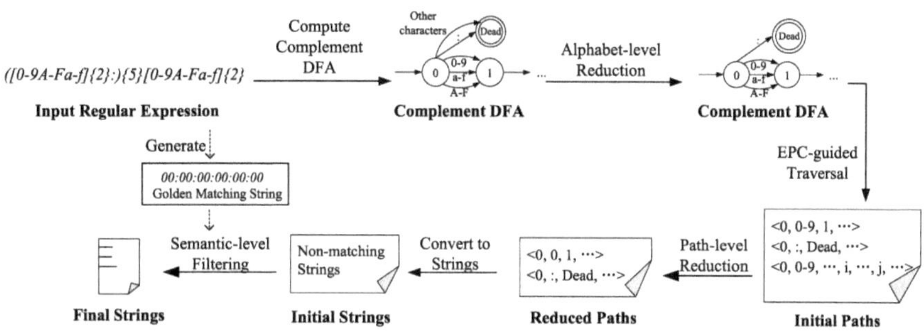

Fig. 1. Generation process of non-matching strings for a given regex.

3.2 Alphabet-Level Reduction

The complement automaton constructed by the Brics library operates over the full Unicode range (from `\u0000` to `\uffff`), introducing a massive number of irrelevant transitions for characters that do not appear in the original regex. This not only expands the solution space but also leads to the generation of numerous semantically meaningless non-matching strings for the regex under test. To eliminate this redundancy, we perform an alphabet-level reduction that restricts the automaton to the set of characters actually used in the regex.

Let Σ_{regex} denote the alphabet of the input regex (i.e., the set of characters that explicitly occur in the regex) supplemented with common intervals such as `a-z` and `A-Z`. For each transition of the complement automaton, we compute the intersection of its original character range R_{old} with Σ_{regex}, denoted as R_{valid}. If $R_{valid} = \emptyset$, this transition is deemed irrelevant and removed. In cases where R_{valid} is a strict subset of R_{old}, the original transition is replaced by a new transition which is labeled with the intervals defined in R_{valid}. This process ensures that the resulting complement automaton operates solely on a meaningful character set derived from the input regex. Take the MAC address regex `([0-9A-Fa-f]2:){5}[0-9A-Fa-f]{2}` as shown in Fig. 1 for example, instead of creating tens of thousands of edges for irrelevant Unicode characters, only transitions labeled with the character ranges `0-9`, `A-F`, `a-f` and the character `:` are retained.

3.3 EPC-Guided Traversal

To systematically generate test paths that satisfy the edge-pair coverage criterion, we first collect the list of all edge-pairs in the complement automaton. This set of edge-pairs serves as the coverage target for the subsequent path generation phase. We then collect a set of paths covering all edge-pairs by performing a modified DFS traversal on the complement automaton. The traversal begins from each edge-pair whose source state is the initial state and uses a traditional backtracking algorithm with certain modifications.

Algorithm 1. EPC-Guided DFS Traversal

```
Input: edge-pairs List, the current edge-pair cur_ep, the current path path, EPC
paths EPCpaths
Output: EPC paths EPCpaths
1: mark cur_ep covered
2: path ← path + cur_ep                //extend the path
3: if cur_ep ends with a final state then
4:     path ← removeCoveredLoops(path)
5:     EPCpaths ← {path} ∪ EPCpaths
6: backtrack ← false
7: next_ep ← detectNextEp(cur_ep) //find next uncovered edge-pair
8: if next_ep not null then
9:     DFS(List, next_ep, path, EPCpaths)
10:    backtrack ← true
11: else          //backtrack
12:    if backtrack = false then
13:        EPCpaths ← {path} ∪ EPCpaths
14:    path ← path − cur_ep
```

Algorithm 1 illustrates the recursive procedure starting from a given edge-pair. The algorithm first marks the current edge-pair as covered and appends it to the current path (lines 1–2). It then checks whether the current edge-pair ends at a final state. If so, it removes any already covered loop transitions from the path to avoid redundancy and adds the processed path to the final test path set *EPCpaths* (lines 4–5). Next, the algorithm attempts to find an uncovered adjacent edge-pair of the current one. If such an edge-pair exists, it recursively traverses from that edge-pair (line 9). If no uncovered adjacent edge-pair is found, the algorithm backtracks and adjusts the path accordingly (line 14). A *backtrack* flag is used to indicate whether the traversal has backtracked from any deeper descendant of the current edge-pair. If the flag remains false, meaning the current edge-pair is the deepest point reached during this traversal, the path is added $EPCpaths$ (line 13).

During the DFS traversal, the exploration may stop at a non-final state when no unvisited edge-pairs can be reached from that point. Since a valid test path must terminate at a final state of the complement automaton (corresponding to a valid non-matching string), we extend such incomplete paths by appending the shortest route from that state to any final state, computed via a breadth-first search (BFS). This ensures that every path in $EPCpaths$ ends at a final state of the complement automaton and represents a valid non-matching string.

3.4 Path-Level Reduction

The set of test paths generated by the DFS traversal and sub-sequent BFS extension (Sect. 3.3) may contain redundancy: multiple paths often cover overlapping edge-pairs, and the extension step can introduce additional paths that do not contribute new coverage. To obtain a compact yet still coverage-adequate test suite, we apply a greedy reduction heuristic that iteratively selects the most cost-effective path, that is, the one that contributes the greatest number of new edge-pairs not yet covered by previously selected paths.

Algorithm 2. Path-Level Reduction

Input: Initial test path set TP, edge-pair list $List$
Output: Reduced test path set $TP_{reduced}$

$TP_{reduced} \leftarrow \emptyset$, $CoveredPairs \leftarrow \emptyset$
while $CoveredPairs \neq List$ **do**
  $p_{best} \leftarrow$ **null**, $maxNewCoverage \leftarrow 0$
  for all path $p \in TP$ **do** //find the *best* path
    $newCoverage \leftarrow |\mathsf{EdgePairs}(p) \setminus CoveredPairs|$
    if $newCoverage > maxNewCoverage$ **then**
      $maxNewCoverage \leftarrow newCoverage$
      $p_{best} \leftarrow p$
  $TP_{reduced} \leftarrow TP_{reduced} \cup \{p_{best}\}$
  $CoveredPairs \leftarrow CoveredPairs \cup \mathsf{EdgePairs}(p_{best})$
  $TP \leftarrow TP \setminus \{p_{best}\}$ //update the candidate path set
return $TP_{reduced}$

Algorithm 2 illustrates the reduction process. Let TS be the set of all candidate paths produced by the previous step. We initialize an empty set $TS_{reduced}$ for the selected paths and a coverage set $CoveredPairs$ to track edge-pairs already covered. While $CoveredPairs$ does not yet contain all edge-pairs of the complement automaton, we examine each remaining path p in TS and compute the number of uncovered edge-pairs it traverses, i.e., $|\mathsf{EdgePairs}(p) \setminus CoveredPairs|$ (line 5). The path with the highest such count is selected, added to $TS_{reduced}$ (line 9), and its edge-pairs are merged into $CoveredPairs$ (line 10). This process repeats until full edge-pair coverage is achieved; any remaining paths are discarded. By construction, the resulting path set is free of redundancy and satisfies the edge-pair coverage criterion with a (typically small) number of paths. This greedy strategy reduces the test suite size while preserving coverage, and it tends to favor paths that contribute diverse edge-pairs early, leading to a compact and informative test set.

3.5 Semantic-Level Filtering

Algorithm 3. Semantic-Level Filtering

Input: Raw test suite T_{raw}, golden sample g_{gold}
Output: Reduced test suite T_{final}

$Reps \leftarrow$ empty map //key of $Reps$: skeleton, value of $Reps$: best string
for all string $str \in T_{\text{raw}}$ **do**
  $skel \leftarrow \mathsf{computeSkeleton}(str)$
  if $skel \notin Reps$ **or** $\mathsf{isBetter}(str, Reps[skel], g_{\text{gold}})$ **then**
    $Reps[skel] \leftarrow str$
$FMap \leftarrow$ empty map //key of $FMap$: first failing position, value of $FMap$: simplest string
$T_{special} \leftarrow \emptyset$
for all string $str \in Reps.values$ **do**
  $idx \leftarrow \mathsf{findFirstDifference}(str, g_{\text{gold}})$
  if $idx = -1$ **then**
    $T_{\text{special}} \leftarrow T_{\text{special}} \cup \{str\}$
  else if $idx \notin FMap.keys$ **or** $\mathsf{isSimpler}(str, FMap[idx])$ **then**
    $FMap[idx] \leftarrow str$
$T_{\text{final}} \leftarrow$ values of $FMap$
if $T_{\text{special}} \neq \emptyset$ **then**
  Sort T_{special} by length in ascending order
  $T_{\text{final}} \leftarrow T_{\text{final}} \cup \{\text{first}(T_{\text{special}}), \text{last}(T_{\text{special}})\}$
return T_{final}

After path-level reduction, the selected paths are concretized into actual string instances: for each transition, if its label is a character range, the first character of that range is used; otherwise, the concrete character itself is taken. We obsearve that although these strings are syntactically distinct, many of them exhibit the same underlying type of error. Consider the regex describing MAC addresses pattern `([0-9A-Fa-f]{2}:){5}[0-9A-Fa-f]{2}` for example, two non-matching strings such as `:A:0:` and `:A:A:` both violate the same core structural rules: they lack the required six groups of two hexadecimal digits, and the colons are misplaced. Presenting all such variants overwhelms users with redundant information and obscures the truly distinct faults. To eliminate this redundancy while preserving diagnostic diversity, we introduce a semantic-level filtering reduction based on two key concepts: *structural skeletons* and a *golden sample.*

- **Structural skeletons.** A structural skeleton abstracts a concrete string by replacing digits with `d`, letters with `w`, and leaving all other symbols unchanged. For instance, `00:00:00` becomes `d:d:d`. This abstraction captures the format of a string while ignoring specific values, enabling the grouping of strings that share the same high-level structure.
- **Golden sample.** The golden sample g_{gold} is a specially constructed string derived from the original regex by *enriching* it to make optional elements mandatory (e.g., converting `{0,}` to `{1,}`, replacing `*` with `+`, and removing `?`). This enrichment ensures that the golden sample embodies the most complete structural form possible. It is obtained by finding the shortest accepting path in the automaton of the enriched regex using the Brics library. For example, the golden sample for `([0-9A-Fa-f]{2}:){5}[0-9A-Fa-f]{2}` is a valid MAC address like `00:00:00:00:00:00`. By using the golden sample as a reference, we can measure how each non-matching string deviates from the matching pattern structure, allowing us to select the most representative example for each distinct error pattern and thus reduce the final test suite.

Algorithm 3 details the filtering process, which proceeds in three phases.

Phase 1: Skeleton-Based Representative Selection (lines 1–5). We iterate over every raw test string, compute its structural skeleton, and maintain a map *Reps* that associates each skeleton with the "best" representative string encountered so far. A string is considered better if it is closer to the golden sample (e.g., shorter edit distance). This step ensures that for each distinct pattern structure, only the most representative candidate is retained.

Phase 2: First Difference Position-Based Filtering (lines 6–13). We further filter the collected representatives by examining the first position where their structural skeletons differ from that of the golden sample. For each candidate string, we compute the first position idx where its skeleton deviates from that of g_{gold} (if the two skeletons are the same, $idx = -1$). A map $FMap$ records, for each distinct first difference position, the simplest string, i.e., the one with the shortest length, that differs at that position. Strings that are structurally identical to g_{gold} are collected into a special set T_{special}.

Phase 3: Final Test Suite Construction (lines 14–17). After processing all candidates, the final reduced test suite T_{final} is constructed as follows: all strings stored in $FMap$ are added because each represents a unique error location. If T_{special} is non-empty, we sort its strings by length and include both the shortest and the longest. The shortest captures the minimal deviation from the golden sample's structure, while the longest may reveal boundary conditions.

This three-phase filtering removes redundant strings that exhibit homogeneous errors, while preserving one concise example for each unique structural error pattern. This further reduces the final test suite size, providing developers with a manageable set of strings that facilitates easier validation.

4 Evaluation

4.1 Research Questions and Baselines

We investigate the following research questions to evaluate our approach:

RQ1 (Fault Detection Ability):
How effective are the non-matching strings generated by our method in detecting faults compared to those produced by existing tools?
RQ2 (Test Suite Compactness): How practical are the test suites generated by our method for real-world usage?
RQ3 (Reduction Strategies): How effective are our proposed reduction strategies in compacting test suites while preserving fault detection capability?
RQ4 (Efficiency): What is the runtime performance of our algorithm, and how does it scale with the complexity of the regexes?

Baselines. We compare our method, denoted as **CEPRex**, against three tools that generate non-matching strings with publicly available source code: EGRET [17], which generates non-matching strings through selective path mutations in a specialized NFA; MutRex [7], which generates non-matching strings via mutations on the regex itself; and RgxGen [4], which relies on random generation.

Metrics. Fault detection ability is measured by the *fault detection rate (FDR)*: the percentage of faulty regexes that are successfully identified. A faulty regex is considered detected if at least one of the generated non-matching strings is accepted by the correct ground truth regex. Test suite compactness is assessed by (i) the number of generated strings and (ii) their lengths. Efficiency is evaluated by measuring total execution time and its correlation with automaton size.

4.2 Dataset

We establish a benchmark grounded in a realistic scenario where LLMs are used to solve real-world regex composition trasks, capturing the specific errors that arise in this process.

Data Source. We leverage three established datasets for real-world regex composition problems:

- (i) RegexEval [23], a benchmark derived from the regex library RegExLib[3], containing 762 manually verified regexes covering real-world scenarios such as email validation, URL parsing, and date formats;
- (ii) StructuredRegex [30], a dataset of structurally complex regexes generated via a probabilistic grammar learned from StackOverflow[4], pairing regexes with crowd-sourced natural language descriptions, and containing 996 items in the test set;
- (iii) Extended Dataset [24], consisting of 189 regexes collected from public forums, representing tasks like password checks and HTML tag matching.

Collectively, these sources provide 1,947 natural language descriptions, each associated with a correct ground truth regex. We use these natural language descriptions as prompts for four LLMs: GPT-4o, DeepSeek-V3, Claude-4, and Qwen-2.5-72B, to generate regexes. Each model produced one regex per task, resulting in a total of 7,788 candidate regexes.

Data Processing. All candidate regexes undergo a multi-stage filtering process. First, we discard any regex that contains syntax errors or unsupported features such as intersection and lookarounds to ensure compatibility with our method and the baseline tools. Second, we compare each candidate against its corresponding ground truth regex using automaton equivalence checking; only those that are semantically different are retained as faulty. Finally, we remove duplicate regexes to avoid bias, leaving 2,269 candidates. We additionally include 662 faulty regexes from the benchmark constructed in [25], which applies a traditional natural-language-to-regex tool to three widely used synthesis datasets. After these steps, the total dataset comprises 2,931 faulty regexes, each paired with its corresponding ground truth regex.

Final Dateset. We further classify the faulty regexes based on their semantic relationship with the ground truth. A faulty regex is considered *overly permissive* if its language is a strict superset of the intended language, i.e., $L(r) \supsetneq L_{\text{truth}}$. Such errors cannot be exposed by non-matching strings, because every string that should be rejected is indeed rejected. Since our work focuses on generation of non-matching test strings, we exclude overly permissive regexes from the evaluation. Among the 2,931 faulty regexes, 1,738 are theoretically detectable by non-matching strings; these form the basis of our experimental analysis. Table 1 summarizes the structural characteristics of these regexes, providing an overview of their complexity and diversity. The reported metrics include length, number of operators, parenthesis nesting depth, as well as the Ehrenfeucht-Zeiger measures [16]: star height and width, which respectively denote the maximum nesting depth of Kleene stars and the maximum branching factor of union operations.

[3] http://regexlib.com/.

[4] https://stackoverflow.com/.

Table 1. Characteristics of 1,738 faulty regexes in experiments

Feature	Faulty Regex				Ground Truth Regex			
	Min	Max	Mean	Median	Min	Max	Mean	Median
Regex length	1	3648	49.76	32	2	733	60.97	38
Operator Number	0	737	12.74	8	0	204	17.27	10
Nesting depth	0	6	1.08	1	0	9	1.58	1
Height	0	3	1.05	1	0	3	1.09	1
Width	1	715	3.21	1	1	59	3.02	2

4.3 Results and Analysis

RQ1: Fault Detection Ability. Table 2 presents the fault detection rate of our method CEPRex and the baseline tools. For a fair comparison, the random baseline RgxGen generated a test set of equal size to ours. The results show that CEPRex achieves the highest performance, detecting 1,191 faults with a detection rate of 68.53%, significantly outperforming MutRex (58.17%), EGRET (24.91%), and RgxGen (5.12%). The lower part of Table 2 further shows the combined detection capability when CEPRex is used alongside other tools: Combining CEPRex with MutRex improves its FDR by 25.26%, while combining with EGRET yields an improvement of 51.04% over EGRET alone. When the three are combined together, the overall detection rate rises to 84.87%, a 21.92% increase over the EGRET+MutRex combination. Interestingly, merging all three tools yields an FDR nearly equivalent to that of CEPRex+MutRex, indicating the poor efficacy of EGRET in this context.

Table 3 illustrates a concrete example of a faulty regex generated by an LLM for a real-world task. Among the non-matching strings produced by our CEPRex, two strings (highlighted in red) are actually accepted by the ground truth regex, thereby exposing that the faulty regex incorrectly rejects valid inputs. In contrast, none of the non-matching strings generated by the baseline tools (EGRET, MutRex, or RgxGen) detected this fault.

Table 2. Fault detection rate (1,738 faulty regexes in total)

Tool	Detected	FDR
CEPRex	**1191**	**68.53%**
MutRex	1011	58.17%
EGRET	433	24.91%
RgxGen	89	5.12%
CEPRex+MutRex	1450	83.43% (↑25.26%)
CEPRex+EGRET	1320	75.95% (↑51.04%)
CEPRex+MutRex+EGRET	1475	84.87% (↑21.92%)

Table 3. Example fault detected by CEPRex while missed by all baselines

<table>
<tr><th>Category</th><th>Content</th></tr>
<tr><td>Description</td><td>The pattern consists of five parts. The first and third parts are either ‘70’ or ‘604’. The second and fourth parts are semi-colons. The last part consists of capital, lowercase, or ‘1’.</td></tr>
<tr><td>Ground truth</td><td>(70|604);(70|604);([A-Z]|([a-z]|1)){1,}</td></tr>
<tr><td>Incorrect regex</td><td>(70|604);(70|604);[a-zA-Z1]*1</td></tr>
<tr><td>CEPRex</td><td>A;, 70A;, 70;70A1, 70;7011, 70;70;AA, 70;70;1AA, ...</td></tr>
<tr><td>EGRET</td><td>70;70;ev4il1, 70;70;61 , 70;70;_1, 70;70;ev_il1 , ...</td></tr>
<tr><td>MutRex</td><td>70;70;[1 , 70;70;)1 , 70;701 , ;70;170;1 , 70;A;1 , ...</td></tr>
<tr><td>RgxGen</td><td>3,AYV992\$[, \~^BGc)*+"3 , 6CI83_Q>4! , ...</td></tr>
</table>

RQ2: Test Suite Compactness. We compare the distribution of test suite size (number of strings) and string length for CEPRex, EGRET, and MutRex, as summarized in Table 4 and visualized in Fig. 2. CEPRex generates an average of 24 strings per regex. We acknowledge that for certain complex regexes, the massive scale of states and transitions in their complement automata results in a higher number of strings even after reduction. Nevertheless, the overall scale remains highly manageable: over 90% of the test suites contain fewer than 54 strings. EGRET produces the fewest strings but also achieves the lowest fault detection rate (24.91%), indicating insufficient test adequacy. In terms of string length, CEPRex and MutRex generate strings of comparable length: the average is $\sim$ 6 characters, with 99% $\leq$ 21, while EGRET tends to produce longer strings. These results demonstrate that CEPRex yields compact yet effective test suites, achieving a balance between size and high fault detection capability.

Table 4. Number and length of generated non-matching strings per regex

Tool	Number						Length					
	Mean	25%	50%	75%	90%	99%	Mean	25%	50%	75%	90%	99%
CEPRex	24	3	9	23	54	268	6	3	5	7	10	21
MutRex	16	7	13	22	30	75	6	2	4	8	11	19
EGRET	5	1	4	8	13	31	7	2	7	11	15	35

RQ3: Reduction Strategies. We evaluate the effectiveness of our three-stage reduction process (alphabet-level, path-level, and semantic-level) by measuring test suite size and fault detection rate at each stage, as summarized in Table 5.

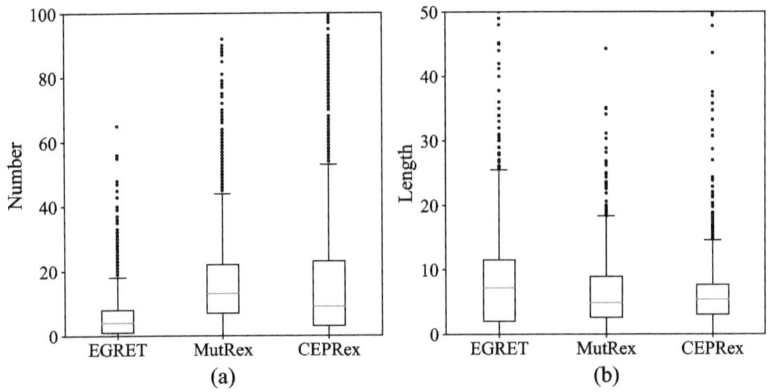

Fig. 2. Number and length of generated non-matching strings per regex.

Before any reduction, the average test suite contains 181 strings with an average length of 7 characters. After applying all three stages, the average suite size drops to 24 strings and average length to 6 characters, achieving a substantial compaction. Among the stages, semantic-level filtering contributes the most, reducing the suite dramatically 94 strings (after path-level reduction) to approximately 24 strings. Importantly, this dramatic reduction in size comes at a minimal cost to fault detection: the detection rate decreases only slightly, from 71.52% before reduction to 68.53% after the full process. These results demonstrate that our multi-stage reduction strategy effectively compacts test suites while preserving most of the fault-detection capability.

Table 5. Test suite size and fault detection rate across reduction stages

Reduction	Number						Length						FDR
	Mean	25%	50%	75%	90%	99%	Mean	25%	50%	75%	90%	99%	
0. Initial	181	34	90	199	468	1381	7	3	5	8	11	48	71.52%
1. Alphabet-Level	142	21	70	152	352	1115	7	3	5	8	10	22	70.83%
2. Path-Level	94	11	40	96	222	870	7	3	5	8	10	22	69.91%
3. Semantic-Level	24	3	9	23	54	268	6	3	5	7	10	21	68.53%

RQ4: Running Time. We evaluate the runtime performance of our implementation by measuring the total time required to generate a complete test suite for each regex[5]. The running for each regex was repeated ten times and the average time is reported. For RgxGen, we measure the time to generate the same number

[5] Experiments were conducted on a machine with an Intel(R) Core(TM) i5-13400 CPU@2.50 GHz, 32 GB of RAM, and a 64-bit Windows operating system.

of strings as produced by our method for each regex. Figure 3 presents a comparison of runtime performance, with regexes sorted by the number of transitions in their complement automaton. CEPRex generally runs faster than MutRex but slower than EGRET and RgxGen. This is expected, as EGRET and RgxGen benefit from their simple automaton traversal and purely random generation strategy, respectively. MutRex incurs high overhead due to expensive mutation analysis involving multiple mutant constructions and comparisons. The runtime of CEPRex scales with the size of the DFA, and its execution time increases accordingly for very large automata. Nevertheless, CEPRex's time cost remains highly practical: the average execution time is 0.7 s per regex, with most cases finishing within 10 s.

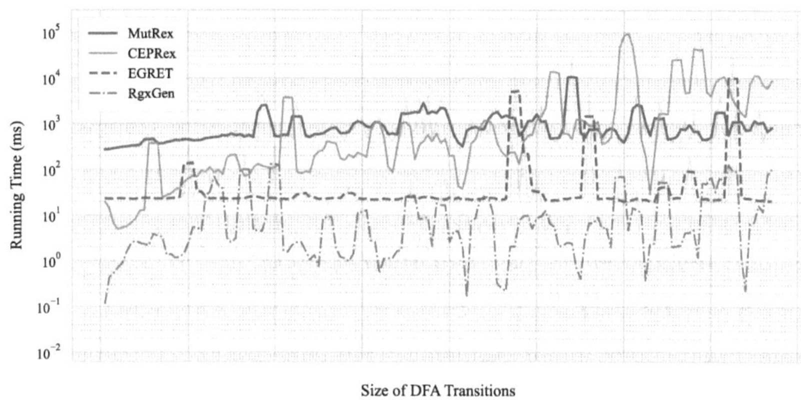

Fig. 3. Running time comparison.

5 Related Work

Automatic generation of strings for regexes is a fundamental issue in formal language theory. Two problems concerning this issue have been studied: generating a uniformly random string of a regular language [10,22] and listing all distinct strings of a regular language or all strings of a given length in some predefined order [5,20]. Some existing string generation tools for regexes, such as Exrex [2], adopt this random or enumeration strategy. For example, Exrex produces all matching strings for a given regex; when the language is infinite, it allows users to restrict the number of repetitions of the Kleene star operator or limit the number of generated strings. However, random generation and enumeration face challenges for practical testing purposes. Random generation lacks coverage guarantees and often misses subtle edge cases, while exhaustive enumeration tends to produce impractically large test suites. Empirical studies report unsatisfactory fault detection rates and/or impractically large test sets for these techniques [7,17,31].

The method proposed in [31] generates test strings based on a pairwise coverage criterion defined directly for regexes, which requires covering all possible combinations of any two concatenated sub-expressions within a regex. The generation proceeds by traversing the regex's abstract syntax tree. Similarly, the approach in [29] also adopts syntax tree traversal and supports extended regex features like lookaround assertions and greedy/lazy matching precedence, yet it lacks explicit coverage criteria to guide the generation process. String constraint solvers based on SMT (Satisfiability Modulo Theories) techniques are also capable of generating strings for regexes [12,19]. These are primarily designed for program verification and symbolic execution to prove satisfiability, rather than for systematically validating the correctness of regex semantics.

The above mentioned methods focus mainly on generating matching strings. EGRET [17] and MutRex [7] are two known tools that support both matching and non-matching strings. EGRET constructs strings from basis paths of an acyclic NFA and produces non-matching strings by adjusting repetition counts. In contrast, our approach generates non-matching strings directly from the complement DFA under a rigorous coverage criterion. MutRex uses mutation testing and extracts strings from the symmetric difference of the mutant and the original regex. It relies on a predefined set of mutation operators, limiting the effectiveness against faults that fall outside modeled error patterns. Our automaton-based approach systematically covers the entire complement language, enabling detection of a broader range of semantic errors. RgxGen [4] also supports non-matching strings but relies on random generation. Our method complements these tools by offering a coverage-guided solution, and can be combined with them to enhance overall regex testing effectiveness.

6 Conclusion

We have presented a novel method for systematically generating non-matching strings to test regexes. Our approach constructs the complement automaton of a given regex and uses graph based edge-pair coverage to guide path exploration, ensuring thorough structural coverage of the complement language. To address the test suite explosion challenge, we introduce a three-level test reduction strategy to reduce test suites while preserving fault detection capability. Experimental evaluation on a large benchmark of faulty regexes demonstrates that our method outperforms existing tools in fault detection effectiveness, while generating test suites compact for practical manual inspection.

Future work includes extending our approach to handle a wider range of regex features such as backreferences and lookarounds, and integrating the testing tool into LLM-based synthesis frameworks to improve the accuracy of LLM-generated regexes. We also plan to explore fault localization techniques that use the generated strings to locate semantic errors in regexes.

Acknowledgments. This work was supported in part by Fundamental Research Funds for the Central Universities (Grant No. ZQN-1010), Natural Science Foundation of Fujian Province (Grant No. 2023J01137) and Xiamen Science and Technology Project (Grant No. 3502Z20251018).

References

1. CWE-20: Improper input validation. https://cwe.mitre.org/data/definitions/20.html
2. EXREX. https://github.com/asciimoo/exrex
3. Regex101. https://regex101.com/
4. RgxGen. https://github.com/curious-odd-man/rgxgen
5. Ackerman, M., Shallit, J.: Efficient enumeration of words in regular languages. Theoret. Comput. Sci. **410**(37), 3461–3470 (2009)
6. Ammann, P., Offutt, J.: Introduction to Software Testing. Cambridge University Press, Cambridge (2017)
7. Arcaini, P., Gargantini, A., Riccobene, E.: Fault-based test generation for regular expressions by mutation. Softw. Test. Verificat. Reliabil. **29**(1–2), e1664 (2019)
8. Bai, G.R., Clee, B., Shrestha, N., Chapman, C., Wright, C., Stolee, K.T.: Exploring tools and strategies used during regular expression composition tasks. In: Proceedings of the 27th International Conference on Program Comprehension (ICPC), pp. 197–208. IEEE (2019)
9. Barlas, E., Du, X., Davis, J.C.: Exploiting input sanitization for regex denial of service. In: Proceedings of the 44th International Conference on Software Engineering, pp. 883–895 (2022)
10. Bernardi, O., Giménez, O.: A linear algorithm for the random sampling from regular languages. Algorithmica **62**, 130–145 (2012)
11. Chapman, C., Stolee, K.T.: Exploring regular expression usage and context in python. In: Proceedings of the 25th International Symposium on Software Testing and Analysis, pp. 282–293 (2016)
12. Chen, T., et al.: Solving string constraints with regex-dependent functions through transducers with priorities and variables. Proc. ACM Program. Lang. (POPL) **6**, 1–31 (2022)
13. Chida, N., Terauchi, T.: On lookaheads in regular expressions with backreferences. IEICE Trans. Inf. Syst. **106**(5), 959–975 (2023)
14. Davis, J.C., Coghlan, C.A., Servant, F., Lee, D.: The impact of regular expression denial of service (ReDoS) in practice: an empirical study at the ecosystem scale. In: Proceedings of the 26th ACM Joint Meeting on European Software Engineering Conference and Symposium on the Foundations of Software Engineering, pp. 246–256 (2018)
15. Eghbali, A., Pradel, M.: No strings attached: an empirical study of string-related software bugs. In: 35th IEEE/ACM International Conference on Automated Software Engineering (ASE), pp. 956–967. IEEE (2020)
16. Ehrenfeucht, A., Zeiger, H.P.: Complexity measures for regular expressions. In: Proceedings of the 6th Annual ACM Symposium on Theory of Computing, pp. 75–79. ACM (1974)
17. Larson, E., Kirk, A.: Generating evil test strings for regular expressions. In: Proceedings of the IEEE International Conference on Software Testing, Verification and Validation (ICST), pp. 309–319. IEEE (2016)

18. Liu, J., Bai, R., Lu, Z., Ge, P., Aickelin, U., Liu, D.: Data-driven regular expressions evolution for medical text classification using genetic programming. In: Proceedings of the IEEE Congress on Evolutionary Computation, pp. 1–8. IEEE (2020)
19. Loring, B., Mitchell, D., Kinder, J.: Sound regular expression semantics for dynamic symbolic execution of javascript. In: Proceedings of the 40th ACM SIGPLAN Conference on Programming Language Design and Implementation, pp. 425–438 (2019)
20. Mäkinen, E.: On lexicographic enumeration of regular and context-free languages. Acta Cybernet. **13**(1), 55–61 (1997)
21. Michael, L.G., Donohue, J., Davis, J.C., Lee, D., Servant, F.: Regexes are hard: decision-making, difficulties, and risks in programming regular expressions. In: Proceedings of the 34th International Conference on Automated Software Engineering (ASE), pp. 415–426. IEEE (2019)
22. Oudinet, J., Denise, A., Gaudel, M.C.: A new dichotomic algorithm for the uniform random generation of words in regular languages. Theoret. Comput. Sci. **502**, 165–176 (2013)
23. Siddiq, M.L., Zhang, J., Roney, L., Santos, J.C.: Re (gEx| DoS) eval: evaluating generated regular expressions and their proneness to DoS attacks. In: Proceedings of the 44th International Conference on Software Engineering: New Ideas and Emerging Results, pp. 52–56 (2024)
24. Tang, Z., Yan, Y., Li, R., Dong, H., Chen, H., Gao, H.: Enhancing multi-modal regular expression synthesis via large language models and semantic manipulations of sub-expressions. In: Dependable Software Engineering. Theories, Tools, and Applications, pp. 122–141. Springer, Singapore (2025). https://doi.org/10.1007/978-981-96-0602-3_7
25. Van Hoan, N., Hung, P.N.: Arext: Automatic regular expression testing tool based on generating strings with full coverage. In: Proceedings of the 13th International Conference on Knowledge and Systems Engineering (KSE), pp. 1–6 (2021)
26. Wang, P., Brown, C., Jennings, J.A., Stolee, K.T.: Demystifying regular expression bugs. Empir. Softw. Eng. **27**(1), 1–35 (2022)
27. Wang, P., Stolee, K.T.: How well are regular expressions tested in the wild? In: Proceedings of the 2018 26th ACM Joint Meeting on European Software Engineering Conference and Symposium on the Foundations of Software Engineering, pp. 668–678 (2018)
28. Wondracek, G., Comparetti, P.M., Krügel, C., Kirda, E.: Automatic network protocol analysis. In: Proceedings of the Network and Distributed System Security Symposium, NDSS. The Internet Society (2008)
29. Yan, Y., et al.: Deducing matching strings for real-world regular expressions. In: Dependable Software Engineering. Theories, Tools, and Applications, pp. 331–350. Springer, Heidelberg (2024). https://doi.org/10.1007/978-981-99-8664-4_19
30. Ye, X., Chen, Q., Dillig, I., Durrett, G.: Benchmarking multimodal regex synthesis with complex structures. In: Proceedings of the 58th Annual Meeting of the Association for Computational Linguistics, pp. 6081–6094 (2020)
31. Zheng, L., Ma, S., Wang, Y., Lin, G.: String generation for testing regular expressions. Comput. J. **63**(1), 41–65 (2020)

Clight2Rust: Translating a Subset of C into Safe Rust with a Small Trusted Runtime

Dongwen Yao, Jinhua Wu, and Yuting Wang(✉)

John Hopcroft Center for Computer Science, School of Computer Science, Shanghai Jiao Tong University, Shanghai 200240, China
yuting.wang@sjtu.edu.cn

Abstract. Memory safety vulnerabilities in C programs remain a critical challenge in systems software. While rewriting legacy code in Rust offers a promising solution, manual migration is error-prone and labor-intensive. Existing automated translation tools either generate `unsafe` Rust or rely on heavy-weight static analysis that struggles with C's flexible pointer arithmetic. We present a lightweight and automated approach to translating C to safe Rust by exploiting dynamic ownership and borrow checking provided by a small trusted runtime built with Rust's smart-pointer primitives. Our method dynamically tracks ownership and borrow boundaries by using a novel pointer structure `Ptr<T>`, enabling the translation of complex C pointer operations—including aliasing and pointer arithmetic—into safe Rust code while confining unavoidable `unsafe` operations (raw pointer dereference/casts and C FFI) to the trusted runtime. We implement our approach for the Clight subset of C, as defined in the CompCert verified compiler. Evaluation on a suite of benchmarks demonstrates that the main test cases in CompCert's test suite are successfully translated. Their functional correctness is validated by comparing with the reference C compilers such as Clang and GCC.

1 Introduction

The systems programming landscape is currently witnessing a paradigm shift from C to Rust. For decades, C has been the lingua franca of operating systems and embedded software due to its performance and low-level control. However, this power comes at a steep cost: memory safety vulnerabilities. Industry reports highlight that approximately 70% of all security vulnerabilities in major software projects—including Microsoft Windows [12] and Google Chrome—are derived from memory safety issues such as buffer overflows and use-after-free errors. Consequently, major organizations like the NSA [13] and the Linux kernel community are actively pushing for the adoption of memory-safe languages.

Rust has emerged as the most viable successor to C. Its unique ownership and borrowing model enforces memory safety at compile-time without the runtime overhead of garbage collection [8]. While writing new components in Rust is

G. De Giacomo et al. (Eds.): TASE 2026, LNCS 16697, pp. 55–72, 2027.
https://doi.org/10.1007/978-3-032-30693-7_4

becoming standard practice [19], the vast ecosystem of legacy C code presents a formidable barrier. Manually rewriting millions of lines of mission-critical C code is not only prohibitively expensive but also risky, as human translation is prone to introducing new logic errors or subtle semantic deviations.

1.1 Challenge for C-to-Rust Translation: the Semantic Gap

Automated source-to-source translation offers a promising solution. However, it faces a fundamental challenge: the mismatch between C's permissive memory model and Rust's strict safety guarantees. On one hand, in C Semantics, pointers are unchecked iterators. They can be freely casted between different types, offsetted arbitrarily, and aliased mutably (i.e., different pointers `*p` and `*q` can mutate the same memory). On the other hand, in Rust Semantics, safe Rust enforces the "aliasing XOR mutability" discipline. At any given point, data can have either multiple immutable references (`&T`) or exactly one mutable reference (`&mut T`), but not both. Bridging this gap requires not just syntactic translation, but a semantic reconstruction of the program's memory behavior.

1.2 Limitations of the State-of-the-Art

Existing translation tools generally fall into the following categories. They either fail to generate safe Rust code, rely on heavy-weight analysis that is not only expensive but also restricts the scope of C programs they can support, or have difficulties to guarantee the soundness of translation because of usage of AI.

1. **Syntactic Transpilers:** Tools like C2Rust [7] prioritize functional equivalence by mapping C pointers to Rust raw pointers (`*mut T`) wrapped in `unsafe` blocks. While this preserves behavior, it fails to deliver the safety benefits that motivate the migration. The resulting code is essentially "C syntax in Rust" and remains vulnerable to memory corruption. Recent works attempt to augment these baseline tools by wrapping their unsafe outputs in neuro-symbolic refinement loops [14], but the underlying reliance on an unsafe fallback remains a structural bottleneck.
2. **Formalized Translators:** Recent works attempt to generate safe Rust based on formal methods [3,5]. However, they often rely on static analysis that rejects valid C programs with complex aliasing (e.g., spaghetti pointers) or restricts to subsets of C (e.g., no re-entrant pointer logic). Moreover, such analysis is usually heavy-weight and can be undesirable in compilation.
3. **LLM-Driven Translators:** The research community has seen a rapid shift toward using Large Language Models (LLMs) to generate more idiomatic Rust. For function-level translation, systems like SACTOR [24], SafeTrans [4], and LAC2R [17] employ static analysis feedback and iterative prompting to refine code. To tackle complex project-level dependencies and global pointer semantics, recent frameworks introduce skeleton-guided parsing like EvoC2Rust [20], knowledge graph integration [23], and dependency-aware workflows like RustMap [2]. Other researchers have proposed combining LLMs

with predefined rule constraints [11], symbolic testing [1], or continuous compilation feedback loops [16] to mitigate semantic hallucinations. While LLMs generate more idiomatic Rust, they face challenges in high-assurance contexts. They often rely on testing to ensure "soft equivalence", therefore lacks a more formal guarantee of correctness. They also frequently require human debugging to resolve semantic mismatches, making fully automated translation elusive.

1.3 Our Approach and Contributions

We propose **Clight2Rust**, a C-to-Rust translation framework that provides a high assurance of translation correctness by leveraging the infrastructure of the formally verified CompCert compiler [9] and that is also lightweight in that it does not depend on complex static analysis.[1]

Our core contribution is a translation strategy that resolves the conflict between C-style pointer arithmetic and the Rust borrow checker. We introduce a smart pointer abstraction, `Ptr<T>`, combined with an improved *Split Tree* algorithm (built on [5]). Unlike prior approaches that purely rely on static splitting, our algorithm adopts a hybrid approach: it uses Split Trees to statically isolate disjoint memory regions where possible, and falls back to dynamic borrow checking (via `RefCell`) to support complex, re-entrant aliasing patterns found in real-world C code.

We implement our approach by utilizing the CompCert compiler, i.e., we use *Clight*—a deterministic subset of C with formal semantics in CompCert—as an intermediate language for our translation and implemented the core translation pass in the Rocq theorem prover [18]. Our specific contributions are:

- **A Safe Pointer Abstraction:** We design the `Ptr<T>` model to encapsulate C-style pointer arithmetic underneath reference counting cells in Rust. This abstraction allows `load`, `store`, and `offset` operations to be translated into calls to a safe runtime API in Rust, maintaining a one-to-one mapping with C behavior while respecting Rust's ownership rules.
- **Improved Split Tree Algorithm:** We propose an enhancement to the Split Tree algorithm to handle the safe conversion of pointers. Our implementation effectively resolves "borrowing hell" issues by intelligently managing disjoint memory slices and leveraging interior mutability.
- **Implementation and Evaluation:** We implemented the complete translation in CompCert (see the directory `clight2rustlight`). We successfully translated all of the test cases in CompCert's test suite. Our evaluation shows that the generated Rust code passes the Rust compiler (`rustc`) checks and produces execution results identical to a reference C compiler (Clang/GCC).

The rest of this paper is organized as follows. Section 2 provides background information and comparison with related work. Section 3 discusses our key ideas. Section 4 gives an overview of our translation system. Section 5 presents our

[1] Our framework is available at https://doi.org/10.5281/zenodo.19815920.

experimental results. Section 6 discusses the limitations of our approach and our plan to lift them. In particular, although our translation is based on CompCert, it does not yet come with a full semantics preservation proof. Section 7 concludes.

2 Background and Related Work

2.1 CompCert and Clight

CompCert [9] is a formally verified compiler that provides a machine-checked proof of semantic preservation from C to Assembly. To facilitate verification, CompCert defines several intermediate representations. Of particular relevance to this work is *Clight*, a deterministic subset of C. Clight simplifies C syntax by separating expressions from statements and explicating side effects, yet it retains the full expressiveness required for systems programming.

In CompCert, a pointer is represented as a pair (b, δ), where b is a block identifier and δ is an integer offset within that block. This explicitly handles pointer provenance, distinguishing different memory regions even if they are adjacent in physical memory. However, Clight permits unrestricted aliasing and arbitrary pointer arithmetic. These features directly conflict with Rust's strict borrowing rules. By targeting Clight rather than raw C Abstract Syntax Trees (ASTs), our translation exploits a precise, disambiguous semantic structure.

2.2 Rustlight

To formally define the translation in Rocq, and to bridge the gap between Clight's memory model and Rust's strict safety guarantees, we make use of *Rustlight* [22]. Rustlight is a formalized intermediate representation for safe Rust that models the core tenets of the Rust type system, including ownership, borrowing, and lifetimes, similar to prior formalizations like RustBelt [8] and Oxide [21]. In our pipeline, Rustlight serves as the target of the translation before being printed into Rust, allowing us to ground our translation rules in a rigorous framework which may enable its formal verification in the future.

2.3 Comparison of Syntax

```
Inductive expr : Type :=
    | Econst_int: int -> type -> expr
    | Econst_float: float -> type -> expr
    | Econst_single: float32 -> type -> expr
    | Econst_long: int64 -> type -> expr
    | Evar: ident -> type -> expr
    | Etempvar: ident -> type -> expr
    | Ederef: expr -> type -> expr
    | Eaddrof: expr -> type -> expr
    | Eunop: unary_op -> expr -> type -> expr
    | Ebinop: bin_op -> expr -> expr -> type -> expr
    | Ecast: expr -> type -> expr
    | Efield: expr -> ident -> type -> expr
    | Esizeof: type -> type -> expr
    | Ealignof: type -> type -> expr
.
```

Listing 1.1. Clight Expressions

```
Inductive pexpr : Type :=
    | Econst_int: int -> type -> pexpr
    | Econst_float: float -> type -> pexpr
    | Econst_single: float32 -> type -> pexpr
    | Econst_long: int64 -> type -> pexpr
    | Eplace: place -> type -> pexpr
    | Eref: origin -> mutkind -> place -> type -> pexpr
    | Ebinop: bin_op -> pexpr -> pexpr -> type -> pexpr
    | Ederef: pexpr -> type -> pexpr
with place : Type :=
    | Plocal : ident -> type -> place
    | Pfield : place -> ident -> type -> place
    | Pderef : place -> type -> place
    | Pdowncast: place -> ident -> type -> place
    | Pparenthesize: ident -> type -> pexpr -> place
    | ParrayIndex : place -> ident -> type -> place.
```

Listing 1.2. Rustlight Expressions

To understand the correspondence in translation, we compare the abstract syntax of expressions in Clight (Listing 1.1) and Rustlight (Listing 1.2). A key difference is that Clight allows arbitrary pointer arithmetic by taking addresses (by `Eaddrof`) and offsetting pointers (by applying `Ebinop` to a pointer and an integer), while Rustlight only allows pointer arithmetic expressed as `places` which are essentially l-values represented as accessing paths. That is, Rustlight explicitly models ownership-related constructs for enforcing borrow checking.

2.4 Related Work

We elaborate on the related work and compare them with our approach. Research on C-to-Rust translation started with *Syntactic Transpilation to Unsafe Rust.* Early tools like Corrode [15] and Citrus [6] attempt to map C constructs to Rust, but development has largely stalled. The current industrial standard is C2Rust [7], which parses C ASTs (via Clang) and emits functionally equivalent Rust code. C2Rust prioritizes compilability and behavior preservation but almost exclusively generates unsafe Rust. It preserves raw pointers (`*mut T`) and manual memory management (`malloc` and `free`). While robust for migrating build systems, the resulting code retains memory safety vulnerabilities of the original C program.

Subsequent research focus on *Post-Translation Refactoring and Lifting.* Recognizing that C2Rust produces unidiomatic and unsafe code, several works focus on automated refactoring to lift this output into safe Rust. Emre et al. conducted a comprehensive study on the sources of unsafety in C2Rust-generated code and proposed techniques to rewrite specific patterns of raw pointers into safe references [3]. Similarly, Laertes [3] and CRustS [10] apply static analysis to promote raw pointers to references. However, these approaches are fundamentally "cleanup" operations; they struggle to reconstruct high-level safe abstractions when the underlying C pointer arithmetic is complex or when the initial transpilation has already erased semantic intents.

The most recent and promising approaches adopt translation based on formal methods. The methodology most aligned with our goals involves formally modeling the translation from C semantics to safe Rust constructs. Fromherz and Protzenko recently proposed a type-directed translation from a subset of C to Safe Rust, formalized in Rocq [5]. A key contribution of their work is the *Split Trees* (or "cell set") analysis. This technique allows the compiler to statically track disjoint slices of memory arrays, enabling the generation of Rust code that uses `split_at_mut` to dynamically partition slices. This effectively maps C's pointer arithmetic to Rust's safe slice operations.

Our Distinction: while our work builds upon the foundational concept of Split Trees [5], we address critical limitations regarding its expressiveness. Previous formal approaches often restrict to subsets of C due to purely static splitting strategies and could easily reject many valid C programs. To solve this issue, we propose a generalized pointer abstraction (`Ptr<T>`) that combines Split Trees with dynamic runtime checks (using `RefCell`). Implemented inside CompCert, our approach leverages Clight's precise semantic information to handle complex control flows and re-entrant pointer logic that purely static approaches reject.

3 Key Ideas

The fundamental challenge for translating C to safe Rust lies in bridging the semantics of C pointers and Rust's strict ownership disciplines. Using the representation of pointers in Clight, a C pointer (b, δ) serves dual purposes: it represents a *owning handler* b (managing memory life cycle) and an *iterator* for traversing memory via arithmetic on δ. Rust separates these concerns into ownership (e.g., `Box`), borrowing (`&`) of places, and slicing (`&[T]`). A naive translation that maps C pointers directly to Rust's standard constructs (e.g., `Box<[T]>` or `&mut [T]`) fails because it cannot simultaneously satisfy three C behaviors: unrestricted aliasing, pointer arithmetic independent of allocation bounds, and dynamic lifetimes. Our key idea is to bridge the semantic gap between C and Rust by establishing a mapping from C pointers to a pointer structure in Rust based on reference counting and interior mutability called `Ptr<T>`, as illustrated in Fig. 1. This design ensures that the abstract pointer provenance (b) and logical offset (δ) are explicitly tracked and guarded by Rust's runtime safety mechanisms.

Below, we first discuss the design of `Ptr<T>`, then present our hybrid technique for translation of C into safe Rust, and finally discuss the critical cases of our translation process.

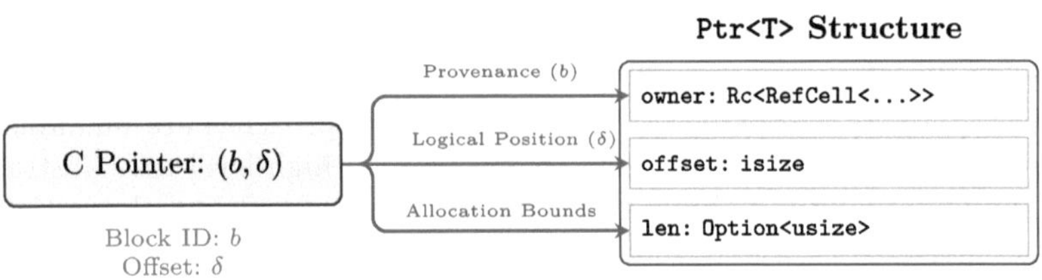

Fig. 1. Mapping from C Pointers to the Unified `Ptr<T>` Abstraction.

3.1 A Unified Pointer Abstraction

We present `Ptr<T>`—the polymorphic Rust structure for representing a pointer to an l-value of type `T`. Its key feature is that it decouples the *view* of memory from the *ownership* of memory. With this, it enables a direct and safe translation of C pointers to Rust by encoding ownership, offset, and bounds information. Formally, this structure is composed of three fields:

- `owner`: `PtrOwner<T>`. This field encodes the backing storage of the pointer: either `Heap(Rc<RefCell<Box<[T]>>>)` for heap-allocated arrays, `Borrowed{base, len, borrow_flag}` for borrowed views (e.g., stack arrays, read-only globals, or FFI-provided buffers), or `Null`.

- `offset: isize`. It encodes the offset to a pointer, indicating that the pointer value is `p + offset` where `p` is the base address of the owned memory.
- `len: Option<usize>`. This is the (dynamic) upper bound of offsets. It is initially derived from `malloc` and may change according to Split Tree analysis.

By definition, `Ptr<T>` encapsulates C pointers under Rust constructs. It also provides the following methods that emulate C pointer semantics safely:

- **Memory Allocation** (`alloc` and `null`). `Ptr::alloc(i)` allocates an array containing `i` elements of type `T` and returns a `Ptr<T>` pointer. This is a safe version of `malloc`. Also, `Ptr::null()` creates and returns a null pointer.
- **Aliasing via cloning** (`clone`). `clone()` returns an aliasing `Ptr<T>` by calling `Rc::clone` internally. Safety of accessing such aliased pointers is enforced at runtime by reference counting in `Rc` and interior mutability in `Refcell`.
- **Pointer Arithmetic** (`offset`). In C, $p + i$ produces a new pointer without affecting the original. The `offset` method mimics this by returning a new `Ptr` instance. Crucially, `offset(i)` updates the `offset` field (by adding `i` to it) without modifying the `owner`. That is, pointer arithmetic is safe by definition, as no memory access occurs at this stage.
- **Memory Access** (`load` and `store`). Dereferencing is where safety is enforced. A single read `load(i)` or write operation `store(i, v)` has the following steps:
  1. **Null Check:** It unwraps the `owner` and panics on `None`. As a result, accessing to null pointers results in a defined behavior (panic).
  2. **Borrow Check:** It enforces Rust's "multiple readers or only one writer" rule dynamically: heap-backed pointers use `RefCell` borrowing, while borrowed pointers use an internal shared borrow flag. If a conflict occurs (e.g., a re-entrant modification), the program panics instead of causing undefined behavior.
  3. **Bound Check:** It verifies that $p + i$ is within the valid range $[0, len)$.
  4. **Access:** Finally, read or write happens on the underlying data. This step uses a small amount of `unsafe` internally in the runtime to dereference raw pointers. It is only reachable after the checks above have been passed.

As we can see, the `Ptr<T>` abstraction effectively acts as a runtime layer that dynamically simulates C pointer semantics within safe Rust. By leveraging `Rc` for liveness and `RefCell` for aliasing, we shift the verification burden from compile-time (which is often impossible for legacy C) to runtime, guaranteeing memory safety without rejecting valid C patterns.

3.2 A Hybrid Approach to C-to-Rust Translation

Our approach to C-to-Rust translation combines static analysis of Split Trees and dynamic ownership enforcement provided by Rust. We discuss its necessity through an example that cannot be handled alone by static analysis in traditional approaches (including Split Trees), and then discuss how we solve this problem by exploiting dynamic ownership provided by `Ptr<T>`.

```
void demonstrate_split_tree(int *arr, int dynamic_offset) {
    // Aliasing analyzable statically
    int *p1 = arr + 0;
    int *p2 = arr + 5;
    *p1 = 10;
    *p2 = 20;

    // Aliasing not statically analyzable due to dynamic offset
    int *p3 = p1 + dynamic_offset;
    *p3 = *p1 + *p2; }
```

Listing 1.3. A C Function with a Dynamic Pointer Offset

Consider the C function in Listing 1.3 which exhibits a common scenario involving pointer arithmetic on both static and dynamic offsets. To translate it into safe Rust, we need to make sure that the write operations through pointers (`*p1 = 10`, `*p2 = 20`, `*p3 = *p1 + *p2`) do not violate Rust's requirement on uniqueness of mutable references. Here, the offsets for `p1` and `p2` are constants. To convert such pointers, a static analyzer could detect the constant offsets and divide a continuous memory into disjoint memory slices. That is, tools based on pure static analysis (e.g., Split Trees [5]) would generate slices by calling a method like `p.split_at_mut(i)`, which is responsible for divide a continuous memory into half at index `i` (i.e., into `p[0..i-1]` and `p[i..]`) and transferring the ownership of divided memory to separate variables. This is shown in Listing 1.4. As a result, `p1` and `p2` now point to disjoint memory and mutation on disjoint memory is allowed by safe Rust's ownership disciplines.

```
fn demonstrate_split_tree_static(arr: *mut i32, dynamic_offset: i32) {
    let (p1_l, p1_r) = arr.split_at_mut(0);
    let (p2_l, p2_r) = p1_r.split_at_mut(5);
    let (p1, p2) = (p2_l, p2_r);
    p1[0] = 10;
    p2[0] = 20;

    // Split tree algorithm cannot tell if the dynamic offset
    // is < 5 or >= 5. Therefore, it cannot decide whether
    // p1 or p2 should be split and how much the offset is.
    let (p3_l, p3_r) = ??.split_at_mut(??); ... }
```

Listing 1.4. Failure to Generate Safe Rust Code by the Split Trees Algorithm

However, this approach cannot be applied to p3 to guarantee the safety of subsequent write operation `*p3 = *p1 + *p2`. Notice that since we do not know the exact value of `dynamic_offset`, we do not know whether `p3` falls into the range of memory owned by `p1` or `p2`. Therefore, we do not know which object or offset `split_at_mut` should be applied to. A purely static approach would simply reject this valid C program at this point and fail to produce any output.

Our framework solves this problem by detecting the boundaries of applicability of static reasoning and selectively falls back to runtime ownership enforced by `Ptr<T>`. For example, if there is no `p3` in Listing 1.3, our algorithm makes use of Split Trees as before. Otherwise, it delegates the aliasing resolution to our `Ptr<T>` abstraction and generates safe Rust code shown in Listing 1.5.

Here, dereferences in C are replaced with safe `load` and `store` operations. Aliasing of pointers is implemented by `clone` operations. If `dynamic_offset`

```
fn demonstrate_split_tree(mut arr: Ptr<i32>, mut dynamic_offset: i32) {
    let mut p1: Ptr<i32> = Ptr::null();
    let mut p2: Ptr<i32> = Ptr::null();
    let mut p3: Ptr<i32> = Ptr::null();

    p1 = arr.clone().offset(0 as isize);
    p2 = arr.clone().offset(5 as isize);
    p1.store(0, 10 as i32);
    p2.store(0, 20 as i32);

    // Fallback to dynamic tracking
    p3 = p1.clone().offset(dynamic_offset as isize);
    p3.store(0, (p1.clone().load(0) as i32 + p2.clone().load(0) as i32)); }
```

Listing 1.5. Corresponding Safe Rust Code Generated by Our Framework

results in p3 overlapping with p1 or p2 during execution, the underlying `RefCell` mechanism will dynamically enforce Rust's borrowing rules to prevent undefined behaviors. This hybrid strategy ensures that even the most unpredictable C idioms can be compiled into safe Rust. Moreover, the translation is straightforward and does not rely on any sophisticated static analysis.

3.3 Critical Cases of Our Translation

Below we discuss the critical cases of our translation algorithm. To motivate their design, we compare it with the existing approaches.

Scenario 1: Mutable Aliasing. C permits multiple pointers to alias the same mutable memory. For example, we have the following C code:

```
int *p = malloc(2 * sizeof(int));
int *q = p; // 'q' is an alias of 'p'
q[0] = 1;   // Modification via 'q'
return p[0]; // Read via 'p', expects 1
```

A direct translation produces code rejected by the Rust compiler because of non-unique mutable aliasing. A naive fix to this problem may not preserve the original semantics. For example, the following code forces a deep copy of `Box` to satisfy the type system, breaking the shared memory semantics.

```
let mut p: Option<Box<[i32]{>}{>} = Some(vec![0; 2].into_boxed_slice());
// ERROR: Box does not support shared ownership.
// Cloning creates a DISTINCT memory block.
let mut q = p.clone();
q.as_mut().unwrap()[0] = 1; // Modifies only q's copy.
return p.as_ref().unwrap()[0]; // Returns 0 (original p is unchanged).
```

Our approach fixes this problem by using `Rc`, i.e., cloning `Ptr` only increments the reference count. Both p and q point to the same `RefCell`.

```
let mut p: Ptr<i32> = Ptr::alloc(2);
let mut q = p.clone();  // Shallow copy. Sharing the same RefCell.
q.store(0, 1);          // Modifies the shared memory.
return p.load(0);       // Correctly returns 1.
```

Scenario 2: Pointer Arithmetic and Memory Ownership. A common C idiom is to use `malloc` to allocate heap memory which should be freed later. Pointers to this heap are used for iteration by pointer arithmetic. For example,

```
int *p = malloc(2 * sizeof(int));
p = p + 1; // p now points to the 2nd element
*p = 42;    // Writes to alloc[1]
... // the original memory should be freed (if we have tracked it)
```

A naive translation using `Box` to manage the ownership allocated memory is problematic. We cannot simply "increment" the box pointer. Using slices (`p[1..]`) as in the Split Tree algorithm destroys the original ownership information, making correct deallocation problematic (equivalent to `free(p+1)` in C, which is Undefined Behavior).

To solve this problem, we have separated the offset (in the `offset` of `Ptr<T>`) from the ownership information (in the `owner` field). As a result, a direct translation is possible as follows where the allocated memory is automatically freed by reference counting when its only pointer `p` goes out of scope.

```
let mut p: Ptr<i32> = Ptr::alloc(2);
p = p.offset(1); // Returns new Ptr { owner: ..., offset: 1 }
p.store(0, 42);  // Internally accesses owner[1 + 0]
// 'p' goes out of scope, Rc's reference counts drops to 0 and Box is freed
```

Scenario 3: Lifetime Extension. In C, pointers can outlive the scope where they were defined if the memory was allocated on the heap. For example,

```
int *p = NULL;
if (cond) {
  p = malloc(10 * sizeof(int)); // Allocation happens in an inner scope
}
if (p != NULL) { p[0] = 7; } // Accessed in another scope
```

A direct translation would try to lift a temporary allocation to an outer scope, violating Rust's borrowing checking and resulting in a compilation error.

```
let mut p: Option<&mut [i32]> = None;
if cond {
    let mut tmp = vec![0; 10].into_boxed_slice();
    // ERROR E0597: 'tmp' is dropped here while still borrowed.
    p = Some(&mut tmp); }
```

With our approach, `Ptr::alloc` creates an `Rc` structure on the heap. Assigning it to `p` (defined in the outer scope) extends the lifetime of the heap data naturally via reference counting.

```
let mut p: Ptr<i32> = Ptr::null();
if cond {
    p = Ptr::alloc(10); // Ownership shared by 'p', lifetime extended
}
if !p.is_null() { p.store(0, 7); } // Valid access
```

Decay and Casting of Arrays. To integrate arrays into our framework, we need to encapsulate their accesses beneath public traits using a minimum amount of unsafe code. As a result, unsafe code will only occur in what we called the "runtime library" (see Sect. 4.2) and will never occur in the generated program logic. For example, in C, arrays implicitly decay to pointers. To emulate this in Rust, where arrays `[T; N]` and pointers are distinct, we introduce the `ArrayPtrCastExt` trait.

```
pub trait ArrayPtrCastExt { fn cast<U>(&self) -> Ptr<U>; }
impl<T, const N: usize> ArrayPtrCastExt for [T; N] {
    fn cast<U>(&self) -> Ptr<U> {
        // Creates a Ptr view from a raw pointer to the stack array.
        Ptr::from_raw_parts(self.as_ptr() as *mut U, N) }}}
```

This allows generated code to seamlessly treat stack arrays as `Ptr` objects, enabling calls like `arr.cast::<i32>().offset(2)`.

Safe Initialization. Safe Rust requires all variables to be initialized before use. Clight allows uninitialized declarations. We bridge this gap using a recursive initialization strategy `array_default`, which internally constructs a zero-initialized array and exposes it safely, satisfying Rust's initialization analysis.

4 Overview of the Framework

Our framework *Clight2Rust* (as shown in Fig. 2) intercepts the compilation pipeline of the CompCert compiler [9] at the *Clight* intermediate representation and redirects the target to *Rustlight* [22]. The core of the system is the translation pass defined in the Rocq file `Clight2Rustlight.v`, which implements a formal transformation that realizes the key ideas in Sect. 3. After that, Rustlight programs are printed into Rust source code and compiled together with our runtime library to generate executable code.

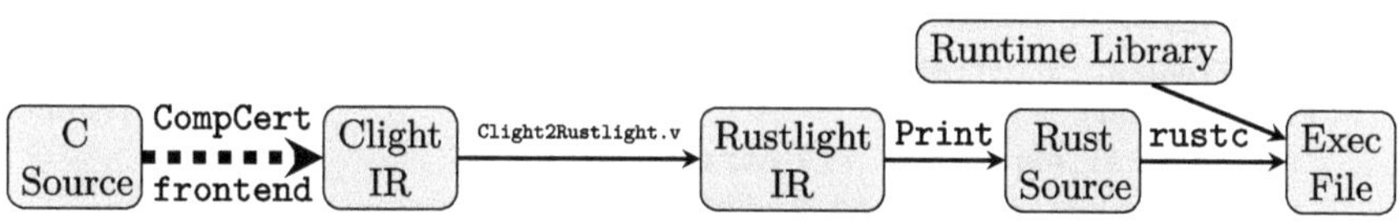

Fig. 2. End-to-end Translation Pipeline of Clight2Rust.

4.1 Translation Architecture

The translation in `Clight2Rustlight.v` is structured as a *bottom-up recursive* function, processing the Clight Abstract Syntax Tree (AST) from the leaves (expressions) to the root (the entire program). This process is implemented with a monadic context (using the `res` error monad in Rocq) to handle potential translation failures and propagate the compilation environment (e.g., type definitions and global symbols). The transformation proceeds in four phases, as follows.

Phase 1: Expressions and Pointers Transformation (`transl_expr`). This is the most critical phase, which materializes the ideas for turning Clight expressions into the `Ptr<T>` API calls formulated in Sect. 3. Clight distinguishes between *l-values* (locations) and *r-values* (values), allowing implicit conversions (decay). In contrast, Rustlight requires explicit method calls for memory accesses. The function `transl_expr` recursively traverses Clight expressions as shown in Algorithm 1. The complex pointer operations are handled as follows:

- **Recursive Composition:** For a nested expression like `**p` (double dereference), the translator first recursively calls `transl_expr(p)` to resolve the inner pointer, producing a Rustlight expression representing a `Ptr<T>`. It then generates a `load` operation on this result to get the inner address, and finally generates another `load` for the outer dereference.
- **Explicit Memory Access:** The translation explicitly distinguishes between pointer arithmetic and memory access.
  - `Ebinop(Oadd, p, i)` is translated to `p.offset(i)`. This merely calculates a new view (updating the offset field) without touching memory.
  - `Ederef(p)` is translated into `p.load(0)`. This forces a runtime borrow check and performs memory read.
  - `Efield(p, id)` (struct access) is translated into `(p.load(0)).id`, effectively loading the struct instance before accessing its field.

Algorithm 1. Core Recursive Translation Steps in `transl_expr`

Require: A Clight expression e
Ensure: A translated Rustlight expression or an error
Function `transl_expr`(e):
match e **with**
 | `Econst_int`(n, _): **return** `OK(Rconst_i32` n`)`;
 | `Etempvar`(id, _): **return** `OK(Rvar` id`)`;
 | `Ebinop(Oadd,` e_1, e_2, _): ▷ Pointer Arithmetic
  $r_1 \leftarrow$ `transl_expr`(e_1); $r_2 \leftarrow$ `transl_expr`(e_2);
  return `OK(Rcall (Rmethod` r_1 `"offset")` [r_2]);
 | `Ederef`(e_1, _): ▷ Dereference
  $r_1 \leftarrow$ `transl_expr`(e_1); **return** `OK(Rcall (Rmethod` r_1 `"load")` [0]);
 | `Efield`(e_1, id, _): ▷ Field Access
  $r_1 \leftarrow$ `transl_expr`(e_1); *struct_val* $\leftarrow$ `Rcall (Rmethod` r_1 `"load")` [0];
  return `OK(Rfield` *struct_val*, id);
 | _: ...
end match

Phase 2: Statement Mapping (`transl_statement`). This phase handles control flow and side effects after translating expressions.

- **Assignments:** An assignment *p = v in C involves evaluating the left-hand side to a location and the right-hand side to a value. Our translator converts this into a method call: p.store(0, v). This ensures all memory writes go through the dynamic safety checks provided by the Ptr<T> abstraction.
- **Control-Flow Normalization:** C loops (e.g., Sloop, Swhile in Clight) are normalized into Rust's infinite loop structure combined with match statements to handle break and continue conditions, bridging the semantic gap between C's structured jumps and Rust's expression-based control flow.

Phase 3: Function Processing (transl_function). The function-level translation creates a local environment and iterates over the function's parameters and local variable declarations.

- **Stack Allocation:** Local arrays and structs in C are identified. The translator generates corresponding Rust initialization code (using array_default) to ensure that all stack variables are initialized before use, satisfying Rust's definite initialization requirement.
- **Signature Matching:** The function signature is transformed, mapping C types to Rustlight types (e.g., int → i32, char* → Ptr<i8>).

Phase 4: Whole-Program Processing (trans_program). Finally, the function trans_program aggregates all translated functions and global variables. A specific detail in our implementation (as in Clight2Rustlight.v) is the explicit injection of external definitions for malloc and free. Since these are built-in primitives in C, our pass checks for their existence and injects the corresponding External function definitions into the Rustlight AST. This ensures that the generated code links correctly against our runtime library.

4.2 Printing and Runtime

To produce Rust source code from Rustlight, we design an OCaml pretty printer (PrintRustlight.ml) to traverse the Rustlight AST and print Rust code, which handles syntactic sugar, module imports, indentation, etc. Moreover, we design a runtime library to provide the concrete implementation of Ptr<T>, malloc, and free, serving as the trusted execution environment for our translation.

5 Evaluation

In this section, we evaluate Clight2Rust to answer the following questions:

- **RQ1 (Compatibility & Correctness):** Can our tool translate diverse C programs into valid safe Rust code, and do they produce correct outputs?
- **RQ2 (Performance):** What is the runtime overhead introduced by our Ptr<T> abstraction and safety checks compared to native C?

5.1 Experimental Setup

Environment. All experiments were conducted on an Apple MacBook Air equipped with an **Apple M4** chip and **16 GB** of RAM, running **macOS 15.2 (Build 25C56)**. The software toolchain includes:

- **C Compiler:** Apple clang version 17.0.0 (targeting `arm64-apple-darwin`).
- **Rust Compiler:** `rustc` version 1.93.0-nightly (2025-10-25).
- **Rocq:** Version 8.12.0.
- **Optimization:** Both C and Rust are compiled with level 2 optimizations (`-O2` for GCC/Clang, `-O` for Rustc) to ensure a fair performance comparison.

Benchmarks. We evaluated our tool on the standard CompCert test suite (`test/c`), which contains 24 benchmarks ranging from computational kernels (e.g., `fft`, `aes`) to data structure manipulations (e.g., `binarytrees`, `lists`).

5.2 Correctness and Compatibility (RQ1)

We consider a translation successful if the generated Rust code compiles without errors and produces output identical to the C reference implementation compiled using a reference C compiler (e.g., Clang/GCC) on representative inputs. As shown in Table 1, our tool successfully translated and executed *all* benchmarks, achieving a success rate of *100%*. Since CompCert's test suite is designed to cover all the C features that CompCert's C subset could support. This demonstrates that our `Ptr<T>` abstraction is capable of handling at least CompCert's subset of C, which includes a wide variety of C constructs, such as pointer arithmetic, recursive structures, and callbacks.

5.3 Performance (RQ2)

Table 1 details the execution time. In this table, the mean overhead for the benchmarks is *1.70x*. We analyze the performance overhead as follows:

- **Comparable Performance** (< 1.0x): surprisingly, benchmarks like `binarytrees`, `bisect` and `mandelbrot` ran faster in Rust (approximately 0.9x). This suggests that for logic dominated by simple arithmetic or recursion, the Rust compiler (LLVM) may perform more aggressive optimizations (e.g., tail-call optimization or inlining) than the reference Clang build, or that our slice-based access allows for better vectorization in specific loops.
- **Moderate Overhead** (1.2x - 2.0x): Most computation-intensive benchmarks (e.g., `aes`, `fft`) fall in this range. The overhead comes from the extra instructions required for `Ptr` offset calculations and the dynamic bounds checks embedded in slice accesses.

Table 1. Translation Results and Performance Comparison

Benchmark	Category	Success	C Time (s)	Rust Time (s)	Overhead
`binarytrees`	Allocation	OK	0.8918	0.6009	0.67×
`bisect`	Control Flow	OK	0.5666	0.5223	0.92×
`mandelbrot`	Fractal	OK	0.4439	0.4334	0.98×
`fib`	Recursion	OK	0.3919	0.3917	1.00×
`integr`	Math	OK	0.3846	0.4016	1.04×
`perlin`	FP Arith	OK	0.4036	0.4744	1.18×
`sha1`	Crypto	OK	0.4447	0.5582	1.26×
`qsort`	Callbacks	OK	0.5000	0.6405	1.28×
`nsieve`	Array Sieve	OK	0.4693	0.6517	1.39×
`aes`	Crypto	OK	0.6035	0.8726	1.45×
`fft`	DSP	OK	0.4805	0.6954	1.45×
`almabench`	Logic	OK	0.4101	0.6054	1.48×
`nsievebits`	Bits	OK	0.5516	0.8283	1.50×
`vmach`	Virtual Mach.	OK	0.4532	0.7730	1.71×
`fftsp`	DSP (Float)	OK	0.4021	0.7527	1.87×
`fftw`	DSP	OK	0.4312	0.8103	1.88×
`siphash24`	Hashing	OK	0.4556	0.8583	1.88×
`spectral`	Math	OK	0.4403	0.8828	2.00×
`knucleotide`	String	OK	0.4560	1.0316	2.26×
`sha3`	Bitwise	OK	0.3838	0.9529	2.48×
`chomp`	Game	OK	0.4822	1.2488	2.59×
`nbody`	Physics	OK	0.4560	1.1994	2.63×
`lists`	Pointers	OK	0.4265	1.1248	2.64×
`fannkuch`	Permutation	OK	0.5414	1.8178	3.36×

– **High Overhead** (> 2.5x): The observed performance degradation (approximately 3x) in benchmarks like `lists`, `chomp`, and `fannkuch` stems from the overhead of safety-encapsulated pointer operations. In C, memory access is a direct pointer dereference. In our translated Rust code, each access through the `Ptr<T>` abstraction results in heavy runtime cost. We conjecture the costs come from (1) Dynamic Borrowing: the use of `Rc<RefCell<Box<[T]>>>` requires pattern matching, index calculation, and `RefCell`'s dynamic borrow counting for every load and store operation, incurring a significant cost in hot loops; (2) Inefficient Field Updates: the current translation for structure fields employs a "load-modify-store" pattern, which triggers unnecessary cloning of the entire structure rather than in-place modification.

5.4 Scope and Interpretation of Our Results

Our benchmarks are drawn from the CompCert test suite, which is designed to exercise the features of its formally verified C subset (Clight). Therefore, the evaluation validates that our translation is correct for this specific, well-behaved subset. It does not constitute a claim of full coverage for arbitrary, GNU-extended C code. Our approach maintains a clear boundary: programs must be expressible in Clight, supported by our translation rules, and compatible with the model of pointers in our runtime library.

5.5 Summary

The evaluation shows that Clight2Rust produces safe Rust code (except for the runtime library) that is functionally correct for standard benchmarks. While the strict enforcement of memory safety introduces an average overhead of 1.70x, this is a reasonable trade-off for memory safety, especially considering that explicit `unsafe` is confined to the small trusted runtime and FFI boundaries.

6 Discussions and Limitations

While our approach successfully bridges significant semantic gaps for a well-defined subset of C, it involves trade-offs in terms of the depth of static guarantees, performance and generality. A key design decision is the introduction of the `Ptr<T>` abstraction. Although this enables direct translation of pointer operations into safe Rust code, the resulting code is not idiomatic Rust. Another drawback is the runtime overhead introduced by reference counting mechanism and runtime borrow checking, as discussed in our evaluation. Our translation pipeline inherits CompCert, which supports all of the MISRA-C 2004 subset of C, plus many features excluded by MISRA (such as recursive functions and dynamic heap memory allocation). Several imperative statements are currently not directly supported and are either rewritten (e.g., `switch` is lowered to `if-else` chains) or explicitly rejected. Those include `goto` statements, taking the address of a unary operation, and some complex l-value casts.

The correctness of our end-to-end pipeline depends on several assumptions. First, we assume that external C standard library functions (e.g., `malloc`, `printf`) behave according to their specifications. Second, the correctness of `unsafe` code within our runtime library (e.g., `runtime/ptr.rs` and `runtime/stdio.rs`) is trusted for safety. For example, `cast` operations between different types (via `ArrayPtrCastExt`) assume compatible memory layouts. A formally verified implementation of these components (using tools like RustBelt [8]) would reduce this trusted computing base.

7 Conclusion

We have presented Clight2Rust, a lightweight framework for translating a subset of C programs into mostly safe Rust by leveraging the precise semantics of CompCert's Clight language and utilizing reference counting and interior mutability in Rust. As a result, we are able to translate a wide range of C programs into safe Rust without relying on complex static analysis, which was not possible before. We have implemented a translation pipeline integrated into CompCert that handles practical challenges like initialization, variadic functions, and FFI callbacks. In the future, we plan to design an even more hybrid approach by integrating aggressive static analysis, in order to turn dynamic borrow checking into static checking, thereby eliminating runtime panics and reducing runtime overhead. We also would like to establish a fully formalized semantic preservation proof from Clight to Rustlight, thereby creating a verified C-to-Rust translator.

Acknowledgments. This work was supported by the National Natural Science Foundation of China (NSFC) under Grant No. W2421088, 62372290, and 62002217.

References

1. Bai, Y., Palit, T.: Rustassure: Differential symbolic testing for llm-transpiled c-to-rust code (2025). https://arxiv.org/abs/2510.07604
2. Cai, X., et al.: Rustmap: towards project-scale c-to-rust migration via program analysis and LLM (2025). https://arxiv.org/abs/2503.17741
3. Emre, M., Schroeder, R., Dewey, K., Hardekopf, B.: Translating c to safer rust. Proc. ACM Program. Lang. **5**, 1–29 (2021). https://doi.org/10.1145/3485498
4. Farrukh, M., Shah, S., Coskun, B., Polychronakis, M.: Safetrans: LLM-assisted transpilation from c to rust (2025). https://arxiv.org/abs/2505.10708
5. Fromherz, A., Protzenko, J.: Scylla: translating an applicative subset of c to safe rust (2026). https://arxiv.org/abs/2412.15042
6. GitLab: Citrus: A C to Rust transpiler (2017). https://gitlab.com/citrus-rs/citrus
7. Immunant, Inc.: C2Rust: Migrating C code to Rust (2023). https://github.com/immunant/c2rust
8. Jung, R., Jourdan, J.H., Krebbers, R., Dreyer, D.: Rustbelt: securing the foundations of the rust programming language. Proc. ACM Program. Lang. (POPL) **2** (2017). https://doi.org/10.1145/3158154
9. Leroy, X.: Formal verification of a realistic compiler. Commun. ACM **52**(7), 107–115 (2009). https://doi.org/10.1145/1538788.1538814
10. Ling, M., Yu, Y., Wu, H., Wang, Y., Cordy, J.R., Hassan, A.E.: In rust we trust – a transpiler from unsafe c to safer rust. In: 2022 IEEE/ACM 44th International Conference on Software Engineering: Companion Proceedings (ICSE-Companion), pp. 354–355 (2022). https://doi.org/10.1145/3510454.3528640
11. Luo, F., et al.: Integrating rules and semantics for LLM-based c-to-rust translation (2025). https://arxiv.org/abs/2508.06926
12. Miller, M.: Trends, challenges, and strategic shifts in the software vulnerability mitigation landscape (2019)
13. Software memory safety, National Security Agency (2022)
14. Nitin, V., Krishna, R., do Valle, L.L., Ray, B.: C2saferrust: transforming c projects into safer rust with neurosymbolic techniques (2025). https://arxiv.org/abs/2501.14257
15. Sharp, J.: Corrode: C to Rust translator (2016). https://github.com/jameysharp/corrode

16. Shiraishi, M., Cao, Y., Shinagawa, T.: Smartc2rust: iterative, feedback-driven c-to-rust translation via large language models for safety and equivalence (2024)
17. Sim, H., Cho, H., Go, Y., Fu, Z., Shokri, A., Ravindran, B.: Large language model-powered agent for c to rust code translation (2025). https://arxiv.org/abs/2505.15858
18. Team, T.R.D.: The Rocq Prover. Inria (2024). https://rocq-prover.org/
19. Vander Stoep, J.: Rust in the Android platform. Google Security Blog (2021)
20. Wang, C., et al.: Evoc2rust: a skeleton-guided framework for project-level c-to-rust translation (2026). https://arxiv.org/abs/2508.04295
21. Weiss, A., Gierczak, O., Patterson, D., Ahmed, A.: Oxide: the essence of rust (2021). https://arxiv.org/abs/1903.00982
22. Wu, J., Wang, Y., Yu, L., Meng, L.: End-to-end compositional verification of program safety through verified and verifying compilation (2025). https://arxiv.org/abs/2510.10015
23. Yuan, Z., et al.: Project-level c-to-rust translation via synergistic integration of knowledge graphs and large language models (2025). https://arxiv.org/abs/2510.10956
24. Zhou, T., et al.: Sactor: LLM-driven correct and idiomatic c to rust translation with static analysis and FFI-based verification (2025). https://arxiv.org/abs/2503.12511

Formal Verification of a Rust-Based Buddy Physical Memory Allocator

Shaojie Wang[1], Yuting Wang[1], Qianying Zhang[1,2](✉), Weituo Dai[3], Tian'ao Xie[3], Shijun Zhao[3], and Yongwang Zhao[2]

[1] College of Information Engineering, Capital Normal University, Beijing, China
qyzhang@cnu.edu.cn

[2] The State Key Laboratory of Blockchain and Data Security, Zhejiang University, Hangzhou, China

[3] Institute of Information Engineering, Chinese Academy of Sciences, Beijing, China

Abstract. The physical memory allocator is a foundational component of an operating system, whose functional correctness is paramount for system reliability. Although Rust provides compile-time memory safety, it cannot guarantee the correctness of allocator-specific implementation logic. This paper presents the formal verification of `UtManager`, a Rust-based buddy physical memory allocator. Leveraging the Verus verification tool, we define state invariants and provide function specifications for the bitmap-based Rust implementation. We prove that operations such as allocation and free preserve these invariants and satisfy their postconditions, while ensuring bounds safety, overflow freedom, and termination. Notably, during verification, we uncovered and fixed a previously unknown control-flow defect in the original code. These results demonstrate that formal methods can enhance the reliability of Rust-based memory management components with zero runtime overhead.

Keywords: Physical memory allocator · Formal verification · Rust · Verus · Buddy allocator

1 Introduction

The physical memory allocator partitions physical address space into manageable units and dynamically processes allocation and free requests. Its correctness directly affects system stability. Among various allocation strategies, the buddy algorithm is widely adopted in Linux and modern microkernels to mitigate external fragmentation and improve merging efficiency. However, practical implementations often employ intricate bitmap operations, free-list maintenance, and complex address arithmetic, making them prone to subtle logical defects such as overlapping allocations, corruption of critical kernel data structures, and

S. Wang and Y. Wang—Contributed equally to this work.

G. De Giacomo et al. (Eds.): TASE 2026, LNCS 16697, pp. 73–80, 2027.
https://doi.org/10.1007/978-3-032-30693-7_5

memory leaks. For instance, formal verification of the buddy memory allocator in Zephyr RTOS revealed a bug that could cause memory block overlap and data corruption [20].

In recent years, Rust has garnered substantial attention in OS development due to its ownership model and strong type system, and has been applied in kernel projects such as Redox OS [17], Tock [16], RedLeaf [12,13], Theseus [3], NrOS [2], and Asterinas [15]. Rust's compile-time checks effectively prevent many memory safety issues common in C, such as null-pointer dereferences and buffer overflows. Nevertheless, these compiler-enforced static guarantees cannot verify the logical correctness of allocator implementations. For example, the Rust compiler cannot determine whether an allocator mistakenly returns the same physical page frame to two different callers or whether buddy block merging satisfies address adjacency constraints.

This paper presents the formal verification of `UtManager`, a Rust-based buddy physical memory allocator. Leveraging Verus [9,10], an SMT-based automated verification tool, we formally define its function specifications and verify the Rust implementation against them without compromising runtime performance. The contributions of this paper are as follows: first, we define state invariants and function specifications for `UtManager`, and verify allocator operations (including allocation, free, and underlying data structure updates); second, we identify and resolve a defect in the original code, and prove that the fixed implementation preserves invariants and satisfies correctness; furthermore, we guarantee bounds safety, overflow freedom, and termination for all verified operations.

2 Preliminaries

2.1 `UtManager`

`UtManager` is a Rust physical memory allocator based on the buddy algorithm. To enhance performance and reduce metadata overhead, it replaces traditional linked lists with a flat, statically indexed array that implicitly maintains the logical buddy tree topology, with a height determined by the total number of physical page frames. Specifically, the allocator utilizes a status array, bitmap: Vec<u8>, where indices correspond to nodes in the buddy tree. Assuming the root node index is 1, for a node at index i, its left child resides at $2i$, its right child at $2i + 1$, and its parent at $i \gg 1$. To accelerate merge checks, each byte in the `bitmap` encodes the allocation status of a node and its children, allowing the allocator to determine mergeability by accessing only the parent's metadata. To accelerate free block lookups, `UtManager` maintains an array of free sets, free_areas: Vec<BTreeSet<usize≫, whose k-th element is the set of free node indices at tree level k. The `BTreeSet` automatically orders elements, ensuring the first element always corresponds to the free block with the lowest physical address at that level. During allocations and frees, `bitmap` and `free_areas` are updated synchronously to maintain structural consistency across node splitting and merging.

2.2 Verus

Verus [9,10] is a formal verification tool for Rust programs. It combines Rust's type system with an SMT solver, allowing specifications and proofs to be written directly in the source code. Verus separates executable code from verification logic through three modes: `exec` code is compiled and executed, while `spec` and `proof` code are used only for verification and erased during compilation. It provides an expressive annotation system where function specifications are defined via `requires` and `ensures` clauses, loop executions are bounded by `invariants`, and the underlying SMT solver is guided through explicit `assert` statements.

3 Verification of `UtManager`

This section presents the formal verification of the `UtManager` allocator. We first introduce the state representation and its invariants, followed by the function specifications and verification of allocator operations.

3.1 State Representation and Invariants

In our verification, the state of the allocator is represented by the `UtManager` structure itself (see Fig. 1). Its fields collectively describe the metadata maintained by the allocator during allocation and free operations. The `base_volume` and `height` fields record the total number of physical page frames and the tree height, respectively. The `bitmap` compactly stores the allocation status of nodes using a `Vec<u8>`. Specifically, the least significant three bits of each byte indicate the free status of the right child node (Bit 0), the left child node (Bit 1), and the node itself (Bit 2), respectively. Meanwhile, `free_areas` explicitly manages the indices of free blocks at each level via `Vec<BTreeSet<usize>>`. Using `BTreeSet` ensures ordered allocation, prioritizing lower-address blocks to adhere to the first-fit strategy.

To ensure the integrity of the underlying data structures, we define the allocator invariant $Invariant(s)$, consisting of two core predicates:

$$Invariant(s) \equiv bitmap\_consistency(s) \wedge hierarchy\_consistency(s).$$

Invariant 1 (Bitmap consistency). *A memory block index appears in `free_areas` at some level if and only if its corresponding bits in the `bitmap` indicate it is free.*

$$bitmap\_consistency(s) \equiv \forall b.\ (\exists d.\ b \in s.\texttt{free\_areas}[d]) \iff status\_free(s, b).$$

Here, $s.\texttt{free\_areas}[d]$ denotes the set of free block indices at level d, and $status\_free$ indicates that the lowest three bits of the corresponding `bitmap` byte are `0b111`. This synchronization prevents erroneous memory allocations and resource leaks.

```
// Allocator State
struct UtManager {
    base_volume: usize,
    height: usize,
    bitmap: Vec<u8>,
    free_areas: Vec<BTreeSet<usize>>,
}

// State Invariant
spec fn inv(&self) -> bool;
```

```
// Allocation Specification
fn alloc(&mut self, size: usize) -> (res: usize)
    requires
        old(self).inv(),
        4096 <= size,
        size <= self.base_volume * 4096,
    ensures
        self.inv(),
        res != 0 ==> (
            self.bitmap[res] == 0b000 &&
            old(self).bitmap[res] == 0b111
        ),
{
    let level = self.size_to_level(size);
    match self.free_areas[level].first() {
        Some(index) => {
            self.update_map_and_split(index);
            proof { ... }
            index
        },
        None => 0,
    }
}
```

Fig. 1. The `UtManager` structure and the `alloc` function specification.

Invariant 2 (Hierarchy consistency). *The child status bits within a parent's* `bitmap` *byte must match the actual free status derived from the child nodes' own* `bitmap` *bytes.*

$$\begin{aligned} \mathit{hierarchy\_consistency}(s) \equiv\ & \forall f, b. \\ & \mathit{is\_lchild}(s, f, b) \implies (\mathit{status\_free}(s, b) \iff \mathit{status\_lfree}(s, f)) \\ \wedge\ & \mathit{is\_rchild}(s, f, b) \implies (\mathit{status\_free}(s, b) \iff \mathit{status\_rfree}(s, f)). \end{aligned}$$

Here, $\mathit{is\_lchild}(s, f, b)$ and $\mathit{is\_rchild}(s, f, b)$ are true if b is a child node of f. The predicates *status_lfree* and *status_rfree* indicate whether the parent node f's `bitmap` byte records the respective child as free. This internal consistency of the metadata is fundamental for correctly performing block split and merge operations.

Proof. We prove that *Invariant* is established initially and preserved by each verified allocator operation. In the initial state, the allocator contains a single free memory region that is consistently recorded in both `bitmap` and `free_areas`; hence, both invariants hold initially. For each verified operation, such as `alloc` or `free`, we reason about the state updates in the function body and use loop invariants for splitting and merging to show that updates to `bitmap` and `free_areas` remain synchronized, and that parent-child status bits are updated consistently. Therefore, the function establishes the postcondition `self.inv()`.

3.2 Specification and Verification of Allocator Operations

We provide Hoare triple specifications for all allocator operations, including `alloc` and `free`. By defining preconditions and postconditions, we ensure that each function correctly manipulates the underlying data structures while preserving the allocator invariants.

Taking the allocation function `alloc` as an example (see Fig. 1), its precondition requires the input state to satisfy the allocator invariants (`old(self).inv()`) and the requested size to be valid. Since the maximum level of the buddy tree corresponds to the smallest allocatable unit (a 4KB page frame), the request `size` is constrained to be at least 4096 bytes and bounded by `self.base_volume` × 4096. Its postcondition constrains the behavior along two properties: 1) invariant preservation, ensuring the returned state `self` satisfies `self.inv()`; 2) state correctness, ensuring that upon successful allocation ($res \neq 0$), the corresponding `bitmap` byte flips from free (`0b111`) to allocated (`0b000`).

During verification, we formally prove all execution paths of `alloc`. For loop structures involving `bitmap` updates, we construct loop invariants to prove that operations preserve *Invariant*. Furthermore, we prove that all array accesses are within bounds, and no arithmetic overflows occur. We also employ `decreases` clauses to establish the termination of all recursive calls and loops.

The specification and verification of the `free` function follow an analogous approach. Its specification requires that the input state satisfy the allocator invariants and that the target block be allocated, and ensures that the `bitmap` and the corresponding set in `free_areas` are updated consistently. During the merge procedure, we construct loop invariants to prove that updates to the `bitmap` and `free_areas` remain synchronized while free buddy blocks are merged.

Ultimately, the verification establishes that all allocator operations preserve the state invariants and satisfy their respective function specifications.

4 Evaluation and Discussion

Verification Effort. We quantify the verification effort by counting the lines of code comprising the verified project. Of the approximately 2,300 total lines of code, specification (`spec`) and proof (`proof`) code account for 1,923 lines, while executable code (`exec`) comprises 349 lines. The verification mainly involves reasoning about bitwise operations and loop invariants. The effort required approximately 2 person-months. On a machine equipped with an Apple M4 processor and 16GB of RAM, the full verification completes in 4.3 s.

Defects Discovered. During the verification process, we uncovered a previously unknown defect in the original implementation: a control-flow error that bypassed metadata updates during specific allocation paths. This issue was corrected and formally verified.

Performance Impact. Runtime performance is critical for operating system components. Verus utilizes ghost code technology to confine all specifications (`spec`), proof-assisting functions (`proof`), and assertions (`assert`) exclusively to the compile-time verification phase. During binary generation, the Rust compiler completely erases this verification logic. Consequently, the formally verified `UtManager` incurs zero runtime overhead compared to its unverified counterpart. This property ensures that the verified code satisfies its specified correctness properties while fully retaining the high-performance benefits of the Rust language.

Trusted Computing Base (TCB). Although formal verification significantly enhances system reliability, the validity of our verification conclusions depends on the correctness of our TCB. Specifically, we assume that the Verus verifier, the underlying Z3 SMT solver, and the Rust compiler are correct.

5 Related Work

Formal Verification of OS Kernels. seL4 [8] and CertiKOS [5] established refinement-based verification for operating systems, but relied on interactive theorem proving with high manual effort. Hyperkernel [14] explored SMT-based automation but imposed strict restrictions on kernel code. Unlike these general OS verification efforts, our work focuses on a Rust-based buddy allocator with complex loops and bitwise operations.

Verification of Memory Management. Memory-management verification includes both code-level and model-level proofs. Code-level verification has been applied to systems such as L4 [18] and Zephyr [20]. Model-level work has verified abstract models of buddy or TLSF (two-level segregated fit) allocators [6,11], but stops short of verifying concrete implementations. Rust verification tools such as RustBelt [7], Prusti [1], Kani [19], and Verus [10] have created new opportunities for systems verification. Rust OS verification has largely focused on page table management [4], while verification of Rust-based physical memory allocators remains scarce. In contrast, our work verifies the Rust implementation of `UtManager`, covering bitmap manipulation, free-block set maintenance, invariant preservation, and memory safety. Unlike traditional proofs in external theorem provers, our verification is carried out within the Verus ecosystem, which allows the source code to be directly verified against its invariants and function specifications, while erasing ghost code and proofs during compilation.

6 Conclusion

This paper presents the formal verification of `UtManager`, a Rust-based buddy physical memory allocator. By establishing preconditions, postconditions, and invariants, we verified the correctness of its flat-indexed implementation, specifically covering bitmap manipulations and free-block set management. Notably, our verification identified a previously unknown defect in the original code. Ultimately, this work demonstrates that formal methods can be effectively applied to Rust-based systems to provide correctness guarantees without compromising performance.

Acknowledgments. This work was supported in part by the Open Research Fund of The State Key Laboratory of Blockchain and Data Security, Zhejiang University, and the National Natural Science Foundation of China (Grant Nos. 62372311, 62272458, 62272323, 62272322, and 62372312).

Disclosure of Interests. The authors have no competing interests to declare that are relevant to the content of this article.

References

1. Astrauskas, V., et al.: The Prusti project: formal verification for Rust. In: Proceedings of the 14th International Symposium on NASA Formal Methods (NFM), pp. 88–108. Springer, Heidelberg (2022). https://doi.org/10.1007/978-3-031-06773-0_5
2. Bhardwaj, A., et al.: NrOS: effective replication and sharing in an operating system. In: Proceedings of the 15th USENIX Symposium on Operating Systems Design and Implementation (OSDI), pp. 295–312. USENIX Association (2021)
3. Boos, K., Liyanage, N., Ijaz, R., Zhong, L.: Theseus: an experiment in operating system structure and state management. In: Proceedings of the 14th USENIX Symposium on Operating Systems Design and Implementation (OSDI), pp. 1–19. USENIX Association (2020)
4. Brun, M., Achermann, R., Chajed, T., Howell, J., Zellweger, G., Lattuada, A.: Beyond isolation: OS verification as a foundation for correct applications. In: Proceedings of the 19th Workshop on Hot Topics in Operating Systems (HotOS), pp. 158–165. ACM (2023). https://doi.org/10.1145/3593856.3595899
5. Gu, R., Shao, Z., Chen, H., Wu, X.N., Kim, J., Sjöberg, V., Costanzo, D.: CertiKOS: An extensible architecture for building certified concurrent OS kernels. In: Proceedings of the 12th USENIX Symposium on Operating Systems Design and Implementation (OSDI), pp. 653–669. USENIX Association (2016)
6. Jiang, K., Sanan, D., Zhao, Y., Kan, S., Liu, Y.: A formally verified buddy memory allocation model. In: Proceedings of the 24th International Conference on Engineering of Complex Computer Systems (ICECCS), pp. 144–153. IEEE (2019). https://doi.org/10.1109/ICECCS.2019.00023
7. Jung, R., Jourdan, J.H., Krebbers, R., Dreyer, D.: RustBelt: securing the foundations of the Rust programming language. Proc. ACM Program. Lang. **2**(POPL), 66:1–66:34 (2017). https://doi.org/10.1145/3158154
8. Klein, G., et al.: seL4: formal verification of an OS kernel. In: Proceedings of the ACM SIGOPS 22nd Symposium on Operating Systems Principles (SOSP), pp. 207–220. ACM (2009). https://doi.org/10.1145/1629575.1629596
9. Lattuada, A., et al.: Verus: a practical foundation for systems verification. In: Proceedings of the ACM SIGOPS 30th Symposium on Operating Systems Principles (SOSP), pp. 438–454. ACM (2024). https://doi.org/10.1145/3694715.3695952
10. Lattuada, A., et al.: Verus: verifying Rust programs using linear ghost types. Proc. ACM Program. Lang. **7**(OOPSLA1), 286–315 (2023). https://doi.org/10.1145/3586037

11. Li, S., Qiao, L., Yang, M.: Memory state verification based on inductive and deductive reasoning. IEEE Trans. Reliab. **70**(3), 1026–1039 (2021). https://doi.org/10.1109/TR.2021.3074709
12. Narayanan, V., Baranowski, M.S., Ryzhyk, L., Rakamarić, Z., Burtsev, A.: RedLeaf: towards an operating system for safe and verified firmware. In: Proceedings of the 17th Workshop on Hot Topics in Operating Systems (HotOS), pp. 37–44. ACM (2019). https://doi.org/10.1145/3317550.3321449
13. Narayanan, V., et al.: RedLeaf: isolation and communication in a safe operating system. In: Proceedings of the 14th USENIX Symposium on Operating Systems Design and Implementation (OSDI), pp. 21–39. USENIX Association (2020)
14. Nelson, L., et al.: Hyperkernel: push-button verification of an OS kernel. In: Proceedings of the 26th Symposium on Operating Systems Principles (SOSP), pp. 252–269. ACM (2017). https://doi.org/10.1145/3132747.3132748
15. Peng, Y., et al.: Asterinas: a Linux ABI-compatible, Rust-based framekernel OS with a small and sound TCB. In: Proceedings of the 2025 USENIX Annual Technical Conference (USENIX ATC), pp. 307–323. USENIX Association (2025)
16. Schuermann, L., Campbell, B., Ghena, B., Levis, P., Levy, A., Pannuto, P.: Tock: from research to securing 10 million computers. In: Proceedings of the ACM SIGOPS 31st Symposium on Operating Systems Principles (SOSP), pp. 36–49. ACM (2025). https://doi.org/10.1145/3731569.3764828
17. The Redox Developers: Redox - your next(gen) OS (2025). https://www.redox-os.org
18. Tuch, H., Klein, G., Norrish, M.: Types, bytes, and separation logic. In: Proceedings of the 34th annual ACM SIGPLAN-SIGACT symposium on Principles of programming languages (POPL), pp. 97–108. ACM (2007). https://doi.org/10.1145/1190216.1190234
19. VanHattum, A., Schwartz-Narbonne, D., Chong, N., Sampson, A.: Verifying dynamic trait objects in Rust. In: Proceedings of the 44th International Conference on Software Engineering: Software Engineering in Practice (ICSE-SEIP), pp. 321–330. ACM (2022). https://doi.org/10.1145/3510457.3513031
20. Zhao, Y., Sanán, D.: Rely-guarantee reasoning about concurrent memory management in Zephyr RTOS. In: Proceedings of the 31st International Conference on Computer Aided Verification (CAV), pp. 515–533. Springer, Heidelberg (2019). https://doi.org/10.1007/978-3-030-25543-5_29

Enhancing LLM-Based Proof Synthesis for Rust Programs via Semantic Chunking and Hierarchical Context Expansion

Yuchen Zhang[1], Cheng Wen[1(✉)], Zhiwu Xu[2], Dugang Liu[2], Jialun Cao[3], Yuwei Liu[4], Shengchao Qin[1], and Cong Tian[1]

[1] Guangzhou Institute of Technology, Xidian University, Guangzhou, China
wencheng@xidian.edu.cn
[2] College of Computer Science and Software Engineering, Shenzhen University, Shenzhen, China
{xuzhiwu,liudugang}@szu.edu.cn
[3] The Hong Kong University of Science and Technology, Sai Kung, China
[4] Institute of Software, Chinese Academy of Sciences, Beijing, China

Abstract. Formal verification of Rust programs using Verus provides rigorous correctness guarantees but demands significant manual effort to craft auxiliary specifications and proofs. While Large Language Model (LLM) agents such as AutoVerus show promise for automating this process, they often fail on non-trivial tasks because generation is undergrounded: the model lacks access to fine-grained, verification-relevant proof patterns. Naïve retrieval-augmented generation (RAG) is also ineffective, since retrieving coarse-grained entire files or functions introduces noise and obscures the fine-grained logical patterns required for verification. To bridge this gap, we present VerusSeek, a retrieval-augmented framework for automated Verus proof synthesis that addresses this granularity mismatch. VerusSeek semantically chunks verified Verus code into proof constructs (*e.g.*, contracts, loop invariants, lemmas, proof blocks, and assertions), performs type-aware retrieval, and applies hierarchical context expansion to provide concise yet logically grounded evidence to the model. We evaluate VerusSeek on 150 VerusBench tasks, showing that our fine-grained approach substantially improves verification success and significantly outperforms both AutoVerus and the RagVerus, with improvements of 76.7% and 43.4%, respectively.

1 Introduction

Rust has become a dominant systems programming language due to its strong memory-safety guarantees and its ability to deliver predictable performance [1–3]. However, in security-critical domains (*e.g.*, aerospace, autonomous driving, and cryptographic libraries), memory safety alone is insufficient; developers must additionally establish functional correctness with respect to precise specifications. Verus [4,5] enables such end-to-end reasoning by allowing programmers to annotate Rust code with mathematical contracts and proofs that are discharged

G. De Giacomo et al. (Eds.): TASE 2026, LNCS 16697, pp. 81–100, 2027.
https://doi.org/10.1007/978-3-032-30693-7_6

by SMT-based verification. In return, Verus can provide rigorous guarantees that the implementation satisfies its specification.

Despite these benefits, the practical adoption of Verus remains constrained by the significant proof burden. To verify even modest programs, users typically must provide auxiliary annotation, such as strengthened pre/post-conditions, loop invariants, supporting lemmas, and localized proof blocks. These annotations are often not obvious from the code alone, must be inductive, and must align closely with the SMT solver's expectations [6,7]. As a result, proof engineering becomes a major bottleneck, where verification effort is dominated not by writing code, but by iteratively discovering and refining proof-relevant structure.

LLM-Based Proof Synthesis and the Context Gap. Recent advances in Large Language Models (LLMs) [8,9] have shown promise in automating code generation and verification tasks [10–17]. Agent-based frameworks, such as AutoVerus [18], leverage LLMs to iteratively generate and refine proofs for Rust programs. While promising, they often fail on non-trivial tasks involving complex loops, quantified properties, and data structures [19–21]. A central reason is that generation is under-grounded, where the model lacks access to the fine-grained, domain-specific proof patterns that are routinely reused by expert verifiers. Consequently, the agent frequently proposes proof annotations that are syntactically correct but fail to discharge the actual proof obligations.

Why naïve RAG is Insufficient. Retrieval-Augmented Generation (RAG) [22,23] is a natural strategy to ground LLMs in external evidence. However, applying standard RAG pipelines to formal verification faces a granularity mismatch. Conventional retrieval units (*e.g.*, entire files, modules, or functions) are too coarse: they mix specifications, invariants, and unrelated implementation details. When injected into prompts, such coarse evidence introduces noise, obscures the local proof structure needed for a failing obligation (*e.g.*, a specific quantified invariant), and reduces the likelihood that the model reuses the precise proof idiom required to complete verification. In our setting, the relevant information is rarely "the whole function"; it is more often a reusable *construct* such as a loop invariant template, a lemma statement, or a short proof block that demonstrates a specific SMT-friendly pattern.

Insight and Proposed Approach. To address these challenges, we propose VerusSeek, a retrieval-augmented framework for automated Verus proof synthesis that grounds LLM generation in verified proof patterns at the right granularity. VerusSeek first *semantically chunks* verified Verus code into proof-bearing constructs (*e.g.*, contracts, loop invariants, lemmas, proof blocks, and assertions), and indexes these constructs for retrieval. Given a program fragment that fails verification, VerusSeek identifies what kind of proof annotation is missing, retrieves the most relevant constructs of that type, and then *expands* each retrieved construct with a small amount of surrounding context (*e.g.*, the enclosing function contract and nearby companion invariants). This produces concise yet logically grounded evidence, which is injected into the prompt to guide the LLM toward verifiable specifications and proofs.

We implement VERUSSEEK and evaluate it on 150 verification tasks from VerusBench [18] spanning four benchmark suites (*i.e.*, CloverBench [24], Diffy [25], MBPP [26], and Misc). VERUSSEEK substantially improves overall verification success rate compared to AutoVerus [18], RagVerus [27] and the coarse-grained retrieval baseline. Specifically, VERUSSEEK reduces the number of repair iterations required on tasks involving loops and quantified specifications.

In summary, this paper makes the following contributions.

- **Semantic proof-construct chunking.** We decompose verified Verus/Rust code into fine-grained proof constructs and index them as retrieval units, enabling construct-level grounding instead of file/function retrieval.
- **Hierarchical context expansion.** We expand retrieved constructs with a bounded amount of surrounding structure to preserve logical dependencies while keeping prompts concise.
- **Open-source toolchain.** We implement VERUSSEEK as an end-to-end, reusable pipeline for chunk extraction, indexing, retrieval, and prompt construction for Verus proof synthesis: https://doi.org/10.5281/zenodo.18769271.
- **Systematic evaluation.** On 150 VerusBench tasks, VERUSSEEK improves verification success and first-shot performance over AutoVerus and the RagVerus method by 76.7% and 43.4%, respectively.

2 Motivation

2.1 A Motivating Example

Figure 1 shows a Rust/Verus implementation of `rotate_right`, which returns `new_list` obtained by rotating an input vector `list` to the right by `n` positions. The specification is naturally stated using the sequence view `list@`: the rotated result is the concatenation of a suffix and a prefix of the original sequence. A helper contract function `rotation_split` (Lines 1–3) defines the split point

$$\texttt{split} \triangleq \texttt{list.len()} - (\texttt{n} \bmod \texttt{list.len()}),$$

and the postcondition (Lines 8–13) requires

$$\texttt{new\_list@} = \texttt{list@.subrange(split, len).add(list@.subrange(0, split))}.$$

The implementation follows the standard two-phase construction: it first appends the suffix `list[split..len)` to `new_list`, then appends the prefix `list[0..split)`. Although the code is straightforward, it is *not* verifiable without proof code (*e.g.*, loop invariants) that explain how `new_list@` relates to the processed portion of `list@` at each iteration. For the first loop, the key relational invariant (Line 23) states that after processing indices `split..index`, the sequence view of `new_list` equals `list@.subrange(split, index)`. For the second loop, the invariant must connect the already-built suffix with the growing prefix (Lines 34–42), yielding an expression of the form

$$\texttt{new\_list@} = \texttt{list@.subrange(split, len).add(list@.subrange(0, index))}.$$

```
spec fn rotation_split(len: usize, n: usize) -> int {          1. Contract: helper function
    len - (n % len)
}

fn rotate_right(list: &Vec<u32>, n: usize) -> (new_list: Vec<u32>)
    requires                                                   2. Contract: pre/post condition
        list.len() > 0,
    ensures
        new_list.len() == list.len(),
        new_list@ == list@.subrange(rotation_split(list.len(), n)
        as int, list@.len() as int).add(
            list@.subrange(0, rotation_split(list.len(), n) as int),
            ),
{
    let rotation = n % list.len();
    let split_index = list.len() - rotation;
    let mut new_list = Vec::with_capacity(list.len());
    let mut index = split_index;
    while index < list.len()
        invariant                                              3. LoopInvariant
            list.len() > 0,                                                        3.1 Bounds
            list.len() == list.len(),
            split_index <= index <= list.len(),
            new_list.len() == index - split_index,                                 3.2 Frame
            new_list@ == list@.subrange(split_index as int, index as int),
            forall k: int 0 <= k < list.len() ==> list@[k] == list@[k],
        decreases list.len() - index                                               3.3 Termination
    {
        new_list.push(list[index]);
        index += 1;
    }
    index = 0;
    while index < split_index
        invariant                                              4. LoopInvariant
            list.len() > 0,                                                        4.1 Bounds
            list.len() == list.len(),
            0 <= split_index <= list.len(),
            0 <= index <= split_index,
            new_list.len() == list.len() - split_index + index,                    4.2 Frame
            new_list@ == list@.subrange(split_index as int, list.len() as int).add(
                list@.subrange(0, index as int)),
            forall k: int 0 <= k < list.len() ==> list@[k] == list@[k],
        decreases split_index - index                                              4.3 Termination
    {
        new_list.push(list[index]);
        index += 1;
    }
    new_list
}
```

Fig. 1. A Motivating Example from the MBPP benchmark.

These invariants require the model to (i) recognize the algorithmic schema (suffix then prefix), and (ii) adapt the postcondition into an inductive statement over the loop index. Even in this small example, missing or slightly misaligned invariants cause the verifier to fail, and repair requires multiple iterations of strengthening bounds, frames, and relational facts.

2.2 Limitation of LLM-Based Methods and the Coarse RAG

LLM-based agents such as AutoVerus [18] attempt to automate Verus proof development by generating candidate invariants and proof snippets and checking them with the verifier in a generate–verify–repair loop. However, their performance is limited by a *context gap*: successful invariants and proof blocks follow domain-specific patterns that are not reliably produced from a small, fixed set of few-shot examples. As a result, the agent often generates invariants that are syntactically plausible but too weak to imply the postcondition, or that omit essential structural components such as index bounds and frame conditions. Our empirical observations indicate that functions like `rotate_right` remain unverifiable when using baseline AutoVerus after three iterations, whereas grounding the model in relevant sequence-processing examples via RAG reduces this overhead to 1 iteration. Figure 2 shows AutoVerus's output for this example.

```
while index < list.len()
    invariant                                       3. LoopInvariant
        list.len() > 0,                                       3.1 Bounds
        list.len() == list.len(),
        index >= 0,
        index <= list.len(),
        new_list.len() == index - split_index,                3.2 Frame
    decreases (list.len() as int - index as int),             3.3 Termination
    ...
```

Fig. 2. Loop invariants produced by AutoVerus (unverified).

```
while index < list.len()
    invariant                                       3. LoopInvariant
        list.len() > 0,                                       3.1 Bounds
        split_index <= index <= list.len(),
        list.len() == list.len(),
        forall k: int 0 <= k < list.len() ==>                 3.2 Frame
            #[trigger] list@.subrange(split_index as int, index as int) =~= new_list@,
    decreases list.len() - index,                             3.3 Termination
    ...
```

Fig. 3. Loop invariants produced by RagVerus (unverified).

RAG is a natural way to provide the model with additional guidance from verified code [22,23]. Yet, in formal verification, RAG retrieving entire files or functions is often ineffective. Coarse retrieval mixes the few lines that matter with large amounts of unrelated implementation detail. This dilutes the relevant proof signal and makes it harder for the LLM to identify and reuse the specific construct required for the current obligation, as shown in RagVerus's output in Fig. 3. In this example, the model does not need another whole sequence-manipulation function; rather, it requires only a small number of *construct-level* patterns: an invariant that characterizes a growing subrange, and an invariant that characterizes the concatenation of a fixed suffix with a growing prefix.

2.3 Our Proposed Construct-Level Retrieval

The rotation task illustrates a broader phenomenon in Verus: proof obligations are typically discharged by short, reusable *proof constructs*, and these constructs must be instantiated with local variables and indices to become inductive. Naïve RAG retrieves entire files or large code blocks, which obscures the specific proof constructs required. Therefore, an effective retrieval mechanism for LLM-based proof synthesis should retrieve and present evidence at the same level of abstraction as the missing artifact.

This motivates our approach: We build a retrieval index over semantically identified proof constructs and reconstruct only the minimal surrounding context needed for correctness, enabling the LLM to reuse verified invariant templates and proof idioms with substantially less noise than file/function-level retrieval, as shown in Fig. 4. VerusSeek addresses this by decomposing verified code into functional units: `Function`, `Lemma`, `Contract`, `LoopInvariant`, `ProofBlock`, and `Assertion`. Using type-aware retrieval, the system identifies when a task requires sequence-based invariants and fetches the most pertinent `LoopInvariant` chunks. These are then expanded with their parent `Contract` to provide a complete logical template. This multi-granularity approach ensures the LLM receives the precise context needed to synthesize correct inductive proofs for complex functions.

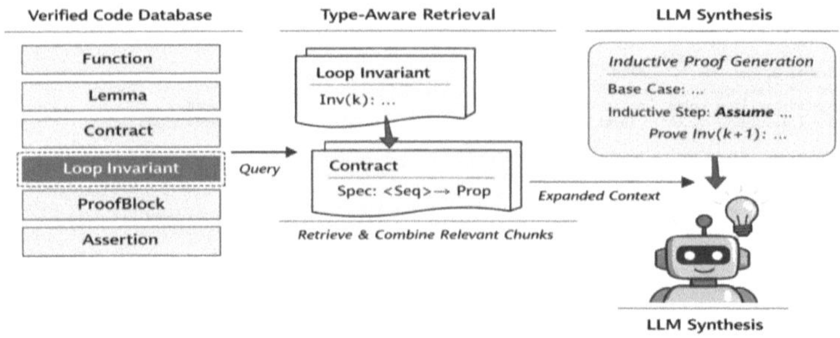

Fig. 4. Construct-Level Retrieval of VERUSSEEK.

3 Methodology

We present VERUSSEEK, a retrieval-augmented framework for automated Verus proof synthesis. Figure 5 presents an overview of the pipeline, which consists of four stages: (1) semantic proof-construct chunking to construct fine-grained retrieval units, (2) type-aware retrieval to select proof-relevant chunks, (3) expands retrieved constructs with a small amount of hierarchical context to recover necessary dependencies; and (4) optionally synthesizes structure-first loop invariant candidates (bounds/frame/termination) that complement retrieval.

The retrieved evidence and synthesized hints are formatted into a single prompt for the LLM, and the verifier feedback drives an iterative generate–verify–repair loop.

3.1 Semantic Proof-Construct Chunking

When manually developing proofs in Verus, practitioners often consult previously verified code and reuse recurring proof patterns to construct specifications and loop invariants. But coarse retrieval units (files/functions) often bury the few lines that determine verification success. VERUSSEEK therefore indexes *proof-bearing constructs* as retrieval units. Concretely, we parse a verified Verus file and extract typed chunks aligned with the constructs that developers typically reuse: `Funtion`, `Specification`, `Lemma`, `LoopInvariant`, `ProofBlock`, and `Assertion`, where the corresponding types are shown in Table 1. Each chunk stores its source span and lightweight metadata (*e.g.*, file, enclosing function, verification status).

During chunking, we build a Chunk Hierarchy Graph $H = (C, R)$ to explicitly capture structural relationships among chunks. The node set C contains semantic units (*e.g.*, `Function`, `Specification`, `Lemma`, `LoopInvariant` ...), and the directed edge set $R \subseteq C \times C$ encodes hierarchical and lateral relations that are later used for context expansion. Each chunk is further annotated with metadata including its type, source span, and formal attributes. In particular, we record:

- *Parent–child links:* edges from enclosing constructs (*e.g.*, a `Function`) to enclosed constructs (*e.g.*, a `LoopInvariant` within that function).

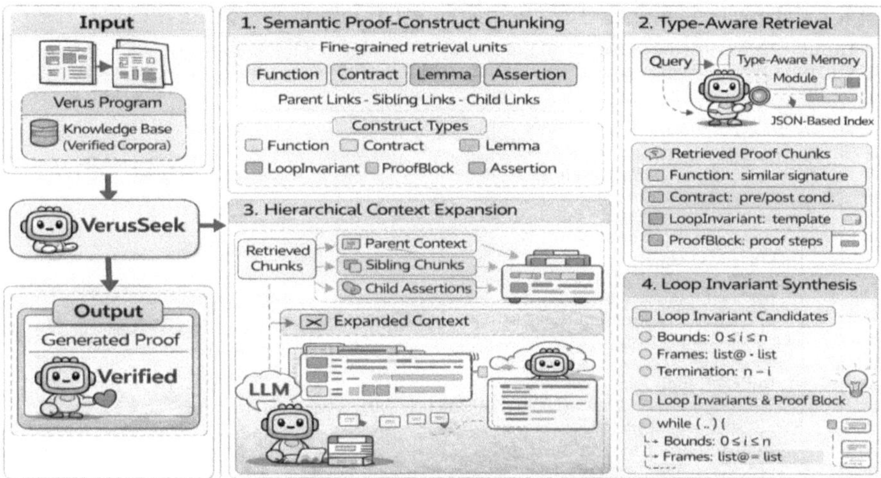

Fig. 5. The overall workflow of our approach.

- *Sibling links:* edges between chunks at the same hierarchy level and of the same kind (*e.g.*, multiple `LoopInvariant` chunks in one function), providing alternative patterns.
- *Context references:* lightweight preceding_context and following_context snippets that preserve local continuity with neighboring code.

Algorithm 1 gives the full extraction routine. It takes as input a Verus source file F and a chunking strategy str, and outputs a Chunked Document that stores (i) a set of typed semantic chunks and (ii) their hierarchical relations.

Table 1. Chunk types used in VERUSSEEK

Chunk Type	Description	Example
`Function`	A complete Verus function body (including signature and body).	`fn sum(arr: Vec<u64>)− > u64`
`Lemma`	A proof lemma or auxiliary proof function.	`proof fn lemma_add_assoc(...)`
`Contract`	Contract clauses attached to a function/lemma.	`requires`, `ensures`, `decreases`
`LoopInvariant`	Invariant block associated with a `while` loop.	`while (...) invariant ... {...}`
`ProofBlock`	A `proof` region containing intermediate reasoning steps.	`proof { assert(...); }`
`Assertion`	A single assertion or check statement.	`assert(i >= 0)`

Algorithm 1: Semantic Proof-construct Chunking for Verified Code

```
Input  : A Verus source file F, and a chunking strategy str.
Output: A ChunkedDocument containing semantic chunks with hierarchical relationships.
begin
    C ← ∅;
    // Phase 1: Extract imports and type definitions.
    C := C∪ extract_imports(F);
    C := C∪ extract_struct_enum(F);
    // Phase 2: Function-based decomposition.
    for each function f in F do
        c_f := create_chunk(FUNCTION, f);
        C := C ∪ {c_f};
        specs := extract_specs(f);
        for each clause s in specs do
            c_s := create_chunk(CONTRACT, s, parent=c_f.id);
            C := C ∪ {c_s};
        // Phase 3: Semantic sub-chunking within functions.
        for each loop l in f do
            c_l := create_chunk(LOOP_INVARIANT, l, parent=c_f.id);
            C := C ∪ {c_l};
        for each proof block p in f do
            c_p := create_chunk(PROOF_BLOCK, p, parent=c_f.id);
            C := C ∪ {c_p};
        for each assertion a in f do
            c_a := create_chunk(ASSERTION, a, parent=c_f.id);
            C := C ∪ {c_a};
        // Phase 4: Link chunks in hierarchy and add context.
        link_parent_child(c_f, C);
        link_siblings(c_f, C);
    // Add preceding and following context for each chunk.
    for each chunk c in C do
        c.preceding_context := get_context(F, c, −200, 0);
        c.following_context := get_context(F, c, 0, 200);
    H := build_hierarchy(C);
    return ChunkedDocument(F, C, H);
```

3.2 Type-Aware Retrieval

The second stage of VERUSSEEK retrieves proof-relevant chunks from the knowledge base conditioned on the query type of the input. Here, the query type characterizes the proof subtask required by the verifier, such as loop-invariant synthesis, contract (pre/post-condition) completion, or construction of a proof block. Because different subtasks demand different evidence, VERUSSEEK performs type-aware retrieval to match the granularity of retrieved context to the target construct. For example, loop-invariant queries benefit most from retrieving existing `LoopInvariant` chunks as reusable templates, whereas contract-related queries typically require broader function-level context (*e.g.*, Contract chunks associated with similar functions).

Query Type Detection. Given an input program, we infer its query type by matching Verus-specific patterns and proof constructs (*e.g.*, presence of while loops, missing invariant blocks, incomplete require/ensures clauses, or proof annotations). Table 2 summarizes the mapping from detected patterns to query types, which then determines the preferred chunk types and retrieval granularity for the subsequent similarity search.

Embedding Index and Scoring. Once the query type t is determined, VERUSSEEK computes an embedding for the input snippet q and performs a similarity search over the JSON-based index that stores precomputed embeddings for all chunks. Concretely, for each chunk c with embedding vector $\mathbf{e}_c$ and query embedding $\mathbf{e}_q$, we compute cosine similarity $\text{sim}(c, q)$ and retrieve an initial candidate set of top-k chunks. We then apply a type-aware scoring function to promote chunks whose types match the preferred set for t, and to slightly favor chunks originating from verified code:

$$\text{score}(c, q) = \text{sim}(c, q) + \alpha \cdot \mathbb{1}[\text{type}(c) \in \text{preferred}(t)] + \beta \cdot \mathbb{1}[\text{verified}(c)], \quad (1)$$

where $\mathbb{1}[\cdot]$ is the indicator function. We set $\alpha = \beta = 0.1$ in this paper unless otherwise stated.

Re-ranking. To break ties and favor locally relevant evidence, we incorporate two lightweight lexical signals: token overlap between the chunk content and the query, and whether the parent context contains query-relevant terms:

$$\text{rerank}(c, q) = \text{score}(c, q) + \gamma \cdot \text{overlap}(\text{content}(c), q) + \delta \cdot \text{parent\_match}(c, q), \quad (2)$$

where $\text{overlap}(\cdot)$ counts matched keywords/tokens (capped to avoid dominating the score), and $\text{parent\_match}(\cdot)$ indicates whether the enclosing parent chunk contains query-relevant terms. We use $\gamma = 0.05$ (with a maximum bonus of 5) and $\delta = 0.02$ by default.

Finally, the top-ranked chunks are formatted into structured in-context evidence (*e.g.*, contract snippets, invariant templates, and proof idioms) and injected into the LLM prompt for proof synthesis.

3.3 Hierarchical Context Expansion

The third stage of VERUSSEEK expands each retrieved chunk with a small amount of hierarchical context to restore the proof-relevant structure that is often omitted by isolated retrieval. While a single chunk (*e.g.*, a loop-invariant template) may match the query semantically, correct proof synthesis frequently depends on surrounding contracts, auxiliary assertions, and companion invariants that appear in the same enclosing function. To capture such dependencies without re-introducing the noise of file-level retrieval, we leverage the Chunk Hierarchy Graph $H = (C, R)$ and selectively attach parent/child/sibling context.

Context Types. For a retrieved chunk c, we consider the context types:

- *Parent chunks* ($\text{Par}(c)$): enclosing constructs that contain c (*e.g.*, the Function chunk containing a Loop_Invariant chunk, or the enclosing Function for a Specification clause), which provide high-level intent and contracts.
- *Child chunks* ($\text{Chi}(c)$): proof-bearing sub-constructs inside c (*e.g.*, Assertion chunks inside a ProofBlock, or Loop_Invariant/ProofBlock chunks inside a Function), which supply fine-grained proof idioms.

Table 2. Query type detection and preferred chunk types

Query Type	Detection Patterns	Preferred Chunk Types
loop	while, for, loop	`Loop Invariant`, `Function`
specification	requires, ensures, invariant	`Contract`, `LoopInvariant`
function	fn, proof fn, spec fn	`Function`, `Lemma`
array	Vec, [], .len(), .push()	`Function`, `Contract`
assertion	assert()	`Assertion`, `ProofBlock`
general	Default	All types

- *Sibling chunks* (Sib(c)): chunks that share the same parent as c and have the same (or closely related) type, which provide alternative patterns (*e.g.*, other Loop_Invariant chunks in the same function, or related Specification clauses such as requires/ensures).

Context Expansion Strategy. Given a query q with detected type t and an initially retrieved chunk c, VERUSSEEK selects a bounded expansion set:

$$\text{Expand}(c,t) \subseteq \text{Par}(c) \ \cup \ \text{Chi}(c) \ \cup \ \text{Sib}(c), \tag{3}$$

where the selection depends on both the query type and the chunk type. Intuitively, we expand towards the context that is most likely to provide missing proof obligations for the target construct:

$$\text{Expand}(c,t) = \begin{cases} \text{Par}(c) \cup \text{Sib}(c) \cup \text{Chi}(c), & \text{if } t = \mathit{loop} \ \wedge \ \text{type}(c) = \mathit{Loop\_Invariant}; \\ \text{Par}(c) \cup \text{Sib}(c), & \text{if } t = \mathit{specification} \ \wedge \ \text{type}(c) = \mathit{Contract}; \\ \text{Chi}(c) \cup \text{Sib}(c), & \text{if } t = \mathit{loop} \ \wedge \ \text{type}(c) = \mathit{Function}; \\ \text{Par}(c), & \text{if type}(c) \in \{\mathit{Assertion}, \mathit{ProofBlock}\}; \\ \emptyset, & \text{otherwise.} \end{cases} \tag{4}$$

We further enforce a small context budget (*e.g.*, maximum number of expanded chunks per retrieved item) to keep the prompt concise. Overall, this strategy preserves proof-relevant dependencies (contracts, companion invariants, and auxiliary assertions) while avoiding the excessive noise of retrieving large, unrelated code regions.

3.4 Loop Invariant Synthesis

Retrieval can fail when the corpus lacks a close match for a loop pattern, and LLMs commonly omit *structural* invariants (bounds/frame/termination) even when they capture the high-level intent. To reduce this failure mode, VERUSSEEK includes a lightweight loop invariant synthesizer that proposes a small "skeleton" of invariants before calling the LLM. Given a loop, it derives: (i) `Bounds` from guards and access sites (e.g., $0 \leq i \leq N$), (ii) `Frames` for quantities not modified (e.g., preservation of `list.len()` and input views), and (iii) a `Termination` measure consistent with the progress variable (denoted by `decrease`). These structure-first candidates are provided as hints; the LLM is instructed to keep them and focus on synthesizing the missing *semantic* relations (*e.g.*, subrange/concatenation facts) guided by retrieved examples.

Running Example. Consider the `rotate_right` function in Fig. 1. The structural invariant candidates produced for its two loops, grouped by category, are shown in Table 3.

Table 3. Structural invariant candidates synthesized for `rotate_right`.

Category	Loop	Candidate Invariant/Measure
Bounds	`index < list.len()`	`split_index <= index <= list.len()`
	`index < split_index`	`0 <= index <= split_index`
	`index < split_index`	`0 <= split_index <= list.len()`
	`index < list.len()`	`list.len() > 0`
Frame	`index < list.len()`	`forall |k:int| 0 <= k < list.len() ==> list@[k] == list@[k]`
	`index < split_index`	`forall |k:int| 0 <= k < list.len() ==> list@[k] == list@[k]`
	`index < split_index`	`list.len() > 0`
Termination	`index < list.len()`	`decreases(list.len() - index)`
	`index < split_index`	`decreases(split_index - index)`

We use a static analyzer that provides structure-first guidance, including canonical index bounds, conservative frame conditions, and termination measures. In this example, it proposes bounds that relate `index` to `split_index` and `list.len()`, frame invariants that preserve the input sequence, and loop-specific decreasing measures (`list.len() - index` and `split_index - index`).

The LLM then combines these structural candidates with semantically relevant proof patterns retrieved from the knowledge base to complete the missing inductive links required by Verus. Concretely, the retrieved evidence helps the model synthesize semantic invariants that characterize the incremental construction of `new_list@` across the two phases of rotation: first matching the suffix subrange `list@.subrange(split_index, index)`, and then matching the concatenation of the suffix with the growing prefix. This complementarity is crucial because the analyzer alone can reliably infer how the loop progresses (bounds/termination), but cannot fully recover what sequence relation must hold to satisfy the rotation specification.

3.5 Prompt Construction and Verification Loop

In each repair round, VERUSSEEK constructs a single prompt consisting of: (i) the failing code snippet and verifier feedback, (ii) expanded construct-level evidence from retrieval, and (iii) (for loops) structure-first invariant hints. The LLM outputs a patch (*e.g.*, new invariants, strengthened contracts, or small

Table 4. VerusBench's Tasks

No.	Dataset	Tasks	Executable LoC	Spec LoC
1	CloverBench	11	175	80
2	Diffy	38	951	265
3	MBPP	78	1333	700
4	Misc	23	390	207
Total		150	2849	1252

Table 5. Per-task characteristics

VerusBench	#Num
Total LoC	32
Spec LoC	8
Proof LoC	10
Loop invariant proof	*8*
Non-loop-inv. proof	*2*
Number of loops	1.6
Number of helper lemmas	0.07

proof blocks), which is immediately checked by Verus. If verification still fails, the new error message is used to re-classify the query type and re-retrieve evidence for the next round. This preserves the generate–verify–repair workflow of prior agents, while substantially improving grounding by retrieving the right *constructs* and reintroducing only the minimal *structure* needed for verification.

4 Evaluation

We implemented a prototype tool VERUSSEEK and conducted a comprehensive evaluation to answer the following research questions:

RQ1. Overall effectiveness. Does VERUSSEEK improve the success rate of Verus proof synthesis compared to the state-of-the-art (SOTA) method?
RQ2. Ablation Study. Do the components of VERUSSEEK contribute to the final effectiveness?
RQ3. Generalization across LLMs. Do the improvements transfer across different backbone LLMs?
RQ4. Qualitative Analysis. What qualitative differences in generated invariants explain successes and failures across methods?

4.1 Experimental Setup

Benchmark. We use all 150 non-trivial verification tasks from VerusBench spanning four suites: CloverBench [24], Diffy [25], MBPP [26], and Misc. These benchmark programs contain Verus-annotated Rust programs with specifications that need to be verified but without proofs. Table 4 and Table 5 summarize the detailed statistical data of the benchmark.

Compared Baselines. We compare VERUSSEEK against several baselines: (1) AutoVerus [18]: an LLM-based agent designed to synthesize proofs for Rust code. It operates in three sequential phases(generation, refinement, and debugging) with static few-shot prompting and no retrieval. (2) RagVerus [27]: a retrieval-augmented LLM baseline for repository-level Verus proof synthesis. It dynamically retrieves project-relevant code/proof context for iterative repair. (3) Basic

RAG: augments generation by retrieving whole verified files as context. (4) Chunked RAG: enables semantic code chunking and further incorporates query-type aware retrieval and hierarchical context expansion, but does not apply invariant enhancement; (5) VERUSSEEK: our proposed full system that additionally strengthens loop-related proof obligations by injecting enhanced invariants.

Metrics. We evaluate all methods using three primary metrics: (1) *verification success rate*: the fraction of tasks verified by Verus without errors within the allowed budget; (2) *first-shot success rate*: the fraction of tasks solved in the first attempt (Step 1), reflecting the quality of the initial proof synthesis; (3) *generate iteration*: the number of generated files executed before verification succeeds. By default, we report the total number of correctly verified tasks obtained after three consecutive runs of VERUSSEEK (*i.e.*, Step 1, Step 2, and Step 3).

Configuration of LLMs. We run all settings with two backbones: *gpt-4o* and *deepseek-v3.2*. We use `max_tokens`=4096 and `temperature`=1.0. Embeddings use *text-embedding-3-small* (1536 dimensions).

Table 6. Evaluation results on VerusBench

Suite	Step	AutoVerus [18]	RagVerus [27]	Basic RAG	Chunked RAG	VERUSSEEK
CloverBench (11)	Step 1	7	3	9	7	8
	Step 2	0	1	0	2	2
	Step 3	0	0	0	0	0
	Total	7/11	4/11	9/11	9/11	10/11
Diffy (38)	Step 1	1	12	2	27	26
	Step 2	2	1	0	4	5
	Step 3	1	4	3	4	1
	Total	4/38	17/38	5/38	35/38	32/38
Misc (23)	Step 1	11	11	12	11	15
	Step 2	0	0	2	3	1
	Step 3	0	0	1	0	1
	Total	11/23	11/23	15/23	14/23	17/23
MBPP (78)	Step 1	34	34	38	27	55
	Step 2	6	12	10	6	5
	Step 3	7	7	1	4	3
	Total	47/78	53/78	49/78	37/78	63/78
All (150)	Step 1	53	60	61	72	104
	Step 2	8	14	12	15	13
	Step 3	8	11	5	8	5
	Total	69/150	85/150	78/150	95/150	122/150

4.2 RQ1: Overall Effectiveness

Table 6 reports the verification performance of four configurations under *gpt-4o* across four benchmark suites. AutoVerus verifies 69/150 tasks (46.0%). RagVerus verifies 85/150 tasks (56.7%). Adding file-level context via Basic RAG improves over AutoVerus to 78/150 (52.0%), suggesting that retrieved examples help but are limited by noise from whole-file retrieval. Replacing coarse retrieval with *construct-level* retrieval yields a larger gain: Chunked RAG verifies 95/150 tasks (63.3%), a +6.6 point improvement over RagVerus, demonstrating that semantic chunking plus query-type aware retrieval and hierarchical context expansion provide substantially more relevant proof evidence. Finally, VERUSSEEK achieves the best overall performance, verifying 122/150 tasks (81.3%), a +35.3 point improvement over AutoVerus and +18.0 points over Chunked RAG, showing that invariant enhancement provides a strong complementary benefit beyond retrieval alone.

Beyond total success, VERUSSEEK improves how quickly proofs are found. It solves 104/150 tasks in Step 1 (69.3%), compared to 53/150 (35.3%) for AutoVerus and 72/150 (48.0%) for Chunked RAG. Among solved tasks, VERUSSEEK generates 1307 verification files to solve 122 tasks, whereas AutoVerus generates 1737 files to solve 69 tasks (10.71 attempts per solved task vs. 25.17 for AutoVerus), suggesting that the initial proofs are closer to what Verus needs, and fewer restarts are required.

Across all metrics, the results show a clear progression: coarse retrieval provides a small benefit, construct-level retrieval provides a large jump, and invariant enhancement delivers an additional substantial gain. Overall, VERUSSEEK yields the strongest end-to-end verification performance and the highest first-shot success.

4.3 Ablation Study

We evaluate four progressively stronger configurations under the same *gpt-4o* setting: (1) AutoVerus (no retrieval), (2) Basic RAG (file-level retrieval), (3) RagVerus (code-level retrieval), (4) Chunked RAG (semantic chunking + query-type aware retrieval + hierarchical context expansion), and (5) VERUSSEEK (Chunked RAG + loop-invariant synthesis).

Table 7. Ablation summary on *gpt-4o*.

Method	Retrieval Unit	Type-aware & Context	Loop Synth.	Success (Overall)
AutoVerus [18]	None	No	No	69/150 (46.0%)
RagVerus [27]	Code/Metadata	No	No	85/150 (56.7%)
Basic RAG	File	No	No	78/150 (52.0%)
Chunked RAG	Chunk	Yes	No	95/150 (63.3%)
VERUSSEEK	Chunk	Yes	Yes	122/150 (81.3%)

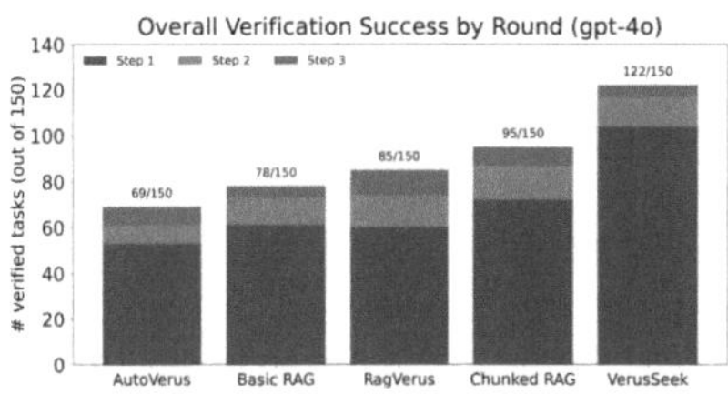

Fig. 6. Distribution of successes across independent restart rounds under *gpt-4o*.

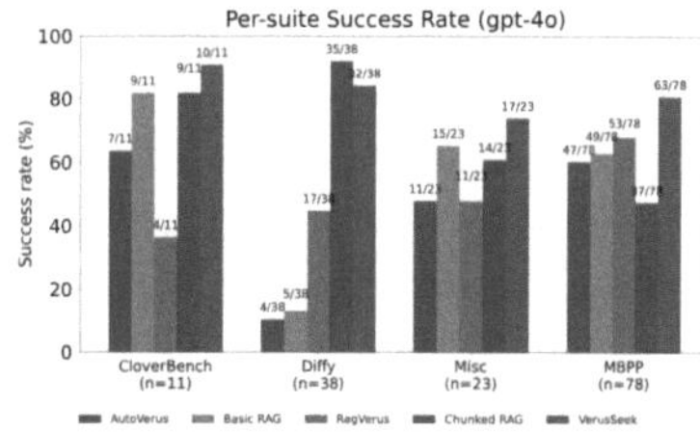

Fig. 7. Per-suite verification success rates under *gpt-4o*.

As shown in Table 7, Basic RAG provides a modest gain over AutoVerus (46.0% → 52.0%), confirming that retrieval is useful even with coarse units, but the improvement is limited by noise from whole-file context. Upgrading to Chunked RAG yields the dominant improvement (52.0% → 63.3%), slightly outperforming RagVerus (56.7%), indicating that *how* context is retrieved and assembled matters: retrieving proof constructs aligned with the current obligation (and expanding them with minimal surrounding structure) supplies more reusable templates than document-level retrieval. Finally, adding loop-invariant synthesis in VerusSeek produces an additional large jump (63.3% → 81.3%), showing that structural invariant hints (bounds, frame conditions, and termination measures) are complementary to retrieval and are especially valuable when the knowledge base lacks a close match.

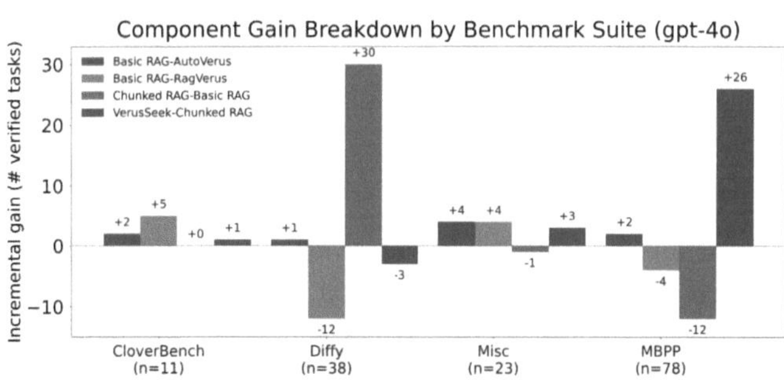

Fig. 8. Incremental gains over AutoVerus under `gpt-4o`.

Since each step is a *fresh restart*, the distribution of successes across Step 1–3 reflects how quickly each method finds a valid proof. Figure 6 shows that stronger configurations shift more successes to earlier rounds, indicating better "first-shot" proof quality. We further visualize the *cumulative* success rate (success by Step k). VerusSeek dominates across all rounds, reaching 81.3% by Step 3, while AutoVerus saturates at 46.0%, highlighting that retrieval +

synthesis substantially increases the probability of finding a correct proof within a small number of restarts.

Figure 7 further explains where the improvements arise. On Diffy, *semantic code chunking* combined with *type-aware retrieval* and *hierarchical context expansion* provides the largest lift for both models, suggesting that Diffy instances benefit most from retrieving loop- and array-specific proof constructs rather than entire files. On MBPP, adding *loop invariant synthesis* yields the largest additional gain for both backbones, consistent with MBPP tasks requiring strong structural obligations (bounds, frame conditions, and termination measures) in addition to semantic proof patterns.

Figure 8 attributes the improvement over AutoVerus to three successive changes: (i) adding Basic RAG, (ii) upgrading to Chunked RAG by incorporating semantic code chunking together with query-type aware retrieval and hierarchical context expansion, and (iii) adding loop invariant synthesis. The largest gain comes from Chunked RAG, showing that retrieving proof constructs at the right granularity and reconstructing minimal surrounding context is the primary driver of verification success. Loop invariant synthesis provides an additional, complementary boost by supplying structural invariants (*e.g.*, `Bounds`, `Frame`, and `Termination`), especially when retrieval does not yield a close matching loop pattern.

Table 8. Overall success rates under different LLM backends (150 tasks in total).

LLM Backend	AutoVerus [18]	RagVerus [27]	Basic RAG	Chunked RAG	VerusSeek
gpt-4o	69/150 (46.0%)	85/150 (56.7%)	78/150 (52.0%)	95/150 (63.3%)	122/150 (81.3%)
deepseek-v3.2	60/150 (40.0%)	62/150 (41.3%)	59/150 (39.3%)	87/150 (58.0%)	116/150 (77.3%)

4.4 Generalization Across LLMs

We further study whether the efficacy of our retrieval-and-synthesis pipeline depends on the choice of the backbone LLM. The same experimental configurations are instantiated using two LLM backends: *gpt-4o* (default in the above experiments) and *deepseek-v3.2*.

Table 8 shows that the same trend holds under both backends: stronger context construction yields higher verification success. With *gpt-4o*, success increases monotonically from AutoVerus (69/150) to Basic RAG (78/150), to RagVerus (85/150), to Chunked RAG (95/150), and reaches the best performance with VerusSeek (122/150). With *deepseek-v3.2*, VerusSeek again achieves the highest success rate (116/150), with Chunked RAG as a strong intermediate variant (87/150). In contrast, Basic RAG is less reliable under *deepseek-v3.2* (59/150) and does not consistently improve over AutoVerus (60/150) or RagVerus (62/150), indicating that coarse file-level retrieval can introduce enough irrelevant context to offset its benefits for a less noise-robust model.

Overall, these results indicate that our retrieval and synthesis components largely transfer across LLM backends; the backbone mainly affects the absolute success ceiling and the tolerance to noisy retrieved context.

4.5 Qualitative Analysis

To understand why verification succeeds or fails under different proof-generation settings, we qualitatively analyze representative Diffy tasks. Figure 9 and Fig. 10 compare the invariants generated by VERUSSEEK. Both attempts typically recover basic structural facts (*e.g.*, bounds and length bookkeeping), but they differ in whether the invariants capture the sequence-level relation required by the postcondition.

```
while (i < N as usize)
    invariant
        N > 0,
        0 <= i <= N as usize,
        a.len() == N,
        sum.len() == 1,
        i > 0 ==> sum[0] <= i as i32,
        forall k: int 0 <= k < a.len() ==> a[k] == 1,
    decreases N as usize - i,
    ...
    ...
```

Fig. 9. Case 1 (verified).

```
while (i < N as usize)
    invariant
        N > 0,
        i <= N as usize,
        a.len() == N,
        sum.len() == 1,
        forall k:
       int 0 <= k < a.len() ==> old(a)[k] == a[k],
        sum[0] == (if i == 0 { 0 } else { sum[0] }),
        sum[0] <= i,
    decreases N as usize - i,
    ...
```

Fig. 10. Case 2 (unverified).

5 Related Work

In this section, we review prior work on LLM-based proof synthesis and position VERUSSEEK relative to these approaches.

LLM-BBased Specification and Proof Generation. There has been substantial interest in applying LLMs to reduce the manual effort of formal verification by automating the creation of specifications, invariants, and proofs. In imperative-language settings (*e.g.*, C and Java), prior work has explored multi-agent collaboration and decomposition to improve specification generation quality and coverage (*e.g.*, AutoSpec [7], SpecGen [28], SLD-Spec [29], ACInv [30], NL2ACSL [31], prompt-engineering strategies for invariant discovery and proof completion [32–34], and reinforcement-learning or feedback-driven fine-tuning to better align generations with verifier requirements (*e.g.*, LIG-SE [35], ReForm [36], Clause2Inv [37]). These efforts highlight a common theme: verification success is often bottlenecked not by producing syntactically valid annotations, but by producing *inductive* and *solver-aligned* proof artifacts (e.g., loop invariants with the right bounds, frames, triggers, and relational content).

LLM-Based Proof Synthesis for Rust. As verification attention shifts toward Rust for security-critical software, recent work has begun to target the Rust verification ecosystem. AutoVerus [18] establishes a generate–verify–repair pipeline; AlphaVerus [6] studies self-improving verified generation via staged refinement; and VeruSAGE [38] shows gains from multi-agent orchestration on larger Rust benchmarks. RagVerus [27] introduces repository-level retrieval-augmented generation and shows that retrieving relevant project context improves proof completion under practical inference budgets. VeriStruct [39] shifts focus from isolated functions to data-structure modules, highlighting the role of structural decomposition in automated verification. VeruSyn [40] addresses data scarcity by synthesizing a large-scale Verus training corpus, showing that scaling seed data can reduce proof-synthesis cost and improve model capability. Collectively, these works demonstrate that LLM-driven generation, iterative repair, and agentic search can substantially improve proof Synthesis in Verus.

In contrast, VerusSeek leverages LLMs to perform semantic proof-construct chunking, type-aware retrieval, hierarchical context expansion, and loop invariant synthesis in a unified pipeline. Moreover, to the best of our knowledge, there is no comparable existing work that drives Verus proof synthesis by using LLMs for semantic proof-construct chunking, type-aware retrieval, hierarchical context expansion, and loop invariant synthesis, which are the key steps of our approach.

6 Conclusion

We have presented VerusSeek, a retrieval-augmented framework for automated Verus proof synthesis that addresses the granularity mismatch of naïve RAG by indexing verification-relevant proof constructs and reconstructing only the minimal surrounding context needed for grounding. Across 150 VerusBench tasks, VerusSeek substantially improves verification success over strong LLM-based baselines, showing that semantic chunking plus hierarchical context expansion is an effective recipe for scaling LLM-assisted verification in Rust/Verus.

Acknowledgements. This work was supported in part by the National Natural Science Foundation of China (Nos. 62472339, 62302375, 62192734), the Basic Research Foundation of Shenzhen City (No. JCYJ20250604184202003), the China Postdoctoral Science Foundation funded project (No. 2023M723736), and the Fundamental Research Funds for the Central Universities.

References

1. Klabnik, S., Nichols, C.: The Rust programming language, No Starch Press (2023)
2. Jung, R., Jourdan, J.-H., Krebbers, R., Dreyer, D.: Rustbelt: securing the foundations of the rust programming language. Proc. ACM Program. Lang. **2**(POPL), 1–34 (2017)
3. Xu, Z., Wu, B., Wen, C., Zhang, B., Qin, S., He, M.: RPG: rust library fuzzing with pool-based fuzz target generation and generic support. In: Proceedings of the IEEE/ACM 46th International Conference on Software Engineering, pp. 1–13 (2024)

4. Lattuada, A., et al.: Verus: verifying rust programs using linear ghost types. Proc. ACM Program. Lang. **7**(OOPSLA1), 286–315 (2023)
5. Lattuada, A., et al.: Verus: a practical foundation for systems verification. In: Proceedings of the ACM SIGOPS 30th Symposium on Operating Systems Principles, pp. 438–454 (2024)
6. Aggarwal, P., Parno, B., Welleck, S.: Alphaverus: bootstrapping formally verified code generation through self-improving translation and treefinement. arXiv preprint arXiv:2412.06176 (2024)
7. Wen, C., et al.: Enchanting program specification synthesis by large language models using static analysis and program verification. In: International Conference on Computer Aided Verification, pp. 302–328. Springer, Cham (2024)
8. Naveed, H., et al.: A comprehensive overview of large language models. ACM Trans. Intell. Syst. Technol. **16**(5), 1–72 (2025)
9. Wen, C., et al.: A survey on static code analysis with large language models. In: International Conference on Knowledge Science, Engineering and Management. Springer, Cham (2026)
10. Cao, J., et al.: From informal to formal–incorporating and evaluating LLMs on natural language requirements to verifiable formal proofs. In: Proceedings of the 63rd Annual Meeting of the Association for Computational Linguistics (Volume 1: Long Papers), pp. 26984–27003 (2025)
11. Ma, Z., et al.: Towards practical requirement analysis and verification: a case study on software ip components in aerospace embedded systems. arXiv preprint arXiv:2404.00795 (2024)
12. Su, J., Deng, L., Wen, C., Qin, S., Tian, C.: CFSTRA: enhancing configurable program analysis through LLM-driven strategy selection based on code features. In: International Symposium on Theoretical Aspects of Software Engineering, pp. 374–391. Springer, Cham (2024)
13. Wen, C., et al.: Automatically inspecting thousands of static bug warnings with large language model: How far are we? ACM Trans. Knowl. Discov. Data **18**(7), 1–34 (2024)
14. Ma, Z., et al.: Automated LTL specification generation from industrial aerospace requirements. In: International Symposium on Formal Methods, pp. 1–20. Springer, Cham (2026)
15. Jiang, C., et al.: Large language models for multilingual code intelligence: a survey. In: International Conference on Knowledge Science, Engineering and Management. Springer, Cham (2026)
16. Lin, Y., et al.: How well does knowledge injection enhance LLM-aided formal protocol modeling? In: 2026 IEEE International Conference on Software Analysis, Evolution and Reengineering (SANER). IEEE (2026)
17. Wang, Y., et al.: Synergizing LLM-driven semantic reasoning with assertion-guided analysis for enhanced vulnerability detection. In: 2026 IEEE International Conference on Software Analysis, Evolution and Reengineering (SANER). IEEE (2026)
18. Yang, C., et al.: Autoverus: automated proof generation for rust code. Proc. ACM Program. Lang. **9**(OOPSLA2), 3454–3482 (2025)
19. Zhang, S., Liu, H., Ma, Z., Liang, X., Wen, C.: Formal verification of aerospace software IP components: a multi-tool case study. In: Proceedings of the 2026 6th International Conference on Computer Network Security and Software Engineering, pp. 1–9 (2026)
20. Ma, Z., Wen, C., Bin, Yu., Jie, S.: Integrating ensemble learning and large language models for efficient formal verification of IP-based aerospace systems. Inf. Fusion **125**, 103466 (2026)

21. Hu, J., et al.: When large language models meet formal theorem proving: a survey. In: International Conference on Knowledge Science, Engineering and Management. Springer, Cham (2026)
22. Lewis, P., et al.: Retrieval-augmented generation for knowledge-intensive NLP tasks. Adv. Neural. Inf. Process. Syst. **33**, 9459–9474 (2020)
23. Gao, Y., et al.: Retrieval-augmented generation for large language models: a survey. arXiv preprint arXiv:2312.10997, 2(1), (2023)
24. Sun, C., Sheng, Y., Padon, O., Barrett, C.: Clover: CLO sed-loop verifiable code generation. In: International Symposium on AI Verification, pp. 134–155. Springer, Cham (2024)
25. Chakraborty, S., Gupta, A., Unadkat, D.: Diffy: inductive reasoning of array programs using difference invariants. In: International Conference on Computer Aided Verification, pp. 911–935. Springer, Cham (2021)
26. Misu, M.R.H., Lopes, C.V., Ma, I., Noble, J.: Towards ai-assisted synthesis of verified Dafny methods. Proc. ACM Softw. Eng. **1**(FSE), 812–835 (2024)
27. Zhong, S.C., Si, X.: Towards repository-level program verification with large language models. In: Proceedings of the 1st ACM SIGPLAN International Workshop on Language Models and Programming Languages, pp. 27–39 (2025)
28. Ma, L., Liu, S., Li, Y., Xie, X., Bu, L.: Specgen: automated generation of formal program specifications via large language models. In: 2025 IEEE/ACM 47th International Conference on Software Engineering (ICSE), pp. 16–28. IEEE (2025)
29. Chen, Z., et al.: Sld-spec: enhancement LLM-assisted specification generation for complex loop functions via program slicing and logical deletion. arXiv preprint arXiv:2509.09917 *arXiv preprint* (2025)
30. Liu, R., Chen, M., Wu, L-I., Ke, J., Li, G.: Enhancing automated loop invariant generation for complex programs with large language models. Sci. Comput. Program. 103387 (2025)
31. Su, W., Wu, X., Zhao, Y.: NL2ACSL: interactively translating natural language to ANSI C specification language with large language models. Knowl. Based Syst. 115177 (2025)
32. Chakraborty, S., et al.: Ranking LLM-generated loop invariants for program verification. In: Findings of the Association for Computational Linguistics: EMNLP 2023, pp. 9164–9175 (2023)
33. Li, J., Li, G., Li, Y., Jin, Z.: Structured chain-of-thought prompting for code generation. ACM Trans. Softw. Eng. Methodol. **34**(2), 1–23 (2025)
34. Beg, A., O'Donoghue, D., Monahan, R.: Evaluating LLM-generated ACSL annotations for formal verification. arXiv preprint arXiv:2602.13851 (2026)
35. Liu, C., Xiwei, W., Feng, Y., Cao, Q., Yan, J.: Towards general loop invariant generation: a benchmark of programs with memory manipulation. Adv. Neural. Inf. Process. Syst. **37**, 129120–129145 (2024)
36. Yan, C., et al.: Re: form–reducing human priors in scalable formal software verification with RL in LLMs: a preliminary study on dafny. *arXiv preprint*arXiv:2507.16331 (2025)
37. Cao, W., et al.: Clause2inv: a generate-combine-check framework for loop invariant inference. Proc. ACM Softw. Eng. **2**(ISSTA), 1009–1030 (2025)
38. Yang, C., Neamtu, N., Hawblitzel, C., Lorch, J.R., Lu, S.: Verusage: a study of agent-based verification for rust systems. arXiv preprint arXiv:2512.18436 (2025)
39. Sun, C., et al.: Veristruct: Ai-assisted automated verification of data-structure modules in verus. arXiv preprint arXiv:2510.25015 (2025)
40. Di, N., et al.: Reducing the costs of proof synthesis on rust systems by scaling up a seed training set. *arXiv preprint*arXiv:2602.04910 (2026)

Towards Accurate Thread Sharing Analysis via Synchronization-Aware Dynamic Tracing

Jun Zhang[1], Xinyin Liao[1], Cheng Wen[1(✉)], Jie Su[1], Zhuohua Li[1], Yuandao Cai[2], Xiaoxue Ma[3], and Shengchao Qin[1(✉)]

[1] Guangzhou Institute of Technology, Xidian University, Xi'an, China
{wencheng,qinshengchao}@xidian.edu.cn
[2] The Hong Kong University of Science and Technology, Hong Kong, China
[3] City University of Hong Kong, Hong Kong, China

Abstract. Understanding which memory locations are truly shared across threads is fundamental for debugging, testing, and analyzing multi-threaded software. Existing static analyses provide broad coverage, but often over-approximate sharing because of aliasing, indirect calls, and complex control flow, which limits their practical usefulness. This paper presents a synchronization-aware dynamic thread-sharing analysis that derives sharing information from concrete executions. Our approach instruments memory accesses and key synchronization events, executes the program under available test cases, and performs an offline analysis to identify source-level thread-sharing points and summarize cross-thread interactions. The analysis further distinguishes thread-local data, observed synchronized sharing, and critical thread sharing points. We implement the approach in an open-source tool, DtTsa, and evaluate it on three benchmark suites (*i.e.*, CVE-Benchmark, DataRaceBench, SCTBench). Results show that DtTsa produces concise, execution-grounded sharing summaries, covers many race-relevant access sites reported by existing tools, directly supports subsequent controlled concurrency testing, and incurs practical overhead.

1 Introduction

Concurrency is a standard technique to improve performance and responsiveness in modern software, but it also makes programs substantially harder to understand, debug, and test [1,2]. In shared-memory multithreaded systems, bugs often arise from unexpected interactions between threads through common data, and even understanding *where* such interaction occurs can be difficult. Prior work on concurrency analysis and race detection has long shown that shared-memory interactions are central to correctness and testing, yet they remain hard to characterize precisely in practice.

A basic question, therefore, matters for both developers and analysis tools: *which memory locations are actually shared across threads, and where in the code does that sharing occur*? The answer is useful for several software engineering

G. De Giacomo et al. (Eds.): TASE 2026, LNCS 16697, pp. 101–120, 2027.
https://doi.org/10.1007/978-3-032-30693-7_7

tasks. It helps developers understand program behavior, inspect synchronization assumptions, narrow debugging effort, and focus concurrency testing on the parts of the code that truly matter. It is also useful for downstream debugging and testing (*e.g.*, controlled concurrency testing), where the effectiveness of schedule exploration depends heavily on selecting good candidate locations [3,4].

However, identifying thread sharing precisely is difficult. In real programs, sharing is often introduced through dynamic allocation, pointer dereferences, aliasing, indirect calls, and runtime-specific parallel constructs [5,6]. Static analyses can provide broad coverage, but they must reason conservatively about heap objects, control flow, and cross-thread reachability. As a result, they often over-approximate the set of potentially shared locations, which can reduce the practical value of their results for debugging and testing. This challenge is widely recognized in prior work on static concurrency and data-sharing analysis [7].

Dynamic techniques provide a different trade-off [8]. Tools such as ThreadSanitizer monitor concrete executions and are highly effective at exposing specific race bugs [9,10]. Yet race detectors mainly report individual conflicting accesses or race pairs, rather than giving developers a compact summary of the broader sharing structure of a program. In practice, developers often need more than a bug report: they need an execution-grounded view of which source locations participate in cross-thread sharing, whether that sharing appears synchronized, and which locations are likely to be relevant for further investigation or testing.

This paper presents *dynamic thread-sharing analysis with synchronization-aware tracing*, a practical approach that summarizes thread sharing using evidence from real executions. The approach follows a simple pipeline. First, we instrument the program to record memory accesses (*e.g.*, reads and writes) together with key synchronization events (*e.g.*, lock acquire/release, wait/signal, and thread fork/join). Each event is linked to source-code locations, allowing trace data to be reported in terms that developers can interpret. Second, we execute the instrumented program using a set of test inputs (and optionally additional runs) and collect traces capturing which threads accessed which memory locations and where. Third, we perform an offline analysis that merges traces and reports a set of *critical points*: source locations and functions associated with memory that is accessed by multiple threads or involved in cross-thread read–write interactions. Using the recorded synchronization events, we also separate data that appears thread-local from shared data whose conflicting accesses appear ordered by observed synchronization. The output is designed to be concise and usable. Rather than exposing raw traces, we group observations by the memory identity used during tracing and summarize the relevant source locations and calling contexts. This format supports program understanding and provides a focused set of locations that can be used to guide further debugging or concurrency testing. In particular, the thread-sharing points can serve as a small, targeted set of scheduling locations for controlled concurrency testing [4,11,12], reducing the search space compared to instrumenting and scheduling at all program locations.

```c
#include<stdio.h>
#include<stdlib.h>

int* counter;

void foo() {
    (*counter)++;
}

int main() {
  counter = (int*) malloc(sizeof(int));
  if (counter== NULL) {
    fprintf(stderr, "malloc() fails\n");
    exit(1);
  }
  *counter = 0;
 #pragma omp parallel
  {
     foo();
  }
  printf("%d \n", *counter);
  free (counter);
  return 0;
}
```

(a) DataRaceBench DRB088.

```c
static void* pipe_write_open(void* arg) {
  ...
  pthread_mutex_lock(&inode->i_mutex);
  ...
  inode->i_pipe->readers++;
  ...
  pthread_mutex_unlock(&inode->i_mutex);
  return NULL;
}
// ... (omitted) ...

static void* involve(void* arg) {
  pthread_mutex_lock(&inode->i_mutex);
  ...
  inode->i_pipe = NULL;
  ...
  pthread_mutex_unlock(&inode->i_mutex);
  return NULL;
}

int main() {
  pthread_create(..., pipe_write_open);
  pthread_create(..., involve);
}
```

(b) CVE-Benchmark CVE-2009-3547.

Fig. 1. Motivating examples

We implement the approach in an open-source tool, DtTsa, and evaluate it on C/C++ multi-threaded programs on three benchmark suites: CVE-Benchmark [4], DataRaceBench [13], and SCTBench [11]. The results show that DtTsa produces concise, execution-grounded sharing summaries, covers many race-relevant access sites reported by existing tools, and incurs practical overhead. More broadly, our goal is to provide developers with a practical middle ground between conservative static over-approximation and low-level dynamic bug reports: a clear summary of where sharing actually happens and how that information can support program understanding and concurrency-focused testing [4,14].

In summary, this paper makes the following contributions.

- We present a synchronization-aware dynamic tracing approach for identifying source-level thread-sharing points from concrete executions.
- We design an offline analysis that merges traces across runs and summarizes thread-local, synchronized, and critical sharing behavior.
- We implement our approach as an open-source tool DtTsa[1]. Our evaluation show that DtTsa is effective, and useful.

2 Motivation

Thread-sharing information is fundamental for understanding concurrent programs and for guiding concurrency testing. If a memory location is accessed by

[1] https://doi.org/10.5281/zenodo.19634158.

multiple threads, then the program may depend on synchronization to ensure correctness, and that location also becomes a natural *schedule point* for exploring interleavings. However, identifying truly shared memory at source-code granularity is difficult in practice, especially when sharing is introduced through dynamic allocation, pointer dereferences, and runtime-specific concurrency constructs. As a result, existing static analyses may miss important sharing sites or report them too imprecisely to be useful for debugging and testing [3,15].

Example 1: Sharing Through Dynamic Allocation and Pointer Dereferences. Figure 1a shows a micro-benchmark in which a global pointer `counter` refers to heap-allocated memory. Inside function `foo`, each thread executes `(*counter)++`. The call to `foo` occurs inside an OpenMP `parallel` region [16, 17], so multiple threads may update the same heap location concurrently. Because the increment is not protected by a lock, atomic operation, or critical section, the writes may interleave and lead to a data race.

This example exposes two practical challenges for static analysis. First, the shared state is not a global scalar variable, but a heap object reached through a pointer. A static tool must therefore reason precisely about dynamic allocation, pointer aliasing, and the propagation of the pointer value across threads. Second, the concurrency boundary is introduced by OpenMP directives and runtime behavior rather than by explicit low-level thread operations in the source code. A tool that does not model these constructs precisely may fail to recognize the increment as a cross-thread access. In our experience, OpenRace [3] and SVF [15] do not report `*counter@8:6:W` as a thread-sharing point, even though that location is exercised by a concrete run. This example shows that static reasoning can miss practically important sharing points even in small programs, thus missing a data race issue.

Example 2: Sharing Points Beyond Plain Data Races. Figure 1b shows a real-world CVE subject (CVE-2009-3547) that illustrates a different kind of concurrency problem. Two threads access the same shared field, `inode->i_pipe`, while synchronizing on the same mutex, `i_mutex`. In `pipe_write_open`, one thread dereferences the shared structure and updates its state through `inode->i_pipe->readers++`. In `involve`, another thread sets `inode->i_pipe = NULL`. Although the accesses are associated with synchronization and may not be reported as a conventional data race, the program can still fail depending on the relative ordering of the two operations. If the invalidation happens before the dereference in a problematic execution, the later access may trigger a NULL-pointer dereference vulnerability.

This example highlights that developers often need more than a race report. They need to know which source-level accesses participate in cross-thread interaction, even when the bug is fundamentally an ordering or state-consistency problem rather than an unsynchronized conflict. Identifying the relevant *thread-sharing points* helps narrow debugging effort and provides natural candidate locations for schedule manipulation during controlled concurrency testing.

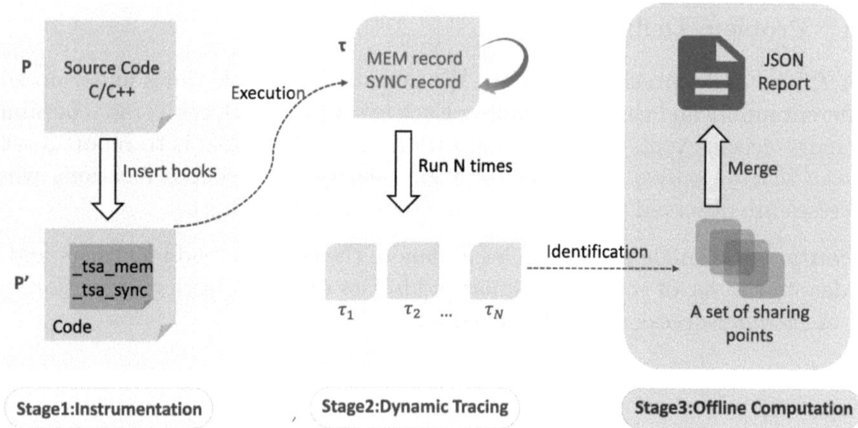

Fig. 2. The Overall Workflow of DtTsa

Implication. These examples motivate an execution-grounded view of thread sharing. A dynamic analysis can directly observe that multiple threads access the same memory location, relate those accesses to source-level statements, and record the synchronization context in which they occur. The resulting thread-sharing points provide a concise summary of where inter-thread interaction actually happens in observed executions. Such information is useful not only for understanding and debugging concurrent code, but also for guiding controlled concurrency testing: instead of perturbing or scheduling at all instructions, the tester can focus on a much smaller set of sharing-relevant locations that are more likely to expose concurrency failures.

3 Methodology

This section presents our methodology for identifying *thread-sharing points* from concrete executions of a multi-threaded C/C++ program. As shown in Fig. 2, the overall workflow has three stages: (1) **instrumentation**, which inserts tracing hooks into the program; (2) **dynamic tracing**, which records memory-access and synchronization events during execution; (3) **offline computation**, which computes per-run sharing summaries and merges them across runs into a source-level report.

The central idea is to recover sharing from *observed executions* rather than from static approximation. We therefore track which threads access which memory locations, associate those accesses with source-code locations, and use synchronization events to interpret whether the observed sharing appears coordinated or potentially unsafe.

3.1 Problem Definition

Let P be a multithreaded program. We execute P multiple times under possibly different inputs and thread schedules. Each execution produces a trace containing memory-access events and synchronization events. Our goal is to report a set of *thread-sharing points* at source-code granularity (*i.e.*, source locations whose accesses are observed to participate in cross-thread sharing).

Events. For a single execution, let $\mathcal{T}$ denote the set of thread identifiers and let $\mathbb{A}$ denote the set of concrete memory addresses observed in that execution.

A *memory-access event* is defined as

$$e = \langle t, k, a, n, \ell, f \rangle, \tag{1}$$

where $t \in \mathcal{T}$ is the thread identifier, $k \in \{\mathsf{R}, \mathsf{W}\}$ is the access kind (read or write), $a \in \mathbb{A}$ is the concrete address, $n \in \mathbb{N}$ is the access size in bytes, $\ell \in \mathcal{L}$ is the source location, and $f \in \mathcal{F}$ is the enclosing function.

A *synchronization event* is defined as

$$s = \langle t, op, x, \ell, f \rangle, \tag{2}$$

where $t \in \mathcal{T}$ is the thread identifier, op is a synchronization operation (*e.g.*, lock acquire, lock release, thread fork, or thread join), x identifies the synchronization object, ℓ is the source location, and f is the enclosing function.

Execution Trace. A trace for one execution is

$$\tau = \langle E, S \rangle, \tag{3}$$

where E is the sequence of memory-access events and S is the sequence of synchronization events recorded during that execution. Across N executions, we obtain a trace set

$$\mathcal{S} = \{\tau_1, \tau_2, \ldots, \tau_N\}. \tag{4}$$

Memory Identity. Concrete addresses usually differ across executions because of allocator behavior, ASLR, and nondeterminism. We therefore define a *memory identity* function

$$\mu : \mathbb{A} \to \mathbb{M}, \tag{5}$$

which maps a concrete address to a comparison unit used within a trace. In the simplest case, $\mu(a) = a$, i.e., the concrete address itself. In practice, μ may also use a coarser-grained unit such as a cache-line bucket, *e.g.*,

$$\mu(a) = \lfloor a/64 \rfloor, \tag{6}$$

to reduce noise from neighboring addresses. For an event e, we write

$$\mathrm{mem}(e) = \mu(a) \tag{7}$$

Thread-Sharing Point in One Trace. Given a trace $\tau = \langle E, S \rangle$, a source location $\ell \in \mathcal{L}$ is a *thread-sharing point* if there exist two memory-access events $e_1, e_2 \in E$ such that

$$\text{loc}(e_1) = \text{loc}(e_2) = \ell, \quad \text{mem}(e_1) = \text{mem}(e_2), \quad \text{tid}(e_1) \neq \text{tid}(e_2). \tag{8}$$

That is, the same source-level access site is observed to access the same memory identity from different threads in the same execution.

We denote the set of thread-sharing points in trace τ by $\mathcal{P}(\tau)$.

Thread-Sharing Points Across Executions. Because sharing may depend on inputs and schedules, we aggregate evidence across runs. The overall reported set of thread-sharing points is the union

$$\mathcal{P} = \bigcup_{i=1}^{N} \mathcal{P}(\tau_i). \tag{9}$$

This union-based definition preserves any location that is observed to participate in cross-thread sharing in at least one execution.

3.2 Stage 1: Instrumentation

The purpose of the instrumentation stage is to insert lightweight tracing hooks that record the runtime evidence needed for later sharing analysis. Starting from the source program P, we compile to LLVM IR and apply an LLVM pass that instruments two categories of operations:

1. *Memory accesses.* We instrument loads and stores whose target memory may be visible across threads.
2. *Synchronization operations.* We instrument operations that create or constrain inter-thread ordering, including lock acquire/release, semaphore wait-/signal, and thread fork/join. For OpenMP programs, we also instrument relevant runtime boundaries.

What is Instrumented. For memory accesses, the pass inserts a call immediately before each selected `load` or `store`. For synchronization, it inserts a call at each recognized synchronization operation. Each inserted call carries source-location and function identifiers derived from LLVM debug information, so that later reports can be mapped back to developer-visible code locations.

Omitting Provably Thread-Local Accesses. Instrumenting all memory accesses would incur unnecessary overhead, especially for stack variables that are guaranteed to remain local to a single thread. We therefore apply a lightweight escape-based filter before instrumentation.

A stack object is treated as *escaping* if its address may become visible outside the current thread, for example, because it is: (i) stored into heap or global memory, (ii) passed to an unknown or unanalyzed function, (iii) returned from the current function, or (iv) passed through a thread creation or OpenMP runtime boundary.

Only accesses to non-stack memory, unknown-base memory, or escaping stack objects are instrumented. Accesses to non-escaping stack locals are omitted. This rule is conservative: if the analysis is unsure whether an object escapes, it is treated as escaping and therefore instrumented.

Instrumentation Interface. The instrumentation pass inserts the following runtime hooks:

- `__tsa_mem(k, addr, size, loc_id, func_id)` for an instrumented memory read or write;
- `__tsa_sync(op, obj_id, loc_id, func_id)` for an instrumented synchronization operation.

Here, `loc_id` and `func_id` are compact identifiers associated with source locations and function names, respectively.

Instrumentation Algorithm. Algorithm 1 shows the static analysis used to decide where tracing hooks should be inserted. The analysis operates on the program's LLVM IR with debug information, but its purpose is not to perform concurrency analysis itself. Instead, it identifies memory accesses and synchronization operations that should be instrumented for later dynamic tracing. To reduce overhead, the analysis excludes stack accesses that are provably thread-local.

Algorithm 1: Static Analysis for Instrumentation

Require: Source program P; spawn API set Spawn; whitelist $\mathsf{NoStore}$
Ensure: Instrumented program P'
1: Compile P to LLVM IR with debug information
2: $\mathsf{Esc} \leftarrow$ FindEscapingStackObjects(IR, Spawn, $\mathsf{NoStore}$)
3: **for** each function F in IR **do**
4:     **for** each instruction I in F **do**
5:         **if** I is `load` or `store` **then**
6:             $o \leftarrow$ BaseObject(I)
7:             **if** o is non-stack or unknown, or $o \in \mathsf{Esc}$ **then**
8:                 Insert `__tsa_mem` before I
9:             **end if**
10:         **end if**
11:         **if** I is a synchronization, thread, or OpenMP runtime operation **then**
12:             Insert `__tsa_sync` at I
13:         **end if**
14:     **end for**
15: **end for**
16: Link the tracing runtime and emit P'
17: **return** P'

The analysis first compiles the source program to LLVM IR with debug information and identifies escaping stack objects (Lines 1–2). It then scans each instruction in the IR (Lines 3–15). For every `load` or `store`, it checks whether the accessed base object is non-stack, unknown, or an escaping stack object; if so, it inserts a `__tsa_mem` hook before the instruction (Lines 5–9). Accesses to non-escaping stack locals are omitted because they are thread-local. For synchronization, thread, and OpenMP runtime operations, it inserts a `__tsa_sync` hook so that the runtime can record ordering-related events (Lines 11–13). Finally, the tracing runtime is linked to produce the instrumented program P' (Line 16).

3.3 Stage 2: Dynamic Tracing

The second stage executes the instrumented program P' and records runtime events. We run P' under the available test cases and, optionally, automatically generated inputs (*e.g.*, fuzzing [18–22]). Each execution produces one trace. Repeating this process yields the trace set $\mathcal{S}$ used by the offline analysis.

What is Recorded. For each instrumented memory access, the runtime records: the executing thread, access kind (read or write), concrete address, access size, source location, and function. For each instrumented synchronization operation, the runtime records: the executing thread, the synchronization operation kind, the synchronization object, source location, and function.

Trace Representation. A trace is stored as a sequence of event records. Conceptually, we use the following record formats:

- MEM record: $(\mathsf{MEM}, tid, epoch, k, addr, size, loc\_id, func\_id)$
- SYNC record: $(\mathsf{SYNC}, tid, epoch, op, obj\_id, loc\_id, func\_id)$

Here, *epoch* is a per-thread monotonically increasing counter used to preserve the local order of events within each thread.

Algorithm 2: Offline Per-trace Analysis

Require: Trace $\tau = \langle E, S \rangle$; memory identity function μ
Ensure: Per-trace summary Σ_τ

$\Sigma_\tau \leftarrow$ empty map
Last $\leftarrow$ empty map from (m, ℓ) to thread ID
for each memory event $e = \langle t, k, a, n, \ell, f \rangle$ in E **do**
  $m \leftarrow \mu(a)$
  add ℓ to $\Sigma_\tau[m]$.lines
  add f to $\Sigma_\tau[m]$.functions
  add t to $\Sigma_\tau[m]$.threads
  if $(m, \ell) \in$ Last and Last$[(m, \ell)] \neq t$ **then**
    mark $\Sigma_\tau[m]$ as Shared
    if $k =$ W **then**
      mark $\Sigma_\tau[m]$ as RW
    end if
  end if
  Last$[(m, \ell)] \leftarrow t$
end for
for each sync event $s = \langle t, op, x, \ell, f \rangle$ in S **do**
  add ℓ to $\Sigma_\tau[x]$.lines
  add f to $\Sigma_\tau[x]$.functions
  mark $\Sigma_\tau[x]$ as Lock/UnLock/Wait/Signal/Fork/Join
end for
return Σ_τ

Why Synchronization Events are Included. Recording memory addresses alone is not sufficient for understanding how sharing is regulated. Two threads may access the same memory location either under disciplined synchronization or in a potentially unsafe way. By recording synchronization events together with memory accesses, the offline analysis can distinguish cross-thread sharing from local behavior and can characterize whether the observed sharing appears associated with lock-based coordination or with unsynchronized read–write interaction.

Multiple Executions. Because the observed sharing set depends on both input coverage and schedule coverage, we do not rely on a single run. Instead, each execution produces a per-run trace $\tau_i = \langle E_i, S_i \rangle$, and the final result is obtained by aggregating evidence across runs.

3.4 Stage 3: Offline Computation

The third stage processes the recorded traces and produces a source-level sharing report. This stage has two steps: (1) compute a per-trace sharing summary for each execution, and (2) merge the per-trace summaries into a global report.

Per-trace Analysis. For one trace $\tau = \langle E, S \rangle$, we group memory-access events by memory identity and source location. The goal is to determine which source-level accesses are observed on the same memory identity from multiple threads.

For each memory identity m, the analysis records: (i) the set of source lines associated with accesses to m, (ii) the set of enclosing functions, (iii) the set of participating thread IDs, and (iv) flags describing whether the observed sharing involves writes and whether related synchronization events were observed.

Algorithm 3: Merge per-trace summaries across runs

Require: Per-trace summaries $\{\Sigma_{\tau 1}, \ldots, \Sigma_{\tau_N}\}$
Ensure: Global report Σ
$\Sigma \leftarrow$ empty map from source location to global record
for each per-trace summary Σ_τ **do**
  for each key u in Σ_τ **do**
    for each source location ℓ in $\Sigma_\tau[u]$.lines **do**
      add ℓ to $\Sigma[\ell]$.lines
      union $\Sigma_\tau[u]$.functions into $\Sigma[\ell]$.functions
      propagate summary flags (RW, Lock, ..., Shared) into $\Sigma[\ell]$
    end for
  end for
end for
assign report IDs and serialize Σ as JSON
return Σ

A memory identity is marked as Shared if accesses to the same (m, ℓ) pair are observed from different threads. If at least one of these accesses is a write, the corresponding record is marked as RW. Synchronization events are recorded separately and linked to their synchronization object and source location, allowing the final summary to retain relevant lock-related context.

Algorithm 2 summarizes one execution trace by grouping events according to memory identity. It first initializes an output map Σ_τ and an auxiliary map Last that records the most recent thread seen for each (m, ℓ) pair (Lines 1–2). For each memory-access event, the algorithm computes the corresponding memory identity $m = \mu(a)$ and records its source line, function, and thread in Σ_τ (Lines 3–7). If the same (m, ℓ) pair was previously accessed by a different thread, the memory object is marked as Shared; if the current access is a write, it is additionally marked as RW (Lines 8–11). The map Last is then updated with the current thread (Line 14). After processing memory accesses, the algorithm records synchronization-related source lines and functions and marks them as Sync (Lines 13–16). The resulting summary captures, for a single run, which memory identities were accessed across threads, where those accesses occurred, and whether they involved writes or synchronization.

Merging Across Traces. The per-trace analysis identifies sharing within one execution. To obtain a global result, we merge all per-trace summaries at the source level.

Because concrete addresses are not stable across executions, we do not attempt to match memory identities from different runs directly. Instead, we aggregate by source location: if a source location is identified as a thread-sharing point in any trace, it is included in the final report. During merging, we union the associated functions and propagate summary tags such as RW or Lock whenever they are observed in any run.

Algorithm 3 combines the per-trace summaries from multiple executions into a single global report. Because concrete addresses are not stable across runs, the merge is performed at the source-location level. For each reported location, the algorithm unions the associated functions and propagates any observed summary tags, such as Shared, RW, and Lock. The final result is then assigned report IDs and serialized as JSON, containing the thread-sharing points identified across all runs. Each report entry contains a unique ID, a summary type (*e.g.*, RW or Lock), and the associated source lines and functions. This report is designed to be directly usable by developers and by downstream tools such as controlled concurrency testing frameworks.

Table 1. Datasets and subject statistics.

Dataset	#Programs	#Tests	LOC (median)	Threads (median)
CVE-Benchmark	10	10	156	3
DataRaceBench	208	208	16	4
SCTBench	41	41	93	3

The methodology intentionally separates evidence collection from analysis. Stage 1 determines *where* to observe the program by instrumenting potentially shared accesses and relevant synchronization operations. Stage 2 records *what happened* in concrete executions. Stage 3 computes *which source locations actually participate in cross-thread sharing* and merges those observations across runs. This design keeps the runtime mechanism simple while producing a concise, execution-grounded summary of thread sharing.

4 Evaluation

Our evaluation studies three research questions:

RQ1 Does DtTsa produce a more compact, execution-grounded set of sharing access sites than a representative static analysis?
RQ2 To what extent do DtTsa's reported sharing sites cover race-relevant access sites reported by existing dynamic race detectors?
RQ3 What overhead does DtTsa incur in runtime, memory usage, and binary size?

4.1 Experimental Setup

Datasets. We evaluate DtTsa on three widely used benchmark suites for concurrent software: CVE-Benchmark [4], which contains real-world vulnerability subjects; DataRaceBench [13], which contains curated OpenMP data-race benchmarks; and SCTBench [11], which contains benchmarks designed for controlled-scheduling and concurrency testing. Table 1 summarizes the datasets.

Baselines. We compare DtTsa against three representative baselines. SVF [15] serves as a representative static analysis that conservatively reports potential cross-thread sharing candidates. OpenRace [3] and ThreadSanitizer (TSan) [9] serve as dynamic race detectors that report concrete racy access pairs. For fairness, we use the same program versions and test suites shipped with each benchmark.

Common Comparison Unit. As the compared tools produce results in different forms, we normalize all outputs to the same representation: *source-level memory access sites* written as `file:line(:col)`. Throughout this section, a "sharing location" refers to an *access site* (*i.e.*, a load/store location), not a declaration line. For SVF, OpenRace, and TSan outputs derived from IR instructions or stack traces, we map each reported access to the innermost user-code frame using debug information and then de-duplicate by exact string match.

Repeated Runs and Aggregation. Since dynamic sharing depends on both inputs and thread schedules, we execute DtTsa multiple times for each program. For a subject program p, let $\mathcal{P}_1, \ldots, \mathcal{P}_N$ denote the per-run sharing sets reported by DtTsa. Unless otherwise stated, we use $N = 100$ runs when feasible. The final dynamic sharing set is the union

$$\mathcal{P}_{\text{dyn}}(p) = \bigcup_{i=1}^{N} \mathcal{P}_i. \tag{10}$$

We also compute the occurrence frequency of each reported site,

$$freq(x) = \frac{|\{i \mid x \in \mathcal{P}_i\}|}{N}, \tag{11}$$

to characterize stability across runs, but we do not filter sites by frequency.

Aggregation and Reporting. All set-based metrics are computed *per program* and then aggregated *per dataset*. Unless stated otherwise, we report *medians across programs*. For multiplicative runtime slowdowns, we report the *geometric mean* across programs.

Environment and Configurations. All experiments are conducted on a machine equipped with an Intel Core i9-14900K processor (24 cores at 3.2 GHz) and 128 GB of memory, running Ubuntu 20.04.6.

4.2 RQ1: Compactness Compared with Static Over-Approximation

For each program p, let $S_{\text{dyn}}(p) = \mathcal{P}_{\text{dyn}}(p)$ be the union sharing set reported by DTTSA across repeated executions, and let $S_{\text{svf}}(p)$ be the normalized sharing-candidate set reported by SVF. Intuitively, S_{dyn} contains source-level access sites that are actually observed to participate in cross-thread sharing during concrete executions, whereas S_{svf} contains statically predicted candidate sites that may be shared under conservative static reasoning. We compare these two sets using their sizes, their overlap,and their differences. In particular, "dyn-only" denotes sites reported only by DTTSA, while "svf-only" denotes sites reported only by SVF. We also compute:

$$J = \frac{|S_{\text{dyn}} \cap S_{\text{svf}}|}{|S_{\text{dyn}} \cup S_{\text{svf}}|} \quad \text{and} \quad R = \frac{|S_{\text{svf}}|}{|S_{\text{dyn}}|}, \tag{12}$$

where J is the Jaccard similarity between the dynamic and static reports. A larger J means that the two tools agree on a larger fraction of normalized sharing sites. R is the static-to-dynamic size ratio. A larger R indicates that SVF reports many more candidate sites than DTTSA, and therefore reflects how much DTTSA reduces the candidate set by focusing on execution-grounded sharing evidence.

Results. Table 2 summarizes the dataset-level medians. Across all three datasets, DTTSA reports fewer sharing sites than SVF. The reduction is most pronounced on CVE subjects ($R = 5.60$), reflecting SVF's over-approximation on real-world code (aliasing/paths/indirect calls), while still retaining a non-trivial overlap ($J = 0.17$), *i.e.*, DTTSA tends to select execution-relevant sites within SVF's broad superset. On DataRaceBench and SCTBench, we also observe a consistent reduction ($R \approx 2$) with similar agreement levels ($J \approx 0.20$–0.24), suggesting that DTTSA's reports remain concise for structured benchmark programs.

Table 2. RQ1 summary per dataset (median across programs).

Dataset	$\lvert S_{\text{dyn}}\rvert$	$\lvert S_{\text{svf}}\rvert$	$\lvert\cap\rvert$	dyn-only	svf-only	J	R
CVE-Benchmark	6.5	37.5	6.5	0.0	31.5	0.17	5.60
DataRaceBench	2.0	5.0	2.0	1.0	4.0	0.20	2.00
SCTBench	3.0	17.0	3.0	0.0	13.0	0.24	2.00

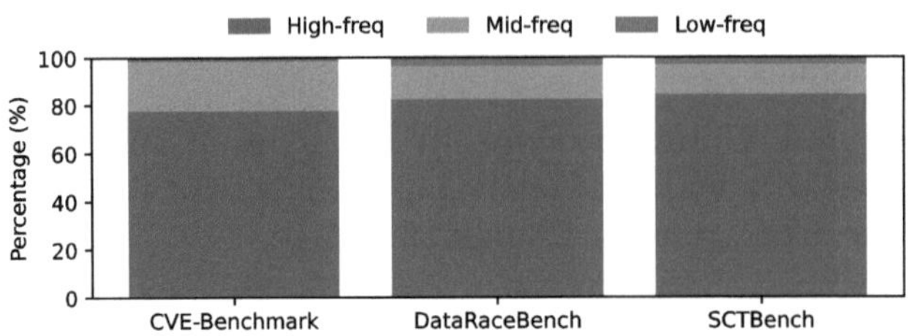

Fig. 3. Stability of the union sharing set across runs (median across programs). High-, mid-, and low-frequency sites are defined as sites with occurrence frequency $freq(x) \geq 0.8$, $0.2 \leq freq(x) < 0.8$, and $freq(x) < 0.2$, respectively.

Stability Across Runs. Figure 3 shows that most sites in the union sharing set are high-frequency sites (77.8%–84.6%), meaning that they appear repeatedly across executions rather than as isolated artifacts. Only a small fraction of sites fall into the low-frequency range (1.4%–3.6%), suggesting that schedule- or input-sensitive sharing exists but does not dominate the reported results.

Answer to RQ1: Overall, DtTSA produces a compact sharing summary that focuses on access sites exercised in real executions. Compared with SVF, it removes a large number of conservative static candidates while preserving meaningful overlap with statically predicted sharing.

4.3 RQ2: Coverage of Race-Relevant Access Sites

For each program p, let $P(p) = \{(a_i, b_i)\}$ denote the set of racy access pairs reported by a reference tool. Let $E(p)$ be the set of unique pair endpoints. We compute coverage only for programs on which the corresponding tool reports at least one race pair.

We report two micro-averaged metrics over all eligible programs:

$$\begin{aligned} \text{Cov}_{end}^{\text{micro}} &= \frac{\sum_p |E(p) \cap S_{\text{dyn}}(p)|}{\sum_p |E(p)|}, \\ \text{Cov}_{pair}^{\text{micro}} &= \frac{\sum_p |\{(a,b) \in P(p) \mid a \in S_{\text{dyn}}(p) \wedge b \in S_{\text{dyn}}(p)\}|}{\sum_p |P(p)|}. \end{aligned} \tag{13}$$

Endpoint coverage measures how many individual race-relevant access sites reported by the reference tool are included in DtTSA's sharing set. It reflects

Table 3. Thread-sharing points coverage per dataset. Coverage values are micro-averaged over all eligible programs.

Dataset	OpenRace			TSan		
	#Pairs	Cov_{end}^{micro}	$\text{Cov}_{pair}^{micro}$	#Pairs	Cov_{end}^{micro}	$\text{Cov}_{pair}^{micro}$
CVE-Benchmark [4]	63	0.60	0.40	12	0.45	0.42
DataRaceBench [13]	269	0.67	0.63	201	0.64	0.61
SCTBench [11]	5	1.00	1.00	14	0.67	0.79

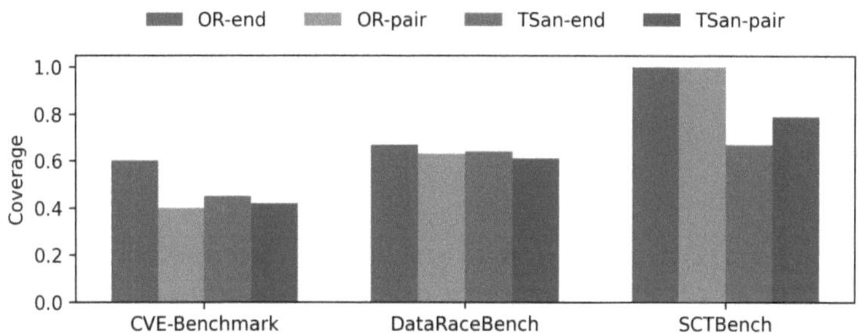

Fig. 4. Micro-averaged endpoint and pair coverage of DtTsa's sharing candidates with respect to OpenRace and TSan.

whether DtTsa can capture program locations that participate in reported races. Pair coverage is stricter: a race pair is counted as covered only when both of its endpoints are included in DtTsa's sharing set. Therefore, high endpoint coverage indicates that DtTsa captures many race-relevant access sites, while high pair coverage indicates that DtTsa captures complete race interactions.

Results. Table 3 and Fig. 4 show that DtTsa covers a substantial fraction of the access sites reported by both OpenRace and TSan. On DataRaceBench, coverage is consistently high for both tools (OpenRace: 0.67 endpoint/0.63 pair; TSan: 0.64 endpoint/0.61 pair), indicating that most benchmark race reports fall within DtTsa's observed sharing set. On CVE-Benchmark, coverage is lower but still meaningful, which is expected given the limited proof-of-concept inputs and the schedule sensitivity of real-world concurrent bugs. On SCTBench, DtTsa covers all OpenRace-reported pairs and most TSan-reported pairs.

Failure Analysis. To understand uncovered cases, we categorize them according to execution status and matching outcomes. Table 4 shows that the dominant causes are: (i) the relevant path or schedule was not exposed in our executions, and (ii) the corresponding subject was not successfully executed. Location-mapping issues are negligible after normalization.

Table 4. Failure Analysis: distribution of uncovered-case causes (percentage)

Dataset	Not executed	Schedule-related	Mapping issue	Other
CVE-Benchmark	0.0	100.0	0.0	0.0
DataRaceBench	50.5	49.5	0.0	0.0
SCTBench	33.3	66.7	0.0	0.0

Table 5. Overhead per dataset. Slowdown is geometric across programs; RSS and binary size are medians across programs. B/D/T denotes Base/DtTsa/TSan

Dataset	Slowdown (DtTsa)	Slowdown (TSan)	Peak RSS B/D/T	Binary (KB) B/D/T
CVE-Benchmark	1.33	5.8	2800/2880/14560	27.5/31.5/33.0
DataRaceBench	4.36	12.5	2880/2881/19840	19.5/19.6/19.6
SCTBench	1.86	6.2	1920/1920/10944	19.9/20.1/20.1

Answer to RQ2: DtTsa, despite not being a race detector, covers many race-relevant access sites reported by existing dynamic tools. This supports the claim that observed thread-sharing points provide a useful approximation of concurrency-relevant program locations.

4.4 RQ3: Performance Overhead

We measure the overhead of DtTsa, compared with three builds of each program: Base (uninstrumented), DtTsa (instrumented with our tracing), and TSan (compiled with ThreadSanitizer). Each configuration is repeated K times (default $K = 5$), and we report medians. Runtime overhead is reported as a slowdown relative to Base, using the geometric mean across programs in each dataset. We also report the memory usage (peak RSS) and binary size (in KB) as medians.

Results. Table 5 shows that DtTsa incurs substantially lower overhead than TSan on all three datasets. On CVE-Benchmark and SCTBench, the runtime slowdown of DtTsa remains modest (1.33× and 1.86×, respectively). On DataRaceBench, the slowdown increases to 4.36×, which is still markedly lower than TSan's 12.5× and is consistent with the heavier memory-access intensity of OpenMP kernels. Peak RSS remains close to the base execution for DtTsa, while TSan incurs much larger memory overhead. Binary-size differences are small in all settings, reflecting that the main cost comes from runtime tracing rather than code growth.

Answer to RQ3: DtTsa achieves practical overhead, especially compared with a full dynamic race detector. This makes it suitable as a lightweight analysis layer for program understanding and as a preprocessing step for downstream testing workflows.

5 Related Work

Our work is most closely related to prior research on (1) static thread-sharing analysis, (2) dynamic race detection and tracing, and (3) controlled concurrency testing. Compared with these lines of work, our goal is not to prove all potentially shared data statically, nor to report only concrete races, but to produce a concise, execution-grounded summary of *where* cross-thread sharing occurs and *how* it is regulated in observed runs.

Static Thread-Sharing Analysis. A large body of prior work uses static analysis to infer which variables or heap objects may be shared among threads [6, 7,15]. Another part of the work further points out potential data races [3,23–28]. These methods are valuable because they provide broad coverage, but they often rely on conservative pointer, heap, and control-flow abstractions [29,30]. As a result, many analyses over-approximate which locations may be shared, especially in the presence of dynamic allocation, aliasing, indirect calls, and runtime-specific parallel constructs. Our work differs in that it does not aim to approximate all *possible* sharing statically; instead, it reports *observed* cross-thread sharing from concrete executions at source-code granularity.

Dynamic Race Detection and Tracing. Dynamic tools such as ThreadSanitizer [9,31] and related race-detection techniques monitor executions to detect conflicting accesses that are not ordered by synchronization [32,33,33]. These tools are highly effective for finding concrete bugs (*e.g.*, FastTrack [34], Race-Hunter [35], Racetrack [36], ConVul [37], UFO [38]), but their main output is typically a set of racy access pairs rather than a compact summary of the overall sharing structure. Prior work on shared-memory dependence tracing also shows the value of runtime evidence for capturing inter-thread interactions precisely [8,39]. In contrast, our goal is broader than race reporting: we summarize where sharing occurs, relate it to source locations, and distinguish thread-local behavior from observed synchronized and potentially unsafe sharing patterns.

Controlled Concurrency Testing. Our work is also related to controlled concurrency testing and schedule exploration, where the choice of scheduling points strongly affects efficiency and bug-finding power [11,12,40]. Existing approaches (*e.g.*, PERIOD [4], Nekara [41], RFF [42], Coyote [43]) often depend on static candidate locations or low-level runtime signals, which can either over-approximate the search space or provide little structural explanation of sharing behavior. Our analysis complements these techniques by producing a compact, execution-grounded set of thread-sharing points that can serve as practical schedule candidates for downstream testing.

6 Conclusion

This paper presented DtTsa, a synchronization-aware dynamic thread-sharing analysis for multithreaded programs. By instrumenting memory accesses and key synchronization operations, collecting traces from real executions, and merging results offline, DtTsa identifies source-level thread-sharing points and summarizes how threads interact through shared memory. Compared with static approaches, DtTsa provides a more compact and execution-grounded view of sharing, while also covering many race-relevant access sites reported by existing dynamic tools.

Acknowledgements. This work was supported in part by the National Natural Science Foundation of China (Nos. 62302375, 62472339, 6240073166, 62192734), the China Postdoctoral Science Foundation funded project (No. 2023M723736), the Basic Research Foundation of Shenzhen City (No. JCYJ20250604184202003), and the Fundamental Research Funds for the Central Universities.

References

1. Chen, Y.A., You, Y.P.: Structured concurrency: a review. In: Workshop Proceedings of the 51st International Conference on Parallel Processing, pp. 1–8 (2022)
2. Hansen, P.B.: The Architecture of Concurrent Programs. Prentice-Hall Inc. (1977)
3. Swain, B., et al.: OpenRace: an open source framework for statically detecting data races. In: 2021 IEEE/ACM 5th International Workshop on Software Correctness for HPC Applications (Correctness), pp. 25–32. IEEE (2021)
4. Wen, C., He, M., Wu, B., Xu, Z., Qin, S.: Controlled concurrency testing via periodical scheduling. In: Proceedings of the 44th International Conference on Software Engineering, pp. 474–486 (2022)
5. Luo, H., Li, P., Ding, C.: Thread data sharing in cache: theory and measurement. ACM SIGPLAN Not. **52**(8), 103–115 (2017)
6. Krishna, A., Samih, A., Solihin, Y.: Data sharing in multi-threaded applications and its impact on chip design. In: 2012 IEEE International Symposium on Performance Analysis of Systems & Software, pp. 125–134. IEEE (2012)
7. Huang, J.: Scalable thread sharing analysis. In: Proceedings of the 38th International Conference on Software Engineering, pp. 1097–1108 (2016)
8. Bo, L., Jiang, S., Qian, J., Wang, R., Yao, Y.: Performance evaluation of data race detection based on thread sharing analysis with different granularities: an empirical study. IEEE Access **7**, 73819–73829 (2019)
9. Serebryany, K., Iskhodzhanov, T.: ThreadSanitizer: data race detection in practice. In: Proceedings of the Workshop on Binary Instrumentation and Applications, pp. 62–71 (2009)
10. Schilling, J., Wendler, A., Görz, P., Bars, N., Schloegel, M., Holz, T.: A binary-level thread sanitizer or why sanitizing on the binary level is hard. In: 33rd USENIX Security Symposium (USENIX Security 24), pp. 1903–1920 (2024)
11. Thomson, P., Donaldson, A.F., Betts, A.: Concurrency testing using controlled schedulers: an empirical study. ACM Trans. Parallel Comput. (TOPC) **2**(4), 1–37 (2016)
12. Mukherjee, S., Deligiannis, P., Biswas, A., Lal, A.: Learning-based controlled concurrency testing. Proc. ACM Program. Lang. **4**(OOPSLA), 1–31 (2020)
13. Liao, C., Lin, P.H., Asplund, J., Schordan, M., Karlin, I.: DataRaceBench: a benchmark suite for systematic evaluation of data race detection tools. In: Proceedings of the International Conference for High Performance Computing, Networking, Storage and Analysis, pp. 1–14 (2017)

14. Huang, J., et al.: Preserving concurrency-revealing seeds in fuzzing of concurrent programs via tuple-based coverage evaluation. In: IEEE International Conference on Software Analysis, Evolution and Reengineering (SANER). IEEE (2026)
15. Sui, Y., Xue, J.: SVF: interprocedural static value-flow analysis in LLVM. In: Proceedings of the 25th International Conference on Compiler Construction, pp. 265–266 (2016)
16. Chandra, R.: Parallel Programming in OpenMP. Morgan Kaufmann (2001)
17. Ayguadé, E., et al.: The design of OpenMP tasks. IEEE Trans. Parallel Distrib. Syst. **20**(3), 404–418 (2008)
18. Jiang, J., Wen, C., Fu, Z., Qin, S.: CtxFuzz: discovering heap-based memory vulnerabilities through context heap operation sequence guided fuzzing. Sci. Comput. Program., 103395 (2025)
19. Wen, C., et al.: MemLock: memory usage guided fuzzing. In: Proceedings of the ACM/IEEE 42nd International Conference on Software Engineering, pp. 765–777 (2020)
20. Fu, Z., Jiang, J., Wen, C., Xu, Z., Qin, S.: MemSpate: memory usage protocol guided fuzzing. In: International Conference on Formal Engineering Methods, pp. 237–256. Springer (2024)
21. Wang, H., et al.: Typestate-guided Fuzzer for discovering use-after-free vulnerabilities. In: Proceedings of the ACM/IEEE 42nd International Conference on Software Engineering, pp. 999–1010 (2020)
22. Xu, Z., Wu, B., Wen, C., Zhang, B., Qin, S., He, M.: RPG: rust library fuzzing with pool-based fuzz target generation and generic support. In: Proceedings of the IEEE/ACM 46th International Conference on Software Engineering, pp. 1–13 (2024)
23. Kahlon, V., Yang, Y., Sankaranarayanan, S., Gupta, A.: Fast and accurate static data-race detection for concurrent programs. In: International Conference on Computer Aided Verification, pp. 226–239. Springer (2007)
24. Kahlon, V., Sankaranarayanan, S., Gupta, A.: Static analysis for concurrent programs with applications to data race detection. Int. J. Softw. Tools Technol. Transfer **15**(4), 321–336 (2013)
25. Kahlon, V., Sinha, N., Kruus, E., Zhang, Y.: Static data race detection for concurrent programs with asynchronous calls. In: Proceedings of the 7th Joint Meeting of the European Software Engineering Conference and the ACM SIGSOFT Symposium on the Foundations of Software Engineering, pp. 13–22 (2009)
26. Chopra, N., Pai, R., D'Souza, D.: Data races and static analysis for interrupt-driven kernels. In: European Symposium on Programming, pp. 697–723. Springer (2019)
27. Wang, W.: MPIRace: a static data race detector for MPI programs. In: International Workshop on Languages and Compilers for Parallel Computing, pp. 73–90. Springer (2022)
28. Chen, L., Ding, X., Emani, M., Vanderbruggen, T., Lin, P.H., Liao, C.: Data race detection using large language models. In: Proceedings of the SC'23 Workshops of the International Conference on High Performance Computing, Network, Storage, and Analysis, pp. 215–223 (2023)
29. Cai, Y., Yao, P., Zhang, C.: Canary: practical static detection of inter-thread value-flow bugs. In: Proceedings of the 42nd ACM SIGPLAN International Conference on Programming Language Design and Implementation, pp. 1126–1140 (2021)

30. Grech, N., Fourtounis, G., Francalanza, A., Smaragdakis, Y.: Shooting from the heap: ultra-scalable static analysis with heap snapshots. In: Proceedings of the 27th ACM SIGSOFT International Symposium on Software Testing and Analysis, pp. 198–208 (2018)
31. Serebryany, K., Potapenko, A., Iskhodzhanov, T., Vyukov, D.: Dynamic race detection with LLVM compiler: compile-time instrumentation for ThreadSanitizer. In: International Conference on Runtime Verification, pp. 110–114. Springer (2011)
32. O'callahan, R., Choi, J.-D.: Hybrid dynamic data race detection. In: Proceedings of the Ninth ACM SIGPLAN Symposium on Principles and Practice of Parallel Programming, pp. 167–178 (2003)
33. Kulkarni, R., Mathur, U., Pavlogiannis, A.: Dynamic data-race detection through the fine-grained lens. arXiv preprint: arXiv:2107.03569 (2021)
34. Flanagan, C., Freund, S.N.: FastTrack: efficient and precise dynamic race detection. ACM Sigplan Not. **44**(6), 121–133 (2009)
35. Gerlits, E.A.: RaceHunter dynamic data race detector. Program. Comput. Softw. **50**(6), 467–481 (2024)
36. Yu, Y., Rodeheffer, T., Chen, W.: RaceTrack: efficient detection of data race conditions via adaptive tracking. In: Proceedings of the Twentieth ACM Symposium on Operating Systems Principles, pp. 221–234 (2005)
37. Meng, R., Zhu, B., Yun, H., Li, H., Cai, Y., Yang, Z.: CONVUL: an effective tool for detecting concurrency vulnerabilities. In: 2019 34th IEEE/ACM International Conference on Automated Software Engineering (ASE), pp. 1154–1157. IEEE (2019)
38. Huang, J.: UFO: predictive concurrency use-after-free detection. In: Proceedings of the 40th International Conference on Software Engineering, pp. 609–619 (2018)
39. Jiang, Y., Li, D., Xu, C., Ma, X., Lu, J.: Optimistic shared memory dependence tracing (T). In: 2015 30th IEEE/ACM International Conference on Automated Software Engineering (ASE), pp. 524–534. IEEE (2015)
40. Fonseca, P., Rodrigues, R., Brandenburg, B.B.: SKI: exposing kernel concurrency bugs through systematic schedule exploration. In: 11th USENIX Symposium on Operating Systems Design and Implementation (OSDI 14), pp. 415–431 (2014)
41. Agarwal, U., et al.: Nekara: generalized concurrency testing. In: 2021 36th IEEE/ACM International Conference on Automated Software Engineering (ASE), pp. 679–691. IEEE (2021)
42. Wolff, D., Shi, Z., Duck, G.J., Mathur, U., Roychoudhury, A.: Greybox fuzzing for concurrency testing. In: Proceedings of the 29th ACM International Conference on Architectural Support for Programming Languages and Operating Systems, vol. 2, pp. 482–498 (2024)
43. Deligiannis, P., Senthilnathan, A., Nayyar, F., Lovett, C., Lal, A.: Industrial-strength controlled concurrency testing for c# programs with coyote. In: International Conference on Tools and Algorithms for the Construction and Analysis of Systems, pp. 433–452. Springer (2023)

A HOL Theorem Proving Interface for C

Yiyuan Cao[1,2], Jiayi Zhuang[1], Jinkai Fan[1], Di Wang[1,2(✉)], and Zhenjiang Hu[1,2]

[1] Key Lab of HCST (PKU), MOE; SCS, Peking University, Beijing, China
[2] Zhongguancun Laboratory, Beijing, China
wangdi95@pku.edu.cn

Abstract. C programmers who wish to perform interactive theorem proving (e.g., when verifying critical code they write) currently face a language barrier: working with existing provers requires familiarity with their own proof languages—usually a custom tactic language or a functional programming language—far removed from the C programming environment and paradigm. To bridge this gap, we present the first higher-order logic (HOL) theorem proving interface for C. Our interface is *comprehensive*: it covers the core data types and operations of HOL theorem proving in the LCF style, readily usable for forward derivation of theorems by invoking existing inference rules. Our interface is *trustworthy*: by extending the LCF architecture with a client-server model, it ensures every theorem constructed by arbitrary C code is necessarily derived from a small trusted proof kernel. Finally, programming derived proof facilities in C is *practical*: we demonstrate this by implementing commonly used tactics for goal-directed reasoning as a library on top of our interface, which utilizes a goal-tree data structure dedicated to the bookkeeping of proof states and applies imperative programming patterns naturally.

Keywords: C programming · HOL theorem proving · LCF architecture

1 Introduction

Interactive theorem proving in expressive higher-order logics (abbreviated as HOL) has been successfully applied by expert teams to verify critical software, including OS kernels [9,12], compilers [13,14], and cryptographic implementations [2,29]. However, this powerful technique remains largely inaccessible to the broader community of systems programmers—despite the clear need for formal proofs, notably when verifying the security and correctness of critical software they write. One crucial barrier is that working in established theorem provers—e.g., Rocq, Isabelle, HOL4, Agda, Lean—requires mastery of custom tactic languages [5,16], declarative proof languages [28], or (dependently-typed)

D. Wang—Corresponding author.

G. De Giacomo et al. (Eds.): TASE 2026, LNCS 16697, pp. 121–139, 2027.
https://doi.org/10.1007/978-3-032-30693-7_8

functional programming languages [6,15,18], out of reach of the typical C programming environment and paradigm.

We envision a world where C programmers can conduct theorem proving in a familiar C development setting, without switching to a foreign proof language and external environment. ust as a developer includes `<gtk/gtk.h>` and links against the GTK library[1] to create a graphical interface, they should be able to include a theorem-proving header to develop theories and derive theorems in C, using operations exposed by the interface. Furthermore, just as developers customize GUI libraries by composing primitive functions into specialized widgets, they should be able to build derived facilities and proof strategies beyond the interface provided, naturally, using C programming techniques. While libraries for domain-specific tasks such as GUI design and database access are routinely used by developers, we are not aware of any comparable interface for theorem proving in C, let alone a usable suite of derived libraries.

The established method for engineering a trustworthy and programmable theorem prover is the LCF approach [6,7]. However, the meta languages of traditional LCF-style provers are ML-like functional languages (e.g., Standard ML and OCaml), featuring support for type abstraction, higher-order functions, and exceptions. Adapting the LCF approach to C presents two fundamental challenges:

(1) C's type system does not enforce type abstraction—unconstrained memory mutation and type casting make it possible to penetrate module boundaries and circumvent the guarded interface of the proof kernel that implements the primitive inference rules of the logic. This undermines the trustworthiness of the proof system: an inadvertent programming mistake or a piece of malicious code can lead to the construction of invalid theorems.

(2) C does not support higher-order functions or exceptions natively. In the LCF tradition, these features are considered essential: not only for defining the kernel interface, but more critically, for building essential proof facilities. The prime example is the notion of tactics for backward (i.e., goal-directed) reasoning [17]. Canonically, tactics are implemented as higher-order functions that return a list of subgoals together with a validation closure for reconstructing forward proofs from solved subgoals. These tactics are combined using tacticals, which compose validators via higher-order combinators; the implementation of tacticals additionally uses exceptions for backtracking the proof state.

We address these challenges in the implementation of our interface as well as in programming proof facilities as derived libraries in C. For the trustworthiness challenge (1), we extend the traditional LCF architecture with a client-server model. The proof kernel runs in a separate server process (we reuse the HOL Light theorem prover [11]). User code on the client side manipulates logical objects only through opaque handles via a core interface, so that process isolation prevents forgery of invalid theorems. For the proof programming challenge (2),

[1] A popular GUI library for C (https://gtk.org/; accessed 2026-02-21).

we adopt C-idiomatic patterns at two levels. At the core interface level, we expose a first-order interface and use status-code error handling. More importantly, at the derived library level, we show that facilities for goal-directed reasoning—traditionally reliant on higher-order functions and exceptions—can be naturally realized in C. Our design uses a goal-tree data structure that explicitly reifies the proof structure and stores validator functions at each internal node, together with imperative control flow for implementing more complex proof strategies.

Contributions. Our contributions are three-fold:

1. **A comprehensive core interface for HOL theorem proving in C** (Sect. 3). It covers term manipulation, inference rules, definitional principles, and proof-search procedures, enabling C developers to readily perform forward derivation of theorems in the LCF-style.
2. **A trustworthy implementation of the core interface** (Sect. 4). Our architecture guarantees that all theorems constructed by arbitrary user-written C code are necessarily derived from a small, trusted proof kernel.
3. **A practical demonstration of proof programming in C** (Sect. 5). Building on the core interface, we program support for goal-directed reasoning as derived proof libraries in C, including subgoaling functionalities and commonly used tactics for HOL reasoning.

Artifact Availability. The source code of the core interface and derived libraries presented in this paper is available online [4].

2 Background

This section reviews the necessary background on higher-order logic and the LCF approach to theorem proving.

2.1 Higher-Order Logic

Higher-order logic (HOL) is the logic underlying a family of modern theorem provers including HOL Light [11], HOL4 [26], and Isabelle/HOL [21]. We briefly describe its syntax. For a full account of its semantics, see Pitts [25].

Types. HOL types are built from type variables (α, β, ...) and type constructors applied to argument types (e.g., natural numbers *num*, finite lists $\mathit{list}(\alpha)$, etc.). Primitive type constructors include the Boolean type *bool* and the function type $\alpha \to \beta$ (written in infix), with their usual set-theoretic interpretations.

Terms. HOL terms are those of a simply-typed lambda calculus, comprising four primitive forms: variables x, constants c, function applications $f\,x$, and lambda abstractions $\lambda x.\,t$. Every term has a type; *formulas* are terms of Boolean type. The most important primitive constant is the (polymorphic) equality predicate $(=) : \alpha \to \alpha \to \mathit{bool}$. Common logical connectives are not built-in primitives but are defined in terms of equality. For example, conjunction and universal quantification (using higher-order abstract syntax [24]) can be defined as [11]:

$$\wedge \stackrel{\text{def}}{=} \lambda p.\, \lambda q.\, (\lambda f.\, f\, p\, q) = (\lambda f.\, f\, \top\, \top) \quad \text{and} \quad \forall \stackrel{\text{def}}{=} \lambda P.\, (P = \lambda x.\, \top)\ .$$

Theorems. A theorem is a provable sequent, represented as $A \vdash p$, where A is a finite set of formulas (the assumptions) and p is a formula (the conclusion). Formally, a proof of a theorem is a sequence of valid applications of primitive inference rules to existing theorems and axioms, ending with the desired sequent. For example, the following primitive inference rule MkComb can be used to prove that two applicative terms are equal, given that their function and argument terms are provably equal and their types are compatible:[2]

$$\frac{\Gamma_1 \vdash f_1 = f_2 : \mathcal{A} \to \mathcal{B} \qquad \Gamma_2 \vdash t_1 = t_2 : \mathcal{A}}{\Gamma_1 \cup \Gamma_2 \vdash f_1\, t_1 = f_2\, t_2 : \mathcal{B}}\ \textsc{MkComb}$$

Higher-order logic contains a minimal set of primitive inference rules (only 10 rules in the HOL Light variant). Together with suitable axioms (e.g., the axiom of choice, excluded middle, etc.), they suffice as an expressive foundation for formal mathematical reasoning [10].

2.2 LCF-Style Theorem Proving

The LCF approach, introduced by Milner and colleagues in the Edinburgh LCF prover [6,7], is the established method for engineering a programmable yet trustworthy theorem prover. It mechanizes the object logic inside a general-purpose programming language (called the *meta language*, traditionally an ML-like functional language[3]). Logical objects (terms, theorems, etc.) are encoded as symbolic data values with predefined operations. For example, predefined constants of the theorem type represent axioms of the logic; and predefined operations that return theorems correspond to primitive inference rules.

Programmability. This approach gives a fully programmable theorem prover. The meta language readily serves as the proof language for users to interact with the prover. Most directly, to prove is just to program code that invokes the predefined operations to perform the inference steps. For example, the following HOL Light code proves $f\ x = x \vdash f\ (f\ x) = x$ by a sequence of rule applications:

```
let th1 = ASSUME `(f:A->A) x = x` in            (* f x = x ⊢ f x = x         *)
let th2 = MK_COMB (REFL `(f:A->A)`, th1) in (* f x = x ⊢ f (f x) = f x   *)
TRANS th2 th1                                   (* f x = x ⊢ f (f x) = x     *)
```

[2] More precisely, it is a rule scheme, since it is parameterized by meta-level type variables $\mathcal{A}$ and $\mathcal{B}$; not to be confused with object-logic type variables α, β, etc.

[3] The ML (an acronym for meta language) language was originally designed specifically for implementing and extending the Edinburgh LCF prover.

Furthermore, derived inference rules and proof facilities can be programmed using the full power of a general-purpose programming language. A facility considered essential since the inception of LCF-style theorem proving [6,7,17] is goal-directed proof strategies, implemented as *tactics*. For example, the following HOL Light code first states the goal to be proved, i.e., commutativity of natural number addition, and proves it by composing a tactic that first applies induction and then discharges the two subgoals by rewriting with the induction hypotheses and the definitional clauses of addition:

```
let ADD_SYM = prove
  (`forall m n:num. m + n = n + m`,
   INDUCT_TAC THEN
   (* subgoal 1: ⊢ ∀n. 0 + n = n + 0  *)
   (* subgoal 2: ∀n. m + n = n + m ⊢ ∀n. (SUC m) + n = n + (SUC m) *)
   ASM_REWRITE_TAC [ADD_CLAUSES])
```

Tactics and tacticals (e.g., `THEN` used in the example) are traditionally implemented using higher-order functions and exceptions in the meta language [17,22].

Trustworthiness. Trustworthiness of this approach relies on the typing discipline enforced by the meta language [6]. The data types for logical objects are encapsulated as *abstract types*, with their primitive operations implemented in a small, trusted module (called the *proof kernel*). Type abstraction ensures that all other code outside the kernel, no matter how complex, must ultimately construct theorems by calling the kernel's operations.

3 Core Interface

This section presents our core interface for HOL theorem proving in C.

3.1 Overview: A Complete Proof in C

To give a big picture of our core interface, we begin with a complete example using the core interface (Fig. 1), which proves a theorem asserting that the right identity of the list-append operation is the empty list. The program includes `hol_prover_client.h` to gain access to the core interface types and functions, and connects to a proof server via `hol_prover_init()` at startup. It demonstrates several components of the core interface—definitional principles, inference rules, rewritings, parsing and printing. The reader need not understand every function used in the proof, but should note that the general structure of forward reasoning in C is the same as in ML-like languages (as shown in Sect. 2.2).

Theory Extension. To introduce a new type for finite lists of natural numbers, it calls `new_datatype_definition` with the clauses of the inductive datatype definition as a string. It derives the induction and recursion theorems returned in the result structure `il`. It then uses `new_rec_definition` to define a recursive function `app` that appends two lists: it takes the list-recursion theorem `il.rec` and the defining equations as input, and returns the defining equation as a theorem.

```c
#include <stdio.h>
#include "hol_prover_client.h"

int main() {
  hol_prover_init();
  /* Step 1: define inductive type nlist */
  new_datatype_definition_results il =
      new_datatype_definition("nlist = Nil | Cons num nlist");
  /* Step 2: define recursive function app */
  thm app_def = new_rec_definition(
      il.rec, parse_term("app Nil l = l &&"
                         "app (Cons h t) l = Cons h (app t l)"));
  /* Step 3: prove !l. app l Nil = l by forward derivation */
  // Base case: |- app Nil Nil = Nil
  thm base_eq = apply_conversion(rewrite_conv(ThmList(app_def)),
                                 parse_term("app Nil Nil"));
  // Inductive step: |- !h t.app t Nil = t ==> app (Cons h t) Nil = Cons h t
  thm ih = assume_rule(parse_term("app t Nil = t"));
  thm step_eq = apply_conversion(rewrite_conv(ThmList(app_def, ih)),
                                 parse_term("app (Cons h t) Nil"));
  step_eq = gen_all_rule(disch_all_rule(step_eq));
  // Combine base and step cases and then apply the induction theorem
  thm ind_thm = beta_rule(spec_rule(parse_term("\\l. app l Nil = l"), il.ind));
  thm result = mp_rule(ind_thm, conj_rule(base_eq, step_eq));
  printf("result theorem: %s\n", string_of_thm(result)); // prints: |- !l. app l Nil = l
  return 0;
}
```

Fig. 1. A complete proof in C using the core interface.

Proving Theorems. After the initial theory extensions, it proves the desired theorem, i.e., $\forall l : \mathit{nlist}.\ \mathit{app}\ l\ \mathit{Nil} = l$. The idea is simple: by induction on the list `l`. Theorems for the base case and the inductive step are established by rewriting using the defining equations for `app` and the induction hypothesis `ih`. After these are established, it specializes the induction theorem `il.ind` to match our goal, and then applies `mp_rule` (modus ponens) to obtain the final theorem.

3.2 Interface Description

The core interface adapts the common HOL API of ML-based provers [1] to C conventions. These form the building blocks for further proof programming in C, which will be demonstrated in Sect. 5.

Core Types. The three kinds of logical objects in HOL—i.e., types, terms, and theorems—are represented as opaque types named `type`, `term`, and `thm`. Users create and inspect them exclusively through functions in the core interface.

Error Handling. Error conditions during interface function calls are communicated through a status-code pattern: a function either succeeds and returns a valid object, or fails and (1) returns an empty value (constants `empty_type`, `empty_term`, `empty_thm` are defined for this purpose), (2) sets a global non-zero error code and an error message. Every function's documentation specifies the conditions for failure ("Fails if ...") or declares it total. For function calls that can fail, the caller should check the code after the call and handle the error appropriately (e.g., reset the code to zero and retry with an alternative proof function) or short-circuit to the upper level in the call stack. For concrete examples of error handling with a goto-based programming pattern, see Sect. 5.

Syntax Manipulation. Recall (Sect. 2.1) that HOL types and terms have a simple structure: types are built from type variables and type constructors, and terms are built from variables, constants, applications, and lambda abstractions. The core interface systematically provides constructors (`mk_*`), destructors (`dest_*`), and discriminators (`is_*`) for these primitive syntactic categories. For example, below are the primitive term constructors:

```
term mk_var(const char* name, type ty);
term mk_const(const char* name, type ty);
term mk_comb(term fn, term arg);  /* fn arg  */
term mk_abs(term v, term body);   /* \v.body */
```

Constructors for standard data types (e.g., `mk_nat`), predicates (e.g., `mk_eq`), and logical connectives (e.g., `mk_forall`) are also provided as derived constructors. Other term manipulations include pattern matching `term_match` and capture-avoiding substitution `subst`. Functions `hyp(th)` and `concl(th)` extract the assumption terms and the conclusion term of a theorem.

Parsing and Printing. It is convenient to construct and display terms using conventional mathematical notation. The core interface provides `parse_term`, `parse_type`, `string_of_term`, `string_of_type` to parse and print terms and types. The sequent representation of a theorem can be printed using `string_of_thm`.

Primitive and Derived Inference Rules. The interface exposes the complete kernel interface to the deductive system of higher-order logic (the HOL Light version [10,11]), comprising 10 primitive inference rules. Table 1 lists them; essentially, they define the meaning of equality and functions. Together with suitable axioms, they suffice to derive all HOL theorems.

Beyond the primitive inference rules, the core interface exposes a rich set of derived rules.[4] These are defined on the server side but outside the proof kernel, and thus not part of the trusted computing base (cf. Sect. 4). From a user's perspective, they are indistinguishable from the primitive ones.

Connective Rules. All usual logical connectives are defined in terms of equality and functions (cf. Sect. 2.1). The interface provides derived introduction and elimination rules for each connective (e.g., `conj_rule` for conjunction introduction, `conjunct1_rule` and `conjunct2_rule` for conjunction elimination).

[4] We expose these derived rules in the core interface to reuse existing implementations from the proof server. Alternatively, they could be re-implemented on the client side, but we do not see clear benefits of doing so.

Table 1. The 10 primitive inference rules of higher-order logic.

C Function Signature	Brief Description (Simplified)
`refl_rule(t)`	Prove $\vdash t = t$ for any term t
`trans_rule(th1, th2)`	From $\vdash s = t$ and $\vdash t = u$, derive $\vdash s = u$
`mk_comb_rule(th1, th2)`	From $\vdash f = g$ and $\vdash x = y$, derive $\vdash f\ x = g\ y$
`abs_rule(x, th)`	From $\vdash s = t$, derive $\vdash \lambda x.\, s = \lambda x.\, t$
`beta_prim_rule(t)`	Prove $\vdash (\lambda x.\, s)\ x = s$
`assume_rule(p)`	Prove $p \vdash p$ for any proposition p
`eq_mp_rule(th1, th2)`	From $\vdash p \Leftrightarrow q$ and $\vdash p$, derive $\vdash q$
`deduct_antisym_rule(th1, th2)`	From $q \vdash p$ and $p \vdash q$, derive $\vdash p \Leftrightarrow q$
`inst_type_rule(ty_pairs, th)`	Instantiate type variables in a theorem
`inst_rule(tm_pairs, th)`	Instantiate free term variables in a theorem

Rewriting and Conversion. Rewriting is ubiquitous in theorem proving, especially in implementing tactics for simplification. The mechanism for rewriting in our interface is *conversions* [22], strategies mapping a term t to a theorem $\vdash t = t'$. Our interface exposes conversions as opaque `conversion` objects, applied via `apply_conversion(conv, tm)`. The built-in conversion `rewrite_conv` is used in the example proof in Fig. 1: it takes a list of equational theorems and produces a conversion that rewrites a term using those equations.

Definitional Principles. The logical theory can be extended conservatively by introducing new type and constant definitions (via `new_basic_definition` and `new_basic_type_definition`) or declarations (via `new_const` and `new_tyconst`). Users may also assert axioms via `new_axiom`, though they are responsible for justifying their validity. Information about the current theory can be queried by functions such as `get_all_axioms`, `get_all_definitions`, and `get_theorem_by_name`.

Atop these basic definition mechanisms, higher-level definitional principles are provided as derived rules: `new_fun_definition` for general recursive functions, `new_datatype_definition` for inductive datatypes, and `new_inductive_definition` for inductively defined relations. Each derives the characteristic theorem(s) from the input equational terms or definition clauses.

Proof-Search Procedures. The interface provides automated provers for several domains, including `arith_rule` for linear arithmetic, `taut_rule` for propositional reasoning, and `meson_solver` for first-order reasoning. These provers take a term and helper lemmas and return a theorem when successful, or fail/loop if the goal cannot be proved. They are useful for finishing simple goals.

4 An Extended LCF Architecture

This section presents the architectural design that makes our core interface trustworthy under unconstrained proof programming in C, and briefly discusses our implementation.

4.1 Architectural Design

The Challenge of Trustworthiness. As reviewed in Sect. 2.2, the trustworthiness of the LCF approach rests on type abstraction provided by the meta language. Specifically, the theorem type is abstract, so only the kernel may construct its values. This ensures that every theorem is necessarily derived from valid applications of the primitive inference rules, a property known as *full expansiveness* [8].

It is immediate that C *does not qualify* as the meta language for the LCF approach: by its low-level nature, C's type system is permissive of pointer arithmetic and type casting; this allows user code to circumvent the kernel interface and forge theorem values by direct memory manipulation. For instance, knowing the concrete layout of theorems in a kernel implementation (e.g., a pointer to a struct with two fields that store the hypothesis list and the conclusion term), a malicious user could mutate the conclusion to fabricate an invalid theorem:

```
struct layout { term* hyps; term concl; };
thm taut = assume_rule(mk_true());          // true |- true
((struct layout*)taut)->concl = mk_false(); // true |- false, unsound!
```

Design: A Client-Server Architecture. Our key observation is that the implementation language of the kernel and the user-facing language for proof programming need not be the same, as long as they can interoperate via a core interface with guards against invalid operations. This deviates from the use of a single meta language for both in the traditional LCF approach. We achieve this through a client-server model (Fig. 2) that extends the LCF architecture, where user code runs in a client process and an LCF prover runs in a server.

The Client. On the client side, a client-interface library implements and exposes the core-interface API to user code. The methods are implemented as remote procedure calls (RPCs) to the server. Importantly, logical objects always live in the server's memory: methods in the core interface manipulate them indirectly through opaque *handles* generated by the server. Because the client has no direct access to the server's memory, arbitrary user proof code—even code written in an unsafe language like C—cannot forge theorem values.

The Server. The server has two main components: a traditional LCF prover and a service handler that manages the interaction between the client and the prover. As required by the LCF approach, the prover is implemented in a language with type abstraction. A *service handler* sits above the LCF prover as a thin wrapper: it maintains the current active logical objects during a proof session in an object store, validates incoming RPC requests, and dispatches them to the prover. The object store associates handles with logical objects: a handle uniquely identifies a logical object in the object store, allowing the client to pass the object around without direct access to its concrete memory representation.

Communication Example. We illustrate the client-server interaction with a concrete example: the user code calls `mp_rule(hdl1, hdl2)`, where `hdl1` and `hdl2` are opaque handles to two theorems. The communication proceeds as follows:

1. *Client → Server.* The client-side `mp_rule` function sends an RPC request carrying `hdl1` and `hdl2` to the server.
2. *Handle resolution.* The service handler looks up the actual theorem objects `thm1` and `thm2` from the object store using the provided handles. If either handle is invalid, the handler immediately signals an error to the client.
3. *Proof computation.* The service handler delegates to the LCF prover by calling the corresponding inference rule, e.g., `MP(thm1, thm2)`. Implementation of `MP` ultimately invokes the primitive inference rules in the kernel, e.g., `EQ_MP`. If any inference fails (e.g., `thm1` is not an implication), the handler signals an error to the client.
4. *Server → Client.* On success, the handler generates a fresh handle for the resulting theorem, stores the association in the object store, and returns the handle to the client for use in subsequent proof steps.

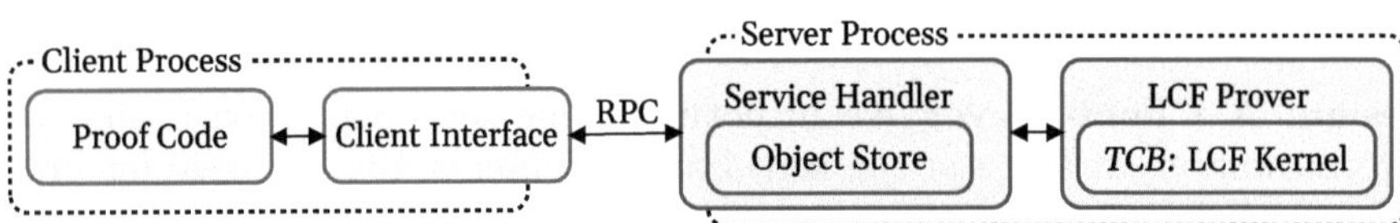

Fig. 2. The extended LCF architecture with a client-server design. The architecture maintains the full expansiveness property of the LCF approach while allowing users to program proofs and derived facilities in an arbitrary language of choice (such as C).

Trustworthiness Guarantee. Our design relies on the assumption that the operating system provides reliable process isolation: user-space processes cannot directly access the memory of other processes. Under this assumption, the architecture ensures that the trusted computing base (TCB) consists solely of the proof kernel. All client-side code (including user-written proof code and the client interface library) is excluded from the TCB by virtue of memory isolation; server-side code beyond the kernel (e.g., the service handler and the derived libraries) is also excluded from the TCB, as guaranteed by type abstraction.

Note that we do not address broader security properties such as access control; for example, a client may forge handles to access theorems created by another user, but this does not compromise soundness, as the forged handles still refer to valid theorems constructed by the kernel.

4.2 Implementation Notes

TCB Size. We implement this architecture in a C client and an OCaml server. For the server side, we choose to reuse the HOL Light theorem prover [11] as the supporting LCF prover. Its kernel is approximately 600 lines of OCaml code that have been widely used and scrutinized by the community.

RPC Implementation. Cross-language RPC between the C client and the OCaml server is handled by Cap'n Proto [27], chosen for its multi-language support. The core interface is defined in Cap'n Proto's schema language, allowing generation of stub code. Handles to logical objects are represented as byte strings, which are the actual payload of the RPC requests. Overall, the client interface comprises ∼7000 lines of C/C++ (mostly auto-generated from the schema) and the service handler comprises ∼4000 lines of OCaml. This shows that our approach is relatively lightweight for supporting proof programming in an arbitrary language of choice.

Memory Management. To avoid manual memory management during proof programming, we employ the Boehm-Demers-Weiser conservative garbage collector [3]: when a handle is reclaimed on the client side, the client interface notifies the server to remove the corresponding object from its store, allowing the OCaml runtime to garbage-collect it as well.

5 Programming Derived Proof Facilities in C

The LCF approach allows users to program additional proof facilities in the meta language as derived libraries atop the kernel. This section demonstrates that *goal-directed reasoning* [17]—the prime example of such facilities, and an integral part of every LCF-style prover—can be programmed idiomatically in C upon our core interface. We first review the traditional ML-based approach to goal-directed reasoning, which relies on higher-order functional programming. We then present our alternative design based on an explicit goal-tree data structure.

5.1 Goal-Directed Reasoning in the LCF Tradition

In LCF-style provers, goal-directed reasoning is expressed in terms of *tactics* that implement basic backward proof steps. These tactics can be composed into full proof strategies by *tacticals*. A *subgoaling package* manages the proof state across individual tactic applications for interactive proof discovery [23].

Tactics and Validation Closures. A *tactic* is an ML function that, given a goal (a sequent to be proved), returns a list of subgoals together with a *validation*—a function that should derive a theorem achieving the goal once theorems for the subgoals are provided. Concretely, the relevant ML types are:

```
type goal = term list * term;
type validation = thm list -> thm;
type tactic = goal -> goal list * validation;
```

For example, read from bottom to top, the following rule for implication introduction (parameterized by any formula p) can be used in goal-directed reasoning to move the antecedent of an implicational goal into the assumptions:

$$\frac{\Gamma \vdash q}{\Gamma \backslash \{p\} \vdash p \Longrightarrow q} \quad \textsc{Disch}(p)$$

This can be implemented in ML as a tactic `DISCH_TAC`:

```
val DISCH_TAC : tactic = fn (asl, conclu) =>
    let val (antece, conseq) = dest_imp conclu (* decomposition *)
    in  ([(antece :: asl, conseq)],     (* singleton subgoal list *)
          fn [th] => DISCH antece th)      (* validation closure *)
    end handle _ => raise Fail "DISCH_TAC"    (* error handling *)
```

Note the validator captures the antecedent `antece` from the environment to create a *closure*. Once the subgoals are solved, the validator can be invoked with the list of theorems for the subgoals (singleton here) to derive the original theorem.

Tacticals and Composite Validators. Most problems cannot be solved by a one-step tactic. *Tacticals* such as `THEN` (sequential composition), `ORELSE` (choice), and `REPEAT` (iteration) are combinators that allow composing tactics into more powerful strategies. (e.g., until they fully solve the problem at hand; cf. the example in Sect. 2.2) Crucially, implementing these tacticals requires assembling individual validators into increasingly larger composite validators by *higher-order functional programming.* For instance, the following ML code implements the `THEN` tactical that applies two tactics sequentially:

```
fun (tac1:tactic) THEN (tac2:tactic) : tactic = fn g =>
  let val (gl,p) = tac1 g
      val (gll,pl) = unzip(map tac2 gl)
  in (flatten gll, (p o mapshape(map length gll) pl)) end;
```

It applies `tac1` to obtain a subgoal list `gl` and a validator `p`, then applies the second tactic `tac2` to each subgoal to obtain a list of subgoal lists `gll` and a list of validators `pl`. After this decomposition phase, it constructs a new validator that chains all of these: the combinator-style code corresponds to first invoking each `pl[i]` on the theorems for the subgoals `gll[i]`, then passing the resulting child theorems to `p` to derive the theorem for the original goal.

Tacticals like `ORELSE` and `REPEAT` additionally rely on *exceptions* for backtracking on the proof state: if a tactic fails (by raising an exception), the tactical catches the exception and either tries an alternative or terminates the iteration.

The Subgoal Package. For proof discovery, users typically make progress by applying small tactics in sequence. To relieve users from bookkeeping of subgoals and calling validators manually, a *subgoal package* manages the proof state across individual tactic applications [23]. It maintains two components: (a) all current unresolved subgoals, and (b) a monolithic validator that incorporates the full chain of composed validators linking the subgoals back to the original goal. Each time the user applies a tactic to one of the open subgoals, the subgoal package updates this monolithic validation by composing the new tactic's validation into the existing chain, similar to the above `THEN` tactical.

5.2 Goal-Directed Reasoning in C

The traditional approach to goal-directed reasoning fundamentally relies on higher-order functional programming (for defining tactics and composing validators), and exceptions (for backtracking in tacticals). C provides none of these natively, motivating the alternative design described next.

```
typedef thm (*validator)(thm* thl, goal g, void *env);

typedef struct goal_node {
  term *asmps, concl;          // goal sequent
  thm solved;                  // theorem proving the goal once solved; empty otherwise

  int num_subgoals;            // number of subgoal nodes
  struct goal_node **subgoals; // array of pointers to subgoal nodes

  validator valid;             // pointer to a validator function
  void *env;                   // custom data for validator
} *GN;                         // GN is short for Goal Node
```

Fig. 3. The `goal_node` structure representing a single node in the goal tree.

Our idea is simple: underlying every goal-directed proof is a tree of goals, where each internal node has been decomposed into subgoals represented by its children; the unsolved leaves constitute the remaining proof obligations.

Instead of making this tree implicit in the composition of validators by higher-order programming, we materialize it as an explicit data structure. The information stored in each node is shown in Fig. 3, including fields for its goal, its child nodes, a validator closure (comprising a function pointer with a user-specified environment), and the theorem to be filled in during proof reconstruction.

Figure 4 schematically presents a (partial) goal tree for proving a goal with conclusion $A \wedge (B \to C)$. The tree results from first applying conjunction introduction to create two nodes with conclusions A and $B \to C$, and then applying an implication introduction tactic to the second node to create a third node with conclusion C. The root node stores a validator `conj_rule(_,_)` that, given theorems for A and $B \to C$, will produce a theorem for $A \wedge (B \to C)$. Its right child stores a validator `disch_rule(B,_)` that, given a theorem for C proved under the extra assumption B, will reconstruct the implication $B \to C$ with the assumption B discharged.

The goal tree serves dual purposes, i.e., subgoaling and validation chaining, *without the need for higher-order programming*. Specifically, for subgoaling, it provides a function `goal_node_get_leaves(gn)` that fetches the unsolved leaves from a node `gn`; for validation chaining, it provides a function `goal_node_prove(gn)` that traverses the tree bottom-up, checks the leaves are solved, and calls each node's validator with the list of theorems for its children. Once this traversal is complete, the final theorem should be available in the node `gn`.

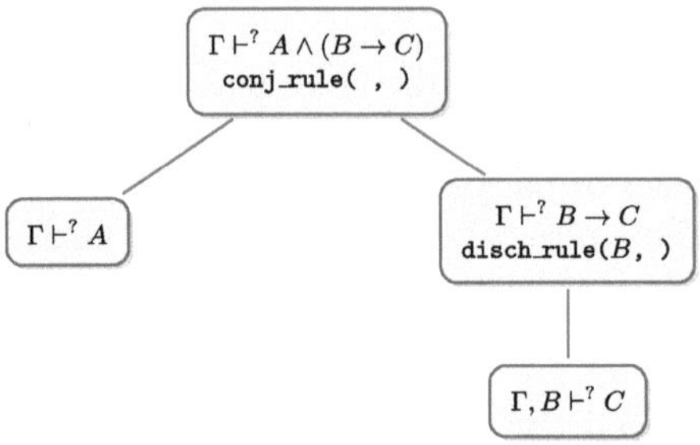

Fig. 4. A schematic partial goal tree for proving $\Gamma \vdash^? A \wedge (B \to C)$. The question mark in $\vdash^?$ is used to indicate that the goal is not yet solved.

Tactics as Tree-Growing Transformations. A tactic in our system is a *tree-growing transformation*: it takes a goal node (usually an unresolved leaf node) and expands it by creating child nodes that represent the decomposed subgoals, storing a validator and its environment in the parent node. A tactic either succeeds (returning the new subgoal nodes) or fails by setting a global error status. As an example, the tactic of implication introduction is implemented as follows:

```
thm DISCH_TAC_VALID(thm_list thl, goal gl, void *antece) {
  return disch_rule(*(term *)antece, thl[0]);
}
GN DISCH_TAC(GN gn) {
  term_list asl = goal_node_get_asmps(gn);
  term conclu = goal_node_get_concl(gn);
  ENSURE_COND(is_imp(conclu), "the conclusion is not an implication"); // error checking
  dest_imp_results dir = dest_imp(conclu); // goal decomposition
  term antece = dir.tm1, conseq = dir.tm2;
  goal_node_set_the_subgoal(gn, terms_append(asl, antece), conseq); // set subgoal nodes
  goal_node_set_validator(
      gn, DISCH_TAC_VALID,       // set validator
      (void *)wrap_term(antece) // allocate memory for the term on heap
  );
  return goal_node_get_the_subgoal(gn); // return the new subgoal node
err: ... /* error handling */
}
```

We have implemented other common HOL tactics following the same pattern: they modify the goal tree, store a validator (plus environment) on the parent node, and return the new subgoal nodes.

Tacticals via C Control Flow. With an explicit goal tree, composite proof strategies (e.g., `THEN`, `ORELSE`, `REPEAT`) can be effectively realized by composing tactics using standard C control flow—loops, conditionals, and `goto` statements. We illustrate the patterns for sequential composition and choice below.

Sequential Composition. We achieve sequential composition by iterating over the list of resulting subgoal nodes:

```
GN gn = GOAL_INIT(parse_term("(A ==> B) /\\ (C ==> D)"));
GN *subgoals = CONJ_TAC(gn);   // the first tactic expands into two subgoal nodes
for (int i = 0; i < 2; i++)
    SOME_TAC(subgoals[i]);    // apply the second tactic to each subgoal node
GN *new_subgoals = goal_node_get_leaves(gn); // collect the unsolved leaves
```

Choice. To implement try-then-else, we attempt the first tactic; if it fails (indicated by error status), we proceed with the second tactic on the same node:

```
GN try_discharge_else_gen(GN gn) {
  GN new_gn = DISCH_TAC(gn);   // attempt using DISCH_TAC
  CHECK_OK_OR_GOTO(after_try); // goto after_try if failed
  return new_gn;               // success, return the new goal node
after_try:
  new_gn = GEN_TAC(gn);        // using GEN_TAC
  ENSURE_OK("both failed");    // ensure success or goto error handling
  return new_gn;               // success, return the new goal node
err: ... /* error handling */
}
```

When the error status is not zero, the macro `CHECK_OK_OR_GOTO(lab)` resets the error code and jumps to `lab`; `ENSURE_OK(msg)` sets the error message to `msg` and jumps to the default error handling label `err`.

```
#include <stdio.h>
#include "hol_prover_client.h"
#include "proof_backward.h" // a library of tactics

int main() {
  hol_prover_init();
  GN root = GOAL_INIT(parse_term("forall m n:num. m + n = n + m"));
  GN* subgoals = NUM_INDUCT_TAC(root); // apply the induction tactic
  for (int i = 0; i < 2; i++)          // apply the rewrite tactic to each subgoal
    subgoals[i] = ASM_REWRITE_TAC(subgoals[i],
                                ThmList(get_theorem_by_name("ADD_CLAUSES")));
  thm result = goal_node_prove(root);  // validate the tree and get the final theorem
  printf("result: %s\n\n", string_of_thm(result));
  return 0;
}
```

Fig. 5. A complete goal-directed proof in C.

A Complete Goal-Directed Proof. Figure 5 shows a complete goal-directed proof in C using our goal-tree based tactics (compare with the ML proof script in Sect. 2.2). It begins with `GOAL_INIT`, which creates a root node from a term. It then applies the tactic `NUM_INDUCT_TAC` to generate two subgoal nodes, and applies `ASM_REWRITE_TAC` to each subgoal to solve them by rewriting. Finally, it validates the tree and returns the final theorem.

6 Related Work

LCF-Style Theorem Proving. The LCF approach [6,7] has been the foundation of a long line of theorem proving systems, especially those in the HOL family [11,23,26]. All of these use an ML-like typed higher-order language as both the implementation language and the user-facing proof language. Our work extends the LCF approach to C: we decouple the kernel implementation language from the proof programming language, ensuring trustworthiness through process isolation while enabling programmers to write proofs and build derived facilities naturally in C.

Supervisionary. Mulligan [20] proposes *Supervisionary*, a proof-checking system for HOL in which the trusted kernel manages logical objects in private heaps, runs at a higher privilege level than untrusted automation, and communicates with user-space through a low-level system-call interface using opaque handles. Our work shares the insight that the proof kernel can be protected by machine-level isolation rather than programming-language mechanisms. In contrast to Supervisionary's approach of building a custom WebAssembly host, our client-server design based on RPC provides a lighter-weight realization that reuses an existing LCF prover. Moreover, Supervisionary does not touch on practical proof programming; our work further demonstrates that goal-directed proof facilities such as tactics can be programmed idiomatically in C.

The Common HOL Platform. Adams [1] defines a standard API for HOL theorem provers, covering syntax utilities, inference rules, parsing and printing, and theory extension commands, with the goal of facilitating source-code and proof portability across the HOL family. Our core interface is partly inspired by this platform: we follow its categorization of components and its design principles of coherence and completeness, while adapting the conventions to C (e.g., replacing ML exceptions with status codes, replacing tuples with monomorphized result structures, and exposing conversions as opaque objects composed via a first-order interface rather than higher-order combinators).

7 Conclusion and Future Work

In this work, we adapt the LCF approach to theorem proving for C, maintaining a small trusted computing base and extending proof programmability to low-level languages without strong type safety guarantees.

One direction for future work is how to support an incremental proof-running experience: currently, proof code is compiled and executed in its entirety, which hinders interactive proof exploration. We also envision this work as a step towards *in-situ* program verification, where implementation code and its correctness proof coexist in the same program. By incorporating a proof-writing interface directly in C, as demonstrated in this paper, it is possible for developers to carry out program-reasoning steps within the same language and toolchain they already use. We leave the design of such a verifier as future work.

Acknowledgments. We thank the anonymous reviewers for their helpful comments; Zixun Guo for his contributions to the implementation; Houjin Chen, Wenbo Xu, Zhiyi Wang, Taofei Guo, Wenkai Xing, Yi Fang, Chengtao Li, Bingjie Duan and Xi He for being the first users of our library; and Qinxiang Cao and Haiyan Zhao for their long-term discussions. This research was partly supported by the National Science and Technology Major Project of the Ministry of Science and Technology of China under Grant No. 2025ZD1503300.

Disclosure of Interests. The authors have no competing interests to declare that are relevant to the content of this article.

References

1. Adams, M.: The common HOL platform. In: Kaliszyk, C., Paskevich, A. (eds.) Proceedings Fourth Workshop on Proof eXchange for Theorem Proving, PxTP 2015, Berlin, Germany, August 2-3, 2015. EPTCS, vol. 186, pp. 42–56 (2015). https://doi.org/10.4204/EPTCS.186.6
2. Appel, A.W.: Verification of a cryptographic primitive: SHA-256. ACM Trans. Program. Lang. Syst. **37**(2), 7:1–7:31 (2015). https://doi.org/10.1145/2701415
3. Boehm, H.J.: Space efficient conservative garbage collection. In: Proceedings of the ACM SIGPLAN 1993 Conference on Programming Language Design and Implementation. PLDI 1993 pp. 197–206. ACM, Albuquerque New Mexico (1993). https://doi.org/10.1145/155090.155109
4. Cao, Y., Zhuang, J., Fan, J., Wang, D., Hu, Z.: Artifact for "A HOL Theorem Proving Interface for C" (2026). https://doi.org/10.5281/zenodo.18887462
5. Delahaye, D.: A tactic language for the system Coq. In: Parigot, M., Voronkov, A. (eds.) LPAR 2000. LNAI, vol. 1955, pp. 85–95. Springer, Heidelberg (2000). https://doi.org/10.1007/3-540-44404-1_7
6. Gordon, M.J.C., Milner, R., Morris, F.L., Newey, M.C., Wadsworth, C.P.: A metalanguage for interactive proof in LCF. In: Aho, A.V., Zilles, S.N., Szymanski, T.G. (eds.) Conference Record of the Fifth Annual ACM Symposium on Principles of Programming Languages, pp. 119–130. ACM Press, Tucson, Arizona, USA (1978). https://doi.org/10.1145/512760.512773
7. Gordon, M.J., Milner, A.J., Wadsworth, C.P.: Edinburgh LCF. LNCS, vol. 78. Springer, Heidelberg (1979). https://doi.org/10.1007/3-540-09724-4
8. Gordon, M.: From LCF to HOL: a short history. In: Plotkin, G.D., Stirling, C., Tofte, M. (eds.) Proof, Language, and Interaction, Essays in Honour of Robin Milner, pp. 169–186. The MIT Press (2000)

9. Gu, R., et al.: CertiKOS: an extensible architecture for building certified concurrent OS kernels. In: Keeton, K., Roscoe, T. (eds.) 12th USENIX Symposium on Operating Systems Design and Implementation, OSDI 2016, Savannah, GA, USA, November 2-4, 2016, pp. 653–669. USENIX Association (2016). https://www.usenix.org/conference/osdi16/technical-sessions/presentation/gu
10. Hales, T.C.: Formal proof. Notices AMS **55**(11), 1370–1380 (2008)
11. Harrison, J.: HOL light: an overview. In: Berghofer, S., Nipkow, T., Urban, C., Wenzel, M. (eds.) TPHOLs 2009. LNCS, vol. 5674, pp. 60–66. Springer, Heidelberg (2009). https://doi.org/10.1007/978-3-642-03359-9_4
12. Klein, G., et al.: seL4: formal verification of an OS kernel. In: Matthews, J.N., Anderson, T.E. (eds.) Proceedings of the 22nd ACM Symposium on Operating Systems Principles 2009, SOSP 2009, Big Sky, Montana, USA, October 11-14, 2009, pp. 207–220. ACM (2009). https://doi.org/10.1145/1629575.1629596
13. Kumar, R., Myreen, M.O., Norrish, M., Owens, S.: CakeML: a verified implementation of ML. In: Jagannathan, S., Sewell, P. (eds.) The 41st Annual ACM SIGPLAN-SIGACT Symposium on Principles of Programming Languages, POPL 2014, San Diego, CA, USA, January 20-21, 2014, pp. 179–192. ACM (2014). https://doi.org/10.1145/2535838.2535841
14. Leroy, X.: Formal verification of a realistic compiler. Commun. ACM **52**(7), 107–115 (2009). https://doi.org/10.1145/1538788.1538814
15. Martin-Löf, P., Cohen, L.J., Łoś, J., Pfeiffer, H.: Constructive mathematics and computer programming. In: Podewski, K.P. (ed.) Logic, Methodology and Philosophy of Science VI, Studies in Logic and the Foundations of Mathematics, vol. 104, pp. 153–175. Elsevier (1982). https://doi.org/10.1016/S0049-237X(09)70189-2
16. Matichuk, D., Murray, T.C., Wenzel, M.: Eisbach: a proof method language for isabelle. J. Autom. Reason. **56**(3), 261–282 (2016). https://doi.org/10.1007/S10817-015-9360-2
17. Milner, R.: The use of machines to assist in rigorous proof. Philos. Trans. R. Soc. London, Series A: Math. Phys. Sci. **312**(1522), 411–422 (1984). https://doi.org/10.1098/rsta.1984.0067
18. Moura, L., Ullrich, S.: The lean 4 theorem prover and programming language. In: Platzer, A., Sutcliffe, G. (eds.) CADE 2021. LNCS (LNAI), vol. 12699, pp. 625–635. Springer, Cham (2021). https://doi.org/10.1007/978-3-030-79876-5_37
19. de Moura, L., Bjørner, N.: Z3: an efficient SMT solver. In: Ramakrishnan, C.R., Rehof, J. (eds.) TACAS 2008. LNCS, vol. 4963, pp. 337–340. Springer, Heidelberg (2008). https://doi.org/10.1007/978-3-540-78800-3_24
20. Mulligan, D.P.: All watched over by machines of loving grace. In: Kesner, D., Pédrot, P. (eds.) 28th International Conference on Types for Proofs and Programs, TYPES 2022, LS2N, University of Nantes, France, June 20-25, 2022. LIPIcs, vol. 269, pp. 1:1–1:23. Schloss Dagstuhl - Leibniz-Zentrum für Informatik (2022). https://doi.org/10.4230/LIPICS.TYPES.2022.1,
21. Nipkow, T., Wenzel, M., Paulson, L.C. (eds.): Isabelle/HOL. LNCS, vol. 2283. Springer, Heidelberg (2002). https://doi.org/10.1007/3-540-45949-9
22. Paulson, L.C.: A higher-order implementation of rewriting. Sci. Comput. Program. **3**(2), 119–149 (1983). https://doi.org/10.1016/0167-6423(83)90008-4
23. Paulson, L.C.: Logic and computation - interactive proof with Cambridge LCF, Cambridge tracts in theoretical computer science, vol. 2, Cambridge University Press, Cambridge (1987)
24. Pfenning, F., Elliott, C.: Higher-order abstract syntax. In: Wexelblat, R.L. (ed.) Proceedings of the ACM SIGPLAN'88 Conference on Programming Language

Design and Implementation (PLDI), Atlanta, Georgia, USA, June 22-24, 1988, pp. 199–208. ACM (1988). https://doi.org/10.1145/53990.54010,

25. Pitts, A.M.: The HOL System: Logic, Trindemossen-2 Edition (2025). https://github.com/HOL-Theorem-Prover/HOL/releases/download/trindemossen-2/trindemossen-2-logic.pdf
26. Slind, K., Norrish, M.: A brief overview of HOL4. In: Mohamed, O.A., Muñoz, C., Tahar, S. (eds.) TPHOLs 2008. LNCS, vol. 5170, pp. 28–32. Springer, Heidelberg (2008). https://doi.org/10.1007/978-3-540-71067-7_6
27. Varda, K.: Cap'n proto. https://capnproto.org/
28. Wenzel, M.: Isar — a generic interpretative approach to readable formal proof documents. In: Bertot, Y., Dowek, G., Théry, L., Hirschowitz, A., Paulin, C. (eds.) TPHOLs 1999. LNCS, vol. 1690, pp. 167–183. Springer, Heidelberg (1999). https://doi.org/10.1007/3-540-48256-3_12
29. Zinzindohoué, J.K., Bhargavan, K., Protzenko, J., Beurdouche, B.: HACL*: a verified modern cryptographic library. In: Thuraisingham, B., Evans, D., Malkin, T., Xu, D. (eds.) Proceedings of the 2017 ACM SIGSAC Conference on Computer and Communications Security, CCS 2017, Dallas, TX, USA, October 30 - November 03, 2017, pp. 1789–1806. ACM (2017). https://doi.org/10.1145/3133956.3134043

CARET Model Checking of Self Modifying Code

Tayssir Touili(✉) and Olzhas Zhangeldinov(✉)

IRIF CNRS and University Paris Cité, Paris, France
{touili,zhangeldinov}@irif.fr

Abstract. Binary analysis is an important issue, especially for malware detection. Pushdown Systems proved to be an effective abstraction to analyse binary programs using model checking. However, malware tends to obfuscate itself using self-modifying instructions. Thus, to model self-modification, we consider Self-Modifying Pushdown Systems (SM-PDS). To define malicious behaviour, one requires an expressive enough language that can talk about the return values of called procedures. Thus, we consider the Temporal Logic of Matching Calls and Returns (CARET) to describe malicious behaviours. We propose an efficient algorithm for CARET model checking of SM-PDS. We have implemented our algorithm in a tool, performed practical experiments, and obtained encouraging results. In particular, our tool is able to detect several self-modifying malware.

1 Introduction

Sometimes, one requires to verify the behaviour of a binary program without having access to the source code. This is the case when the subject of verification is a proprietary software or a potential malware. However, binaries are often obfuscated using different techniques, such as self-modification.

In this work, we consider verification of *self-modifying* binaries. First, let us demonstrate how self-modification hinders binary analysis. Consider the binary code in Listing 1.1 that consists of three columns. The first column shows the addresses of the binary, the second column shows the bytecodes stored at the corresponding addresses, and the third column contains the assembly instructions corresponding to the bytecodes. The execution of the code starts at address `0x04`, which contains the binary sequence `eb00`. This binary code corresponds to the assembly instruction `jmp 0x06` that jumps to the address `0x06` to execute the next instruction. The address `0x06` contains the bytecode `c6050500000009`, which is the bytecode of the instruction `mov [0x05], 0x09`. This instruction sets the byte stored at the address `0x05` to `0x09`. Note that the address `0x05` corresponds to the byte `00` inside the bytecode `eb00` of the instruction `jmp 0x06`. Therefore, the `mov [0x5], 0x09` instruction will change the bytecode from

This work was partially funded by the french ANR grant Defmal "ANR-22-PECY-0007".

G. De Giacomo et al. (Eds.): TASE 2026, LNCS 16697, pp. 140–156, 2027.
https://doi.org/10.1007/978-3-032-30693-7_9

```
# Address   Bytecode             Assembly
  0x04      eb00                 jmp    0x06
  0x06      c6050500000009       mov    [0x05], 0x09
  0x0d      ebf5                 jmp    0x04
  0x0f      6a00                 push   0x00
  0x11      ff1500000000         call   [GetModuleFileNameA]
```

Listing 1.1. Example of self-modifying code.

```
# Address   Assembly
  0x04      jmp    0x06          #-- executing  -> jmp 0x0f
                                 # mov    [0x05], 0x09
  0x06      mov    [0x05], 0x09
  0x0d      jmp    0x04
  0x0f      push   0x00
  0x11      call   [GetModuleFileNameA]
```

Listing 1.2. Example from Listing 1.1 after self-modification.

`eb00` to `eb09`, and the bytecode `eb09` corresponds to the assembly instruction `jmp 0x0f`. In other words, the `mov [0x5], 0x09` instruction is a self-modifying instruction and it replaces the `jmp 0x06` instruction with a new instruction `jmp 0x0f`. The program after the self-modification is presented in Listing 1.2. Next, address `0x0d` contains the bytecode `ebf5`, which corresponds to the assembly instruction `jmp 0x04` that jumps to the address `0x04`, which now contains the modified instruction `jmp 0x0f`. It jumps to the address `0x0f`, where the bytecode is `6a00` and it corresponds to the instruction `push 0x00`, which pushes 0 onto the stack. Then, the address `0x11` contains `ff1500000000`, which corresponds to the instruction `call [GetModuleFileNameA]`. It calls the Windows function *GetModuleFileNameA*, which returns the filename of the current program if the first value on the stack is 0. This is a typical malicious behaviour, as viruses can use the filename returned by *GetModuleFileNameA* to insert it into the registry or to copy itself to other computers on the network. However, if we do not consider self-modification, standard static analysis would only identify the infinite loop at addresses `0x04`, `0x06`, and `0x0d`. Thus, it would fail to discover that the *GetModuleFileNameA* function is called during the execution. Therefore, it is important to consider self-modification when we analyse a binary code.

We consider model checking, since it allows to explore the behaviours of the program without executing it. In particular, model checking of binary programs proved to be effective in malware detection [13,17]. However, for model checking, one needs an adequate model to represent binary programs. Pushdown System (PDS) is a natural abstraction for binary code [17] because it can directly model the execution stack. To deal with self-modification, we consider Self-Modifying Pushdown Systems (SM-PDS) introduced by [19]. This is a kind of PDS that can change its own transition rules during execution. Touili and Ye [18–20] previously proposed model checking of SM-PDS using reachability analysis, LTL, and CTL. However, some malicious behaviours cannot be described using LTL or CTL. In particular, let us consider the code injection behaviour used by trojans. The malware calls the Windows function $OpenProcess$ to find a legitimate process to inject itself into. $OpenProcess$ returns a handle h to the target process. Then, trojans call function $WriteProcessMemory$ to inject the malicious payload into the target process. In order to do that, the first argument of the $WriteProcessMemory$ function must be h (the handle returned by $OpenProcess$). LTL and CTL cannot describe such behaviour because it requires that the return value of the $OpenProcess$ function is used as an argument for the $WriteProcessMemory$ function. Such behaviour can be naturally described with the Temporal Logic with matching Calls and Returns (CARET) [2] using a formula of the form $F^g\big(call(OpenProcess) \wedge X^a eax = h \wedge F^g(call(WriteProcessMemory) \wedge h\Gamma^*)\big)$, where F^g is the standard LTL operator F, and X^a denotes the return point of the current procedure. The subformula $F^g(call(OpenProcess) \wedge X^a eax = h)$ expresses that in the future, $OpenProcess$ is called and the value of the `eax` register is equal to h at the return location, i.e. $OpenProcess$ returns h. Then, the subformula $F^g(call(WriteProcessMemory) \wedge h\Gamma^*)$ means that in the future, function $WriteProcessMemory$ will be called and h will be on top of the stack (i.e. h is the parameter passed to the function $WriteProcessMemory$ since parameter passing is done through stack in assembly). However, existing CARET model checking approaches do not consider self-modifications. We go one step further and present a *direct* and *efficient* algorithm for CARET model checking Self-Modifying Pushdown Systems, which is a natural abstraction for self-modifying binaries. The proposed algorithm reduces the model checking problem of an SM-PDS $\mathcal{P}$ against a CARET formula ψ into the emptiness problem of a Self-Modifying *Büchi* Pushdown System (SM-BPDS), which is a kind of product between $\mathcal{P}$ and ψ. The emptiness problem of the SM-BPDS can be efficiently solved by the algorithm proposed by [19]. A naive approach to this problem would be to construct a standard non self-modifying PDS that is equivalent to the given SM-PDS, and then apply the CARET model checking algorithm for standard PDS proposed by [15]. However, the experiments show that our *direct* algorithm is much more efficient and can handle larger models. Moreover, our approach allows CARET formulas with regular valuations, where atomic propositions match the stack contents against regular languages. Regular valuations are needed to describe malicious behaviours.

We have implemented the proposed algorithm in a tool that performs CARET model checking of binary programs. We then expressed several malicious behaviours by CARET formulas and applied the tool to detect the malicious behaviours in binary programs. Our results are encouraging since our tool is able to detect malicious behaviour in many different self-modifying malwares.

Related Works. Model checking binary programs has been studied by [4–6,13,17]. However, these studies do not consider self-modifying binaries. To handle self-modifications formally, [8–10] proposed abstract models for a self-modifying code. However, these models attempt to represent the program's memory accurately, which makes modelling real-world binaries too complex. Other research [3,7] provided techniques to obtain the control flow graph of the self-modifying code. However, these works ignore the execution stack.

Pushdown Systems were considered for malware detection by [17]. Later, [18–20] introduced Self-Modifying Pushdown Systems (SM-PDS) to model self-modifications and proposed efficient model checking algorithms for reachability analysis, LTL and CTL. However, the model proposed can only modify one transition at a time. Whereas our SM-PDS allows modification of *multiple* transitions, which occurs in real binary code. Moreover, we propose model checking against CARET.

To describe the relations between calls and returns, [2] introduced the Temporal Logic of Nested Calls and Returns (CARET). CARET model checking of PDS was proposed by [15] and this technique proved to be useful for malware detection [14]. However, [15] did not consider self-modifying code.

Outline. Section 2 introduces base concepts used throughout this paper. Section 3 presents the main contribution - a direct and efficient CARET model checking algorithm of SM-PDS. In Sect. 4, we describe the results of practical experiments, including malware detection using CARET model checking.

2 Preliminaries

2.1 Self-Modifying Pushdown Systems

Definition 1. *A Labelled Self-Modifying Pushdown System (SM-PDS) is a tuple $\mathcal{P} = (P, \Gamma, \Delta, \Delta^c)$, such that P is a finite set of control locations, Γ is a stack alphabet, Δ is a finite set of rules of the forms: (1) $p\gamma \overset{int}{\hookrightarrow} p_1\omega_1$, (2) $p\gamma \overset{call}{\hookrightarrow} p_1\gamma_1\gamma_2$, and (3) $p\gamma \overset{ret}{\hookrightarrow} p_1$, where $p, p_1 \in P$, $\gamma, \gamma_1, \gamma_2 \in \Gamma$, $\omega_1 \in \Gamma^*$; Δ^c is a finite set of self-modifying rules of the form $p \overset{(\rho_1,\rho_2)}{\hookrightarrow} p_1$, where $\rho_1, \rho_2 \subseteq \Delta \cup \Delta^c$. A Labelled Pushdown System (PDS) is an SM-PDS, such that $\Delta^c = \emptyset$.*

For an SM-PDS $\mathcal{P} = (P, \Gamma, \Delta, \Delta^c)$, a *configuration* $c \in Conf = P \times \Gamma^* \times 2^{\Delta \cup \Delta^c}$ of $\mathcal{P}$ is a tuple of the form $(\langle p, \omega \rangle, \theta)$, where $p \in P$ is the current control location, $\omega \in \Gamma^*$ is the current stack content, and $\theta \subseteq \Delta \cup \Delta^c$ is the current phase. For configurations c, c', and a label $t \in \{call, int, ret\}$, the successor relation $c \overset{t}{\Longrightarrow} c'$ is defined as follows. For any $p, p' \in P$, $\omega \in \Gamma^*$, and $\theta, \theta', \rho, \rho' \subseteq \Delta \cup \Delta^c$:

1. if there is a rule $r = p\gamma \overset{int}{\hookrightarrow} p'\omega' \in \theta$, then $(\langle p, \gamma\omega \rangle, \theta) \overset{int}{\Longrightarrow} (\langle p', \omega'\omega \rangle, \theta)$,
2. if there is a rule $r = p\gamma \overset{call}{\hookrightarrow} p'\gamma_1\gamma_2 \in \theta$, then $(\langle p, \gamma\omega \rangle, \theta) \overset{call}{\Longrightarrow} (\langle p', \gamma_1\gamma_2\omega \rangle, \theta)$,
3. if there is a rule $r = p\gamma \overset{ret}{\hookrightarrow} p' \in \theta$, then $(\langle p, \gamma\omega \rangle, \theta) \overset{ret}{\Longrightarrow} (\langle p', \omega \rangle, \theta)$,
4. if there is a rule $r = p \overset{(\rho,\rho')}{\hookrightarrow} p' \in \theta$ and $\rho \subseteq \theta$, then $(\langle p, \omega \rangle, \theta) \overset{int}{\Longrightarrow} (\langle p', \omega \rangle, \theta')$, where $\theta' = (\theta \backslash \rho) \cup \rho'$.

To express the self-modifying behaviour of SM-PDS, we introduce the notion of *phase* $\theta \subseteq \Delta \cup \Delta^c$, which is the current set of rules that can be applied. Intuitively, a rule of the form $p\gamma \overset{int}{\hookrightarrow} p_1\omega_1$ pops γ from the stack, pushes the word ω_1 onto the stack (ω_1 can be empty), and changes the current control location from p to p_1. A rule of the form $p\gamma \overset{call}{\hookrightarrow} p_1\gamma_1\gamma_2$ often corresponds to a call statement of the form $\gamma \xrightarrow{call\ proc} \gamma_2$, where *proc* is the name of the called procedure, γ is the location of the call statement, γ_1 is the entry point of *proc*, γ_2 is the return location, and p, p_1 represent global states. This rule pops γ from the stack, changes the control location from p to p_1, and pushes $\gamma_1\gamma_2$ onto the stack. A rule of the form $p\gamma \overset{ret}{\hookrightarrow} p_1$ corresponds to a return statement. It pops γ from the stack and changes the control location from p to p_1. A self-modifying rule of the form $p \overset{(\rho_1,\rho_2)}{\hookrightarrow} p_1$ changes the control location from p to p_1, removes every rule of ρ_1 from the current phase θ, and adds every rule from ρ_2 to it.

A *run* $\pi = (c_0, t_0)(c_1, t_1)\dots$ on $\mathcal{P}$ is an infinite sequence of labelled configurations, where for any $i \geq 0$, $c_i \in Conf$, $t_i \in \{call, int, ret\}$, and $c_i \overset{t_i}{\Longrightarrow} c_{i+1}$. We denote by $\pi(i)$ the i-th pair (c_i, t_i) of π. We say that π *starts* at c_0.

2.2 CARET formulas

Let $\pi = (c_0, t_0)(c_1, t_1)\dots$ be a run on an SM-PDS $\mathcal{P} = (P, \Gamma, \Delta, \Delta^c)$, such that for $i \geq 0$, $\pi(i) = (c_i, t_i) = \big(((\langle p_i, \omega_i\rangle, \theta_i), t_i\big)$, where $p_i \in P$, $\omega_i \in \Gamma^*$, $\theta_i \subseteq \Delta \cup \Delta^c$, and $t_i \in \{call, int, ret\}$. For any $i \geq 0$, the configuration c_i at index i on π may have three types of successors:

- the *global successor*, $next^g_\pi(i) = i + 1$;
- the *abstract successor*, $next^a_\pi(i)$, depends on the label t_i:
  - if $t_i = call$, then $next^a_\pi(i)$ is the next index after the matching *ret*,
  - if $t_i = int$, then $next^a_\pi(i) = i + 1$, and
  - if $t_i = ret$, then $next^a_\pi(i) = \bot$;
- the *caller successor*, $next^c_\pi(i)$, is the index of the nearest unmatched *call* ($next^c_\pi(i) < i$), otherwise $next^c_\pi(i) = \bot$.

A sequence $s_0 s_1 \dots$, s.t. for each $j \geq 0$, $s_{j+1} = next^a_\pi(s_j)$, is called an *abstract path*. Intuitively, the global successor is the "standard" successor. The abstract successor depends on the nature of the action $c_i \overset{t_i}{\Longrightarrow} c_{i+1}$. If it is a call, then the abstract successor is its corresponding "return" point k ($c_{k-1} \overset{ret}{\Longrightarrow} c_k$), if it is an internal transition, then the abstract successor is the global successor, and if it is a return, then the abstract successor does not exist (it is $\bot$). The caller successor corresponds to the call location of the current procedure. Since there is no call location for the topmost procedure, which contains the entry location, we say that there is no caller successor for configurations at the topmost procedure, i.e. the caller successor is $\bot$.

Given a set of atomic propositions AP, we define a CARET formula ψ:

Definition 2. *A CARET formula ψ is ($e \in AP \cup \{call, ret, int\}$):*

$$\psi ::= e \mid \neg\psi \mid \psi \vee \psi \mid X^g\psi \mid X^a\psi \mid X^c\psi \mid \psi U^g \psi \mid \psi U^a \psi \mid \psi U^c \psi$$

Intuitively, X^g corresponds to the global successor, X^a corresponds to the abstract successor, X^c corresponds to the caller successor, U^g is the standard *until* operator, U^a is the until operator using only *abstract successors*, and U^c is the until operator using only *caller successors*.

For a CARET formula ψ, let λ be a labelling function $\lambda : P \to 2^{AP}$ that labels each control location with a set of atomic propositions. Formally, we write $(\pi, i) \models \psi$ if π satisfies ψ at the i-th step. The satisfaction is defined as follows:

1. $(\pi, i) \models e$, where $e \in AP \cup \{call, ret, int\}$, if $e \in \lambda(p_i)$ or $e = t_i$,
2. $(\pi, i) \models \neg\psi$ if $(\pi, i) \not\models \psi$,
3. $(\pi, i) \models \psi_1 \vee \psi_2$ if $(\pi, i) \models \psi_1$ or $(\pi, i) \models \psi_2$,
4. $(\pi, i) \models X^b\psi$, where $b \in \{g, a, c\}$, if $next^b_\pi(i) \neq \perp$ and $(\pi, next^b_\pi(i)) \models \psi$,
5. $(\pi, i) \models \psi_1 U^b \psi_2$, where $b \in \{g, a, c\}$, if there exists a sequence $s = s_0 s_1 \ldots s_k$, s.t. $s_0 = i$, for j, $0 \leq j < k$, $s_{j+1} = next^b_\pi(s_j)$, $(\pi, s_j) \models \psi_1$, and $(\pi, s_k) \models \psi_2$.

We say that $\pi \models \psi$ if $(\pi, 0) \models \psi$. For a configuration c of $\mathcal{P}$, $c \models \psi$ iff there exists a run π on $\mathcal{P}$ starting from c, s.t. $\pi \models \psi$. Let $Cl(\psi)$ be the closure of ψ defined as follows:

1. $\psi \in Cl(\psi)$ and $\{call, int, ret\} \subseteq Cl(\psi)$,
2. if $\neg\psi' \in Cl(\psi)$, then $\psi' \in Cl(\psi)$,
3. if $\psi' \in Cl(\psi)$, s.t. $\psi' \neq \neg\psi''$, then $\neg\psi' \in Cl(\psi)$,
4. if $\psi_1 \vee \psi_2 \in Cl(\psi)$, then $\psi_1 \in Cl(\psi)$ and $\psi_2 \in Cl(\psi)$,
5. if $X^b\psi' \in Cl(\psi)$, where $b \in \{g, a, c\}$, then $\psi' \in Cl(\psi)$,
6. if $\psi_1 U^b \psi_2 \in Cl(\psi)$, where $b \in \{g, a, c\}$, then $\psi_1 \in Cl(\psi)$, $\psi_2 \in Cl(\psi)$, and $X^b(\psi_1 U^b \psi_2) \in Cl(\psi)$.

A subset $A \subseteq Cl(\psi)$ is an *atom* if:

1. For every $\psi' \in Cl(\psi)$: $\psi' \in A$ iff $\neg\psi' \notin A$,
2. For every $\psi_1 \vee \psi_2 \in Cl(\psi)$: $\psi_1 \vee \psi_2 \in A$ iff $\psi_1 \in A$ or $\psi_2 \in A$,
3. For every $\psi_1 U^b \psi_2 \in Cl(\psi)$, where $b \in \{g, a, c\}$: $\psi_1 U^b \psi_2 \in A$ iff $\psi_2 \in A$ or $\psi_1 \in A$ and $X^b(\psi_1 U^b \psi_2) \in A$, and
4. $A \cap \{call, int, ret\}$ is exactly one element.

The set of all atoms of ψ is denoted by $Atoms(\psi)$. For two atoms $A, A' \in Atoms(\psi)$:

1. $GlNext(A, A')$ iff $\forall X^g\psi' \in Cl(\psi) : X^g\psi' \in A$ iff $\psi' \in A'$.
2. $AbsNext(A, A')$ iff $\forall X^a\psi' \in Cl(\psi) : X^a\psi' \in A$ iff $\psi' \in A'$.
3. $CallerNext(A, A')$ iff $\forall X^c\psi' \in Cl(\psi) : X^c\psi' \in A$ iff $\psi' \in A'$.

Let $Forms_{X^c}(A) = \{X^c\psi' \in A\}$ and $Forms_{X^a}(A) = \{X^a\psi' \in A\}$. We define the well-known CARET operators: $F^g\psi = (True\ U^g\ \psi)$, $F^a\psi = (True\ U^a\ \psi)$, $F^c\psi = (True\ U^c\ \psi)$, $G^g\psi = \neg F^g\neg\psi$, $G^a\psi = \neg F^a\neg\psi$, and $G^c\psi = \neg F^c\neg\psi$.

3 CARET Model Checking of SM-PDSs

This section presents our main contribution. We propose a *direct* algorithm for model checking SM-PDSs against CARET formulas. We fix an SM-PDS $\mathcal{P} = (P, \Gamma, \Delta, \Delta^c)$ and a CARET formula ψ defined over a set of atomic propositions AP with a labelling function $\lambda : P \to 2^{AP}$.

3.1 Self-Modifying Generalized Büchi Pushdown Systems

First, we construct an SM-GBPDS BP_G - a kind of product between $\mathcal{P}$ and ψ, which accepts runs of $\mathcal{P}$ that satisfy ψ.

Definition 3. *A Self-Modifying Generalized Büchi Pushdown System (shortly, SM-GBPDS) is a tuple $BP_G = (P', \Gamma', \Delta', \Delta^{c\prime}, F)$, where $(P', \Gamma', \Delta', \Delta^{c\prime})$ is a Self-Modifying Pushdown System, and $F \subseteq 2^{P'}$ is a finite set of sets of accepting control locations. A Self-Modifying Büchi Pushdown System (SM-BPDS) is an SM-GBPDS $BP = (P', \Gamma', \Delta', \Delta^{c\prime}, F)$, s.t. $|F| = 1$.*

Let $F = \{F_1, \ldots, F_n\}$, where for $i, 1 \leq i \leq n$, F_i is a set of control locations. A run π' on BP_G is *accepting* if it visits some control locations from every set $F_1, \ldots, F_n$ infinitely many times. BP_G accepts a configuration $c = (\langle p, \omega \rangle, \theta)$, where $p \in P'$, $\omega \in \Gamma'^*, \theta \subseteq \Delta' \cup \Delta^{c\prime}$, if there is an accepting run starting from c. We denote by $\mathcal{L}(BP_G)$ the set of all configurations accepted by BP_G. We can show that:

Theorem 1. *For any SM-GBPDS BP_G, we can effectively construct an SM-BPDS BP, s.t. $\mathcal{L}(BP_G) = \mathcal{L}(BP)$.*

Theorem 2. *[19] We can efficiently solve the emptiness problem of SM-BPDS.*

3.2 From CARET Model Checking of SM-PDS to the Emptiness Problem of SM-GBPDS

We show how we can construct an SM-GBPDS that will accept configurations that satisfy ψ. The idea is to encode the atoms of ψ into the control locations of the SM-GBPDS in a way that when the SM-GBPDS is executed, it tracks which subformulas of ψ are satisfied at each control location. Therefore, the problem of model checking is reduced to the emptiness problem of the SM-GBPDS.

Let $BP_G = (P', \Gamma', \Delta', \Delta^{c\prime}, F)$ be an SM-GBPDS, such that $P' = P \times Atoms(\psi) \times \{exit, unexit\}$ is a set of control locations of the form $[p, A, l]$, $\Gamma' = \Gamma \cup (\Gamma \times Atoms(\psi) \times \{exit, unexit\})$ is the stack alphabet, $F = F_1 \cup F_2 \cup F_3$, where:

- $F_1 = \{P \times Atoms(\psi) \times \{unexit\}\}$,
- $F_2 = \bigcup_{\psi' U^g \psi'' \in Cl(\psi)} \{P \times A_{\psi' U^g \psi''} \times \{exit, unexit\}\}$, where $\forall \psi' U^g \psi'' \in Cl(\psi)$, $A_{\psi' U^g \psi''} = \{A \in Atoms(\psi) \mid \psi' U^g \psi'' \in A \text{ implies } \psi'' \in A\}$,
- $F_3 = \bigcup_{\psi' U^a \psi'' \in Cl(\psi)} \{P \times A_{\psi' U^a \psi''} \times \{unexit\}\}$, where $\forall \psi' U^a \psi'' \in Cl(\psi)$, $A_{\psi' U^a \psi''} = \{A \in Atoms(\psi) \mid \psi' U^a \psi'' \in A \text{ implies } \psi'' \in A\}$.

And $\Delta' = prod(\Delta) \cup sync(\Delta)$, $\Delta^{c'} = prod(\Delta^c)$, where for a set of rules $\theta \subseteq \Delta \cup \Delta^c$ of $\mathcal{P}$, $prod(\theta)$ and $sync(\theta)$ are defined as follows:

(α_1) For $r = p\gamma \xhookrightarrow{call} p'\gamma_1\gamma_2 \in \theta$, $A, A' \in Atoms(\psi)$, $l, l' \in \{exit, unexit\}$, s.t.:
$(\alpha_{1.1})$ $A \cap \{call, int, ret\} = \{call\}$,
$(\alpha_{1.2})$ $A \cap AP = \lambda(p)$,
$(\alpha_{1.3})$ $GlNext(A, A')$,
$(\alpha_{1.4})$ $CallerNext(A', A)$,
$(\alpha_{1.5})$ $l' = unexit$ implies $l = unexit$ and $Forms_{X^a}(A) = \emptyset$,
add $[p, A, l]\gamma \hookrightarrow [p', A', l']\gamma_1 \lfloor \gamma_2, A, l \rfloor \in prod(\theta)$;
(α_2) For every $r = p\gamma \xhookrightarrow{ret} p' \in \theta$:
$(\alpha_{2.1})$ For every $A, A' \in Atoms(\psi)$, $l \in \{exit, unexit\}$, s.t.:
(β_1) $A \cap \{call, int, ret\} = \{ret\}$,
(β_2) $A \cap AP = \lambda(p)$,
(β_3) $GlNext(A, A')$,
(β_4) $Forms_{X^a}(A) = \emptyset$,
add $[p, A, exit]\gamma \hookrightarrow [p', A', l] \in prod(\theta)$;
$(\alpha_{2.2})$ For every $\gamma_0 \in \Gamma$, $A, A' \in Atoms(\psi)$, $l \in \{exit, unexit\}$, s.t.:
(ξ_1) $AbsNext(A, A')$,
(ξ_2) $Forms_{X^c}(A') = Forms_{X^c}(A)$
add $[p', A', l]\lfloor \gamma_0, A, l \rfloor \hookrightarrow [p', A', l]\gamma_0 \in sync(\theta)$;
(α_3) For every $r = p\gamma \xhookrightarrow{int} p'\omega \in \theta$, $A, A' \in Atoms(\psi)$, $l \in \{exit, unexit\}$, s.t.:
$(\alpha_{3.1})$ $A \cap \{call, int, ret\} = \{int\}$,
$(\alpha_{3.2})$ $A \cap AP = \lambda(p)$,
$(\alpha_{3.3})$ $GlNext(A, A')$,
$(\alpha_{3.4})$ $AbsNext(A, A')$,
$(\alpha_{3.5})$ $Forms_{X^c}(A) = Forms_{X^c}(A')$,
add $[p, A, l]\gamma \hookrightarrow [p', A', l]\omega \in prod(\theta)$.
(α_4) For every $r = p \xhookrightarrow{(\rho,\rho')} p' \in \theta$, $A, A' \in Atoms(\psi)$, $l \in \{exit, unexit\}$, s.t.:
$(\alpha_{4.1})$ $A \cap \{call, int, ret\} = \{int\}$,
$(\alpha_{4.2})$ $A \cap AP = \lambda(p)$,
$(\alpha_{4.3})$ $GlNext(A, A')$,
$(\alpha_{4.4})$ $AbsNext(A, A')$,
$(\alpha_{4.5})$ $Forms_{X^c}(A) = Forms_{X^c}(A')$,
add $[p, A, l] \xhookrightarrow{(prod(\rho), prod(\rho'))} [p', A', l] \in prod(\theta)$.

Intuitively, *prod* translates rules from Δ and Δ^c in $\mathcal{P}$ to their corresponding rules in Δ' and $\Delta^{c'}$ in BP_G. A phase θ in $\mathcal{P}$ corresponds to a phase $\beta(\theta) = prod(\theta) \cup sync(\Delta)$ in BP_G (rules from *sync* do not depend on the phase). Roughly speaking, we construct BP_G in such a way that if there is a run π of $\mathcal{P}$ from $(\langle p, \omega\rangle, \theta)$, s.t. $\pi \models \psi$, then there is an accepting run π' starting from $(\langle [p, A, unexit], \omega\rangle, \beta(\theta))$ in BP_G, s.t. $\psi \in A$. Let $\pi(i) = \big((\langle p_i, \omega_i\rangle, \theta_i), t_i\big)$. Intuitively, we can project π onto π', such that $\pi'(i) = \big(\langle [p_i, A_i, l_i], \omega_i\rangle, \beta(\theta_i)\big)$, where for every $\phi \in Cl(\psi)$, $\phi \in A_i$ iff $(\pi, i) \models \phi$, and l_i is a label guessing whether the current procedure will return ($l_i = exit$) or not ($l_i = unexit$).

The initial configuration $(\langle[p, A, unexit], \omega\rangle, \beta(\theta))$ of BP_G implies that the entry location $(\langle p, \omega\rangle, \theta)$ of $\mathcal{P}$ belongs to the topmost procedure of the run π that never returns ($l_0 = unexit$). For the i-th step on π, if $\mathcal{P}$ used a rule $r \in \theta_i$ to obtain the transition $(\langle p_i, \omega_i\rangle, \theta_i) \xrightarrow{t_i}_{\mathcal{P}} (\langle p_{i+1}, \omega_{i+1}\rangle, \theta_{i+1})$, then BP_G uses a rule $r' \in prod(\{r\}) \subseteq \beta(\theta_i)$ to obtain the transition $(\langle[p_i, A_i, l_i], \omega_i\rangle, \beta(\theta_i)) \Longrightarrow_{BP_G} (\langle[p_{i+1}, A_{i+1}, l_{i+1}], \omega_{i+1}\rangle, \beta(\theta_{i+1}))$. Conditions $(\alpha_{1.1})$, (β_1), $(\alpha_{3.1})$, and $(\alpha_{4.1})$ ensure that A_i contains the correct label t_i of the transition in π (*call*, *ret*, or *int*). Conditions $(\alpha_{1.2})$, (β_2), $(\alpha_{3.2})$, and $(\alpha_{4.2})$ ensure that A_i contains only atomic propositions that are in $\lambda(p_i)$. Conditions $(\alpha_{1.3})$, (β_3), $(\alpha_{3.3})$, and $(\alpha_{4.3})$ express that $X^g\phi \in A_i$ iff $\phi \in A_{i+1}$. The case of $X^a\phi \in A_i$ is non-trivial and depends on the nature of t_i:

- If $t_i = call$, then there are two cases depending on whether this call has a corresponding return in the run π or not:
  1. If t_i does not have a corresponding return, i.e. $next^a_\pi(i) = \bot$. Then, $(\pi, i) \not\models X^a\phi$ for any ϕ since i does not have an abstract successor. Thus, we must ensure that $X^a\phi$ is not in A_i. We solve this by encoding labels $l_i \in \{exit, unexit\}$ into the control locations of BP_G, where $l_{i+1} = exit$ means that the called procedure will return, and $l_{i+1} = unexit$ means that the called procedure will never terminate. The rules $(\alpha_{2.1})$ in BP_G obtained from *ret* rules in $\mathcal{P}$ ensure that each return is labelled by *exit*, and rules (α_1), $(\alpha_{2.2})$, (α_3), (α_4) ensure that the *exit* label is carried along the abstract path. Thus, condition $(\alpha_{1.5})$ ensures that if there is no corresponding return for the call at the i-th step, then A_i does not contain $X^a\phi$ (i.e. $Forms_{X^a}(A_i) = \emptyset$).
  2. If t_i has a corresponding return, say at position k. In this case, $l_{i+1} = l_k = exit$ (since as explained above, *exit* means the current procedure returns). Then, let the *call* rule corresponding to the step i be of the form $p_i\gamma \xhookrightarrow{call} p_{i+1}\gamma_1\gamma_2$, and let $p_k\gamma' \xhookrightarrow{ret} p_{k+1}$ be its corresponding return. I.e. let $(\langle p_i, \gamma\omega\rangle, \theta_i) \xRightarrow{t_i = call} (\langle p_{i+1}, \gamma_1\gamma_2\omega\rangle, \theta_{i+1})$ and $(\langle p_k, \gamma'\gamma_2\omega\rangle, \theta_k) \xRightarrow{ret} (\langle p_{k+1}, \gamma_2\omega\rangle, \theta_{k+1})$ be in π. Then, in the run π' of BP_G, there are corresponding transitions $(\langle[p_i, A_i, l_i], \gamma\omega\rangle, \beta(\theta_i)) \Longrightarrow (\langle[p_{i+1}, A_{i+1}, exit], \gamma_1 \lfloor\gamma_2, A_i, l_i\rfloor\omega\rangle, \beta(\theta_{i+1}))$, and $(\langle[p_k, A_k, exit], \gamma'\lfloor\gamma_2, A_i, l_i\rfloor\omega\rangle, \beta(\theta_k)) \Longrightarrow (\langle[p_{k+1}, A_{k+1}, l_{k+1}], \lfloor\gamma_2, A_i, l_i\rfloor\omega\rangle, \beta(\theta_{k+1}))$ (obtained from rules that are constructed by (α_1) and $(\alpha_{2.1})$). Thus, we need to ensure that $X^a\phi \in A_i$ iff $\phi \in A_{k+1}$. Rule (α_1) encodes A_i into the return location $\lfloor\gamma_2, A_i, l_i\rfloor$ at the i-th step on π', s.t. π' carries $\lfloor\gamma_2, A_i, l_i\rfloor$ until the corresponding return k, and then a rule added by $(\alpha_{2.2})$ validates A_i over A_{k+1}. At $\pi'(k+1)$, only rules added by $(\alpha_{2.2})$ to $sync(\Delta)$ can be applied. Condition (ξ_1) ensures that there is $(\langle[p_{k+1}, A_{k+1}, l_{k+1}], \lfloor\gamma_2, A_i, l_i\rfloor\omega\rangle, \beta(\theta_{k+1})) \Longrightarrow (\langle[p_{k+1}, A_{k+1}, l_{k+1}], \gamma_2\omega\rangle, \beta(\theta_{k+1}))$ only if A_i and A_{k+1} are such that $X^a\phi \in A_i$ iff $\phi \in A_{k+1}$. Additionally, l_i is also carried on the stack and validated over l_{k+1} because both steps i and $k+1$ correspond to the same procedure.

- If $t_i = int$, then $(\langle p_i, \omega_i \rangle, \theta_i) \stackrel{int}{\Longrightarrow} (\langle p_{i+1}, \omega_{i+1} \rangle, \theta_{i+1})$. Therefore, $next_\pi^a(i) = i+1$ and thus, conditions $(\alpha_{3.4})$ and $(\alpha_{4.4})$ ensure that $X^a\phi \in A_i$ iff $\phi \in A_{i+1}$.
- If $t_i = ret$, then $(\langle p_i, \omega_i \rangle, \theta_i) \stackrel{ret}{\Longrightarrow} (\langle p_{i+1}, \omega_{i+1} \rangle, \theta_{i+1})$. Therefore, $next_\pi^a(i) = \perp$ and thus, condition (β_4) ensures that $X^a\phi$ cannot be in A_i.

Another non-trivial case is $X^c\phi \in A_i$. Let $k = next_\pi^c(i) < i$ be the caller successor of i. Since the caller successor is always a call, there is a transition of the form $(\langle p_k, \omega_k \rangle, \theta_k) \stackrel{t_k = call}{\Longrightarrow} (\langle p_{k+1}, \omega_{k+1} \rangle, \theta_{k+1})$ in π. Then, (α_1) construct a rule, s.t. there is $(\langle [p_k, A_k, l_k], \omega_k \rangle, \beta(\theta_k)) \Longrightarrow (\langle [p_{k+1}, A_{k+1}, l_{k+1}], \omega_{k+1} \rangle, \beta(\theta_{k+1}))$ in π', and condition $(\alpha_{1.4})$ ensures that $X^c\phi \in A_{k+1}$ iff $\phi \in A_k$. Then, $X^c\phi$ is carried over the path (using rules $(\alpha_{3.5})$ and $(\alpha_{4.5})$) until the run reaches the corresponding return t_h at step h of the call t_k. As previously, rules (α_1) and (ξ_2) ensure that $X^c\psi' \in A_{h+1}$ iff $X^c\psi' \in A_k$.

Let us explain the Büchi acceptance conditions $F = F_1 \cup F_2 \cup F_3$. Since the run π is infinite, π either loops inside of some procedure (including the topmost one) that never returns, or π performs an infinite recursion, i.e. calls infinitely many procedures without returning from them. Thus, F_1 ensures that either of these cases happens in π'. Then, F_2 (resp. F_3) ensures that $(\pi, i) \models \psi' U^g \psi''$ (resp. $\psi' U^a \psi''$) iff either it satisfies ψ'', or i has a global (resp. abstract) successor k, such that $(\pi, k) \models \psi' U^g \psi''$ (resp. $\psi' U^a \psi''$). Note that F_3 contains only control locations labelled by *unexit* to ensure that these control locations belong to the same procedure that never returns. We can show that:

Theorem 3. *For an SM-PDS $\mathcal{P}$ and a CARET formula ψ, we can compute an SM-GBPDS BP_G, s.t. for a configuration $(\langle p, \omega \rangle, \theta)$ of $\mathcal{P}$, $(\langle p, \omega \rangle, \theta) \models \psi$ iff there exists $A \in Atoms(\psi)$, s.t. $\psi \in A$ and $\big(\langle [p, A, unexit], \omega \rangle, \beta(\theta)\big) \in \mathcal{L}(BP_G)$.*

Thus, we can reduce the problem of CARET model checking of SM-PDS to the emptiness problem of SM-GBPDS. From Theorems 1, 2, and 3 we get:

Theorem 4. *We can effectively model check an SM-PDS $\mathcal{P}$ against a CARET formula ψ.*

3.3 Model Checking with Regular Valuations

It is often useful to reason about stack contents in the CARET formula, as will be shown in Sect. 4.2.

Definition 4. *For an SM-PDS $\mathcal{P} = (P, \Gamma, \Delta, \Delta^c)$, a set of configurations W is regular if: $(\langle p, \omega \rangle, \theta) \in W$ iff $\omega \in L_p$, where $L_p \subseteq \Gamma^*$ is a regular set for each $p \in P$.*

A *regular* valuation is a function $\nu : AP \to 2^{Conf}$ that assigns to each atomic proposition a regular set of configurations. We extend the construction algorithm in Sect. 3.2 in order to facilitate regular valuation functions. Let $\mathcal{M}_p$ be a finite automaton that accepts L_p. We follow the lines of [12] and encode the states of $\mathcal{M}_p$ for each $p \in P$ into the stack alphabet. Thus, we can show that:

Theorem 5. *We can effectively model check SM-PDS against a CARET formula with regular valuations.*

Table 1. Comparison of performance of our approach vs. PDS approach ($|\Delta$— + $|\Delta^c|$ are numbers of standard and self-modifying rules respectively, $|\psi|$ is the size of CARET formula, OOM - out of memory).

		Our approach		PDs approach	
$\|\Delta\| + \|\Delta^c\|$	$\|\|\psi\|$	**Time, s**	**Memory**	**T, s**	**Memory**
424 + 14	12	15.70 s	342.18 MB	32.31 s	531.10 MB
396 + 10	13	15.94 s	323.82 MB	39.50 s	514.41 MB
170 + 12	9	17.36 s	493.68 MB	24.21 s	719.71 MB
335 + 11	8	18.88 s	632.72 MB	26.84 s	1.01 GB
182 + 10	9	19.50 s	651.02 MB	28.82 s	956.58 MB
174 + 14	7	20.32 s	724.01 MB	24.99 s	1.05 GB
432 + 2	13	21.59 s	677.05 MB	32.03 s	1.00 GB
355 + 4	8	21.65 s	544.16 MB	37.59 s	806.35 MB
432 + 0	10	23.23 s	389.59 MB	23.42 s	408.28 MB
158 + 15	11	28.25 s	713.96 MB	62.47 s	1.08 GB
191 + 7	9	34.80 s	431.88 MB	69.37 s	612.59 MB
273 + 19	10	44.45 s	929.47 MB	136.41 s	1.39 GB
216 + 9	10	46.74 s	1.60 GB	61.70 s	2.38 GB
442 + 0	11	50.46 s	354.53 MB	50.05 s	363.63 MB
286 + 8	10	53.41 s	710.29 MB	99.59 s	967.96 MB
426 + 19	10	55.47 s	1.47 GB	114.56 s	2.40 GB
417 + 23	9	84.97 s	5.45 GB	OOM	OOM
393 + 5	**10**	**90.28 s**	**996.36 MB**	**289.85 s**	**1.47 GB**
65 + 5	9	108.03 s	4.55 GB	121.76 s	5.01 GB
177 + 18	11	108.56 s	1.93 GB	318.29 s	2.89 GB
384 + 13	11	118.37 s	3.41 GB	264.82 s	5.17 GB
331 + 6	11	119.31 s	1.32 GB	388.12 s	1.96 GB
203 + 14	**11**	**120.36 s**	**2.60 GB**	**409.88 s**	**3.97 GB**
495 + 8	11	127.17 s	3.76 GB	235.79 s	5.51 GB
446 + 8	9	128.22 s	3.07 GB	354.83 s	4.81 GB
325 + 23	11	137.59 s	8.23 GB	OOM	OOM
350 + 10	11	171.42 s	6.03 GB	OOM	OOM
299 + 18	8	199.11 s	5.47 GB	OOM	OOM
473 + 14	8	211.84 s	5.46 GB	OOM	OOM
335 + 18	10	215.39 s	6.08 GB	OOM	OOM
441 + 16	8	243.92 s	7.41 GB	OOM	OOM
491 + 24	10	275.03 s	6.01 GB	OOM	OOM
496 + 19	7	277.60 s	7.69 GB	OOM	OOM
220 + 21	11	447.65 s	7.48 GB	OOM	OOM
325 + 23	13	492.37 s	6.99 GB	OOM	OOM
496 + 7	**14**	**586.11 s**	**2.00 GB**	**2456.74 s**	**2.97 GB**
185 + 13	16	821.05 s	2.81 GB	1809.80 s	3.76 GB
574 + 14	12	994.21 s	5.65 GB	timeout	timeout
279 + 8	17	1045.79 s	2.89 GB	timeout	timeout
507 + 18	14	1097.46 s	5.79 GB	timeout	timeout
412 + 7	17	1650.58 s	2.86 GB	timeout	timeout
301 + 0	16	1808.21 s	1.62 GB	1786.20 s	1.69 GB
572 + 2	15	2369.35 s	1.75 GB	timeout	timeout
373 + 14	18	2579.33 s	3.15 GB	timeout	timeout

4 Experiments

4.1 SM-PDS vs PDS

An SM-PDS can be translated into an equivalent non self-modifying PDS by encoding the phases into the control locations [18]. Therefore, the naive CARET model checking approach would consist in translating the given SM-PDS into a PDS, and then applying the algorithm proposed by [15]. However, this approach is not efficient compared to our direct approach because it results in a blow-up of the control locations and rules. We have implemented both approaches using the Zig programming language and applied them on random SM-PDS models and CARET formulas. The comparison was run on a machine with Intel Core i3-4150 CPU @ 3.50 GHz with 10 GB available memory. The results of the comparison are presented in Table 1. We highlighted some of the significant rows. Implementation of our algorithm performed much better than the naive approach, finishing in general twice as fast and requiring less memory. For example, in the case when there are 496 standard rules and 7 self-modifying rules, our algorithm finished in 10 min, while the naive implementation required 40 min. In many cases the naive approach ran out of memory and time, while our direct approach generally finished in few minutes.

4.2 Applications for Malware Detection

We created a tool that performs CARET model checking on binary self-modifying programs. We focus on binaries that target x86 architecture under Windows system since it is the most common target for malware. The tool obtains the program's Control Flow Graph (CFG) using ANGR [16] and translates the CFG into an SM-PDS $\mathcal{P}$ using the translation proposed by [19]. Shortly, binary addresses of instructions are control locations of $\mathcal{P}$ and instructions correspond to rules in $\mathcal{P}$. If an instruction is a `call`, then it corresponds to a *call* rule, if the instruction is a `return`, then it corresponds to a *ret* rule, if it is a self-modifying instruction, then it corresponds to a self-modifying rule, and otherwise it corresponds to an *int* rule. Then, we described malicious behaviours using CARET formulas. If the binary satisfies one of the formulas, the tool marked the binary as malicious. We were able to detect 255 different malwares taken from public malware databases such as Virusshare [11] and Malware Bazaar [1]. Table 2 shows some of the detected malwares, where the column ψ contains the satisfied CARET formulas. In what follows, we describe the malicious behaviours' CARET formulas used in our experiments.

Registry Key Injection. A commonly used by malware technique is the registry key injection. The malware injects its own filename into the Windows registry specifying startup programs, in order to start the malware at boot time. To obtain its filename, the malware calls the $GetModuleFileNameA$ function with 0 as parameter. Then, it calls function $RegSetValueExA$ to modify the registry with the obtained filename. Registry key injection could be described by the LTL

Table 2. Malware detection results.

Malware	# of rules	ψ	Time
Trojan-Downloader.Win32.Harnig.c.exe	3168	ψ_{rq}	146.73 s
Trojan.Win32.KillAV.db.exe	2460	ψ_{th}	516.18 s
Trojan-Spy.Win32.Haxspy.d.exe	3341	ψ_{ci}	459.87 s
Trojan.Win32.StartPage.rg.exe	254	ψ_{rki}	0.86 s
Trojan-Dropper.Win32.Delf.eh.exe	16421	ψ_{rki}	792.63 s
Backdoor.Win32.SdBot.rs.exe	16964	ψ_{rki}	437.52 s
Trojan-PSW.Win32.Kesk.b.exe	1195	ψ_{rq}	42.73 s
Trojan-Downloader.Win32.Small.cho.exe	659	ψ_{rq}	16.39 s
Backdoor.Win32.Agent.pl.exe	2763	ψ_{ci}	273.54 s
Backdoor.Win32.Dumador.c.exe	1052	ψ_{rq}	112.15 s
Backdoor.Win32.Afbot.a.exe	763	ψ_{w}	116.88 s
Worm.Win32.Chainsaw.b.exe	1341	ψ_{w}	54.27 s
Backdoor.Win32.Bossat.exe	4662	ψ_{rq}	195.21 s
Trojan-Downloader.Win32.Small.bdw.exe	1563	ψ_{rki}	13.65 s
Trojan-Downloader.Win32.Agent.js.exe	2286	ψ_{th}	614.18 s
Trojan-Downloader.Win32.Small.hj.exe	1729	ψ_{rq}	89.39 s
Trojan-Downloader.Win32.Small.afq.exe	3217	ψ_{rki}	18.44 s
Backdoor.Win32.Pipes.exe	1413	ψ_{w}	67.48 s
Trojan-Downloader.Win32.Agent.lx.exe	4351	ψ_{th}	467.29 s
Trojan-PSW.Win32.Lmir.iz.exe	14619	ψ_{rki}	493.96 s
Trojan-Spy.Win32.Qukart.s.exe	1119	ψ_{th}	215.71 s
Trojan-Downloader.Win32.Vidlo.ag.exe	889	ψ_{ci}	123.51 s
Trojan-Downloader.Win32.Small.bdc.exe	539	ψ_{rq}	23.80 s
Trojan-Proxy.Win32.Mitglieder.al.exe	1655	ψ_{rki}	20.73 s
Trojan.Win32.KillAV.bx.exe	457	ψ_{w}	26.00 s
Trojan-Downloader.Win32.Small.xg.exe	743	ψ_{rq}	15.73 s
Trojan-Downloader.Win32.Agent.jm.exe	396	ψ_{rki}	4.96 s
Trojan-PSW.Win32.QQPass.jk.exe	8192	ψ_{rki}	641.58 s
Trojan-Downloader.Win32.Small.e.exe	664	ψ_{w}	22.60 s
Trojan-Downloader.Win32.Small.ht.exe	2743	ψ_{rki}	30.69 s
Trojan-Downloader.Win32.Delf.uk.exe	6559	ψ_{rki}	444.45 s
Trojan-Dropper.Win32.Djoiner.11.exe	1095	ψ_{w}	102.88 s
Backdoor.Win32.Small.e.exe	656	ψ_{rki}	5.74 s
Backdoor.Win32.Beastdoor.200.e.exe	15783	ψ_{rki}	967.40 s
Trojan-Downloader.Win32.Agent.iu.exe	396	ψ_{rki}	4.09 s
Trojan-Downloader.Win32.Tiny.bo.exe	394	ψ_{rq}	11.74 s
Backdoor.Win32.Nucledor.11.b.exe	720	ψ_{w}	82.55 s
Backdoor.Win32.Delf.app.exe	9008	ψ_{rki}	690.00 s
Trojan.Win32.Harnig.b.exe	4272	ψ_{rq}	409.93 s
Trojan-Downloader.Win32.Druser.b.exe	389	ψ_{rki}	5.05 s
Email-Worm.Win32.Bagle.e.g.exe	799	ψ_{rki}	4.35 s
Backdoor.Win32.BNLite.exe	2168	ψ_{rki}	23.52 s
Trojan.Win32.StartPage.ho.exe	2610	ψ_{th}	589.66 s
Trojan-Clicker.Win32.Agent.bx.exe	364	ψ_{rki}	1.61 s
Trojan-Proxy.Win32.Webber.p.exe	410	ψ_{rki}	1.54 s
Email-Worm.Win32.Bagle.ef.exe	799	ψ_{th}	373.42 s
Virus.Win32.Belod.b.exe	353	ψ_{w}	15.51 s

formula $F(call(GetModuleFileNameA) \wedge 0\Gamma^* \wedge F\ call(RegSetValueExA))$ that expresses that first, *GetModuleFileNameA* is called with 0 on top of the stack (i.e. with 0 as parameter), and then, function *RegSetValueExA* is called. This represents perfectly the above behaviour if we consider "standard" programming policies. However, malware writers usually try to obfuscate their code, and instead of making a "standard" call, they would use obfuscation techniques like:

```
d0:   push 0
d1:   call [d]
d2:   ...
d :   jmp [GetModuleFileNameA]
```

Where: (1) there is no direct call to *GetModuleFileNameA*, and (2) at point `d`, the topmost symbol on the stack is the return address `d2`, and not 0. Indeed, the parameter 0 is guaranteed to be on top of the stack when the call is made, i.e. at address `d1`. Thus, registry key injection can be more precisely described by the following CARET formula:

$$\psi_{rki} = \mathbf{F^g}(GetModuleFileNameA \wedge (\mathbf{X^c} 0\Gamma^*) \wedge F^g RegSetValueExA)$$

The subformula $GetModuleFileNameA \wedge (\mathbf{X^c} 0\Gamma^*)$ states that 0 is on top of the stack (is the argument) at the call location (here `d1`) of *GetModuleFileNameA*. Indeed, $\mathbf{X^c}$ expresses the caller successor. The caller successor refers to `call [GetModuleFileNameA]` if it is a "standard" call or, if the binary is obfuscated, to `call [d]`, depending on how the function *GetModuleFileNameA* was called.

Email Worm Behaviour. Email worms operate by copying themselves. A worm calls *GetModuleFileNameA* with the second parameter being some address d, into which the wormn's filename is saved. Then, the worm calls *CopyFileA* with d as parameter. This behaviour can be described by the following CARET formula, where $\bigvee_{d \in \Gamma}$ is taken over all possible memory addresses d pushed onto the stack:

$$\psi_w = \bigvee_{d \in \Gamma} \mathbf{F^g}\Big(GetModuleFileNameA \wedge (\mathbf{X^c} 0d\Gamma^*) \wedge \mathbf{F^g}\big(CopyFileA \wedge (\mathbf{X^c} d\Gamma^*)\big)\Big)$$

As explained previously, The subformula $GetModuleFileNameA \wedge (\mathbf{X^c} 0d\Gamma^*)$ states that the function *GetModuleFileNameA* is called with 0 as its first parameter and d as its second parameter. Then, the subformula $\mathbf{F^g}\big(CopyFileA \wedge (\mathbf{X^c} d\Gamma^*)\big)$ states that the *CopyFileA* function will be called with the same d as parameter. The subformula $(\mathbf{X^c} d\Gamma^*)$ ensures that the copied file is the one returned by *GetModuleFileNameA*.

Process Iteration. Some malwares scan currently running programs on the host machine. The malware first calls function *CreateToolhelp32Snapshot* that returns a snapshot d of the system in the `eax` register. Then, the malware reads the first running program by calling function *Process32First* with d as parameter. After that, the malware reads the next running program in a loop. To read the next process, the loop calls $Process32Next$ with d as parameter. This behaviour can be described as:

$$\psi_{th} = \bigvee_{d\in\Gamma} \mathbf{F^g}\Big(CreateToolhelp32Snapshot \wedge (\mathbf{X^c}\mathbf{X^a}eax = d)\wedge$$

$$\mathbf{F^g}\big(Process32First \wedge (\mathbf{X^c}d\Gamma^*) \wedge \mathbf{X^c}\mathbf{G^a}\mathbf{F^g}(Process32Next \wedge [\mathbf{X^c}d\Gamma^*])\big)\Big)$$

The subformula $CreateToolhelp32Snapshot \wedge (\mathbf{X^c}\mathbf{X^a}eax = d)$ states that function $CreateToolhelp32Snapshot$ is called and at the abstract successor $\mathbf{X^a}$ of the call, the value of the eax register is equal to d. $\mathbf{X^c}\mathbf{X^a}$ refers to the return location of the current function, and this subformula means that the return value of $CreateToolhelp32Snapshot$ is d. Then, the subformula $Process32First \wedge (\mathbf{X^c}d\Gamma^*)$ expresses that the $Process32First$ function is called with d as parameter. Then, the subformula $\mathbf{X^c}\mathbf{G^a}\mathbf{F^g}(Process32Next \wedge [\mathbf{X^c}d\Gamma^*])$ expresses a loop, which calls $Process32Next$ with d as parameter. We use the caller successor $\mathbf{X^c}$ together with the abstract version $\mathbf{G^a}$ of the standard LTL operator $\mathbf{G^g}$ to express that the loop happens after $Process32First$ returns.

Code Injection. Malware uses code injection to hide from antivirus software by making another program execute the malicious payload. Malware obtains a handle h of the target program using the return value of either function $CreateProcess$ or $OpenProcess$. Then, the malware allocates new memory in the target program by calling $VirtualAllocEx$ with h as parameter. Then, the malware writes the payload into the memory of the target program by calling $WriteProcessMemory$ with h as parameter. This can be described as:

$$\psi_{ci} = \bigvee_{h\in\Gamma} \mathbf{F^g}\Big((CreateProcess \vee OpenProcess) \wedge (\mathbf{X^c}\mathbf{X^a}eax = h)\wedge$$

$$\mathbf{F^g}\big(VirtualAllocEx \wedge [\mathbf{X^c}h\Gamma^*] \wedge \mathbf{F^g}(WriteProcessMemory \wedge [\mathbf{X^c}h\Gamma^*])\big)\Big)$$

This formula states that the program will call $CreateProcess$ or $OpenProcess$, and the return value is h. Then, the formula expresses that a call will be made to $VirtualAllocEx$ with parameter h, and then, $WriteProcessMemory$ is called with parameter h.

Listening for Outside Connections. Some malware receives commands from the Command and Control server to manipulate the infected system remotely. This is performed by opening an external socket and receiving connections on the opened socket. This behaviour is described as:

$$\psi_{rq} = \bigvee_{d\in\Gamma} \mathbf{F^g}\Big(socket \wedge (\mathbf{X^c}\mathbf{X^a}eax = d) \wedge \mathbf{G^g}\mathbf{F^g}\big(recv \wedge (\mathbf{X^c}d\Gamma^*)\big)\Big)$$

This formula states that the program will call the $socket$ function, which opens a socket, and the socket handle is returned into eax. Then, the program will call the $recv$ function infinitely many times ($\mathbf{G^g}\mathbf{F^g}$).

5 Conclusion

In this paper, we proposed a direct and efficient algorithm for model checking SM-PDS over CARET formulas. Our algorithm is faster than the naive approach that consists in translating the SM-PDS into a non self-modifying PDS. We implemented our technique in a tool and we obtained interesting results. In particular, we were able to detect different types of malware by performing model checking of SM-PDS obtained from binary programs over CARET formulas specifying malicious behaviours.

References

1. abuse.ch: Malware Bazaar. https://bazaar.abuse.ch/about/. Accessed 15 Nov 2025
2. Alur, R., Etessami, K., Madhusudan, P.: A temporal logic of nested calls and returns. In: International Conference on Tools and Algorithms for the Construction and Analysis of Systems, pp. 467–481. Springer, Cham (2004)
3. Anckaert, B., Madou, M., De Bosschere, K.: A model for self-modifying code. In: Information Hiding: 8th International Workshop, IH 2006, Alexandria, VA, USA, July 10-12, 2006. Revised Selcted Papers 8, pp. 232–248. Springer, Cham (2007)
4. Battista, P., Mercaldo, F., Nardone, V., Santone, A., Visaggio, C.A.: Identification of android malware families with model checking. In: ICISSP, pp , 542–547 (2016)
5. Beaucamps, P., Gnaedig, I., Marion, J.Y.: Abstraction-based malware analysis using rewriting and model checking. In: Computer Security–ESORICS 2012: 17th European Symposium on Research in Computer Security, Pisa, Italy, September 10-12, 2012. Proceedings 17, pp. 806–823. Springer, Cham (2012)
6. Blackham, B., Heiser, G.: Sequoll: a framework for model checking binaries. In: IEEE 19th Real-Time and Embedded Technology and Applications Symposium (RTAS), pp. 97–106. IEEE (2013)
7. Blazy, S., Laporte, V., Pichardie, D.: Verified abstract interpretation techniques for disassembling low-level self-modifying code. J. Autom. Reason. **56**, 283–308 (2016)
8. Bonfante, G., Marion, J.Y., Reynaud-Plantey, D.: A computability perspective on self-modifying programs. In: Seventh IEEE International Conference on Software Engineering and Formal Methods, pp. 231–239. IEEE (2009)
9. Cai, H., Shao, Z., Vaynberg, A.: Certified self-modifying code. In: Proceedings of the 28th ACM SIGPLAN Conference on Programming Language Design and Implementation, pp. 66–77 (2007)
10. Coogan, S.K., Debray, K.P., Townsend, G.M.: On the semantics of self-unpacking malware code. Citeseer. Technical report (2008)
11. Corvus Forensics: Virus Share. https://virusshare.com/about. Accessed 15 Nov 2025
12. Esparza, J., Kučera, A., Schwoon, S.: Model checking LTL with regular valuations for pushdown systems. Inf. Comput. **186**(2), 355–376 (2003)
13. Kinder, J., Katzenbeisser, S., Schallhart, C., Veith, H.: Detecting malicious code by model checking. In: Detection of Intrusions and Malware, and Vulnerability Assessment: Second International Conference, DIMVA 2005, Vienna, Austria, July 7-8, 2005. Proceedings 2, pp. 174–187. Springer, Cham (2005)

14. Nguyen, H.V., Touili, T.: CARET model checking for malware detection. In: Proceedings of the 24th ACM SIGSOFT International SPIN Symposium on Model Checking of Software, pp. 152–161 (2017)
15. Nguyen, H.V., Touili, T.: CARET model checking for pushdown systems. In: Proceedings of the Symposium on Applied Computing, pp. 1393–1400 (2017)
16. Shoshitaishvili, Y., et al.: SoK:(state of) the art of war: offensive techniques in binary analysis. In: 2016 IEEE Symposium on Security and Privacy (SP), pp. 138–157. IEEE (2016)
17. Song, F., Touili, T.: Efficient malware detection using model-checking. In: International Symposium on Formal Methods, pp. 418–433. Springer, Cham (2012)
18. Touili, T., Ye, X.: Reachability analysis of self modifying code. In: 2017 22nd International Conference on Engineering of Complex Computer Systems (ICECCS), pp. 120–127. IEEE (2017)
19. Touili, T., Ye, X.: LTL model checking of self modifying code. Formal Methods Syst. Des. **60**(2), 195–227 (2022)
20. Touili, T., Ye, X.: SMODIC: a model checker for self-modifying code. In: Proceedings of the 17th International Conference on Availability, Reliability and Security, pp. 1–6 (2022)

QCP: A Practical Separation Logic-Based C Program Verification Tool

Xiwei Wu[1], Yueyang Feng[1], Xiaoyang Lu[1], Tianchuan Lin[1], Kan Liu[1], Zhiyi Wang[2], Shushu Wu[1], Lihan Xie[1], Chengxi Yang[1], Hongyi Zhong[1], Zihan Zhang[1], Juanru Li[1], Naijun Zhan[2], Zhenjiang Hu[2], and Qinxiang Cao[1(✉)]

[1] Shanghai Jiao Tong University, Shanghai, China
caoqinxiang@gmail.com
[2] Peking University, Beijing, China

Abstract. As software systems increase in size and complexity dramatically, ensuring their correctness, security, and reliability becomes an increasingly formidable challenge. Despite significant advancements in verification techniques and tools, their practical application to complex, real-world systems is often hindered by critical gaps in both automation and expressiveness. To address these difficulties, this paper presents **Qualified C Programming Verifier (QCP)**, a novel verification tool that integrates annotation-based automatic verification with interactive proving using Rocq. QCP employs symbolic execution and a separation logic entailment solver to automatically discharge many verification obligations, while deferring more complex obligations to Rocq for manual proof. Furthermore, QCP includes a VS Code extension designed to enhance proof efficiency and support a deeper understanding of both the program behavior and verification outcomes.

Keywords: Program Verification · Programming Languages · Separation Logic

1 Introduction

Software verification tools have made significant advancements, providing robust frameworks to ensure program correctness. Existing verification tools can be primarily classified into three predominant categories: (1) fully automated systems (e.g. Infer [3]) that focus on shape properties, such as memory safety and the absence of specific faults like null pointer dereferences, using built-in heuristics and algorithms for predefined predicates; (2) annotation-based systems (e.g., VeriFast [10], Viper [15], Hip/Sleek [17] and Smallfoot [1]) which verify not only shape properties but also some functional correctness properties by leveraging built-in SMT solvers and user-provided annotations; (3) interactive systems (e.g., VST [4], Iris [11] using Rocq) capable of verifying complex functional correctness but requiring substantial manual effort to write proof code in proof assistants.

Y. Feng and X. Lu—These authors contributed equally to this work.

G. De Giacomo et al. (Eds.): TASE 2026, LNCS 16697, pp. 157–173, 2027.
https://doi.org/10.1007/978-3-032-30693-7_10

Ideally, a verification tool should achieve the following:

(A) Support the verification of complex functional correctness properties, comparable to interactive proof assistants.
(B) Minimize human intervention to the greatest extent possible, similar to fully automated and annotation-based tools. For simple programs and safety properties, verification should be achievable solely by writing annotations, without requiring manual proof construction in a proof assistant.
(C) Provide real-time feedback during development. For example, immediately following the input of a precondition and a line of code, the tool should run symbolic execution and show the results before further code is written. If the execution fails, the tool should highlight the problematic line and report the error.

Existing tools either only support (A) or (B); quite a few of them support (A) and (B) simultaneously, let alone (C) (to the best of our knowledge, none of them support (C)). This paper introduces **Qualified C Programming (QCP)**, a C program verification tool that targets all three requirements above.

For (A) and (B), QCP adopts well-established design elements from existing tools. Specifically, (1) QCP handles the memory manipulation of the C language using separation logic, which introduces an additional connective logic separating conjunction ($*$). $P * Q$ asserts that P and Q hold for the disjoint heap regions. (2) It allows users to annotate programs with assertions outlining a proof skeleton, enabling separation-logic-based symbolic execution to generate verification conditions automatically. (3) For C function calls, QCP requires users to provide function specifications that describe the functions' behavior. During symbolic execution, QCP verifies that the preconditions of callee functions are satisfied and derives the postconditions for the calling context. (4) To automate the process of checking verification conditions, users can employ QCP's built-in SMT solver or add customized separation logic heuristics. (5) QCP allows users to manually write Rocq proof code to fill proof gaps, which are about user-defined predicates that cannot be verified automatically by an SMT solver. Therefore, QCP can combine the advantages of annotation-based and interactive-based verifiers.

However, regarding requirement (C), conventional verification tools typically require users to provide a fully annotated program before initiating the verification process. This approach presupposes that developers possess thorough familiarity with both the program code and the tool's internal verification mechanisms-specifically, the ability to anticipate whether a given program can be automatically verified under the current assertions. In contrast, QCP introduces a Visual Studio Code extension and a web interface that visualize intermediate verification states and partial results during the verification process. This functionality provides users with insight into program behavior and the underlying verification process, enabling them to incrementally develop and refine annotations, which is especially useful when working with complex or unfamiliar code.

Outline. This paper makes two primary contributions: (1) a novel integration of annotation-based and interactive verification methodologies (Sect. 2), (2) an incremental verification support via a Visual Studio Code (VS Code) extension or a web interface (Sect. 3). Additionally, Sect. 4 presents the implementation of QCP. Section 5 presents comprehensive evaluation results of QCP across diverse sample programs. Section 6 discusses related work, including comparative analysis with existing verification tools to demonstrate QCP's efficacy and practical utility, while Sect. 7 concludes with findings and suggests directions for future research.

2 Overview of QCP

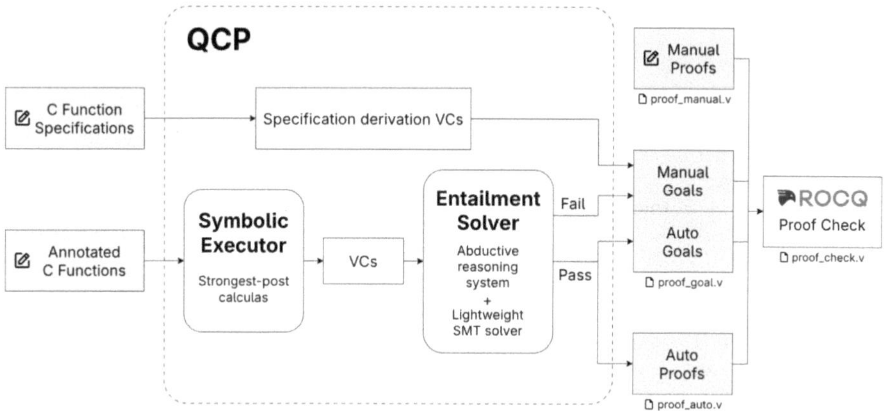

Fig. 1. The components of QCP.

QCP takes annotated C code as input and generates verification conditions. The straightforward conditions are discharged automatically, as shown in Fig. 1, while the complex ones are left for manual proof within the expressive logic of the Rocq proof assistant.

2.1 C Module Verification

QCP supports C module verification. In other words, we can verify all functions defined in a C file against their specifications, assuming that any function merely declared in that file—but implemented elsewhere—satisfies its own specification. In such cases, QCP requires that each function be accompanied by at least one function specification. Figure 2 is a minimal example of C module verification in QCP: `free_node_list` is only declared in this module and probably implemented elsewhere, and `sll_free` is implemented in this module. Both functions are attached with their specifications. The predicate `listrep`, conventionally used to describe the structural properties of singly-linked lists, is defined as follows:

```
listrep(x) = x == NULL && emp ||
    exists v y, x != NULL && x -> next == y && x -> data == v &&
        listrep(y)
```

The `listrep` predicate specifically characterizes that pointer `x` references a singly-linked list, without concerning itself with the list's contents or other attributes. Here, the expression `x->next` indicates that we hold both the permission for `x` and the access permission to its `next` field. The syntax of QCP is designed to make sure that the .c file is still a legal C program that can pass typical compiler checks like gcc. Indeed, this file says, if `free_node_list(x)` correctly frees the memory permission of `x -> data` and `x -> next`, then the implementation of `sll_free(x)` is also correct w.r.t. its own specification, i.e., `sll_free(x)` frees all elements in the linked list with head point `x`.

```
// The function free_list_node and the definition of struct list
// are imported via the header file (.h).
struct list {
   int data;
   struct list *next;
};

void free_list_node(struct list * x)
/*@ With d n
    Require x -> data == d && x -> next == n
    Ensure emp */;

void sll_free(struct list * x)
/*@ Require listrep(x)
    Ensure emp */
{
  /*@ Inv listrep(x) */
  while (x != NULL) {
    /*@ exists v n, x -> data == v && x -> next == n && listrep(n) */
    struct list *y = x -> next;
    free_list_node(x);
    x = y;
  }
}
```

Fig. 2. example of `sll_free`. The predicate `listrep` describes the structural properties of singly-linked lists.

In practical software verification, it is often necessary to reason about functions at different levels of abstraction. A function may be equipped with both a concrete, implementation-oriented specification and more abstract specifications that capture its high-level behavior. To handle this, QCP mandates that each function be assigned one primitive function specification, which is used directly in verifying the function itself. Any other function specifications associated with it can be derived from this primitive specification and utilized in verifying functions that call it. QCP automatically generates verification conditions for function specification derivation, guaranteeing that all secondary specifications logically follow from the primary one, thereby maintaining consistency and completeness at the module level.

```
typedef struct LOS_DL_LIST {
  int pstData;
  struct LOS_DL_LIST * pstPrev, * pstNext;
} LOS_DL_LIST;

void LOS_ListAdd(LOS_DL_LIST *list, LOS_DL_LIST *node)
/*@ primitive_spec
  With (x: Z) (a: Z)
  Require list -> pstNext == x && x -> pstPrev == list &&
      node -> pstData == a &&
      has_permission(&(node -> pstPrev)) * has_permission(&(node -> pstNext))
  Ensure  x -> pstPrev == node && node -> pstNext == x &&
      list -> pstNext == node && node -> pstPrev == list &&
      node -> pstData == a */;

void LOS_ListAdd(LOS_DL_LIST *list, LOS_DL_LIST *node)
/*@ head_insert_spec <= primitive_spec
  With (a: Z)
  Require node -> pstData == a && store_dll(list) *
    has_permission(&(node -> pstPrev)) * has_permission(&(node -> pstNext))
  Ensure store_dll(list) */
{
  node->pstNext = list->pstNext;
  node->pstPrev = list;
  list->pstNext->pstPrev = node;
  list->pstNext = node;
}

void LOS_ListTailInsert(LOS_DL_LIST *list, LOS_DL_LIST *node)
/*@ With (a: Z)
  Require node -> pstData == a && store_dll(list) *
    has_permission(&(node -> pstPrev)) * has_permission(&(node -> pstNext))
  Ensure store_dll(list)
*/
{  LOS_ListAdd(list->pstPrev,node); }
```

Fig. 3. Specification of `LOS_ListAdd` and `LOS_ListTailInsert` from LiteOS. The predicate `store_dll(x)` represents a circular doubly-linked list storage structure, where `x` denotes the sentinel node.

For example, Fig. 3 demonstrates the multiple specification case of the `LOS_ListTailInsert` function from LiteOS [8], a lightweight operating system based on a real-time kernel. To simplify the description, we have reduced the original polymorphic doubly-linked list to a circular doubly-linked list where each node stores an integer. Figure 4 illustrates the simplified definition of

LOS_DL_LIST, which consists of only a previous pointer (pstPrev), a next pointer (pstNext), and a data pointer (pstData). The predicate store_dll(x) represents a circular doubly-linked list storage structure, where x denotes the sentinel node. In this context, our focus is solely on the overall shape property, while the actual data list is disregarded.

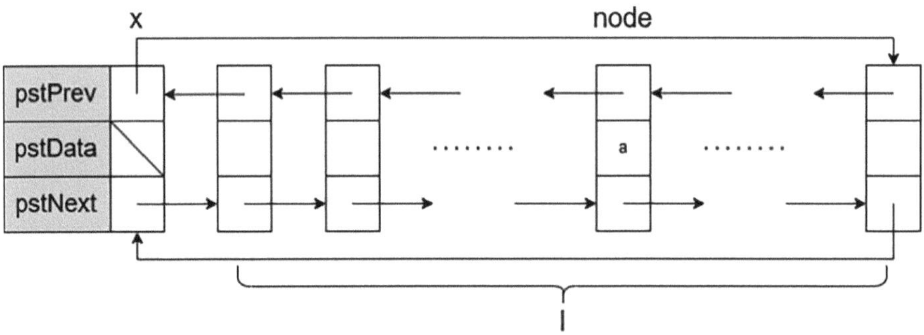

Fig. 4. The definition of LOS_DL_LIST in LiteOS. The node x serves as a sentinel node, and its pstData field remains unused.

In this case, the LOS_ListAdd function is equipped with two specifications. The primitive_spec is used for the verification of LOS_ListAdd itself as well as the LOS_ListTailInsert function. Meanwhile, since LOS_ListAdd can also function as a routine for inserting a node at the head, an additional head_insert_spec is provided to describe this high-level behavior. QCP then requires the user to prove that head_insert_spec can be derived from primitive_spec, thereby eliminating the need for a separate, redundant verification of LOS_ListAdd against head_insert_spec.

2.2 C Function Verification

As shown in previous examples in Figs. 2 and 3, users can use assertion annotations to verify a C function against its primitive specification. Given an input annotated C function, QCP performs symbolic execution to compute the strongest postcondition and generates corresponding verification conditions (VCs). These VCs are then processed by an entailment solver, which automatically discharges some verification conditions. The entailment solver integrates a rule-based abductive reasoning system (similar to the one used in VeriFast) and a lightweight SMT solver. Any remaining VCs are exported to Rocq for manual proof construction. This design combines the strengths of existing verification tools: it retains Rocq's expressiveness and proving power through manual proof engineering, while enhancing automation and efficiency through the entailment solver.

We now proceed to demonstrate the QCP verification process using the function in Fig. 2. Throughout the verification, it must be guaranteed that x->next remains properly accessible for the store operation at line 14, which requires solving the following entailment:

```
x != NULL && listrep(x) |-- exists v R, x->next == v && R
```

At line 19, the user introduces a new assertion annotation to unfold the `listrep (x)` predicate, ensuring that the symbolic execution of the read operation on `x->next` at line 19 can proceed correctly. For this user-introduced annotation, QCP generates the following verification condition:

```
    x != NULL && listrep(x)
|-- exists v n, x -> next == n && x -> data == v && listrep(n)
```

This verification condition can be automatically discharged by our entailment solver. As symbolic execution progresses, the verification process generates multiple VCs, comprising both invariant validity checks and function call verifications. These VCs are systematically organized into four distinct output files:

- `proof_goal.v`: Contains statements of all generated VCs, including the derivation of function specifications and VCs generated during the symbolic execution of function bodies.
- `proof_auto.v`: Contains proof of all automatically verified VCs
- `proof_manual.v`: Contains proof goals of VCs requiring manual verification.
- `proof_check.v`: Ensuring all VCs present in `proof_goal.v` are properly accounted for in either `proof_auto.v` or `proof_manual.v`

The files `proof_goal.v`, `proof_auto.v`, and `proof_check.v` are automatically generated and require no user modification. The file `proof_manual.v` contains only the VCs to be proved, which require manual completion of the proofs. In practice, we achieve full automatic verification for this example in Fig. 2.

3 Integration of Development and Incremental Verification

Notably, our tool supports incremental verification and simultaneous development of a program and its correctness proof-it operates not only on fully annotated code but also presents intermediate verification results and program states through its VS Code IDE integration and web interface QIDE. The interested readers could access https://ide.qua.codes to test it. Although the two interfaces differ slightly in layout, they present identical verification information. The following explanation will be based on the VS Code IDE version.

As shown in the screenshot of Fig. 5, which corresponds to the `sll_free` function in Fig. 2, the current symbolic state is displayed on the right-hand side. To enhance usability for developers with varying levels of expertise, we provide multiple assertion formats that allow users to customize how the current state is visualized and interpreted. Such detailed feedback helps users better understand program behavior and the verification process, thereby assisting them in completing annotations-or refining unfinished programs-more effectively. Green highlighting indicates code segments that have passed preliminary checks and are ready for symbolic execution to generate verification conditions. This demonstrates how our VS Code plugin allows users to seamlessly incorporate verification into their development workflow, offering real-time validation during code writing.

Fig. 5. Live verification during code editing in VS Code.

As for failure scenarios, Fig. 6 illustrates a case in which an incorrect implementation of the `sll_free` function leads to a use-after-free error. In this situation, symbolic execution fails due to the inability to retain permission for `x->next` after the memory has been freed. Within the VS Code interface, the affected code segment is highlighted in red on the left, while the right-hand panel displays the error message: "Cannot derive the precondition of Memory Read." It is worth noting that the code in Fig. 6 is not yet complete. Even in such cases, QCP is able to provide intuitive and actionable error feedback, assisting users in diagnosing and correcting such faults.

Fig. 6. Failure case for live verification during code editing in VS Code.

For those cases that pass symbolic execution but cannot be fully solved automatically, we use yellow highlighting to distinguish them from failure cases. The corresponding code lines will be marked in yellow.

In summary, QCP features an integrated development interface that provides immediate visual feedback during the verification process. This significantly enhances the user's understanding of program behavior and proof status, thereby facilitating more efficient annotation writing and error debugging.

4 Implementation

4.1 Symbolic Execution

QCP's frontend decomposes complete or incomplete C programs into what we term partial statements, which subsequently serve as the input to QCP's symbolic executor. Figure 7 illustrates the decomposition of an incomplete function into its constituent partial statements, with different types of partial statements distinguished by color. These include: one program variable declaration (`struct list *y`); two singleton statements (specifically, the assignments `y = x->next` and the function call `free_list_node(x)`; two annotation statements; one control-flow statement (`break`); one conditional statement(`if (x -> data == 0)`); one iteration statement (`while`); two block begin and a block end. The complete grammar for partial statements is provided in Fig. 8.

```
/*@ Inv listrep(x) */
while (x != NULL) {
    /*@ exists v n, x -> data == v && x -> next == n && listrep(n) */
    struct list *y;   y = x->next;
    if (x -> data == 0) { break; }
    free_list_node(x);
```

Fig. 7. Example illustrating symbolic state during partial program execution, with different types of partial statements distinguished by color.

Partial Statement *ps* ::=	*s*	singleton statement
	| *asrt*	annotation statement
	| break | continue	control-flow statement
	| return | return *e*	return statement
	| if (*e*) | else	conditional-if/else
	| switch(*e*) | case *e*: | default:	switch-case-default
	| while (*e*) | do | for(*s*;*e*;*s*)	iteration
	| { | }	block begin/end
	| *ctype* var_name	program variable declaration

Fig. 8. Syntax of C partial statements. Singleton statements encompass assignments, increment/decrement operations, and function calls.

The symbolic execution over partial statements follows conventional methodologies. During execution, QCP maintains a symbolic state stack. Figure 7 shows a partial program example: when execution reaches point `free_list_node(x);`, the stack contains two nodes as shown by two rectangular blocks. Within the inner block, QCP maintains both a `Normal` assertion (when `x -> data` does not store 0) and a `Break` assertion (when `x -> data` stores 0). Similarly, `continue` and `return` statements generate `Continue` and `Return` assertions, respectively. These states are visualized in real-time within the QIDE environment (see Fig. 5). Upon loop exit, the four types of inner assertions-`Normal`, `Break`, `Continue`, and `Return`-are merged with the outer assertion before symbolic execution continues with subsequent instructions.

4.2 Entailment Solver

To efficiently discharge verification conditions, QCP employs a custom entailment solver at its core. This solver is specifically designed to automate the reasoning process within our verification framework. As shown in Fig. 1, the solver integrates an abductive reasoning system with a lightweight SMT solver.

The reasoning system is a rule-based separation logic engine responsible for eliminating spatial constraints in separation logic formulas. It supports user-defined predicates and corresponding elimination rules while simultaneously generating soundness proofs for each deduction step. QCP's implementation builds upon the Stellis framework [21].

Our SMT solver implements decision procedures for two fundamental theories: **Linear Integer Arithmetic (LIA)** [6] and **Uninterpreted Functions (UF)** [18]. The solver architecture follows the Nelson-Oppen framework [14] for theory combination, ensuring soundness when processing formulas containing mixed LIA and UF constraints. Currently, the solver does not support quantified formulas; such cases require manual user intervention.

4.3 Rocq Library

QCP formalizes a C memory model and develops a separation logic library upon it. This library includes a C-specific assertion language, support for relational reasoning, and a suite of specialized proof tactics. The library employs C-style notations that closely resemble front-end C assertions, while being expressed in standard separation logic form. For example, the verification condition discussed in Sect. 2.2 is presented as follows:

```
forall (x: Z),
  [| (x <> 0) |] && (listrep x)
|-- EX (v: Z) (n: Z),
  [| (x <> 0) |] && ((&((x) # "list" -> "next")) # Ptr mapsto n)
  ** (listrep n) ** ((&((x) # "list" -> "data")) # Int mapsto v)
```

To efficiently manage the proof burden associated with separation logic, QCP provides a suite of specialized proof tactics. These tactics handle the tedious aspects of reasoning about spatial assertions, such as:

- `Intros/Exists`: Introduces or instantiates existentially quantified variables, and improves the organization of canonical preconditions.
- `entailer!`: Automatically cancels common spatial predicates on both sides of the entailment by leveraging the associativity and commutativity of the separating conjunction.
- `sep_apply`: Performs separation logic transformations by applying lemmas; it automatically collects the left spatial predicates of a lemma against those in the entailment's left side, replacing them with the lemma's right side.

Furthermore, QCP incorporates relational verification capabilities through Shushu Wu's new discovery that can encode forall-exists relational Hoare logic into standard Hoare logic [22]. This design allows users to write relational specifications for conducting refinement proofs and algorithm consistency verification within the same framework. The system smoothly supports standard Hoare logic, relational Hoare logic, and even hybrid reasoning styles, providing flexibility for diverse verification requirements. Several verification examples demonstrating these capabilities will be presented in our long version [23].

5 Evaluation

5.1 Performance of QCP

We evaluated QCP across 155 functions spanning five domains: arithmetic (Arith), typical data structures (Typical DS, covering sll/dll/trees/arrays), typical algorithm implementations (Typical alg, covering merge sort, Knuth-Morris-Pratt algorithm, etc.), LiteOS microkernel components (mainly for doubly-linked lists), QCP implementation components (QCP Impl, covering FourierMotzkin elimination algorithm [6], Typeinfer algorithm, etc.).

Our evaluation[1] focuses on QCP's ability to verify imperative implementations that exhibit typical programming patterns rather than verificationoriented implementations. The supported C features (see Sect. 5.4) are representative of these patterns and are exercised across all benchmark examples. The functions in QCP implementation components represent a codebase that evolved organically over a year of QCP's development, providing a case study of verifying non-verification-oriented software; details are provided in our long version [23].

Table 1 reveals two key trends: (1) The code-to-annotation ratio ranges from 1:0.6 for arithmetic programs (159 code vs. 98 annotations) to 1:2.3 for QCP implementation components (QCP Impl), reflecting the intrinsic specification needs of imperative programming; (2) QCP automates 74.3% of verification conditions (1964 auto vs. 679 manual VCs), achieving high automation in arithmetic checks while reserving expert effort in LiteOS (60.3% automation).

[1] https://github.com/QinxiangCao/QualifiedCProgramming/releases/tag/v1.0.

Table 1. Evaluation results for QCP, including annotation lines, the number of verification conditions (Auto VCs and Manual VCs), symbolic-execution time per function (SE Time), and Rocq checking time per function (Rocq Time).

Type	Functions	Annotations (Lines)	Total Code (Lines)	Auto VCs	Manual VCs	SE Time (s)	Rocq Time (s)
Arithm	12	98	159	84	39	0.07	1.43
Typical DS	67	954	1135	716	192	0.40	2.38
Typical alg	19	574	339	214	101	0.06	3.23
QCP Impl	36	1757	755	859	287	2.01	16.48
LiteOS DLL	21	493	584	91	60	0.02	11.00
Total	155	3876	2972	1964	679	0.65	6.85

Table 2. Automatically verified results for QCP

File	Type	Functions	Annotations (Lines)	Total Code (Lines)	Auto VCs	SE Time (s)
add	Arith	5	27	27	18	< 0.01
max3	Arith	1	9	14	4	0.01
sll_auto	Typical DS	6	45	110	48	0.02
dll_auto	Typical DS	9	66	187	81	0.16
avl_insert	Typical DS	8	99	116	250	2.84
array_auto	Typical DS	9	68	85	81	0.03

Several examples in our evaluation are verified fully automatically, and the results for these cases are presented in Table 2. In these cases, QCP achieves automated verification with an average code-to-annotation ratio of 1:0.5.

5.2 Comparison with Separation-Logic-Based Annotation Verifiers

Real-world programs often involve complex memory structures that necessitate the use of separation logic. However, some annotation-based verification tools, such as Frama-C [12], do not support separation logic. For this reason, our evaluation is limited to a comparison with other separation logic-based verifiers. Tables 3 and 4 present a comparative evaluation of QCP against VeriFast and Hip/Sleek on a suite of fully automatic verification cases, measuring the number of required annotations and verification time. The data, drawn from their respective benchmarks, show that QCP achieves verification times comparable to VeriFast and Hip/Sleek in the fully automatic mode.

Table 3. Comparison of verification effort and verification checking time (Annotation Lines, Proof Lines, and Time in s) between QCP and VeriFast.

			QCP		VeriFast	
Program	Functions	LoC	Anno.	Time(s)	Anno.	Time(s)
arraylist	7	74	33	0.37	31	0.10
strlib	4	38	31	0.14	17	0.10
sll_stack	9	77	40	0.09	46	0.17

Table 4. Comparison of verification checking time between QCP and Hip/Sleek.

Program	Functions	LoC	Anno.	Hip/Sleek Time(s)	QCP Time(s)
Singly linked list	16	139	32	0.93	0.05
Doubly linked list	15	181	34	0.90	0.14
Sort algorithms	10	110	20	1.52	0.05

5.3 Comparison with Interactive Verifiers

To the best of our knowledge, limited prior research has integrated annotation-based and interactive verification methodologies such as QCP. Among existing approaches, VST-A is the most relevant. We evaluate the performance of QCP against both VST-A and VST using the VST-A benchmark (see Table 5). The benchmark data are sourced directly from the original publication [24]. We recorded the number of annotations, proof codes, and verification checking time for each tool, including both the time required to generate Rocq code and the time to execute the Rocq proof.

In terms of proof effort, QCP also significantly reduces the required proof lines by 52.8% compared to VST-A (457 vs. 969) and 62.3% compared to VST (457 vs. 1212), which is attributed to its use of an entailment solver that automates significant portions of the proof process. As observed in Table 1, the symbolic execution time in QCP is notably lower than the corresponding Rocq verification time. Therefore, reducing proof length directly contributes to shorter Rocq execution time. For example, in the SLL category, QCP achieves a 95.4% reduction in execution time compared to VST-A (16.11 s vs. 349.75 s) and an 83.3% reduction compared to VST (16.11 s vs. 96.39 s).

It should be noted that QCP requires a larger number of annotations than VST-A. This is because QCP utilizes annotations to drive assertion transformations-effectively shifting the separation logic transformations that would traditionally be done within proofs into the annotation phase. Despite this increase in annotations, the combined total of annotation lines and proof lines in QCP remains lower than that of VST-A. This result demonstrates that QCP not only provides a more intuitive proving experience by allowing users to perform assertion transformations through manual annotations, but also achieves an overall reduction in the total verification effort.

Table 5. Comparison of verification effort and verification checking time (Annotation Lines, Proof Lines, and Time in s) among QCP, VST-A, and VST.

			QCP			VST-A			VST	
Program	Function	Codes	Anno.	Proofs	Time(s)	Anno.	Proofs	Time(s)	Proofs	Time(s)
Basics	8	78	59	8	0.65	61	84	84.36	156	15.90
SLL	18	350	209	457	16.11	140	969	349.75	1212	96.39
DLL	4	95	36	70	4.33	32	171	155.25	213	29.91
BST	4	115	93	169	13.62	67	202	190.35	364	33.83

5.4 Supported C Features

QCP provides comprehensive support for standard C types, encompassing integers, pointers, arrays, enumerated types, `struct`, `union`, and `typedef`. The unsupported features consist of floating-point types, function pointers, and bit-fields.

Regarding expression handling, QCP accommodates most C expressions, including: postfix operators (like array subscripting and structure member selection), arithmetic operators (both value and pointer arithmetic), bitwise and logical operators, conditional operator, and assignment operators. The system strictly enforces C-standard implicit type conversions and implements short-circuit evaluation for all expressions. Notable unsupported features include string literals, the comma operator, and compound operators (e.g., (int [ ]){2, 4}).

For control flow, QCP supports all standard C control flow statements including conditional branches (`if-else`), iteration constructs (`while`, `for`, and `do-while`), and selection statements (`switch-case`). The only non-supported control flow feature is the `goto` statement.

6 Related Work

C Module Verification: Multiple Specifications in Other Tools. Multiple specification verification is valuable in real-world program verification, and many verifiers have recognized this need and introduced relevant support. For instance, Frama-C [12] and VeriFast [10] allow multiple specifications to be verified simultaneously within a single function, without requiring these specifications to be derivationally related-an approach that is particularly suitable for independent multiple specifications. Although similar effects can be encoded through specification derivation, QCP will also incorporate such functionality in future development. Similar to specification derivation, VSU [2] enables specification multiplicity between modules via subsumption, yet each module internally maintains only one specification. In this regard, Hip/Sleek [16] goes further: it supports simultaneous symbolic execution for multiple specifications and specification derivation [5]. But it requires all derivations to be automatically verified-a constraint that can become a bottleneck in complex correctness proofs. In contrast, QCP offers more flexible support for specification derivation by allowing manual proof of the derivation verification conditions.

C Function Verification: Fully Automated Systems. Tools like CBMC [13] employ bounded model checking to verify memory safety and undefined behavior, yet their reliance on solvers like Z3 leads to non-negligible false positives. Similarly, abstract interpretation tools such as SPARTA [7] and MemCAD [9] utilize various abstract domains to verify numerical and basic memory properties efficiently. While these fully automated tools excel at proving a wide range of simple properties, they generally fall short in establishing the full functional correctness of real-world programs.

C Function Verification: Annotation-Based System. VeriFast [10] and Hip/Sleek [16] are separation logic-based annotation verifiers, and CN [19] is a separation logic-based refinement type annotation verifier. All three tools incorporate specialized annotations designed to assist in the symbolic execution process. They rely on SMT solvers or type checkers to discharge verification conditions, and for moderately complex cases, VeriFast and Hip/Sleek further allow users to supply lemma functions to aid the SMT solver. While this approach can support automated proofs of functional correctness to a certain extent, it remains insufficient for more complex verification scenarios. As demonstrated in Tables 3 and 4, QCP achieves verification automation comparable to that of VeriFast and Hip/Sleek. Moreover, by enabling manual proofs for verification conditions that cannot be resolved automatically, QCP can address more complex verification tasks.

As for Frama-C [12], it is built upon first-order logic and does not support separation logic. While Frama-C excels at scalable, automated analysis of runtime errors and functional properties within its supported logic fragment, it is not convenient for verifying complex data structures and algorithms.

C Function Verification: Interactive Systems. VST-A [24] decomposes the entire annotated program into multiple straight-line programs in Rocq, requiring users to perform manual symbolic execution proofs using tactics. The entire system is built on CompCert, with corresponding tactics and decomposition operations formally verified for soundness in Rocq. In contrast, QCP only requires users to prove specific VCs while leveraging entailment solvers to automatically resolve others. This approach significantly reduces the user's workload and enhances verification efficiency.

RefinedC [20] translates annotated C programs directly into Rocq. It employs typing rules to drive execution and generate typing derivation VCs, which are mostly discharged through a library of Rocq tactics-though unresolved cases still require manual intervention. However, its lack of SMT-based automation limits proof power, while its full implementation within Rocq results in lower verification efficiency and higher usability overhead compared to QCP.

7 Conclusion

In this work, we presented QCP, a verification tool designed to efficiently verify complex program properties. By leveraging separation logic, QCP provides a flexible and intuitive framework for symbolic execution and verification condition generation. QCP integrates both entailment solvers and Rocq, balancing automation with the ability to handle intricate proofs manually when necessary. Our evaluation demonstrates QCP's effectiveness in verifying programs with common data structures and highlights its ability to reduce manual effort.

Looking ahead, we aim to extend QCP to support advanced language features such as function pointers and goto statements. We also plan to enhance its usability for developers-for instance, by enabling integrated verification of multiple specifications. QCP represents a significant step forward in making program verification more accessible and practical for real-world software development.

Acknowledgements. This work was supported by the NSF China (No. 62472274).

References

1. Berdine, J., Calcagno, C., O'Hearn, P.W.: Smallfoot: modular automatic assertion checking with separation logic. In: Proceedings of the 4th International Conference on Formal Methods for Components and Objects, FMCO'05, pp. 115–137. Springer-Verlag, Berlin (2005). https://doi.org/10.1007/11804192_6
2. Beringer, L.: Verified software units. In: Programming Languages and Systems: 30th European Symposium on Programming, ESOP 2021, Held as Part of the European Joint Conferences on Theory and Practice of Software, ETAPS 2021, Luxembourg City, Luxembourg, March 27 – April 1, 2021, Proceedings, pp. 118–147. Springer-Verlag, Berlin (2021). https://doi.org/10.1007/978-3-030-72019-3_5
3. Calcagno, C., Distefano, D.: Infer: an automatic program verifier for memory safety of C programs. In: Proceedings of the Third International Conference on NASA Formal Methods, NFM'11, pp. 459–465. Springer-Verlag, Berlin (2011)
4. Cao, Q., Beringer, L., Gruetter, S., Dodds, J., Appel, A.W.: VST-Floyd: a separation logic tool to verify correctness of C programs. J. Autom. Reason. **61**(1), 367–422 (2018). https://doi.org/10.1007/s10817-018-9457-5
5. Chin, W.N., David, C., Nguyen, H.H., Qin, S.: multiple pre/post specifications for heap-manipulating methods. In: 10th IEEE High Assurance Systems Engineering Symposium (HASE'07), pp. 357–364 (2007). https://doi.org/10.1109/HASE.2007.19
6. Dantzig, G.B., Curtis Eaves, B.: Fourier-Motzkin elimination and its dual. J. Comb. Theory, Ser. A **14**(3), 288–297 (1973). https://doi.org/10.1016/0097-3165(73)90004-6
7. Facebook: SPARTA: a library of software components designed for building high-performance static analyzers based on the theory of abstract interpretation. https://github.com/facebook/SPARTA. gitHub repository
8. Huawei LiteOS: LiteOS kernel. https://github.com/LiteOS/LiteOS
9. Illous, H., Lemerre, M., Rival, X.: A relational shape abstract domain. In: Barrett, C., Davies, M., Kahsai, T. (eds.) NASA Formal Methods, pp. 212–229. Springer International Publishing, Cham (2017)

10. Jacobs, B., Smans, J., Philippaerts, P., Vogels, F., Penninckx, W., Piessens, F.: VeriFast: a powerful, sound, predictable, fast verifier for C and Java. In: Bobaru, M., Havelund, K., Holzmann, G.J., Joshi, R. (eds.) NASA Formal Methods, pp. 41–55. Springer, Berlin, Heidelberg (2011)
11. Jung, R., Krebbers, R., Birkedal, L., Dreyer, D.: Higher-order ghost state. SIGPLAN Not. **51**(9), 256–269 (2016). https://doi.org/10.1145/3022670.2951943
12. Kirchner, F., Cuoq, P., Correnson, L., Prevosto, V., Signoles, J.: Frama-C: a software analysis perspective. Formal Aspects Comput. **27**(3), 573–609 (2015). https://doi.org/10.1007/s00165-014-0326-7
13. Kroening, D., Schrammel, P., Tautschnig, M.: CBMC: the C bounded model checker (2023). https://arxiv.org/abs/2302.02384
14. Kroening, D., Strichman, O.: Decision Procedures: An Algorithmic Point of View, 1st edn. Springer Publishing Company, Incorporated, Cham (2008)
15. Müller, P., Schwerhoff, M., Summers, A.J.: Viper: a verification infrastructure for permission-based reasoning. In: Jobstmann, B., Leino, K.R.M. (eds.) Verification, Model Checking, and Abstract Interpretation (VMCAI). LNCS, vol. 9583, pp. 41–62. Springer-Verlag (2016). https://doi.org/10.1007/978-3-662-49122-5_2
16. Nguyen, H.H., David, C., Qin, S., Chin, W.N.: Automated verification of shape and size properties via separation logic. In: Proceedings of the 8th International Conference on Verification, Model Checking, and Abstract Interpretation, VMCAI'07, pp. 251–266. Springer-Verlag, Berlin (2007)
17. Nguyen, Q.L., David, C., Chin, W.N.: Hip/Sleek: verification system for heap-manipulating programs (Splice example) (2023). https://github.com/hipsleek/hipsleek/blob/master/benchmark/SV-COMP/list_properties/splice.ss. gitHub repository, benchmark example: `splice.ss`
18. Nieuwenhuis, R., Oliveras, A.: Proof-producing congruence closure. In: Proceedings of the 16th International Conference on Term Rewriting and Applications,. RTA'05, pp. 453–468 Springer-Verlag, Berlin (2005). https://doi.org/10.1007/978-3-540-32033-3_33
19. Pulte, C., Makwana, D.C., Sewell, T., Memarian, K., Sewell, P., Krishnaswami, N.: CN: verifying systems C code with separation-logic refinement types. Proc. ACM Program. Lang. **7**(POPL) (2023). https://doi.org/10.1145/3571194
20. Sammler, M., Lepigre, R., Krebbers, R., Memarian, K., Dreyer, D., Garg, D.: RefinedC: automating the foundational verification of C code with refined ownership types. In: Proceedings of the 42nd ACM SIGPLAN International Conference on Programming Language Design and Implementation (PLDI 2021), pp. 158–174. ACM, New York (2021). https://doi.org/10.1145/3453483.3454060
21. Wang, Z., et al.: Stellis: a strategy language for purifying separation logic entailments (2025). https://arxiv.org/abs/2512.05159
22. Wu, S., Wu, X., Cao, Q.: Encode the ∀∃ relational Hoare logic into standard Hoare logic. Proc. ACM Program. Lang. **9**(OOPSLA2) (2025). https://doi.org/10.1145/3763138
23. Wu, X., et al.: QCP: a practical separation logic-based C program verification tool (2026). https://arxiv.org/abs/2505.12878
24. Zhou, L., Qin, J., Wang, Q., Appel, A.W., Cao, Q.: VST-A: a foundationally sound annotation verifier. Proc. ACM Program. Lang. **8**(POPL) (2024). https://doi.org/10.1145/3632911

Formal Specification-Based Code Review via LLMs

Jiandong Li[1] and Shaoying Liu[2](✉)

[1] Peking University, Beijing 100871, China
jiandong.li@pku.edu.cn
[2] East China Normal University, Shanghai 200062, China
syliu@sei.ecnu.edu.cn

Abstract. Code review is widely employed to verify software functionality against requirements. Increasing evidence suggests that adopting formal specifications can enhance the process and quality of traditional code review by introducing greater rigorS. A high level of automation in formal specification-based code review is desirable, as the process is time-consuming and labor-intensive. Additionally, the program reading techniques used in the existing formal specification-based review methods, such as checklist-based reading, provide little guidance for reviewers on how to detect faults or the inconsistencies, relying on the reviewer's experience and personal skills. In this paper, we address these problems by proposing an improved method for formal specification-based code review, leveraging the remarkable capabilities of LLMs to automatically review code against the formal specification to identify potential discrepancies and produce review report. A tool is developed to support it. Experiments are conducted to evaluate its performance by using the public BuggyJava + JML dataset comprising 586 buggy programs after processing. The result demonstrates that the proposed method integrating GPT-5.4 is effective, attaining an 85.84% recall in identifying the code-specification inconsistencies (bugs), which encompasses a diverse set of mutants produced by PITest that were formally verified and confirmed by OpenJML. The findings also indicate that integrating LLMs-based techniques is a promising strategy for streamlining the efforts involved in formal specification-based code reviews, leading to improvements in software quality.

Keywords: Formal Specification-Based Code Review · Verification · Code Inspection · Conformance checking · Software Quality Assurance

1 Introduction

Code review is a widespread practice essential for identifying faults, verify adherence to requirements and ensuring software quality [1–3]. To enhance its rigor, researchers have introduced formal specification-based code review techniques [4–6]. However, these approaches remain primarily manual, labor-intensive, and heavily reliant on the reviewer's personal experience. Existing reading techniques, such as ad hoc or checklist-based methods, provide overly general guidelines (e.g., merely asking if a function is implemented) and lack specific, actionable hints for detecting defects.

G. De Giacomo et al. (Eds.): TASE 2026, LNCS 16697, pp. 174–179, 2027.
https://doi.org/10.1007/978-3-032-30693-7_11

To address these limitations, we propose an automated formal specification-based code review method leveraging Large Language Models (LLMs). While LLMs have demonstrated remarkable efficacy across various software engineering tasks [7–9], including security reviews, functional validation, and specification synthesis, their potential for rigorous code review against formal specifications remains largely unexplored. Our approach utilizes LLMs to automatically review source code with its formal specifications, generating detailed review reports that pinpoint exact defect line numbers and provide natural language explanations for the violations. To support this method, we developed a dedicated tool integrated with GPT-5.4.

We evaluated our approach using the public BuggyJava + JML dataset [10], comprising 586 buggy Java programs after processing. Each program's correct behavior is defined by a JML specification. The ground truth for code-specification inconsistencies was strictly defined by the exact physical lines where mutations were injected via PITest, rather than relying on the symptomatic warning locations reported by the OpenJML verifier. A detection is considered successful only if the LLM's predicted line numbers intersect with these actual mutated lines. Experiment results demonstrate the effectiveness of our GPT-5.4-powered method, achieving an 85.84% recall rate in detecting these verified specification violations.

2 Formal Specification-Based Code Review

In this section, we formalize the problem of improving automation in formal specification-based code review.

2.1 Code Review Based on Formal Specifications

A formal specification defines the intended behavior of software, detailing necessary operations and their constraints. In contract-based specification languages (e.g., JML), an operation S is typically governed by a contract defined by a precondition *Pre* and a postcondition *Post*. In model-based formal specifications, an operation S in the specification can be represented as a four-tuple $< iv, ov, pre, post >$, where iv denotes the set of input variables, ov denotes the set of output variables, and pre and $post$ represent the pre-condition and post-condition, respectively. Let P be the code implementation of S. To ensure that P correctly implements S, the verification condition is as follows:

$$\forall_{\sim\sigma\in\nabla} \cdot Pre(\sim \alpha) \Rightarrow Post(\sim \alpha, P(\sim \alpha)) \quad (1)$$

Here, ∇ denotes all the possible initial and final states of S. In this expression, program P is the refinement of the operation (specification) S and defines a relationship between initial state $\sim \alpha$ before the execution of the program P and final state $\alpha(= P(\sim \alpha))$ after executing program P. Condition (1) requires that, for any initial state $\sim \alpha$ satisfying the precondition pre, the final state α resulting from the execution of P must satisfy the postcondition *Post*.

To verify this condition (1) and identify the discrepancies between the specification and its implemented programs, while ensuring code quality, we can employ the technique of formal specification-based code review.

In the general process of conducting code reviews against the formal specification, the reviewer begins by reading the formal specification to grasp the requirements. Using the specification as a reference, the reviewer then analyzes the code to verify that whether the formal specification is correctly implemented in the corresponding code. The reviewer then compiles a review report to highlight any defects discovered. Applying the general specification-based code review in practice is costly, tedious, and labor-intensive. Besides, the performance of code review against the specification is significantly affected by the knowledge and experience of the reviewers, as they are not provided with directions or guidelines on identifying defects.

2.2 Problem Statement

The goal of this research is to work out a systematic and effective way to automatically review code based on formal specification or provide reviewers with better guidance for detecting the inconsistencies between the code and the specification during the review process. This aims to alleviate the burden on reviewers, make the review process more user-friendly for reviewers, and ultimately improve the overall quality of reviews.

We are concerned with the following problem: Given a formal specification S and its corresponding code implementation P, how can the inspection of P be automated to verify its compliance with S and identify the violations?

3 LLM-Powered Code Review Against Formal Specification

We propose to advance formal specification-based code review by leveraging the remarkable capabilities of LLMs, such as ChatGPT. The review process takes the formal specification and its corresponding code implementation as input, analyze them to assess whether the formal specification is correctly implemented by the code and to identify potential discrepancies. Upon completing the analysis, the LLM generates a report, including the identified defects, the line number where the defect occurs, along with explanations of how the code violates the specification.

We develop a tool to support the proposed formal specification-based code review approach integrating with GPT-5.4. The software tool is developed as an interactive web application using Python3 and Streamlit. To facilitate reproducibility and support future research, the complete source code of the tool, along with the specific system prompts utilized for the code review process, has been made publicly available [11]. After running the Streamlit app locally with the command 'streamlit run app.py' in the console, the users can access it through their local browsers at http://localhost:8501/.

4 A Controlled Experiment and Evaluation

This section describes a controlled experiment validating the effectiveness of the proposed formal specification-based code review method, presents the results obtained.

4.1 Experiment Setup

To evaluate the performance of our proposed method, we utilized the public BuggyJava + JML dataset [10]. Originally, this dataset comprises 597 Java programs, each seeded with a single defect generated via PITest, and accompanied by a formal JML specification describing its correct behavior. During our automated preprocessing, one instance was excluded due to an invalid or missing verification log. Crucially, for each target buggy program, rather than relying on symptomatic OpenJML warnings the definitive ground truth was rigorously established by comparing the original clean source files against the generated buggy programs to extract the exact physical line numbers where mutations were injected. These process results in a final curated dataset of 586 valid programs for our experiments. To adapt the LLM for formal specification-based code review, we engineered a specialized system prompt that instructs the model to act as a formal verification expert. The tool feeds the target Java code and its embedded JML specifications into the LLM (GPT-5.4 in our case) via an API endpoint.

4.2 Research Questions and Experiment Results

To evaluate the proposed specification-based review method, we are concerned with the following question:

- How effective is our proposed method in identifying the code violations flagged by the formal verification tool? (RQ1)

During the evaluation, the LLM is tasked with identifying the buggy lines based solely on the source Java code and the embedded JML specifications. An LLM detection is classified as a *True Positive (Pass)* if and only if there is an intersection between the set of line numbers predicted by the LLM and the ground truth generated by comparing the original clean source files against the generated buggy programs. This strict, file-level matching criterion ensures that the LLM is genuinely identifying the same violations flagged by the formal verifier, allowing us to accurately calculate the recall rate of our proposed approach.

Table 1 illustrates the experiment results for RQ1. Metric *recall* is used to evaluate the performance of LLMs in the task of formal specification-based code review. The LLM-based approach achieved a recall rate of 85.84%. *Recall* denotes the ratio of the number of bugs found by LLMs of the total number of bugs in the dataset, which is calculated using the following formula:

$$Recall = \frac{number\ of\ correctly\ identified\ bugs\ byLLMs}{total\ numbers\ of\ bugs\ in\ the\ dataset} \tag{2}$$

Table 1. The experiment result for RQ1.

The Dataset	*Number of Bugs Correctly found by LLMs*	*Total Number of Bugs in the Dataset*	*Recall*
BuggyJava+JML	503	586	85.84% (503/586)

5 Related Work

How to use the formal specification to facilitate the inspection of programs have been explored by several scholars. Parnas et al. proposed a document driven inspection (DDI) technique to detecting the discrepancies between the code and the requirements [6]. Wassyng and Lawford developed an inspection approach by the adoption of both the formally described requirements and the design documents. Jin proposed a code inspection method supporting the verification of concurrent programs by extending DDI. Taking advantages of the formal specifications, Liu and Chen et al. proposed a formal specification-based inspection (FSBI) method that establishes a static, systematic, and rigorous inspection process for program verification [4]. Liu and Li et al. putted forward a code inspection method by reversing engineering [12].

Large language models (LLMs) have demonstrated strong potential across a wide range of software engineering tasks [7–9], with recent studies specifically exploring their use in code review [1–3]. These studies can be broadly categorized into two areas: identifying security vulnerabilities in code and validating code functionality (i.e., ensuring it meets its intended purpose). Zhou et al. evaluated GPT-3.5 and GPT-4 on coarse-grained binary classification tasks to detect unspecified security defects using various prompt [14]. Almeida et al. developed an IntelliJ IDEA plugin leveraging GPT-3.5 to enhance automated code review support and identify potential code issues [2]. Lu and Yu introduced LLaMA-Reviewer, a novel framework utilizing LLaMA for modern code review tasks to explore its effectiveness [1]. Yu et al. compared the performance of six LLMs using five different prompts against state-of-the-art static analysis tools like CppCheck, Bandit, CodeQL, and SonarQube for detecting and analyzing security flaws [13]. Additionally, Jensen et al. explored how LLMs can determine whether code meets its intended functionality without execution [3].

6 Conclusion

We present a new formal specification-based code review method for detecting the inconsistences between the code and the formal specification by leveraging LLMs. The faults (violations) are expected to be found by LLMs to automatically review the code against the formal specification. Our method shifts the paradigm of formal verification from rigid mathematical checking to an intelligent review process. Specific techniques for LLM-powered code review are discussed. We also develop a tool to support the method. Further, we conduct an evaluation of the proposed approach on the public BuggyJava+JML dataset and present our findings. We demonstrate that the GPT-5.4 achieves an 85.84% recall in identifying verified code-specification inconsistencies.

References

1. Lu, J., Yu, L., Li, X., Yang, L., Zuo, C.: LLaMA-reviewer: advancing code review automation with large language models through parameter-efficient fine-tuning. In: 2023 IEEE 34th International Symposium on Software Reliability Engineering (ISSRE), pp. 647–658. IEEE (2023)
2. Almeida, Y., et al.: AICodeReview: advancing code quality with AI-enhanced reviews. SoftwareX **26**, 101677 (2024)
3. Jensen, R.I.T., Tawosi, V., Alamir, S.: Software vulnerability and functionality assessment using LLMs. In: 2024 IEEE/ACM International Workshop on Natural Language-Based Software Engineering (NLBSE), pp. 25–28. IEEE (2024)
4. Liu, S., Chen, Y., Nagoya, F., McDermid, J.A.: Formal specification-based inspection for verification of programs. IEEE Trans. Software Eng. **SE-38**(5), 1100–1122 (2012)
5. Li, J., Liu, S., Liu, A., Huang, R.: Knowledge graph construction for SOFL formal specifications. Int. J. Software Eng. Knowl. Eng. **32**(04), 605–644 (2022)
6. Parnas, D.L., Madey, J., Iglewski, M.: Precise documentation of well-structured programs. IEEE Trans. Software Eng. **20**(12), 948–976 (1994)
7. Hou, X., et al.: Large language models for software engineering: a systematic literature review. ACM Trans. Softw. Eng. Methodol. (2023)
8. Wen, C., et al.: Enchanting program specification synthesis by large language models using static analysis and program verification. In: International Conference on Computer Aided Verification, pp. 302–328. Springer, Cham (2024)
9. Rong, G., et al.: Code comment inconsistency detection and rectification using a large language model. In: 2025 IEEE/ACM 47th International Conference on Software Engineering (ICSE), pp. 432–443. IEEE Computer Society (2024)
10. Nilizadeh, A., Leavens, G.T., Le, X.-B.D., Păsăreanu, C.S., Cok, D.R.: Exploring true test overfitting in dynamic automated program repair using formal methods. In: 2021 14th IEEE Conference on Software Testing, Verification and Validation (ICST), Porto de Galinhas, Brazil, pp. 229–240 (2021)
11. The source code. https://app.box.com/s/bd542m2tkov33a4f4vcw38j8se07h8sv
12. Liu, S., Li, H., Jiang, Z., Li, X., Liu, F., Zhong, Y.: Rigorous code review by reverse engineering. Inf. Softw. Technol. **133**, 106503 (2021)
13. Yu, J., et al.: An insight into security code review with LLMs: capabilities, obstacles and influential factors. arXiv preprint arXiv:2401.16310 (2024)
14. Zhou, X., Zhang, T., Lo, D.: Large language model for vulnerability detection: emerging results and future directions. arXiv preprint arXiv:2401.15468 (2024)

RealSanitizer: Detecting Floating-Point Errors via a Dynamic Precision Oracle

Yuantao Hu[1,3(✉)], Shizhong Zhao[1,2], Yun Wang[3,4], and Mingyuan Xia[3]

[1] East China Normal University, Shanghai, China
71265902093@stu.ecnu.edu.cn, szzhao@sei.ecnu.edu.cn
[2] Shanghai Key Laboratory for Trustworthy Computing, Shanghai, China
[3] UltraRISC Technology, Shanghai, China
yunwang94@sjtu.edu.cn, xiamy@ultrarisc.com
[4] Shanghai Jiao Tong University, Shanghai, China

Abstract. Floating-point numerical errors are a major threat to software reliability. Existing oracle-based dynamic analysis tools typically use a statically configured precision oracle, forcing a trade-off between accuracy and overhead. We present RealSanitizer, an instrumentation tool with an ISREAL-based dynamic precision oracle that adjusts precision per operation while bounding oracle error by a user-specified threshold. On 42 reported GSL error-triggering cases, RealSanitizer detects 39 (93%), outperforming ATOMU and approaching FPCC.

Keywords: Floating-point · Shadow execution · Instrumentation · Dynamic analysis

1 Introduction

Floating-point computation is pervasive, but finite precision makes each floating-point value only an approximation of a real number. This approximation introduces roundoff and cancellation, while limited range also causes overflow, underflow, and Not-a-Number (NaN) results. Such numerical errors have contributed to severe failures [11,12].

Many dynamic floating-point analysis tools [2–4,14] rely on a statically configured high precision. While simple, this strategy has clear limits in both cost and accuracy. High precision arithmetic is usually implemented in software and can be much slower than native floating-point execution [9]. More importantly, a single fixed precision cannot serve as a reliable reference for all operations. Most operations are numerically stable, but expressions with large magnitude differences may require much higher precision. For example, although $(e^{256}+1)-e^{256}$ is mathematically equal to 1, a 128-bit reference may lose the intermediate 1, and 512 bits may be needed to recover the exact result.

To address these limitations, we make three contributions. First, we propose a dynamic precision oracle for shadow execution, extending ISREAL with a general Adaptive Interval Search for monotonic functions and a direct error-forwarding

G. De Giacomo et al. (Eds.): TASE 2026, LNCS 16697, pp. 180–187, 2027.
https://doi.org/10.1007/978-3-032-30693-7_12

rule for Lipschitz-1 functions, reducing both implementation complexity and working precision. Second, we implement an LLVM-based instrumentation tool, RealSanitizer, to bring this oracle into dynamic analysis of real programs. Third, we evaluate our approach on GSL and show that it detects numerical errors effectively.

To support reproducibility, the code and experimental setup used in this work are publicly available at: https://github.com/HttoHu/real-sanitizer.

2 The Dynamic Precision Oracle

We build our dynamic precision oracle on top of ISREAL [19]. For each expression during execution, we distinguish three values: the real value x, the runtime value $\tilde{x}$ produced by the original program, and the shadow value $\hat{x}$ maintained by the oracle. The oracle associates each expression with a state $(\hat{x}, \epsilon_x)$ such that $|x - \hat{x}| \leq \epsilon_x$.

For an operation $y = f(x_1, \ldots, x_n)$ and a target tolerance $\mathcal{T}$, the oracle derives input requirements $\delta_1, \ldots, \delta_n$ under which it can construct a shadow state $(\hat{y}, \epsilon_y)$ satisfying $\epsilon_y \leq \mathcal{T}$. If the current operand states already satisfy $\epsilon_i \leq \delta_i$, the oracle certifies the target tolerance for the current operation. Otherwise, it recursively requests tighter operand states and recomputes the corresponding subexpressions at higher precision. In this way, complex expressions are handled recursively over the dynamic expression DAG until reaching leaves, namely program inputs and constants which the oracle idealizes as exact values with zero error.

For most arithmetic and elementary operations, we directly reuse the derivation rules from ISREAL. Since the correctness of these rules has already been established in the original ISREAL work, we treat them as the basic cases of our oracle. We further introduce two simplifications. For monotonic continuous functions such as exp and log, we use an interval search method that usually requires lower working precision than the original ISREAL treatment. For functions with Lipschitz constant at most 1 on the relevant domain, such as sin and cos, the oracle simply forwards the input error bound.

Common Method for Monotonic Functions. Let $I \subseteq \mathbb{R}$ be an interval, let $f : I \to \mathbb{R}$ be continuous and monotonic, let $\hat{x} \in I$ be an input estimate, and let $\mathcal{T} > 0$ be a target output tolerance. Our goal is to find $\delta > 0$ such that $[\hat{x} - \delta, \hat{x} + \delta] \subseteq I$ and the variation of f over this interval is at most $\mathcal{T}$, i.e.,

$$\sup_{x \in [\hat{x}-\delta, \hat{x}+\delta]} \mathrm{f(x)} - \inf_{x \in [\hat{x}-\delta, \hat{x}+\delta]} \mathrm{f(x)} \leq \mathcal{T}.$$

Since f is monotonic, the extrema over a closed interval are attained at the endpoints. Hence, the above condition is equivalent to

$$|f(\hat{x} + \delta) - f(\hat{x} - \delta)| \leq \mathcal{T}.$$

Based on this observation, we iteratively shrink δ from an initial value δ_{init} until the endpoint difference satisfies the target tolerance, and then return the midpoint of the resulting output interval.

Algorithm 1: Adaptive Interval Search (AIS)

Input: Function f, input estimate $\hat{x}$, target error $\mathcal{T}$, initial bound δ_{init}
Output: Input bound δ, output estimate $\hat{y}$

$\delta \leftarrow \delta_{\text{init}}$;
$y_l \leftarrow f(\hat{x} - \delta)$;
$y_h \leftarrow f(\hat{x} + \delta)$;
while $|y_h - y_l| > \mathcal{T}$ **do**
    $\delta \leftarrow \delta/2$;
    $\hat{x} \leftarrow \text{ISREAL}(\hat{x}, \delta)$;
    $y_l \leftarrow f(\hat{x} - \delta)$;
    $y_h \leftarrow f(\hat{x} + \delta)$;
$\hat{y} \leftarrow (y_l + y_h)/2$;
return $\delta, \hat{y}$;

By monotonicity, the midpoint $\hat{y} = (y_l + y_h)/2$ satisfies $|f(x) - \hat{y}| \leq \mathcal{T}/2$ whenever $x \in [\hat{x} - \delta, \hat{x} + \delta]$, and the algorithm terminates in finitely many iterations by continuity of f.

3 Implementation

We implement our approach in RealSanitizer, which consists of an instrumentation tool and a runtime library (rsan-rt). The instrumentation tool is implemented as a LLVM ModulePass. At compile time, it instruments user-provided programs by inserting calls to shadow execution functions in rsan-rt after floating-point instructions. Figure 1 shows the framework of our approach.

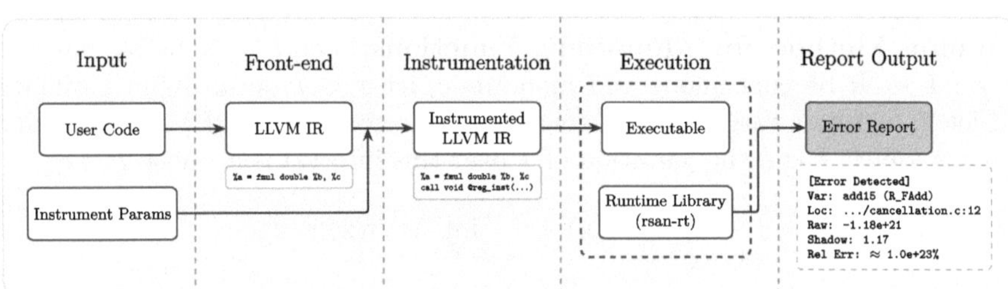

Fig. 1. Framework of RealSanitizer

Module Instrumentation Pass: The pass iterates over all functions in the module and assigns two identifiers to each floating-point operation. The `inst_id` identifies the static LLVM IR instruction site, while `entry_id` identifies its dynamic execution instance.

Shadow Execution: The instrumentation pass injects calls to rsan-rt after floating-point instructions. At critical sinks such as stores and conversions, it initiates recomputation over the operation DAG managed by rsan-rt. The runtime implements the dynamic precision oracle and performs a post-order traversal to bound absolute errors. It recursively recalculates operands only when higher precision is required. Similar to the temporary space of EFTSanitizer [5], rsan-rt bounds memory overhead by maintaining a sliding queue of recent shadow values, with each instrumentation-provided `entry_id` mapped to a unique slot. When a slot is overwritten by a newer value, the previous shadow value is discarded, which may cause some errors to go undetected. In return, memory usage remains bounded, enabling long-running dynamic analysis.

We also propose a novel numeric representation instead of relying on MPFR to represent shadow value. The representation encodes each value using a high-precision integer significand and an integer exponent. The exponent determines the precision, while the significand stores the scaled value exactly. This design allows rsan-rt to refine shadow values by adjusting the exponent and recomputing the significand, without maintaining a separate explicit error field.

After the shadow execution of a floating-point operation completes, rsan-rt compares the original value with the shadow value. If the absolute or relative error exceeds a specified threshold, it reports the source file location, the raw floating-point value, and the shadow value.

4 Experimental Evaluation

We evaluate RealSanitizer on GSL, a standard benchmark for floating-point error detection. The experiments were conducted on an AMD Ryzen 7 9700X (8-core) machine with 32 GB RAM running Ubuntu 22.04. The results show that RealSanitizer detects substantially more problematic cases than prior dynamic approaches while also providing error-path traces for debugging.

We use the 42 error-triggering inputs reported by DEMC [17], which are also adopted by ATOMU [20] and FPCC [18]. This makes the comparison direct. We use the same relative error threshold, 10^{-3}. To make runtime dependencies explicit, we evaluate an inlined subset of GSL, denoted gsl-lite. We also implement gsl-lite-py with mpmath as a tunable-precision reference. However, we preserve the original GSL formulas instead of replacing them with mpmath's native functions, because our goal is to expose floating-point errors in the GSL implementation rather than algorithmic approximation gaps caused by different formulas.

RealSanitizer detects 39 of the 42 problematic functions (93%). As shown in Table 1, this result is close to FPCC (42) and clearly better than ATOMU (28) and DEMC (20). The three missed cases are `gsl_sf_lambert_W0`,

Table 1. Data on the 42 functions with significant errors

Function Name	Error Triggering Input	Detected by RealSanitizer	Detected by DEMC	Detected by ATOMU
gsl_sf_airy_Ai	-4.042852549222488e+11	✓	✓	✓
gsl_sf_airy_Bi	-7.237129918123468e+11	✓	✓	✓
gsl_sf_airy_Ai_scaled	-3.073966210399579e+11	✓	-	-
gsl_sf_airy_Bi_scaled	-8.002750158072251e+11	✓	-	-
gsl_sf_airy_Ai_deriv	-1.018792971647468e+00	✓	✓	✓
gsl_sf_airy_Bi_deriv	-2.294439682614124e+00	✓	✓	✓
gsl_sf_airy_Ai_deriv_scaled	-1.018792971647467e+00	✓	-	-
gsl_sf_airy_Bi_deriv_scaled	-2.294439682614120e+00	✓	-	-
gsl_sf_bessel_J0	2.404825557695774e+00	✓	✓	✓
gsl_sf_bessel_J1	3.831705970207514e+00	✓	✓	✓
gsl_sf_bessel_Y0	3.957678419314854e+00	✓	✓	✓
gsl_sf_bessel_Y1	2.197141326031017e+00	✓	✓	✓
gsl_sf_bessel_j1	-7.725251836937709e+00	✓	-	-
gsl_sf_bessel_j2	9.095011330476359e+00	✓	-	-
gsl_sf_bessel_y0	2.585919463588284e+17	✓	-	-
gsl_sf_bessel_y1	9.361876298934626e+16	✓	-	-
gsl_sf_bessel_y2	1.586407411088372e+17	✓	-	-
gsl_sf_clausen	1.252935780352301e+14	✓	✓	✓
gsl_sf_dilog	1.259517036984501e+01	✓	-	✓
gsl_sf_expint_E1	-3.725074107813663e-01	✓	-	✓
gsl_sf_expint_E2	-1.347155251069168e+00	✓	-	✓
gsl_sf_expint_E1_scaled	-3.725074107813663e-01	✓	-	-
gsl_sf_expint_E2_scaled	-2.709975303391678e+228	✓	-	-
gsl_sf_expint_Ei	3.725074107813668e-01	✓	✓	✓
gsl_sf_expint_Ei_scaled	3.725074107813666e-01	✓	-	-
gsl_sf_Chi	5.238225713898647e-01	✓	✓	✓
gsl_sf_Ci	2.311778262696607e+17	✓	✓	✓
gsl_sf_lngamma	-2.457024738220797e+00	✓	-	✓
gsl_sf_lambert_W0	1.666385643189201e-41	-	-	✓
gsl_sf_lambert_Wm1	1.287978304826439e-121	-	-	-
gsl_sf_legendre_P2	-5.773502691896254e-01	✓	✓	✓
gsl_sf_legendre_P3	7.745966692414830e-01	✓	✓	✓
gsl_sf_legendre_Q1	8.335565596009644e-01	✓	✓	✓
gsl_sf_psi	-6.678418213073426e+00	✓	✓	✓
gsl_sf_psi_1	-4.799999999999998e+01	✓	✓	✓
gsl_sf_sin	-5.037566598712291e+17	✓	-	✓
gsl_sf_cos	-1.511080519199221e+17	✓	-	✓
gsl_sf_sinc	3.050995817918706e+15	✓	-	✓
gsl_sf_lnsinh	8.813735870195427e-01	✓	✓	✓
gsl_sf_zeta	-9.999999999999984e+00	✓	✓	✓
gsl_sf_zetam1	-1.699999999999999e+02	-	-	-
gsl_sf_eta	-9.999999999999989e+00	✓	✓	✓

`gsl_sf_lambert_Wm1`, and `gsl_sf_zetam1`. The two Lambert cases have extremely small absolute values below 10^{-40}, which are difficult for our oracle to distinguish. For `gsl_sf_zetam1`, the high-precision reference remains within the reporting threshold, with a relative error of about 0.0003, so no alarm is expected.

We also compare the produced shadow values with gsl-lite-py at 500-bit precision. In 23 cases, the two results agree directly. The remaining mismatches are mainly explained by error-induced branch flips or swapped-out intermediate shadow value queue slots. These effects can prevent exact path-by-path alignment even when RealSanitizer still identifies the root cause operation.

We use the GSL Chi function as a representative debugging example.

$$\mathrm{Chi}(x) = \gamma + \ln(x) + \int_0^x \frac{\cosh(t) - 1}{t} dt$$

For input 5.238225713898647e-01, GSL returns 6.106226635438361e-16, while gsl-lite-py returns 6.4463921621e-16. Figure 2 shows the error DAG reported by RealSanitizer. The dominant source is catastrophic cancellation at node #396. The two operands are nearly equal, so the subtraction discards most significant digits and yields a local relative error of 5.2%.

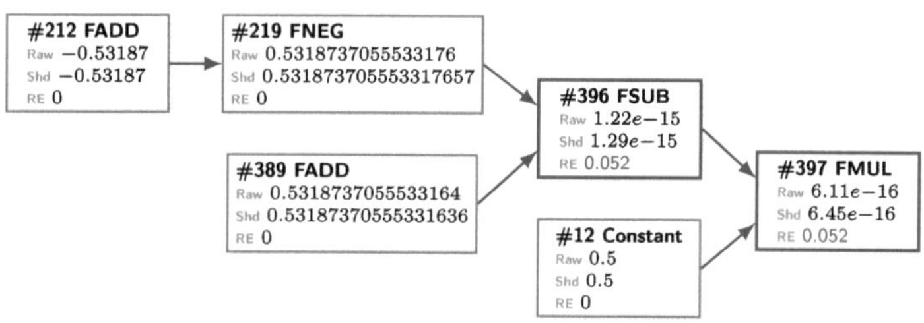

Fig. 2. Chi error path DAG trace. Raw denotes the original values calculated by gsl-lite. Shd denotes the shadow values calculated by RealSanitizer. RE denotes the relative error between Raw and Shd.

We also evaluated the runtime overhead of RealSanitizer by measuring the execution time of the SPEC CPU2006FP C++ benchmarks under the test input workload before and after instrumentation. The results show that RealSanitizer introduces around 100x overhead. We also used the same instrumentation infrastructure to implement shadow execution with statically configured high precision using MPFR. For SPEC CPU2006FP floating-point benchmarks with 128-bit precision, rsan-rt maintains a slightly lower overhead.

5 Related Work

We review related work on floating-point error detection methods, including static error-bound analysis and dynamic analysis.

Static error-bound analysis includes Gappa [7], Fluctuat [8], FPTaylor [15], PRECiSA [16], and VCFloat2 [1]. These tools provide formal guarantees, but they often produce conservative bounds and face scalability issues on large programs.

Dynamic analysis detects errors during execution. Early systems such as FPDebug [2], Herbgrind [14], FPSanitizer [3], and PFPSanitizer [4] compare native execution with high-precision shadow values. To reduce the runtime overhead, oracle-free methods such as EFTSanitizer [5], ATOMU [20], and FPCC [18] diagnose instability without relying on high-precision shadow value. Separately, some work in high performance computing focuses on hardware-level floating-point exceptions [6,10,13].

References

1. Appel, A., Kellison, A.: VCfloat2: floating-point error analysis in Coq. In: Proceedings of the 13th ACM SIGPLAN International Conference on Certified Programs and Proofs, CPP 2024, pp. 14–29. Association for Computing Machinery, New York (2024). https://doi.org/10.1145/3636501.3636953
2. Benz, F., Hildebrandt, A., Hack, S.: A dynamic program analysis to find floating-point accuracy problems. In: Proceedings of the 33rd ACM SIGPLAN Conference on Programming Language Design and Implementation, PLDI 2012, pp. 453–462. Association for Computing Machinery, New York (2012). https://doi.org/10.1145/2254064.2254118
3. Chowdhary, S., Lim, J.P., Nagarakatte, S.: Debugging and detecting numerical errors in computation with posits. In: Proceedings of the 41st ACM SIGPLAN Conference on Programming Language Design and Implementation, PLDI 2020, pp. 731–746. Association for Computing Machinery, New York (2020). https://doi.org/10.1145/3385412.3386004
4. Chowdhary, S., Nagarakatte, S.: Parallel shadow execution to accelerate the debugging of numerical errors. In: Proceedings of the 29th ACM Joint Meeting on European Software Engineering Conference and Symposium on the Foundations of Software Engineering, ESEC/FSE 2021, pp. 615–626. Association for Computing Machinery, New York (2021). https://doi.org/10.1145/3468264.3468585
5. Chowdhary, S., Nagarakatte, S.: Fast shadow execution for debugging numerical errors using error free transformations. Proc. ACM Program. Lang. **6**(OOPSLA2) (2022). https://doi.org/10.1145/3563353
6. Dinda, P., Bernat, A., Hetland, C.: Spying on the floating point behavior of existing, unmodified scientific applications. In: Proceedings of the 29th International Symposium on High-Performance Parallel and Distributed Computing, HPDC 2020, pp. 5–16. Association for Computing Machinery, New York (2020). https://doi.org/10.1145/3369583.3392673
7. de Dinechin, F., Lauter, C.Q., Melquiond, G.: Assisted verification of elementary functions using Gappa. In: Proceedings of the 2006 ACM Symposium on Applied Computing, SAC 2006, pp. 1318–1322. Association for Computing Machinery, New York (2006). https://doi.org/10.1145/1141277.1141584
8. Goubault, E., Putot, S., Baufreton, P., Gassino, J.: Static analysis of the accuracy in control systems: principles and experiments. In: Leue, S., Merino, P. (eds.) FMICS 2007. LNCS, vol. 4916, pp. 3–20. Springer, Heidelberg (2008). https://doi.org/10.1007/978-3-540-79707-4_3

9. Larsson, P.: Exploring quadruple precision floating point numbers in GCC and ICC (2013). https://www.nsc.liu.se/~pla/blog/2013/10/17/quadruple-precision. Accessed 27 Jan 2026
10. Li, X., Laguna, I., Fang, B., Swirydowicz, K., Li, A., Gopalakrishnan, G.: Design and evaluation of GPU-FPX: a low-overhead tool for floating-point exception detection in NVIDIA GPUs. In: Proceedings of the 32nd International Symposium on High-Performance Parallel and Distributed Computing, HPDC 2023, pp. 59–71. Association for Computing Machinery, New York (2023). https://doi.org/10.1145/3588195.3592991
11. Lions, J.L.: Flight 501 failure. Report by the Inquiry Board 190 (1996)
12. Marshall, E.: Fatal error: how patriot overlooked a scud. Science **255**(5050), 1347–1347 (1992)
13. Miao, D., Laguna, I., Rubio-González, C.: FloatGuard: efficient whole-program detection of floating-point exceptions in AMD GPUs. In: Proceedings of the 34th International Symposium on High-Performance Parallel and Distributed Computing, HPDC 2025. Association for Computing Machinery, New York (2025). https://doi.org/10.1145/3731545.3731586
14. Sanchez-Stern, A., Panchekha, P., Lerner, S., Tatlock, Z.: Finding root causes of floating point error. In: Proceedings of the 39th ACM SIGPLAN Conference on Programming Language Design and Implementation, PLDI 2018, pp. 256–269. Association for Computing Machinery, New York (2018). https://doi.org/10.1145/3192366.3192411
15. Solovyev, A., Baranowski, M.S., Briggs, I., Jacobsen, C., Rakamarić, Z., Gopalakrishnan, G.: Rigorous estimation of floating-point round-off errors with symbolic Taylor expansions. ACM Trans. Program. Lang. Syst. **41**(1) (2018). https://doi.org/10.1145/3230733
16. Titolo, L., Feliú, M.A., Moscato, M., Muñoz, C.A.: An abstract interpretation framework for the round-off error analysis of floating-point programs. In: VMCAI 2018. LNCS, vol. 10747, pp. 516–537. Springer, Cham (2018). https://doi.org/10.1007/978-3-319-73721-8_24
17. Yi, X., Chen, L., Mao, X., Ji, T.: Efficient automated repair of high floating-point errors in numerical libraries. Proc. ACM Program. Lang. **3**(POPL) (2019).https://doi.org/10.1145/3290369
18. Yi, X., Yu, H., Chen, L., Mao, X., Wang, J.: FPCC: detecting floating-point errors via chain conditions. Proc. ACM Program. Lang. **8**(OOPSLA2) (2024). https://doi.org/10.1145/3689764
19. Zhao, S.: A reliable computing algorithm and its software application ISReal for arithmetic expressions(in Chinese). SCIENTIA SINICA Inform. **46**, 698–713 (2016). https://doi.org/10.1360/N112015-00061
20. Zou, D., Zeng, M., Xiong, Y., Fu, Z., Zhang, L., Su, Z.: Detecting floating-point errors via atomic conditions. Proc. ACM Program. Lang. **4**(POPL) (2019). https://doi.org/10.1145/3371128

Random Generation of Small Quantitative Automata for Algorithm Debugging

Mikael Bisgaard Dahlsen-Jensen(✉) and Jaco van de Pol

Aarhus University, Aarhus, Denmark
{mikael,jaco}@cs.au.dk

Abstract. Analysis algorithms for quantitative automata are complex and hard to validate. Existing approaches—benchmarks, mutation testing, uniform random generation—each fail to expose subtle implementation bugs. We present a framework that repeatedly 1) generates random quantitative automata that are non-degenerate by construction, 2) tests each against a target property, and 3) shrinks any violation to a local minimum, yielding a small, actionable counterexample. We implement the framework for parametric timed automata (PTA) and apply it to IMITATOR, a mature model checker for PTA, uncovering 5 previously unknown bugs, one of which was exposed by a counterexample with just 2 locations and 1 transition.

1 Introduction

Quantitative automata (timed, parametric, weighted, probabilistic) underpin a wide range of formal verification tools. Their analysis algorithms are complex and subject to continuous optimisation: as tools mature and acquire new features, subtle bugs can accumulate in corner cases that standard benchmark suites never exercise. Small, actionable counterexamples are crucial for debugging such bugs, but manually crafting them is difficult when the nature of the fault is unknown.

We propose a semantics-respecting random generation framework that avoids degenerate models—unsatisfiable guards, unreachable locations—by construction, paired with a shrinking procedure that iteratively removes structure while verifying the target property is preserved, yielding a small, human-readable witness. While we instantiate the framework for parametric timed automata (PTAs) [1], the design is not specific to them.

We demonstrate that the framework produces small, actionable counterexamples automatically: applying it to IMITATOR [2], a mature model checker for PTAs, it uncovered 5 previously unknown bugs. One counterexample consists of just two locations and one transition, yet it exposes a fault in the unavoidability synthesis algorithm that had gone undetected until now.

This work was supported by Innovationsfonden Danmark's DIREC project SIoT (Secure Internet of Things).

G. De Giacomo et al. (Eds.): TASE 2026, LNCS 16697, pp. 188–205, 2027.
https://doi.org/10.1007/978-3-032-30693-7_13

Existing approaches fall short in different ways. Benchmark suites [4] of curated models rarely stress edge cases. Mutation testing requires a collection of good seeds, but any bias in those seeds risks missing entire classes of faults; and when the nature of the bugs is unknown, there is no principled basis for selecting them. Uniform random generation avoids this bias but produces mostly degenerate models with unsatisfiable constraints or unreachable locations that no algorithm can meaningfully distinguish.

Related Work. Property-based testing [6] introduced the generate-and-shrink paradigm for automated counterexample finding. Random generation to stress-test analysis tools is well-established: compiler testing [13] and SMT solver fuzzing [5] demonstrate that random inputs reliably surface subtle implementation faults. Random NFA generation [12] has been used to benchmark algorithm performance rather than find bugs: performance evaluation tolerates degenerate inputs and has no need for small witnesses, goals orthogonal to ours. Most closely related is the work of Manini et al. [8], who generate random timed automata and derive a problem-specific oracle automatically; however, constructing such an oracle requires non-trivial problem-specific theory, limiting applicability to problems where one is available, and they perform no counterexample minimisation. We sidestep the oracle problem entirely via differential testing [9], comparing two algorithm variants on the same input, and reduce any witness to a minimal non-witness example through property-preserving shrinking.

Contributions

- A semantics-respecting random PTA generator that produces non-degenerate models by construction
- A shrinker that reduces witnesses to a local minimum while preserving the target property, yielding small actionable counterexamples
- An implementation as a meta-tool within IMITATOR
- An empirical evaluation uncovering 5 previously unknown bugs in a mature tool

2 Background

2.1 Parametric Timed Automata

A Parametric Timed Automaton (PTA) is a structure based on timed automata (TA). Like classical automata, it has locations connected by discrete transitions. It also has clocks. Locations are associated a condition on clock valuations (invariant) that must be satisfied while staying in the location. An action in a timed automaton is either to take a discrete transition or to let some time pass. Discrete transitions have a guard that must be satisfied in order to take the transition, and a set of clocks to reset. In a parametric setting, these conditions use linear terms over clocks and parameters. Parameters are unspecified but constant during a run.

Throughout this paper, we let X denote a set of real-valued clocks and P a set of rational parameters.

Definition 1 (parametric guards). *A* linear term *over P has the form k or kp or a sum thereof, where $k \in \mathbb{Q}$ and $p \in P$. The set of* parametric guards *$\mathcal{G}(X, P)$ is defined by the grammar:*

$$\phi := \top \mid \phi \wedge \phi \mid x \bowtie \tau \mid \tau' \bowtie \tau$$

where $x \in X$, $\bowtie \in \texttt{Cmp} := \{<, \leq, =, \geq, >\}$, and τ, τ' are linear terms over P.

In this paper, parametric guards are treated as syntactic objects. Their semantics will be defined in terms of the set of valuations that satisfy them (Definition 6).

Definition 2 (atomic sub-expressions). *Let $\phi \in \mathcal{G}(X, P)$ be a parametric guard. The multiset of* atomic sub-expressions *of ϕ, denoted $\texttt{subexpr}(\phi)$, is the multiset of sub-expressions of ϕ that are of the form $x \bowtie \tau$ or $\tau' \bowtie \tau$.*

Example 1. Consider the parametric guard $\phi = (x \leq p + 5) \wedge (y > 2p) \wedge (x \leq p + 5)$. The multiset of atomic sub-expressions of ϕ is:

$$\texttt{subexpr}(\phi) = \{x \leq p + 5, x \leq p + 5, y > 2p\}.$$

Definition 3 (Parametric Timed Automaton). *A* Parametric Timed Automaton *is a tuple of the form $\mathcal{A} = (L, X, P, T, \ell_0, Inv)$ such that*

- *L, X, P are disjoint sets of* locations, clocks, parameters.
- *$T \subseteq L \times \mathcal{G}(X, P) \times 2^X \times L$ is the set of* transitions *of the form (ℓ, g, Y, ℓ') where: ℓ, ℓ' are source and target locations, g is the parametric guard, Y the set of clocks to reset. We write $\ell \xrightarrow{g,Y} \ell'$ to denote a transition and $\ell \rightarrow \ell'$ when the guard and resets are unimportant.*
- *ℓ_0 is the initial location.*
- *$Inv : L \rightarrow \mathcal{G}(X, P)$ associates an* invariant *with each location.*

Definition 4 (valuations). *A* clock valuation *is a function $v_X \in \mathbb{R}_{\geq 0}^X$ assigning a non-negative real value to each clock in X. A* parameter valuation *$v_P \in \mathbb{Q}_{\geq 0}^P$ assigns a non-negative rational value to each parameter in P. A* valuation *is a pair $v = (v_X, v_P)$. The set of all valuations of a PTA with clocks X and parameters P is denoted $V = \mathbb{R}_{\geq 0}^X \times \mathbb{Q}_{\geq 0}^P$. Since X and P are disjoint, we write $v(y)$ for $v_X(y)$ if $y \in X$ and $v_P(y)$ if $y \in P$.*

Definition 5 (clock update). *For $Y \subseteq X$ and $v \in V$, write $v[Y \mapsto 0]$ for the valuation that maps each $x \in Y$ to 0 and each $x \notin Y$ to $v(x)$. For $Z \subseteq V$, write $Z[Y \mapsto 0]^{-1} := \{v \mid v[Y \mapsto 0] \in Z\}$, i.e., the set of valuations that land in Z after resetting the clocks in Y.*

Definition 6 (satisfaction of guards). *Let $g \in \mathcal{G}(X, P)$ be a parametric guard, and $v = (v_X, v_P)$ a valuation. We say that v* satisfies *g, denoted $v \models g$, if g evaluates to true when each clock $x \in X$ is replaced by $v_X(x)$ and each parameter $p \in P$ is replaced by $v_P(p)$. Let $[\![g]\!]$ denote the set of valuations satisfying g:*

$$[\![g]\!] = \{v \in V \mid v \models g\}.$$

2.2 Multigraphs

We recall the standard notion of directed multigraphs, which we use to describe the graph structure of generated automata.

Definition 7 (multigraph). *A directed multigraph is a pair $G = (L, M)$, where L is a finite set of locations and $M : L \times L \to \mathbb{N}$ is an edge multiplicity function. For $\ell, \ell' \in L$, let the value $M(\ell, \ell')$ be the number of directed edges from ℓ to ℓ'.*

The outgoing degree of a location $\ell \in L$ (counting multiplicities) is defined as

$$\deg_M^+(\ell) \triangleq \sum_{\ell' \in L} M(\ell, \ell').$$

2.3 Probability Distributions

We use probability distributions to describe and parameterize the random generation of automata.

Definition 8 (Distribution). *For a countable set A, $\mathcal{D}(A)$ denotes the set of probability distributions over A, i.e. functions $\mu : A \to [0,1]$ with $\sum_{a\in A} \mu(a) = 1$. We write $X \sim \mu$ to denote that X is sampled according to μ.*

We now introduce several standard constructions on distributions that we use to describe our generation algorithms.

Definition 9 (Standard distributions). *We use the following standard distributions on countable sets.*

- *Uniform(A): uniform over a non-empty finite set A, assigning probability $1/|A|$ to each element.*
- *Bern(p): Bernoulli, $p \in [0, 1]$: taking 1 with probability p and 0 with $1 - p$.*
- *Choose$_k$(A): uniform over k-element subsets of finite set A, for $0 \leq k \leq |A|$.*
- *δ_a is the Dirac distribution: a point mass at a, with $\delta_a(a) = 1$.*
- *Geom$_{\leq m}$(q): Capped Geometric, for $q \in (0, 1)$ and $m \in \mathbb{N}_{\geq 1}$, the distribution on $\{1, \dots, m\}$ with $P(K{=}k) = (1 - q)q^{k-1}$ for $k < m$ and $P(K{=}m) = q^{m-1}$.*

Definition 10 (Pushforward). *Let $f : A \to B$ and $\mu \in \mathcal{D}(A)$. The pushforward distribution $f_*(\mu) \in \mathcal{D}(B)$ is defined by*

$$f_*(\mu)(b) = \sum_{a\in A\,:\, f(a)=b} \mu(a).$$

Equivalently, if $X \sim \mu$ then $f(X) \sim f_*(\mu)$.

Definition 11 (Dependent sampling). *Let $\mu \in \mathcal{D}(A)$ and $f : A \to \mathcal{D}(B)$. The distribution $\mu \circledast f \in \mathcal{D}(B)$ is defined by*

$$(\mu \circledast f)(b) = \sum_{a\in A} \mu(a)\, f(a)(b).$$

Equivalently, sample $a \sim \mu$ and then sample b from $f(a)$.

Definition 12 (Product distribution). *Let* $\mu \in \mathcal{D}(A)$ *and* $\nu \in \mathcal{D}(B)$. *Their product* $\mu \otimes \nu \in \mathcal{D}(A \times B)$ *is defined by*

$$(\mu \otimes \nu)(a, b) = \mu(a)\nu(b).$$

Equivalently, sample independently from μ *and* ν.

Definition 13 (n-fold product). *Let* $\mu \in \mathcal{D}(A)$, $n \in \mathbb{N}$, *and write* $Fin(n) := \{0, \ldots, n-1\}$. *The* n*-fold product* $\mu^{\otimes n} \in \mathcal{D}(A^{Fin(n)})$ *is defined by*

$$\mu^{\otimes n}\big((a_i)_{i \in Fin(n)}\big) := \prod_{i \in Fin(n)} \mu(a_i).$$

Equivalently, $\mu^{\otimes n}$ *samples* n *independent values from* μ.

Definition 14 (Geometric subset choice). *For* $q \in (0, 1)$ *and a finite set* S, *define*

$$ChooseGeom(q, S) \triangleq Geom_{\leq |S|}(q) \circledast (\lambda k.\ Choose_k(S)).$$

Equivalently, draw a random size k *from* $Geom_{\leq |S|}(q)$ *and return a uniformly random* k*-element subset of* S.

3 Framework

The framework consists of two components: a semantics-respecting random generator (Sect. 4) and a property-preserving shrinker (Sect. 5). Together they form the VALIDATOR (Algorithm 1), searching for a small counterexample to a property φ.

A *model specification* $\mathcal{M}$ is a user-supplied configuration controlling the intended size and structure of generated PTAs, and a *generator schema* Σ is a structured collection of probability distributions over PTA components; both are defined formally in Sect. 4. The generator comprises two high-level procedures: CONSTRUCTSCHEMA (Algorithm 5), which translates $\mathcal{M}$ into Σ, and AUTOMATONGEN (Algorithm 2), which draws a PTA from Σ. The shrinker is SHRINK (Sect. 5), which iteratively removes structure from a violating PTA while preserving the violation. Section 4 establishes formal requirements for the generator and describes the algorithms that satisfy them by construction; Sect. 5 presents the staged shrinking pipeline and its design principles.

Algorithm 1. VALIDATOR: bounded random search for a minimal witness

Require: Model specification $\mathcal{M}$, property φ, bound $r \in \mathbb{N}$
Ensure: A minimal witness $\mathcal{A}$ with $\neg\varphi(\mathcal{A})$, or $\bot$
$\Sigma \leftarrow$ CONSTRUCTSCHEMA($\mathcal{M}$)
for $i \leftarrow 1$ **to** r **do**
    $\mathcal{A} \sim$ AUTOMATONGEN(Σ)
    if $\neg\varphi(\mathcal{A})$ **then**
        return SHRINK($\mathcal{A}, \varphi$)
return $\bot$

4 Semantics-Respecting Generator

This section develops the semantics-respecting PTA generator in three steps: we first state formal requirements that any meaningful generator must satisfy (Sect. 4.1), then introduce the generation scheme and AUTOMATONGEN, which samples a PTA from a given schema (Sect. 4.2), and finally show how CONSTRUCTSCHEMA builds a schema from a model specification so that all requirements are met by construction (Sect. 4.3).

4.1 Generator Requirements

We adopt a *principle of meaningfulness*: all components of the generated PTA should be **meaningful**. This means that we want to avoid generating components that are trivial, unreachable, unsatisfiable, or redundant. We now outline the specific design goals we have for the generator.

Graph Structure. The shape of the underlying graph of the generated PTA is an important aspect of generation. A completely random graph structure has a high likelihood of being disconnected or having locations that are unreachable from the initial location. Following the principle of meaningfulness, this is unacceptable as it leads to meaningless locations.

We therefore require all locations to be reachable from the initial location via discrete transitions.

Requirement 1 (Graph Reachability). *The underlying directed graph of the generated PTA is such that all locations are reachable from the initial location via discrete transitions, ignoring guards, invariants and time elapsing:*

$$\psi_{Graph}(\mathcal{A} = (L, X, P, T, \ell_0, Inv)) \triangleq \forall \ell \in L, \ell_0 \rightarrow^* \ell$$

where $\rightarrow^*$ is the transitive closure of $\rightarrow$.

Invariants. Invariants are important components of timed automata as they restrict the time that can be spent in a location. However, if an invariant is unsatisfiable, then the location becomes meaningless as no time can be spent there. Following the principle of meaningfulness, we want to avoid generating locations with unsatisfiable invariants.

Requirement 2 (Invariant Satisfiability) *Every invariant is satisfiable:*

$$\psi_{InvSat}(\mathcal{A} = (L, X, P, T, \ell_0, Inv)) \triangleq \forall \ell \in L, [\![Inv(\ell)]\!] \neq \emptyset$$

Furthermore, we want to ensure that the initial location invariant is satisfiable for the initial clock valuation where all clocks are set to 0. This ensures that the system can start executing from the initial location. In a sense, this is the most important requirement for invariants, as if this is not satisfied, the generated PTA is completely meaningless from the start.

Requirement 3 (Initial Invariant Satisfiability). *The initial invariant holds when all clocks are zero:*

$$\psi_{InvInit}(\mathcal{A} = (L, X, P, T, \ell_0, Inv)) \triangleq [\![\bigwedge_{x \in X} x = 0]\!] \subseteq [\![Inv(\ell_0)]\!]$$

Guards. Similar to invariants, a guard is only meaningful if it is satisfiable, so this is a nice starting point. We can strengthen this even more: even if a guard is satisfiable for *some valuations*, it might not be satisfiable in any *context* where the guard is used i.e. on a transition between two locations with certain invariants. There are three components to consider here: the source location invariant, the guard itself, and the target location invariant (after resetting the appropriate clocks). Thus, a first attempt at a meaningfulness requirement for guards is that each guard should be satisfiable within the context of the source location invariant and the target location invariant (after resetting the appropriate clocks):

$$\begin{aligned}\psi_{GuardSatAttempt}(\mathcal{A} = (L, X, P, T, \ell_0, Inv)) \triangleq \forall (\ell_1, g, Y, \ell_2) \in T,\\ [\![g]\!] \cap [\![Inv(\ell_1)]\!] \cap [\![Inv(\ell_2)]\!][Y \mapsto 0]^{-1} \neq \emptyset\end{aligned}$$

However, this requirement on guards imposes a significant restriction on invariants. Invariant generation is no longer a local problem, since now all pairs of invariants connected by a transition must have a non-empty intersection (taking into account resets). This makes invariant generation significantly more complex, as we can no longer generate invariants independently for each location. Instead, we must consider the entire graph structure and the transitions between locations when generating invariants, introducing a graph exploration aspect to invariant generation. A good middleground between meaningfulness and feasibility is to only consider the source location invariant when checking guard satisfiability. This way, we ensure that the guard is meaningful in the context of where it is used, without overly complicating invariant generation. Thus, we require the following:

Requirement 4 (Guard Satisfiability). *All guards in the generated PTA are satisfiable within the context of the source location invariant:*

$$\begin{aligned}\psi_{GuardSat}(\mathcal{A} = (L, X, P, T, \ell_0, Inv)) \triangleq \forall (\ell_1, g, Y, \ell_2) \in T,\\ [\![g]\!] \cap [\![Inv(\ell_1)]\!] \neq \emptyset\end{aligned}$$

Redundant Sub-expressions. A guard or invariant may contain redundant sub-expressions that do not contribute to the overall meaning of the constraint. For example, the guard $x \leq 5 \wedge x \leq 10$ contains the redundant sub-expression $x \leq 10$ since it is implied by $x \leq 5$. Following the principle of meaningfulness, we want to avoid generating guards and invariants with redundant sub-expressions. We define a helper predicate over $\mathcal{G}(X, P)$ to capture the absence of redundant sub-expressions:

$$\psi_{NoRed}(\phi) \triangleq \forall \phi_1, \phi_2 \in \texttt{subexpr}(\phi), [\![\phi_1]\!] \not\subseteq [\![\phi_2]\!]$$

and then require that all guards and invariants in the generated PTA satisfy this property:

Requirement 5 (No Redundant Sub-expressions). *No guard or invariant contains redundant sub-expressions:*

$$\psi_{Redundant}(\mathcal{A} = (L, X, P, T, \ell_0, Inv)) \triangleq \forall \ell \in L, \psi_{NoRed}(Inv(\ell)) \wedge \\ \forall (\ell_1, g, Y, \ell_2) \in T, \psi_{NoRed}(g)$$

4.2 Generation Scheme

To describe the generator, we first introduce the notion of a generation schema, which is a collection of probability distributions over the components of a PTA. A generation schema defines how to sample each simple component of a PTA, such as the set of locations, clocks, parameters, the graph structure, invariants, guards, and resets.

Definition 15 (generation schema). *A* generation schema *is a tuple* $\Sigma = (\mathfrak{L}, \mathfrak{X}, \mathfrak{P}, \mathfrak{G}, \mathfrak{I}, \mathfrak{Z}, \mathfrak{Y})$ *where:*

- $\mathfrak{L}$ *is a probability distribution over finite sets of locations* L,
- $\mathfrak{X}$ *is a probability distribution over finite sets of clocks* X,
- $\mathfrak{P}$ *is a probability distribution over finite sets of parameters* P,
- $\mathfrak{I}(L, X, P)$ *is a probability distribution over invariant functions* $Inv : L \to \mathcal{G}(X, P)$,
- $\mathfrak{G}(L)$ *is a probability distribution over multigraphs over* L,
- $\mathfrak{Z}(X, P)$ *is a probability distribution over* $\mathcal{G}(X, P)$,
- $\mathfrak{Y}(X)$ *is a probability distribution over* 2^X.

Since the types of locations, clocks, and parameters are not fixed, we use canonical tagged carriers whose sizes are supplied dynamically.

Definition 16 (Tagged canonical carriers for generation). *Let* $Tag := \{\mathtt{Loc}, \mathtt{Clock}, \mathtt{Param}\}$ *be a set of tags. For each* $\alpha \in Tag$ *and* $n \in \mathbb{N}$, *define the tagged carrier* $Fin^{\mathtt{Loc}}(\alpha) := Fin(n) \times \{\alpha\}$. *Distinct tags ensure pairwise disjointness, allowing unambiguous distinction of locations, clocks, and parameters in guards. We write* ℓ_n, x_n, p_n *as shorthands for* $(n, \mathtt{Loc})$, $(n, \mathtt{Clock})$, $(n, \mathtt{Param})$*; the initial location is fixed as* $\ell_0 = (0, \mathtt{Loc})$.

AutomatonGen (Algorithm 2) samples PTA components in dependency order. The sets L, X, P are drawn first, since all remaining distributions are parameterized by them. Invariants are sampled before the transition structure, so

Algorithm 2. AutomatonGen

Require: Generation schema $\Sigma = (\mathfrak{L}, \mathfrak{X}, \mathfrak{P}, \mathfrak{G}, \mathfrak{I}, \mathfrak{Z}, \mathfrak{Y})$
Ensure: A randomly generated automaton $\mathcal{A}$

$(L, X, P) \sim (\mathfrak{L} \otimes \mathfrak{X} \otimes \mathfrak{P})$ ▷ *sample components that parameterize the rest*
$Inv \sim \mathfrak{I}(L, X, P)$
$M \sim \mathfrak{G}(L)$
$T \leftarrow \emptyset$
for all $\ell, \ell' \in L$ **do**
  for $i = 1$ to $M(\ell, \ell')$ **do**
    $g \sim \mathfrak{Z}(X, P, Inv, \ell)$
    $Y \sim \mathfrak{Y}(X)$
    $T \leftarrow T \cup \{(\ell, g, Y, \ell')\}$
return $(L, X, P, T, \ell_0, Inv)$

that the already-sampled source invariant $Inv(\ell)$ can be passed to $\mathfrak{Z}$ as context—a dependency that an appropriately instantiated $\mathfrak{Z}$ can exploit to satisfy Requirement 4.

The distributions in Σ are left abstract. The next subsection defines a model specification and the ConstructSchema procedure that instantiates them to satisfy the design goals by construction.

4.3 Instantiation of Generation Schema

We now instantiate the abstract generation schema: we define two subprocedures, GraphGen and GuardGen, that enforce the structural requirements, and show how ConstructSchema uses them to assemble a complete, requirements-satisfying schema from a model specification.

Graph Structure. To satisfy Requirement 1, $\mathfrak{G}$ must only produce graphs where all locations are reachable from ℓ_0. GraphGen (Algorithm 3) achieves this

Algorithm 3. GraphGen

Require: Set of locations L and an outdegree mapping $K : L \to \mathbb{N}_{\geq 1}$
Ensure: A directed graph multigraph $G = (L, M)$ where all locations are reachable from ℓ_0

$A \leftarrow \{\ell_0\}$ ▷ *locations already in the spanning tree*
$M := \{(u, v) \mapsto 0 \mid u, v \in L\}$ ▷ $M : L \times L \to \mathbb{N}$
for all $\ell \in L \setminus \{\ell_0\}$ **do** ▷ *build spanning tree from* ℓ_0
  $\ell' \sim \text{Uniform}(A);\; M(\ell', \ell) \leftarrow 1;\; A \leftarrow A \cup \{\ell\}$
for all $\ell \in L$ **do**
  while $\deg^+_M(\ell) < K(\ell)$ **do**
    $\ell' \sim \text{Uniform}(L)$
    $M(\ell, \ell') \leftarrow M(\ell, \ell') + 1$
$G = (L, M)$
return G

by first building a spanning tree rooted at ℓ_0 (guaranteeing reachability), then adding random edges until the desired per-location outdegree is met.

Guard Generation. Guards must intersect the invariant of their source location (Requirement 4), but a uniformly random guard is almost certainly disjoint from any fixed invariant. We therefore restrict generation to *Coupled Interval Guards* (CIGs), a class of guards structured as interval-and-coupling triples that admit efficient witness-based sampling guaranteeing intersection by construction.

Throughout this section, an *interval* denotes a closed, open, or half-open interval with non-negative integer endpoints: $[l, u]$, $(l, u]$, $[l, u)$, or (l, u) with $l, u \in \mathbb{Z}_{\geq 0} \cup \{+\infty\}$. Write $\mathbb{Z}(I)$ for the set of non-negative integers in I; for example, $\mathbb{Z}([2, 5)) = \{2, 3, 4\}$ and $\mathbb{Z}((3, 4)) = \emptyset$.

Definition 17 (Coupled Interval Guard (CIG)). *Let X be a finite set of clocks and P a finite set of parameters. A* Coupled Interval Guard *(CIG) over (X, P) is a triple*

$$C = (B_X, B_P, \kappa)$$

where:

- $B_X : X \to \mathbb{I}_{\geq 0}$ *assigns to each clock $x \in X$ an interval $B_X(x)$ (closed, open, or half-open) with $l_x, u_x \in \mathbb{Z}_{\geq 0} \cup \{+\infty\}$,*
- $B_P : P \to \mathbb{I}_{\geq 0}$ *assigns to each parameter $p \in P$ an interval $B_P(p)$ (closed, open, or half-open) with $l_p, u_p \in \mathbb{Z}_{\geq 0} \cup \{+\infty\}$,*
- $\kappa : X \rightharpoonup (P \times \texttt{Cmp})$ *is a partial function (the* coupling map*), where* $\texttt{Cmp} = \{<, \leq, >, \geq\}$.

Interpretation. Every CIG $C = (B_X, B_P, \kappa)$ induces a parametric guard $\phi_C \in \mathcal{G}(X, P)$ by interpreting its components as conjunctions of atomic constraints. Hence CIGs form a syntactic subclass of parametric guards.

In particular, CIGs restrict the guard language to: (i) interval bounds over individual clocks and parameters (closed endpoints give $\leq/\geq$ constraints; open endpoints give $</>$ constraints), and (ii) at most one clock-parameter comparison per clock. No clock-clock comparisons and no comparisons between linear parameter terms are permitted. From now on, we freely identify a CIG with its induced parametric guard.

Example 2. Let $X = \{x\}$, $P = \{p\}$, and let $C = (B_X, B_P, \kappa)$ with $B_X(x) = [0, 5)$, $B_P(p) = [0, 3]$, and $\kappa(x) = (p, <)$. The induced guard is $x \geq 0 \wedge x < 5 \wedge p \geq 0 \wedge p \leq 3 \wedge x < p$. We use this CIG as a running example below.

A CIG C is *integer-satisfiable* if $[\![C]\!]$ contains a witness whose clock and parameter values are all non-negative integers. Note that for open intervals with integer endpoints, integer-satisfiability is strictly stronger than real-satisfiability: $(3 < x < 4)$ is satisfiable over $\mathbb{R}$ but not integer-satisfiable. Throughout, we require all CIGs arising in the generation pipeline to be integer-satisfiable.

Definition 18 (tight CIG). *A CIG $C = (B_X, B_P, \kappa)$ is* tight *if*

- *for every clock $x \in X$, $\mathbb{Z}(B_X(x)) = \{ v(x) \mid v$ integer witness of $C \}$,*
- *for every parameter $p \in P$, $\mathbb{Z}(B_P(p)) = \{ v(p) \mid v$ integer witness of $C \}$.*

Intuitively, the integer points of each box exactly span the values the variable takes across all integer witnesses of C.

Example 3. The CIG C from the previous example is not tight. The strict coupling $x < p$ and the bound $p \leq 3$ force $v(x) \leq 2$ for every integer witness (since $v(x) < v(p) \leq 3$ and $v(x) \in \mathbb{Z}_{\geq 0}$), so $\{v(x) \mid v$ is an integer witness of $C\} = \{0, 1, 2\} \neq \{0, 1, 2, 3, 4\} = \mathbb{Z}(B_X(x))$.

Tightening. Given a CIG $C = (B_X, B_P, \kappa)$, we write tighten(C) for a *bound-tightened* form of C whose integer witnesses are exactly those of C. It is defined whenever C is integer-satisfiable, and the result is itself integer-satisfiable: any integer witness of C satisfies the coupling constraints and therefore also satisfies the tightened bounds. In our restricted setting, tightening is local and bidirectional: for each coupled clock with $\kappa(x) = (p, \bowtie)$, the bound of $B_X(x)$ in the direction of $\bowtie$ is tightened to match the corresponding bound of $B_P(p)$ (closed endpoint for $\leq/\geq$, open for $</>$); symmetrically, the opposing bound of $B_P(p)$ is tightened to exclude parameter values for which no compatible integer clock value exists.

Example 4. Tightening C yields tighten(C) $= (B'_X, B'_P, \kappa)$ with $B'_X(x) = [0, 3)$ and $B'_P(p) = [1, 3]$. In the forward direction, $\kappa(x) = (p, <)$ propagates p's upper bound 3 as an open upper endpoint on x. In the backward direction, $p = 0$ is excluded from B'_P because no integer $x \geq 0$ satisfies $x < 0$; the smallest parameter value with a compatible integer clock is $p = 1$ (witnessed by $x = 0$).

Witness Generation. For integer-satisfiable $C = (B_X, B_P, \kappa)$, WitnessGen(C) is the distribution over integer witnesses $v = (v_X, v_P) \in [\![C]\!]$ defined by first computing $C' = \text{tighten}(C)$, then drawing each $v_P(p)$ uniformly from $\mathbb{Z}(B'_P(p))$, and each $v_X(x)$ uniformly from the integers in the (possibly coupling-restricted) interval $B'_X(x)$. The joint tight condition on B'_P ensures that every sampled $n_p \in \mathbb{Z}(B'_P(p))$ has at least one compatible integer n_x in the coupling-restricted interval, so the distribution is well-defined; $v \in [\![C]\!]$ holds by construction, and every integer witness has positive probability.

GuardGen (Algorithm 4) generates guards satisfying Requirements 2 to 5 by construction. It samples a witness valuation $v = (v_X, v_P) \in [\![C]\!]$ via WitnessGen(C) (which tightens C internally). Using this witness, a *maximal candidate* $C_{\max}$ is constructed: for each clock and parameter, an interval (with randomly chosen open or closed endpoints) is sampled around the corresponding witness value, and for each clock a clock-parameter comparison is chosen such that it is satisfied by v. Since v is an integer witness, any combination of open or closed endpoints is valid: an open lower bound samples strictly below v, and an open upper bound samples strictly above v, so v always lies in the resulting interval. By construction, every atomic constraint in $C_{\max}$ is satisfied by v.

The final guard is obtained by sampling a geometrically sized random subset of $\texttt{subexpr}(C_{\max})$. Since all atomic constraints in $C_{\max}$ are satisfied by v, any conjunction of a subset of them is also satisfied by v. Hence, for the returned guard G, $[\![C]\!] \cap [\![G]\!] \neq \emptyset$. In particular, when the procedure is instantiated with the invariant of the source location as seed CIG, Requirement 4 holds.

When instantiated with the trivial seed guard $\top$, the procedure produces satisfiable guards, establishing Requirement 2. Instantiating the initial location invariant with $\bigwedge_{x \in X} x = 0$ ensures that the generated invariant intersects the all-zeros valuation, establishing Requirement 3. Finally, the guards induced by CIGs contain no redundant sub-expressions, since they are conjunctions of atomic constraints that are not implied by each other, ensuring Requirement 5.

Algorithm 4. GuardGen

Require: X, P, $N \geq 1$, integer-satisfiable CIG $C = (B_X, B_P, \kappa)$
Ensure: Parametric guard G with $[\![C]\!] \cap [\![G]\!] \neq \emptyset$

$v \sim$ WitnessGen(C)
for all $y \in X \uplus P$ **do** ▷ *build* $B^{\max}$ *(*$t_{l/u}$*=1: open, 0: closed)*
  $t_l, t_u \leftarrow 0, 0$
  if $v(y) > 0$ **then**
    $t_l \sim \text{Bern}(1/2)$
  if $v(y) < N$ **then**
    $t_u \sim \text{Bern}(1/2)$
  $l_y \sim \text{Uniform}(\{0, \ldots, v(y) - t_l\})$
  $u_y \sim \text{Uniform}(\{v(y) + t_u, \ldots, N\})$
  $B^{\max}(y) \leftarrow$ interval $[l_y, u_y]$ with endpoint types t_l, t_u
for all $x \in X$ **do** ▷ *build* $\kappa^{\max}$
  $p \sim \text{Uniform}(P)$
  $\bowtie \sim \text{Uniform}(\{\bowtie \in \texttt{Cmp} \mid v(x) \bowtie v(p)\})$
  $\kappa^{\max}(x) \leftarrow (p, \bowtie)$
$C_{\max} \leftarrow (B^{\max}|_X,\ B^{\max}|_P,\ \kappa^{\max})$
return $\bigwedge_{\phi \in \text{ChooseGeom}(0.5, \texttt{subexpr}(C_{\max}))} \phi$

Model Specification. A *model specification* is a user-supplied configuration controlling the intended size and density of generated PTAs; it is the input to ConstructSchema. Here $\mathbb{I}_{\geq 1}$ denotes the set of non-empty closed intervals $[a, b]$ with $a, b \in \mathbb{N}_{\geq 1}$, used to specify size ranges.

Definition 19 (model specification). *A* model specification *is a tuple* $\mathcal{M} = (I_L, I_X, I_P, I_K, p_{Inv}, p_g, p_R, N)$ *where:*

- $I_L \in \mathbb{I}_{\geq 1}$ *is the size interval for locations,*
- $I_X \in \mathbb{I}_{\geq 1}$ *is the size interval for clocks,*
- $I_P \in \mathbb{I}_{\geq 1}$ *is the size interval for parameters,*
- $I_K \in \mathbb{I}_{\geq 1}$ *is the size interval for outgoing transitions per location,*

- $p_{Inv} \in [0,1]_{\mathbb{R}}$ *is the probability of a non-trivial location invariant,*
- $p_g \in [0,1]_{\mathbb{R}}$ *is the probability of a non-trivial transition guard,*
- $p_R \in [0,1]_{\mathbb{R}}$ *is the probability of a clock reset on a transition,*
- $N \in \mathbb{N}_{\geq 1}$ *is the maximum constant in linear terms.*

Schema Assembly. ConstructSchema (Algorithm 5) assembles the component distributions into a generator schema Σ, wiring each parameter of $\mathcal{M}$ to the appropriate distribution constructor.

Algorithm 5. ConstructSchema

Require: Model specification $\mathcal{M} = (I_L, I_X, I_P, I_K, p_{Inv}, p_g, p_R, N)$
Ensure: A generator schema Σ
1: $\mathfrak{L}, \mathfrak{X}, \mathfrak{P} \leftarrow \mathrm{Fin}_*^{\texttt{Loc}}(\mathrm{Uniform}(I_L)), \mathrm{Fin}_*^{\texttt{Clock}}(\mathrm{Uniform}(I_X)), \mathrm{Fin}_*^{\texttt{Param}}(\mathrm{Uniform}(I_P))$
2: $\mathfrak{G} \leftarrow \lambda L.\ \mathrm{Uniform}(I_K)^{\otimes |L|} \circledast (\lambda K.\ \textsc{GraphGen}(L, K))$
3: $I \leftarrow \lambda X, P.\ \mathrm{Bern}(p_{Inv}) \circledast [0 \mapsto \delta_\top, 1 \mapsto \textsc{GuardGen}(X, P, N, \top)]$
4: $I_0 \leftarrow \lambda X, P.\ \mathrm{Bern}(p_{Inv}) \circledast [0 \mapsto \delta_\top, 1 \mapsto \textsc{GuardGen}(X, P, N, \bigwedge_{x \in X} x = 0)]$
5: $\mathfrak{I} \leftarrow \lambda L, X, P.\ I_0(X, P) \otimes I(X, P)^{\otimes(|L|-1)}$
6: $\mathfrak{Z} \leftarrow \lambda X, P, Inv, \ell.\ \mathrm{Bern}(p_g) \circledast [0 \mapsto \delta_\top, 1 \mapsto \textsc{GuardGen}(X, P, N, Inv(\ell))]$
7: $\mathfrak{Y} \leftarrow \lambda X.\ \mathrm{Bern}(p_R) \circledast [0 \mapsto \delta_\emptyset, 1 \mapsto \mathrm{ChooseGeom}(1/2, X)]$
8: **return** $(\mathfrak{L}, \mathfrak{X}, \mathfrak{P}, \mathfrak{G}, \mathfrak{I}, \mathfrak{Z}, \mathfrak{Y})$

The set distributions $\mathfrak{L}, \mathfrak{X}, \mathfrak{P}$ sample finite sets from the specified size intervals. The graph distribution $\mathfrak{G}$ first samples per-location outdegrees, then delegates to GraphGen. The invariant distributions encode the initial-location constraint (Requirement 3) by instantiating GuardGen with $\bigwedge_{x \in X} x = 0$ at the initial location and $\top$ elsewhere. The guard distribution instantiates GuardGen with the invariant of the source location $Inv(\ell)$, ensuring guard–invariant intersection (Requirement 4) by construction. Clock resets complete the schema.

5 Property-Preserving Shrinking

Once a PTA violating the target property has been identified, the framework applies a shrinking phase inspired by delta debugging [14] and test-case reduction [11]: the model is iteratively reduced while verifying that the target property is preserved. The goal is to quickly obtain a small and comprehensible witness suitable for inspection and debugging, rather than to compute a formally minimal automaton.

The shrinker is intentionally agnostic to the nature of the target property, which is treated as an external oracle. Unlike generation, which enforces global semantic constraints by construction, shrinking is inherently heuristic and oracle-guided. We therefore present the shrinker in terms of design principles and a staged shrinking procedure.

5.1 Shrinker Design Goals

We adopt a *principle of parsimony*: the shrinker aims to eliminate components of a witness PTA that are not relevant to satisfying the target property. Parsimony is not understood as formal minimality, but as a practical criterion for removing unnecessary structure while preserving the property of interest.

Preservation of Target Property. Every accepted shrinking step must preserve the target property; a shrunk PTA that no longer witnesses the violation is useless.

Monotonic Progress. Each shrinking step strictly decreases a chosen measure of model size or complexity, such as the number of locations, transitions, clocks, or constraints. This guarantees progress and termination, and enforces parsimony by ensuring each accepted step removes structure rather than rearranging it.

Well-Formedness Preservation. Every operator yields a well-formed PTA, avoiding ill-defined models such as PTAs with inconsistent clock constraints or syntactically invalid components. This ensures parsimony does not produce degenerate or semantically meaningless witnesses.

Locality and Modularity. The shrinker is structured as a collection of local and independent operators, each targeting a specific aspect of the PTA. This modular design supports parsimony through fine-grained elimination of unnecessary components without globally restructuring the model.

5.2 Shrinking Procedure

The shrinker applies a staged, deterministic shrinking pipeline, where each stage enforces parsimony at a different structural level. Each stage is applied repeatedly until no further shrinking steps are found; the procedure does not backtrack or reorder stages. The overall procedure is as follows:

1. **Transition Removal.** Transitions are removed one at a time, accepting a removal only if the target property is preserved.
2. **Reachability Normalization.** After transition removals, all unreachable locations are deterministically eliminated (not property-dependent).
3. **Invariant and Guard Simplification.** Guards and invariants are simplified by removing conjuncts, provided the target property remains satisfied.
4. **Location Coalescing.** Locations are merged when possible while preserving well-formedness and satisfaction of the target property.
5. **Variable Cleanup.** Unused clocks and parameters (not appearing in guards, invariants, or resets) are removed in a final cleanup step.

6 Implementation and Evaluation

We instantiate the framework as a differential testing tool [9] for PTA analysis algorithms: two configurations of the same algorithm—or two algorithms whose outputs should agree on a shared model class—are run on each generated PTA, and disagreement serves as the target property φ. Concretely, given two analysis procedures Π_1 and Π_2, we define

$$\varphi(\mathcal{A}) \triangleq \Pi_1(\mathcal{A}) = \Pi_2(\mathcal{A}).$$

Whenever φ is violated, the shrinking procedure reduces the witness to a local minimum, yielding a small and actionable counterexample. This strategy is especially effective for testing optimizations and implementation-specific heuristics: if Π_2 is a trusted reference and Π_1 an optimized variant, any counterexample to φ pinpoints a semantic inconsistency introduced by the optimization.

6.1 Implementation Details

The framework is implemented as a meta-tool within the IMITATOR model checker [2]. The generator is realized as a custom random PTA generator adhering to the design principles of Sect. 4, while the reducer implements the property-preserving shrinking procedure described in Sect. 5.[1]

IMITATOR provides multiple PTA analysis procedures; in this section, we focus on three relatively recent additions: a parametric timed game (PTG) algorithm [7], currently under active development; an unavoidability (AF) synthesis algorithm [3], an experimental implementation of an established theory; and an NDFS algorithm [10] for detecting accepting cycles, a mature and well-tested procedure. All three expose numerous toggleable optimizations and features, making them suitable candidates for differential validation.

6.2 Experimental Setup

All experiments were conducted on a single core of a computer with an Intel Core i5-1135G7 CPU @ 2.40 GHz with 16 GB of RAM running Ubuntu 22.04.5 LTS. Each experiment ran with r = 100,000 random iterations per seed, repeated over 5 seeds, with a per-run time limit of 0.1 s. Each experiment compares two configurations of IMITATOR on the same randomly generated PTA; a disagreement in their outputs triggers the shrinking procedure. Seeds that did not find a counterexample within r iterations are included in the average count with a value of r, giving a conservative estimate. Table 1 summarizes the results.

If a bug was found and later fixed, the experiment is run on an older version of IMITATOR and the counterexample is confirmed as fixed on the latest version. Three experiments—**PTG-Closed-Clock-Bug**, **PTG-Explore-Bug**, and **PTG-Invariant-Bug**—target distinct bugs in the PTG algorithm by comparing the base implementation against a version with a new convex hull abstraction. The bugs themselves were found to be unrelated to the abstraction, but the difference in state space size and exploration order makes each bug manifest in the comparison. **PTG-Double-Inclusion-Bug** targets a bug in the double inclusion (two-way subsumption) check of the PTG algorithm, comparing

[1] Available at github.com/imitator-model-checker/imitator.

the base implementation against one with the check enabled. This check is still experimental and the bug has not yet been fixed. **AF-Bug** compares the PTG and AF synthesis algorithms on the same models, exploiting the fact that their outputs should agree on a subclass of PTA; it finds a bug in the AF algorithm that has not yet been fixed. The final two experiments, **NDFS-Check** and **AF-Double-Inclusion-Check**, serve as negative controls.

Table 1. Results of differential validation experiments on IMITATOR. Columns: "Avg. count" = mean PTAs generated before a counterexample; "Seeds" = seeds (of 5) finding a witness; "Reduction" = percentage reduction in locations/transitions after shrinking; "Final size" = shrunk counterexample size in locations/transitions; "Fixed" = confirmed fixed in latest IMITATOR.

Experiment	Seeds	Avg. count	Reduction	Final size	Fixed
PTG-Closed-Clock-Bug	4/5	58624	21%/48%	4/4	Yes
PTG-Explore-Bug	3/5	68081	36%/54%	5/6	Yes
PTG-Double-Inclusion-Bug	5/5	853	20%/60%	3/5	No
PTG-Invariant-Bug	3/5	54374	42%/66%	4/4	Yes
AF-Bug	5/5	14	67%/93%	2/1	No
NDFS-Check	0/5	–	–	–	–
AF-Double-Inclusion-Check	0/5	–	–	–	–

6.3 Discussion

The framework finds bugs reliably; the wide variance in average PTA count (14–68081) reflects differences in bug rarity: **AF-Bug** triggers on a common structural pattern, whereas **PTG-Explore-Bug** requires a more specific feature combination. Shrinking consistently yields substantial reductions: up to 93% of transitions and 67% of locations. The two unfixed bugs (**PTG-Double-Inclusion-Bug** and **AF-Bug**) were confirmed in the current IMITATOR release at time of writing; the counterexamples are small and informative enough to be directly actionable for debugging—for instance, the **AF-Bug** counterexample is just 2 locations and 1 transition, likely an unhandled edge case. The negative-control experiments produced no counterexamples, confirming no spurious disagreements.

7 Conclusion

The experiments confirm that analysis algorithms under active development harbour corner-case bugs that benchmarks miss. The generate-and-shrink framework surfaces such bugs reliably and reduces any witness to a small, actionable counterexample; the smallest found consists of just two locations and one transition, yet exposes a fault that had gone undetected in IMITATOR until now.

The framework has three main limitations. First, differential testing requires the compared algorithms to produce deterministic output. Second, the shrinker finds a locally rather than globally minimal witness. Third, the generator is heuristic and offers no formal coverage guarantee: the distribution, shaped by the model specification and CIG-based guard sampling, under-represents guards outside the CIG family and atypical graph structures.

As a cheap, oracle-free development tool, the framework transfers readily beyond PTAs: the graph generator and shrinker carry over to any quantitative-automata class; only model-specific sampling requires adaptation, with CIG-based guard and invariant sampling arguably the hardest case. We leave concrete instantiations to future work.

Acknowledgments. Parts of this paper used generative AI tools (Claude by Anthropic) to assist with editing for style and clarity.

Disclosure of Interests. The authors have no competing interests to declare that are relevant to the content of this article.

References

1. Alur, R., Henzinger, T.A., Vardi, M.Y.: Parametric real-time reasoning. In: STOC, pp. 592–601. ACM (1993)
2. André, É.: IMITATOR 3: synthesis of timing parameters beyond decidability. In: Silva, A., Leino, K.R.M. (eds.) CAV 2021. LNCS, vol. 12759, pp. 552–565. Springer, Cham (2021). https://doi.org/10.1007/978-3-030-81685-8_26
3. André, É., Lime, D., Roux, O.H.: Integer-complete synthesis for bounded parametric timed automata. In: Bojańczyk, M., Lasota, S., Potapov, I. (eds.) RP 2015. LNCS, vol. 9328, pp. 7–19. Springer, Cham (2015). https://doi.org/10.1007/978-3-319-24537-9_2
4. André, É., Marinho, D., van de Pol, J.: A benchmarks library for extended parametric timed automata. In: Loulergue, F., Wotawa, F. (eds.) TAP 2021. LNCS, vol. 12740, pp. 39–50. Springer, Cham (2021). https://doi.org/10.1007/978-3-030-79379-1_3
5. Brummayer, R., Biere, A.: Fuzzing and delta-debugging SMT solvers. In: Proceedings of the 7th International Workshop on Satisfiability Modulo Theories, SMT 2009, pp. 1–5. Association for Computing Machinery, New York (2009)
6. Claessen, K., Hughes, J.: QuickCheck: a lightweight tool for random testing of Haskell programs. In: ICFP, pp. 268–279. ACM (2000)
7. Dahlsen-Jensen, M.B., Fievet, B., Petrucci, L., van de Pol, J.: On-the-fly algorithm for reachability in parametric timed games (extended version) (2024)
8. Manini, A., Rossi, M., San Pietro, P.: Random testing of model checkers for timed automata with automated oracle generation. In: Rümmer, P., Wu, Z. (eds.) TASE 2025. LNCS, vol. 15841, pp. 343–360. Springer, Cham (2026). https://doi.org/10.1007/978-3-031-98208-8_20
9. McKeeman, W.M.: Differential testing for software. Digit. Tech. J. **10**(1), 100–107 (1998)

10. Nguyen, H.G., Petrucci, L., van de Pol, J.: Layered and collecting NDFS with subsumption for parametric timed automata. In: ICECCS, pp. 1–9. IEEE Computer Society (2018)
11. Regehr, J., Chen, Y., Cuoq, P., Eide, E., Ellison, C., Yang, X.: Test-case reduction for C compiler bugs. In: PLDI, pp. 335–346. ACM (2012)
12. Tabakov, D., Vardi, M.Y.: Experimental evaluation of classical automata constructions. In: Sutcliffe, G., Voronkov, A. (eds.) LPAR 2005. LNCS (LNAI), vol. 3835, pp. 396–411. Springer, Heidelberg (2005). https://doi.org/10.1007/11591191_28
13. Yang, X., Chen, Y., Eide, E., Regehr, J.: Finding and understanding bugs in C compilers. In: PLDI, pp. 283–294. ACM (2011)
14. Zeller, A.: Yesterday, my program worked. Today, it does not. Why? In: Nierstrasz, O., Lemoine, M. (eds.) ESEC/SIGSOFT FSE -1999. LNCS, vol. 1687, pp. 253–267. Springer, Heidelberg (1999). https://doi.org/10.1007/3-540-48166-4_16

Learning-Based Quantitative Evaluation of GR(1) Temporal Properties upon Partial Data Traces

Jianing Chen, Wanwei Liu(✉), and Ji Wang

College of Computer Science and Technology, National University of Defense Technology, Changsha, Hunan 410073, China
{chenjianing,wwliu,wj}@nudt.edu.cn

Abstract. Temporal logics are widely used to specify and reason about system behaviors over time. However, classical temporal logic reasoning often relies on explicit system models or complete execution traces and typically yields Boolean satisfaction results, which limits its applicability in data-driven settings where only partial observational traces are available. To address this issue, we propose a neural-symbolic framework for learning-based quantitative evaluation of GR(1) temporal properties upon partial data traces. The core idea is to treat elementary temporal formulas as learnable primitives that predict confidence values for future satisfaction of atomic propositions. Confidence values of more complex formulas are then derived using compositional rules. We apply the framework to a real-world academic collaboration prediction task on a temporal collaboration network. Experimental results demonstrate that the proposed approach effectively captures future collaboration patterns and supports temporal logic evaluation in real-world settings. This work bridges classical temporal logic reasoning and data-driven prediction, enabling quantitative temporal reasoning under partial observation.

Keywords: Linear Temporal Logic · Formal Methods · Neural-Symbolic Methods · Temporal Reasoning

1 Introduction

Temporal logics, especially Linear Temporal Logic (LTL), are fundamental formalisms in formal methods and software engineering for specifying and reasoning about the temporal behavior of systems [1]. They provide a rigorous and expressive language for describing how system properties evolve over time, including event ordering, eventual satisfaction of goals, and safety or liveness constraints over execution traces. As a result, these formalisms have been widely studied in specification, verification, and synthesis of reactive systems, and have been successfully applied to robotics and autonomous systems, distributed and embedded systems, and software system design [2–4]. In particular, the GR(1) fragment of

G. De Giacomo et al. (Eds.): TASE 2026, LNCS 16697, pp. 206–222, 2027.
https://doi.org/10.1007/978-3-032-30693-7_14

LTL has received considerable attention due to its favorable balance between expressive power and algorithmic tractability [5].

In traditional formal verification, temporal properties are commonly analyzed through model checking and runtime verification. Model checking usually relies on an explicit system model, such as a transition system or a Kripke structure, and verifies whether temporal logic formulas hold over all possible execution traces by exhaustively exploring the system state space [6,7]. Runtime verification, in contrast, monitors actual execution traces and determines whether the observed behaviors satisfy the specified properties [8]. These approaches provide rigorous mechanisms and strong correctness guarantees when accurate models or concrete execution traces are available.

However, explicit system models are difficult or even impossible to obtain in many real-world scenarios. Instead, system behavior is often observed indirectly through execution traces, event logs, or monitoring data. Such observations are typically incomplete, noisy, limited to past executions, and often generated at a coarse temporal granularity through discrete sampling or periodic updates, which further limits the timeliness and continuity of the available information. For instance, academic publication records are updated periodically, user behaviors are recorded at discrete time points, and environmental events are monitored at fixed intervals. As a consequence, traditional formal verification methods cannot be directly applied, since they fundamentally rely on sufficiently complete system models or execution traces. Furthermore, for properties involving future behaviors, Boolean satisfaction is often insufficient to reflect the likelihood or confidence of satisfaction under uncertainty.

In parallel, data-driven learning approaches have been widely used to predict future events or system outcomes from historical observations [9–11]. These methods can learn statistical patterns from observed data and provide probabilistic estimates for individual events or short-term trends, showing advantages in handling incomplete data and capturing complex nonlinear relationships. Nevertheless, they are not inherently designed for structured temporal reasoning, making it difficult to answer queries such as whether a property will eventually hold or continue to hold over time. Moreover, since they mainly focus on individual-event prediction, corresponding to atomic propositions, they lack the symbolic semantics and compositional rules required for directly evaluating complex temporal logic formulas.

This gap highlights a fundamental challenge: how to reason about temporal logic properties in systems where explicit models are unavailable and future behaviors must be inferred from observational data. Such data typically consist of timestamped records of events occurring within a limited observation window, providing only partial traces of the system's behavior. Addressing this challenge requires combining the expressive power of temporal logic with the predictive capabilities of learning-based methods.

In this paper, we propose a neural-symbolic framework for learning-based quantitative evaluation of GR(1) temporal properties upon partial data traces. Our approach integrates symbolic temporal composition with learnable evaluation of future-oriented temporal primitives, enabling the computation of confidence values for complex formulas. The key idea is to treat the eventually operator applied to atomic propositions, i.e., formulas of the form $\mathbf{F}p$ with $p \in \mathcal{P}$, as a learnable primitive learned from partial observational traces. Based on this learnable foundation, temporal properties in the GR(1) fragment are evaluated compositionally using symbolic temporal operators and Boolean connectives.

The main contributions of this work are:

1. We propose a neural-symbolic framework for quantitative evaluation of GR(1) temporal properties over partial observational data. The framework combines data-driven prediction with symbolic temporal reasoning by modeling future-oriented primitive formulas, such as $\mathbf{F}p$, as learnable confidence functions, thereby enabling temporal logic evaluation beyond classical model-based Boolean semantics.
2. We provide a compositional quantitative semantics for the complete GR(1) fragment. By combining learnable primitive evaluations with symbolic temporal operators and Boolean connectives, the proposed formalization supports systematic and interpretable evaluation of complex temporal logic formulas under partial observation.
3. We instantiate the proposed framework in a real-world academic collaboration prediction task. By using a learning-based predictor to estimate the confidence of future collaborations and further composing derived temporal formulas, the case study demonstrates the applicability of the framework in data-driven settings.

The remainder of this paper is organized as follows. Section 2 introduces the necessary background on temporal logic and learning-based methods. Section 3 presents the proposed neural-symbolic framework. Section 4 reports the experimental evaluation, and finally, Sect. 5 concludes the paper.

2 Preliminaries

2.1 LTL and GR(1)

LTL is a formalism for specifying temporal properties of discrete-time systems. We fix a countable set $\mathcal{P}$ of atomic propositions. All temporal logic formulas are interpreted with respect to a starting time $i \in \mathbb{T} = \{0, 1, 2, \ldots\}$, unless otherwise specified.

In LTL, the execution of a system is usually modeled as an infinite trace that evolves over time. Such a trace reflects which atomic propositions are satisfied at each discrete time point, thereby characterizing the changes of system states over time. Formally, a trace can be represented as an infinite sequence over the set of atomic propositions, transforming system behavior into the temporal evolution of proposition truth values. Specifically, an infinite trace $\pi \in (2^{\mathcal{P}})^\omega$ is an ω-word over the alphabet $2^{\mathcal{P}}$, where each position $\pi(i) \subseteq \mathcal{P}$ represents the set of atomic propositions that are true at time i.

(1) Syntax of LTL. Formulas are constructed from atomic propositions in $\mathcal{P}$, Boolean connectives ($\neg, \wedge, \vee, \rightarrow$), and temporal operators such as $\mathbf{X}$ (next) and $\mathbf{U}$ (until). The syntax of LTL formulas is defined recursively as

$$\varphi ::= \ \mathrm{p} \mid \neg\varphi \mid \varphi_1 \rightarrow \varphi_2 \mid \mathbf{X}\varphi \mid \varphi_1 \mathbf{U} \varphi_2$$

The operator $\mathbf{X}$ specifies that a formula holds at the next time point, while $\mathbf{U}$ expresses that one property holds until another becomes true.

Then, the Boolean connectives of disjunction, conjunction, and equivalence can be expressed in terms of negation and implication:

$$\begin{aligned} \varphi_1 \vee \varphi_2 &\equiv \neg\varphi_1 \rightarrow \varphi_2 \\ \varphi_1 \wedge \varphi_2 &\equiv \neg(\neg\varphi_1 \vee \neg\varphi_2) \\ \varphi_1 \leftrightarrow \varphi_2 &\equiv (\varphi_1 \rightarrow \varphi_2) \wedge (\varphi_2 \rightarrow \varphi_1) \end{aligned}$$

Similarly, the temporal operators $\mathbf{F}$ (eventually) and $\mathbf{G}$ (globally) can be derived from the "until" operator:

$$\mathbf{F}\varphi \equiv \top \mathbf{U} \varphi \qquad \mathbf{G}\varphi \equiv \neg\mathbf{F}\neg\varphi$$

$\mathbf{F}\varphi$ indicates that the formula φ eventually holds at some future time point, while $\mathbf{G}\varphi$ indicates that φ holds at all future time points from the current position onward. These temporal operators are widely used in the specification and analysis of temporal logic properties.

(2) (Qualitative) Semantics of LTL. Given a trace π and a position $i \in \mathbb{N}$, the satisfaction relation $\pi, i \models \varphi$ is defined inductively as follows:

$$\begin{aligned} &\pi, i \models p \iff p \in \pi(i) \\ &\pi, i \models \neg\varphi \iff \pi, i \not\models \varphi \\ &\pi, i \models \varphi_1 \rightarrow \varphi_2 \iff \pi, i \models \neg\varphi_1 \text{ or } \pi, i \models \varphi_2 \\ &\pi, i \models \mathbf{X}\varphi \iff \pi, i+1 \models \varphi \\ &\pi, i \models \varphi_1 \mathbf{U} \varphi_2 \iff \exists j \geq i \text{ s.t. } \pi, j \models \varphi_2 \text{ and } \forall k,\ i \leq k < j,\ \pi, k \models \varphi_1 \end{aligned}$$

Then, according to the above definitions, the semantics of the derived operators are given as follows:

$$\begin{aligned} \pi, i \models \mathbf{F}\varphi &\iff \exists j \geq i \text{ s.t. } \pi, j \models \varphi \\ \pi, i \models \mathbf{G}\varphi &\iff \forall j \geq i,\ \pi, j \models \varphi \end{aligned}$$

(3) GR(1) Fragment of LTL. Although LTL can express rich temporal properties, its general form often leads to high computational complexity in automated reasoning and system synthesis. To achieve a balance between expressive power and computational efficiency, several syntactically restricted yet efficiently tractable fragments of LTL have been proposed. Among them, GR(1) is one of the most representative fragments.

The GR(1) fragment is constructed from the following basic temporal formulas and their Boolean combinations:

$$\mathbf{F}p, \quad \mathbf{G}p, \quad \mathbf{GF}p, \quad \mathbf{FG}p, \quad \text{where } p \in \mathcal{P}.$$

These formulas capture typical temporal properties of system behavior:

- $\mathbf{F}p$ indicates that p will eventually hold at some future time point;
- $\mathbf{G}p$ means that p holds permanently from the current position onward;
- $\mathbf{GF}p$ describes that p holds infinitely often;
- $\mathbf{FG}p$ describes that there exists a time point after which p always holds.

These patterns cover requirements such as eventual reachability, persistent satisfaction, repeated occurrence, and eventual stabilization, and can be combined to construct rich system specifications.

Since the GR(1) fragment preserves important temporal expressiveness while maintaining favorable computational tractability, it has been widely applied in formal verification and reactive system synthesis. In this work, we focus on GR(1) for describing temporal properties of system behavior.

2.2 Learning-Based Prediction Methods

Compared with traditional formal verification methods, another important line of research is to model and predict system behavior based on observational data. Learning-based prediction methods extract patterns from historical data and estimate future behaviors using statistical learning or neural network models. Such methods have been widely applied in complex system analysis, recommender systems, and time-series data modeling.

In general, a data-driven prediction problem can be formulated as a function mapping from input features to target variables. Specifically, given an input feature vector $\mathbf{x}$ extracted from observational data, a parameterized model f_θ is used to predict the target variable:

$$\hat{y} = f_\theta(\mathbf{x}) \in [0, 1]$$

where θ denotes the learnable parameters of the model, and the output $\hat{y}$ can be interpreted as the probability or confidence that the target event will occur.

Traditional machine learning methods, such as logistic regression, support vector machines, and decision trees, typically rely on manually designed features for classification or regression tasks. With the development of deep learning, neural network-based models have achieved significant progress in complex data modeling and prediction tasks. For example, feedforward neural networks learn nonlinear mappings between input features and target variables [12], while recurrent neural networks further enhance the ability to model sequential data [13].

Furthermore, in many practical scenarios, observational data are not limited to independent events or entities, but often contain rich relational structures among entities, such as user interactions in social networks and citation relationships in academic networks. Such data can be naturally represented as graphs, where nodes represent entities and edges represent relationships between entities, which motivates representation learning methods that can explicitly model structural dependencies. Graph representation learning methods, with graph neural networks (GNNs) as a representative example, provide an effective way to model relational data [14–16]. A generic GNN layer can be described as follows:

$$\mathbf{h}_v^{(l+1)} = \sigma\left(\sum_{u \in \mathcal{N}(v) \cup \{v\}} \mathbf{W}^{(l)} \mathbf{h}_u^{(l)} \right), \quad v \in V$$

where $\mathbf{h}_v^{(l)}$ is the embedding of entity v at layer l, $\mathcal{N}(v)$ denotes the set of neighbors of v, $\mathbf{W}^{(l)}$ is a learnable weight matrix for layer l, and σ is a nonlinear activation function, e.g., ReLU or tanh.

Overall, data-driven prediction methods can effectively learn from observational data and estimate the occurrence of future events, showing advantages in scenarios with incomplete observations. In our work, such predictive capabilities can be further combined with temporal logic reasoning to enable learnable evaluation of complex temporal properties.

3 Learning-Based Quantitative Evaluation of GR(1) Properties

3.1 Problem Formalization

In many real-world applications, system behavior is collected and stored as timestamped event sequences that describe how system states evolve over time. Due to limitations in observation scope, sampling frequency, and data update cycles, the available data cover only a finite time interval, making it necessary to define a trace-based representation compatible with temporal logic semantics.

Moreover, future-oriented temporal properties cannot be directly evaluated from current observations. This motivates a quantitative semantics that represents formula satisfaction by confidence values under incomplete future information.

Let $\mathcal{P}$ be a set of atomic propositions, and let $\mathbb{T} = \{0, 1, 2, \ldots\}$ be a discrete time domain.

Partial Data Traces. In LTL, system behavior is usually modeled as an infinite trace. A complete execution trace $\pi \in (2^{\mathcal{P}})^\omega$ is represented as an infinite sequence

$$\pi = \pi(0), \pi(1), \pi(2), \ldots$$

where each $\pi(t) \subseteq \mathcal{P}$ denotes the set of atomic propositions that hold at time t. In a partial-observation setting, what is actually available is only a finite prefix of π over the time interval $[0, T]$:

$$\pi[0{:}T] = \pi(0), \pi(1), \ldots, \pi(T),$$

where $T \in \mathbb{T}$ is the latest observable time point. This finite sequence describes system behavior over $[0, T]$, while states after T cannot be directly observed.

Quantitative Semantics. Classical LTL semantics assigns Boolean satisfaction values to formulas over complete traces. Under partial observation, however, formulas involving future behaviors require confidence-valued evaluation.

To address this limitation, we introduce a quantitative semantics for temporal logic formulas. For a temporal logic formula φ, its quantitative semantics at time i is defined as:

$$[\![\varphi]\!]_\pi(i) \in [0,1],$$

which extends the value domain of formulas from $\{0,1\}$ to the interval $[0,1]$. We refer to $[\![\varphi]\!]_\pi(i)$ as the *confidence value*, which quantifies the degree to which available observations support the satisfaction of φ at time i. In what follows, we omit π from the subscript whenever the context is clear.

For an atomic proposition $p \in \mathcal{P}$, its confidence value at time i is directly determined by the observed truth value:

$$[\![p]\!](i) \in \{0,1\},$$

where the value is 1 if p holds at time i, and 0 otherwise.

The semantics is defined recursively over formula structure. Boolean connectives combine the confidence values of their subformulas as follows:

$$\begin{aligned}
[\![\neg\varphi]\!](i) &= 1 - [\![\varphi]\!](i) \\
[\![\varphi_1 \wedge \varphi_2]\!](i) &= \min([\![\varphi_1]\!](i), [\![\varphi_2]\!](i)) \\
[\![\varphi_1 \vee \varphi_2]\!](i) &= \max([\![\varphi_1]\!](i), [\![\varphi_2]\!](i))
\end{aligned}$$

The semantics of temporal operators is constructed in the following subsections together with the data-driven prediction mechanism. This quantitative interpretation lifts classical Boolean semantics to a data-driven setting, enabling principled reasoning over partially observed traces.

3.2 Framework for Quantitative Evaluation

We propose a neural-symbolic quantitative evaluation framework that introduces data-driven prediction into formal semantics, thereby modeling the uncertainty of future behaviors. The core idea is to preserve the structured expressiveness of temporal logic while using learning-based methods to estimate unobservable future information. Data-driven models estimate future events from observations, while compositional semantics recursively evaluates complex temporal formulas.

Given a target GR(1) formula φ, the proposed framework evaluates its confidence value compositionally according to the syntactic structure of the formula:

- Observable atomic propositions are evaluated from data;

- Eventuality formulas $\mathbf{F}p$ involving future behavior are evaluated by learnable predictive models;
- Compositional formulas are recursively computed from previously obtained confidence values using compositional rules.

In the considered GR(1) fragment, operators such as **G**, **GF**, and **FG** can be constructed through combinations of the eventually operator **F** and Boolean operations. Therefore, the quantitative modeling of **F** serves as the key bridge between data-driven prediction and symbolic reasoning in the proposed framework. Based on this observation, we first define the learning-based semantics of the eventually operator and then construct the semantics of other temporal operators accordingly, resulting in a modular and interpretable evaluation framework.

Learnable Eventually Operator F. In classical LTL semantics, the formula $\mathbf{F}p$ means that, for a given starting time i, there exists some future time $j \geq i$ such that the atomic proposition p holds. However, when only partial data traces of a system execution are available, evaluating the satisfaction of $\mathbf{F}p$ requires predictive reasoning. The semantic definitions in this work are given over a partial trace $\pi[0{:}T]$. Accordingly, all time indices are restricted to $[0, T]$, and any evaluation starting time i satisfies $0 \leq i \leq T$.

Let $p \in \mathcal{P}$ be an atomic proposition and $i \in \mathbb{T}$ be a starting time. We define a *learnable prediction function* for the eventually operator:

$$\mathcal{O}_F : \mathcal{P} \times \mathbb{T} \rightarrow [0, 1],$$

where $\mathcal{O}_F(p, i)$ returns a confidence value representing the likelihood that p will hold at some future time $j \geq i$, evaluated from starting time i. Then, the confidence value of the temporal formula $\mathbf{F}p$ at time i is given by:

$$[\![\mathbf{F}p]\!](i) = \mathcal{O}_F(p, i).$$

This definition transforms the existential question in classical temporal logic into a prediction problem, thereby enabling the uncertainty of future events to be modeled in a data-driven manner. In particular, the prediction function $\mathcal{O}_F$ is instantiated by a predictive model that estimates the eventual occurrence of the atomic proposition p using the observations available from time i onward, i.e., the information contained in the trace segment $\pi[i{:}T]$. If information prior to time i were also used, it would introduce observations irrelevant to the forward temporal interpretation of the eventually operator at the current evaluation point. This keeps the quantitative semantics consistent with the forward-looking interpretation of **F**, capturing the overall tendency that "p will occur at some future time" rather than merely extrapolating from historical observations.

Given the finite prefix $\pi[0{:}T]$, the segment used for evaluation at starting time i is $\pi[i{:}T] = \pi(i), \pi(i+1), \ldots, \pi(T)$, which contains the observations available from time i onward. Through a feature extraction function $\varPhi$, the observational information relevant to the atomic proposition p is mapped into a feature space, yielding the vector representation:

$$\mathbf{x}_i^{(p)} = \Phi(\pi[i{:}T], p),$$

where $\mathbf{x}_i^{(p)} \in \mathbb{R}^d$ encodes the contextual information relevant to p for estimating the confidence value of $\mathbf{F}p$. Here, the atomic proposition $p \in \mathcal{P}$ represents a target event to be predicted, whose specific meaning depends on the application scenario. It may denote an event involving a single entity, or a relation involving multiple entities. For example, in behavioral data, p may represent whether a certain user action occurs; in system monitoring, p may indicate whether an anomalous event appears; and in relational networks, p may describe whether a certain relation holds. Accordingly, $\mathbf{x}_i^{(p)}$ encodes event-relevant patterns, such as attribute, frequency-based, or structural features, obtained through feature engineering or representation learning.

The extracted feature vector is then fed into a learning model f_θ, which outputs the probability that the event represented by proposition p will eventually occur from starting time i onward, i.e., the value of the prediction function $\mathcal{O}_F$:

$$\mathcal{O}_F(p, i) = f_\theta(\mathbf{x}_i^{(p)}),$$

where θ denotes the learnable parameters of the model f_θ. The predictive model can be instantiated in various ways, such as multi-layer perceptrons, recurrent neural networks, Transformer-based models, or graph neural networks for relational data [12,14,17,18]. Following the standard machine learning paradigm, the training process learns a general predictive model f_θ that captures the semantics of the eventually operator, rather than a separate model for each individual trace. During inference, the learned model parameters are fixed. For each starting time $i \leq T$, the model takes $\mathbf{x}_i^{(p)}$ extracted from $\pi[i{:}T]$ as input and computes the confidence value $[\![\mathbf{F}p]\!](i)$.

This design is flexible, allowing different predictive models to be integrated for different data types and tasks without changing the semantic framework.

Derived Temporal Operators. After defining the quantitative semantics of the eventually operator $\mathbf{F}$, we further construct the semantics of other temporal operators in the GR(1) fragment.

The confidence value of the temporal formula $\mathbf{G}p$ at time i is defined as

$$[\![\mathbf{G}p]\!](i) = 1 - [\![\mathbf{F}\neg p]\!](i).$$

This definition follows the LTL equivalence $\mathbf{G}p \equiv \neg\mathbf{F}\neg p$ and extends it to confidence-valued semantics.

The confidence value of the temporal formula $\mathbf{GF}p$ at time i is defined as

$$[\![\mathbf{GF}p]\!](i) = \min_{i \leq j \leq T} [\![\mathbf{F}p]\!](j).$$

The above definition computes the confidence value of $\mathbf{GF}p$ at time i by taking the minimum of $[\![\mathbf{F}p]\!](j)$ over all time points j with $i \leq j \leq T$. This aggregation reflects the universal temporal requirement inherent in $\mathbf{GF}p$: from any future evaluation point, the eventuality $\mathbf{F}p$ should hold with sufficiently high confidence. Moreover, this construction induces a monotonicity property with respect to time:

$$[\![\mathbf{GF}p]\!](i) \leq [\![\mathbf{GF}p]\!](i+1).$$

For a finite observation trace, this monotonicity follows because moving the starting time forward removes earlier evaluation points from the minimum. Consequently, the confidence value of $\mathbf{GF}p$ is non-decreasing over time. This design aligns the quantitative semantics with the classical LTL interpretation of $\mathbf{GF}$ as a persistent liveness property, where low confidence at any future evaluation point cannot be compensated by higher confidence at earlier ones.

The confidence value of the temporal formula $\mathbf{FG}p$ at time i is defined as

$$[\![\mathbf{FG}p]\!](i) = 1 - [\![\mathbf{GF}\neg p]\!](i).$$

This definition follows the LTL equivalence $\mathbf{FG}p \equiv \neg\mathbf{GF}\neg p$, allowing the eventually-always operator to be evaluated compositionally from $\mathbf{GF}$.

Together with the Boolean connectives defined in Sect. 3.1, the above derived temporal operators enable the evaluation of all temporal formulas in the GR(1) fragment of Linear Temporal Logic. This design enables modular and interpretable evaluation of complex temporal properties by combining data-driven prediction with symbolic temporal reasoning.

3.3 Algorithmic Realization of Quantitative Evaluation

This section presents the computational realization of the quantitative semantics defined above. Given a temporal logic formula φ and a starting time $i \in \mathbb{T}$, our goal is to compute a confidence value $[\![\varphi]\!](i) \in [0, 1]$.

We design a structured evaluation algorithm that recursively computes confidence values along the syntactic structure of the formula. To ensure consistent evaluation, the input formula is first rewritten into a normal form according to classical equivalences. Specifically, $\mathbf{G}p$ is rewritten as $\neg\mathbf{F}\neg p$, and $\mathbf{FG}p$ is rewritten as $\neg\mathbf{GF}\neg p$. The normalized formula is then parsed into a syntax tree and evaluated in a bottom-up manner.

Algorithm 1 summarizes the overall evaluation procedure. The algorithm normalizes the input formula, parses it into a syntax tree, and maintains a map $\mathcal{C}$ for subformula confidence values. For atomic propositions, the confidence value is directly determined by observational data. For formulas of the form $\mathbf{F}p$, the prediction function $\mathcal{O}_F$ is invoked to estimate the corresponding confidence value. For the remaining formulas, the confidence values are computed according to compositional rules by the function EVALDERIVED shown in Algorithm 2.

Algorithm 2 presents the implementation of the function EVALDERIVED. Since the input formula has been normalized in the main algorithm, it only needs to process Boolean combinations and basic temporal patterns in the normal form, without revisiting the original formula structure. The eventually operator $\mathbf{F}$ is implemented by the prediction function $\mathcal{O}_F$. To illustrate the learnable

Algorithm 1. Evaluation of Temporal Logic Formulas

Require: GR(1) temporal formula φ, starting time i
Ensure: Confidence value $[\![\varphi]\!](i) \in [0, 1]$
Rewrite φ into a normal form according to classical equivalences
Parse the normalized formula into a syntax tree
Initialize confidence map $\mathcal{C}$
for each subformula ψ in bottom-up order **do**
  if ψ is an atomic proposition p **then**
    $\mathcal{C}[\psi] \leftarrow [\![p]\!](i)$
  else if ψ is of the form $\mathbf{F}p$ **then**
    $\mathcal{C}[\psi] \leftarrow \mathcal{O}_F(p, i)$
  else
    $\mathcal{C}[\psi] \leftarrow$ EvalDerived$(\psi, i, \mathcal{C})$
  end if
end for
return $\mathcal{C}[\varphi]$

Algorithm 2. Evaluation of Derived Temporal Formulas (EvalDerived)

Require: Formula ψ in normal form, starting time i, confidence map $\mathcal{C}$
Ensure: Confidence value $\mathcal{C}[\psi]$
if $\psi = \neg\varphi$ **then**
  $\mathcal{C}[\psi] \leftarrow 1 - \mathcal{C}[\varphi]$
else if $\psi = \varphi_1 \wedge \varphi_2$ **then**
  $\mathcal{C}[\psi] \leftarrow \min(\mathcal{C}[\varphi_1], \mathcal{C}[\varphi_2])$
else if $\psi = \varphi_1 \vee \varphi_2$ **then**
  $\mathcal{C}[\psi] \leftarrow \max(\mathcal{C}[\varphi_1], \mathcal{C}[\varphi_2])$
else if $\psi = \mathbf{GF}p$ **then**
  $\mathcal{C}[\psi] \leftarrow \min_{i \leq j \leq T} \mathcal{O}_F(p, j)$
end if
return $\mathcal{C}[\psi]$

component, we instantiate $\mathcal{O}_F$ with a GNN-based model for graph-structured data.

Algorithm 3 summarizes the computation procedure. Given finite timestamped observational data $\mathcal{D}$, the algorithm first constructs a graph representation relevant to the target atomic proposition p, including the required node types and relation schema. The data $\mathcal{D}$ are then organized into a temporal graph sequence to capture the evolution of system behavior. Node features $\mathbf{x}$ are constructed by incorporating both intrinsic node attributes and interaction information. The learning process consists of two phases: training and inference. During training, the model parameters are learned from training data following the standard machine learning paradigm, yielding a predictive model that captures the semantics of the eventually operator $\mathbf{F}$. During inference, node features $\mathbf{x}_i$ are constructed from the graph sequence starting at time i and fed into the trained GNN model. Through multi-layer message passing and neighborhood aggregation, the model obtains node embeddings that incorporate local neigh-

Algorithm 3. GNN-based Computation of $\mathcal{O}_F(p, i)$

Require: Timestamped data $\mathcal{D}$, atomic proposition p, starting time i
Ensure: Confidence value $\mathcal{O}_F(p, i) \in [0, 1]$

```
Determine the graph schema according to p
Organize the data D into a graph sequence
Construct node features x
// Training phase
Initialize GNN parameters
for each training epoch do
    Feed the training data into the GNN
    Perform multi-layer message passing and neighborhood aggregation
    Map the node embeddings to prediction scores
    Compute loss and update parameters
end for
// Inference phase
Construct node features x_i from the graph sequence starting at time i
Feed the features into the trained model for forward propagation
Obtain the predicted confidence value O_F(p, i)
return O_F(p, i)
```

borhood information. Finally, node embeddings are mapped to scalar outputs, yielding the confidence estimate $\mathcal{O}_F(p, i) \in [0, 1]$ that p will hold in the future from starting time i.

4 Experimental Evaluation

4.1 Experimental Setup

Task Instantiation. We instantiate the proposed neural-symbolic framework on a link prediction task over an academic collaboration network. The dataset is constructed from publicly available academic publications and online resources, containing profiles of 5,508 experts with metadata such as research areas and publication records. Given partial historical observations, the task is to quantitatively evaluate temporal logic properties of future collaborations between experts.

The experimental setup follows the framework described in Sect. 3. Time is discretized by year, with each time step corresponding to a calendar year. Each expert is modeled as a node, and an undirected edge is created between two nodes if the corresponding experts co-author at least one paper in a given year. This yields a temporal collaboration network from 2014 to 2024, with 123504 edges in total. We denote the discrete time steps by $t = 0, 1, \ldots, T$, where $t = 0$ corresponds to 2014 and $t = T$ corresponds to 2024. For any starting time i, the available observation is the graph sequence $G[i], G[i+1], \ldots, G[T]$ over the interval $[i, T]$.

We define the atomic proposition $p(a, b)$ to be true at time step t if experts a and b collaborate at that time. Accordingly, $\mathbf{F}p(a, b)$ represents that experts

a and b will collaborate at some future time step from a given starting time i. This formulation enables the evaluation of temporal properties of co-authorship behavior within the proposed framework.

Eventually Operator Implementation. We instantiate the quantitative evaluation of the temporal formula $\mathbf{F}p(a,b)$ using a GNN-based predictive model. Given a starting time i, the model takes the collaboration graph sequence over $[i,T]$ as input and outputs the confidence value of $\mathbf{F}p(a,b)$ at time i, representing the likelihood that experts a and b will collaborate in the future.

Graph Representation Learning. Predicting collaborations between experts requires capturing both node attributes and structural patterns in the network.

Node2Vec [19] can capture structural roles and network connectivity patterns through biased random walks, but the original algorithm does not explicitly incorporate node attributes. Since research interests strongly influence future co-authorship, we derive semantic attributes from experts' publications. Specifically, we embed paper titles and abstracts into semantic vectors and average the vectors of all papers authored by each expert to represent their research interests. Structural embeddings are then obtained using a modified Node2Vec algorithm. Let t denote the previous node in a random walk, v the current node, and x a candidate next node. The structural bias term $\alpha_{pq}(t,x)$ is defined as

$$\alpha_{pq}(t,x) = \begin{cases} \frac{1}{p}, & d_{tx} = 0 \\ 1, & d_{tx} = 1 \\ \frac{1}{q}, & d_{tx} = 2 \end{cases}$$

where d_{tx} denotes the shortest path distance between nodes t and x, and p and q control the trade-off between breadth-first and depth-first exploration.

To incorporate collaboration strength and semantic similarity, we define the unnormalized transition probability as

$$\pi(v,x) = \alpha_{pq}(t,x) \cdot w(v,x) \cdot \big(1 + \lambda \cdot \mathrm{sim}(v,x)\big),$$

where $w(v,x)$ is the time-decayed edge weight between v and x, $\mathrm{sim}(v,x)$ is the cosine similarity between their semantic attribute vectors, and λ controls the influence of semantic similarity. The normalized transition probability is then given by

$$P(v \to x) = \frac{\pi(v,x)}{\sum_{x' \in \mathcal{N}(v)} \pi(v,x')}.$$

Based on the above transition probabilities, random walk sequences are generated and the model is trained using the Skip-gram objective, yielding node embeddings $\mathbf{z}_v$ that integrate both graph structural and semantic information.

The final node representation is obtained by concatenating the Node2Vec embedding with the attribute vector. This representation is used as the input feature for the subsequent GNN model.

GNN Model. We use GraphSAGE [16] to compute node embeddings by aggregating features from local neighborhoods:

$$\mathbf{h}_v^{(l+1)} = \sigma\left(\mathbf{W}^{(l)} \cdot \mathrm{AGG}\big(\{\mathbf{h}_u^{(l)} : u \in \mathcal{N}(v)\} \cup \{\mathbf{h}_v^{(l)}\}\big)\right),$$

where $\mathrm{AGG}(\cdot)$ is a permutation-invariant aggregation function.

The learned node embeddings are then used to predict collaboration likelihoods. The computation consists of two phases: training and inference. During training, we adopt a chronological data split, using records from 2014 to 2022 for training, 2023 for validation, and 2024 for testing. After training, the model parameters are fixed. During inference, observations from different starting times are fed into the trained model to obtain confidence estimates for $\mathbf{F}p(a,b)$.

Derived Temporal Formulas Computation. We further evaluate derived temporal formulas, focusing on $\mathbf{GF}p(a,b)$, which characterizes persistent collaboration potential between experts a and b.

According to the proposed semantics, given a starting time i, the confidence value of $\mathbf{GF}p(a,b)$ is computed by taking the minimum confidence of $\mathbf{F}p(a,b)$ over time steps $t \geq i$. Under the above temporal setting, we fix the starting time as $i = 0$, corresponding to the year 2014, and select representative time steps $\{0, 2, 4, 6, 8\}$, corresponding to 2014, 2016, 2018, 2020, and 2022, to approximate

$$[\![\mathbf{GF}p(a,b)]\!](0) = \min_{t \geq 0} [\![\mathbf{F}p(a,b)]\!](t).$$

Basic temporal properties can also be combined to characterize more complex collaboration patterns. For example, $\mathbf{F}p(a,b) \wedge \mathbf{F}p(a,c)$ indicates that expert a may collaborate with both b and c in the future, capturing potential multi-party collaboration. In contrast, $\mathbf{F}p(a,b) \vee \mathbf{F}p(a,c)$ indicates that expert a may collaborate with at least one of the two experts, which can be used to model alternative collaboration relationships.

4.2 Experimental Results

Eventually Operator Evaluation. We first evaluate the predictive quality of the model using standard link prediction metrics, including Area Under the ROC Curve (AUC) and Average Precision (AP), which indirectly assesses the quality of $\mathbf{F}p(a,b)$ evaluation.

We compare our approach with several baselines, including: (1) Heuristic Methods such as Adamic–Adar and Jaccard Coefficient, (2) Traditional Node2Vec Method, (3) Graph Convolutional Network (GCN), and (4) Standard GraphSAGE Model. For GCN and GraphSAGE, we use original Node2Vec embeddings combined with node attributes as input, whereas the proposed method uses the improved embeddings described above. All methods are trained and evaluated under identical experimental settings.

As shown in Table 1, the proposed approach achieves the best performance across all metrics. This improvement can be attributed to the integration of

Table 1. Performance comparison on the collaboration prediction task.

Method	AUC	AP
Adamic–Adar	0.5804	0.5812
Jaccard Coefficient	0.5803	0.5799
Node2Vec	0.9334	0.9428
GCN	0.9510	0.9584
GraphSAGE	0.9620	0.9698
Proposed	0.9657	0.9731

richer structural and attribute-aware representations, which enables the model to capture collaboration patterns more effectively.

After training, the model is used to compute $[\![\mathbf{F}p(a,b)]\!](i)$ for different starting times i, and we further analyze the consistency between the predicted confidence values and the ground-truth collaboration outcomes. Taking $i = 0$ as an example, Fig. 1 shows the confidence distributions of positive and negative samples. Instances where the eventuality is satisfied (label $= 1$) concentrate in higher confidence ranges, while instances without eventual satisfaction (label $= 0$) are assigned lower confidence values. This separation indicates that the learned confidence scores are consistent with the intended notion of eventual satisfaction under partial observations.

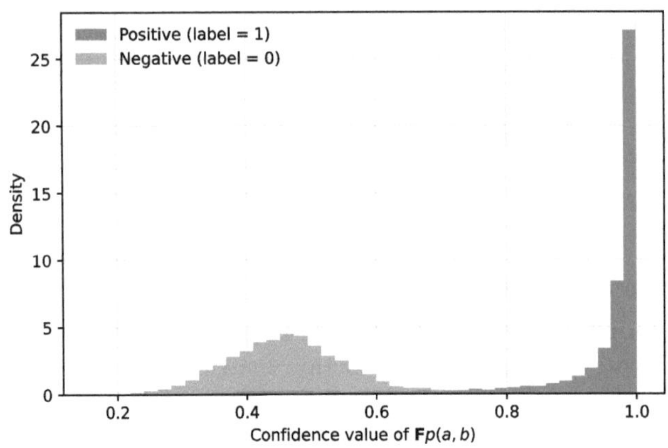

Fig. 1. Confidence distribution of $\mathbf{F}p(a,b)$.

Derived Temporal Formulas Evaluation. As described above, we further compute the temporal formula $[\![\mathbf{GF}p(a,b)]\!](i)$, taking $i = 0$ as an example.

For qualitative analysis, expert pairs are grouped into three categories according to their collaboration patterns: *long-term* pairs with repeated collaborations over multiple years, *sporadic* pairs with occasional collaborations, and *never* pairs with no recorded collaborations. For each category, we randomly sample 1000 pairs to ensure a balanced comparison and sufficient statistical support.

Figure 2 presents the confidence distributions across the three categories. As expected, long-term pairs have confidence values concentrated near 1, reflecting stable interaction patterns and high eventuality satisfaction. Sporadic pairs show a broader distribution, typically between 0.8 and 1.0, indicating substantial potential for future collaboration. Never pairs generally receive lower confidence values, although some obtain higher scores due to shared affiliation, overlapping research interests, or incomplete observations. Overall, the separation among the three categories is consistent with intuitive collaboration patterns, suggesting that the proposed framework can compositionally derive and evaluate higher-level temporal properties from learned atomic predicates.

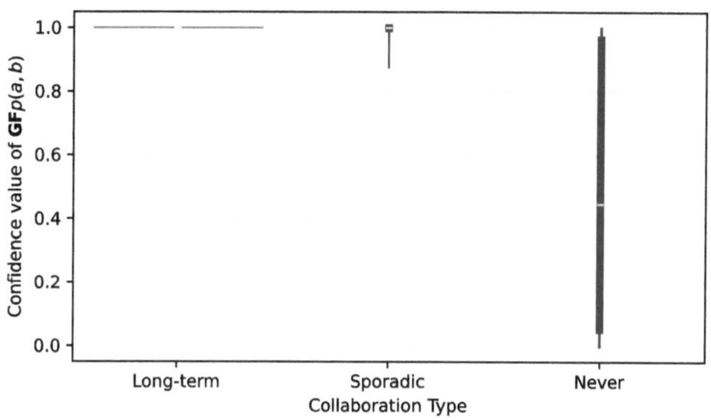

Fig. 2. Confidence distribution of $\mathbf{GF}p(a, b)$ by collaboration type.

5 Conclusion

This paper presented a neural-symbolic framework for learning-based quantitative evaluation of GR(1) temporal properties upon partial data traces. The framework treats the eventually operator as a learnable primitive, allowing temporal properties to be evaluated in a confidence-valued manner. Derived temporal operators in the GR(1) fragment are constructed symbolically, enabling principled evaluation of more complex temporal specifications. By combining data-driven prediction with symbolic temporal composition, the proposed framework supports interpretable reasoning about temporal properties under partial observation.

Experimental results on a real-world academic collaboration prediction task demonstrate the practical applicability and effectiveness of the framework in supporting meaningful data-driven temporal reasoning. Future work may apply the framework to a broader range of domains. Another direction is to extend the framework to more expressive temporal logics beyond GR(1) to support richer temporal specifications.

Acknowledgments. This work is supported by the National Key R&D Program of China No. 2022YFA1005101, the National Natural Science Foundation of China under Grant No. 61872371 and No. 62032024.

References

1. Pnueli, A.: The temporal logic of programs. In: 18th Annual Symposium on Foundations of Computer Science (SFCS 1977), pp. 46–57. IEEE (1977)
2. Kupferman, O., Vardi, M.Y.: Model checking of safety properties. Formal Methods Syst. Design **19**(3), 291–314 (2001)
3. Kress-Gazit, H., Fainekos, G.E., Pappas, G.J.: Temporal-logic-based reactive mission and motion planning. IEEE Trans. Rob. **25**(6), 1370–1381 (2009)
4. Bloem, R., Jobstmann, B., Piterman, N., Pnueli, A., Sa'ar, Y.: Synthesis of reactive (1) designs. J. Comput. Syst. Sci. **78**(3), 911–938 (2012)
5. Piterman, N., Pnueli, A., Sa'ar, Y.: Synthesis of reactive(1) designs. In: Emerson, E.A., Namjoshi, K.S. (eds.) VMCAI 2006. LNCS, vol. 3855, pp. 364–380. Springer, Heidelberg (2005). https://doi.org/10.1007/11609773_24
6. Clarke, E.M.: Model checking. In: Ramesh, S., Sivakumar, G. (eds.) FSTTCS 1997. LNCS, vol. 1346, pp. 54–56. Springer, Heidelberg (1997). https://doi.org/10.1007/BFb0058022
7. Baier, C., Katoen, J.-P.: Principles of Model Checking. MIT Press (2008)
8. Leucker, M., Schallhart, C.: A brief account of runtime verification. J. Logic Algebraic Program. **78**(5), 293–303 (2009)
9. Murphy, K.P.: Machine Learning: A Probabilistic Perspective. MIT Press (2012)
10. Bengio, S., Vinyals, O., Jaitly, N., Shazeer, N.: Scheduled sampling for sequence prediction with recurrent neural networks. Adv. Neural. Inf. Process. Syst. **28** (2015)
11. Lipton, Z.C., Kale, D.C., Elkan, C., Wetzel, R.: Learning to diagnose with LSTM recurrent neural networks. arXiv preprint arXiv:1511.03677 (2015)
12. Rumelhart, D.E., Hinton, G.E., Williams, R.J.: Learning representations by back-propagating errors. Nature **323**(6088), 533–536 (1986)
13. Hochreiter, S., Schmidhuber, J.: Long short-term memory. Neural Comput. **9**(8), 1735–1780 (1997)
14. Scarselli, F., Gori, M., Tsoi, A.C., Hagenbuchner, M., Monfardini, G.: The graph neural network model. IEEE Trans. Neural Netw. **20**(1), 61–80 (2008)
15. Kipf, T.N.: Semi-supervised classification with graph convolutional networks. arXiv preprint arXiv:1609.02907 (2016)
16. Hamilton, W., Ying, Z., Leskovec, J.: Inductive representation learning on large graphs. Adv. Neural. Inf. Process. Syst. **30** (2017)
17. Schmidhuber, J., Hochreiter, S., et al.: Long short-term memory. Neural Comput. **9**(8), 1735–1780 (1997)
18. Vaswani, A., et al.: Attention is all you need. Adv. Neural. Inf. Process. Syst. **30** (2017)
19. Grover, A., Leskovec, J.: node2vec: scalable feature learning for networks. In: Proceedings of the 22nd ACM SIGKDD International Conference on Knowledge Discovery and Data Mining, pp. 855–864 (2016)

Learn by Analogy: Distribution-Aware Fuzz Testing for DNNs via Cross-Modal Generation

Boli Huang[1], Tianlin Li[2], Ming Hu[1], Ziming Zhao[3], and Mingsong Chen[1](✉)

[1] East China Normal University, Shanghai, China
51275902020@stu.ecnu.edu.cn, mschen@sei.ecnu.edu.cn
[2] Beihang University, Beijing, China
[3] Zhejiang University, Hangzhou, China

Abstract. Deep Neural Networks (DNNs) have gained widespread use in safety-critical systems, underscoring the importance of reliability testing in system development. Existing methods typically generate test cases by directly mutating training data, which inherently assumes that valid inputs fall within the training data distribution. However, due to practical data-collection challenges, DNNs frequently encounter target distributions that extend well beyond their training scope, rendering these mutation-based tests inadequate. Moreover, directly mutating training data further restricts generation diversity, as the process remains constrained by task-irrelevant features like color, background, and posture. To address these issues, we propose a novel distribution-aware fuzz testing framework leveraging fully trained AI-Generated Content (AIGC) models. Specifically, our method first uses cross-modal AIGC technologies to transform the original training data into intermediate data in an abstract modality, preserving general semantic features while disregarding task-irrelevant ones. Subsequently, we generate diverse test cases based on this intermediate abstract data. To ensure the quality of the generated test cases, we introduce a cluster-based data cleaning mechanism to filter out invalid inputs. Comprehensive experimental results demonstrate that, compared with state-of-the-art DNN test methods, our approach achieves up to 39.47% coverage improvement and finds more errors. Furthermore, our approach achieves better accuracy on test sets than baselines.

Keywords: AI-Generated Content · Cross-Modal · Data Augmentation · Deep Learning · Software Testing

1 Introduction

Deep Neural Networks (DNNs) present significant advantages in various tasks and are widely deployed in safety-critical systems, such as autonomous driving [8] and healthcare [21]. However, due to poor robustness, the reliability of DNN-based applications is seriously threatened. Adequate testing is essential to

G. De Giacomo et al. (Eds.): TASE 2026, LNCS 16697, pp. 223–242, 2027.
https://doi.org/10.1007/978-3-032-30693-7_15

evaluate the reliability of DNN applications. Typically, DNN testing needs sufficient test cases to cover the distribution of a valid input space. However, the vast input space of DNNs poses a challenge for testing engineers in collecting a comprehensive test dataset that covers the distribution of real-world data. This difficulty is further exacerbated by strict data protection regulations and escalating privacy concerns, which significantly increase the costs of real-world data collection.

To efficiently test DNNs with limited data, automated test case generation technologies have been widely adopted. Typically, the goal of the generation methods is to generate *valid* and *diverse* test cases to evaluate the reliability of DNNs. Existing methods [30,33] primarily employ simple mutation strategies (e.g., flip, rotation, scale, and translation). Since these methods assume valid inputs strictly adhere to the original training distribution, they are heavily constrained to generating test cases that follow the distribution of training data [3,14].

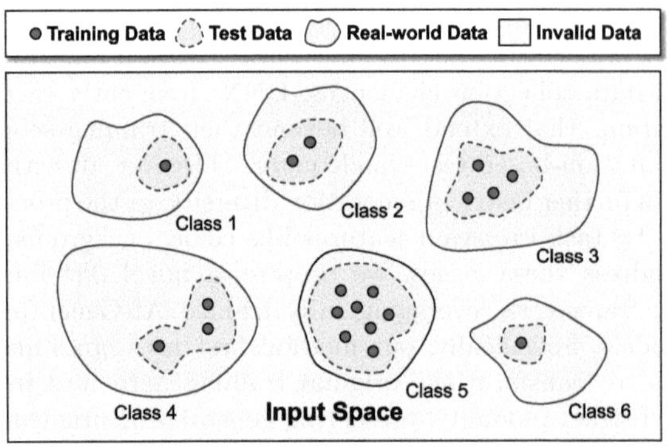

Fig. 1. Illustration of a motivating example.

However, due to limited data-collection capacity, training data cannot fully represent the real-world data distribution. In DNN applications, the distribution of collected data is often imbalanced, such as a long-tail distribution, where some classes have abundant data while the majority have only a limited amount. As shown in Fig. 1, the training data collected can cover only a limited distribution of valid inputs. Although existing methods can generate various test cases, the discrepancy between the training data and the actual target data distributions means that the generated in-distribution data represents only a limited portion of the valid input space. For example, as shown in Fig. 1, because the training data for Class 5 are more diverse, they can cover a wider range of real-world data distributions. Therefore, the test data generated from Class 5 data has higher testing quality. Due to the lack of adequate and diverse data samples, the data of classes 1, 4, and 6 can only cover a limited part of the real-world data distribution. Due to limited knowledge of valid data, existing methods struggle to generate additional high-quality test cases that cover unknown real-world data distributions. Therefore, the diversity of generated test cases is severely limited by the quality of training data.

To generate more diverse valid data, the state-of-the-art method DistXplore [31] attempts to use various mutation operations to generate out-of-distribution data between the distributions of two classes. However, since it is still based on the original training data and lacks exposure to real-world data, the diversity of the generated data remains severely limited. For example, as illustrated in Fig. 1, DistXplore can generate data between the training sets of Classes 4 and 5. However, it cannot generate data in the left region of the training data for Class 4.

In addition, since existing methods generate test cases by modifying the original training data, the features of the generated data are constrained by the task-irrelevant features of the training data, such as color and posture. Consequently, the diversity of the generated test cases is seriously limited. These limitations are severely exacerbated when scaling to high-quality, high-resolution datasets (e.g., ImageNet) required for modern safety-critical domains. Training samples in such datasets are highly dispersed in the feature space and possess complex, high-level semantics that simple low-level mutations cannot effectively diversify. Therefore, *how to deal with the problem caused by the limited amount and uneven distribution of training data and generate valid and diverse test data, particularly when dealing with complex and high-resolution datasets, is an important challenge for DNN testing.*

To generate more diverse and valid test data, the generation method should be based on more general features, avoid being constrained by specific attributes, and leverage more knowledge of real-world data. Advancements in AI-Generated Content (AIGC) technologies [5] have enabled data generation across various modalities, including image-to-text and text-to-image. By mapping images into a textual embedding space, we can capture their general conceptual features while ignoring many instance-specific details. Typically, a general AIGC model requires massive real-world data for training. Since AIGC models learn from real-world data, they can generate high-quality data. By leveraging these learned embeddings to guide the generative model, we can use the AIGC model's encoded knowledge to generate test cases. Moreover, by adding constraint text that delineates the DNN model's scope, we can guide it to generate more valid images.

Inspired by the above intuition, we present a novel cross-modal generation-based, distribution-aware DNN fuzz testing framework named *CMGFuzz*, which first captures the shared semantics from limited data and transforms them into an abstract modality, then leverages the learned abstract representations to generate diverse and distribution-aware test cases. To break free from pixel-level constraints, CMGFuzz utilizes Textual Inversion [11] to transform limited training images into abstract textual embeddings. These embeddings capture complex, high-level semantics, guiding a text-to-image model to synthesize semantically rich and highly diverse test cases. To ensure the validity of the generated cases, CMGFuzz employs a cluster-based data-cleaning mechanism to filter out data points that are far from cluster centers. Moreover, to efficiently test DNN models, CMGFuzz adaptively generates test cases based on the distribution of training and test data. Specifically, CMGFuzz prefers to generate more data for categories with less data in the training and test datasets. Experimental results demonstrate that, compared to state-of-the-art methods, CMGFuzz can generate more diverse test cases and achieve four coverage improvements. The main contributions of the paper are as follows:

- We propose CMGFuzz, a novel distribution-aware DNN fuzz testing framework tailored for high-resolution image data, which adopts AIGC models to convert training and test data into abstract textual embeddings, and then generate more diverse test cases based on these learned representations.
- We present an adaptive test case generation strategy that efficiently generates test cases based on the original training and test data distributions.
- To ensure the validity of generated test cases, we present a cluster-based data cleaning mechanism to filter invalid data.
- We conducted extensive empirical evaluations on well-known datasets and representative models to demonstrate the effectiveness of the CMGFuzz.

2 Preliminaries and Problem Definition

2.1 Preliminaries

Deep Neural Network. A DNN can be modeled as a function $f : X \rightarrow Y$, where X and Y denote the input and output spaces, respectively. Typically, a DNN consists of multiple layers. Given an input $x \in X$, the network produces an output $y = f(x)$ through a composition of L layers, i.e., $f = l_L \circ \cdots \circ l_1$, where each layer transforms its input representation to a higher-level feature space.

Data Validity. Assume that D_r is a dataset of all real-world data that the target DNN model needs to handle. A sample d is considered valid if $d \in D_r$. Since D_r is practically unobservable in its entirety, existing methods generate synthetic data while constraining it to remain close to D_r. Typically, an L_p distance constraint [22] is imposed, i.e., a generated sample d_r is valid if $\exists d \in D_r$ such that $||d_r - d||_p < b$, where b is a bound to control the safe distance between the generated data and the real-world data.

Data Distributions. Assume that D_T is the training dataset and D_R is the set of all valid real-world data. In practice, D_T provides only a partial approximation to D_R, leading to a distributional gap between the training data and real-world scenarios. Existing methods implicitly assume that D_T sufficiently represents D_R and thus focus on exploring variations within D_T. However, due to limited data-collection capabilities, this assumption may not hold, thereby limiting test performance. To address this issue, this paper attempts to leverage real-world data knowledge in AIGC models to generate valid data for D_R.

2.2 Problem Definition

This paper evaluates the reliability of DNN models through three objectives: diversity of test cases, model coverage, and error analysis.

Diversity. Our testing strategy aims to generate a broader, more varied set of valid test cases that reflect a wider spectrum of real-world data distributions. Because training data distributions often differ from those observed in practice, the data generation process focuses on producing additional data that more fully represent the range of real-world distributions.

Coverage. To measure the thoroughness of the generated test suite, we adopt four multi-granularity criteria. Let b_u and b_l denote the upper and lower activation bounds of a target neuron observed during training. We employ: *k-multisection Neuron Coverage (KMNC)* [34], which divides $[b_l, b_u]$ into k equal sections to measure activation distribution; *Neuron Boundary Coverage (NBC)* [18] and *Strong Neuron Activation Coverage (SNAC)* [34], which measure the ratio of activations falling outside $[b_l, b_u]$ and strictly above b_u, respectively; and *Top-k Neuron Coverage (TKNC)* [34], which measures the ratio of the number of neurons that have once been the most active k neurons on each layer.

Error. An important metric for evaluating a testing method is its ability to identify errors within the target software. Therefore, an important goal of our DNN test is to find as many errors as possible. For DNN testing, an error case is a test case misclassified by the target DNN. To evaluate the effectiveness of test methods, we count the number of errors found within a specified time.

3 Methodology

3.1 Overview

Figure 2 illustrates the *CMGFuzz* workflow, which comprises three core components: an abstract modality generator maintains a data abstraction technology to convert the training data into intermediate data in an abstract modal; a test case generator that adopts AIGC model to generate diverse test cases according to the generated intermediate data and the distribution of training data; and a data cleaner that filters invalid inputs based on their similarity to original training samples. In this paper, we implement CMGFuzz to test DNNs for image classification tasks and adopt the text modal as the abstract modality for intermediate data generation.

As shown in Fig. 2, the abstract modality generator operates in two main steps: data clustering and image-to-text abstraction. Initially, training data are clustered to select representative samples. Notably, variations in style, color, or shape may result in multiple clusters even within a single class. Subsequently, CMGFuzz employs textual inversion [11] to encode the selected samples into a compact textual embedding space that captures their semantic essence. Our

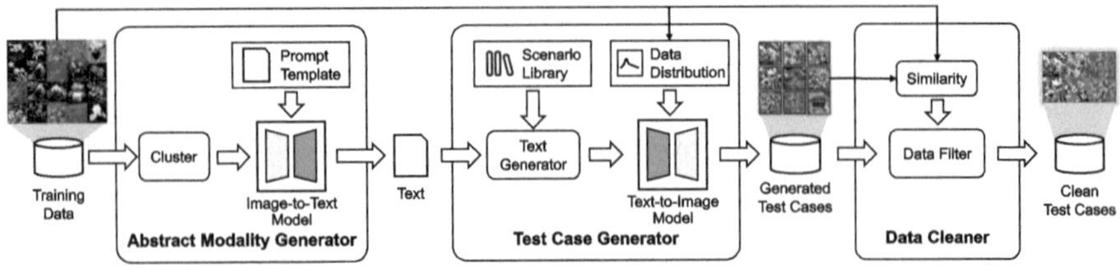

Fig. 2. Framework and workflow of CMGFuzz.

implementation utilizes a prompt template, e.g., "a photo of $\langle S^* \rangle$", where $\langle S^* \rangle$ is a learnable token which encodes the cluster-specific visual semantics.

The test case generator performs two steps, i.e., text generation and distribution-aware test case generation. The text generation step aims to produce multiple text samples based on the abstract modality generator's output. To facilitate diverse test case generation, the text generator applies a mutation strategy to the scenario description generated from the abstract modality generator. Specifically, the test case generator maintains a scenario library that stores the various scenario descriptions provided by requirement engineers. By adding the scenario description to the intermediate text, along with items from the scenario library, the test case generator can produce diverse intermediate data for generating test cases. Note that all scenario descriptions in the library are based on specific requirements and the expertise of requirements engineering. In the distribution-aware test case generation step, the generator uses a text-to-image model to produce multiple images based on the generated text. Since the data samples and distributions of each class in the training dataset differ, the generator prefers to generate more data for classes with fewer training samples to effectively generate test cases.

The data cleaner aims to filter the generated invalid test cases. Specifically, it calculates the similarity between the generated test cases and all cluster centers within the training data. Test cases that exceed a predefined threshold distance from all cluster centers will be filtered out. Note that to maintain an adequate supply of test cases, after the data cleaning process, CMGFuzz triggers the test case generator to generate additional test cases to replenish the filtered data.

3.2 Abstract Modality Data Generation

To generate diverse test cases, CMGFuzz aims to extract more general features and filter task-irrelevant features. Based on this motivation, CMGFuzz captures the shared semantics within limited data and transforms them into an abstract modality. Compared to the original modality, the abstract modality can preserve general features of the training data while ignoring specific, detailed features.

To efficiently generate test cases, CMGFuzz prefers to select representative data rather than all the training data for abstract modality generation. This is because training data often contains numerous similar samples. When generating the abstract modality, these similar samples may produce nearly identical results. Therefore, it suffices to use a representative subset of the data rather than the entire training data. To select representative data samples (i.e., seeds), we first cluster training data into multiple groups. We perform the k-means [15] clustering strategy to cluster training data. Specifically, given a DNN f and the set of samples of class c $(x_1, x_2, ..., x_n)$, we aim to partition the n samples into $k(\leq n)$ sets S=$(S_1, S_2, ..., S_k)$ so as to minimize:

$$\arg\min_{S} \sum_{i=1}^{k} \sum_{x \in S_i} \|f_l(x) - \mu_i\|^2, \tag{1}$$

where f_l is the output of layer l and μ_i is the mean of the outputs of layer l with inputs S_i, i.e.,

$$\mu_i = \frac{1}{|S_i|} \sum_{x \in S_i} f_l(x). \tag{2}$$

This way, data samples of a specific class can be clustered into multiple groups based on their similarity. We select n seeds from each cluster to construct a seed set for test case generation, where n is determined by the test's resource constraints (e.g., time and memory). Here, we select multiple seeds per group rather than a single seed for text generation. This is because our aim is to guide the image-to-test model in generating descriptions that capture the general features of the data in the clustered group. Note that a small value of n may cause the model to generate unique features specific to individual images.

We employ an image-to-text abstraction approach based on Textual Inversion [11] to learn a new token embedding for each cluster of seed images. Specifically, we introduce a newly learnable token $\langle S^*(C)\rangle$. By forcing a frozen text-to-image model to reconstruct the cluster's seed images using the prompt "a photo of $\langle S^*(C)\rangle$", we exclusively optimize this token's embedding. Consequently, $\langle S^*(C)\rangle$ captures the essential visual semantics of the cluster, serving as an abstract textual identifier for prompt-guided generation.

3.3 Distribution-Aware Test Case Generation

Given the generated text modality, CMGFuzz uses a text-to-image model to generate test cases. To guarantee the diversity and validity of test cases, CMGFuzz supports requirement engineers to add multiple scenario descriptions to enhance the generated text. Based on these scenario descriptions, CMGFuzz mutates the original text data to generate multiple inputs. To improve efficiency in test case generation, CMGFuzz leverages the training data distribution to regulate the number of test cases generated per class.

Input Generation. The scope of a DNN model is defined by the scenarios in which it is used. To thoroughly test the DNN model, CMGFuzz maintains a scenario library containing textual descriptions of scenarios provided by requirements engineers. Specifically, requirements engineers use their expertise to manually extract scenario descriptions from requirements. In addition, many existing

Natural Language Processing (NLP) algorithms [6] can automatically extract relevant descriptions from requirement documents. To generate more diverse test cases, CMGFuzz attempts to mutate the generated text data using scenario descriptions. To ensure the validity of the mutated data, each scenario description should specify which data classes it applies to. For each text generated by the abstract modality generator, CMGFuzz selects k relevant scenarios, duplicates the text k times, and inserts one scenario into each duplicate to yield k distinct inputs (e.g., forming "a dog in grass" for "a dog"). To prevent over-constraining the generation, empty strings are also included in the scenario descriptions. Note that initializing the placeholder simply as "$\langle S^* \rangle$" causes the model to learn it as an isolated concept disconnected from its class. Thus, before mutation, we modify the base prompt to "$\langle S^* \rangle$, a kind of C", where C is the actual class name of the image input.

Distribution-Aware Generation. CMGFuzz adopts a text-to-image model to generate test cases according to the generated inputs. Note that due to the inherent randomness of image generation, identical inputs can yield similar but distinct images. Given constraints on test time and hardware, the total number of generated test cases is limited. Since DNNs typically exhibit poorer classification performance on minority classes due to insufficient training, CMGFuzz prefers to generate more test cases for classes with limited training data to efficiently detect potential errors. Assume the target DNN classifies m classes. Let $N = \{n_{c_1}, ..., n_{c_m}\}$ denote the set of training sample counts per class, where n_{c_i} is the sample count for the ith class. Let $NG = \{ng_{c_1}, ..., ng_{c_m}\}$ indicate the number of generated test cases for each class. Assuming *CMGFuzz* aims to generate a total of N_T test cases (with $N_T \geq m$ to ensure at least one per class), the generation budget ng_{c_x} for class c_x is calculated as:

$$ng_{c_x} = \frac{(N_T - m)(\max(N) - n_{c_x})}{\sum_{m}^{i=1} \max(N) - n_{c_i}} + 1, \quad (3)$$

where $\max(N)$ represents the maximum training sample count among all classes.

3.4 Data Cleaning Mechanism

To ensure the validity of the generated test cases, CMGFuzz employs a cluster-based data filtering mechanism to eliminate potentially invalid test cases. Specifically, we first input each training data sample ts and test case tc into a pre-trained model f and extract the output vector of a specific layer as a feature vector. Here, for a data sample d, its feature vector can be denoted by $v_d = f_l(d)$. In this way, we can obtain two sets of feature vectors, i.e., F_{ts} and F_{tc} for the training data and the generated test cases, respectively. Then we cluster the feature vectors in F_{ts} into K groups. For each group, we calculate its cluster center. Here, we use the notation ct_i to denote the cluster center of the ith group. Next, for each test case, we calculate the similarity of its feature value with all cluster centers and select the minimum value as its deviation degree, which can be defined as follows:

$$d_{tc} = \min_{i=1}^{K} \|f_l(tc) - ct_i\|, \tag{4}$$

where tc denotes the test case and $\|\cdot\|$ indicates the Euclidean distance. Note that a lower value of d_{tc} indicates that tc is closer to one of the training data cluster centers. Based on the calculated deviation value, CMGFuzz filters the test cases far away from all the cluster centers as follows:

$$S_{filter} = \{s_i \in S_{tc} | d_i > Bar(S_{tc}, l(s_i), x)\}, \tag{5}$$

where S_{filter} denotes the set of filtered test cases, $l(s_i)$ denotes the class (i.e., label) of s_i, the function $Bar(\cdot)$ selects the threshold of deviation degree with the control of x, $x \in [0, 1.0]$ is a hyperparameter to control the proportion of clean data, and t is the distance threshold between clean data and original data. Specifically, $Bar(\cdot)$ first sorts the test cases for each class according to their deviation degree, and then for a class c, $Bar(\cdot)$ selects the deviation degree of $\lfloor x|S_{tc}^c|\rfloor^{th}$ test case as a threshold.

4 Evaluation

We implemented CMGFuzz using Python 3.11 and the PyTorch framework (version 2.2.1). To demonstrate the effectiveness of our CMGFuzz approach, we conducted experiments to answer the following four research questions (RQs), where RQ1 is to present the effectiveness of CMGFuzz in test case generation, RQ2 and RQ3 demonstrate the effectiveness of CMGFuzz on DNN model evaluation and repair, and RQ4 evaluates the effectiveness of components in CMGFuzz.

- **RQ1:** How effective is *CMGFuzz* for generating diverse data?
- **RQ2:** How effective is *CMGFuzz* for error detection?
- **RQ3:** How effective are testing cases generated by *CMGFuzz* in model repair?
- **RQ4:** How effective are the clustering and data cleaning strategies in improving the performance of *CMGFuzz*?

All experiments were performed on an Ubuntu workstation equipped with an Xeon Platinum 8336C CPU, 128 GB memory, and four NVIDIA RTX 4090 GPUs.

4.1 Experimental Setup

Settings of Datasets and Models. To assess the effectiveness of our approach, we conducted experiments on the Oxford Flowers-17-LT (OF17-LT) [23], Food-101-LT (Food101-LT) [4], ImageNet100-LT (IN100-LT) [9], and STL-10-LT (STL10-LT) [7] datasets. We constructed these by randomly selecting subsets via an Imbalanced Factor (IF), defined as the ratio of the largest class size (SS) to the smallest class size ($\frac{SS}{IF}$). More details of the datasets in our experiments are summarized in Table 1. To better compare and understand the performance of these testing methods, we categorized classes by sample count into many-shot (> 50 images), medium-shot (10-50), and few-shot (< 10). We constructed Food-101-FEW and ImageNet100-FEW (IN100-FEW) with exactly 20 images per class to simulate uniform data scarcity. For model selection, we select ResNet50 [13] for IN100, Food101, and OF17, and MobileNet [28] and AlexNet [16] for STL10. We adopted Stable Diffusion V2 [27] as the text-to-image model in CMGFuzz, which can be directly accessed in [1]. We employed a pre-trained Inception-V3 [29] network for data cleaning.

Table 1. Settings of long-tailed distribution.

Dataset	# of Classes	# of Images	Imbalance Factor
Oxford Flowers-17-LT	17	385	20
Food-101-LT	101	12K	200
ImageNet100-LT	100	25K	200
STL-10-LT	10	11K	200

Settings of CMGFuzz. We clustered the training dataset into three clusters, with four images per cluster selected as seeds to generate test cases ($SS/3$ test cases per cluster). To avoid removing too many valid test inputs of a class, we set the threshold to 0.3, meaning that up to 30% of the test inputs are removed from each class. For each CMGFuzz run, we limited the generative model's training to 500 steps. The number of iterations of the data cleaning phase is limited to 30. These specific hyperparameters were empirically determined through a grid search on a small validation subset to strike an optimal balance between generation quality and computational efficiency. More details can be found on our website [2]. For a class c with sample size S_c, we randomly select $SS - S_c$ from the cleaned test inputs of this class. In our evaluation, the scenario library is constructed using a combination of manually curated generic phrases and dataset-specific descriptions to ensure high diversity and relevance.

Settings of Baselines. To evaluate the effectiveness of CMGFuzz, we followed DistXplore to compare CMGFuzz against four state-of-the-art baselines: two adversarial attacks, BIM [17] and PGD [20]; a robustness-oriented method, SENSEI [12], using genetic algorithms based on empirical loss; and the distribution-aware technique, DistXplore, which utilizes genetic algorithms to generate test suites representing specific distributions by accounting for inter-class distribution differences. We implemented the two classic adversarial attacks using foolbox 3.3.4 [26]. We performed untargeted attacks on these attacks to generate test inputs. For SENSEI, we implemented it in PyTorch 2.2.1 [24], ran it for 25 epochs, and selected the top 10 individuals for each seed at each epoch. For DistXplore, we followed its default configurations to generate test cases. For all baselines, we generated test inputs and randomly selected an equal number to those generated by CMGFuzz. For seed selection, we randomly selected 100 seeds per class from the training dataset for BIM, PGD, and DistXplore, and used the entire training dataset as seed inputs for SENSEI, as described in [12].

Settings of Different RQs. RQ1: To assess the generation diversity of CMGFuzz, we evaluated testing coverage using four test coverage criteria: K-Multisection Neuron Coverage (KMNC) [34], Neuron Boundary Coverage (NBC) [18], Strong Neuron Activation Coverage (SNAC) [34], and Top-K Neuron Coverage (TKNC) [34]. Higher coverage indicates that the generated test cases are more effective in exploring the model's state space. **RQ2:** To evaluate the efficiency of CMGFuzz for error detection and the strength of errors, we counted and compared all errors found in the few-shot, medium-shot, and many-shot classes within a specified time. **RQ3:** For a fair comparison, we analyzed the model's performance on various test datasets generated by the mentioned baseline methods, following the setting in DistXplore [31]. **RQ4:** We removed either the cluster module or the CMGFuzz data cleaning module, and again performed RQ1 to RQ3 on the Oxford Flowers-17 dataset.

4.2 Experimental Results for Data Diversity (RQ1)

To evaluate the diversity of the generated data, we created visualizations to highlight differences between the data generated by CMGFuzz and the baselines. In particular, we randomly selected 1600 samples from the test cases generated by each method and computed the distances between these test cases and the training datasets. Based on the calculated distance, we visualized the distribution of test cases using tSNE [19].

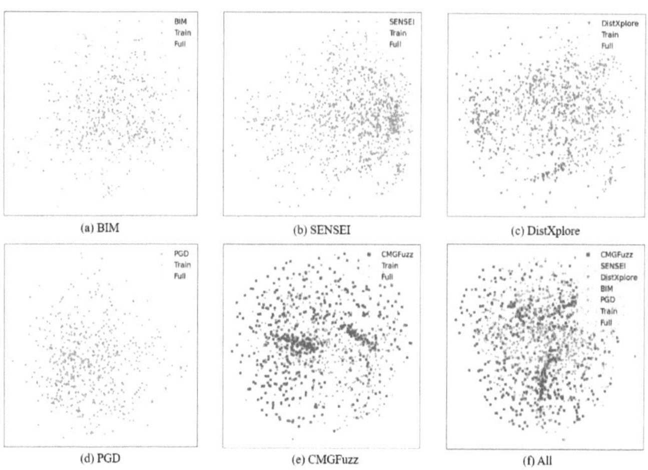

Fig. 3. Diversity of generated test cases with training data and full-dataset.

As shown in Fig. 3, CMGFuzz covers the largest area, surpassing the boundaries of original training data while remaining within the full dataset. In contrast, as shown in Fig. 3(b), test cases generated by SENSEI clusters narrowly around the training distribution, and while BIM, DistXplore, and PGD improve diversity, they remain more constrained than CMGFuzz. From Fig. 3(f), we can observe that, compared to the test cases generated by the baselines, the ones generated by CMGFuzz cover the largest area. In other words, CMGFuzz can generate the most diverse test cases. To further support the observation above, we present some examples of test cases generated by each method. As shown in Fig. 4, CMGFuzz produces superior semantic variations in the shapes and backgrounds of objects without losing structural integrity.

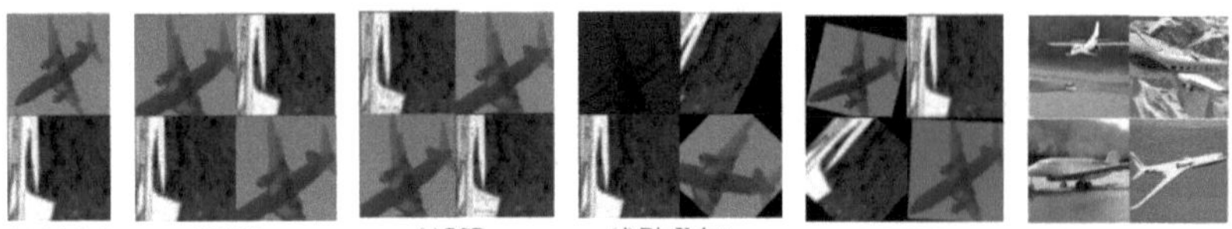

Fig. 4. Comparison between STL10 samples and those generated by each method.

To better evaluate the effectiveness of all five methods, we compute four coverage criteria from the generated test cases. Table 2 presents the coverage of CMGFuzz and four baselines on four coverage criteria. Table 2 summarizes the coverage metrics across four datasets. On Food101, CMGFuzz outperformed the best baselines by 23.97%, 19.46%, 5.00%, and 1.94% in NBC, SNAC, KMNC, and TKNC, respectively. On OF17, it achieves up to 17.88% improvement in SNAC. We observed that all methods achieved 100% NBC on OF17, likely because the dataset's small size limits the need for out-of-distribution generalization. Similar gains on IN100 and STL10 confirm that CMGFuzz consistently enhances NBC and SNAC, indicating more effective exploration of the model's state space compared to baselines. Table 2 indicates that CMGFuzz substantially increases NBC and SNAC, while generally yielding higher KMNC and lower TKNC values in most cases.

Answer to RQ1: Compared to the four baselines, CMGFuzz can achieve the highest coverage across all four criteria on the three datasets, highlighting the diversity of generation.

4.3 Experimental Results for Found Errors (RQ2)

To evaluate the effectiveness of CMGFuzz, we count the unique number of errors found in the test cases generated in RQ2. Since BIM and PGD focus on pixel-level perturbations with limited diversity, we primarily compared *CMGFuzz* against SENSEI and DistXplore across few-shot ($<$ 10 training samples), medium-shot

Table 2. Coverage of CMGFuzz and four baselines (LT).

Dataset	Method	NBC (%)	SNAC (%)	KMNC (%)	TKNC (%)
Food101	BIM	56.01	58.84	89.76	20.22
	SENSEI	46.14	49.32	86.33	19.34
	DistXplore	56.88	59.21	90.27	20.13
	PGD	53.93	55.49	87.63	19.67
	CMGFuzz	**80.81**	**78.67**	**95.27**	**22.16**
OF17	BIM	**100.00**	39.12	59.27	5.16
	SENSEI	**100.00**	54.89	80.91	7.28
	DistXplore	**100.00**	60.71	78.75	6.85
	PGD	**100.00**	39.23	59.49	5.15
	CMGFuzz	**100.00**	**78.59**	**86.57**	**10.18**
IN100	BIM	50.09	51.49	**91.00**	22.02
	SENSEI	33.63	34.17	84.46	19.65
	DistXplore	47.95	47.13	87.47	20.71
	PGD	41.69	41.64	87.71	22.03
	CMGFuzz	**58.70**	**55.43**	90.09	**22.29**
STL10 (MobileNet)	BIM	20.81	23.75	65.43	20.67
	SENSEI	32.84	30.67	76.84	24.60
	DistXplore	51.20	44.39	80.54	**26.64**
	PGD	35.57	32.18	78.71	16.99
	CMGFuzz	**57.60**	**50.32**	**82.28**	19.20
STL10 (AlexNet)	BIM	9.07	17.29	35.62	16.47
	SENSEI	31.05	59.74	71.27	29.55
	DistXplore	29.34	54.56	58.94	26.21
	PGD	30.32	59.65	76.01	19.79
	CMGFuzz	**49.06**	**95.71**	**89.33**	**47.46**

(10-50), and many-shot (> 50) classes. Table 3 presents the unique number of errors found by CMGFuzz and baselines. Note that because OF17 rarely contains many-shot classes, we do not provide results on the number of detected errors for many-shot classes in OF17. As shown in Table 3, CMGFuzz significantly outperforms all baselines in all scenarios. Notably, on Food101 and IN100, CMGFuzz identified 43,764 and 47,516 unique errors, respectively, exceeding the best baselines by nearly fivefold. We can observe that all methods detect more errors in few-shot classes, as DNNs exhibit lower inference performance on sparse training data. Due to differences in testing efficiency, SENSEI detects more errors per unit time than DistXplore under identical hardware configurations.

Table 3. Unique Number of found errors within a specified time (LT).

Dataset	Method	Few	Medium	Many	Total
Food101	**CMGFuzz**	**24234**	**9086**	**10444**	**43764**
	DistXplore	3712	1188	1068	5968
	SENSEI	5599	1893	1995	9487
OF17	**CMGFuzz**	**471**	**52**	/	**523**
	DistXplore	99	5	/	104
	SENSEI	167	4	/	171
IN100	**CMGFuzz**	**22723**	**9537**	**15256**	**47516**
	DistXplore	3064	1651	3104	7819
	SENSEI	4481	1554	2018	8053
STL10 (MobileNet)	**CMGFuzz**	**2421**	**709**	**36**	**3166**
	DistXplore	400	137	18	555
	SENSEI	622	152	12	786
STL10 (AlexNet)	**CMGFuzz**	**2128**	**488**	**103**	**2719**
	DistXplore	317	107	32	456
	SENSEI	450	103	28	581

Answer to RQ2: Compared to all baselines, CMGFuzz can find more errors with greater diversity.

4.4 Experimental Results for Repair Performance (RQ3)

To evaluate the repair performance of the test methods, we split the data generated by all five methods into training and test sets. Then, after retraining the model on a balanced dataset (a mixture of generated and original training data), we analyze its performance across different test datasets.

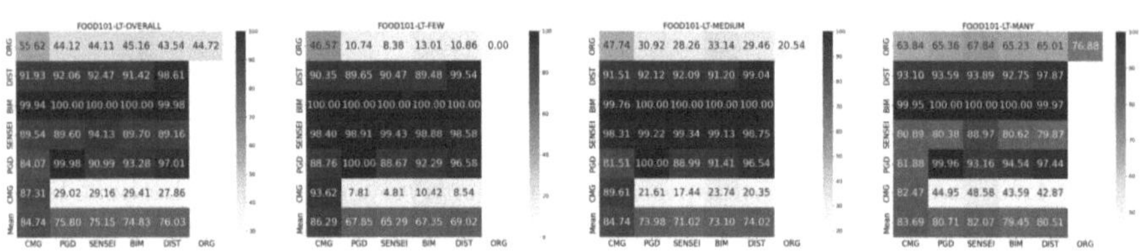

(a) Overall (b) Few (c) Medium (d) Many

Fig. 5. Repair performance of different methods on Food101-LT.

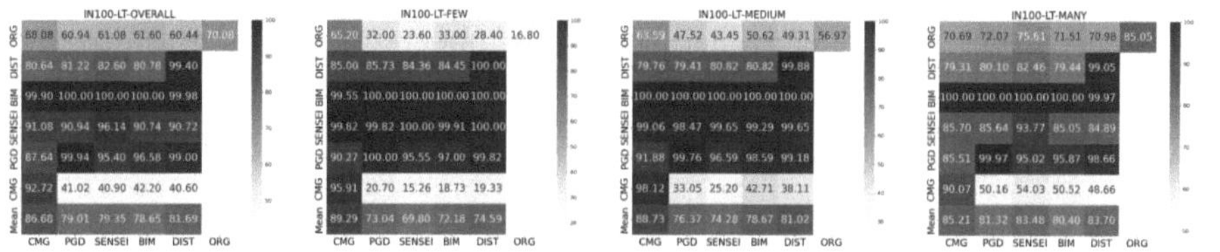

(a) Overall (b) Few (c) Medium (d) Many

Fig. 6. Repair performance of different methods on IN100-LT.

Figure 5 and Fig. 6 present the cross-evaluation matrix for the representative high-resolution Food101-LT and IN100-LT datasets, respectively. In each plot, each column represents the classification accuracy of models retrained on the training dataset produced by a specific method, while each row shows the classification accuracy of these models on the test dataset generated by a specific method. In the figure, we denote CMGFuzz, PGD, SENSEI, BIM, and DistXplore as *CMG*, *PGD*, *SENSEI*, *BIM*, and *DIST*, respectively. The performance of the original model, evaluated on the original test set, is denoted *ORG*. We also report the mean performance of each method across all datasets, labeled as *Mean*.

From the figures, we observe that CMGFuzz achieves the highest overall accuracy on the original test sets across all datasets. Furthermore, in cross-evaluation, CMGFuzz demonstrates superior generalization: on Food101-LT, it achieves at least 87.31% accuracy against test data generated by baselines, whereas models retrained by baselines peak at only 29.41% accuracy on CMGFuzz-generated data. These results confirm that CMGFuzz generates valid data that covers a broader, more challenging distribution, effectively exposing model vulnerabilities. Across varying levels of data availability, all methods tend to boost accuracy for both few-shot and medium-shot classes, but CMGFuzz achieves markedly superior performance. This underscores CMGFuzz's capacity to effectively learn from highly imbalanced data distributions.

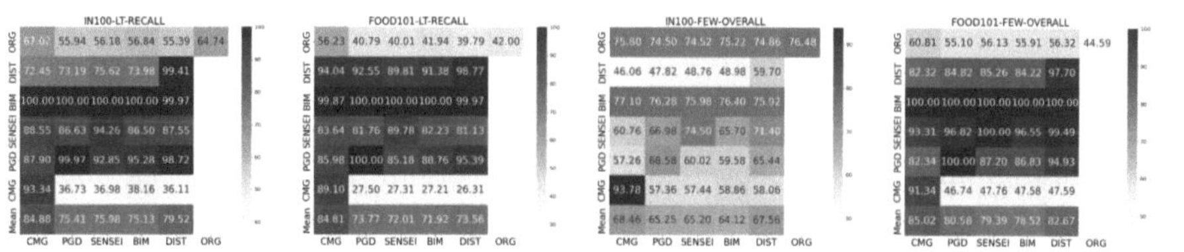

(a) IN100-LT (b) FOOD101-LT (c) IN100-FEW (d) FOOD101-FEW

Fig. 7. (a) and (b) show the recall rates of different methods on many-shot classes. (c) and (d) present the repair performance of different methods on few-version datasets.

While all retrained models exhibit slight declines in accuracy on many-shot classes, recall analysis (Fig. 7) reveals that the original model's high initial accuracy stems from overfitting rather than true understanding of the distribution. Naive mutation-based baselines exacerbate this overfitting. For instance, on Food101-LT, the original model yields a 42.00% recall rate, which baselines further degrade (peaking at only 41.94% for BIM). In stark contrast, CMGFuzz significantly increases recall to 56.23%, indicating that the model enhanced by CMGFuzz exhibits greater robustness and generalization for many-shot classes. We can also observe similar trends on the IN100-LT dataset.

For few-version datasets, we also evaluated the models on the corresponding balanced test sets, as shown in Figure 7. As in long-tail scenarios, CMGFuzz continues to perform best across all test sets, and the test data it generates is also more difficult to predict. The data generated by different methods cover varying distributions, depending on their generation strategies. All of this data could potentially serve as input in real-world deployment, and the data generated by CMGFuzz covers the widest distribution.

Answer to RQ3: Compared to all four baselines, CMGFuzz can generate test cases with diverse distributions, which can identify more unseen data for further model enhancement.

4.5 Experimental Results for Ablation Study (RQ4)

To evaluate the effectiveness of the clustering strategy and the data cleaning mechanism of CMGFuzz, we consider two variants of CMGFuzz (i.e., "w/o Clu" not using the clustering strategy, and "w/o DC" not adopting the data cleaning mechanism) and evaluate their test performance on the OF17 dataset using the same settings as **RQ1–RQ3**.

Table 4. Ablation study results of CMGFuzz variants.

Configuration	Coverage (%)				Found Errors				Repair (%)			
	NBC	SNAC	KMNC	TKNC	Few	Medium	Many	Total	Few	Medium	Many	Overall
CMGFuzz	**100.0**	78.6	86.6	**10.2**	483	**87**	1	571	**80.0**	96.0	**100.0**	**87.1**
w/o Clu	**100.0**	74.0	85.8	9.3	484	42	0	526	71.0	**100.0**	**100.0**	82.9
w/o DC	**100.0**	**80.6**	**88.6**	10.2	**512**	77	**4**	**593**	77.0	98.0	**100.0**	85.9

Table 4 summarizes the coverage, error detection, and repair performance. Compared to variant "w/o Clu", CMGFuzz achieves higher coverage, confirming that the clustering strategy improves feature extraction and diversity. The variant "w/o DC" achieves the highest raw coverage by retaining all generated samples, since the data cleaning mechanism filters out data that are less valuable or even invalid for model repair. Similarly, CMGFuzz detects more errors than the variant "w/o Clu" but fewer than the variant "w/o DC". However, CMGFuzz achieves the highest classification accuracy, especially in few-shot classes. These results suggest that the clustering strategy and the data cleaning mechanism facilitate the extraction of task-relevant features and the generation of more valid data for classes with few samples, thereby benefiting model repair.

Answer to RQ4: Our proposed clustering strategy and data cleaning mechanism can improve test performance, especially for few-shot classes.

5 Threats to Validity

Diffusion models introduce a level of randomness during the image generation process, which can affect the consistency and reproducibility of the generated images. This randomness is a double-edged sword; it allows for the generation of diverse images from textual descriptions but can also lead to variability in the quality and characteristics of the output. The selection of datasets plays a crucial role in determining the CMGFuzz's capability to generate diverse and realistic images. An unrepresentative or biased training dataset can impart similar biases to the evaluation of the generated images. The choice of image classification models for evaluation significantly influences the interpretation of test results. Different models have varying capacities to handle noise, artifacts, and image quality variations, which are prevalent in images generated by diffusion models.

6 Related Work

To assess DNN reliability, many DNN testing methods have been proposed. They generate diverse test cases and fall into two categories: coverage-guided and distribution-aware methods.

Coverage-Guided DNN Testing. Coverage-guided DNN testing extends traditional software testing criteria to neural networks by defining neuron-level and path-level coverage metrics [18,25,32,33]. These approaches guide test generation toward maximizing structural activation coverage. However, they rely solely on low-level mutation strategies (e.g., rotation, flipping) and do not model the input data distribution, which may lead to unrealistic or low-quality test inputs.

Distribution-Aware DNN Testing. Distribution-aware methods attempt to leverage the distribution of training data to generate more valid data to achieve more effective DNN testing. Mainstream distribution-aware methods assume that valid test cases must follow the distribution of the training data. Based on this assumption, they focus on generating in-distribution data. For example, Dola et al. [10] adopt Variational Autoencoders (VAEs) to generate in-distribution data. BIM [17] and PGD [20] adopt adversarial generative technologies to generate in-distribution test cases. However, due to a lack of knowledge about valid out-of-distribution (OOD) data, none of the aforementioned methods can effectively address scenarios involving low-quality training data resulting from limited data-collection capabilities. The most recent work, *DistXplore*, attempts to generate OOD data by transforming the data to follow a specific distribution.

Although *DistXplore* can generate more diverse data compared to conventional test methods, its mutation strategy remains constrained by the distribution of the original training data. Consequently, when faced with scenarios with low-quality training data, the diversity of the data generated by *DistXplore* remains severely limited.

7 Conclusion

Due to low-quality training data stemming from limited data-collection capabilities, existing DNN test methods suffer from inadequate testing. To address this problem, this paper presents a novel cross-modal generation-based fuzz testing approach, named *CMGFuzz*. Using knowledge learned from AIGC models, *CMGFuzz* can generate more valid test cases based on real-world data. To guarantee the diversity of generated test cases, *CMGFuzz* first converts training data into an abstract modality and then uses the converted data for the generation of test cases. Experimental results show the superiority of *CMGFuzz* in DNN testing.

Acknowledgments. This research is supported by the Natural Science Foundation of China (62272170). All data and source code are available on our website [2].

References

1. Stable diffusion v2 (2024). https://huggingface.co/stabilityai/stable-diffusion-2
2. CMGFuzz (2025). https://sites.google.com/view/cmgfuzz
3. Berend, D., et al.: Cats are not fish: deep learning testing calls for out-of-distribution awareness. In: Proceedings of International Conference on Automated Software Engineering (ASE), pp. 1041–1052 (2020)
4. Bossard, L., Guillaumin, M., Van Gool, L.: Food-101 – mining discriminative components with random forests. In: Proceedings of European Conference on Computer Vision (ECCV), pp. 446–461 (2014)
5. Cao, Y., et al.: A comprehensive survey of AI-generated content (AIGC): a history of generative AI from GAN to ChatGPT. arXiv preprint arXiv:2303.04226 (2023)
6. Chowdhary, K.R.: Natural language processing. Fundam. Artif. Intell. 603–649 (2020)
7. Coates, A., Ng, A., Lee, H.: An analysis of single-layer networks in unsupervised feature learning. In: Gordon, G., Dunson, D., Dudík, M. (eds.) Proceedings of the Fourteenth International Conference on Artificial Intelligence and Statistics. Proceedings of Machine Learning Research, vol. 15, pp. 215–223. PMLR, Fort Lauderdale (2011). https://proceedings.mlr.press/v15/coates11a.html
8. Cui, Y., et al.: Deep learning for image and point cloud fusion in autonomous driving: a review. IEEE Trans. Intell. Transp. Syst. (TITS) **23**(2), 722–739 (2021)
9. Deng, J., Dong, W., Socher, R., Li, L.J., Li, K., Fei-Fei, L.: ImageNet: a large-scale hierarchical image database. In: Proceedigns of IEEE Conference on Computer Vision and Pattern Recognition (CVPR), pp. 248–255 (2009)

10. Dola, S., Dwyer, M.B., Soffa, M.L.: Distribution-aware testing of neural networks using generative models. In: Proceedings of International Conference on Software Engineering (ICSE), pp. 226–237 (2021)
11. Gal, R., et al.: An image is worth one word: personalizing text-to-image generation using textual inversion (2022). https://arxiv.org/abs/2208.01618
12. Gao, X., Saha, R.K., Prasad, M.R., Roychoudhury, A.: Fuzz testing based data augmentation to improve robustness of deep neural networks. In: Proceedings of International Conference on Software Engineering (ICSE), pp. 1147–1158 (2020)
13. He, K., Zhang, X., Ren, S., Sun, J.: Deep residual learning for image recognition. In: Proceedings of IEEE Conference on Computer Vision and Pattern Recognition (CVPR), pp. 770–778 (2016)
14. Huang, W., Zhao, X., Banks, A., Cox, V., Huang, X.: Hierarchical distribution-aware testing of deep learning. ACM Trans. Softw. Eng. Methodo. (TOSEM) **33**(2), 1–35 (2023)
15. Krishna, K., Murty, M.N.: Genetic k-means algorithm. IEEE Trans. Syst. Man Cybern. Part B **29**(3), 433–439 (1999)
16. Krizhevsky, A., Sutskever, I., Hinton, G.E.: ImageNet classification with deep convolutional neural networks. Commun. ACM **60**(6), 84–90 (2017). https://doi.org/10.1145/3065386
17. Kurakin, A., Goodfellow, I.J., Bengio, S.: Adversarial examples in the physical world. In: Artificial Intelligence Safety and Security, pp. 99–112. Chapman and Hall/CRC (2018)
18. Ma, L., et al.: DeepGauge: multi-granularity testing criteria for deep learning systems. In: Proceedings of International Conference on Automated Software Engineering (ASE), pp. 120–131 (2018)
19. van der Maaten, L., Hinton, G.: Visualizing data using t-SNE. J. Mach. Learn. Res. (JMLR) **9**(86), 2579–2605 (2008)
20. Madry, A., Makelov, A., Schmidt, L., Tsipras, D., Vladu, A.: Towards deep learning models resistant to adversarial attacks (2017). https://arxiv.org/abs/1706.06083
21. Miotto, R., Wang, F., Wang, S., Jiang, X., Dudley, J.T.: Deep learning for healthcare: review, opportunities and challenges. Brief. Bioinform. **19**(6), 1236–1246 (2018)
22. Money, A., Affleck-Graves, J.F., Hart, M., Barr, G.D.I.: The linear regression model: LP norm estimation and the choice of p. Commun. Stat.-Simul. Comput. **11**(1), 89–109 (1982)
23. Nilsback, M.E., Zisserman, A.: A visual vocabulary for flower classification. In: Proceedigns of IEEE Conference on Computer Vision and Pattern Recognition (CVPR), pp. 1447–1454 (2006)
24. Paszke, A., et al.: Pytorch: An imperative style, high-performance deep learning library. In: Proceedings of Advances in Neural Information Processing Systems (NeurIPS), pp. 8024–8035 (2019)
25. Pei, K., Cao, Y., Yang, J., Jana, S.: DeepXplore: automated whitebox testing of deep learning systems. In: Proceedings of the 26th Symposium on Operating Systems Principles (SOSP), pp. 1–18 (2017)
26. Rauber, J., Brendel, W., Bethge, M.: FoolBox: a python toolbox to benchmark the robustness of machine learning models. In: Reliable Machine Learning in the Wild Workshop, 34th International Conference on Machine Learning (2017). http://arxiv.org/abs/1707.04131
27. Rombach, R., Blattmann, A., Lorenz, D., Esser, P., Ommer, B.: High-resolution image synthesis with latent diffusion models. In: Proceedings of the IEEE/CVF

Conference on Computer Vision and Pattern Recognition (CVPR), pp. 10684–10695 (2022)
28. Sandler, M., Howard, A., Zhu, M., Zhmoginov, A., Chen, L.C.: MobileNetv2: inverted residuals and linear bottlenecks (2019). https://arxiv.org/abs/1801.04381
29. Szegedy, C., Vanhoucke, V., Ioffe, S., Shlens, J., Wojna, Z.: Rethinking the inception architecture for computer vision (2015). https://arxiv.org/abs/1512.00567
30. Tian, Y., Pei, K., Jana, S., Ray, B.: DeepTest: automated testing of deep-neural-network-driven autonomous cars. In: Proceedings of International Conference on Software Engineering (ICSE), pp. 303–314 (2018)
31. Wang, L., et al.: DistXplore: distribution-guided testing for evaluating and enhancing deep learning systems. In: Proceedings of ACM Joint European Software Engineering Conference and Symposium on the Foundations of Software Engineering (FSE), pp. 68–80 (2023)
32. Xie, X., et al.: NPC: neuron path coverage via characterizing decision logic of deep neural networks. ACM Trans. Softw. Eng. Methodol. (TOSEM) **31**(3), 1–27 (2022)
33. Xie, X., et al.: DeepHunter: a coverage-guided fuzz testing framework for deep neural networks. In: Proceedings of International Symposium on Software Testing and Analysis (ISSTA), pp. 146–157 (2019)
34. Yang, Z., Shi, J., Asyrofi, M.H., Lo, D.: Revisiting neuron coverage metrics and quality of deep neural networks. In: Proceedings of International Conference on Software Analysis, Evolution and Reengineering (SANER), pp. 408–419 (2022)

A Formal Quantitative Approach for Evaluating Safety-Critical Driving Scenarios via Statistical Model Checking

Xinyu Liang and Qin Li(✉)

Software Engineering Institute, East China Normal University, Shanghai, China
qli@sei.ecnu.edu.cn

Abstract. Safety-critical scenarios are fundamental to the safety validation of Autonomous Driving Systems (ADS). Common approaches for identifying such high-value scenarios involve manual expert assessment or post-simulation analysis, which respectively suffer from human subjectivity and prohibitive computational overhead. To address this, we propose a formal framework for evaluating the risk level of a driving scenario via statistical model checking (SMC). The framework contains: (1) an automated conversion module that transforms a scenario subject to OpenSCENARIO standard into a probabilistic Timed Automata model; (2) a SMC module that verifies the formal model with a TTC-based quantitative metrics aligned with ISO 34502 standard and assigns the scenario a score to indicate its safety criticality. This framework provides an end-to-end objective evaluation approach for assessing safety criticality of driving scenarios, thereby improving efficiency. Experiments successfully scored 20 nondeterministic scenarios that are hard for humans to assess and achieved a 45- to 50-fold speedup compared to post-simulation evaluation, further saving labor and enabling rigorous automated safety scoring and scenario prioritization.

Keywords: Autonomous Driving · Scenario Criticality Assessment · OpenSCENARIO · UPPAAL-SMC

1 Introduction

Safety verification of autonomous driving technology is a critical bottleneck for its industrial deployment [15]. Rigorous validation requires a wide range of diverse traffic scenarios to assess the system's decision-making and execution capabilities in complex environments [11]. Simulation-based testing has therefore become an indispensable pillar of ADS development, effectively overcoming the prohibitive costs and extremely limited scenario coverage of real-world road testing [23]. To address the lack of unified scenario description standards, the OpenSCENARIO [22] standard was formally released by ASAM in 2020. It has gained significant industrial traction and enabled efficient virtual simulation across platforms. Despite its advantages, ensuring the safety of an autonomous

G. De Giacomo et al. (Eds.): TASE 2026, LNCS 16697, pp. 243–260, 2027.
https://doi.org/10.1007/978-3-032-30693-7_16

driving system within a single scenario still requires massive simulation testing, which consumes enormous computational resources. Therefore, mining high-value scenarios, which are those with higher risk levels that are more likely to expose system defects and thus warrant prioritized testing [27], has emerged as a critical challenge in current autonomous driving validation.

Current validation workflows are increasingly hindered by the prohibitive human effort required for scenario construction and risk evaluation. Manual risk assessment by safety experts is inherently labor-intensive, subjective, and error-prone [16], with even simple maneuvers requiring substantial domain expertise and suffering from inconsistent scoring criteria [5]. Existing automated approaches rely on fixed thresholds and deterministic equations that often fail to capture the complex, context-dependent nature of driving risks [19,21]. These methods typically provide only binary (safe/unsafe) or coarse-grained classifications without probabilistic understanding, resulting in redundant testing of nominal behaviors while failing to provide exhaustive guarantees against edge-case failures [9].

To overcome the subjectivity and inconsistency of manual scenario classification, as well as its inherent limitations when dealing with non-deterministic scenarios, while simultaneously reducing the substantial time and computational overhead of purely simulation-based methods, this work proposes a rigorous, interpretable criticality assessment framework grounded in formal verification and established automotive safety standards. Model checking offers a rigorous alternative by abstracting systems into finite-state machines and exhaustively exploring the state space [26,28]. In this work, we employ UPPAAL [3], which utilizes Timed Automata (TA) to model real-time processes and enables formal verification of properties expressed in Timed Computation Tree Logic (TCTL) [18]. Beyond qualitative "yes/no" safety assertions, the UPPAAL-SMC (Statistical Model Checking) [4] extension allows for quantitative evaluation of safety degrees, providing probabilistic insights into system performance under uncertainty. Our scoring criteria are derived from ISO 34502 [14], adopting a three-tier taxonomy (Safe, Critical, Collision) as inspired by its Annex E and mapping it to quantitative metrics including collision probability, danger probability, and risk coefficient.

The primary objective of this research is to bridge the gap between scenario descriptions in OpenSCENARIO and formal safety verification by providing an objective, quantifiable, and repeatable criticality assessment framework based on model checking. The main contributions of this paper are as follows:

- We propose a formal criticality assessment framework that objectively evaluates OpenSCENARIO files by combining formal model verification with statistical analysis. Central to this is an automated transformation strategy that systematically maps OpenSCENARIO semantics to formal Timed Automata. To the best of our knowledge, this is the first automated formal conversion of the OpenSCENARIO standard, enabling formal verification of

safety-critical properties. This framework mitigates the subjectivity of manual expert evaluations and substantially reduces the computational demands of post-simulation assessments.
- We extended the verification framework to include Statistical Model Checking (SMC) for the quantitative evaluation of autonomous driving scenarios. Unlike traditional qualitative assertions, this module computes a probabilistic "Risk Coefficient" under uncertain environments, enabling a granular and numerical analysis of system risks. This approach provides comparable risk scores that allow for direct comparison across different scenarios, establishing a rigorous standard for safety grading beyond simple binary results.
- Experimental evaluation across 20 critical scenarios demonstrates the framework's efficiency and utility. This framework enables automated and objective safety evaluations of non-deterministic scenarios that are challenging for manual assessments. Crucially, compared to high-fidelity simulators (e.g., esmini with Monte Carlo methods), our method achieves a 45- to 50-fold speedup in coverage efficiency. This high-throughput solution provides a robust and efficient means for automated safety scoring and scenario prioritization in ADS development.

2 Related Work

The validation of Autonomous Driving Systems (ADS) has shifted from functional testing to scenario-based evaluation. This section situates our work within the evolving landscape of simulation, criticality analysis, and formal verification.

High-fidelity simulators like CARLA [8] and LGSVL [24] predominantly focus on deterministic execution of specific trajectories. However, as highlighted in the comprehensive survey by Riedmaier et al. [23], a "scenario" is fundamentally a non-deterministic parameter space rather than a single simulation run. Traditional "point-based" testing fails to capture the risks inherent in environmental uncertainties. Our work treats the non-deterministic scenario itself as the research object, abstracting physical complexity into timed automata to evaluate the entire uncertain space.

Identifying "high-value" scenarios—those most likely to expose safety defects—is a central theme in recent research. CCTest [16,17] utilizes scenario decomposition to uncover autopilot defects, while S-TaLiRo [2] and Breach [7] employ falsification methods based on Signal Temporal Logic (STL) to find counter-examples. Furthermore, reinforcement learning-based approaches [9] and LLM-driven generation (e.g., TARGET [5]) have been used to explore the scenario space. However, these methods primarily focus on failure discovery; they search for individual critical points but lack the exhaustive coverage required to classify the safety boundaries of an entire non-deterministic range.

Formal methods offer mathematical guarantees that simulation cannot provide. Responsibility-Sensitive Safety (RSS) [25] defines a logic-based safety envelope, but it is often hard to integrate with dynamic maneuver standards. While CommonUppRoad [10] bridges CommonRoad [1] and UPPAAL, its capability is restricted to binary safety judgments (safe vs. unsafe) and it lacks native support for industry-standard OpenSCENARIO. Our framework distinguishes itself by providing a direct, semantic-preserving mapping from OpenSCENARIO to UPPAAL NTA. By Statistical Model Checking, we significantly reduce the subjectivity and time costs associated with manual expert evaluation in uncertain environments.

3 Preliminaries

3.1 OpenSCENARIO Standard

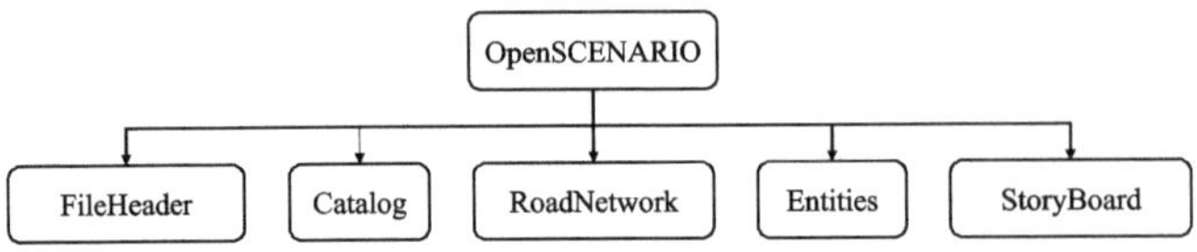

Fig. 1. The overall framework of OpenSCENARIO

OpenSCENARIO employs a hierarchical architecture (Fig. 1) where RoadNetwork establishes geometry via external files (e.g., OpenDRIVE) and Entities define dynamic participants. As the industry standard (ASAM v1.0), it is extensively supported by simulators such as VTD [20] and CARLA.

Building upon this static foundation, the Storyboard governs the dynamic execution of the scenario through a nested hierarchy (Story → Act → ManeuverGroup → Maneuver → Event → Action). Each Storyboard element follows a deterministic lifecycle; as depicted in Fig. 2, elements transition from **Standby** (initial idle state awaiting activation) to **Running** (active execution phase where actions or sub-elements are performed) and **Complete** (terminal state indicating successful fulfillment of conditions) based on specific triggers, such as start conditions (e.g., temporal or spatial events) or stop/end conditions that lead to premature termination (e.g., via skip or abort).

3.2 UPPAAL

UPPAAL is an integrated tool environment for modeling, simulation, and verification of real-time systems as Networks of Timed Automata (NTA), whose formal definitions and semantics are detailed in the tutorial by Behrmann et al. [3]. By leveraging symbolic reachability analysis and state-space reduction, UPPAAL mitigates the 'state-space explosion' problem, making it effective for evaluating the safety-criticality of autonomous driving scenarios. UPPAAL verifies system properties expressed in Timed Computation Tree Logic (TCTL). The state-space is explored to satisfy formulas defined by the following Backus-Naur Form (BNF):

$$\varphi ::= p \mid \neg\varphi \mid \varphi_1 \vee \varphi_2 \mid \forall\Box\varphi \mid \forall\Diamond\varphi \mid \exists\Box\varphi \mid \exists\Diamond\varphi \mid \varphi_1 \longrightarrow \varphi_2$$

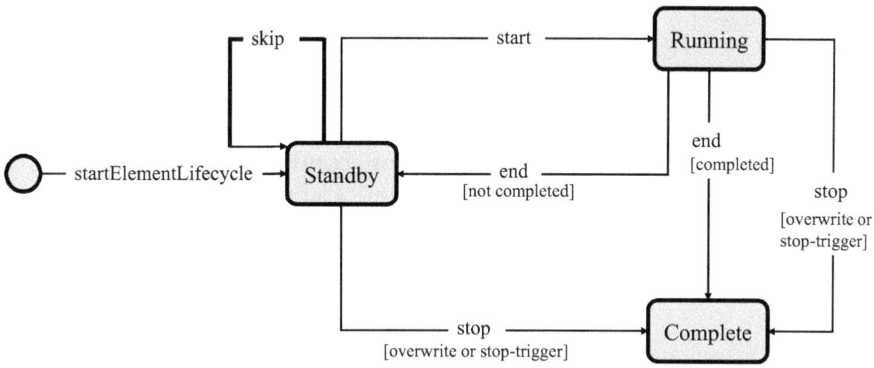

Fig. 2. State Machine for a runtime instantiation of a StoryboardElement

TCTL distinguishes between state formulas, which describe properties of individual states, and path formulas, which quantify the execution paths of the model.

Complementing standard verification, UPPAAL-SMC [4] enables quantitative safety analysis by replacing exhaustive state-space exploration with statistical estimation based on simulations. This extension allows for evaluating the probability that a property φ is satisfied within a time bound T:

$$Pr[\leq T](\Diamond\varphi)$$

Furthermore, it can estimate the expected value of a specific expression (e.g., risk coefficient) over N simulation runs:

$$E[\leq T; N](\text{max: expr})$$

Given the stochastic nature of autonomous driving, which is manifested in non-deterministic scenarios that defy evaluation by human experts, SMC provides a necessary mechanism to compute granular safety degrees rather than binary "safe/unsafe" assertions.

4 Methodology

We define the transformation from OpenSCENARIO to UPPAAL as a semantic-preserving mapping function $\Phi : \mathcal{S}_{osc} \to \overline{TA}$. This function is designed to translate hierarchical scenario instances into a verifiable Network of Timed Automata (NTA), ensuring that the execution logic and temporal constraints of the original scenario are precisely reflected in the formal model.

4.1 Transformation Architecture

As illustrated in Fig. 3, the framework operates between two distinct domains: the syntactic domain of OpenSCENARIO ($\mathcal{S}_{osc}$) and the semantic domain of

UPPAAL (targeting $\overline{TA}$). We formally abstract an OpenSCENARIO instance as a tuple $M_{osc} = \langle \mathcal{L}, \mathcal{T}, \mathcal{E} \rangle$, where:

- $\mathcal{L}$(Logic Hierarchy): Represents the **Storyboard**, a hierarchical logic tree governing the scenario lifecycle (Story → Act → Maneuver → Event).
- $\mathcal{T}$(Triggers): Denotes the set of **activation conditions** (e.g., spatial proximity or relative velocities) that initiate state transitions.
- $\mathcal{E}$: Represents the set of **Participants** (e.g., vehicles) and their associated **state variables** (e.g., position, speed) that are updated during the execution of actions.

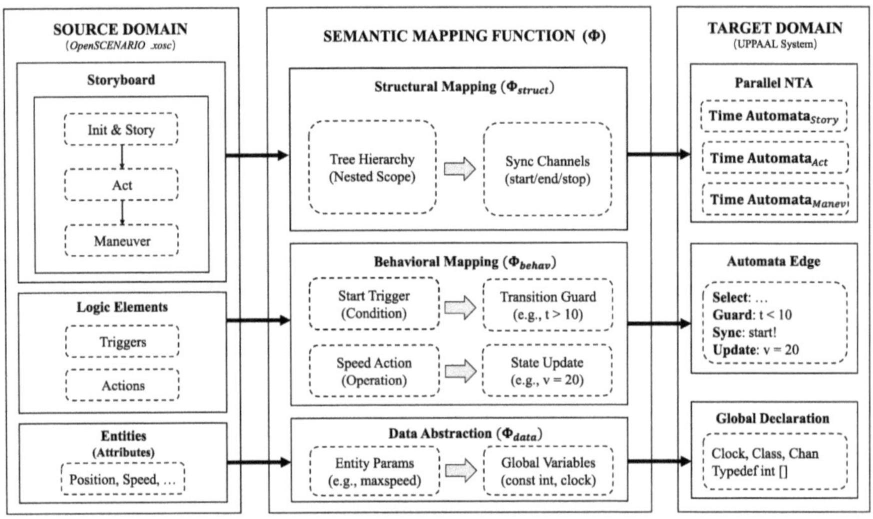

Fig. 3. The proposed formal transformation framework. The function Φ maps the hierarchical OpenSCENARIO syntax ($\mathcal{S}_{osc}$) into a parallel Network of Timed Automata ($\overline{TA}$) through structural, behavioral, and data mappings.

To resolve the impedance mismatch between the nested structure of XML and the flat, parallel nature of NTA, we decompose the mapping function Φ into three specialized sub-functions:

$$\Phi(M_{osc}) = \Phi_{struct}(\mathcal{L}) \parallel \Phi_{behav}(\mathcal{T}) \parallel \Phi_{data}(\mathcal{E})$$

- Φ_{struct} (Structural Mapping): Addresses the impedance mismatch between the nested XML tree and the flat parallel NTA. It flattens the **Storyboard** into a set of collaborating automaton templates, utilizing synchronization channels to simulate parent-child lifecycle management.
- Φ_{behav} (Behavioral Mapping): Converts **Triggers** into transition guards and synchronization signals, ensuring that the system state switches at the precise logical moment.

- Φ_{data} (Data Mapping): Maps **entities** and their **physical attributes** into global variables or bounded intervals ($int[min, max]$), facilitating symbolic exploration of the non-deterministic parameter space during verification.

The result of the transformation is a network of timed automata $\overline{TA} = TA_1 \parallel TA_2 \parallel \cdots \parallel TA_n$. The validity of this framework hinges on semantic preservation, ensuring that the execution logic defined in M_{osc} is captured within the state space of TA. By abstracting the scenario into this formal representation, we can leverage TCTL to exhaustively verify safety properties and liveness properties.

4.2 Hierarchical Structural and Behavior Mapping

The OpenSCENARIO standard defines scenario execution through a strictly nested hierarchy (Storyboard → Story → Act → ManeuverGroup → Maneuver → Event →Action). However, UPPAAL NTA operates on a flat network of parallel automata. To address this structural mismatch, we employ a 'Decouple and Synchronize' strategy that maps each hierarchical element in OpenSCENARIO to corresponding UPPAAL constructs, ensuring one-to-one correspondence in structure, behavior, and synchronization mechanisms.

In the subsequent automata models, we adhere to the UPPAAL synchronization semantics. A transition label suffixed with '!' (e.g., `start!`) indicates a signal emission, serving as a command or trigger, while a label suffixed with '?' (e.g., `start?`) indicates signal reception, representing a passive reaction or conditional wait.

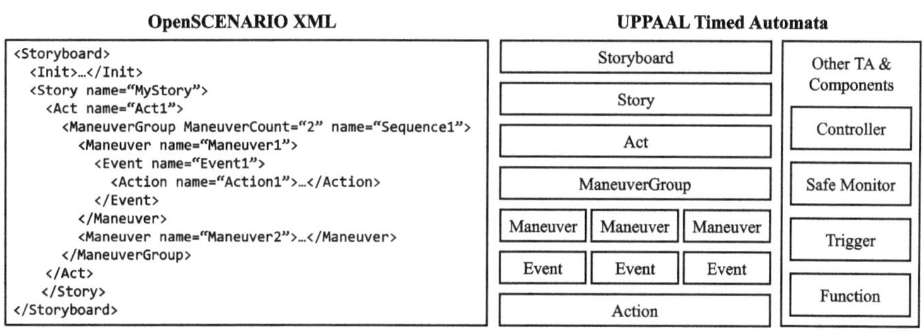

Fig. 4. Structural correspondence mapping the hierarchical OpenSCENARIO XML schema to a parallel network of UPPAAL Timed Automata.

Structural Mapping. Every logical node in the OpenSCENARIO nested XML hierarchy is mapped to a collaborative automaton template. As illustrated in Fig. 4, the hierarchical schema, ranging from the top-level `<Storyboard>` down to the lowest `<Action>`, corresponds strictly to a parallel composition of specific UPPAAL automata.

To demonstrate this structural mapping, the ManeuverGroup automaton acts as a dispatcher managing child structures (shown in Fig. 5). In OpenSCENARIO, a ManeuverGroup orchestrates multiple maneuvers. Correspondingly, in our UPPAAL framework, it resides in the *Standby* state until it receives a `startManeuverGroup?` signal from its parent Act. Upon activation, it transitions to *Running* and immediately broadcasts `startManeuver!` to activate its child nodes. It uses a **ManeuverCount** variable to manage the iterative execution of these child maneuvers. To ensure zero-time propagation, the activation and downward signaling pass through an atomic Committed Location (C), while the `stopTrigger?` channel enables immediate preemption from any state.

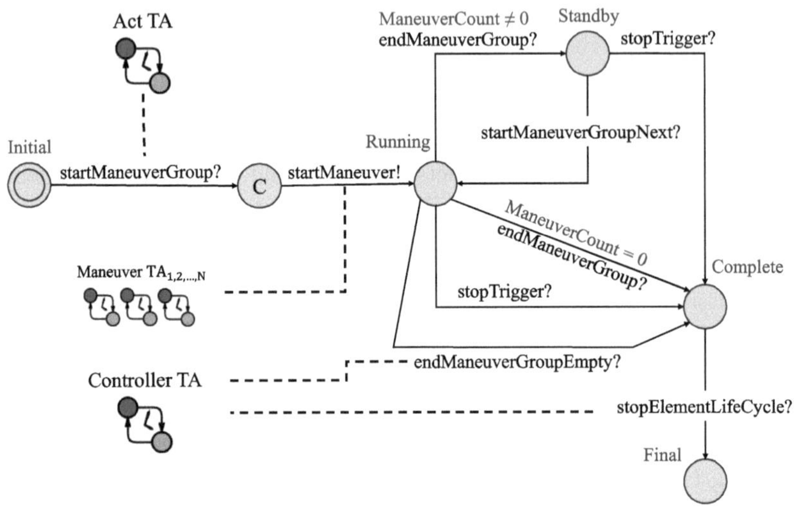

Fig. 5. Automaton Template for ManeuverGroup: A logical dispatcher managing child maneuver lifecycles via synchronization channels.

Behavior Mapping. While the structural mapping defines the skeleton, the behavioral mapping populates the specific kinematic and logical operations. Here, OpenSCENARIO `<Condition>` and `<Action>` elements are translated into UPPAAL transition guards and state updates. As depicted in Fig. 6, the Action automaton encapsulates specific maneuver logic. Initially, the system operates in a normal driving state by receiving the `keepRun?` signal after successfully passing condition and safety checks. The automaton actively evaluates the environment against the defined `<Condition>`. Once the condition is met, the `<StartTrigger>` forces a state transition via synchronization channels. For instance, it emits `startJudge!` to initiate safety evaluations with the Safe Monitor. The corresponding automaton then transitions from a *Standby* state to a *Running* state. Specific parameters defined in the OpenSCENARIO source code, such as a target speed factor defined within the `<SpeedAction>`, are mapped directly to variables within the globally defined vehicle entity structure rather than simple edge labels.

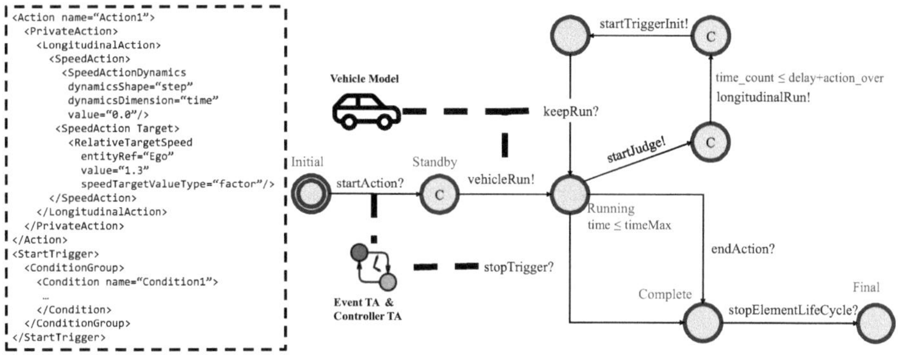

Fig. 6. Automaton Template for Action: A behavioral state machine mapping logical triggers to vehicle state updates.

To execute these mapped behaviors dynamically, the system operates within a closed-loop reactive architecture as illustrated in Fig. 7. The behavioral intent formalized in the Action TA does not exist in isolation. It directly interacts with the global Vehicle entity and the Safe Monitor. During execution, the vehicle updates its discrete physical states via a kinematic function. Simultaneously, the StartTrigger TA and Safe Monitor observe these states. When a trigger condition is met, a synchronization signal is broadcast to the Action TA. The Action TA then feeds specific operational commands back to the global vehicle structure. This feedback loop ensures that static behavioral mappings accurately translate into dynamic and verifiable discrete vehicle responses.

Synchronization Mechanisms. Since UPPAAL employs a flat parallel network of timed automata, preserving the original hierarchical execution order of OpenSCENARIO requires robust synchronization and strict state constraints. We address this through three complementary mechanisms:

- **Logical Atomicity:** To eliminate propagation delays in hierarchical signaling, we extensively exploit UPPAAL's committed locations. Transitions through these locations consume zero time, ensuring that a trigger issued at the top level (e.g., Storyboard) reaches the bottom-level Action instantaneously and thereby faithfully preserves the original timing semantics.
- **Guards and Invariants:** Behavioral execution is further constrained by transition guards (e.g., $v > 10$) and location invariants (e.g., $t \leq \text{timeMax}$). Guards act as enabling conditions that fire only when kinematic or logical prerequisites are satisfied, while invariants enforce strict upper time bounds, guaranteeing liveness and preventing states from lingering indefinitely.

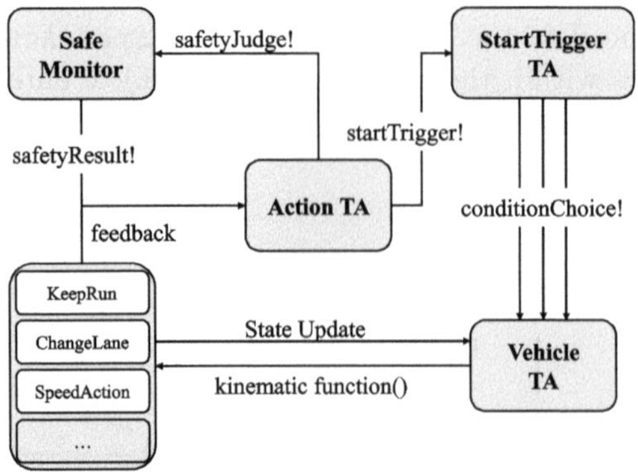

Fig. 7. The Closed-Loop Reactive Architecture: A synchronized feedback loop coordinating discrete vehicle state updates, safety monitoring, and action execution.

- **Global Controller:** For complex scenarios involving preemptive conditions (e.g., emergency stops), we introduce a dedicated Controller TA together with the Safe Monitor. The controller handles forced lifecycle termination via the `stopElementLifeCycle?` channel and purges stalled automata, eliminating deadlock risks and ensuring all liveness properties hold during verification.

4.3 Runtime Execution and Discrete Abstraction

While Sect. 4.2 established the structural and behavioral mappings (Φ_{struct} and Φ_{behav}), the runtime execution phase requires additional mechanisms to bridge the gap between the continuous physical dynamics of OpenSCENARIO scenarios and UPPAAL's discrete semantics. Therefore, in alignment with the data mapping strategy (Φ_{data}), we introduce integer-based time discretization together with symbolic range abstraction to ensure the verifiability of the resulting model.

Integer-Based Time Abstraction. Standard model checking algorithms struggle with non-linear differential equations. To render the verification decidable, we abstract the continuous kinematic evolution into discrete integer steps.

- **Time Discretization:** We define a global synchronization step Δt (mapped to the logical clock x_{clock}). The Vehicle Automaton executes a state update transition exactly when $x_{clock} == \Delta t$, ensuring synchronized evolution across all parallel components.
- **Integer Scaling Strategy:** Since UPPAAL restricts data variables to integers, we apply a global scaling factor K (e.g., $K = 100$) to all physical parameters. This integer-based abstraction introduces a quantization error when discretizing continuous kinematic equations. Given the scaling factor K, the maximum truncation error per discrete step Δt is strictly bounded by $\epsilon \leq \frac{1}{K}$. For example, with $K = 100$, the single-step deviation is limited

to 0.01 units, which remains negligible compared to standard safety margins (e.g., collision buffers $> 0.5\,\mathrm{m}$) in typical short-duration scenarios.

Symbolic Range Abstraction. Moving beyond point-based testing with fixed values, we introduce non-deterministic range abstraction for critical scenario variables. Parameters such as initial velocities and trigger positions are modeled using UPPAAL's bounded interval type (`int[min, max]`), comprehensively capturing the relative state space between vehicles. The resolution of this space is governed by the integer scaling factor K (e.g., yielding a $0.01\,\mathrm{m/s}$ granularity when $K = 100$). During statistical model checking, values from these intervals are sampled uniformly, guaranteeing an unbiased evaluation of the parameter space without relying on prior empirical distributions. Consequently, the model checker evaluates a continuous density of configurations, providing safety assessments across an entire range of conditions rather than isolated setups.

4.4 Verification Queries

We define some TCTL and Statistical Model Checking (SMC) queries as follows, that will be used in the experiments in Sect. 5. Before assessing safety, we must ensure the scenario logic is sound and executable. The following liveness properties verify that the simulation proceeds without deadlocks.

- φ_1 (Scenario Liveness): $\forall\Diamond Storyboard.Final$ This query ensures the scenario storyboard eventually reaches its final state.
- φ_2 (Maneuver Completeness): $\forall\Diamond Vehicle.Complete$This query ensures the vehicle eventually completes its assigned maneuver.

We define a Risk Coefficient (RC) based on ISO 34502 to quantify the risk level within non-deterministic scenarios. While the standard defines four levels, we adopt a three-tier classification: Safe, Critical, and Collision. The TTC thresholds are derived from established traffic conflict research: TTC $< 1.5\,\mathrm{s}$ is widely recognized as the critical conflict threshold requiring immediate driver action [13], while TTC $< 3\,\mathrm{s}$ serves as the warning-level threshold for urban scenarios [12,21]. We consolidate the 'Critical' and 'Hazardous' levels because both necessitate immediate active safety intervention, differing primarily in temporal urgency rather than the fundamental nature of the risk. We discretize the continuous state space into three distinct safety levels:

- Level 0 (Safe): $RC = 0$. The vehicle maintains a safe distance/TTC (Time-To-Collision) greater than the comfort threshold (TTC $\geq 3\,\mathrm{s}$). The system is in a nominal state.
- Level 1 (Critical/Warning): $RC = 1$. The vehicle breaches the safety threshold (TTC $< 3\,\mathrm{s}$) but no collision has occurred. This corresponds to the "Controllable Avoidance" phase in ISO standards, where emergency braking is required.

- Level 2 (Collision): $RC = 2$. Physical overlap occurs between entities. This represents the "Uncontrollable" hazardous event.

Based on this classification, we propose the following SMC queries to generate the final scenario score:

- φ_3 (Collision Probability): $\Pr[\leq T](\Diamond Vehicle.Collision)$ This query estimates the collision probability (RC = 2) within time T.
- φ_4 (Hazard Probability): $Pr[\leq T](\Diamond Vehicle.Danger)$ This query estimates the probability of entering the critical warning state ($RC = 1$).
- φ_5 (Maximal Risk Coefficient): $E[\leq T; N](\max : RiskCoefficient)$ This query calculates the expected maximum risk level reached during the scenario. The result is a value in the range $[0, 2]$. This metric serves as a unified "Risk Index", where a higher value directly indicates greater risk. It allows us to automatically rank scenarios from safe to extremely dangerous without manual labeling.

5 Experiment

The evaluation is conducted using simulation platform specification, e.g., esmini integrated with OpenSCENARIO. Our scenario library comprises 20 critical traffic situations selected from the ASAM OpenSCENARIO official catalog and extended with esmini. The subsequent analysis is structured as follows: Sect. 5.1 investigates the impact of behavioral dynamics and non-deterministic factors on scenario safety assessment. Building on this, Sect. 5.2 categorizes the full scenario library into risk tiers based on formal verification properties and evaluates computational overhead. This demonstrates that the proposed method not only accurately identifies risk categories but also achieves significant computational efficiency compared to traditional simulation platforms.

5.1 Case Study

Sensitivity to Behavioral Dynamics. This case study examines how post-maneuver velocity profiles affect safety outcomes within identical geometric configurations. We analyze two variants of a cut-in scenario (shown in Fig. 8).

Scenario A depicts Car A (red) merging from the left-adjacent lane into the ego vehicle's (blue) lane. After merging, Car A maintains its longitudinal velocity v_A. With the ego vehicle maintaining a slower cruising speed v_{ego} ($v_A > v_{ego}$), a natural safe gap is established.

Scenario B shares the identical initial merge trajectory. However, upon completing the lane change, Car A gradually decelerates to 0 m/s. This creates a dynamic "closing velocity", forcing the ego vehicle to compensate for both the initial gap reduction and an actively shrinking safety margin.

Based on the queries in Sect. 4.4, we can obtain the results presented in Table 1. In Scenario A, due to standardized lane-changing conditions and safe

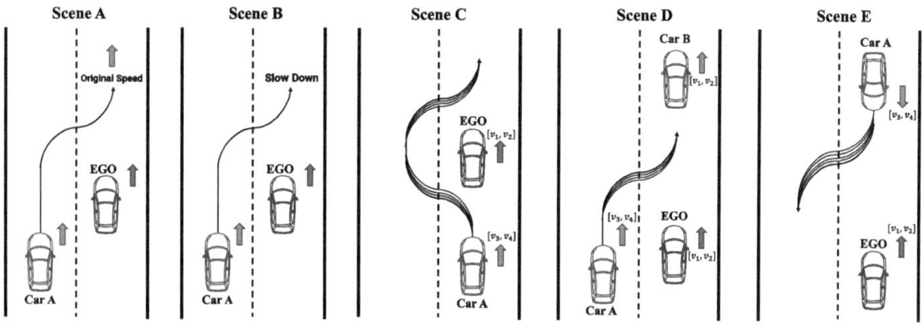

Fig. 8. Variants of the cut-in scenario (Scenes A, B) and representative interaction patterns (Scenes C, D, E). Car A and Car B denote environmental vehicles; EGO denotes the autonomous vehicle. Velocity ranges are indicated in brackets where applicable.

driving, the probability of collision and being in a dangerous situation is almost zero; whereas in Scenario B, emergency braking by the preceding vehicle will result in an average probability of 71% for collision, with a 75% probability of being in a dangerous state, and the corresponding risk coefficient is as high as 1.408. With 2000 simulation runs, unobserved events are reported with probability $\leq 0.37\%$ (95% confidence interval). Note that the liveness properties φ_1 and φ_2 hold for all scenarios in subsequent experiments and are therefore omitted from further tables.

Table 1. TCTL and SMC Results for Behavioral Dynamics Comparison

Queries	Scenario A (Constant Speed)	Scenario B (Deceleration)
φ_1	✓	✓
φ_2	✓	✓
φ_3	≤ 0.0037	0.71 ± 0.028
φ_4	≤ 0.0037	0.75 ± 0.027
φ_5	0	1.408 ± 0.057

This case study illustrates the substantial impact of dynamic behaviors on scenario safety. Furthermore, it demonstrates the strong applicability of our method to same-type scenarios with varying kinematic profiles, while offering precise probabilistic metrics and risk coefficients for accurate safety assessment.

Evaluation of Non-deterministic Scenarios. While Sect. 5.1 examined parametric variations within a single topology, introducing non-deterministic factors across distinct spatial configurations creates a level of complexity where human experts struggle to make accurate or intuitive risk assessments. To systematically quantify these intrinsic risk hierarchies, we analyze three canonical interaction patterns with increasing geometric complexity (shown in Fig. 8).

Scenario C (Overtake): Car A overtakes and returns to the ego vehicle's lane. This single-agent interaction primarily poses lateral proximity risks during the merge, after which Car A safely maintains its forward momentum.

Scenario D (Sandwich Cut-in): Car A merges between the ego and a lead vehicle (Car B). This multi-agent coupling forces the ego to simultaneously monitor Car A's potential deceleration and Car B's presence, severely limiting gap adjustment options.

Scenario E (Opposite-Direction Conflict): An oncoming vehicle (Car A) directly enters the ego's path. This "head-on" scenario presents severe asymmetric risk due to high relative velocity ($v_{rel} = v_A + v_{ego}$) and critically constrained lateral escape routes.

We verify properties capturing both collision probability and severity, which shown in Table 2. The results establish a risk hierarchy: Scenario C $\approx$ Scenario D $<$ Scenario E. In Scenario E, due to the oncoming vehicle significantly reducing the distance for collision, the average probability of collision occurring in this scenario is 86%, with a probability of being in danger being 93%, and the risk coefficient reaching 1.81.

Table 2. SMC Results for Three Non-Deterministic Scenarios

Queries	Scenario C	Scenario D	Scenario E
φ_3	≤ 0.0037	≤ 0.0037	0.86 ± 0.022
φ_4	0.19 ± 0.025	0.21 ± 0.025	0.93 ± 0.017
φ_5	0.215 ± 0.026	0.223 ± 0.026	1.81 ± 0.032

Owing to speed uncertainty, each scenario spans a range of possible trajectories rather than fixed paths. This complexity renders direct risk comparison by human experts particularly difficult. In particular, dangerous conditions in Scenario C caused by excessive overtaking speeds are frequently overlooked. These findings highlight the distinct advantage of our framework in providing systematic and quantitative evaluation for non-deterministic scenarios that defy intuitive manual assessment.

5.2 Comprehensive Classification and Computational Analysis

Scenario Library Classification. Building upon the risk indicators identified in the preceding case studies, Table 3 presents representative scenarios together with their risk metrics. We categorize the entire scenario library into three risk-based **priority levels**: Low-Value, Middle-Value, and High-Value. Higher-value levels are assigned to scenarios with higher risk (i.e., greater probability of collision or danger), which are more likely to expose defects in autonomous driving systems, and thus warrant prioritized testing and validation.

1. Low-Value Scenarios: The probability of collision(φ_3) and the probability of being in danger(φ_4) are **both less than 0.4**.
2. Middle-Value Scenarios: The probability of collision(φ_3) is less than 0.4 and the probability of being in danger(φ_4) is greater than 0.4. Or the sum of the two is greater than 0.4.
3. High-Value Scenarios: The probability of collision(φ_3) and the probability of being in danger(φ_4) are **both greater than 0.4**.

Table 3. Representative Scenarios and Their Risk Priority Levels

Scenario Description	φ_3	φ_4	φ_5	Priority Level
cut-in constant	≤ 0.0037	≤ 0.0037	0	Low
cut-in sandwich	≤ 0.0037	0.21 ± 0.025	0.223 ± 0.026	Low
cut-in brake	0.71 ± 0.028	0.75 ± 0.027	1.408 ± 0.057	High
overtake constant	≤ 0.0037	0.19 ± 0.025	0.215 ± 0.026	Low
overtake adventure	≤ 0.0037	0.51 ± 0.031	0.513 ± 0.031	Middle
overtake head-on	0.86 ± 0.022	0.93 ± 0.017	1.81 ± 0.032	High
lane weaving car-free	≤ 0.0037	≤ 0.0037	0	Low
lane weaving in-out	0.23 ± 0.026	0.26 ± 0.027	0.413 ± 0.049	Middle

Computational Overhead Comparison. We compare the efficiency of UPPAAL statistical model checking against simulation platform (esmini [6]) with Monte Carlo method. We selected two high-value scenarios and one low-value scenarios from Table 3 as the targets for computational overhead comparison, each undergoing 100 simulation runs and 10 times UPPAAL model check. The results are shown in Table 4.

Table 4. Computational Efficiency Comparison: esmini Monte Carlo Simulation vs. UPPAAL-SMC

Scenario	Method	Execution Time	Iterations	Collision prob.
overtake constant	esmini	1423 s	100	0/100
	UPPAAL	30.2 s	10	0.37%
cut-in brake	esmini	1373 s	100	52/100
	UPPAAL	27.8 s	10	71.2%
overtake head-on	esmini	983 s	100	34/100
	UPPAAL	20.5 s	10	86.2%

The results in Table 4 highlight the significant efficiency and efficacy of our formal framework. While esmini requires 983 s to 1423 s per scenario, our approach completes the assessment in just 20.5 s to 30.2 s, achieving a 45- to 50-fold speedup. Crucially, our framework successfully identifies collision risks (e.g., in the "overtake head-on" scenario) that discrete simulations might under-report or miss. This proves that symbolic range exploration can rigorously confirm the existence of boundary violations and high-value corner cases, overcoming the limitations of computationally expensive simulations with substantially lower overhead.

6 Discussion

In this work, our framework targets multi-vehicle interactions in structured lane-based environments, covering representative maneuvers such as cut-ins, overtakes, and braking under non-deterministic kinematic variations. The current evaluation considers interactions involving up to three vehicles. This scope supports systematic risk assessment over well-defined traffic topologies and remains extensible to curved roads and intersections. By constraining abstraction errors through the scaling factor and update interval, numerical deviations remain at the inverse-scaling level, preserving consistent relative risk rankings.

Our SMC-based approach complements tools such as S-TaLiRo and Breach, which are commonly used for STL-based falsification and parameter synthesis to identify violating trajectories or critical parameter settings. In contrast, this work uses SMC as a scenario-level evaluation mechanism to estimate unified probabilistic risk metrics for criticality assessment and prioritization. A current limitation is scalability to high-density traffic, where the state space grows rapidly with additional participants. Future work will explore guided exploration techniques, such as reinforcement learning-driven SMC, that steer the model checker toward high-risk parameter combinations while maintaining computational tractability in high-dimensional scenarios without sacrificing quantitative rigor.

7 Conclusion

We propose a formal quantitative framework for evaluating safety-critical driving scenarios in Autonomous Driving Systems, addressing the subjectivity and labor costs of manual expert methods in nondeterministic settings, as well as the computational overhead of simulation-based approaches. Our method automatically transforms OpenSCENARIO descriptions into nondeterministic UPPAAL timed automata via semantic-preserving mappings, enabling statistical model checking for probabilistic risk assessment with objective metrics including collision probability, hazard probability, and ISO-derived Risk Coefficient. Experiments on 20 critical scenarios uncover hidden risks that humans struggle to assess, while delivering a 45- to 50-fold speedup over high-fidelity simulators like esmini. Future work will integrate this verification engine with autonomous driving algorithms to enforce real-time safety constraints and improve ADS decision-making reliability in complex environments.

Acknowledgment. This work was supported by the National Natural Science Foundation of China (NSFC) under Grant No. 92582203 and 62272165.

References

1. Althoff, M., Koschi, M., Manzinger, S.: CommonRoad: composable benchmarks for motion planning on roads. In: 2017 IEEE Intelligent Vehicles Symposium (IV), pp. 719–726. IEEE (2017)
2. Annpureddy, Y., Liu, C., Fainekos, G., Sankaranarayanan, S.: S-TaLiRo: a tool for temporal logic falsification for hybrid systems. In: Abdulla, P.A., Leino, K.R.M. (eds.) TACAS 2011. LNCS, vol. 6605, pp. 254–257. Springer, Heidelberg (2011). https://doi.org/10.1007/978-3-642-19835-9_21
3. Behrmann, G., David, A., Larsen, K.G.: A tutorial on UPPAAL. In:Formal Methods for the Design of Real-Time Systems, pp. 200–236 (2004)
4. David, A., Larsen, K.G., Legay, A., Mikučionis, M., Poulsen, D.B.: UPPAAL SMC tutorial. Int. J. Softw. Tools Technol. Transf. **17**(4), 397–415 (2015)
5. Deng, Y., Tu, Z., Yao, J., Zhang, M., Zhang, T., Zheng, X.: TARGET: Traffic rule-based test generation for autonomous driving systems. IEEE Trans. Software Eng. (2025)
6. esmini Developers: esmini: a basic openscenario player (2024). https://github.com/esmini/esmini. Accessed 02 Feb 2026
7. Donzé, A.: Breach, a toolbox for verification and parameter synthesis of hybrid systems. In: Touili, T., Cook, B., Jackson, P. (eds.) CAV 2010. LNCS, vol. 6174, pp. 167–170. Springer, Heidelberg (2010). https://doi.org/10.1007/978-3-642-14295-6_17
8. Dosovitskiy, A., Ros, G., Codevilla, F., Lopez, A., Koltun, V.: Carla: An open urban driving simulator. In: Conference on Robot Learning, pp. 1–16. PMLR (2017)
9. Feng, S., Yan, X., Sun, H., Feng, Y., Liu, H.X.: Intelligent driving intelligence test for autonomous vehicles with naturalistic and adversarial environment. Nat. Commun. **12**(1), 748 (2021)
10. Gu, R., Tan, K., Høeg-Petersen, A.H., Feng, L., Larsen, K.G.: CommonUppRoad: a framework of formal modelling, verifying, learning, and visualisation of autonomous vehicles. In: Margaria, T., Steffen, B. (eds.) ISoLA 2024. LNCS, vol. 15221, pp. 385–404. Springer, Cham (2024). https://doi.org/10.1007/978-3-031-75380-0_22
11. Guo, J., Kurup, U., Shah, M.: Is it safe to drive? An overview of factors, metrics, and datasets for driveability assessment in autonomous driving. IEEE Trans. Intell. Transp. Syst. **21**(8), 3135–3151 (2019)
12. Hirst, S., Graham, R.: The format and presentation of collision warnings. In: Ergonomics and Safety of Intelligent Driver Interfaces, pp. 203–219. CRC Press (2020)
13. van der Horst, A.R.A.: A time-based analysis of road user behaviour in normal and critical encounters. Ph.D. thesis, Delft University of Technology, Delft, The Netherlands (1990)
14. ISO: Road vehicles—test scenarios for automated driving systems—scenario based safety evaluation framework. Standard ISO 34502:2022, International Organization for Standardization, Geneva, Switzerland (2022)
15. Koopman, P., Wagner, M.: Challenges in autonomous vehicle testing and validation. SAE Int. J. Transp. Saf. **4**(1), 15–24 (2016)

16. Li, C., Sifakis, J., Yan, R., Zhang, J.: CCTest: critical configuration testing for autonomous driving systems. In: Proceedings of the 33rd ACM International Conference on the Foundations of Software Engineering, pp. 1203–1207 (2025)
17. Li, C., Sifakis, J., Yan, R., Zhang, J.: A comprehensive evaluation of four end-to-end ai autopilots using CCTest and the Carla leaderboard. arXiv preprint arXiv:2501.12090 (2025)
18. Lukács, G., Bartha, T.: Construction of formal models and verifying property specifications through an example of railway interlocking systems. Pollack Periodica **14**(2), 39–50 (2019)
19. Mahmud, S.S., Ferreira, L., Hoque, M.S., Tavassoli, A.: Application of proximal surrogate indicators for safety evaluation: a review of recent developments and research needs. IATSS Res. **41**(4), 153–163 (2017)
20. Menzel, T., Bagschik, G., Isensee, L., Schomburg, A., Maurer, M.: Detailing a keyword based scenario description for execution in a simulation environment using the example of scenarios on german highways. In: Workshop Fahrerassistenzsysteme und automatisiertes Fahren, vol. 12, pp. 15–26 (2018)
21. Minderhoud, M.M., Bovy, P.H.: Extended time-to-collision measures for road traffic safety assessment. Accid. Anal. Prevent. **33**(1), 89–97 (2001)
22. OpenSCENARIO, A.: Asam openscenario. Standardization Automat. Measuring Syst. (ASAM), Munich, Germany (2020)
23. Riedmaier, S., Ponn, T., Ludwig, D., Schick, B., Diermeyer, F.: Survey on scenario-based safety assessment of automated vehicles. IEEE Access **8**, 87456–87477 (2020)
24. Rong, G., et al.: LGSVL simulator: A high fidelity simulator for autonomous driving. In: 2020 IEEE 23rd International Conference on Intelligent Transportation Systems (ITSC), pp. 1–6. IEEE (2020)
25. Shalev-Shwartz, S., Shammah, S., Shashua, A.: On a formal model of safe and scalable self-driving cars. arXiv preprint arXiv:1708.06374 (2017)
26. Siron, F.: Methodology for the formal verification of temporal properties for real-time safety-critical applications based on logical time. Ph.D. thesis, Université Côte d'Azur (2023)
27. Song, Q., Tan, K., Runeson, P., Persson, S.: Critical scenario identification for realistic testing of autonomous driving systems. Software Qual. J. **31**(2), 441–469 (2023)
28. Strauss, M., Mitsch, S.: Slow down, move over: a case study in formal verification, refinement, and testing of the responsibility-sensitive safety model for self-driving cars. In: Prevosto, V., Seceleanu, C. (eds) TAP 2023. LNCS, vol. 14066, pp. 149–167. Springer, Cham (2023). https://doi.org/10.1007/978-3-031-38828-6_9

Semantics-Based Verification of an Implemented Shor Oracle for ECDLP in Qrisp

Lei Zhang(✉) and Zhiyuan Chen

Department of Information Systems, University of Maryland, Baltimore County, Catonsville, MD, USA
{leizhang,zhchen}@umbc.edu

Abstract. Shor-style quantum algorithms for the elliptic-curve discrete logarithm problem (ECDLP) are highly sensitive to the exact semantics of their group-operation oracles. Consequently, minor implementation choices can invalidate the intended mathematical model and lead to misleading conclusions. This paper introduces a semantics-first verification perspective for an end-to-end, compilable ECDLP implementation built on Qrisp. We specify the implemented oracle at the level of program semantics, derive refinement-style verification obligations for its key components, and provide a high-level complexity argument for the resulting oracle family. A small case study highlights that (i) the core point-update primitive agrees with a classical reference on well-formed inputs, yet (ii) controlled execution may violate the expected control law under the evaluated toolchain, despite a passing trivial control sanity check. These results position semantic auditing as a practical prerequisite for trustworthy ECDLP-oriented quantum software.

Keywords: elliptic-curve cryptography · Shor's algorithm · program semantics · quantum software engineering · quantum software verification

1 Introduction

Shor-style quantum algorithms threaten widely deployed public-key cryptosystems [1,16,17]. Quantum programming frameworks such as Qrisp [12] provide high-level abstractions and compilation infrastructure, including support for Shor-style implementations [10]. Compared to integer factorization, Shor-style approaches to the elliptic-curve discrete logarithm problem (ECDLP) are less mature in terms of end-to-end implementations and require more substantial oracle constructions for elliptic-curve group arithmetic [2–4].

This paper focuses on quantum software verification for Shor-style ECDLP implementations. Existing work has developed formal methods and program logics for quantum programs [5,14], including certified end-to-end verification of Shor's factoring algorithm [9]. However, ECDLP implementations often rely

G. De Giacomo et al. (Eds.): TASE 2026, LNCS 16697, pp. 261–268, 2027.
https://doi.org/10.1007/978-3-032-30693-7_17

on specialized group-arithmetic gadgets, encodings, and sign conventions, leaving a gap between the mathematical oracle specified in an algorithmic description and the oracle realized after decomposition, control construction, ancilla management, and compilation. This gap is critical because the ECDLP oracle determines the algebraic relation recovered from the final measurements.

We address this gap by treating the implemented ECDLP oracle as a program-semantic object rather than only as an abstract mathematical function. Testing alone is insufficient: small sign or representation mismatches can invalidate the intended model and yield misleading interference patterns [6–8]. Moreover, because large-scale fault-tolerant hardware capable of threatening modern RSA and ECC parameters is not yet available, current evaluation relies mainly on mathematical reasoning, formal analysis, and small-scale simulation.

We distinguish three layers of correctness: (i) the standalone point-update primitive, (ii) its mathematically controlled version, and (iii) the controlled operation generated by the programming framework and compiler. This distinction matters because a primitive may behave correctly in isolation, while its controlled realization may fail to satisfy the identity branch required by the standard control law. We study these layers in an end-to-end, compilable ECDLP implementation built on Qrisp [10], focusing on the semantic contracts for point update and controlled oracle construction. Our artifacts are available on Zenodo [15].

This paper makes three contributions. First, we specify the implemented oracle as a state transformer on computational basis states. Second, we state refinement obligations for the in-place point-update gadget and the controlled scalar-multiplication-and-add routine. Third, we give a structural complexity argument showing that the oracle family is polynomial under standard assumptions on reversible modular arithmetic.

2 Preliminaries and Formal Model

ECDLP and Shor-Style Oracles. Let p be a prime and let $E(\mathbb{F}_p)$ be an elliptic-curve group over $\mathbb{F}_p$. Let $G \in E(\mathbb{F}_p)$ generate a cyclic subgroup of order r, and let $P = \ell G$ for an unknown $\ell \in \mathbb{Z}_r$. A Shor-style ECDLP oracle uses two n-qubit quantum registers with computational-basis values $x_1, x_2 \in \mathbb{Z}_{2^n}$, which index scalar multiples of G and P. The oracle computes a group expression, such as $x_1G + x_2P$, into an accumulator point register before the inverse quantum Fourier transform [13] extracts a linear constraint. The exact oracle semantics matters: if the implementation realizes $x_1G + x_2P$ while the analysis assumes $x_1G - x_2P$, the induced relation and classical post-processing differ by a sign.

Points and Registers. Let $\mathcal{O}$ denote the identity of $E(\mathbb{F}_p)$. The accumulator encodes a point $R \in E(\mathbb{F}_p)$ using two modular registers for affine coordinates; in the case study (Sect. 4), $(0, 0)$ encodes $\mathcal{O}$. We write $|x_1\rangle|x_2\rangle|R\rangle$ for a computational basis state.

Implemented Oracle. Figure 1 summarizes the compiled oracle as two sequential scalar-multiplication-and-add updates of the accumulator, controlled bitwise by x_1 and x_2. Let $f_{\text{impl}}(x_1, x_2) = x_1 G \oplus x_2 P$ denote the point-valued function computed into the accumulator by the implementation. The implemented oracle is

$$\mathcal{O}_{\text{impl}} : |x_1\rangle|x_2\rangle|R\rangle \mapsto |x_1\rangle|x_2\rangle|R \oplus x_1 G \oplus x_2 P\rangle, \quad (1)$$

where $\oplus$ denotes the elliptic-curve group operation as realized by the implementation's point encoding. Substituting $P = \ell G$ gives $f_{\text{impl}}(x_1, x_2) = x_1 G \oplus x_2 P = (x_1 + \ell x_2)G$.

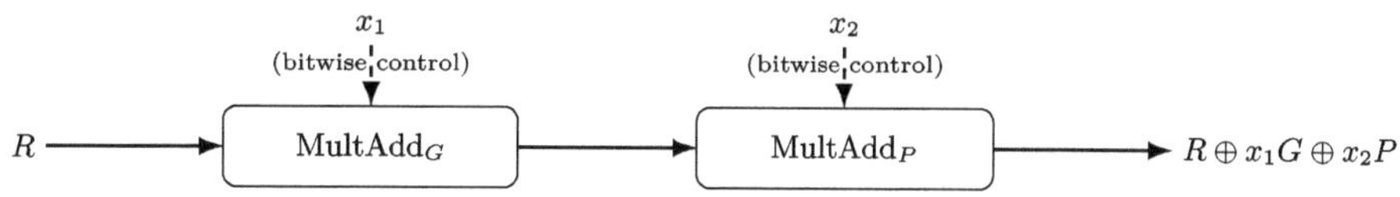

Fig. 1. Oracle composition in the implementation. The accumulator R is updated by two scalar-multiplication-and-add routines, controlled bitwise by x_1 and x_2, yielding $R \oplus x_1 G \oplus x_2 P$. Here $\oplus$ denotes the elliptic-curve group operation under the implementation's point encoding, not bitwise XOR.

Refinement Notion. Let C be a circuit acting on registers (x_1, x_2, R). We write $[\![C]\!]$ for its denotation on computational basis states. We say C *refines* $\mathcal{O}_{\text{impl}}$ (written $C \sqsubseteq \mathcal{O}_{\text{impl}}$) if, for all basis states $|x_1\rangle|x_2\rangle|R\rangle$ satisfying a well-formedness predicate $\mathsf{WF}(x_1, x_2, R)$, the action of C on the point register equals (1), and all ancillas are returned to their initial states.

Well-Formedness. We parameterize our specifications by a predicate WF that excludes exceptional inputs for the affine gadget, such as division by zero in slope computation, adding inverse points, or invalid intermediate encodings of $\mathcal{O}$. In this pilot study, WF is treated as an explicit precondition; handling exceptional cases is left to future work.

3 Semantic Verification Obligations and Complexity

This section states the refinement obligations induced by the implemented oracle and derives a structural bound on the oracle's circuit size. The obligations reflect the three-layer distinction introduced in Sect. 1: standalone primitive correctness, controlled-operation correctness, and correctness after framework-level generation and compilation.

3.1 In-Place Point Update (Correctness Obligation)

Let AddInpl_G denote the implementation's in-place point-update gadget for adding a fixed base point G over modulus p. Its intended behavior is

$$|R\rangle \mapsto |R \oplus G\rangle.$$

Here *in-place* means that the accumulator register storing R is overwritten with $R \oplus G$, up to ancillas that are uncomputed, rather than writing the result to a separate output register. The first verification obligation is a partial-correctness statement for this standalone primitive.

Lemma 1 (In-place point update (partial correctness)). *For any basis state* $|R\rangle$ *such that* $\mathsf{WF}(R, G)$ *holds,* $[\![\mathrm{AddInpl}_G]\!](|R\rangle) = |R \oplus G\rangle$*, and the gadget returns all ancillas to* $|0\rangle$*.*

Lemma 1 is an algebraic verification task: the gadget computes slope-like values using reversible modular arithmetic, including the fixed-round Kaliski-style inversion routine used in Qrisp ECDLP [10], then updates affine coordinates and uncomputes temporaries. We treat it as an explicit obligation for future mechanization or symbolic validation.

3.2 Controlled Scalar Multiplication-and-Add

Let $\mathrm{MultAdd}_G$ denote the scalar-multiplication-and-add routine that processes an n-qubit register k bitwise and conditionally applies $\mathrm{AddInpl}_{2^i G}$, where the doubles $2^i G$ are generated classically. Its intended effect is

$$(k, R) \mapsto (k,\ R \oplus kG),$$

i.e., it accumulates kG into R via conditional additions of precomputed doubles.

Lemma 2 (Scalar multiplication-and-add (refinement)). *Assume Lemma 1 holds for all constants in the doubling schedule, the controlled invocations satisfy the standard control law, and* WF *holds for all intermediate accumulator states. Then, for any basis state* $|k\rangle|R\rangle$ *with* $k \in \mathbb{Z}_{2^n}$*,*

$$[\![\mathrm{MultAdd}_G]\!](|k\rangle|R\rangle) = |k\rangle|R \oplus kG\rangle.$$

Proof. By induction on the loop index i. After i iterations, the accumulator is $R \oplus \sum_{j<i} k_j(2^j G)$. At iteration i, the controlled invocation of $\mathrm{AddInpl}_{2^i G}$ adds $2^i G$ iff $k_i = 1$ and otherwise acts as identity. Thus the invariant is extended to $j \le i$. After n iterations, the accumulator is $R \oplus \sum_{j<n} k_j(2^j G) = R \oplus kG$.

3.3 Oracle Refinement and Polynomial Complexity

By composing two instances of Lemma 2 (for G and P), the implementation refines $\mathcal{O}_{\mathrm{impl}}$ in (1) under WF and the stated controlled-correctness assumptions.

We now argue that the implementation's oracle circuit family is polynomial in the field-size parameter $m = \lceil \log_2 p \rceil$.

Lemma 3 (Structural cost bound). *Let* $\mathrm{Cost}_{\mathrm{Add}}(m)$ *be a cost measure (e.g., gate count or* T*-count) for* $\mathrm{AddInpl}_G$ *on* m*-bit modular registers. Then* $\mathrm{MultAdd}_G$ *has cost at most* $n \cdot \mathrm{Cost}_{\mathrm{Add}}(m) + O(n)$*, and the oracle* $\mathcal{O}_{\mathrm{impl}}$ *has cost at most* $2n \cdot \mathrm{Cost}_{\mathrm{Add}}(m) + O(n)$*.*

Proof. MultAdd_G iterates exactly n times and performs at most one controlled invocation of AddInpl per iteration; the remaining work is constant overhead and classical constant updates. The oracle composes two such calls.

Theorem 1 (Polynomial oracle family (under standard arithmetic assumptions)). *Assume the modular arithmetic primitives used in* AddInpl_G *compile to uniform reversible circuits of size polynomial in* m*, the modular inversion subroutine uses a bounded number of iterations polynomial in* m*, and the scalar-register size* n *is polynomially bounded in* m*. Then the oracle circuit family realizing* $\mathcal{O}_{\text{impl}}$ *is uniform and polynomial in* m*.*

Theorem 1 excludes prototype constructions that hide exponential advice in hard-coded encodings or bespoke permutations; in our setting, the cost is explicit in reversible modular arithmetic and polynomial in the register size.

4 Case Study: Semantic and Complexity Witnesses

For the case study, we use the short Weierstrass curve $E : y^2 \equiv x^3 + ax + b \pmod p$ over the prime field $\mathbb{F}_p$, with parameters $p = 5$, $a = 3$, and $b = 3$. We measure the oracle components from the Qrisp-based ECDLP implementation [10]. As in the reference code, we adopt the convention that $(0, 0)$ encodes the identity element $\mathcal{O}$.

WF Filtering and a Semantic Witness for Lemma 1. Because the in-place addition gadget is derived for a generic affine case, we first filter accumulator inputs using a lightweight well-formedness screen that avoids immediate singular intermediates induced by the gadget's initial normalization steps, e.g., values that make $R_x - G_x \equiv 0 \pmod p$ or $R_y - G_y \equiv 0 \pmod p$. For this instance, the filter yields a single candidate point $R_0 = (4, 3)$ with constant point $G = (3, 2)$. On this input, a basis-state simulation witness confirms that the in-place gadget computes the expected group update:

$$\text{AddInpl}_G(R_0) = (4, 2) = R_0 \oplus G,$$

matching the classical reference implementation. This provides a concrete witness supporting Lemma 1 under WF.

Control-Law Anomaly for the Elliptic-Curve Gadget. Shor-style ECDLP oracles require controlled invocations of the point-update gadget. We therefore test the standard control law: when the control qubit is set to $|0\rangle$, the controlled operation should act as the identity on the target. Let c be a control qubit, and consider the externally controlled invocation of AddInpl_G on the accumulator register encoding $R = (4, 3)$, implemented using the Qrisp control context control(c). With $c = |1\rangle$, the update behaves as expected and maps $(4, 3) \mapsto (4, 2)$. However, with $c = |0\rangle$, the accumulator changes from $(4, 3)$ to $(3, 3)$ in our environment, violating the expected identity behavior for a controlled operation. To rule out a global control malfunction, we additionally validate a trivial controlled-X sanity test under $c = |0\rangle$, which yields deterministic measurements {00 : 256}, confirming that basic control works and that the anomaly is specific to the elliptic-curve gadget's controlled execution/compilation. This observation motivates treating controlled-oracle correctness as an explicit refinement obligation rather than an assumption.

Table 1. Compilation metrics for AddInpl and Ctrl-AddInpl on the prototype instance

Circuit	#Qubits	Depth	T-count	CX-count
AddInpl	6	39,130	13,652	36,261
Ctrl-AddInpl	7	39,196	13,709	36,406

Compilation Metrics (Evidence for Lemma 3). Table 1 reports compilation metrics for the prototype instance. These data should be interpreted only as a concrete compilation witness showing that the studied implementation produces finite circuits for the selected parameters and that adding control introduces limited overhead in this small instance. They are not intended as empirical scaling evidence across field sizes. The polynomial-family claim in Theorem 1 instead follows from the structural form of the implementation: scalar multiplication invokes a point-addition routine once per scalar bit, and each point addition is reduced to reversible modular arithmetic over m-bit registers. Therefore, under the stated assumption that the underlying modular arithmetic and fixed-round inversion routines compile to uniform polynomial-size reversible circuits, the resulting oracle family is polynomial in m.

To summarize, our case study shows that the in-place point-update gadget matches the classical reference under WF, but controlled execution violates the expected control law under the evaluated toolchain, indicating a semantic gap that must be treated as an explicit verification obligation. The case study is therefore intended as a semantic witness and bug-finding demonstration, rather than a broad empirical validation across curves or field sizes.

5 Conclusion and Future Work

In this paper, we present a semantics-based specification of the implemented ECDLP oracle and a refinement-based framework for reasoning about its correctness and complexity. Our case study provides concrete evidence that (i) the in-place point-update gadget can match a classical reference on well-formed inputs, and (ii) controlled execution can violate the expected control law even when basic controlled-X behavior is correct. Together, these results highlight the need to treat controlled-oracle correctness as an explicit verification obligation in ECDLP-oriented quantum software.

Future work will (i) mechanize the core refinement obligations (e.g., Lemmas 1–2) in a proof assistant or via symbolic reasoning over $\mathbb{F}_p$, (ii) extend

WF to cover exceptional cases (e.g., point-at-infinity and inverse-point additions) using complete point representations such as projective coordinates, and (iii) establish sufficient conditions—or a verified compilation path—under which controlled oracle components satisfy the standard control law, enabling an end-to-end refinement argument for the full oracle and the associated classical post-processing.

Acknowledgments. We thank Dr. Tan Teik Guan (CEO and Co-founder of pQCee [11]) for early discussions that inspired the direction of this study.

Disclosure of Interests. The authors have no competing interests to declare that are relevant to the content of this article.

References

1. Ahmed, N., Zhang, L., Gangopadhyay, A.: A survey of post-quantum cryptography support in cryptographic libraries. In: 2025 IEEE International Conference on Quantum Computing and Engineering (QCE), vol. 1, pp. 906–917. IEEE (2025)
2. Albuainain, A., Alansari, J., Alrashidi, S., Alqahtani, W., Alshaya, J., Nagy, N.: Experimental implementation of Shor's quantum algorithm to break RSA. In: 2022 14th International Conference on Computational Intelligence and Communication Networks (CICN), pp. 748–752. IEEE (2022)
3. Bhatia, V., Ramkumar, K.: An efficient quantum computing technique for cracking RSA using Shor's algorithm. In: 2020 IEEE 5th International Conference on Computing Communication and Automation (ICCCA), pp. 89–94. IEEE (2020)
4. Larasati, H.T., Kim, H.: Quantum cryptanalysis landscape of Shor's algorithm for elliptic curve discrete logarithm problem. In: Kim, H. (ed.) WISA 2021. LNCS, vol. 13009, pp. 91–104. Springer, Cham (2021). https://doi.org/10.1007/978-3-030-89432-0_8
5. Lewis, M., Soudjani, S., Zuliani, P.: Formal verification of quantum programs: theory, tools, and challenges. ACM Trans. Quantum Comput. **5**(1), 1–35 (2023)
6. Miranskyy, A., Campos, J., Mjeda, A., Zhang, L., de Guzmán, I.G.R.: On the feasibility of quantum unit testing. arXiv preprint arXiv:2507.17235 (2025)
7. Miranskyy, A., Zhang, L.: On testing quantum programs. In: 2019 IEEE/ACM 41st International Conference on Software Engineering: New Ideas and Emerging Results (ICSE-NIER), pp. 57–60. IEEE (2019)
8. Miranskyy, A., Zhang, L., Doliskani, J.: On testing and debugging quantum software. arXiv preprint arXiv:2103.09172 (2021)
9. Peng, Y., et al.: A formally certified end-to-end implementation of Shor's factorization algorithm. Proc. Natl. Acad. Sci. **120**(21), e2218775120 (2023)
10. Polimeni, D., Seidel, R.: End-to-end compilable implementation of quantum elliptic curve logarithm in Qrisp. arXiv preprint arXiv:2501.10228 (2025)
11. pQCee Ltd: (2026). https://www.pqcee.com
12. Seidel, R., et al.: Qrisp: a framework for compilable high-level programming of gate-based quantum computers. arXiv preprint arXiv:2406.14792 (2024)
13. Weinstein, Y.S., Pravia, M., Fortunato, E., Lloyd, S., Cory, D.G.: Implementation of the quantum Fourier transform. Phys. Rev. Lett. **86**(9), 1889 (2001)

14. Yu, N., Palsberg, J.: Quantum abstract interpretation. In: Proceedings of the 42nd ACM SIGPLAN International Conference on Programming Language Design and Implementation, pp. 542–558 (2021)
15. Zhang, L.: Semantics-based verification pilot for ECDLP Shor oracle in Qrisp (2026). https://doi.org/10.5281/zenodo.18865658
16. Zhang, L., Miranskyy, A., Rjaibi, W.: Quantum advantage and the Y2K bug: a comparison. IEEE Softw. **38**(2), 80–87 (2020)
17. Zhang, L., Miranskyy, A., Rjaibi, W., Stager, G., Gray, M., Peck, J.: Making existing software quantum safe: a case study on IBM Db2. Inf. Softw. Technol. **161**, 107249 (2023)

Reachable Completeness Theorem of Order Sorted Equational Logic with Infinite Proofs

Taeseung Sohn(✉) and Tsubasa Takagi(✉)

Japan Advanced Institute of Science and Technology, Nomi, Japan
{taeseung.sohn,tsubasa}@jaist.ac.jp

Abstract. Order-sorted equational logic is sound and complete with respect to all models, but it cannot prove inductive theorems because they are not necessarily satisfied by unreachable models. We propose OEqID^{ω}, an extended order-sorted equational logic that permits infinite proofs, and has a case-split inference rule corresponding to the structural induction, which is sound and complete with respect to all reachable models, thereby enabling the proof of all inductive theorems.

Although the case-split rule is defined with respect to a constructor family in a many-sorted specification, an order-sorted specification (1) might not allow the case-split rule for some constructor family, or (2) the rule may require redundant premises. In OEqID^{ω}, we introduce the notion of *constructor cover* to address these two issues.

Keywords: Order-Sorted Equational Logic · Reachable Completeness Theorem · Infinite Proof · Structural Induction

1 Introduction

Equational logic provides the theoretical foundation for algebraic specification [10]. The properties of various data structures in computer science can be expressed as equational formulas. More precisely, any computable data types can be algebraically specified by a finite set of many-sorted equations [1]. However, equational logic is a restricted proof system that lacks the inherent ability to prove *inductive theorems*. A famous example of inductive theorems is an (implicitly) universally qualified equation `M + N = N + M` that represents the commutativity of addition in an equational specification for natural numbers [9, Section 6.2]. This equation is not provable, despite the fact that all ground instances of this equation, namely $t_1 + t_2 = t_2 + t_1$ where t_1 and t_2 are ground terms (terms containing no variables), are provable. In fact, such inductive theorems have *unreachable* counter-models, which contain elements that cannot be represented by ground terms. Because equational logic is sound with respect to *all* models, it cannot prove such inductive theorems.

Such unreachable models are often unintended models of a given specification. For proving inductive theorems, unreachable models must be excluded, and the equational logic should be extended to a sound and (desirably) complete proof

G. De Giacomo et al. (Eds.): TASE 2026, LNCS 16697, pp. 269–285, 2027.
https://doi.org/10.1007/978-3-032-30693-7_18

system with respect to only *reachable* models, not all models. An example is the ω-rule, also called infinite induction, an inference rule which derives an equation from all ground instances of the equation. It is known that equational logic with the ω-rule can prove all inductive theorems [13, Theorem 3.1.4]. However, because it requires an infinite number of premises, the ω-rule is impractical for machine implementation.

An alternative approach proposed in [11] is an *infinite* proof system EqID^ω with structural induction. EqID^ω is an extended many-sorted equational logic with an inference rule called the *case-split rule*, which corresponds to structural induction. Moreover, the proof system admits proof trees of infinite length, while exploiting the principle of proof by infinite descent to ensure soundness with respect to all reachable models. It was shown that EqID^ω can also prove all inductive theorems. Because the case-split rule only requires finite premises for a finite specification, the infinite proof approach takes practical advantages over the ω-rule; one can take the subset of infinite proofs having only finite numbers of distinct subtrees and obtain a *cyclic proof system* [2,3] that can be finitely encoded and thus machine implementation-friendly. This result was inspired by an infinite proof system LKID^ω [2,3] for first-order logic with inductive predicates.

In this paper, we extend EqID^ω in two aspects. First, we introduce a subsort relation between sorts, which enables rich expressions such as hierarchies of data structures and the subsort polymorphism between them [4]. For example, one can declare a subsort relation as `Nat < Int < Rat`, reflecting $\mathbb{N} \subset \mathbb{Z} \subset \mathbb{Q}$, and define addition and multiplication for each sort. Second, we extend equations to *conditional* equations, namely equations that hold only when certain equational conditions are satisfied. It is known that equational specifications that allow conditional equations are strictly more expressive than specifications with only (unconditional) equations [12].

In particular, we propose OEqID^ω, an order-sorted conditional equational logic that allows infinite proofs and has the case-split rule. Although the case-split rule in EqID^ω is uniquely defined from a constructor family of the many-sorted specification, it cannot apply directly to some order-sorted specifications. Thus, we introduce the notion of *constructor cover* in Definition 30 to uniquely determine the case-split rule for order-sorted specifications, as in Definition 32.

2 Preliminaries

Definition 1 (Sequences). *A* ***sequence*** *on a set L is a function $I \to L$ for some interval $I \subseteq \mathbb{N}$, denoted by $\{e_i\}_{i\in I}$. An empty sequence is denoted by $\varepsilon : \emptyset \to L$. A finite sequence $\{e_i\}_{0\le i<n}$ is identified with a tuple $(e_0, \cdots, e_{n-1}) \in L^n$. We write the concatenation of finite sequences p, p' as pp'. The set of finite sequences and (finite or infinite) sequences on L are denoted by L^* and $L^{*,\omega}$, respectively.*

Definition 2 (S-set). *For a set S, an* ***S-set*** *is an S-indexed family of sets $A = \{A_s\}_{s\in S}$. For $w = (s_0, \cdots, s_{n-1}) \in S^*$, we define $A_w := A_{s_0} \times \cdots \times A_{s_{n-1}}$. If A is an S-set, then we shortly write $a \in A$ iff $a \in A_s$ for some $s \in S$.*

Definition 3 (**S-function**). *For a set S, an S-**function** is an S-indexed family of functions $g = \{g_s : A_s \to B_s\}_{s\in S}$ between two S-sets A and B. For $w = (s_0, \cdots, s_{n-1}) \in S^*$, we define $g_w : A_w \to B_w$ by $g_w(a_0, \cdots, a_{n-1}) := (g_{s_0}(a_0), \cdots, g_{s_{n-1}}(a_{n-1}))$. If the context is clear, we simply write $g : A \to B$.*

*For two S-functions $g : A \to B$ and $h : B \to C$, the **composition** $h \circ g : A \to C$ is an S-function defined as $h \circ g := \{h_s \circ g_s : A_s \to C_s\}_{s\in S}$.*

Definition 4 (Inclusion). *For two sets T and U satisfying $T \subseteq U$, denote the inclusion function $\iota_{T\hookrightarrow U} : T \hookrightarrow U$. For two S-sets A, B, we write $A \subseteq B$ iff $A_s \subseteq B_s$ for all $s \in S$, where an S-function $\iota_{A\hookrightarrow B} := \{\iota_{A_s\hookrightarrow B_s}\}_{s\in S}$ is associated with the inclusion.*

Definition 5 (Locally Filtered Poset). *A **poset** is a pair $(S, \leq)$ where $\leq$ is a partial order on the set S. The reflexive, transitive, and symmetric closure of $\leq$ is denoted as $\equiv_\leq$. Each $s \in S$ is associated with its equivalence class $[s]_\leq := \{s' \in S : s \equiv_\leq s'\} \in S/{\equiv_\leq}$, called the **connected component** of s.*

*A poset $(S, \leq)$ is said to be **locally filtered** iff, whenever $[s]_\leq = [s']_\leq$, there exists a common supersort $s'' \geq s, s'$ in S.*

Fact 1. *The partial order $\leq$ can be extended to a binary relation on S^*:*

$$(s_0, \cdots, s_{n-1}) \leq (s'_0, \cdots, s'_{n'-1}) :\Leftrightarrow n = n' \text{ and } s_i \leq s'_i \ (\forall i = 0, \cdots, n-1) .$$

This $\leq$ is a partial order on S^*. If $(S, \leq)$ is locally filtered, then so is $(S^*, \leq)$.

Definition 6 (**$(S, \leq)$-set**). *For a locally filtered poset $(S, \leq)$, an S-set $A = \{A_s\}_{s\in S}$ is called an $(S, \leq)$-**set** iff $s \leq s'$ implies $A_s \subseteq A_{s'}$.*

Definition 7 (**$(S, \leq)$-function**). *For a locally filtered poset $(S, \leq)$, an S-function $g : A \to B$ between two $(S, \leq)$-sets A and B is called an $(S, \leq)$-**function**, iff $g_s(a) = g_{s'}(a)$ holds whenever $s \leq s'$ and $a \in A_s$. It is clear that the composition of two $(S, \leq)$-functions is also an $(S, \leq)$-function.*

Definition 8 (**Local $(S, \leq)$-equivalence**). *For a locally filtered poset $(S, \leq)$ and an $(S, \leq)$-set A, a **local** $(S, \leq)$-**equivalence** on A is an $(S/{\equiv_\leq})$-indexed family $\sim = \{\sim_c \subseteq A_c \times A_c\}_{c\in S/\equiv_\leq}$, where each $\sim_c$ is an equivalence relation on $A_c := \bigcup_{s\in c} A_s$. For each $c \in S/{\equiv_\leq}$, define the **quotient of** A **by** $\sim$ as an S-set $A/{\sim} = \{(A/{\sim})_s\}_{s\in S}$, where $(A/{\sim})_s$ is the image of $A_s \subseteq A_{[s]_\leq}$ under the projection $a \mapsto [a]_{\sim_{[s]_\leq}}$. The **projection of** A **by** $\sim$ is an S-function,*

$$\pi_\sim := \{\pi_{\sim,s} : A_s \twoheadrightarrow (A/{\sim})_s\}_{s\in S}, \quad \text{where} \quad \pi_{\sim,s}(a) := [a]_{\sim_{[s]_\leq}} .$$

Fact 2. *In Definition 8, $A/{\sim}$ is an $(S, \leq)$-set, and $\pi_\sim : A \twoheadrightarrow A/{\sim}$ is an $(S, \leq)$-function.*

3 Review of Order-Sorted Equational Logic

We follow the foundational work in [4] for order-sorted equational specifications and algebra, except for some modifications to reflect the widely accepted conventions of order-sorted algebra [8]: monotonicity and regularity can be weakened, respectively, to inheritance (Definition 9) [6,7] and preregularity (Definition 10).

3.1 Order-Sorted Signature and Algebra

Definition 9 (OSS). *An* ***order-sorted signature(OSS)*** *is a tuple* $\Sigma = (S, \leq, F)$*, where* $(S, \leq)$ *is a locally filtered poset, and* F *is an* $(S^* \times S)$*-indexed family of sets satisfying the following:*

(Inheritance Condition) $F_{w,s} \cap F_{w',s'} \neq \emptyset$ *and* $w \equiv_{\leq} w'$ *jointly imply* $s \equiv_{\leq} s'$*.*

S and F are called the ***sort set*** *and the* ***family of function symbols*** *of Σ, respectively. We assume that both S and F are at most countable. For a function symbol $f \in F_{w,s}$, it is said that f has* ***rank*** *(w, s),* ***arity*** *w, and* ***coarity*** *s.*

$f_{w,s}$ indicates a pair $(f, (w, s))$ of a function symbol f and its rank (w, s). If there is no confusion, we also call $f_{w,s}$ a ***rank****.*

Remark 1. We abuse the notation and let F indicate either $(S^* \times S)$-indexed family of sets, or the set of all ranks $\bigcup_{(w,s)\in S^* \times S}\{f_{w,s} : f \in F_{w,s}\}$. The two concepts can be identified with each other; in particular $f_{w,s} \in F \Leftrightarrow f \in F_{w,s}$.

Remark 2. A **many-sorted signature** (S, F) is an OSS where the order $\leq$ is the identity on S.

Definition 10 (Preregularity of Σ). *Consider an OSS $\Sigma = (S, \leq, F)$. For $w \in S^*$, a rank $f_{w',s'} \in F$ is called a w-**lower bounded rank of** f iff $w \leq w'$. Σ is called* ***preregular*** *iff, for each $w \in S^*$, if a function symbol f has a w-lower bounded rank, then f has a w-lower bounded rank with the least coarity.*

Definition 11 (Σ-algebra). *For an OSS $\Sigma = (S, \leq, F)$, a* ***Σ-prealgebra*** *is a structure $\mathcal{A}$ equipped with an $(S, \leq)$-set $|\mathcal{A}|$, called the* ***carrier*** *of $\mathcal{A}$, together with a function $f^{\mathcal{A}}_{w,s} : |\mathcal{A}|_w \to |\mathcal{A}|_s$ for each rank $f_{w,s} \in F$, satisfying the following:*

(Inheritance Condition) *If $f \in F_{w,s} \cap F_{w',s'}$ and $w \equiv_{\leq} w'$, $f^{\mathcal{A}}_{w,s}(\alpha) = f^{\mathcal{A}}_{w',s'}(\alpha)$ holds for each $\alpha \in |\mathcal{A}|_w \cap |\mathcal{A}|_{w'}$.*

A ***Σ-algebra*** *is a Σ-prealgebra $\mathcal{A}$ which additionally satisfies the following:*

(Inhabitedness) *For each sort $s \in S$, $|\mathcal{A}|_s$ is nonempty.*

Definition 12 (Σ-homomorphism). *For an OSS $\Sigma = (S, \leq, F)$, a* ***Σ-homomorphism*** *between two Σ-algebras $\mathcal{A}$ and $\mathcal{B}$ is an $(S, \leq)$-function $g : |\mathcal{A}| \to |\mathcal{B}|$ satisfying the following:*

(Homomorphism Condition) *For each $f_{w,s} \in F$, $g_s \circ f^{\mathcal{A}}_{w,s} = f^{\mathcal{B}}_{w,s} \circ g_w$.*

It is clear that the composition of two Σ-homomorphisms $g : \mathcal{A} \to \mathcal{B}$ and $h : \mathcal{B} \to \mathcal{C}$ (as $(S, \leq)$-functions) is also a Σ-homomorphism $h \circ g : \mathcal{A} \to \mathcal{C}$.

Definition 13 (Σ-term Algebra). *For an OSS $\Sigma = (S, \leq, F)$, the family of* ***Σ-terms*** *is defined as the least $(S, \leq)$-set $|\mathcal{T}_\Sigma|$, which satisfies the following: if $(t_0, \cdots, t_{n-1}) \in |\mathcal{T}_\Sigma|_w$ and $f \in F_{w,s}$, then the juxtaposition $f(t_0, \cdots, t_{n-1})$ of f and the terms $t_0, \cdots, t_{n-1}$, is in $|\mathcal{T}_\Sigma|_s$. Then there is a Σ-prealgebra $\mathcal{T}_\Sigma$ having $|\mathcal{T}_\Sigma|$ as the carrier, and each rank $f_{w,s} \in F$ is associated with the function $f^{\mathcal{T}_\Sigma}_{w,s} : |\mathcal{T}_\Sigma|_w \to |\mathcal{T}_\Sigma|_s$ which maps $(t_0, \cdots, t_{n-1}) \in |\mathcal{T}_\Sigma|_w$ to $f(t_0, \cdots, t_{n-1})$.*

If $\mathcal{T}_\Sigma$ is inhabited, then $\mathcal{T}_\Sigma$ is a Σ-algebra, called the ***Σ-term algebra****. An OSS Σ is called* ***inhabited*** *iff $\mathcal{T}_\Sigma$ is inhabited.*

Lemma 1 (Least Sort). *If an OSS $\Sigma = (S, \leq, F)$ is preregular, for every Σ-term $t \in |\mathcal{T}_\Sigma|$ there is the least sort $s \in S$ for t, denoted $\mathrm{LS}(t)$, such that $t \in |\mathcal{T}_\Sigma|_s$. This can be extended as the* ***least sort function*** *$\mathrm{LS} : \bigcup_{w \in S^*} |\mathcal{T}_\Sigma|_w \to S^*$, defined as $\mathrm{LS}(t_0, \cdots, t_{n-1}) := (\mathrm{LS}(t_0), \cdots, \mathrm{LS}(t_{n-1}))$.*

Proof. Analogous to [4, Proposition 2.10]. □

Corollary 1. *For a preregular OSS Σ and its term $t = f(u_0, \cdots, u_{n-1}) \in |\mathcal{T}_\Sigma|$, there is a $\mathrm{LS}(u_0, \cdots, u_{n-1})$-lower bounded rank $f_{w,\mathrm{LS}(t)} \in F$ for some $w \in S^*$.*

Theorem 1 (Initiality of $\mathcal{T}_\Sigma$). *If an OSS Σ is preregular, for each Σ-algebra $\mathcal{A}$ there is a unique Σ-homomorphism $[\![\cdot]\!]^{\mathcal{A}}_\Sigma : \mathcal{T}_\Sigma \to \mathcal{A}$. In other words, $\mathcal{T}_\Sigma$ is the* ***initial Σ-algebra****.*

Proof. Analogous to [4, Theorem 2.12]. □

Definition 14 (Reachable Σ-algebra). *For a preregular OSS $\Sigma = (S, \leq, F)$, a Σ-algebra $\mathcal{A}$ is* ***reachable*** *iff $[\![\cdot]\!]^{\mathcal{A}}_{\Sigma,s}$ is surjective for each $s \in S$.*

Definition 15 (Variables). *A family X of* ***variables*** *applicable to an OSS $\Sigma = (S, \leq, F)$ is an S-indexed family of at most countable, pairwise disjoint sets $X = \{X_s\}_{s \in S}$, such that each X_s is disjoint with F. The* ***variable extension*** *of Σ by X is an OSS $\Sigma(X) = (S, \leq, F(X))$ with the extended set of ranks $F(X) := F \sqcup \{x_{\varepsilon,s} : s \in S, x \in X_s\}$, where $\sqcup$ indicates a disjoint union.*

Remark 3. Let $\varnothing_S$ be the S-set consisting of only empty sets. $\Sigma(X)$ reduces to $\Sigma = \Sigma(\varnothing_S)$ when $X = \varnothing_S$. To emphasize that the terms in $\mathcal{T}_\Sigma$ do not contain any variables, $\mathcal{T}_\Sigma$ is called the **ground Σ-term algebra**, and its terms are called **ground Σ-terms**.

Lemma 2. *Let $\Sigma = (S, \leq, F)$ be an OSS and $\Sigma(X)$ be its variable extension.*

1. *If Σ is inhabited, then $\Sigma(X)$ is also inhabited.*
2. *If Σ is preregular, then $\Sigma(X)$ is also preregular.*

Proof. 1. $\emptyset \neq |\mathcal{T}_\Sigma|_s \subseteq |\mathcal{T}_{\Sigma(X)}|_s$ for each $s \in S$.

2. The only cases to be checked are the variables. If $x \in X_s$ has a w-lower bounded rank in $F(X)$, the only possible case is $w = \varepsilon$ and the rank $x_{\varepsilon,s}$.

□

Remark 4. Any $\Sigma(X)$-algebra is a Σ-algebra. In particular, the $\Sigma(X)$-term algebra $\mathcal{T}_{\Sigma(X)}$ is a Σ-algebra, provided that $\Sigma(X)$ is inhabited.

Definition 16 (Assignment). *Let Σ be an OSS, $\Sigma(X)$ be its variable extension, and $\mathcal{A}$ be a Σ-algebra. An* ***assignment*** *for X in $\mathcal{A}$ is an S-function $\theta : X \to |\mathcal{A}|$.*

Theorem 2 (Freeness of $\mathcal{T}_{\Sigma(X)}$). *For an inhabited and preregular OSS $\Sigma = (S, \leq, F)$ and its variable extension $\Sigma(X)$, let $\mathcal{A}$ be any Σ-algebra. Then a Σ-homomorphism $\hat{\theta} : \mathcal{T}_{\Sigma(X)} \to \mathcal{A}$ is in one-to-one correspondence with an assignment $\theta : X \to |\mathcal{A}|$, such that $\hat{\theta} \circ \iota_{X \hookrightarrow |\mathcal{T}_{\Sigma(X)}|} = \theta$.*

Proof. Analogous with [4, Theorem 2.13]. □

Remark 5. A Σ-homomorphism $\hat{\theta} : \mathcal{T}_{\Sigma(X)} \to \mathcal{A}$ is called an **interpretation**. When $\mathcal{A} = \mathcal{T}_{\Sigma(Y)}$ for a variable family Y, then $\hat{\theta}$ is also called a **substitution**.

We simply write $\hat{\theta}(t)$ for $\hat{\theta}_{\mathrm{LS}(t)}(t)$, as $\hat{\theta}_s(t)$ is defined only when $t \in |\mathcal{T}_{\Sigma(X)}|_s$, which implies $s \geq \mathrm{LS}(t)$ and $\hat{\theta}_s(t) = \hat{\theta}_{\mathrm{LS}(t)}(t)$. Similarly, write $\hat{\theta}(v)$ for $\hat{\theta}_{\mathrm{LS}(v)}(v)$.

Definition 17 (Σ-congruence). *For an OSS $\Sigma = (S, \leq, F)$ and a Σ-algebra $\mathcal{A}$, a* ***Σ-congruence*** *$\sim$ on $\mathcal{A}$ is a local equivalence on $|\mathcal{A}|$, satisfying the following:*

(**Congruence Condition**) *If $f \in F_{w,s} \cap F_{w',s'}$ and $[w]_{\leq} = [w']_{\leq}$, for $\alpha \in |\mathcal{A}|_w$ and $\alpha' \in |\mathcal{A}|_{w'}$, $\pi_{\sim,w}(\alpha) = \pi_{\sim,w'}(\alpha')$ implies $\pi_{\sim,s}(f^{\mathcal{A}}_{w,s}(\alpha)) = \pi_{\sim,s'}(f^{\mathcal{A}}_{w',s'}(\alpha'))$.*

Theorem 3 (Quotient Σ-algebra). *For an OSS $\Sigma = (S, \leq, F)$, a Σ-algebra $\mathcal{A}$ and a Σ-congruence $\sim$ on $\mathcal{A}$, there is a Σ-algebra $\mathcal{A}/\!\sim$, called the* ***quotient Σ-algebra*** *of $\mathcal{A}$ by $\sim$, which has $|\mathcal{A}/\!\sim| := |\mathcal{A}|/\!\sim$ as the carrier, and each $f \in F_{w,s}$ associated with the function $f^{\mathcal{A}/\sim}_{w,s} : (|\mathcal{A}|/\!\sim)_w \to (|\mathcal{A}|/\!\sim)_s$ satisfying:*

$$f^{\mathcal{A}/\sim}_{w,s}(\pi_{\sim,w}(\alpha)) := \pi_{\sim,s}(f^{\mathcal{A}}_{w,s}(\alpha)).$$

Proof. From Fact 2 and the congruence condition of $\sim$, $f^{\mathcal{A}/\sim}_{w,s}$ is well-defined, and the inheritance condition for $\mathcal{A}/\!\sim$ is straightforward. Since each $|\mathcal{A}|_s$ is nonempty, its image $|\mathcal{A}/\!\sim|_s = (|\mathcal{A}|/\!\sim)_s$ under $\pi_{\sim,s}$ is also nonempty, hence $\mathcal{A}/\!\sim$ is inhabited. □

Lemma 3 (Projection as Σ-homomorphism). *In Definition 17, the S-function of projections $\pi_\sim : |\mathcal{A}| \to |\mathcal{A}|/\!\sim$ is a Σ-homomorphism $\pi_\sim : \mathcal{A} \to \mathcal{A}/\!\sim$.*

Proof. From Fact 2 and Theorem 3. □

Theorem 4 (Factorization). *For an OSS $\Sigma = (S, \leq, F)$ and its variable extension $\Sigma(X)$, let $\mathcal{A}$ be a Σ-algebra and $\sim$ be a Σ-congruence on $\mathcal{A}$. For any interpretation $\hat{\theta} : \mathcal{T}_{\Sigma(X)} \to \mathcal{A}/\!\sim$, there is $\hat{\bar{\theta}} : \mathcal{T}_{\Sigma(X)} \to \mathcal{A}$ such that $\hat{\theta} = \pi_\sim \circ \hat{\bar{\theta}}$.*

Proof. Apply Theorem 2, and for each $x \in X$, choose a representative $\bar{\theta}(x)$ from the quotient $\theta(x) \subseteq |\mathcal{A}|_{\mathrm{LS}(x)}$. □

3.2 Order-Sorted Conditional Equational Specifications

We distinguish the object-level equation symbol $\doteq$, from its meta-level counterpart $=$.

Definition 18 (Conditional $\Sigma(X)$-equations). *For an inhabited and preregular OSS $\Sigma = (S, \leq, F)$ and its variable extension $\Sigma(X)$, an* ***(unconditional) $\Sigma(X)$-equation*** *is a pair (t, t'), denoted $t \doteq t'$, in the set*

$$\mathbf{Eq}_{\Sigma(X)} := \bigcup_{c \in S/\equiv_{\leq}} (|\mathcal{T}_{\Sigma(X)}|_c \times |\mathcal{T}_{\Sigma(X)}|_c).$$

For a substitution $\hat{\sigma} : \mathcal{T}_{\Sigma(X)} \to \mathcal{T}_{\Sigma(X)}$, we write $\hat{\sigma}(t \doteq t') := (\hat{\sigma}(t) \doteq \hat{\sigma}(t'))$.

A ***conditional $\Sigma(X)$-equation*** *is a pair $(\{u_k \doteq u'_k\}_{k \in I}, u \doteq u')$, denoted $(u \doteq u' \Leftarrow \{u_k \doteq u'_k\}_{k \in I})$, in the set $\mathbf{CEq}_{\Sigma(X)} := (\mathbf{Eq}_{\Sigma(X)})^{*,\omega} \times \mathbf{Eq}_{\Sigma(X)}$.*

Definition 19 (Variables in $\Sigma(X)$-terms and $\Sigma(X)$-equations). *For a preregular OSS Σ and its variable extension $\Sigma(X)$, the finite set $\mathbf{Var}(t)$ of variables appearing in a term $t \in |\mathcal{T}_{\Sigma(X)}|$, is defined inductively:*

1. *If $x \in V$, then $\mathbf{Var}(x) := \{x\}$.*
2. *If $t = f(t_0, \cdots, t_{n-1})$ for some $f \in F$ and $t_0, \cdots, t_{n-1} \in |\mathcal{T}_{\Sigma(X)}|$, then $\mathbf{Var}(t) := \bigcup_{k=0}^{n-1} \mathbf{Var}(t_k)$. For the edge case when $n = 0$, define $\mathbf{Var}(t) := \emptyset$.*

The set of variables in $t \doteq t' \in \mathbf{Eq}_{\Sigma(X)}$ is $\mathbf{Var}(t \doteq t') := \mathbf{Var}(t) \cup \mathbf{Var}(t')$.

Definition 20 (Satisfaction of a Conditional $\Sigma(X)$-equation). *For an inhabited and preregular OSS Σ and its variable extension $\Sigma(X)$, let $\mathcal{A}$ be a Σ-algebra and $\hat{\theta} : \mathcal{T}_{\Sigma(X)} \to \mathcal{A}$ be an interpretation.*

A $\Sigma(X)$-equation $t \doteq t'$ is ***satisfied by $\hat{\theta}$****, denoted $\hat{\theta} \vDash t \doteq t'$, iff $\hat{\theta}(t) = \hat{\theta}(t')$. A conditional $\Sigma(X)$-equation $(t \doteq t' \Leftarrow \{u_k \doteq u'_k\}_{k \in I})$ is* ***satisfied by $\hat{\theta}$****, iff $\hat{\theta} \vDash u_k \doteq u'_k$ for each $k \in I$ implies $\hat{\theta} \vDash t \doteq t'$. A $\Sigma(X)$-equation or a conditional $\Sigma(X)$-equation is* ***satisfied by $\mathcal{A}$****, iff it is satisfied by every $\hat{\theta} : \mathcal{T}_{\Sigma(X)} \to \mathcal{A}$. The statement that a $\Sigma(X)$-equation $t \doteq t'$ is satisfied by $\mathcal{A}$ is denoted $\mathcal{A} \vDash t \doteq t'$.*

Definition 21 (OSCES). *An* ***order-sorted conditional equational specification(OSCES)*** *is a tuple $\mathsf{SP} = (\Sigma, V, E)$, where $\Sigma = (S, \leq, F)$ is an inhabited and preregular OSS, V is a family of countable sets of variables which is applicable to Σ, and $E \subseteq \mathbf{CEq}_{\Sigma(V)}$ is a set of conditional $\Sigma(V)$-equations, called the* ***axioms*** *of SP.*

Definition 22 (SP-model and Reachable SP-model). *For an OSCES $\mathsf{SP} = (\Sigma, V, E)$, a Σ-algebra $\mathcal{A}$ is an* ***SP-model****, iff all axioms in E are satisfied by $\mathcal{A}$. Furthermore, $\mathcal{A}$ is a* ***reachable SP-model****, iff $\mathcal{A}$ is an SP-model and is reachable.*

Definition 23 (Tree). *For a given set L, a* ***L-tree*** *is a partial function $\tau : \mathbb{N}^* \rightharpoonup L$ satisfying the following:*

1. *$\tau(\varepsilon)$ is defined; $(\varepsilon, \tau(\varepsilon))$ is called the* ***root node*** *of τ.*

2. *For $p \in \mathbb{N}^*$ and $n \in \mathbb{N}$, if $\tau(pn)$ is defined, then $\tau(p)$ is defined, and there is an interval $I \subseteq \mathbb{N}$ such that $\tau(pm)$ is defined iff $m \in I$. $(p, \tau(p))$ is called the* ***parent*** *of $(pn, \tau(pn))$.*

For a given L-tree τ, a ***node*** *is a pair $(p, \tau(p))$ of a position $p \in \mathbb{N}^*$ and the value $\tau(p)$ defined at p, or just $\tau(p)$ when p is contextually implied. A node $\tau(p)$ is called an* ***ancestor*** *of another node $\tau(p')$ iff p is a prefix of p'.*

Each node $\tau(p)$ is associated with a sequence $\{\tau(pk)\}_{k\in I}$ of child nodes, called the ***children*** *of $\tau(p)$. A* ***leaf*** *of τ is a node of τ with empty children.*

A ***path*** *of an L-tree τ is a sequence $\{\tau(p_l)\}_{l\in I}$ of nodes, such that $\tau(p_l)$ is the parent of $\tau(p_{l+1})$. A* ***finite L-tree*** *is an L-tree that has no infinite paths.*

Definition 24 (Graft). *Let τ, τ' be L-trees, and $(p, \tau(p))$ be a node of τ. A* ***graft*** *of τ' on τ at position $p \in \mathbb{N}^*$, denoted $\tau[p \leftarrow \tau']$, is an L-tree that maps $q \in \mathbb{N}^*$ to $\tau'(p')$, if $q = pp'$ for some $p' \in \mathbb{N}^*$, and $\tau(q)$ otherwise.*

Definition 25 (Inference Rule). *For a given set L, an* ***inference rule*** *$\mathfrak{R}$ on L is a subset of $L^{*,\omega} \times L$. For $(\{e_k\}_{k\in I}, e') \in \mathfrak{R}$, $\{e_k\}_{k\in I}$ is called the* ***premises****, and e' is called the* ***conclusion****.*

An L-tree τ is said to be ***partially derived from*** *$\mathfrak{R}$, iff each node $\tau(p)$ either has children $\{\tau(pk)\}_{k\in I}$ such that $(\{\tau(pk)\}_{k\in I}, \tau(p)) \in \mathfrak{R}$, or is a leaf. A leaf node $\tau(p)$ such that $(\varepsilon, \tau(p)) \notin \mathfrak{R}$ is called a* ***bud****. An L-tree τ is said to be* ***derived from*** *$\mathfrak{R}$, iff τ is partially derived from $\mathfrak{R}$ and τ has no buds.*

Definition 26 (Finite SP-proof Tree). *For an OSCES $\mathsf{SP} = (\Sigma, V, E)$, a* ***finite*** *SP****-proof tree*** *is a finite $\mathbf{Eq}_{\Sigma(V)}$-tree τ, derived from the following rules:*

- **(Axiom; $\hat{\sigma}$)** *A conclusion $\hat{\sigma}(u = u')$ from premises $\{\hat{\sigma}(u_k = u'_k)\}_{k\in I}$, where $\hat{\sigma} : \mathcal{T}_{\Sigma(V)} \to \mathcal{T}_{\Sigma(V)}$ is a substitution and $(u = u' \Leftarrow \{u_k = u'_k\}_{k\in I}) \in E$.*
- **(Refl)** *A conclusion $t = t$ from empty premises, where $t \in |\mathcal{T}_{\Sigma(V)}|$.*
- **(Symm)** *A conclusion $t' = t$ from a premise $t = t'$, where $t, t' \in |\mathcal{T}_{\Sigma(V)}|$.*
- **(Trans)** *A conclusion $t = t''$ from two premises $t = t'$ and $t' = t''$, where $t, t', t'' \in |\mathcal{T}_{\Sigma(V)}|$.*
- **(Cong)** *A conclusion $f(t_0, \cdots, t_{n-1}) = f(t'_0, \cdots, t'_{n-1})$ from n premises $t_0 = t'_0$, $\cdots$, $t_{n-1} = t'_{n-1}$, where f is a function symbol having an arity in S^n.*

The visualization of these inference rules are provided as in Table 1.

A $\Sigma(V)$-equation $t = t'$ is ***finitely*** *SP****-provable****, denoted $\mathsf{SP} \vdash t = t'$, iff there is a finite SP-proof tree τ whose root node is $(\varepsilon, t = t')$.*

Theorem 5 (Soundness for Finite SP-proofs). *For an OSCES $\mathsf{SP} = (\Sigma, V, E)$ and $t = t' \in \mathbf{Eq}_{\Sigma(V)}$, $\mathsf{SP} \vdash t = t'$ implies $\mathcal{A} \vDash t = t'$ for any SP-model $\mathcal{A}$.*

Proof. Straightforward. □

Theorem 6 (Finite SP-proof Congruence). *For an OSCES $\mathsf{SP} = (\Sigma, V, E)$ where $\Sigma = (S, \leq, F)$, and a variable family $X \subseteq V$, the $(S/\equiv_{\leq})$-indexed family $\equiv_{\mathsf{SP}(X)} = \{\equiv_{\mathsf{SP}(X),c}\}_{c\in S/\equiv_{\leq}}$ of binary relations $\equiv_{\mathsf{SP}(X),c}$ on $|\mathcal{T}_{\Sigma(X)}|_c$, defined as $t \equiv_{\mathsf{SP}(X),c} t' :\Leftrightarrow \mathsf{SP} \vdash t = t'$, is a Σ-congruence on $\mathcal{T}_{\Sigma(X)}$.*

Table 1. Finite SP-proof Tree Inference Rules in Definition 26.

$$\text{(Refl)}\ \frac{}{t = t} \qquad \text{(Symm)}\ \frac{t = t'}{t' = t} \qquad \text{(Trans)}\ \frac{t = t' \qquad t' = t''}{t = t''}$$

$$\text{(Cong)}\ \frac{t_0 = t'_0 \qquad \cdots \qquad t_{n-1} = t'_{n-1}}{f(t_0, \cdots, t_{n-1}) = f(t'_0, \cdots, t'_{n-1})} \qquad \text{(Axiom; } \hat{\sigma}\text{)}\ \frac{\{\hat{\sigma}(u_k = u'_k)\}_{k \in I}}{\hat{\sigma}(u = u')}$$

Proof. For each $c \in S/\equiv_{\leq}$, the inference rules (Refl), (Symm), (Trans) ensures that $\equiv_{\mathsf{SP}(X),c}$ is an equivalence relation on $|\mathcal{T}_{\Sigma(X)}|_c$. The inference rule (Cong) gives the congruence condition for $\equiv_{\mathsf{SP}(X)}$. □

Remark 6. We denote $\equiv_{\mathsf{SP}}$ for $\equiv_{\mathsf{SP}(\varnothing_S)}$.

Definition 27 (Quotient $\Sigma(X)$-term Algebra). *For an OSCES* $\mathsf{SP} = (\Sigma, V, E)$ *and* $X \subseteq V$ *a variable family, the quotient* Σ*-algebra* $\mathcal{T}_{\Sigma(X)}/\equiv_{\mathsf{SP}(X)}$ *is called* ***the quotient*** $\Sigma(X)$***-term algebra modulo*** SP. *Particularly in* $X = \varnothing_S$ *case,* $\mathcal{T}_\Sigma/\equiv_{\mathsf{SP}}$ *is called* ***the quotient ground*** Σ***-term algebra modulo*** SP.

Theorem 7 (Model Existence). *For an OSCES* $\mathsf{SP} = (\Sigma, V, E)$ *and a variable family* $X \subseteq V$, $\mathcal{T}_{\Sigma(X)}/\equiv_{\mathsf{SP}(X)}$ *is an* SP*-model.*

Proof. Sufficient to show that each axiom $(u = u' \Leftarrow \{u_k = u'_k\}_{k \in I}) \in E$ is satisfied by each $\hat{\theta} : \mathcal{T}_{\Sigma(V)} \to \mathcal{T}_{\Sigma(X)}/\equiv_{\mathsf{SP}(X)}$. From Theorem 4, take $\hat{\hat{\theta}} : \mathcal{T}_{\Sigma(V)} \to \mathcal{T}_{\Sigma(X)}$ such that $\hat{\theta} = \pi_{\equiv_{\mathsf{SP}(X)}} \circ \hat{\hat{\theta}}$. Note that $\mathsf{SP} \vdash \hat{\hat{\theta}}(t = t')$ iff $\hat{\theta} \models t = t'$. From the inference rule (Axiom; $\hat{\hat{\theta}}$), $\hat{\theta} \models u_k = u'_k$ for all $k \in I$ implies $\hat{\theta} \models u = u'$. □

Theorem 8 (Completeness for Finite SP-proofs). *For an OSCES* $\mathsf{SP} = (\Sigma, V, E)$ *and* $t = t' \in \mathbf{Eq}_{\Sigma(V)}$, *if* $\mathcal{A} \models t = t'$ *for every* SP*-model* $\mathcal{A}$, *then* $\mathsf{SP} \vdash t = t'$.

Proof. Take $\mathcal{A} = \mathcal{T}_{\Sigma(V)}/\equiv_{\mathsf{SP}(V)}$, a verified SP-model from Theorem 7. We have $\mathcal{T}_{\Sigma(V)}/\equiv_{\mathsf{SP}(V)} \models t = t'$, particularly $\pi_{\equiv_{\mathsf{SP}(V)}} \models t = t'$. $\mathsf{SP} \vdash t = t'$ follows. □

Theorem 9 (Reachable Model Existence). $\mathcal{T}_\Sigma/\equiv_{\mathsf{SP}}$ *is a reachable* SP*-model.*

Proof. $\mathcal{T}_\Sigma/\equiv_{\mathsf{SP}}$ is already an SP-model from Theorem 7, taking $X = \varnothing_S$. From the initiality of $\mathcal{T}_\Sigma$, two Σ-homomorphisms $[\![\cdot]\!]_\Sigma^{\mathcal{T}_\Sigma/\equiv_{\mathsf{SP}}}, \pi_{\equiv_{\mathsf{SP}}} : \mathcal{T}_\Sigma \to \mathcal{T}_\Sigma/\equiv_{\mathsf{SP}}$ are identical, and each $\pi_{\equiv_{\mathsf{SP}},s}$ is surjective. Hence, $\mathcal{T}_\Sigma/\equiv_{\mathsf{SP}}$ is reachable. □

Remark 7. $\mathcal{T}_\Sigma/\equiv_{\mathsf{SP}}$ is also known as the **initial model** of SP [7].

4 Constructor Cover

In many-sorted equational specifications, the induction rule is defined dependently to a certain constructor family [11]. However in OSCES, some constructor family might not admit the corresponding induction rule, or the rule may contain redundant premises. These issues emerge because OSCES admits subsort polymorphism, while the standard definition of constructor is *sort-agnostic.* Hence, we need a refined definition of constructor family, which is always eligible to structure induction, and redundant premises are avoidable.

4.1 Sort-Aware Constructor Family

Definition 28 (Subsignature). *For an OSS $\Sigma = (S, \leq, F)$, a $(S^* \times S)$-indexed family $C \subseteq F$ corresponds to a* ***subsignature*** *of Σ, defined as $\Sigma_C := (S, \leq, C)$. This Σ_C is an OSS as the inheritance condition holds from $C \subseteq F$.*

Definition 29 (Sort-aware Constructor Family). *Consider an OSCES* $\mathtt{SP} = (\Sigma, V, E)$ *and a subsignature Σ_C of Σ. We call the $(S^* \times S)$-family C a* ***constructor family*** *of* SP, *iff the following two conditions hold:*

- **(Inhabitedness)** *Σ_C is inhabited.*
- **(Sufficient Completeness)** *For each $t \in |\mathcal{T}_\Sigma|$, there is $t' \in |\mathcal{T}_{\Sigma_C}|$ such that* $\mathtt{SP} \vdash t = t'$.

If C is a constructor family of SP, *ground terms of Σ_C are called* ***constructor ground terms*** *of the family C. Similarly, we call C a* ***sort-aware constructor family*** *of* SP, *iff the following condition holds:*

- **(Sort-aware Sufficient Completeness)** *For each $s \in S$ and $t \in |\mathcal{T}_\Sigma|_s$, there is $t' \in |\mathcal{T}_{\Sigma_C}|_s$ such that* $\mathtt{SP} \vdash t = t'$.

Lemma 4. *A sort-aware constructor family C of an OSCES* $\mathtt{SP} = (\Sigma, V, E)$ *is also a constructor family of* SP.

Proof. Straightforward. □

Remark 8. Any OSCES $\mathtt{SP} = (S, \leq, F, V, E)$ has a trivial sort-aware constructor family, namely F itself.

Example 1. Consider an OSCES $\mathtt{EX} = (\Sigma_{\mathtt{EX}}, V_{\mathtt{EX}}, E_{\mathtt{EX}}) = (S_{\mathtt{EX}}, \leq_{\mathtt{EX}}, F_{\mathtt{EX}}, V_{\mathtt{EX}}, E_{\mathtt{EX}})$, described as in Fig. 1. Since we have no axioms ($E_{\mathtt{EX}} = \emptyset$), $\mathcal{T}_{\Sigma_{\mathtt{EX}}}/{\equiv_{\mathtt{EX}}}$ is isomorphic to $\mathcal{T}_{\Sigma_{\mathtt{EX}}}$.

```
obj EX is
  sorts ChildA ChildB Parent .
  subsorts ChildA ChildB < Parent .
  op a : -> ChildA .                  op b : -> ChildB .
  op f : ChildA ChildA -> ChildA .    op f : ChildB ChildB -> ChildB .
  op f : Parent Parent -> Parent .
endo
```

Fig. 1. OBJ-style [5] description of OSCES EX. `sorts` declares the sort set $S_{\mathtt{EX}} = \{\mathtt{ChildA}, \mathtt{ChildB}, \mathtt{Parent}\}$ and `subsorts` the generators of the order $\leq_{\mathtt{EX}}$ on $S_{\mathtt{EX}}$. `op` declares the family of function symbols $F_{\mathtt{EX}}$. Dynamically generated variable family $V_{\mathtt{EX}}$ and the empty axiom set $E_{\mathtt{EX}}$ are omitted.

Among the ground $\Sigma_{\mathtt{EX}}$-terms are `f(a,a)`, `f(b,b)`, `f(a,b)` whose least sort is `ChildA`, `ChildB`, and `Parent`, respectively. It is easily observable that a rank set

Table 2. A non-working (a) and a working (b) attempt to define an induction rule for a variable $\mathtt{A} : \mathtt{ChildA}$, respectively based on non-sort-aware $C_{\mathtt{EX.1}}$ and sort-aware $F_{\mathtt{EX}}$. The variables are $\mathtt{P1}, \mathtt{P2} : \mathtt{Parent}$ and $\mathtt{A1}, \mathtt{A2} : \mathtt{ChildA}$.

$$\frac{(\widehat{\{\mathtt{A} \mapsto \mathtt{a}\}})(t = t') \quad (\widehat{\{\mathtt{A} \mapsto \mathtt{f(P1,P2)}\}})(t = t')}{t = t'}\,(\mathrm{a}) \qquad \frac{(\widehat{\{\mathtt{A} \mapsto \mathtt{a}\}})(t = t') \quad (\widehat{\{\mathtt{A} \mapsto \mathtt{f(A1,A2)}\}})(t = t')}{t = t'}\,(\mathrm{b})$$

$C \subseteq F_{\mathtt{EX}}$ is a constructor family of $\mathtt{EX}$, if and only if C is a superset of $C_{\mathtt{EX.1}} := \{\mathtt{a}_{\varepsilon,\mathtt{ChildA}}, \mathtt{b}_{\varepsilon,\mathtt{ChildB}}, \mathtt{f}_{\mathtt{ParentParent},\mathtt{Parent}}\}$. Note that $C_{\mathtt{EX.1}}$ is not sort-aware, because $\mathtt{f(a,a)}$ is not of sort $\mathtt{ChildA}$ in $(\Sigma_{\mathtt{EX}})_{C_{\mathtt{EX.1}}}$.

Table 2 (a) shows a failing induction on a variable $\mathtt{A} : \mathtt{ChildA}$, based on non-sort-aware $C_{\mathtt{EX.1}}$. The rule should handle terms like $\mathtt{f(a,a)}$, which are of sort $\mathtt{ChildA}$ in $\Sigma_{\mathtt{EX}}$. However, the only rank of $\mathtt{f}$ in $C_{\mathtt{EX.1}}$ is $\mathtt{f}_{\mathtt{ParentParent},\mathtt{Parent}}$, and the rule requires a premise corresponding to an invalid assignment $\{\mathtt{A} \mapsto \mathtt{f(P1,P2)}\}$.

The *correct* form of induction is given in Table 2 (b), based on sort-aware $F_{\mathtt{EX}}$. The two assignments $\{\mathtt{A} \mapsto \mathtt{a}\}$ and $\{\mathtt{A} \mapsto \mathtt{f(A1,A2)}\}$ for variables $\mathtt{A1}, \mathtt{A2} : \mathtt{ChildA}$ precisely corresponds to the entire constructor ground terms of sort $\mathtt{ChildA}$.

4.2 Constructor Cover

Example 2. Consider $\mathtt{EX}$ from Example 1, and try to define an induction rule for $\mathtt{Parent}$, based on the sort-aware constructor family $F_{\mathtt{EX}}$.

Table 3. Attempts to define an induction rule for a variable $\mathtt{P} : \mathtt{Parent}$ based on the sort-aware constructor family $F_{\mathtt{EX}}$, with redundancy (a) and without redundancy (b). The variables are $\mathtt{P1}, \mathtt{P2} : \mathtt{Parent}$, $\mathtt{A1}, \mathtt{A2} : \mathtt{ChildA}$, and $\mathtt{B1}, \mathtt{B2} : \mathtt{ChildB}$.

$$\frac{(\widehat{\{\mathtt{P} \mapsto \mathtt{a}\}})(t = t') \quad (\widehat{\{\mathtt{P} \mapsto \mathtt{b}\}})(t = t') \quad (\widehat{\{\mathtt{P} \mapsto \mathtt{f(P1,P2)}\}})(t = t') \quad (\widehat{\{\mathtt{P} \mapsto \mathtt{f(A1,A2)}\}})(t = t') \quad (\widehat{\{\mathtt{P} \mapsto \mathtt{f(B1,B2)}\}})(t = t')}{t = t'}\,(\mathrm{a})$$

$$\frac{(\widehat{\{\mathtt{P} \mapsto \mathtt{a}\}})(t = t') \qquad (\widehat{\{\mathtt{P} \mapsto \mathtt{b}\}})(t = t') \qquad (\widehat{\{\mathtt{P} \mapsto \mathtt{f(P1,P2)}\}})(t = t')}{t = t'}\,(\mathrm{b})$$

The induction rule in Table 3 (a) is *sound*, whose exact meaning will be discussed later in Theorem 11. However, this soundness costs three premises corresponding to $\{\mathtt{P} \mapsto \mathtt{f(P1,P2)}\}$, $\{\mathtt{P} \mapsto \mathtt{f(A1,A2)}\}$, and $\{\mathtt{P} \mapsto \mathtt{f(B1,B2)}\}$ for the same symbol $\mathtt{f}$, where $\{\mathtt{P} \mapsto \mathtt{f(P1,P2)}\}$ covers the others.

We want a rule as in Table 3 (b), which only requires necessary premises: $\{\mathtt{P} \mapsto \mathtt{f(P1,P2)}\}$ as well as $\{\mathtt{P} \mapsto \mathtt{a}\}$ and $\{\mathtt{P} \mapsto \mathtt{b}\}$. However, no sort-aware constructor family corresponds to this rule; removing redundant ranks from $F_{\mathtt{EX}}$ reduces to non-sort-aware $C_{\mathtt{EX.1}}$, as in Example 1. An alternative approach is to *selectively remove* redundant ranks for inductions on the sort $\mathtt{Parent}$, while keeping the rank $\mathtt{f}_{\mathtt{ChildAChildA},\mathtt{ChildA}}$ present for inductions on the sort $\mathtt{ChildA}$.

Definition 30 (Constructor Cover). *For an OSCES* $\mathtt{SP} = (S, \leq, F, V, E)$, *a **constructor cover** of* SP *is an* S*-indexed family* $D = \{D^{\mathfrak{s}}\}_{\mathfrak{s} \in S}$ *of* $(S^* \times S)$*-indexed families* $D^{\mathfrak{s}} = \{D^{\mathfrak{s}}_{w,s}\}_{(w,s) \in S^* \times S} \subseteq F$ *, satisfying the following:*

1. $D^{\mathfrak{s}}_{w,s} \neq \emptyset$ *implies* $s \leq \mathfrak{s}$.
2. $\tilde{D} := \{\bigcup_{\mathfrak{s} \in S} D^{\mathfrak{s}}_{w,s}\}_{(w,s) \in S^* \times S} \subseteq F$ *is a sort-aware constructor family of* SP.
3. *If* $f_{w,s} \in \tilde{D}$, *then for each* $\mathfrak{s} \geq s$, *there is a* w*-lower bounded rank* $f_{w',s'} \in D^{\mathfrak{s}}$.

Remark 9. For a given sort-aware constructor family C of an OSCES SP, there is a **trivial constructor cover** D such that $\tilde{D} = C$, taking $D^{\mathfrak{s}}_{w,s} := C_{w,s}$ if $s \leq \mathfrak{s}$, and $D^{\mathfrak{s}}_{w,s} := \emptyset$ otherwise.

Remark 10. If an OSCES SP has no order structure (many-sorted), any constructor family is sort-aware. Moreover, a constructor cover D is in one-to-one correspondence with a constructor family $\tilde{D}$, because $D^{\mathfrak{s}}_{w,s}$ can be nonempty only if $\mathfrak{s} = s$.

Example 3. Again, consider EX from Example 1. Define $D_{\mathtt{EX.3}}$ as:

$$(D_{\mathtt{EX.3}})^{\mathtt{ChildA}} := \{\mathtt{a}_{\varepsilon,\mathtt{ChildA}}, \mathtt{f}_{\mathtt{ChildAChildA},\mathtt{ChildA}}\},$$
$$(D_{\mathtt{EX.3}})^{\mathtt{ChildB}} := \{\mathtt{b}_{\varepsilon,\mathtt{ChildB}}, \mathtt{f}_{\mathtt{ChildBChildB},\mathtt{ChildB}}\},$$
$$(D_{\mathtt{EX.3}})^{\mathtt{Parent}} := \{\mathtt{a}_{\varepsilon,\mathtt{ChildA}}, \mathtt{b}_{\varepsilon,\mathtt{ChildB}}, \mathtt{f}_{\mathtt{ParentParent},\mathtt{Parent}}\}.$$

$D_{\mathtt{EX.3}}$ is a non-trivial constructor cover with $\tilde{D}_{\mathtt{EX.3}} = F_{\mathtt{EX}}$. Now, $(D_{\mathtt{EX.3}})^{\mathtt{ChildA}}$ corresponds to the induction in Table 2 (b) for ChildA, and $(D_{\mathtt{EX.3}})^{\mathtt{Parent}}$ corresponds to the induction in Table 3 (b) for Parent.

Each component $D^{\mathfrak{s}}$ of a constructor cover D corresponds to an induction rule for the sort $\mathfrak{s} \in S$. This correspondence is formalized in Definition 32.

Definition 31 (CCCES). *A **constructor-covered conditional equational specification (CCCES)** is a pair* $(\mathtt{SP}, D)$ *of an OSCES* SP *and its constructor cover* D.

Definition 32 (Case-Split Rule). *For a CCCES* $(\mathtt{SP}, D)$ *where* $\mathtt{SP} = (\Sigma, V, E)$, *fix a* $\Sigma(V)$*-equation* $t \doteq t'$, *and a variable* $x \in \mathbf{Var}(t \doteq t') \cap V_{\mathfrak{s}}$ *of sort* $\mathfrak{s} \in S$. *Consider a sequence* $\{(f_j)_{w_j,s_j}\}_{j \in J}$ *enumerating all ranks in* $D^{\mathfrak{s}}$. *The **case-split rule** is an inference rule on* $\mathbf{Eq}_{\Sigma(V)}$ *defined as the following:*

(Case; x**)** *A conclusion* $t \doteq t'$ *from premises* $\{\hat{\varphi}_j(t \doteq t')\}_{j \in J}$, *where each* $\hat{\varphi}_j : \mathcal{T}_{\Sigma(V)} \to \mathcal{T}_{\Sigma(V)}$ *is given as* $\varphi_j := \{x \mapsto f_j(y_0, \cdots, y_{n-1})\}$.
Here, $y_0, \cdots, y_{n-1} \in V$ *are distinct variables of sorts* $\mathrm{LS}(y_0, \cdots, y_{n-1}) = w_j$. *Furthermore, each* y_i *should be fresh; formally,* $y_i \notin \mathbf{Var}(t \doteq t') \setminus \{x\}$.

5 Order-Sorted Equational Logic with Infinite Proof

Our proof system OEqID^{ω} runs on a CCCES $(\mathtt{SP}, D)$, and accepts a $(\mathtt{SP}, D)$-proof tree which is a (possibly infinite) tree derived from all previous inference rules plus the case-split rule. Completeness Theorem with respect to the reachable models of SP and $(\mathtt{SP}, D)$-proof trees is demonstrated. As OEqID^{ω} is an order-sorted extension of EqID^{ω} [11], the core ideas and proofs are analogous to EqID^{ω} except for the soundness of the case-split rule (Theorem 10) which additionally requires the sort-aware sufficient completeness for the constructor family.

5.1 Provability

Definition 33 (($\texttt{SP}, D$)-**preproof Tree**). *For a CCCES* $(\texttt{SP}, D)$ *where* $\texttt{SP} = (\Sigma, V, E)$, *an* $(\texttt{SP}, D)$-***preproof tree*** *is an* $\mathbf{Eq}_{\Sigma(V)}$*-tree, which is derived from the union of the rules (Axiom;* $\hat{\sigma}$*), (Refl), (Symm), (Trans), (Cong) defined for* $\texttt{SP}$ *in Definition 26, and (Case;* x*) in Definition 32. An* ***open*** $(\texttt{SP}, D)$-***preproof tree*** *is an* $\mathbf{Eq}_{\Sigma(V)}$*-tree which is partially derived from the above rules.*

Definition 34 (Trace). *For a CCCES* $(\texttt{SP}, D)$ *such that* $\texttt{SP} = (\Sigma, V, E)$, *let* τ *be an* $(\texttt{SP}, D)$*-preproof tree. A* ***trace*** *of a path* $\{(p_i, t_i \doteq t'_i)\}_{i \in I}$ *in* τ *is a sequence* $\{(p_i, z_i)\}_{i \geq m, i \in I} \subseteq \mathbb{N}^* \times V$ *for some* $m \in I$, *satisfying the following:*

1. $z_i \in \mathbf{Var}(t_i \doteq t'_i)$ *for each* $i \in I$ *such that* $i \geq m$.
2. *If the inference rule for the node* $(p_i, t_i \doteq t'_i)$ *is (Case;* z_i*), and the child node on the given path is* $(p_{i+1}, \hat{\sigma}(t_i \doteq t'_i))$ *where* $\sigma = \{z_i \mapsto f(y_0, \cdots, y_{n-1})\}$, *then* $z_{i+1} \in \{y_0, \cdots, y_{n-1}\}$. *Such* p_i *is called a* ***progress point*** *of the given trace.*
3. *If the inference rule for* $(p_i, t_i \doteq t'_i)$ *is other than (Case;* z_i*), then* $z_{i+1} = z_i$.

Definition 35 (($\texttt{SP}, D$)-**proof Tree**). *For a CCCES* $(\texttt{SP}, D)$, *an* $(\texttt{SP}, D)$-***proof tree*** *is an* $(\texttt{SP}, D)$-***preproof tree*** τ *satisfying the following:*

(Global Trace Condition) Each infinite path $\{(p_i, t_i \doteq t'_i)\}_{i \geq 0}$ *of* τ *has a trace with infinitely many progress points.*

A $\Sigma(V)$*-equation* $t \doteq t'$ *is* $(\texttt{SP}, D)$-***provable***, *denoted* $(\texttt{SP}, D) \Vdash t \doteq t'$, *iff there is an* $(\texttt{SP}, D)$*-proof tree* τ *whose root node is* $(\varepsilon, t \doteq t')$.

Remark 11. Any finite $\texttt{SP}$-proof tree is vacuously an $(\texttt{SP}, D)$-proof tree.

5.2 Reachable Soundness

Lemma 5. *Let* $\Sigma = (S, \leq, F)$ *be an OSS and* $\Sigma(X)$ *be its variable extension. If an interpretation* $\hat{\theta} : \mathcal{T}_{\Sigma(X)} \to \mathcal{A}$ *satisfies* $\hat{\theta}(x) = \hat{\theta}(u)$ *for some* $x \in X_s$, $u \in |\mathcal{T}_{\Sigma(X)}|_s$, *and* $s \in S$, *then* $\hat{\theta}(t) = \hat{\theta}((\widehat{\{x \mapsto u\}})(t))$ *holds for each* $t \in |\mathcal{T}_{\Sigma(X)}|$.

Proof. Structural induction for t. □

Lemma 6. *Let* $(\texttt{SP}, D)$ *be a CCCES such that* $\texttt{SP} = (\Sigma, V, E)$, τ *be an* $(\texttt{SP}, D)$*-preproof tree with the root* $\tau(\varepsilon) = (t_0 \doteq t'_0)$, *and* $\mathcal{A}$ *be a reachable model of* $\texttt{SP}$. *If an interpretation* $\hat{\theta}_0 : \mathcal{T}_{\Sigma(V)} \to \mathcal{A}$ *satisfies* $\hat{\theta}_0 \nvDash t_0 \doteq t'_0$, *then there is an infinite path* $\{(p_i, t_i \doteq t'_i)\}_{i \geq 0}$ *of* τ, *with an infinite sequence of 'counterexample' interpretations* $\{\hat{\theta}_i : \mathcal{T}_{\Sigma(V)} \to \mathcal{A}\}_{i \geq 0}$, *which satisfy the following:*

1. *For each* $i \geq 0$, $\hat{\theta}_i \nvDash t_i \doteq t'_i$.
2. *For each* $s \in S$ *and* $a \in |\mathcal{A}|_s$, *define* $T_{(\texttt{SP},D)}(a, s) := \{t \in |\mathcal{T}_{\Sigma_{\hat{D}}}|_s : [\![t]\!]^{\mathcal{A}}_{\Sigma} = a\}$.

For an arbitrary trace $\{(p_i, z_i)\}_{i \geq m}$, *let* $T_i := T_{(\texttt{SP},D)}(\hat{\theta}_i(z_i), \mathrm{LS}(z_i))$ *and* $d_i := \min_{t \in T_i} \mathbf{depth}(t)$. *Such* d_i *is well-defined, and* $d_i \geq d_{i+1}$ *holds for each* $i \geq m$, *particularly* $d_i > d_{i+1}$ *whenever* p_i *is the progress point of the trace.*

Proof. Analogous to [11, Lemma 4.2].

We first show $T_{(\mathsf{SP},D)}(a,s) \neq \emptyset$ for any $s \in S$ and $a \in |\mathcal{A}|_s$. Since $\mathcal{A}$ is reachable, there is $t \in |\mathcal{T}_\Sigma|_s$ such that $[\![t]\!]^{\mathcal{A}}_\Sigma = a$. From the sort-aware sufficient completeness of $\tilde{D}$, there exists $t' \in |\mathcal{T}_{\Sigma_{\tilde{D}}}|_s$ such that $\mathsf{SP} \vdash t = t'$. Theorem 5 implies $\mathcal{A} \models t = t'$, which reads $[\![t]\!]^{\mathcal{A}}_\Sigma = [\![t']\!]^{\mathcal{A}}_\Sigma$ for ground terms t and t'. Hence $t' \in T_{(\mathsf{SP},D)}(a,s)$. The well-definedness of each d_i follows.

For each $l \in \mathbb{N}$, inductively construct a finite path $\{(p_i, t_i = t'_i)\}_{0\leq i\leq l}$ with counterexamples $\{\hat{\theta}_i : \mathcal{T}_{\Sigma(V)} \to \mathcal{A}\}_{0\leq i\leq l}$ which satisfy the finite version of Condition 1 and 2. The desired infinite path and the counterexample sequence can be taken respectively as their unions.

The initial conditions are trivial. Now suppose $(p_l, t_l = t'_l)$ and $\hat{\theta}_l$ are defined, find $t_{l+1} = t'_{l+1}$ and $\hat{\theta}_{l+1}$ to append, depending on the inference rule for $t_l = t'_l$.

(Axiom; $\hat{\sigma}$) There exists $\hat{\sigma} : \mathcal{T}_{\Sigma(V)} \to \mathcal{T}_{\Sigma(V)}$ and $(u = u' \Leftarrow \{u_k = u'_k\}_{k\in I}) \in E$, such that $(t_l = t'_l) = \hat{\sigma}(u = u')$, and its premises are $\{\hat{\sigma}(u_k = u'_k)\}_{k\in I}$. $\hat{\theta}_l \not\models t_l = t'_l$ implies $\hat{\theta}_l \circ \hat{\sigma} \not\models u = u'$. Since $\mathcal{A}$ satisfies the axiom, there should be at least one premise $u_k = u'_k$ such that $\hat{\theta}_l \circ \hat{\sigma} \not\models u_k = u'_k$. Define:

$$(p_{l+1}, t_{l+1} = t'_{l+1}) := (p_l k, \hat{\sigma}(u_k = u'_k)), \quad \hat{\theta}_{l+1} := \hat{\theta}_l,$$

then Condition 1 is automatic. For a trace $\{(p_i, z_i)\}_{m\leq i\leq l+1}$, it should be $z_{l+1} = z_l$. Then $\hat{\theta}_l(z_l) = \hat{\theta}_{l+1}(z_{l+1})$, which implies $T_l = T_{l+1}$ and $d_l = d_{l+1}$.

(Refl),(Symm),(Trans),(Cong) Straightforward, similar to (Axiom; $\hat{\sigma}$).

(Case; x) Let $T := T_{(\mathsf{SP},D)}(\hat{\theta}_l(x), \mathrm{LS}(x)) \subseteq |\mathcal{T}_{\Sigma_{\tilde{D}}}|_{\mathrm{LS}(x)}$. Since $T \neq \emptyset$, there is a term $t \in T \subseteq |\mathcal{T}_{\Sigma_{\tilde{D}}}|_{\mathrm{LS}(x)}$ with the minimum depth $d := \mathbf{depth}(t)$ among T. $\hat{\theta}_l(x) = [\![t]\!]^{\mathcal{A}}_\Sigma = \hat{\theta}_l(t)$ holds. Now, suppose t is in the form $t = f(u_0, \cdots, u_{n-1})$. Because D is a constructor cover, $f \in D^{\mathrm{LS}(x)}_{w,s}$ for some $w \geq \mathrm{LS}(u_0, \cdots, u_{n-1})$ and $s \leq \mathrm{LS}(x)$. Hence, among premises of $t_l = t'_l$, there is $\hat{\varphi}_j(t_l = t'_l)$ of some index j, in the form $\varphi_j = \{x \mapsto f(y_0, \cdots, y_{n-1})\}$ with variables $y_0, \cdots, y_{n-1} \notin \mathbf{Var}(t_l = t'_l) \setminus \{x\}$ and $w = \mathrm{LS}(y_0, \cdots, y_{n-1}) \geq \mathrm{LS}(u_0, \cdots, u_{n-1})$. Define an assignment $\phi := \{y_0 \mapsto u_0, \cdots, y_{n-1} \mapsto u_{n-1}\} : X \to |\mathcal{T}_{\Sigma_{\tilde{D}}}|$, and

$$(p_{l+1}, t_{l+1} = t'_{l+1}) := (p_l j, \hat{\varphi}_j(t_l = t'_l)), \quad \hat{\theta}_{l+1} := \hat{\theta}_l \circ \hat{\phi}.$$

Observe that $\hat{\phi} \circ \hat{\varphi}_j$ corresponds to the assignment

$$\hat{\phi} \circ \varphi_j = \{x \mapsto f(u_0, \cdots, u_{n-1}) = t, y_0 \mapsto u_0, \cdots, y_{n-1} \mapsto u_{n-1}\},$$

where if $y_k = x$ for some $k = 0, \cdots, n-1$, $y_k \mapsto u_k$ should be omitted. Since $\{y_0, \cdots, y_{n-1}\}$ and $\mathbf{Var}(t_l) \setminus \{x\}$ are disjoint, $(\hat{\phi} \circ \hat{\varphi}_j)(t_l) = (\widehat{\{x \mapsto t\}})(t_l)$. Combined with Lemma 5, we have:

$$\hat{\theta}_{l+1}(t_{l+1}) = (\hat{\theta}_l \circ \hat{\phi} \circ \hat{\varphi}_j)(t_l) = \hat{\theta}_l((\widehat{\{x \mapsto t\}})(t_l)) = \hat{\theta}_l(t_l).$$

Analogously $\hat{\theta}_{l+1}(t'_{l+1}) = \hat{\theta}_l(t'_l)$; hence $\hat{\theta}_l \not\models t_l = t'_l$ implies $\hat{\theta}_{l+1} \not\models t_{l+1} = t'_{l+1}$.

Take an arbitrary trace $\{(p_i, z_i)\}_{m \le i \le l+1}$. It can be either $z_l \neq x$ and $z_{l+1} = z_l$, or $z_l = x$ and $z_{l+1} = y_k$ for some $k = 0, \cdots, n-1$.
For the former case, $z_l \neq y_k$ for each k, since $z_l \in \mathbf{Var}(t_l \doteq t'_l) \setminus \{x\} \not\ni y_k$. This gives $\hat{\phi}(z_{l+1}) = z_l$, and $\hat{\theta}_{l+1}(z_{l+1}) = \hat{\theta}_{l+1}(\hat{\phi}(z_l)) = \hat{\theta}_l(z_l)$. Hence $d_l = d_{l+1}$.
The latter case is the progress point. From the definition of ϕ,

$$\hat{\theta}_{l+1}(z_{l+1}) = \hat{\theta}_{l+1}(y_k) = \hat{\theta}_l(\hat{\phi}(y_k)) = \hat{\theta}_l(u_k) = [\![u_k]\!]^{\mathcal{A}}_{\Sigma}.$$

Combined with $u_k \in |\mathcal{T}_{\Sigma_{\tilde{D}}}|_{\mathrm{LS}(z_{l+1})}$, we have $u_k \in T_{l+1}$. Also notice that $d_l = d$, because $T_l = T_{(\mathtt{SP},D)}(\hat{\theta}_l(z_l), \mathrm{LS}(z_l)) = T$. The below inequality follows:

$$\begin{aligned} d_l = d = \mathbf{depth}(t) &= \mathbf{depth}(f(u_0, \cdots, u_{n-1})) \\ &> \mathbf{depth}(u_k) \ge \min_{u \in T_{l+1}} \mathbf{depth}(u) = d_{l+1}. \end{aligned}$$

□

Theorem 10 (Reachable Soundness for $(\mathtt{SP}, D)$**-proofs).** *For a CCCES* $(\mathtt{SP}, D)$ *such that* $\mathtt{SP} = (\Sigma, V, E)$, *and for any* $(t \doteq t') \in \mathbf{Eq}_{\Sigma(V)}$, *if* $(\mathtt{SP}, D) \Vdash t \doteq t'$ *then* $\mathcal{A} \models t \doteq t'$ *for any reachable* $\mathtt{SP}$*-model* $\mathcal{A}$.

Proof. Assume $\mathcal{A} \not\models t \doteq t'$ for some reachable $\mathtt{SP}$-model $\mathcal{A}$. Take an $(\mathtt{SP}, D)$-preproof tree τ of $t \doteq t'$. From Lemma 6, there is an infinite path $\{(p_i, t_i \doteq t'_i)\}_{i \ge 0}$ of τ, such that for each trace $\{(p_i, z_i)\}_{i \ge m}$ there is a monotonically decreasing sequence of natural numbers $\{d_i\}_{i \ge m}$, which strictly decreases at each progress point p_i. Now suppose that τ is a $(\mathtt{SP}, D)$-proof tree. From the global trace condition, there is a trace with infinitely many progress points $p_{i_0}, p_{i_1}, \cdots$, and an infinitely decreasing sequence of natural numbers $d_{i_0} > d_{i_1} > \cdots$, which contradicts the well-foundedness of $\mathbb{N}$. □

5.3 Initial and Reachable Completeness

Lemma 7. *Let* $\Sigma = (S, \le, F)$ *be a preregular OSS, and* $\Sigma(V)$ *be its variable extension. For* $\hat{\sigma} : \mathcal{T}_{\Sigma(V)} \to \mathcal{T}_{\Sigma(V)}$ *and* $t, t' \in |\mathcal{T}_{\Sigma(V)}|$, *if* $\mathbf{Var}(\hat{\sigma}(t) \doteq \hat{\sigma}(t')) = \emptyset$, *then there is* $\hat{\sigma}' : \mathcal{T}_{\Sigma(V)} \to \mathcal{T}_{\Sigma}$ *such that* $\hat{\sigma}(t \doteq t') = \hat{\sigma}'(t \doteq t')$.

Proof. For each $x \in V_s$, let σ'_s maps $x \in V_s$ into $\sigma_s(x)$ if $x \in \mathbf{Var}(t \doteq t')$, and into an arbitrary chosen element $t_s \in |\mathcal{T}_\Sigma|_s (\neq \emptyset)$ otherwise. From structural induction $\hat{\sigma}(u) = \hat{\sigma}'(u)$ can be shown for all $u \in |\mathcal{T}_{\Sigma(V)}|$, particularly for $u = t, t'$. □

Lemma 8. *For a CCCES* $(\mathtt{SP}, D)$, *let* τ *be an open* $(\mathtt{SP}, D)$*-preproof tree with an infinite path* $\{(p_i, t_i \doteq t'_i)\}_{i \ge 0}$. *If each node* $t_i \doteq t'_i$ *is a conclusion of (Case) rules in* τ, *then this path has a trace with infinitely many progress points.*

Proof. See [11, Lemma 5.3]. The proof involves König's Lemma. □

Theorem 11 (Initial Completeness for $(\mathtt{SP}, D)$**-proofs).** *For a CCCES* $(\mathtt{SP}, D)$ *with* $\mathtt{SP} = (\Sigma, V, E)$, *and* $t \doteq t' \in \mathbf{Eq}_{\Sigma(V)}$, $\mathcal{T}_\Sigma / {\equiv_{\mathtt{SP}}} \models t \doteq t'$ *implies* $(\mathtt{SP}, D) \Vdash t \doteq t'$.

Proof. Following [11, Theorem 5.6], construct a monotonic sequence $\tau_0 \subseteq \tau_1 \subseteq \cdots$ of open $(\mathtt{SP}, D)$-preproof trees inductively, such that each bud in each τ_i is in the form $\hat{\sigma}(t = t')$ for some $\hat{\sigma} : \mathcal{T}_{\Sigma(V)} \to \mathcal{T}_{\Sigma(V)}$.

Start with $\tau_0 := \{(\varepsilon, t = t')\}$. Construct τ_{i+1} from τ_i as following: take a bud $(p, \hat{\sigma}(t = t'))$ of τ_i with the least $\mathbf{enc}(p)$, where the encoding $\mathbf{enc} : \mathbb{N}^* \hookrightarrow \mathbb{N}$ may be any injection that linearly orders all positions.

1. If τ_i has no buds, then $\tau_{i+1} := \tau_i$.
2. Suppose that the chosen bud $(p, \hat{\sigma}(t = t'))$ has no variables. From Lemma 7, we can take $\hat{\sigma}' : \mathcal{T}_{\Sigma(V)} \to \mathcal{T}_{\Sigma}$ such that $\hat{\sigma}(t = t') = \hat{\sigma}'(t = t')$, and from $\mathcal{T}_{\Sigma}/{\equiv_{\mathtt{SP}}} \models t = t'$ we have $\pi_{\equiv_{\mathtt{SP}}} \circ \hat{\sigma}' \models t = t'$ i.e. $\mathtt{SP} \vdash \hat{\sigma}'(t = t')$. Choose a finite $\mathtt{SP}$-proof τ' for $\hat{\sigma}'(t = t')$, and define τ_{i+1} as a graft $\tau[p \leftarrow \tau']$.
3. If the chosen bud $(p, \hat{\sigma}(t = t'))$ contains variables, choose one $x \in \mathbf{Var}(\hat{\sigma}(t) = \hat{\sigma}(t'))$ and append $(p, \hat{\sigma}(t = t'))$ with its premises in (Case; x).

Now take an open $(\mathtt{SP}, D)$-preproof tree $\tau := \bigcup_{i \geq 0} \tau_i$. Each bud $(p, \tau_i(p))$ is eventually chosen in τ_j for some $j \leq \mathbf{enc}(p) + 1$ and no longer a bud henceforth. Therefore, τ has no buds, and is an $(\mathtt{SP}, D)$-preproof tree.

For any infinite path $\{(p_i, t_i = t_i')\}_{i \geq 0}$ in τ, only (Case) rule is allowed from the consturction, and has a trace with infinitely many progress points from Lemma 8. Therefore, τ is a $(\mathtt{SP}, D)$-proof tree of $t = t'$. □

Definition 36 (Inductive Theorem of $\mathtt{SP}$**).** *For an OSCES* $\mathtt{SP} = (\Sigma, V, E)$*, an equation* $(t = t') \in \mathbf{Eq}_{\Sigma(V)}$ *is called an* ***inductive theorem*** *of* $\mathtt{SP}$*, iff* $\mathtt{SP} \vdash \hat{\sigma}(t = t')$ *for each ground term substitution* $\hat{\sigma} : \mathcal{T}_{\Sigma(V)} \to \mathcal{T}_{\Sigma}$.

Corollary 2 (Reachable Completeness for $(\mathtt{SP}, D)$**-proofs).** *For a CCCES* $(\mathtt{SP}, D)$ *such that* $\mathtt{SP} = (\Sigma, V, E)$*, and* $(t = t') \in \mathbf{Eq}_{\Sigma(V)}$*, if* $\mathcal{A} \models t = t'$ *for every reachable* $\mathtt{SP}$*-model* $\mathcal{A}$*, then* $(\mathtt{SP}, D) \Vdash t = t'$.

Proof. From Theorem 9, $\mathcal{T}_{\Sigma}/{\equiv_{\mathtt{SP}}}$ is a reachable $\mathtt{SP}$-model. Reachable completeness directly follows from Theorem 11. □

Corollary 3 (Provability of Inductive Theorems). *For a CCCES* $(\mathtt{SP}, D)$*, if an equation* $t = t'$ *is an inductive theorem of* $\mathtt{SP}$*, then* $(\mathtt{SP}, D) \Vdash t = t'$.

Proof. From Theorem 11, it is sufficient to show that $\mathcal{T}_{\Sigma}/{\equiv_{\mathtt{SP}}} \models t = t'$. Take any interpretation $\hat{\theta} : \mathcal{T}_{\Sigma(V)} \to \mathcal{T}_{\Sigma}/{\equiv_{\mathtt{SP}}}$. From Theorem 4, we have a factorization $\hat{\theta} = \pi_{\equiv_{\mathtt{SP}}} \circ \hat{\hat{\theta}}$ for some substitution $\hat{\hat{\theta}} : \mathcal{T}_{\Sigma(V)} \to \mathcal{T}_{\Sigma}$. By assumption $\mathtt{SP} \vdash \hat{\hat{\theta}}(t = t')$, which is equivalent to $\hat{\theta}(t) = \pi_{\equiv_{\mathtt{SP}}}(\hat{\hat{\theta}}(t)) = \pi_{\equiv_{\mathtt{SP}}}(\hat{\hat{\theta}}(t')) = \hat{\theta}(t')$. □

6 Conclusion and Future Work

The key results of this paper are Theorem 10, Corollary 2, and Corollary 3. Combining these statements shows that (1) our proof system OEqID$^\omega$ is sound and complete with respect to all reachable models, and (2) OEqID$^\omega$ can prove all inductive theorems.

However, this result only implies that an OEqID$^{\omega}$ proof of an inductive theorem always exists: it tells nothing about how such a proof can be constructed because the proof might be infinitely long and non-repeating. A practical implementation would be to restrict OEqID$^{\omega}$ and accept only cyclic proofs. Although cyclic proofs form only a subset of all possible proofs, this restriction would enable automated proof construction for inductive theorems in many practical specifications.

Additionally, automated optimization and verification of a constructor cover from a given OSCES can be another area of future work to support such an application.

References

1. Bergstra, J.A., Tucker, J.V.: Algebraic specifications of computable and semicomputable data structures. Theor. Comput. Sci.: J. EATCS **50**(2), 137–181 (1987)
2. Brotherston, J.: Sequent calculus proof systems for inductive definitions. PhD Thesis (2006)
3. Brotherston, J., Simpson, A.: Sequent calculi for induction and infinite descent. J. Log. Comput. **21**(6), 1177–1216 (2011)
4. Goguen, J.A., Meseguer, J.: Order-sorted algebra I: equational deduction for multiple inheritance, overloading, exceptions and partial operations. Theor. Comput. Sci. **105**(2), 217–273 (1992)
5. Goguen, J.A., Winkler, T., Meseguer, J., Futatsugi, K., Jouannaud, J.P.: Introducing OBJ. In: Goguen, J., Malcolm, G. (eds.) Software Engineering with OBJ. Advances in Formal Methods, LNCS, vol. 2, pp. 3–167. Springer, Boston, MA (2000). https://doi.org/10.1007/978-1-4757-6541-0_1
6. Loeckx, J., Ehrich, H., Wolf, M.: Specification of Abstract Data Types. Wiley Teubner on Applicable Theory in Computer Science, Wiley, Hoboken (1996)
7. Meseguer, J.: Membership algebra as a logical framework for equational specification. In: Presicce, F.P. (ed.) WADT 1997. LNCS, vol. 1376, pp. 18–61. Springer, Heidelberg (1998). https://doi.org/10.1007/3-540-64299-4_26
8. Meseguer, J.: Generalized rewrite theories and coherence completion. In: Rusu, V. (ed.) Rewriting Logic and Its Applications. WRLA 2018. LNCS, vol. 11152, pp. 164–183. Springer, Cham (2018). https://doi.org/10.1007/978-3-319-99840-4_10
9. Ölveczky, P.C.: Designing Reliable Distributed Systems. Springer, Cham (2017). https://doi.org/10.1007/978-1-4471-6687-0
10. Sannella, D., Tarlecki, A.: Foundations of Algebraic Specification and Formal Software Development. Springer, Cham (2012). https://doi.org/10.1007/978-3-642-17336-3
11. Shimanuki, R., Aoto, T.: Towards a proof system EqIDω with infinite derivation trees for inductive theorem proving in equational logic. Trans. Program. **18**(2), 2 (2025). https://cir.nii.ac.jp/crid/1050867344087082112
12. Thatcher, J.W., Wagner, E.G., Wright, J.B.: Data type specification: parameterization and the power of specification techniques. In: Proceedings of the Tenth Annual ACM Symposium on Theory of Computing, pp. 119–132 (1978)
13. Wirsing, M.: Algebraic Specification, pp. 675—-788. MIT Press, Cambridge (1991)

LLM-Guided Requirement Scenario-Based Testing for Simulink Models

Ling Qin[1], Jincao Feng[2(✉)], and Weikai Miao[1(✉)]

[1] Software Engineering Institute, East China Normal University, Shanghai, China
{wkmiao,wkmiao}@sei.ecnu.edu.cn
[2] Shanghai Kong'an Intelligent Technology Software Co., Ltd., Shanghai, China
jincaofeng@foxmail.com

Abstract. Requirement-driven testing of Simulink models is crucial for ensuring safety early in development, yet domain engineers often struggle to construct comprehensive test cases or translate natural-language requirements into formal specifications. To address this challenge, we propose LLM-guided Requirement Scenario-Based Testing (RST-LLM), where an LLM serves as a semantic transformer that converts requirements into structured testing artifacts rather than directly producing test cases. We introduce a hierarchical Action–Scenario abstraction. The LLM extracts typical actions with signal-level constraints and composes requirement-related scenarios as ordered action sequences. The scenarios are first enhanced and instantiated, and executable test cases are subsequently generated through constraint-guided search. Experimental results show that RST-LLM improves model coverage and achieves stronger fault-detection capability compared with adaptive random testing and direct LLM-based test generation.

Keywords: Simulink models · requirement-based testing · LLMs

1 Introduction

Simulink [17] is a modeling environment widely used in model-based development (MBD), particularly for embedded and safety-critical systems. In industrial practice, Simulink models serve as high-level design artifacts that describe system behavior before code implementation [6]. This paradigm enables validation and verification through simulation at early development stages, reducing downstream debugging costs and improving development efficiency. Testing Simulink models has therefore become an important activity in engineering workflows [8]. Developing scalable testing techniques at the model level is therefore critical to ensuring behavioral correctness prior to deployment.

Existing model-level testing techniques typically rely on formal specifications or precisely defined property/input languages. For example, Simulink Design Verifier [16] (SLDV) performs formal verification for detection of design errors, and S-TaLiRo [1] searches for counterexamples guided by temporal logics such as

G. De Giacomo et al. (Eds.): TASE 2026, LNCS 16697, pp. 286–304, 2027.
https://doi.org/10.1007/978-3-032-30693-7_19

Signal Temporal Logic (STL). Other frameworks require engineers to specify system behaviors using specialized synchronous or constraint-based languages [19] (e.g., Lustre). However, a persistent challenge in practice is that system requirements are often written in natural language at a high level of abstraction, whereas testing tools require highly formalized inputs and properties [24]. This semantic gap forces domain engineers to manually translate informal requirements into tool-compatible specifications, which is labor-intensive, error-prone, and may fail to accurately capture the original intent, ultimately undermining test effectiveness.

Recently, Large Language Models (LLMs) have demonstrated strong capabilities in natural language understanding and semantic reasoning [4], creating new opportunities for requirement-driven testing [30]. Compared with rule-based or template-based approaches, LLMs can interpret high-level requirements [15] and infer implicit constraints. These capabilities enable the automated transformation of informal requirements into structured testing artifacts, thereby reducing manual effort and supporting more systematic and scalable requirement-driven testing.

Motivated by the observations mentioned earlier, we propose LLM-guided Requirement Scenario-Based Testing (RST-LLM) for Simulink models. In our approach, the LLM acts as a semantic transformer that converts natural-language requirements into structured testing artifacts through a hierarchical Action-Scenario abstraction. In this abstraction, an action captures a typical input behavior with explicit signal-level constraints derived from requirements, while a scenario represents an ordered sequence of actions describing a possible evolution of system behaviors. Given a requirement document, the LLM first extracts typical actions and then composes requirement-related scenarios as ordered action sequences. The generated scenarios are first enhanced to increase behavioral diversity, then instantiated into temporally structured scenario templates, and finally converted into executable test cases through robustness-guided search, which searches for input signals satisfying the constraints associated with each action and scenario. The resulting test cases are executed on Simulink models to evaluate system behaviors.

We implement the proposed approach and evaluate it on four benchmarks from the Lockheed Martin CPS (LMCPS) dataset [19], and compare it with adaptive random testing and direct LLM-based test generation. The results show that RST-LLM consistently improves testing effectiveness compared with Adaptive Random Testing (ART) and direct LLM-based test generation. On average, RST-LLM improves condition, decision, and MC/DC coverage by 17.5%, 7.5%, and 21.7% over ART, and by 12.5%, 15.2%, and 48.5% over direct LLM-based test generation, respectively. It also improves the fault-revealing rate by 43.8% over ART and 32.8% over the direct LLM-based test generation.

The main contributions of this work are as follows:

1) We introduce a hierarchical Action–Scenario abstraction to bridge the semantic gap between natural-language requirements and model-level test inputs.

2) We design an LLM-based automated pipeline that derives requirement-related actions and scenarios from natural-language requirements.
3) We present a test generation method that instantiates scenarios into executable test cases by integrating scenario-driven constraints with robustness-guided search.
4) We conduct a systematic evaluation on four benchmarks to demonstrate the effectiveness of the proposed method.

The remainder of this paper is organized as follows. Section 2 gives a running example. Section 3 introduces key concepts. Section 4 presents the methodology. Section 5 discusses the experimental evaluation. Section 6 presents related work. Section 7 concludes the paper.

2 Running Example: Triplex Signal Monitor

To illustrate the key concepts used in our approach, we present a running example based on the Triplex Signal Monitor challenge problem from the Lockheed Martin CPS benchmark [19]. The complete automated workflow of RST-LLM will be introduced in Sect. 4. The Triplex benchmark provides a requirement document containing (i) a model description, (ii) input and output specifications, and (iii) a set of natural-language requirement items describing expected system behaviors.

2.1 Problem Overview

The Triplex Signal Monitor models a redundancy management (RM) system for airborne applications. Three redundant input signals, denoted as ia, ib, and ic, are continuously monitored to detect discrepancies and prevent error propagation. Each pair of signals is compared against a configurable threshold $Tlevel$. The model produces four outputs: the persistence counter PC, the totalizer counter TC, the latched fault code FC, and the selected value set_val. If a miscompare persists longer than the persistence limit $PClimit$, a failure is latched and reflected in FC. In our testing process, actions and scenarios constrain the input behaviors, whereas the output traces are checked by requirement oracles: PC records persistence, TC records totalized state information, FC reports latched failures, and set_val is the main observable value for checking the expected selection behavior in RM-002 and RM-004 (Fig. 1).

In this system, the following requirement item must be satisfied:

- **[RM-001]** In the no-fail state, a miscompare that lasts longer than the persistence limit shall be reported as a failure.
- **[RM-002]** In the no-fail state, the selected value shall be the mid-value.
- **[RM-003]** In the single-fail state, the selected value shall be the good channel average.
- **[RM-004]** If a second failure is in progress, the selected value shall remain unchanged.

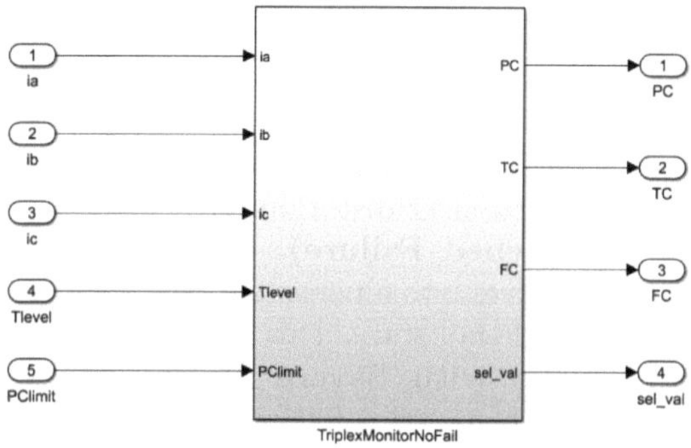

Fig. 1. Triplex Signal Monitor

2.2 From Requirement Document to Actions

Instead of directly specifying raw input signals, input behaviors can be described using *actions*, where each action represents a class of input patterns satisfying certain signal relations and temporal conditions. Following the action-extraction step of RST-LLM, the LLM derives action candidates from the signal relations and temporal conditions in the requirement document. The listed actions are the normalized form of the LLM-generated actions after checking that they use declared signals and valid constraints.

For the Triplex model, the normalized actions are defined based on the relationships among the three signals ia, ib, and ic relative to the threshold $Tlevel$. They represent normal, transient, persistent, and severe divergence patterns implied by the requirements.

- **A1 (All signals consistent):** *Input constraint:* $|ia - ib| \leq Tlevel \wedge |ia - ic| \leq Tlevel \wedge |ib - ic| \leq Tlevel$. *Temporal constraint: true.*
- **A2 (Transient miscompare between** ib **and** ic**):** *Input constraint:* $|ia - ib| \leq Tlevel \wedge |ia - ic| \leq Tlevel \wedge |ib - ic| > Tlevel$. *Temporal constraint:* $duration \leq PClimit$.
- **A3 (Persistent miscompare between** ib **and** ic**):** *Input constraint:* $|ia - ib| \leq Tlevel \wedge |ia - ic| \leq Tlevel \wedge |ib - ic| > Tlevel$. *Temporal constraint:* $duration > PClimit$.
- **A4 (All-pairs miscompare):** *Input constraint:* $|ia - ib| > Tlevel \wedge |ia - ic| > Tlevel \wedge |ib - ic| > Tlevel$. *Temporal constraint:* $duration \leq PClimit$.

2.3 From Actions to Scenarios

While actions describe local input behaviors over a time interval, *scenarios* represent higher-level behavioral flows by combining actions into ordered sequences. Using the actions introduced above, different scenarios can be constructed to represent typical system behaviors.

- **S1 (Transient Disturbance with Recovery).** The action sequence is $[A1, A2, A1]$. The system transitions from a consistent state to a transient miscompare and then returns to normal operation. Since the disturbance does not exceed the persistence limit, no failure is latched. This scenario supports checking RM-002 under transient disturbance.
- **S2 (Escalation to Latched Failure).** Action sequence: $[A1, A2, A3]$. A transient miscompare evolves into a persistent one, leading to failure latching and transition to the single-fail state. This scenario is related to RM-001.
- **S3 (Persistent Failure with Severe Divergence).** Action sequence: $[A3, A4]$. A persistent miscompare is followed by all-pairs divergence beyond the trip level. This scenario exercises failure behavior related to RM-001 and RM-004.
- **S4/S5 (Single-fail output checking).** The complete generated scenario set also contains scenarios for RM-003 and RM-004.

  For example, $[A1, A2, A3, A1]$ checks that the selected value becomes the good channel average after a single failure, and $[A1, A2, A3, A4]$ checks that *set_val* remains unchanged when a second failure is in progress.

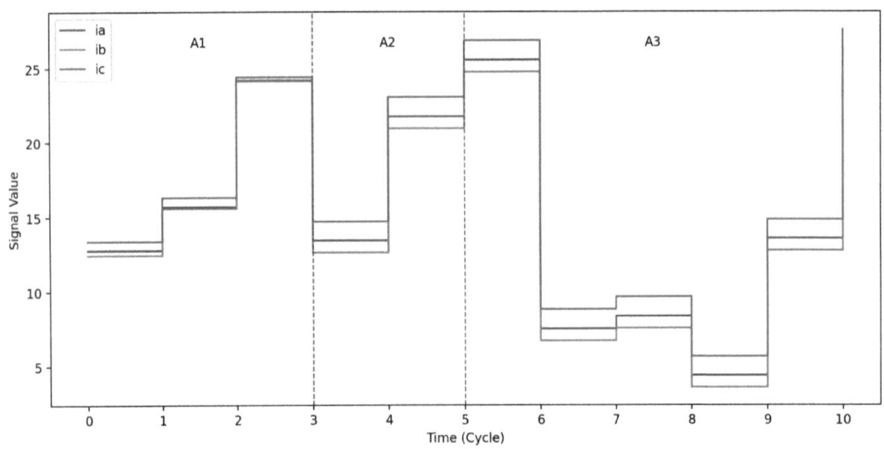

Fig. 2. Test cases for $[A1, A2, A3]$

2.4 From Scenarios to Executable Test Cases

Once scenarios are constructed, they are instantiated into concrete input signals for the Triplex model. Consider Scenario S2 with action sequence $[A1, A2, A3]$. This sequence represents normal operation, followed by a transient miscompare, and finally a persistent miscompare that exceeds the persistence limit.

Given a specific test configuration: $0 \leq ia, ib, ic \leq 30$, $PClimit = 2, Tlevel = 1$, $Simulationtime = 10$, our tool will instantiate $[A1, A2, A3]$ into executable test cases as shown in Fig. 2. Specifically, the interval $t \in [0, 3]$ corresponds to Action A1, during which all three signals remain within the trip level. The interval $t \in [3, 5]$ corresponds to Action A2, where a short-duration miscompare occurs. Since this segment lasts two time steps, it does not exceed the persistence limit $PClimit = 2$. Finally, the interval $t \in [5, 10]$ corresponds to Action A3, in which the miscompare persists for more than $PClimit$, thereby triggering a latched failure according to RM-001.

3 Formal Definitions

An action captures a semantic input behavior over a time interval. It specifies both the constraints that input signals must satisfy and the admissible duration of that behavior.

Definition 1 (Action). *Let $u : \mathbb{R}_{\geq 0} \to U$ denote the system input signal. Let φ denote a semantic input constraint defined over u, $\mathcal{I}_T \subseteq \mathbb{R}_{>0}$ denote the admissible duration set, and let Σ denote the semantic description space. An* action *is defined as a tuple*

$$\mathcal{A} = (\varphi, \mathcal{I}_T, \sigma),$$

where $\sigma \in \Sigma$ denotes the semantic description consistent with the action.

In this paper, Σ is not a mathematical state space of the Simulink model; it denotes the space of textual or structured semantic descriptions used for traceability. The description σ can be a short phrase such as "persistent miscompare between *ib* and *ic*". The admissible duration set $\mathcal{I}_T$ is represented as an interval or a finite union of intervals over positive real time, e.g., $(0, PClimit]$ or $(PClimit, T_{sim}]$.

While an action specifies input constraints and admissible duration, it is also necessary to determine when such an action occurs in a signal trace. This is particularly important when different actions share the same signal constraint but differ in their temporal constraints. In the Triplex running example, both transient and persistent miscompare actions satisfy $|ib - ic| > Tlevel$, but they are distinguished by whether the miscompare duration is no greater than or exceeds $PClimit$. To capture when both the signal constraint and temporal requirement are satisfied, we introduce the notion of *action occurrence*. We use the standard STL globally operator $\mathbf{G}_{[t_1,t_2]}(\varphi)$ to denote that constraint φ holds for all time points in interval $[t_1, t_2]$.

Definition 2 (Occurrence of an Action). *Given an input signal u, an action $\mathcal{A} = (\varphi, \mathcal{I}_T, \sigma)$ is said to* occur *in u if and only if there exist $t_1, t_2 \in \mathbb{R}_{\geq 0}$ such that*

$$u \models \mathbf{G}_{[t_1,t_2]}(\varphi), \quad t_2 - t_1 \in \mathcal{I}_T.$$

For example, the Triplex action A3 can be represented as

$$\mathcal{A}_3 = (\varphi_3, (PClimit, T_{sim}], \sigma_3),$$

where $\varphi_3 = |ia - ib| \leq Tlevel \wedge |ia - ic| \leq Tlevel \wedge |ib - ic| > Tlevel$, and σ_3 is "persistent miscompare between *ib* and *ic*".

Definition 3 (Action Set). *Let $\mathbb{A}$ denote a collection of actions, where each action $\mathcal{A}_i \in \mathbb{A}$ is defined as*

$$\mathcal{A}_i = (\varphi_i, \mathcal{I}_T^i, \sigma_i).$$

The action set *is defined as*

$$\mathbb{A} = \{\mathcal{A}_1, \mathcal{A}_2, \ldots, \mathcal{A}_N\},$$

where $N \in \mathbb{N}$ denotes the cardinality of the action set.

In requirement engineering, *scenario* is a broadly used concept whose meaning may vary across studies. In our approach, a scenario denotes an ordered sequence of actions that represents a requirement-related behavioral evolution.

Definition 4 (Scenario). *Let $\mathbb{A}$ denote a finite action set. A* scenario *is defined as a tuple*

$$\mathcal{S} = (\mathbf{A}, \sigma_S, \rho),$$

where:

- *$\mathbf{A} = \langle \mathcal{A}_1, \mathcal{A}_2, \ldots, \mathcal{A}_K \rangle$ is an ordered sequence of actions, with $\mathcal{A}_k \in \mathbb{A}$;*
- *$\sigma_S \in \Sigma$ denotes the semantic description of the scenario;*
- *ρ denotes the identifier of the related requirement(s), represented by requirement IDs such as RM-001 or by a set of such IDs.*

Definition 5 (Occurrence of a Scenario). *Given an input signal u and a scenario $\mathcal{S} = (\mathbf{A}, \sigma_S, \rho)$, the scenario is said to* occur *in u if there exist time intervals*

$$[t_1^1, t_2^1], [t_1^2, t_2^2], \ldots, [t_1^K, t_2^K]$$

such that:

1. *each action $\mathcal{A}_k$ occurs in u over $[t_1^k, t_2^k]$;*
2. *the temporal order is preserved:*

$$t_2^k \leq t_1^{k+1}, \quad \forall k = 1, \ldots, K-1.$$

The non-strict order permits unconstrained gaps in the general definition. In our implementation, however, Scenario Instantiation allocates contiguous intervals whose union covers $[0, T_{sim}]$, so consecutive actions satisfy $t_2^k = t_1^{k+1}$.

Definition 6 (Scenario Set). *Let $\mathbb{A}$ denote a finite action set. A* scenario set *is defined as a finite collection of scenarios*

$$\mathbb{S} = \{\mathcal{S}_1, \mathcal{S}_2, \ldots, \mathcal{S}_M\},$$

where each scenario

$$\mathcal{S}_i = (\mathbf{A}_i, \sigma_{S_i}, \rho_i)$$

consists of an ordered action sequence $\mathbf{A}_i = \langle \mathcal{A}_{i,1}, \ldots, \mathcal{A}_{i,K_i} \rangle$, with $\mathcal{A}_{i,k} \in \mathbb{A}$, a semantic description σ_{S_i}, and an associated requirement identifier ρ_i.

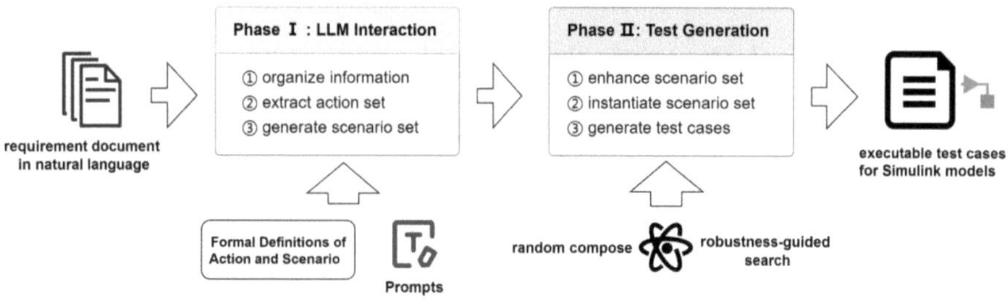

Fig. 3. Overview of RST-LLM

4 LLM-Guided Requirement Scenario-Based Testing Framework

Figure 3 presents an overview of RST-LLM. The input is the requirement document for Simulink model. To generate executable test cases, the document must include model input/output configuration, model descriptions, requirement items and test configuration. The output is executable test cases. The workflow is composed of a LLM-interaction phase and a test-generation phase.

4.1 LLM-Interaction Phase

The LLM-interaction phase consists of three prompt-based steps, as illustrated in Fig. 3.

Step 1: Organize Information. We first instruct the LLM to extract and organize key information from the requirement document, including the model description, input/output signals, requirement items, and test configuration. This step ensures that the LLM obtains a basic understanding of the target system.

Step 2: Extract the Action Set. Next, we include the formal definition of *Action* in the prompt and instruct the LLM to analyze the requirement document to derive the action set for the target system. Each action in the action set is characterized by four attributes: *name*, *description*, *input constraint*, and *temporal constraint*. The input constraint specifies conditions that the input signals must satisfy, while the temporal constraint describes the admissible duration of the action.

To improve reliability, generated actions must follow a predefined schema, use only declared input signals, and express constraints in STL. We do not assume every raw LLM output is well formed: constraints are checked by the STL parser and against the declared signal set, and malformed outputs are rejected, regenerated, or normalized before test generation.

Continuous Signal Parameterization. The motivating example in Sect. 2 illustrates the workflow using piecewise-constant signals for simplicity. In practice, RST-LLM also supports continuous signal representations through signal parameterization. Whether a signal is parameterized and which parameterization mode is used are specified in the test configuration provided in the requirement document. In our implementation, the signal within an action interval is parameterized using three control values $\mathbf{x} = (x_1, x_2, x_3)$, which represent the signal values at the beginning, middle, and end of the action duration.

Two parameterization modes are supported. In the *pconst* mode, the signal is generated as a sequence of constant segments determined by the parameters. In the *pchip* mode, a smooth signal segment is constructed using cubic Hermite interpolation:

$$x(t) = \text{pchip}(x_1, x_2, x_3).$$

The values x_1, x_2, x_3 are not fixed by users or generated by the LLM; they are decision variables sampled and optimized during robustness-guided test generation. Users specify bounds and the parameterization mode, while the LLM generates constraints, actions, and scenarios.

Step 3: Generate the Scenario Set. Finally, we include the formal definition of *Scenario* in the prompt and instruct the LLM to generate a scenario set based on the requirement items and the previously derived action set. Each scenario contains four attributes: *name*, *description*, *action sequence*, and *related requirement*. Similarly, the generated scenario set must follow the predefined format, use only actions from the extracted action set, and correspond to at least one requirement item. We additionally check that each referenced action exists and that each scenario remains traceable to at least one requirement ID.

4.2 Test-Generation Phase

The Test-Generation phase consists of three steps, as illustrated in Fig. 3. The action set, scenario set, and test configurations produced in the LLM-interaction phase serve as inputs to this phase.

Algorithm 1. Scenario Enhancement via Validated Random Composition

Require: Original scenario set $\mathbb{S} = \{\mathcal{S}_1, \ldots, \mathcal{S}_M\}$; maximum combination count $C_{\max}$; maximum sampling attempts $R_{\max}$.
Ensure: Enhanced scenario set $\mathbb{S}_{\text{enh}}$.

```
S_enh ← ∅
for i = 1 to M do
    Initialize composition list C with S_i
    Sample c ~ Uniform{2, ..., C_max}; r ← 0
    while |C| < c and r < R_max do
        Randomly sample S_j ∈ S; r ← r + 1
        if COMPATIBLE(C, S_j) then
            Append S_j to C
    A ← ⟨ ⟩
    for all S ∈ C do
        A ← CONCAT(A, action sequence of S)
    Construct S_{i,enh} ← (A, σ_{S_i}, ρ_i)
    S_enh ← S_enh ∪ {S_{i,enh}}
return S_enh
```

Algorithm 2. Scenario Instantiation

Require: Enhanced scenario set $\mathbb{S}_{\text{enh}}$; simulation time T_{sim}.
Ensure: Instantiated scenario set $\mathbb{S}^+$.

```
S+ ← ∅
for all S_enh = (A, σ, ρ) ∈ S_enh do
    d[1, ..., |A|] ← ALLOCATEDURATIONS(A, T_sim)
    t ← 0;  I ← ⟨ ⟩
    for k = 1 to |A| do
        t_s ← t;  t_e ← t + d[k]
        Append [t_s, t_e] to I
        t ← t_e
    S+ ← (A, I, σ, ρ)
    S+ ← S+ ∪ {S+}
return S+
```

Step 1: Enhance the Scenario Set. To increase behavioral diversity, original scenarios are randomly composed into longer sequences. Algorithm 4.1 fixes the first scenario as the corresponding original scenario and samples the remaining ones. The composition is not accepted unconditionally: COMPATIBLE checks shared input/output configuration, feasible temporal allocation within T_{sim}, requirement traceability, and, when available, state-mode compatibility.

Step 2: Instantiate the Scenario Set. After enhancement, each scenario is instantiated into a temporally structured scenario according to the test configuration. Algorithm 2 performs this step. In particular, the total simulation time is partitioned into a sequence of contiguous time intervals corresponding to the actions in the scenario. Each action is assigned a duration sampled from the admissible temporal interval defined by its temporal constraint, and the sum of all assigned durations equals the total simulation time. As a result, the instantiated scenario satisfies both the action ordering and the temporal requirements.

In some cases, the generated scenario composition may contain too many actions to be feasibly instantiated within the simulation time. In such cases, Algorithm 4.1 and Algorithm 2 are repeated up to a bounded number of attempts until a valid instantiated scenario is obtained.

Algorithm 3. Robustness-Guided Test Generation

Require: Instantiated scenario set $\mathbb{S}^+$, input bounds B, candidate pool size P, maximum iterations $I_{\max}$, and simulation time T_{sim}.
Ensure: Executable test suite $\mathbb{T}$.

$\mathbb{T} \leftarrow \emptyset$
for all $\mathcal{S}^+ = (A, \mathbf{I}, \sigma, \rho) \in \mathbb{S}^+$ **do**
  Initialize $u(\cdot)$ on $[0, T_{\text{sim}}]$
  for $k = 1$ **to** $|A|$ **do**
    $a \leftarrow A[k]$; $[t_s, t_e] \leftarrow \mathbf{I}[k]$
    Initialize candidate parameter pool $\mathcal{P}$ by sampling within B
    bestRob $\leftarrow -\infty$; $u^\star(\cdot) \leftarrow \bot$; iter $\leftarrow 0$
    repeat
      Generate candidates by resampling or perturbing parameter vectors in $\mathcal{P}$
      for all $u_{\text{cand}}(\cdot) \in \mathcal{P}$ **do**
        $rob \leftarrow$ Robustness($u_{\text{cand}}(\cdot), a$)
        if $rob >$ bestRob **then**
          bestRob $\leftarrow rob$; $u^\star(\cdot) \leftarrow u_{\text{cand}}(\cdot)$
      iter $\leftarrow iter + 1$
    until bestRob ≥ 0 **or** $iter = I_{\max}$
    Overwrite $u(\cdot)$ on $[t_s, t_e]$ with $u^\star(\cdot)$
  Construct test case $tc \leftarrow (u(\cdot), \rho)$
  $\mathbb{T} \leftarrow \mathbb{T} \cup \{tc\}$
return $\mathbb{T}$

Step 3: Generating Executable Test Cases. Finally, executable test cases are generated through robustness-guided search. For each action interval, candidates are produced by sampling signal-segment parameters within declared bounds: pconst parameters define constant segment values, while pchip parameters define beginning, middle, and ending control values. The pool is refreshed by resampling or perturbing the current best candidate and evaluated using STL robustness. Search terminates when *bestRob* ≥ 0 or $I_{\max}$ is reached; otherwise the best candidate is retained for the attempt or the scenario is regenerated within the retry budget. Robustness is computed using `rtamt` [20].

5 Experimental Evaluation

This section empirically evaluates RST-LLM by answering the following research questions:

RQ1: How effective are the test cases generated by RST-LLM?
RQ2: Does the Action–Scenario abstraction improve LLM-based test generation?
RQ3: To what extent can RST-LLM detect faults that violate requirement-related behaviors?

5.1 Benchmark

Our benchmark contains four industrial Simulink models. Each model has its corresponding requirement document. Four models (TRI, FSM, TUI, and NN) are selected from the Ten Lockheed Martin Challenge Problems (LMCPS) [19].

LMCPS contains ten industrial Simulink models and corresponding natural-language requirements developed by domain experts. The requirement documents include 1) model description; 2) model input/output configuration; 3) a set of requirement items. The models of LMCPS are inspired by flight control and vehicle management systems, and LMCPS is widely used in requirement and formal verification research. The documents do not include test configurations for simulation, like input signal scope, simulation time. We write test configurations for each model according to former research [3,12,19]. Table 1 present basic information of these four models.

All the experiments are performed on the same environment (Windows 11, Intel i9-13900H CPU, 32 GB RAM). We use DeepSeek [7] as the underlying LLM for our approach. The benchmarks and experimental data are available in the repository https://github.com/FishMoun/RST-LLM.

Table 1. Model Information (NoB: Number of Blocks NoR: Number of Requirement Items)

Model	Description	NoB	NoR
TRI	A redundancy management system	479	4
FSM	An abstraction of an advanced autopilot system interacting with an independent sensor platform	279	13
TUI	A flight software utility for computing the integration of a signal	45	4
NN	A two-input single-output predictor neural network	699	4

5.2 RQ1: Effectiveness

To evaluate the effectiveness of RST-LLM, we compare it with Adaptive Random Testing (ART) under identical experimental settings. ART randomly generates test inputs while attempting to evenly distribute test cases in the input space. For each benchmark model, we conduct 10 independent runs to reduce the influence of randomness in test generation. In each run, both approaches generate the same number of test cases to ensure a fair comparison. For RST-LLM, test cases are obtained by instantiating requirement-related scenarios derived from the requirement document.

We evaluate three structural coverage metrics: condition coverage, decision coverage, and MC/DC coverage. Table 2 summarizes the coverage results.

Overall, RST-LLM achieves coverage that is consistently comparable to or higher than ART across all evaluated models. The improvement is particularly clear on models with complex control logic, such as TRI and FSM. On TRI, RST-LLM increases condition coverage from 97.87% to 99.95%, decision coverage from 91.49% to 95.74%, and MC/DC coverage from 52.75% to 90.20%. On FSM, RST-LLM also improves all three metrics, with condition coverage increasing from 93.44% to 93.75%, decision coverage from 93.54% to 93.75%, and MC/DC coverage from 74.00% to 80.00%. These results indicate that the scenario-based abstraction helps guide test generation toward more diverse logical combinations and state transitions, which is especially beneficial for satisfying stricter criteria such as MC/DC.

For models with simpler structures, RST-LLM still demonstrates an advantage over ART. On TUI, condition coverage improves substantially from 50.00% to 100%, and decision coverage increases from 79.00% to 100%. On NN, although only decision coverage is applicable, RST-LLM still achieves the highest result, improving from 88.12% to 92.66%. These results show that even when the model behavior is relatively simple, requirement-guided scenario generation remains effective in improving structural coverage.

Answer to RQ1: RST-LLM generates test cases that achieve consistently comparable or higher structural coverage than Adaptive Random Testing across all evaluated models, demonstrating its effectiveness. On average, RST-LLM improves condition coverage by approximately 17.5%, decision coverage by 7.5%, and MC/DC coverage by 21.7%.

Table 2. Coverage Comparison Across Models (mean over 10 independent runs). "–" indicates that the corresponding coverage metric is not applicable for the model.

Model	Coverage	ART (RQ1)	LLM (RQ2)	RST-LLM
TRI	Condition	97.87	85.50	**99.95**
	Decision	91.49	72.77	**95.74**
	MC/DC	52.75	18.24	**90.20**
FSM	Condition	93.44	90.62	**93.75**
	Decision	93.54	89.06	**93.75**
	MC/DC	74.00	55.00	**80.00**
TUI	Condition	50.00	80.00	**100**
	Decision	79.00	70.00	**100**
	MC/DC	–	–	–
NN	Condition	–	–	–
	Decision	88.12	89.41	**92.66**
	MC/DC	–	–	–

5.3 RQ2: Impact of the Action–Scenario Abstraction

RQ2 investigates whether introducing the Action–Scenario abstraction improves the effectiveness of LLM-based test generation compared with directly generating test cases using an LLM.

Both approaches use the same underlying language model and decoding configuration. The direct LLM-based test generation directly generates executable test cases from the requirement document without explicitly defining intermediate abstractions. In contrast, RST-LLM first derives semantically structured actions and requirement-related scenarios, which are then instantiated into executable test cases.

As shown in Table 2, RST-LLM consistently achieves higher coverage than the direct LLM-based test generation on several models. The improvement is particularly evident on TRI and FSM in terms of MC/DC coverage. For example, on TRI the MC/DC coverage increases significantly from 18.24% to 90.20%, while on FSM it improves from 55.00% to 80.00%. RST-LLM also improves condition and decision coverage on TRI, increasing condition coverage from 85.50% to 99.95% and decision coverage from 72.77% to 95.74%. These results suggest that explicitly structuring the input space through actions and scenarios enables the testing process to systematically explore diverse logical combinations and temporal behaviors, which are difficult to achieve when test cases are generated directly by the LLM. For models with simpler control structures, such as TUI and NN, the difference between the two approaches is smaller, although RST-LLM still achieves comparable or higher coverage.

Answer to RQ2: Compared with direct LLM-based test generation, RST-LLM achieves consistently higher coverage on the evaluated models, demonstrating the effectiveness of introducing the Action–Scenario abstraction. On average, RST-LLM improves condition coverage by approximately 12.5%, decision coverage by 15.2%, and MC/DC coverage by 48.5% .

Table 3. Injected faults and their related requirements

Model	Fault	Related Requirement Item
TRI	If a second failure is in progress, the selected value will change from the previous selected value	If a second failure is in progress, the selected value shall remain unchanged from the previous selected value
FSM	Exceeding sensor limits will not latch an autopilot pullup when the pilot is not in control (not standby) and the system is supported without failures (not apfail)	Exceeding sensor limits shall latch an autopilot pullup when the pilot is not in control (not standby) and the system is supported without failures (not apfail)
TUI	Added a constant error of $1 \cdot 10^{-10}$ to the integral	The Output (y_{out}) shall be bounded by the provided Top and Bottom limits (TL and BL)
NN	Values for both input signals close to 0 at the same time lead the Deep Neural Network to output values above 1.1	The maximum value of the NN output, z, shall always be less than or equal to 1.1, regardless of the input values

5.4 RQ3: Requirement-Related Fault Detection

RQ3 evaluates the ability of RST-LLM to reveal faults that violate requirement-related behaviors. The injected faults in Table 3 are requirement-oriented rather than arbitrary syntactic mutations. For each model, we select one representative requirement item with an STL oracle and manually modify the model behavior so that the requirement may be violated under specific input conditions, without changing the model interface, input ranges, or simulation configuration. A test is fault-revealing if its trace violates the oracle [2]; all methods are compared on the same fault-seeded model and oracle.

We conduct 10 independent runs for each injected-fault setting. In each run, RST-LLM targets one requirement item and generates 10 scenarios, each instantiated into one executable test case (i.e., 10 test cases per run). For a run producing n test cases, among which v violate the oracle, the fault-revealing rate (FRR) is defined as

$$FRR = \frac{v}{n}.$$

The final FRR reported for each model is the mean value over the 10 runs.

Table 4 reports the FRR results. Overall, RST-LLM consistently achieves the highest FRR across all evaluated models. It reaches 95% on TRI, 100% on FSM, and 99% on TUI, all substantially higher than those of ART and direct LLM-based test generation. Even on the more challenging NN model, RST-LLM still achieves an FRR of 13%, while both baselines remain at 0%. The NN fault is more difficult because the injected violation is triggered only when both inputs fall into a narrow region close to zero. ART and direct LLM generation rarely hit this corner condition, whereas RST-LLM improves the chance by explicitly constructing requirement-related scenarios; its FRR is still lower than on the other models because the triggering region is small. These results indicate that requirement-related scenarios generated by RST-LLM are more effective at triggering requirement-related faults.

Answer to RQ3: RST-LLM achieves the highest fault-revealing rate across all evaluated models. On average, it improves the FRR by approximately 43.8% over ART and 32.8% over direct LLM-based test generation, demonstrating stronger capability in detecting requirement-related faults.

Table 4. Fault-Revealing Rate (FRR) for Injected Faults (mean over 10 independent runs)

Model	ART (%)	LLM (%)	RST-LLM (%)
TRI	44.00	70.00	**95.00**
FSM	46.00	56.00	**100**
TUI	42.00	50.00	**99.00**
NN	0	0	**13.00**

5.5 Threats to Validity

We discuss several potential threats to the validity of our experimental evaluation.

Internal Validity. Threats may arise from the implementation of scenario generation, signal instantiation, and robustness evaluation. We mitigate this risk by using established tools such as `rtamt` and by running all compared approaches under the same environment. RST-LLM does not formally guarantee complete LLM extraction of all requirement-implied actions; output schemas, declared-signal checks, STL parseability checks, and requirement traceability reduce this risk, but completeness remains a limitation.

Construct Validity. We use structural coverage and FRR, which are common in model-based testing and CPS verification. We do not systematically report raw LLM constraint-generation success rates or scenario-composition validity rates; such measurements are left for future work.

External Validity. The results may depend on the selected benchmarks and LLM. We evaluate four LMCPS Simulink models and use DeepSeek as the underlying model; cross-model and cross-LLM evaluation is future work. The baselines isolate randomness and direct LLM generation, but do not cover all Simulink falsification and model-based testing techniques. Ordered action sequences fit sequential behavior, whereas branching or concurrent requirements may require scenario graphs or automata.

6 Related Work

Our work leverages LLMs to generate requirement-driven tests for Simulink models. Existing Simulink testing approaches include random-search-based, constraint-solving-based, and falsification-based techniques. Random-search methods [5,18,26] explore the input space and may use coverage feedback. However, they are not explicitly guided by natural-language requirements.

Constraint-solving approaches [13,14] and falsification techniques [1,9,27] are effective when formal properties, STL/MTL formulas, input constraints, or coverage objectives are available. Signal feature coverage [3] similarly relies on variables appearing in property formulas.

In contrast, RST-LLM uses the LLM to transform natural-language requirements into structured actions and scenarios, which are then instantiated by robustness-guided search.

Requirement-based and scenario-based test generation have also been widely studied. Prior approaches often derive tests from formal requirement models, UML/use-case specifications, or manually maintained scenario descriptions [11,21,23,28]. These methods provide strong traceability but usually require substantial manual formalization.

Recent LLM-based testing studies [10,22,25,29] show the potential of LLMs for generating properties or scenarios, but structured integration of requirement semantics into Simulink model-level testing remains limited.

RST-LLM differs from direct LLM test generation by introducing the intermediate Action–Scenario abstraction. We do not claim an exhaustive experimental comparison with all Simulink testing methods; our baselines isolate the benefit of requirement-guided scenario abstraction over random generation and direct LLM generation.

7 Conclusion and Future Work

This paper presents RST-LLM, an LLM-guided requirement scenario-based testing framework for Simulink models. RST-LLM introduces a hierarchical Action–Scenario abstraction that bridges natural-language requirements and executable model-level inputs. In our framework, the LLM serves as a semantic transformer that converts natural-language requirements into structured testing artifacts, including actions with explicit signal and temporal constraints and requirement-related scenarios represented as ordered action sequences.

We evaluated RST-LLM on four industrial benchmark models and compared it with Adaptive Random Testing (ART) and a direct LLM-based test generation baseline. The results show that RST-LLM achieves structural coverage that is comparable to or higher than the baselines, with particularly clear improvements in MC/DC coverage on models with complex control logic. Compared with directly generating test cases using an LLM, the proposed Action–Scenario abstraction enables more systematic exploration of model behaviors. In addition, RST-LLM achieves higher fault-revealing rates for requirement-related faults, suggesting that using an LLM to transform natural-language requirements into structured Action–Scenario artifacts enables more effective requirement-driven test generation for Simulink models.

In future work, we plan to extend the approach to more complex and large-scale industrial systems, conduct broader empirical studies with additional benchmarks and multiple large language models, and further investigate automated techniques for improving action completeness and scenario validity.

We also plan to support richer scenario structures, such as branching or concurrent scenario graphs. In addition, we plan to compare RST-LLM more broadly with Simulink falsification and model-based testing techniques.

References

1. Annpureddy, Y., Liu, C., Fainekos, G., Sankaranarayanan, S.: S-taliro: a tool for temporal logic falsification for hybrid systems. In: Abdulla, P.A., Leino, K.R.M. (eds.) Tools and Algorithms for the Construction and Analysis of Systems. TACAS 2011. LNCS, vol. 6605, pp. 254–257. Springer, Berlin, Heidelberg (2011). https://doi.org/10.1007/978-3-642-19835-9_21
2. Bartocci, E., Mariani, L., Ničković, D., Yadav, D.: Property-based mutation testing. In: 2023 IEEE Conference on Software Testing, Verification and Validation (ICST), pp. 222–233. IEEE (2023)

3. Bartocci, E., Mariani, L., Nickovic, D., Yadav, D.: Signal feature coverage and testing for cps dataflow models. ACM Trans. Softw. Eng. Methodol. **34**(7), 1–37 (2025)
4. Brown, T., et al.: Language models are few-shot learners. Adv. Neural Inf. Process. Syst. **33**, 1877–1901 (2020)
5. Cleaveland, R., Smolka, S.A., Sims, S.T.: An instrumentation-based approach to controller model validation. In: Broy, M., Krüger, I.H., Meisinger, M. (eds.) Model-Driven Development of Reliable Automotive Services. ASWSD 2006. LNCS, vol. 4922, pp. 84–97. Springer, Berlin, Heidelberg (2006). https://doi.org/10.1007/978-3-540-70930-5_6
6. Dajsuren, Y., van den Brand, M.G., Serebrenik, A., Roubtsov, S.: Simulink models are also software: modularity assessment. In: Proceedings of the 9th International ACM Sigsoft Conference on Quality of Software Architectures, pp. 99–106 (2013)
7. DeepSeek-AI: Deepseek: Large language model (2024). https://www.deepseek.com/. Accessed 22 Feb 2026
8. Elberzhager, F., Rosbach, A., Bauer, T.: Analysis and testing of matlab simulink models: a systematic mapping study. In: Proceedings of the 2013 International Workshop on Joining AcadeMiA and Industry Contributions to Testing Automation, pp. 29–34 (2013)
9. Ernst, G., Sedwards, S., Zhang, Z., Hasuo, I.: Falsification of hybrid systems using adaptive probabilistic search. ACM Trans. Model. Comput. Simul. (TOMACS) **31**(3), 1–22 (2021)
10. Etemadi, K., Sirjani, M., Helali Moghadam, M., Strandberg, P., Pettersson, P.: Llm-based property-based test generation for guardrailing cyber-physical systems. In: Steffen, B. (ed.) Bridging the Gap Between AI and Reality. AISoLA 2025. LNCS, vol. 16220, pp. 18–46. Springer, Cham (2025). https://doi.org/10.1007/978-3-032-07132-3_3
11. Farooq, M., Tahreem, T.: Requirement-based automated test case generation: systematic literature review. VFAST Trans. Softw. Eng. **10**(2), 133–142 (2022)
12. Formica, F., Fan, T., Rajhans, A., Pantelic, V., Lawford, M., Menghi, C.: Simulation-based testing of simulink models with test sequence and test assessment blocks. IEEE Trans. Softw. Eng. **50**(2), 239–257 (2023)
13. Hamon, G., et al.: Simulink design verifier-applying automated formal methods to simulink and stateflow. In: Third Workshop on Automated Formal Methods (2008)
14. He, N., Rümmer, P., Kroening, D.: Test-case generation for embedded simulink via formal concept analysis. In: Proceedings of the 48th Design Automation Conference, pp. 224–229 (2011)
15. Leong, I.T., Barbosa, R.: Translating natural language requirements to formal specifications: a study on gpt and symbolic nlp. In: 2023 53rd Annual IEEE/IFIP International Conference on Dependable Systems and Networks Workshops (DSN-W), pp. 259–262. IEEE (2023)
16. MathWorks: Simulink design verifier. https://www.mathworks.com/products/sldesignverifier.html. Accessed 26 Feb 2026
17. MathWorks: Simulink: Simulation and model-based design. https://www.mathworks.com/products/simulink.html. Accessed 26 Feb 2026
18. Matinnejad, R., Nejati, S., Briand, L.C., Bruckmann, T.: Simcotest: a test suite generation tool for simulink/stateflow controllers. In: Proceedings of the 38th International Conference on Software Engineering Companion, pp. 585–588 (2016)
19. Mavridou, A., et al.: The ten lockheed martin cyber-physical challenges: formalized, analyzed, and explained. In: 2020 IEEE 28th International Requirements Engineering Conference (RE), pp. 300–310. IEEE (2020)

20. Ničković, D., Yamaguchi, T.: Rtamt: online robustness monitors from STL. In: Hung, D.V., Sokolsky, O. (eds.) Automated Technology for Verification and Analysis. ATVA 2020. LNCS, vol. 12302, pp. 564–571. Springer, Cham (2020). https://doi.org/10.1007/978-3-030-59152-6_34
21. Offutt, J., Abdurazik, A.: Generating tests from uml specifications. In: France, R., Rumpe, B. (eds.) UML '99 — The Unified Modeling Language. UML 1999. LNCS, vol. 1723, pp. 416–429. Springer, Berlin, Heidelberg (1999). https://doi.org/10.1007/3-540-46852-8_30
22. Petrovic, N., et al.: Llm-driven testing for autonomous driving scenarios. In: 2024 2nd International Conference on Foundation and Large Language Models (FLLM), pp. 173–178 (2024)
23. Rodrigues, A., Vilela, J., Silva, C.: A systematic mapping study on techniques for generating test cases from requirements. IoTBDS, pp. 141–148 (2024)
24. Rozier, K.Y.: Specification: the biggest bottleneck in formal methods and autonomy. In: Blazy, S., Chechik, M. (eds.) Verified Software. Theories, Tools, and Experiments. VSTTE 2016. LNCS, vol. 9971, pp. 8–26. Springer, Cham (2016). https://doi.org/10.1007/978-3-319-48869-1_2
25. Sami, A.M., Rasheed, Z., Waseem, M., Zhang, Z., Tomas, H., Abrahamsson, P.: A tool for test case scenarios generation using large language models. arXiv preprint arXiv:2406.07021 (2024)
26. Satpathy, M., Yeolekar, A., Ramesh, S.: Randomized directed testing (redirect) for simulink/stateflow models. In: Proceedings of the 8th ACM International Conference on Embedded Software, pp. 217–226 (2008)
27. Waga, M.: Falsification of cyber-physical systems with robustness-guided black-box checking. In: Proceedings of the 23rd International Conference on Hybrid Systems: Computation and Control, pp. 1–13 (2020)
28. Wang, C., Pastore, F., Goknil, A., Briand, L., Iqbal, Z.: Automatic generation of system test cases from use case specifications. In: Proceedings of the 2015 International Symposium on Software Testing and Analysis, pp. 385–396 (2015)
29. Wang, J., Huang, Y., Chen, C., Liu, Z., Wang, S., Wang, Q.: Software testing with large language models: survey, landscape, and vision. IEEE Trans. Softw. Eng. **50**(4), 911–936 (2024)
30. Yang, Z., Huang, R., Cui, C., Niu, N., Towey, D.: Requirements-based test generation: a comprehensive survey. ACM Trans. Softw. Eng. Methodol. (2025)

PAT2PRISM: Bridging Qualitative Correctness and Quantitative Resilience for IoT Protocols

Zihan Tang[1], Sini Chen[1(✉)], Lili Xiao[2], and Huibiao Zhu[1(✉)]

[1] Shanghai Key Laboratory of Trustworthy Computing, East China Normal University, Shanghai, China
{51285902038,52265902002}@stu.ecnu.edu.cn, hbzhu@sei.ecnu.edu.cn
[2] School of Information and Intelligent Science, Donghua University, Shanghai, China
xiaolili@dhu.edu.cn

Abstract. The formal verification of IoT security protocols is often split into two largely independent domains. Qualitative analysis establishes logical correctness against active intruders, whereas quantitative analysis evaluates performance metrics such as latency and energy consumption. Maintaining separate models for these purposes is both labor-intensive and prone to semantic drift, leading to a recurring mismatch: protocols that appear secure in theory may fail once exposed to stochastic constraints of real-world networks. To address this gap, we propose a unified framework anchored by Pat2Prism, a novel tool that automates the translation of CSP-based specifications into probabilistic models. Beyond mere automation, we establish a rigorous theoretical foundation for this transformation. We define a formal mapping from Process Analysis Toolkit (PAT)'s Labeled Transition Systems (LTSs) to PRISM's Markov Decision Processes (MDPs) and prove that it preserves trace semantics and safety properties, ensuring quantitative insights are drawn from a behaviorally faithful refinement of the verified specification.

We evaluate the framework on the CoAP-EAP protocol and its lightweight variant, Lo-CoAP-EAP. Although both pass qualitative verification, quantitative results expose a critical trade-off: the 7.87% reduction in communication cost achieved by Lo-CoAP-EAP comes at the price of markedly reduced robustness under packet loss and imperfect anti-replay protection. This illustrates how aggressive optimizations can introduce hidden reliability risks in IoT protocols. By unifying logical proofs with probabilistic reasoning, our work delivers a principled, tool-supported methodology for designing protocols that are not only theoretically secure but also robust against the uncertainties of physical deployment.

Keywords: Formal Verification · IoT Security Protocols · Probabilistic Model Checking · Quantitative Resilience · Automated Tool

G. De Giacomo et al. (Eds.): TASE 2026, LNCS 16697, pp. 305–323, 2027.
https://doi.org/10.1007/978-3-032-30693-7_20

1 Introduction

The rapid deployment of Internet of Things (IoT) devices in safety-critical infrastructure—ranging from industrial control systems [23] to medical telemetry [29]—relies on lightweight protocols such as the Constrained Application Protocol (CoAP) [3], Extensible Authentication Protocol (EAP) [28], Datagram Transport Layer Security (DTLS) [19], and Object Security for Constrained RESTful Environments (OSCORE) [14] to exchange security-critical messages. Ensuring that these protocols behave correctly poses a dual challenge [4]. On the one hand, they must satisfy rigorous logical properties, including authentication, secrecy, and replay protection, in the presence of active adversaries. On the other hand, the same event-driven handshakes must remain robust under severe resource constraints and stochastic network conditions, providing quantifiable guarantees on latency, energy consumption, and message delivery reliability.

Against this backdrop, a fundamental gap remains in the formal analysis of security protocols: the split between qualitative security reasoning and quantitative performance modeling. Protocols are typically described in high-level process algebras (e.g., CSP, applied π-calculus) [1] and analysed with symbolic model checkers or theorem provers [15,25]. These tools are effective at uncovering logical flaws under an abstract Dolev-Yao intruder, but they deliberately abstract away the probabilistic behaviour of real deployments. Conversely, probabilistic model checkers based on Markov Decision Processes (MDPs) or Continuous-time Markov chains (CTMCs) [20] provide precise analysis of loss rates, delays, and adversarial schedulers, yet their state-centric formalisms struggle to capture the rich event-driven structure of real protocols. This divergence is reflected in existing tools: PAT, grounded in CSP#, offers strong support for detecting logical inconsistencies such as divergence or nondeterminism, whereas PRISM provides exact probabilistic verification, but its modeling language requires labor-intensive remodeling when translating from process-algebraic specifications. UPPAAL SMC [13] attempts to bridge the two domains, but its simulation-based semantics provide only statistical guarantees and therefore lack the coverage and exactness offered by PAT and PRISM. Consequently, system architects often face the burden of maintaining two parallel models: one for security proofs and another for performance estimation.

Manual translation between the two domains is time-consuming and invites semantic drift, where the performance model inadvertently simplifies or distorts the original security logic [5]. Moreover, existing attempts to combine logical and probabilistic verification often rely on ad-hoc simulation pipelines rather than formally justified refinement steps, so there is no rigorous guarantee that quantitative results preserve the safety properties established in the qualitative phase. This gap motivates a verification approach that explicitly bridges logical correctness with quantitative robustness, enabling engineers to reason about security properties and performance trade-offs within a single framework.

To address this issue, we propose a unified verification framework specifically targeted at network security protocols that bridges the semantic gap between the

PAT and the PRISM model checker. Our key observation is that the labeled transition system semantics of CSP#—widely used to model sequential processes and message-passing behavior—can be mapped systematically to the nondeterministic choices of an MDP, while probabilistic aspects are factored into an explicit environment model. Building on this, we design PAT2PRISM, an automated translation tool that turns verified CSP# protocol specifications into PRISM MDP skeletons. As illustrated in Fig. 1, the framework operates in three layers: (1) qualitative verification in PAT; (2) PAT2PRISM translation via semantic mapping and syntactic translation; (3) quantitative verification in PRISM with parameters P_{loss}, P_{vuln}. The translation preserves *trace equivalence* (proved by formalized rules), guaranteeing behavioral consistency between the probabilistic model and the logical specification. This ensures that safety properties established qualitatively are preserved in quantitative analysis. This paper makes the following contributions:

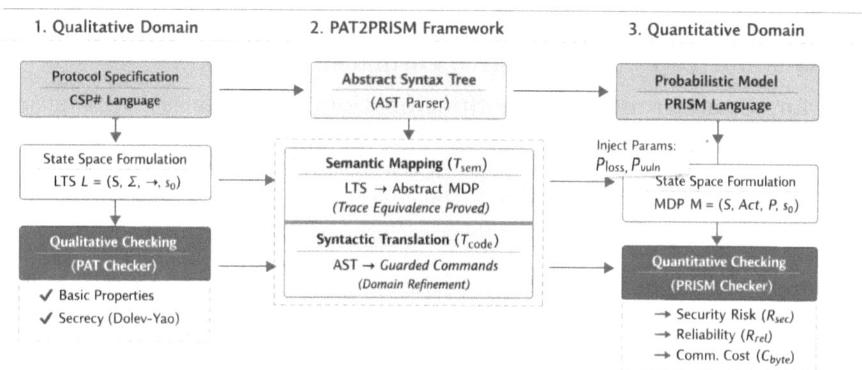

Fig. 1. Overview of the PAT2PRISM unified verification framework.

- **Formal Semantics Mapping:** We establish a rigorous theoretical mapping between CSP# LTS and PRISM MDPs, proving that the transformation preserves the trace semantics required for valid security analysis.
- **Automated Translation Tool:** We develop PAT2PRISM, a protocol-agnostic translator that automatically converts CSP# specifications into PRISM MDP skeletons. It preserves correct control-flow logic while enabling experts to inject deployment parameters, thereby eliminating semantic drift, reducing modeling effort, and ensuring broad applicability across IoT protocols.
- **Empirical Insights:** Through a comparative case study of the CoAP-EAP and Lo-CoAP-EAP protocols, we demonstrate that our framework uncovers critical trade-offs: lightweight optimizations, while efficient, exhibit disproportionate sensitivity to implementation flaws, which are undetectable by qualitative verification alone.

The remainder of this paper is organized as follows. Section 2 reviews the theoretical foundations and introduces the CoAP-EAP protocol family. Section 3 discusses related work and research gap. Section 4 presents the formal semantics mapping and the corresponding syntactic translation strategy. Section 5 describes the design of our automated translation tool. Section 6 reports empirical results from case studies on representative IoT protocols. Finally, Sect. 7 concludes the paper and outlines directions for future research.

2 Background

This section outlines the formal foundations of our framework, leveraging CSP for concurrency and MDPs for probabilistic reasoning. We first review the formalisms that enable rigorous evaluation and then introduce the CoAP-EAP protocol family, which serves as the primary case study for evaluating our approach.

2.1 Qualitative vs. Quantitative Formalisms

CSP for Concurrent System Specification. Communicating Sequential Processes (CSP) [16] provides a rigorous algebra for specifying concurrent system behavior, widely adopted in hardware/software co-design for its compositionality. We utilize the CSP# dialect [21], which extends classical CSP with data-rich features essential for modeling complex security protocols:

- **Shared Variables**: Enable the modeling of global state (e.g., channel buffers, cryptographic nonces) and atomic updates.
- **Rich Data Types**: Support complex message structures (e.g., arrays, user-defined records) required for cryptographic protocols.
- **Channel Communication**: Facilitates the modeling of diverse interaction patterns, including point-to-point synchronization and broadcast.

A process P is defined by the grammar:

$$P, Q ::= \text{Skip} \mid \text{Stop} \mid a \rightarrow P \mid P\,;Q \mid P \parallel Q \mid P \,\Box\, Q \mid [b]P$$

where a denotes atomic events, $\parallel$ parallel composition, and $[b]P$ guarded execution. The operational semantics is a Labeled Transition System (LTS) $\mathcal{L} = (S, \Sigma, \rightarrow, s_0)$. We employ the PAT to verify qualitative properties on these models, ensuring functional correctness such as deadlock freedom and secrecy. However, while PAT excels at logical verification [8], it provides no quantitative performance metrics—a critical gap for resource-constrained IoT systems where timing and energy are first-class design constraints.

MDPs for Quantitative Performance Analysis. To support performance modeling, we lift LTS semantics to MDPs $\mathcal{M} = (S, \mathrm{Act}, \mathbf{P}, s_0)$. Unlike standard LTS or Discrete Time Markov Chains (DTMCs) [18], MDPs explicitly distinguish between **nondeterminism** (system-controlled choices like scheduling or attacker strategies) and **probability** (environment-driven uncertainty like channel errors). This separation is critical for performance analysis as it allows exploring worst-case scenarios under adversarial conditions while simultaneously modeling realistic probabilistic workloads.

We employ PRISM [20] to analyze these models. Its guarded-command language encodes probabilistic transitions:

$$[\mathrm{act}]\ \mathrm{guard}\ \rightarrow\ \lambda_1 : \mathrm{update}_1\ +\ \ldots\ +\ \lambda_k : \mathrm{update}_k;$$

Furthermore, PRISM's **reward structures** facilitate the computation of quantitative metrics such as expected latency ($\mathbb{E}[\mathrm{steps}]$), energy consumption ($\mathbb{E}[\sum \mathrm{costs}]$), and probabilistic guarantees ($P_{max}[\Diamond_{\leq K}\mathrm{goal}]$).

However, a key challenge lies in the semantic gap between high-level protocols and PRISM's low-level input language: PRISM relies on simple integer-based state encoding and lacks support for complex data structures (e.g., pointers, dynamic arrays) found in CSP#. This discrepancy creates a significant barrier to modeling complex systems, highlighting the need for automated abstraction mechanisms that can bridge these two formalisms.

2.2 The CoAP-EAP Protocol Family

The CoAP-EAP framework [12] adapts the Extensible Authentication Protocol (EAP) [28] for constrained IoT networks by encapsulating EAP payloads within CoAP messages. As illustrated in Fig. 2, the protocol involves a multi-phase interaction between a Smart Object, a Controller, and a AAA Server. The standard workflow proceeds through (I) Triggering, (II) Nonce Exchange for replay protection, (III) Identity Exchange, (IV) EAP Method Execution (e.g., EAP-PSK), and (V) Final Completion.

To minimize communication overhead in Low-Power Wide-Area Networks (LP-WANs) [24], the Lo-CoAP-EAP variant introduces aggressive cross-layer optimizations. As highlighted in the figure, it employs (i) **message consolidation**, merging the bootstrapping and identity phases to reduce round-trips; (ii) **implicit acknowledgments** via CoAP's "No-Response" option to save control traffic; and (iii) **piggybacked success** notifications.

While these architectural changes promise significant efficiency gains, they fundamentally alter the protocol's reliability dynamics. By removing explicit handshake steps, the design reduces the "safety margin" against network nondeterminism. The absence of a formal performance model leaves a critical gap: it is unknown whether these optimizations compromise the protocol's resilience to packet loss or active adversarial interference. This necessitates a rigorous, quantitative analysis to determine the safe operating boundaries of the low-power variant.

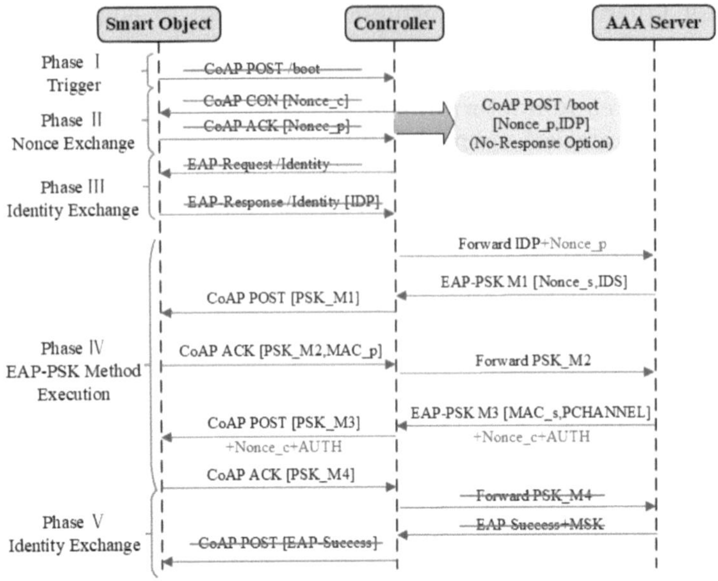

Fig. 2. Workflow of the CoAP-EAP protocol and the Lo-CoAP-EAP optimizations (highlighted in green). (Color figure online)

3 Related Work and Research Gap

The verification of IoT application-layer protocols has attracted increasing attention. Surveys such as [17] advocate for the formal modeling of protocols like CoAP and MQTT to prevent safety-critical failures. However, existing efforts typically operate at a high level of abstraction, focusing on generic service workflows rather than detailed cryptographic handshakes.

Attempts to bridge the gap between qualitative and quantitative analysis include Probabilistic CSP (PCSP) [22] and statistical model checking tools like UPPAAL SMC [10]. However, PCSP implementations often lack the mature ecosystem of PRISM for complex reward-based analysis, while UPPAAL SMC relies on statistical simulation, which provides asymptotic confidence rather than the exact probabilistic guarantees required for critical security proofs.

In the specific context of linking CSP and PRISM, Conserva Filho et al. [9] pioneered the "WatchDog Transformation" to verify probabilistic refinement for robotic controllers. While this work validates the theoretical compatibility of the two formalisms, its methodology is tailored to refinement assertions for control logic. To the best of our knowledge, no analogous framework currently exists for the security protocol domain that addresses the specific requirements of Dolev-Yao attacker modeling and message-passing semantics.

Our framework fills this void by providing a unified, automated translation from CSP# to PRISM. Unlike prior approaches, PAT2PRISM is designed specifically for network security protocols, enabling a sound transition from qualitative correctness proofs in PAT to quantitative robustness analysis in PRISM with minimal manual re-implementation and without semantic drift.

4 Formal Transformation Methodology

To bridge qualitative CSP# specifications and quantitative PRISM analysis, we propose a two-layer transformation (Fig. 3).

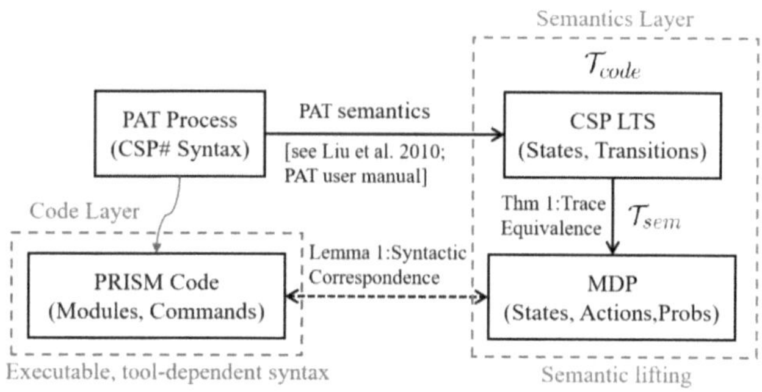

Fig. 3. Overall two-layer transformation architecture from CSP# to PRISM.

1. **Semantic Layer:** a mapping $\mathcal{T}_{sem}$ from CSP# LTS semantics to an abstract MDP.
2. **Syntactic Layer:** a translation $\mathcal{T}_{code}$ realizing the abstract MDP in PRISM's guarded-command language.

Crucially, since the operational semantics of the PAT model checker are formally defined via LTSs [27], we adopt the LTS as the ground truth for the source model.

4.1 Semantic Mapping and Trace Equivalence

We first define the semantic transformation $\mathcal{T}_{sem}$. Formally, this mapping lifts the nondeterministic, event-labeled transitions of a CSP process to the state-based, action-labeled transitions of an MDP, while preserving the sequential and concurrent structures of the protocol.

Abstract Transformation Rules. The transformation rules for the core CSP fragment used in our MDP models are summarized in Table 1. We adopt the following notation: An MDP is a quadruple $M = (S, s_0, AP, \Delta)$ equipped with a labelling function $L : S \to 2^{AP}$. For each CSP term P we write

$$\mathcal{T}_{sem}(P) = (S_P, s_P^0, AP_P, \Delta_P)$$

where S_P is the state space, s_P^0 the initial state, AP_P the set of atomic propositions, and $\Delta_P : S_P \times \Sigma \to \mathcal{D}(S_P)$ the transition function. We use δ_s for the Dirac distribution on state s and $\Delta|_{S'}$ for the restriction of Δ to a subset $S' \subseteq S$. The symbol $\uplus$ denotes disjoint union of sets. Note that R5 introduces $p \in (0,1)$ as a symbolic probability (later instantiated in PRISM) for the internal choice.

Table 1. Abstract Transformation Rules of $\mathcal{T}_{sem}$

Rule	CSP Term	Abstract MDP Semantics
R1–R2	skip, stop	$\mathcal{T}_{sem}(X) = (\{s_0\}, s_0, AP, \Delta),\ X \in \{\texttt{skip}, \texttt{stop}\},\ \forall\alpha.\ \Delta(s_0,\alpha) = \bot,$ $(X = \texttt{skip} \Rightarrow \mathit{term} \in L(s_0)) \wedge (X = \texttt{stop} \Rightarrow \mathit{dead} \in L(s_0))$
R3	$a \to P$	$\dfrac{\mathcal{T}_{sem}(a \to P) = (S_P \cup \{s_0\},\ s_0,\ AP_P,\ \Delta)}{\Delta(s_0, a) = \delta_{s_P^0},\ \Delta\|_{S_P} = \Delta_P}$
R4	$P \Box Q$	$\dfrac{\mathcal{T}_{sem}(P \Box Q) = (S_P \uplus S_Q \uplus \{s_0\},\ s_0,\ AP,\ \Delta)}{\Delta(s_0,\alpha) = \Delta_P(s_P^0,\alpha) \cup \Delta_Q(s_Q^0,\alpha)}$
R5	$P \sqcap Q$	As in R4, except $\Delta(s_0,\tau) = p\cdot\delta_{s_P^0} + (1-p)\cdot\delta_{s_Q^0}$ for fixed $0 < p < 1$
R6	$c!m \to P$	$\dfrac{\mathcal{T}_{sem}(c!m \to P) = (S_P \cup \{s_0\}, s_0, AP_P, \Delta)}{\Delta(s_0, c!m) = \delta_{s_P^0[\mathsf{ch}:=\mathsf{enc}(m)]},\ \Delta\|_{S_P} = \Delta_P}$
R7	$c?x \to P$	$\dfrac{\mathcal{T}_{sem}(c?x \to P) = (S_P \cup \{s_0\}, s_0, AP_P, \Delta)}{\forall m.\ \mathsf{ch}(s_0) = \mathsf{enc}(m) \Rightarrow \Delta(s_0, c?m) = \delta_{s_P^0[x\mapsto m]},\ \Delta\|_{S_P} = \Delta_P}$
R8	$[b]P$	$\dfrac{\mathcal{T}_{sem}([b]P) = (S_P \cup \{s_0\}, s_0, AP_P, \Delta)}{b(s_0) = \text{true} \Rightarrow \Delta(s_0,\tau) = \delta_{s_P^0},\quad b(s_0) = \text{false} \Rightarrow \forall\alpha.\Delta(s_0,\alpha) = \bot}$
R9	$\{x := e\} \to P$	As in R3, $\Delta(s_0,\tau) = \delta_{s_P^0[x\mapsto e(s_0)]},\ \Delta\|_{S_P} = \Delta_P$.
R10	$P_1 \,\|\, P_2$	$\dfrac{\mathcal{T}_{sem}(P_1 \| P_2) = (S_1 \times S_2,\ (s_1^0, s_2^0),\ AP_1 \cup AP_2,\ \Delta_{\|})}{\forall (s_1,s_2),\alpha.\ \Delta_{\|}((s_1,s_2),\alpha) = \Delta_1(s_1,\alpha) \times \delta_{s_2}\ \cup\ \delta_{s_1} \times \Delta_2(s_2,\alpha)}$
R11	$P_1 \,\|_A\, P_2$	As in R10, except that for $a \in A$, $\Delta_{\|}$ enables only joint transitions $(s_1,s_2) \xrightarrow{a} (s_1',s_2')$ where $s_i \xrightarrow{a} s_i'$ in $\mathcal{T}_{sem}(P_i)$, while actions $\alpha \notin A$ interleave as in R11.

Trace Preservation. Defining transformation rules is necessary but not sufficient; we must also rigorously prove that this mapping preserves the system's behavior. We now show that $\mathcal{T}_{sem}$ preserves observable behavior in the sense of *trace equivalence.* Let

$$Traces_{\mathrm{CSP}}(P) = \{\sigma \in \Sigma^* \mid \exists P'.\ P \xrightarrow{\sigma} P'\}$$

denote the set of finite traces of a CSP process P [16], where $P \xrightarrow{\sigma} P'$ means P evolves to P' via action sequence σ. For an MDP M, let $Traces_{\mathrm{MDP}}(M)$ denote the traces of M under all schedulers [20]:

$$Traces_{\mathrm{MDP}}(M) = \bigcup_{\mathfrak{S}} \{\,\sigma \in \Sigma^* \mid \exists\pi.\ \mathbb{P}_M^{\mathfrak{S}}(\pi) > 0,\ \mathit{trace}(\pi) = \sigma\,\}.$$

where $trace(\pi)$ extracts the action sequence from path π, $\mathfrak{S}$ ranges over all schedulers, and π over finite paths.

Theorem 1 (Trace Equivalence). *For every process P in the supported fragment,*

$$Traces_{\mathrm{CSP}}(P) = Traces_{\mathrm{MDP}}(\mathcal{T}_{sem}(P)).$$

The equivalence is proved by structural induction on P. The abstract rules in Table 1 are not ad hoc: they are directly derived from the standard SOS rules of CSP. Consequently, for every CSP subterm Q with LTS initial state q^0 and $\mathcal{T}_{sem}(Q) = (S_Q, s_Q^0, Trans_Q, L_Q)$, the construction satisfies the following invariants.

Invariant. One for enabledness and one for successor correspondence.
(I1) α is enabled at q^0 iff $Trans_Q(s_Q^0, \alpha) \neq \varnothing$.
(I2) For each visible α:

- (completeness) for every CSP step $Q \;\Rightarrow^{\alpha}\; Q'$ there exist $\mu \in Trans_Q(s_Q^0, \alpha)$ and $s' \in \mathrm{supp}(\mu)$ with $Traces_{\mathrm{MDP}}((S_Q, s', AP_Q, Trans_Q)) = Traces_{\mathrm{CSP}}(Q')$;
- (soundness) for every $\mu \in Trans_Q(s_Q^0, \alpha)$ and every $s' \in \mathrm{supp}(\mu)$ there exists Q' with $Traces_{\mathrm{MDP}}((S_Q, s', AP_Q, Trans_Q)) = Traces_{\mathrm{CSP}}(Q')$.

Compact Proof Sketch. Using (I1)–(I2) we show two inclusions.

(1) $Traces_{\mathrm{CSP}}(P) \subseteq Traces_{\mathrm{MDP}}(\mathcal{T}_{\mathrm{sem}}(P))$. Given a finite CSP trace σ from P, follow its CSP derivation stepwise. By completeness (I2) choose at each visible step a $\mu \in Trans$ and $s' \in \mathrm{supp}(\mu)$ that encodes the CSP continuation; for internal choices use any μ in the nonempty $Trans(s, \tau)$. This yields a finite MDP path whose projection equals σ and which has positive probability under the scheduler that always selects the chosen $Trans$-elements (finite-length construction).
(2) $Traces_{\mathrm{MDP}}(\mathcal{T}_{\mathrm{sem}}(P)) \subseteq Traces_{\mathrm{MDP}}(P)$. Let σ arise from a finite MDP path under some scheduler. By induction on $|\sigma|$, the first visible step must come from a rule in the table; by soundness (I2) the MDP successor corresponds to a CSP continuation, and the suffix of the path gives, by induction hypothesis, a CSP trace of that continuation. Hence $\sigma \in Traces_{\mathrm{MDP}}(P)$.

A short scheduler-correspondence remark suffices: for finite traces one can construct a scheduler that implements the nondeterministic selections required to follow any given CSP derivation (and conversely any scheduler's finite path choices correspond to some CSP branch by (I2)). Combining (1) and (2) yields equality. □

Crollary. Since safety properties in CSP are trace-closed, trace preservation implies preservation of safety properties and any finite "bad" trace excluded by the CSP model is also excluded by the MDP under all schedulers.

4.2 Syntactic Translation and Implementation Correctness

The second layer, $\mathcal{T}_{code}$, operationalizes the abstract semantics by mapping CSP constructs to executable PRISM code. This translation is designed to be a direct syntactic realization of $\mathcal{T}_{sem}$. We map each PAT abstract syntax tree (AST) construct to a PRISM code pattern, as summarized in Table 2.

Table 2. Syntactic Translation $\mathcal{T}_{code}$: Mapping PAT Constructs to PRISM Code

Rule ID	PAT Construct (AST Node)	Generated PRISM Code Pattern
R1–R2	`SKIP` / `STOP`	`[] s=END -> (s'=END);`
R3	Event $a \to P$	`[a] s=l -> (s'=l');`
R4–R5	Choice operators ($\sqcap, \Box$)	`[] s=l -> 0.5:(s'=l1) + 0.5:(s'=l2);`
R6–R7	Messages	`const int MSG_m = 1;`
	Send / Receive ($c!m, c?x$)	`global c; [] s=l & c=MSG_m -> (c'=0)...`
R8	Guard $[b]\, a \to P$	`[a] s=l & b -> (s'=l');`
R9	Assignment $x := e$	`[] s=l -> (x'=e) & (s'=l');`
R10	Parallel $P \parallel Q$	`module P ... endmodule module Q ...`
R11	Synchronization on a	`[a] s_P=...` and `[a] s_Q=...`

To ensure the fidelity of our implementation, we establish a structural correspondence between the generated code and the abstract semantics.

Lemma 1 (Syntactic Correspondence). *Let P be a CSP# process. The PRISM model generated by $\mathcal{T}_{code}(P)$ induces an MDP $\mathcal{M}_{PRISM}$ that is isomorphic to the abstract MDP $\mathcal{T}_{sem}(P)$.*

Proof. We define a bijection $\beta : S_{PRISM} \to S_{abs}$ mapping the program counter values (and variable valuations) in the PRISM model to the abstract states in $\mathcal{T}_{sem}(P)$. The proof proceeds by structural induction on P. Consider the prefix case $P = a \to Q$. The abstract rule R3 defines a transition $\delta(s_0, a) = \delta_{s_P^0}$. The corresponding code generation rule produces a command `[a] s=l -> (s'=l');`. Under β, where $\beta(l) = s_0$ and $\beta(l') = s_P^0$, this command induces exactly the transition required by R3. Similar bijective correspondences hold for choice and parallel constructs, where the PRISM synchronization mechanism (matching action labels) faithfully implements the intersection of transition relations defined in R11. Thus, $\mathcal{M}_{PRISM}$ and $\mathcal{T}_{sem}(P)$ are isomorphic up to state relabeling. □

Correctness Guarantee. Combining Theorem 1 with the Syntactic Correspondence Lemma, we conclude that the PRISM models analyzed in our quantitative experiments are behaviorally equivalent to the CSP# specifications used for qualitative verification.

5 The PAT2PRISM Tool

To make the transformation $\mathcal{T}_{code}$ from Sect. 4 applicable to realistic protocol specifications, we implemented it in the open-source PAT2PRISM tool.[1] The implementation is released under an MIT-style license.

5.1 Architecture and Rule-Guided Implementation

The architecture of PAT2PRISM, illustrated in Fig. 4, is designed as a multi-stage pipeline that bridges the gap between PAT's expressive syntax and PRISM's finite-state requirements. The pipeline consists of a *Preprocessor* for syntax normalization, an *ANTLR4-based Parser* for AST construction, and an *Enhanced IR Builder* that performs static analysis before final code generation.

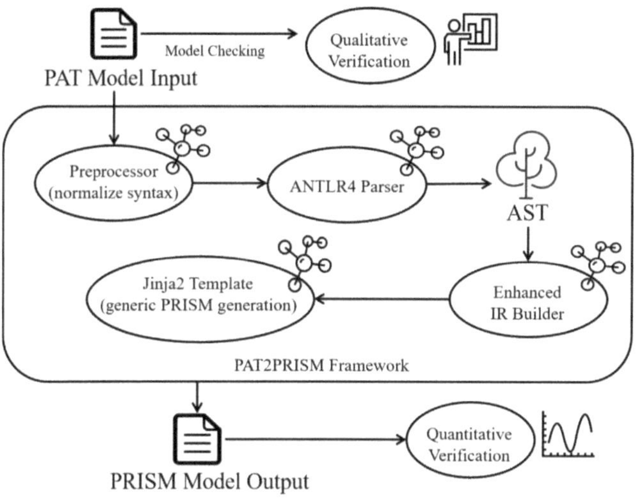

Fig. 4. Overall architecture of the PAT2PRISM translation pipeline.

Crucially, the core compilation engine is designed to strictly adhere to the formal transformation rules $\mathcal{T}_{code}$ defined in Sect. 4. Since the syntactic translation rules (Table 2) have already been established as a faithful realization of the semantics, the tool traverses the PAT AST and emits the corresponding PRISM guarded commands for each node type.

5.2 Algorithmic Translation and Optimization

To ensure scalability and correctness, we formalize the translation logic via two key optimizations: *Control Flow Linearization* and *Abstract Domain Refinement*.

[1] Repository: https://github.com/hanfeny7/pat2prism.

Recursive Control Flow Linearization. Standard translation often exacerbates state explosion when flattening hierarchical processes. We employ a *continuation-passing linearization* strategy, inspired by classical compilation techniques [7]. This approach recursively constructs a **Control Flow Graph (CFG)** by propagating a target program counter (PC). Unlike naive flattening with $O(n^2)$ complexity, our approach runs in linear time $O(n)$ and eliminates redundant ϵ-transitions. The resulting CFG serves as the compact intermediate representation for the subsequent optimization phase.

Abstract Domain Refinement. To further mitigate state explosion, we implement *Abstract Interpretation* [26] over the **generated CFG**. As detailed in Algorithm 1, we perform a fixed-point iteration over the Interval Lattice L_{Int}. This analysis infers tight finite bounds for all state variables (e.g., counters, buffer indices), effectively minimizing the bit-width required for the final MDP encoding. The algorithm's termination is guaranteed by the monotonicity of the transfer function (Tarski's Fixed Point Theorem) [11].

Algorithm 1. Fixed-Point Interval Analysis

Require: CFG Transitions $\mathcal{T}$, Variables $\mathcal{V}$
Ensure: Abstract Environment Γ (Variable Ranges)
$\Gamma \leftarrow \{v \mapsto [-\infty, +\infty] \mid v \in \mathcal{V}\}$ ▷ Initialize to Top
$Worklist \leftarrow \mathcal{T}$
while $Worklist \neq \emptyset$ **do** ▷ Chaotic Iteration
    $\tau \leftarrow Worklist.\text{pop}()$
    $\Gamma_{in} \leftarrow \Gamma$
    $\Gamma_{out} \leftarrow \text{TRANSFER}(\tau, \Gamma_{in})$ ▷ Apply assignment & guard
    if $\Gamma_{out} \sqsubset \Gamma$ **then** ▷ Refinement Check
        $\Gamma \leftarrow \Gamma \sqcap \Gamma_{out}$ ▷ Meet in Lattice
        $Worklist.\text{add}(\text{SUCCESSORS}(\tau))$
    end if
end while
return Γ

5.3 Parameterized Model Generation and Configuration

A key feature of PAT2PRISM is its support for **Design Space Exploration**. Instead of generating a static model, the tool produces a *parameterized template*. This allows system architects to perform sensitivity analysis by varying key environmental parameters without recompiling the model.

Specifically, the tool automatically injects:

- **Channel Reliability (p_{loss}):** Transforms deterministic communication into probabilistic transitions. This allows evaluating protocol performance under varying network conditions (e.g., 5% vs 20% packet loss).

- **Vulnerability Probability (p_{vuln}):** Simulates implementation imperfections (e.g., weak RNGs). This parameter enables the quantification of the "Security Margin"—how robust the protocol is against implementation flaws.

This parameterization is essential for the trade-off analysis presented in the following case study.

6 Case Study: CoAP-EAP vs. Lo-CoAP-EAP

To evaluate the capabilities of our unified verification framework, we conduct a comparative case study on the two IOT authentication standards: the standard **CoAP-EAP** and its low-power optimization, **Lo-CoAP-EAP**. Both protocols are critical for securing resource-constrained IoT devices. However, their authentication workflows differ markedly in structure and efficiency, making them ideal candidates to demonstrate how PAT2PRISM quantifies the trade-offs between architectural complexity and performance resilience.

6.1 CSP Modeling and Intruder Formalization

We model the CoAP-EAP and Lo-CoAP-EAP protocols in CSP# as a system of concurrent entities (*SmartObject*, *Controller*, *AAA Server*) communicating over abstract channels. Figure 5 illustrates the logic optimization in Lo-CoAP-EAP, where the standard multi-round handshake is consolidated into a single piggybacked exchange, directly reducing the state space for subsequent analysis.

To verify security, we employ a Dolev-Yao intruder model capable of intercepting, modifying, and injecting messages. The intruder is formalized as a recursive process $Intruder(F)$ that evolves its knowledge set F through learning from traffic and injecting derivable messages. Its behavior is captured by the following core recurrence:

$$\begin{aligned} Intruder(F) \widehat{=}\ & \underbrace{\Box_{m \in \Sigma}(\text{intercept}(m) \rightarrow Intruder(F \cup \{m\}))}_{\text{Learn}} \\ & \Box\ \underbrace{\Box_{F \vdash m}(\text{inject}(m) \rightarrow Intruder(F))}_{\text{Masquerade}} \end{aligned}$$

where $\vdash$ denotes the deduction relation based on cryptographic primitives. Secrecy is verified by asserting that the intruder cannot deduce the Master Session Key (MSK) from F (i.e., checking reachability of a *DataLeak* event).

6.2 Qualitative Verification via PAT

Before quantitative analysis, we formally verify the logical correctness of the system using PAT by modeling the system as the parallel composition of protocol entities and a Dolev-Yao intruder:

$$System() = SmartObject() \parallel Controller() \parallel AAA\_Server() \parallel Intruder()$$

Listing 1.1. Standard CoAP-EAP

```
SmartObject() =
  // Standard Handshake
 ComSC!CoAP_POST ->
 ComSC?CoAP_ACK.N_C ->
 Generate_Nonce() ->
 ComSC!CoAP_POST ->
 ComSC?CoAP_ACK.N_P ->
 ComSC?EAP_Req_Id ->
 ComSC!EAP_Resp_Id.ID_P ->
  // EAP Authentication
  ComSC?EAP_Req_PSK_M1.N_S.ID_S ->
  call(Compute_AK, PSK, N_S, N_P) ->
  ComSC!EAP_Resp_PSK_M2.MAC_P ->
  ComSC?EAP_Req_PSK_M3.MAC_S ->
  ComSC!EAP_Resp_PSK_M4 ->
 ComSC?EAP_Success.MSK ->
  Skip();
```

Listing 1.2. Optimized Lo-CoAP-EAP

```
SmartObject() =
  // Optimized: Piggybacked Identity
 ComSC!LO_CoAP_POST.ID_P.N_P ->
  // Direct transition to Auth
  ComSC?EAP_Req_PSK_M1.N_S.ID_S ->
  call(Compute_AK, PSK, N_S, N_P) ->
  ComSC!EAP_Resp_PSK_M2.MAC_P ->
  ComSC?EAP_Req_PSK_M3.MAC_S ->
  ComSC!EAP_Resp_PSK_M4 ->
 ComSC?MSK ->
  Skip();
```

Fig. 5. Side-by-side comparison of SmartObject CSP# models in PAT.

Table 3 summarizes these properties, their formal assertions, and the verification results. Both standard CoAP-EAP and Lo-CoAP-EAP satisfy all requirements. This confirms that the structural optimizations in Lo-CoAP-EAP do not introduce logical flaws (e.g., livelocks or ambiguity) or compromise security, providing a sound baseline for the subsequent quantitative analysis.

Table 3. Qualitative Verification Objectives, Assertions, and Results

Property	**Description & PAT Assertion**	**Result**
Divergence Freeness	Ensures the system is free from livelocks. `#assert System() divergencefree;`	Valid
Determinism	Confirms the protocol specification is unambiguous. `#assert System() deterministic;`	Valid
Data Accessibility	The SmartObject eventually receives the Master Session Key. `#assert System() reaches data_access==true;`	Valid
Data Reliability	Entities correctly detect injected messages with invalid MICs. `#assert System() reaches auth_check!=false;`	Valid
Data Security	The intruder never deduces the MSK (LTL safety property). `#assert System() |= []!key_leak;`	Valid

6.3 Quantitative Verification via PRISM

While qualitative verification (Sect. 6.2) confirms security under ideal conditions, real-world IoT deployments suffer from resource constraints (e.g., weak RNGs, limited memory, etc.). To quantify robustness against these realities, we utilize the MDP skeleton generated by PAT2PRISM (Fig. 6) and extend it with a novel probabilistic adversary model.

Performance Metrics. We define three key performance indicators (KPIs) using Probabilistic Computation Tree Logic (PCTL):

- **Reliability (P_{succ}):** Defined as the maximum probability of completing authentication within a bounded number of steps ($K = 50$), capturing the protocol's robustness against packet loss:

$$P_{succ} \triangleq P_{\max=?}[F^{\leq K} \texttt{"auth\_complete"}]$$

- **Security Risk (P_{risk}):** Measures the maximum probability that an attacker successfully derives the session key or injects a valid message within the session bound:

$$P_{risk} \triangleq P_{\max=?}[F^{\leq K} \texttt{"security\_breach"}]$$

- **Energy Efficiency (E_{cost}):** Quantifies the expected communication overhead (in bytes) required to complete a session, modeled using PRISM's reward structures:

$$E_{cost} \triangleq R\{byte\_cost\}_{=?}[F \texttt{"auth\_complete"}]$$

Environmental Parameters. Leveraging the parameterized model structure, we perform a dual-dimension sensitivity analysis to simulate realistic IoT environments. We vary two independent parameters:

- **Network Quality ($p_{loss} \in [0, 0.2]$):** Models network degradation by representing the probability of packet loss per transmission, simulating congested wireless channels such as LoRaWAN or NB-IoT [2].
- **Implementation Quality ($p_{vuln} \in [0, 0.1]$):** Captures cryptographic imperfections where security checks fail due to hardware limitations, such as weak RNGs or side-channel leakage [6].

This setup allows us to quantify the **Security Margin**—defined as the minimum implementation quality required to sustain security guarantees under degraded network conditions.

6.4 Quantitative Trade-Off Analysis

The qualitative verification results in Table 3 confirm that all specifications are satisfied. Based on it, We conducted experiments using PRISM 4.9 to compare standard CoAP-EAP and optimized Lo-CoAP-EAP. The results (Fig. 7) reveal a nuanced trade-off between efficiency and implementation sensitivity that qualitative verification alone could not detect.

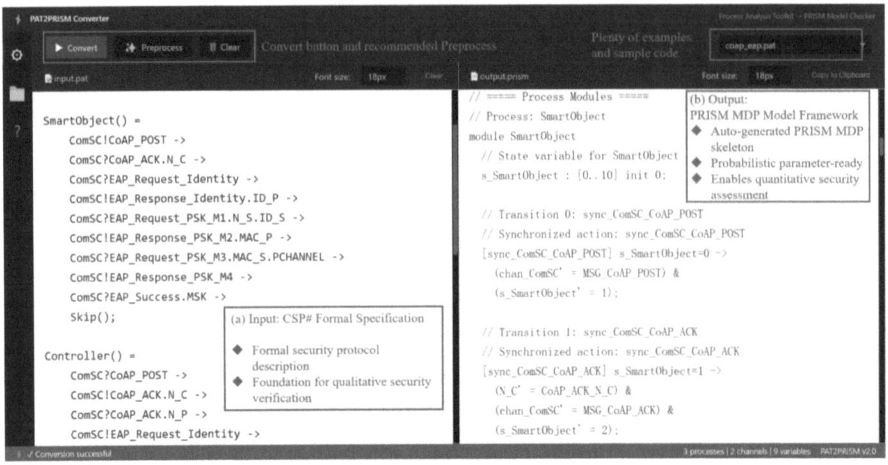

Fig. 6. Screenshot of the PAT2PRISM interface converting the Lo-CoAP-EAP model.

Efficiency vs. Robustness in Lossy Networks. Our analysis reveals a critical performance inversion under adverse network conditions. While Lo-CoAP-EAP is designed for efficiency, achieving a **7.87% reduction** in byte overhead (Fig. 7c, d), it also demonstrates superior resilience to channel noise.

As shown in Fig. 7b, at a packet loss rate of $p_{loss} = 0.2$, the optimized variant maintains an authentication success rate of **56%**, outperforming the standard protocol's **50%**. This counter-intuitive result stems from the reduction in handshake round-trips; by consolidating messages, Lo-CoAP-EAP minimizes the "exposure time" to stochastic packet loss. This insight, derived from the exhaustive exploration of the MDP state space, highlights the non-obvious benefit of structural simplification for energy-harvesting devices in unstable environments.

Security Sensitivity Analysis. The improvement in efficiency comes at the cost of architectural fragility. We analyzed the security risk (P_{risk}) as a function of implementation vulnerability (p_{vuln}), simulating defects such as weak random number generation.

Figure 7a highlights a non-linear degradation in security for the optimized protocol. While both variants are secure under ideal conditions, Lo-CoAP-EAP exhibits heightened sensitivity to implementation flaws: at $p_{vuln} = 0.1$, its risk probability spikes to **6.50%**, compared to just **2.65%** for the standard protocol. This indicates that the standard CoAP-EAP's multi-stage handshake provides a form of "defense-in-depth", where redundant nonces mask partial entropy failures. In contrast, the consolidated design of Lo-CoAP-EAP creates a single point of failure, requiring stricter hardware assurance for safe deployment.

Implications. These findings highlight a critical architectural insight: Lo-CoAP-EAP achieves its lightweight goals but requires stricter adherence to secure coding practices. For system architects, this implies that Lo-CoAP-EAP is

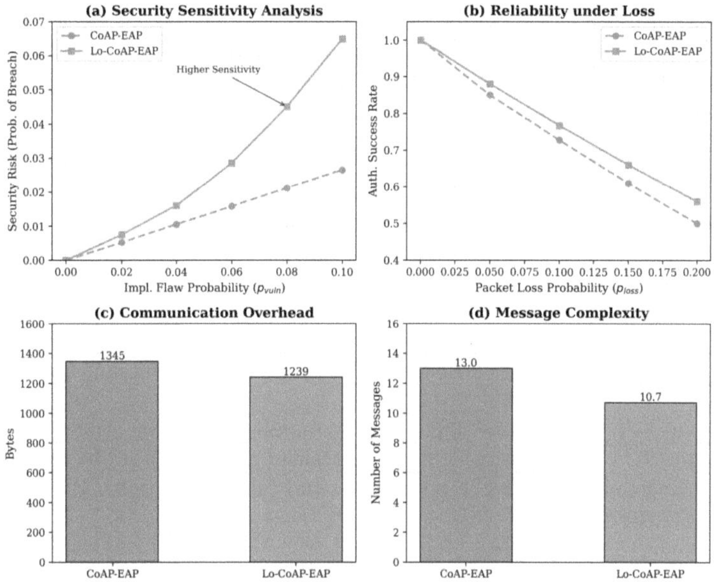

Fig. 7. Quantitative comparison.

the superior choice for high-quality hardware deployments, whereas the standard protocol offers a safer margin of error for legacy devices. This subtle trade-off validates the power of our unified framework: by bridging CSP modeling with MDP analysis, we expose risks that are invisible to qualitative verification alone.

7 Conclusion

We presented a unified verification framework that bridges qualitative security analysis and quantitative performance evaluation for IoT protocols. By formalizing a semantics-preserving mapping from CSP# LTSs to PRISM MDPs, PAT2PRISM enables the automated translation of logically verified PAT models into probabilistic models suitable for quantitative analysis. This provides a sound basis for combining functional correctness with resilience evaluation in a single workflow.

Our study of CoAP-EAP and Lo-CoAP-EAP demonstrates the value of this approach. Although both protocols satisfy qualitative security requirements, quantitative analysis reveals a clear efficiency–robustness trade-off: the lightweight variant reduces communication cost but is more sensitive to implementation flaws. This result highlights the importance of integrating qualitative and quantitative verification for resource-constrained IoT systems. Future work will extend the framework to CTMC-based timing analysis, counterexample-guided abstraction refinement, and larger protocols such as TLS 1.3 and 5G AKA.

Acknowledgements. This work was partially supported by the National Key Research and Development Program of China (No. 2022YFB3305102), the National Natural Science Foundation of China (No. 62032024), and the Open Project of Shanghai Key Laboratory of Trustworthy Computing.

References

1. Abadi, M., Blanchet, B., Fournet, C.: The applied pi calculus: mobile values, new names, and secure communication. J. ACM **65**(1), 1–41 (2018)
2. Adelantado, F., Vilajosana, X., Tuset-Peiro, P., Martinez, B., Melia-Segui, J., Watteyne, T.: Understanding the limits of lorawan. IEEE Commun. Mag. **55**, 34–40 (2017)
3. Akpakwu, G.A., Mathonsi, T.E., Tshilongamulenzhe, T.M., Maswikaneng, S.P., Muchenje, T.: Congestion control in constrained application protocol for the internet of things: state-of-the-art, challenges, and future directions. IEEE Access **13**, 33733–33767 (2025)
4. Al-Fuqaha, A., Guizani, M., Mohammadi, M., Aledhari, M., Ayyash, M.: Internet of things: a survey on enabling technologies, protocols, and applications. IEEE Commun. Surv. Tutor. **17**(4), 2347–2376 (2015)
5. Ameur-Boulifa, R., Lugou, F., Apvrille, L.: SysML model transformation for safety and security analysis. In: Hamid, B., Gallina, B., Shabtai, A., Elovici, Y., Garcia-Alfaro, J. (eds.) Security and Safety Interplay of Intelligent Software Systems. CSITS ISSA 2018 2018. LNCS, vol. 11552, pp. 35–49. Springer, Cham (2019). https://doi.org/10.1007/978-3-030-16874-2_3
6. Bernstein, D.J., et al.: Factoring rsa keys from certified smart cards: coppersmith in the wild. In: Sako, K., Sarkar, P. (eds.) Advances in Cryptology - ASIACRYPT 2013. ASIACRYPT 2013. LNCS, vol. 8270, pp. 341–360. Springer, Berlin, Heidelberg (2013). https://doi.org/10.1007/978-3-642-42045-0_18
7. Beyer, D., Cavalcanti, A.: From mechanized semantics to verified compilation: the clight semantics of compcert. In: Beyer, D., Cavalcanti, A. (eds.) Fundamental Approaches to Software Engineering. FASE 2024. LNCS, vol. 14573, pp. 1–21. Springer, Cham (2024). https://doi.org/10.1007/978-3-031-57259-3_1
8. Chen, S., Li, R., Zhu, H.: Formalization and verification of enhanced group communication coap. Int. J. Softw. Eng. Knowl. Eng. **34**, 301–330 (2024)
9. Conserva Filho, M.S., Marinho, R., Mota, A., Woodcock, J.: Analysing robochart with probabilities. In: Massoni, T., Mousavi, M. (eds.) Formal Methods: Foundations and Applications. SBMF 2018. LNCS, vol. 11254, pp. 198–214. Springer, Cham (2018). https://doi.org/10.1007/978-3-030-03044-5_13
10. David, A., Larsen, K.G., Legay, A., Mikučionis, M., Poulsen, D.B.: Uppaal smc tutorial. Int. J. Softw. Tools Technol. Transf. **17**(4), 397–415 (2015)
11. Fearnley, J., P'alv"olgyi, D., Savani, R.: A faster algorithm for finding Tarski fixed points. ACM Trans. Algorithms 1–23 (2022)
12. Garcia-Carrillo, D., Marin-Lopez, R., Kandasamy, A., Pelov, A.: A coap-based network access authentication service for low-power wide area networks: Lo-coap-eap. Sensors **17**(11), 2646 (2017)
13. González, A., Cristiá, M., Luna, C.: Verification of quantitative temporal properties in RealTime-DEVS. SIMULATION **101**(10), 1057–1076 (2025)

14. Gunnarsson, M., Brorsson, J., Palombini, F., Seitz, L., Tiloca, M.: Evaluating the performance of the oscore security protocol in constrained iot environments. Internet Things (Amsterdam, Online) **13**, 100333 (2021)
15. Haase, B., Labrique, B.: Aucpace: efficient verifier-based pake protocol tailored for the iiot. IACR Trans. Cryptogr. Hardw. Embed. Syst. (2019)
16. Hoare, C.A.R.: Communicating sequential processes. Commun. ACM **26**(1) (1985)
17. Hofer-Schmitz, K., Stojanović, B.: Towards formal verification of iot protocols: a review. Comput. Netw. **174**, 107233 (2020)
18. Kumar, A., Martinez-Bauset, J., Li, F.Y., Florea, C., Dobre, O.A.: Understanding inter- and intra-cluster concurrent transmissions for iot uplink traffic in mimo-noma networks: a dtmc analysis. IEEE Internet Things J. **11**, 14328–14343 (2024)
19. Kumar, P.M., Gandhi, U.D.: Enhanced dtls with coap-based authentication scheme for the internet of things in healthcare application. J. Supercomput. **76**(6), 3963–3983 (2020)
20. Kwiatkowska, M., Norman, G., Parker, D.: PRISM 4.0: verification of probabilistic real-time systems. In: Gopalakrishnan, G., Qadeer, S. (eds.) CAV 2011. LNCS, vol. 6806, pp. 585–591. Springer, Heidelberg (2011). https://doi.org/10.1007/978-3-642-22110-1_47
21. Liu, Y., Sun, J., Dong, J.S.: Developing model checkers using PAT. In: Bouajjani, A., Chin, W.N. (eds.) Automated Technology for Verification and Analysis. ATVA 2010. LNCS, vol. 6252, pp. 371–377. Springer, Berlin, Heidelberg (2010). https://doi.org/10.1007/978-3-642-15643-4_30
22. Morgan, C., McIver, A., Seidel, K., Sanders, J.W.: Refinement-oriented probability for CSP. Form. Aspects Comput. **8**(6), 617–647 (1996). https://doi.org/10.1007/BF01213492
23. Pastorek, A., Tundis, A.: Navigating the landscape of iot security and associated risks in critical infrastructures. In: Proceedings of the 19th International Conference on Availability, Reliability and Security, pp. 1–7 (2024)
24. Sanchez-Iborra, R., Cano, M.D.: State of the art in lp-wan solutions for industrial iot services. Sensors **16**, 708 (2016)
25. Schmidt, B., Meier, S., Cremers, C., Basin, D.: Automated analysis of diffie-hellman protocols and advanced security properties. IEEE (2012)
26. Stein, B., Chang, B.Y.E., Sridharan, M.: Interactive abstract interpretation with demanded summarization. ACM Trans. Program. Lang. Syst. **46**(1), 1–40 (2024)
27. Sun, J., Liu, Y., Dong, J.S., Pang, J.: PAT: towards flexible verification under fairness. In: Bouajjani, A., Maler, O. (eds.) CAV 2009. LNCS, vol. 5643, pp. 709–714. Springer, Heidelberg (2009). https://doi.org/10.1007/978-3-642-02658-4_59
28. Yadav, A.K., Misra, M., Pandey, P.K., Liyanage, M.: An eap-based mutual authentication protocol for wlan-connected iot devices. IEEE Trans. Ind. Inf. **19**(2), 1343–1355 (2023)
29. Zhou, X., Wang, S., Wen, K., Hu, B., Tan, X., Xie, Q.: Security-enhanced lightweight and anonymity-preserving user authentication scheme for iot-based healthcare. IEEE Internet Things J. **11**(6), 9599–9609 (2024)

From Monolithic to Compositional: A Compositional Operational Semantics for Crystality

Ziyun Xu[1], Hao Wang[2], and Meng Sun[1](✉)

[1] School of Mathematical Sciences, Peking University, Beijing, China
{xuziyun,sunm}@pku.edu.cn
[2] International Digital Economy Academy (IDEA), Shenzhen, China
wanghao2020@idea.edu.cn

Abstract. Parallel execution has become a key approach to improving blockchain scalability, but the lack of formal semantics for smart contract languages in such settings makes rigorous reasoning difficult. Crystality is a smart contract language designed for parallel EVMs, supporting scoped state and asynchronous relay across execution engines. This paper introduces a compositional operational semantics for Crystality. Unlike the original monolithic semantics, the new semantics decomposes the system into engine components and a global component, making the structure of parallel execution explicit. The compositional formulation enables simple proofs of key structural properties, including locality, global isolation, and strong commutativity of independent local steps. Furthermore, we prove that the compositional semantics is semantically equivalent to the original one via a transaction-level bisimulation theorem based on encoding and decoding functions between configurations, and two code-level bisimulation theorems for local and global execution.

Keywords: Operational Semantics · Compositional Semantics · Blockchain · Smart Contracts · Parallel Execution · Bisimulation

1 Introduction

Smart contracts enable decentralized applications to operate autonomously on blockchain platforms. As the demand for scalability intensifies [27], parallel execution environments, such as parallel Ethereum Virtual Machines (EVMs) [1,3,4], have emerged as a promising solution to overcome the inherent throughput limitations of sequential smart contract execution [7,9,13,14,26]. However, the lack of formal semantics [18,29] for smart contract languages in these parallel settings poses new challenges, particularly in capturing cross-engine interactions and reasoning about distributed state updates.

Crystality [28] is a smart contract programming language designed for parallel EVMs. It introduces two key abstractions: *Programmable Contract Scope*, which enables fine-grained state partitioning, and *Asynchronous Functional*

G. De Giacomo et al. (Eds.): TASE 2026, LNCS 16697, pp. 324–342, 2027.
https://doi.org/10.1007/978-3-032-30693-7_21

Relay, which supports deferred cross-engine interactions, thereby enabling parallel execution and decentralized control flow.

In [30], we presented an operational semantics [25] for Crystality that formally defined its behavior and enabled the verification of basic correctness properties via Rocq/Coq [19]. While this semantics establishes the first formal foundation for Crystality, it has a key limitation: the semantics is *monolithic*: the entire system state, including engine states, mempools, and the global state, is encoded in a single configuration. As a result, local and global effects are tightly intertwined in the semantic rules. The behavior of an individual engine cannot be described independently of the global system configuration. This design makes it difficult to reason modularly about the behavior of individual engines or to establish system-level properties that depend on the separation between local and global computations.

To address this limitation, this paper introduces a *compositional operational semantics* [5,10,24] for Crystality. In the new semantics, the system configuration is decomposed into a collection of *local components*, each representing an engine, together with a distinct *global component* responsible for global transactions. Relay transactions are represented explicitly and propagated through the mempool, while system-level execution composes the behavior of the components. This design exposes the modular structure of Crystality programs and enables local reasoning about engine behavior.

A crucial requirement for such a redesign is that it preserves the meaning of programs. To establish this formally, we define encoding and decoding functions that translate configurations between the original and the compositional semantics. Using these mappings, we prove a *transaction-level bisimulation* theorem which shows that the two semantics are equivalent.

In addition to the equivalence result, we prove several structural properties of the compositional semantics. These include locality of local steps, isolation of global execution, and strong commutativity of independent local steps. These properties are difficult to express directly in the original monolithic semantics but follow naturally from the compositional structure.

The contributions of this paper can be summarized as follows:

- We introduce a compositional operational semantics for Crystality.
- We prove a transaction-level bisimulation theorem establishing semantic equivalence between the original non-compositional operational semantics and the proposed compositional operational semantics.
- We show that the compositional semantics enables clear statements and proofs of key properties such as locality, global isolation, and strong commutativity of independent local steps.

The rest of the paper is organized as follows. Section 2 introduces the core features of Crystality. Section 3 presents the compositional operational semantics and demonstrates several properties that are transparent in the compositional framework. Section 4 establishes its correspondence with the original semantics via bisimulation. Section 5 discusses related work, and Sect. 6 concludes.

2 Crystality

Crystality is a programming language designed for parallel execution of smart contracts across multiple engines. Instead of assuming a sequential execution context, the language distinguishes different scopes of computation and provides two mechanisms that structure interactions in a concurrent environment.

Scoped State. Crystality programs manipulate state variables that belong to different *scopes*. The language distinguishes three scopes:

- **Address scope**. State associated with a specific user address. Such variables can be read and updated only by functions executed for that address.
- **Engine scope**. State locally shared in an engine. These variables are visible only within the corresponding engine.
- **Global scope**. State shared by all engines. Global variables represent system-wide information and can be modified only by global functions.

The scope discipline restricts how state can be accessed. Local computations may read global variables but cannot modify them directly.

Relay Mechanism. Crystality provides a primitive `relay@target f(args)` that asynchronously schedules a function invocation at another scope. Depending on the target, the relay may generate a transaction to be executed by another address, another engine, or at the global level. The relay mechanism allows a local computation to trigger subsequent actions without blocking the current execution. Relay-generated transactions are placed into mempools associated with the engines and then be selected and executed in subsequent blocks.

Execution in Crystality proceeds in blocks, where each block contains a sequence of transactions. Since Crystality does not support user-initiated `global` transactions, any `global` transaction must be relayed from a previous transaction. Relay transactions needed to be executed first. Therefore, a key convention of Crystality is that `global` transactions are executed before any `address` or `engine` transactions in the same block. The execution of a block therefore follows two phases.

- **Global phase**. The global component executes global transactions. The global state may change and the updated global state is propagated to all engines. The mempools may grow due to newly generated relay transactions.
- **Local phase**. Once the global transactions of the block have been completed, the global component remains unchanged, while the engines execute their local transactions independently in an interleaving manner.

Figure 1 shows a simplified banking contract that maintains account balances and records a global aggregate of transferred funds. Each user account has an instance of variable `balance` recording the funds associated with the user's address. The global variable `total` aggregates the amounts transferred across the entire system. The function `transfer` is executed in the `address` scope. It

```
contract Bank {
  int @address balance;
  int @global total;
  function transfer(address payee, int amount) @address {
    if (amount <= balance) then {
      balance := balance - amount;
      relay @ payee deposit(amount);
      relay @ global updateTotal(amount);
    } else { skip }
  }
  function deposit(int amount) @address {
    balance := balance + amount;
  }
  function updateTotal(int amount) @global {
    total := total + amount;
  }
}
```

Fig. 1. A simplified banking contract.

deducts tokens from the sender's `balance` and relays two operations: a `deposit` to the recipient and an update to the global variable `total`.

Assume there are two execution engines. Let `a,d` be addresses managed by engine `1`, and `b,c` be addresses managed by engine `2`. Suppose the current block contains exactly two user-initiated transactions: `transfer(b,3)` sent by `a` and `transfer(d,2)` sent by `c`. When they execute, each `transfer` deducts tokens from the sender and produces two relay calls. As a result, relay transactions for `deposit` and `updateTotal` are generated and placed into the mempools of the corresponding engines.

In the next block, these relay transactions are executed in two phases. First, the global transactions are executed which update the global variable `total`. After all global transactions finish, the local transactions are executed which update the balances of the corresponding users.

This example highlights two central aspects of Crystality's execution model: the separation between local computation and global state updates, and the deferred execution of relay-generated transactions. These characteristics motivate the design of compositional operational semantics presented in the next section.

3 Compositional Operational Semantics

We present the compositional operational semantics of Crystality at two levels. The first level presents the semantics of components. Since the execution of transactions within each engine is independent of other engines, each engine can be treated as a relatively autonomous component. Additionally, we treat the global state as a distinct component and refer to it as the 'global component'.

Global state variables and global functions are exclusively associated with this global component. The second level encompasses the semantics of the entire system. We have defined compositional rules that integrate the semantics of individual components, thereby deriving the overall system semantics.

In the following, we first introduce the notations used throughout the semantics. We then present the rules for statement execution, expression evaluation, and transaction execution. Finally, we describe how the semantic rules of components are composed to yield the overall semantics of the entire system.

3.1 Notations

Let n and k denote the number of execution engines and the number of addresses managed by each engine. The set $\mathbb{A}$ represents all possible memory addresses, while $\mathbb{B}$ denotes the set of byte values. A mapping of the form $\mathbb{A} \rightarrow \mathbb{B}$ is used to model storage, associating each memory address with its stored byte contents. $\mathbb{ID}$ refers to the set of all variable identifiers and $\mathbb{IDF}$ denotes the set of function identifiers. Additionally, $\mathbb{T}$ stands for the collection of all variable types.

We define the overall configuration of the system as $(\Gamma, \Omega, \gamma_G)$, where $\Gamma = (\gamma_1, ..., \gamma_n)$. Each $\gamma_i = (\sigma_i, Prog_i)$ represents the configuration of the i-th engine, and $\gamma_G = (\sigma_G, Prog_G)$ denotes the configuration of the global component.

$Prog_i$ and $Prog_G$ are the sets of program to be executed. The state of the i-th engine is given by $\sigma_i = (\Psi_i, M_i, G_i)$, where Ψ_i captures the storage of state variables (including `engine` variables and `address` variables) , M_i is the memory stack used for function calls and temporary variables, and G_i corresponds to the view of the storage of `global` state variables G from the i-th engine's perspective. We introduce G_i To allow each engine to access the global state variables while preserving the relative independence of engines executing in parallel. The state of the global component is defined as $\sigma_G = (G, M_G)$, where $G : \mathbb{A} \rightarrow \mathbb{B}$ is the storage of `global` state variables, and M_G is the memory stack used by the global component. Ψ_i within each engine further decomposes into $\Psi_i = (\Psi_{i,1}, \Psi_{i,2}, ..., \Psi_{i,k}, \Psi_{i,s})$, where $\Psi_{i,j} : \mathbb{A} \rightarrow \mathbb{B}\,(j = 1, ..., k)$ holds `address` state variables specific to the j-th address within the i-th engine, and $\Psi_{i,s} : \mathbb{A} \rightarrow \mathbb{B}$ represents `engine` state variables within the i-th engine.

The memory stack M_i maintains temporary variables of the i-th engine, which contains a stack to model new scopes when calling a function. M_i is a stack of functions, each modeled as a mapping $\mathbb{A} \rightarrow \mathbb{B}$. The top layer of the stack indicates the memory available in the current function. The stack provides operations such as $top(M_i)$ to access the top layer, $removetop(M_i)$ to remove it, and $addtop(M_i, Y)$ to push a new layer Y to M_i. Every layer carries associated contextual information, including a scope attribute denoted by $.scope$ and a return variable identifier denoted by $.rt$, both of which must be defined when a layer is added.

We define the memory pool (mempool) configuration $\Omega = (\Omega_1, ..., \Omega_n, \Omega_G)$, where each mempool Ω_i is associated with the i-th engine and contains pending relay transactions, while Ω_G is the virtual mempool handling global relay transactions.

Finally, we use $\mathcal{E}[\![(\sigma_\iota, exp_\iota)]\!]$ for the evaluation of expressions within a given state, where the subscript ι can refer to any engine index from 1 to n or to the global component G.

For each memory or storage mapping $f : \mathbb{A} \rightarrow \mathbb{B}$, we define two auxiliary functions: the name space $N_f : \mathbb{ID} \rightarrow \mathbb{A} \cup None$, which maps variable identifiers to their corresponding memory addresses (or indicates that an identifier is undefined), and the type space $T_f : \mathbb{ID} \rightarrow \mathbb{T} \cup None$, which associates each identifier with its declared type. To retrieve the value stored at a particular position, we use the notation $[addr]^{size}_{store}$, which denotes the value of length $size$ located at position $addr$ within the storage $store$. The size of variables of type t is given by $size(t)$.

Additionally, for function identifiers, we introduce several auxiliary functions that retrieve relevant information about the function.

- $\Lambda_{scope} : \mathbb{IDF} \rightarrow \{global, engine, address\}$ determines the declared scope of a function.
- $\Lambda_{paraname} : \mathbb{IDF} \rightarrow \mathbb{ID}^*$ returns the ordered list of parameter names associated with each function identifier.
- $\Lambda_{paratype} : \mathbb{IDF} \rightarrow \mathbb{T}^*$ specifies the types of those parameters.
- $\Lambda_{body} : \mathbb{IDF} \rightarrow Prog$ maps each function identifier to its program body.
- $\Lambda_{rttype} : \mathbb{IDF} \rightarrow \mathbb{T} \cup None$ indicates the return type of the function, if any.

Given a state σ, the notation σ' represents the state after applying a particular transformation to σ. In addition, symbols such as $\hat{\sigma}$, $\bar{\sigma}$, or indexed forms like $\sigma^{(1)}$ and $\sigma^{(2)}$ denote intermediate states arising during a sequence of modifications. The name space and type space associated with a function are auxiliary but integral components of its definition. Consequently, any change to the name space or type space also implies a change in the function itself.

Furthermore, there is an implicit 'zooming' mechanism in the notation. For example, if a component such as $\Psi_{i,s}$ is updated to $\Psi'_{i,s}$, then the enclosing state σ_i is implicitly updated to σ'_i, while all other components remain unchanged. This convention allows the formal definitions to remain concise and more readable without requiring explicit expansion of all nested structures each time a modification is described.

In the semantic rules, the arrows are annotated with superscripts and subscripts. There are two types of subscripts: l and g, indicating whether the rule is executed in a single engine or by the global component. The superscripts on the arrows also come in two forms: τ and $?(\omega_1, ..., \omega_n, \omega_G)$ which differentiate whether the corresponding step involves interaction with other components. τ indicates that the step does not generate any relay calls, while $?(\omega_1, ..., \omega_n, \omega_G)$ signifies that the step sends relay transactions to various memory pools.

3.2 Semantic Rules of Statements

We now present the first-level rules defining the compositional operational semantics. We begin by describing how state variables are declared during contract deployment.

When a state variable is declared with `address` scope, the system creates a separate instance of that variable for every valid address managed by each engine. Storage space is allocated for each instance according to the variable's declared type. In rule SVDA, the first premise asserts that, prior to initialization, the `address` variable named *id* is undefined in σ_i. The second premise updates the type space in the resulting state σ_i', recording that *id* has the specified type *Type*. The third step allocates memory for *id* in the name space of σ_i'. Finally, the fourth step initializes the allocated memory with the default value corresponding to *Type*. Because there is one such instance per address, these operations must be performed for all k addresses within the engine.

$$\text{SVDA}\ \frac{\begin{array}{c} N_{\Psi_{i,j}}(id) = None,\ 1 \leq j \leq k \qquad T_{\Psi'_{i,j}}(id) = Type,\ 1 \leq j \leq k \\ N_{\Psi'_{i,j}}(id) = allocate\_new(Type, \Psi_{i,j}),\ 1 \leq j \leq k \\ [N_{\Psi'_{i,j}}(id)]^{size(Type)}_{\Psi'_{i,j}} = init(Type),\ 1 \leq j \leq k \end{array}}{(\sigma_i, @address\ Type\ id;) \rightarrow^{\mathcal{T}}_{l} (\sigma_i', \cdot)}$$

The rule SVDG requires special attention. In the compositional semantics, we conceptualize accesses to `global` state variables and invocations of `global` functions as operating within an independent, virtual component separate from any specific engine. This abstraction is a modeling convenience for clarity and modularity, and does not necessarily correspond to the system's implementation.

$$\text{SVDG}\ \frac{\begin{array}{c} N_G(id) = None \qquad T_{G'}(id) = Type \\ N_{G'}(id) = allocate\_new(Type, G) \qquad [N_{G'}(id)^{size(Type)}_{G'}] = init(Type) \end{array}}{(\sigma_G, @global\ Type\ id;) \rightarrow^{\mathcal{T}}_{g} (\sigma_G', \cdot)}$$

The rules for declaring temporary variables require a distinction based on the location where they occur. A statement is local if it is within an `address` or `engine` function, affecting the memory stack of the corresponding engine. Conversely, if the statement is within a `global` function, it should affect the memory of the global component.

$$\text{TVDL}\ \frac{\begin{array}{c} top(M_i).scope \neq global \qquad N_{top(M_i)}(id) = None \\ T_{top(M_i)'}(id) = Type \qquad N_{top(M_i)'}(id) = allocate\_new(Type, top(M_i)) \\ [N_{top(M_i)'}(id)]^{size(Type)}_{top(M_i)'} = init(Type) \end{array}}{(\sigma_i, Type\ id;) \rightarrow^{\mathcal{T}}_{l} (\sigma_i', \cdot)}$$

$$\text{TVDG}\ \frac{\begin{array}{c} top(M_G).scope = global \\ N_{top(M_G)}(id) = None \qquad T_{top(M_G)'}(id) = Type \\ N_{top(M_G)'}(id) = allocate\_new(Type, top(M_G)) \\ [N_{top(M_G)'}(id)]^{size(Type)}_{top(M_G)'} = init(Type) \end{array}}{(\sigma_G, Type\ id;) \rightarrow^{\mathcal{T}}_{g} (\sigma_G', \cdot)}$$

We illustrate assignment statements using the rule SASSIGNAA. The rule checks the scope of the function performing the assignment and the scope of the state variable, and applies when both scopes are `address` . The expression exp here may be a function call with a return value. The states σ_i and $\hat{\sigma_i}$ denote the configuration of the current engine before and after the evaluation of exp, respectively.

$$\text{SASSIGNAA}\ \frac{\begin{array}{c}\mathcal{E}[\![(\sigma_i, exp)]\!] \rightarrow_l^{?(\omega_1,...,\omega_n,\omega_G)} (\hat{\sigma_i}, v) \\ top(M_i).scope = (address, j) \qquad top(\hat{M_i}).scope = (address, j) \\ N_{\hat{\Psi_{i,j}}}(id) \neq None \qquad [N_{\hat{\Psi_{i,j}}'}(id)]_{\hat{\Psi_{i,j}}'}^{size(T_{\hat{\Psi_{i,j}}'}(id))} = v\end{array}}{(\sigma_i, id = exp;) \rightarrow_l^{?(\omega_1,...,\omega_n,\omega_G)} (\hat{\sigma_i}', \cdot)}$$

We use rule IFUNGG as an example for function calls. The key point is to 'record' any relay calls generated during the process, and to ensure that all these steps are marked as global. By treating the global environment as a separate component, we can more easily define the rules for `global` function calls than in the original semantics. All state changes will occur within the global component because `global` function is not allowed to modify `engine` or `address` variables.

$$\text{IFUNGG}\ \frac{\begin{array}{c}\Lambda_{scope}(idf) = global \qquad top(M_G).scope = global \\ \Lambda_{rettype}(idf) = None \qquad \Lambda_{body}(idf) = Block \\ \Lambda_{paraname}(idf) = (id_1, ..., id_t) \qquad \Lambda_{paratype}(idf) = (T_1, ..., T_t) \\ M_G^{(1)} = addtop(M_G, top(M_G)) \qquad top(M_G^{(1)}).scope = global \\ top(M_G^{(1)}).rt = None \qquad M_G^{(3)} = removetop(M_G^{(2)}) \\ (\sigma_G^{(1)}, T_1\ id_1 = exp_1; ...; T_t\ id_t = exp_t; Block) \rightarrow_g^{?(\omega_1,...,\omega_n,\omega_G)} (\sigma_G^{(2)}, \cdot)\end{array}}{(\sigma_G, idf(exp_1, ..., exp_t)) \rightarrow_g^{?(\omega_1,...,\omega_n,\omega_G)} (\sigma_G^{(3)}, \cdot)}$$

We separate all memory pools from the state of each engine, treating them as distinct components. Since transactions in the memory pool do not affect the execution of the current transaction, this separation allows for a clearer representation of Crystality's semantics.

The engine or global component generating the relay transactions 'sends' them out. In practice, the relay transactions are propagated through the network, selected by nodes, and stored in memory pools, which is a process that may involve some delay. Therefore, we separate the sending and receiving of relay transactions into different rules.

We use the rule RELAYAL as an example for relay calls. It handles the case where the relay target is a specific address. Evaluating the expression exp yields a result (r, j), which identifies the j-th address managed by the r-th engine. The function idf, along with its provided arguments, is then encapsulated into a relay transaction and dispatched to the engine responsible for the target address.

$$\text{RELAY}_{\text{AL}}\ \frac{\begin{array}{c} top(M_i).scope \neq global \qquad \Lambda_{scope}(idf) = address \\ \mathcal{E}[\![(\sigma_i, exp)]\!] \rightarrow_l^{\mathcal{T}} (\sigma_i, (r, j)) \qquad \mathcal{E}[\![(\sigma_i, exp_l)]\!] \rightarrow_l^{\mathcal{T}} (\sigma_i, v_l), 1 \leq l \leq t \\ \omega_r = \{(address, j, idf(v_1, ..., v_t))\} \qquad \omega_\iota = \emptyset, \forall \iota \neq r \end{array}}{(\sigma_i, relay@exp\ idf(exp_1, ..., exp_t);) \rightarrow_l^{?(\omega_1, ..., \omega_n, \omega_G)} (\sigma_i, \cdot)}$$

The sending of relay transactions is denoted by $?(\omega_1, ..., \omega_n, \omega_G)$, while the receiving is denoted by $!(\omega_1, ..., \omega_n, \omega_G)$.

$$\text{RELAY}_{\text{O}}\ \frac{}{(\Omega_1, ..., \Omega_n, \Omega_G) \rightarrow^{!(\omega_1, ..., \omega_n, \omega_G)} (\Omega_1 \cup \omega_1, ..., \Omega_n \cup \omega_n, \Omega_G \cup \omega_G)}$$

Due to space limitations, we present only the representative rules here. The complete set of semantic rules, auxiliary definitions, and detailed proofs is available in the extended version of this paper [31].

3.3 Semantic Rules of Evaluations

The rules for evaluating expressions are also provided compositionally. We use ESIDAG and ESIDGG as examples. In Crystality, the `address` and `engine` function can read `global` state variables. Therefore, when modeling the behavior of each engine, it is necessary to bind a space corresponding to all `global` variables within the state of each engine. However, we model `global` variables and `global` functions within a separate, virtual component. As a result, the corresponding entity within each engine's state is essentially what that engine perceives as 'G', namely G_i for the i-th engine. In the first level of the compositional semantics, we do not guarantee that the perceived G_i across different engines, as well as the actual G, are identical. However, in the second level of the semantics, which concerns the overall system semantics, we define a corresponding composition operation that ensures they are identical.

$$\text{ESID}_{\text{AG}}\ \frac{\begin{array}{c} top(M_i).scope = (address, j) \\ N_{G_i}(id) \neq None \qquad [N_{G_i}(id)]_{G_i}^{size(T_{G_i}(id))} = v \end{array}}{\mathcal{E}[\![(\sigma_i, id)]\!] \rightarrow_l^{\mathcal{T}} (\sigma_i, v)}$$

ESIDGG corresponds to the case where a `global` function reads a `global` state variable. This can be directly accessed from G. In contrast to ESIDAG, there is no need to go through the G_i perceived by some engine.

$$\text{ESID}_{\text{GG}}\ \frac{\begin{array}{c} top(M_G).scope = global \\ N_G(id) \neq None \qquad [N_G(id)]_G^{size(T_G(id))} = v \end{array}}{\mathcal{E}[\![(\sigma_G, id)]\!] \rightarrow_g^{\mathcal{T}} (\sigma_G, v)}$$

3.4 Semantic Rules of Transactions

Defining transaction semantics is central to smart contract languages. We model transactions as function calls (T-functions), abstracting away gas and signatures.

Since we first present the semantics at the component level, the rules for a transaction only involve the engine where the transaction occurs (or the global component if it is a `global` transaction). We introduce a subscript t on the arrow to indicate that this step represents the complete execution of a transaction, specifically a T-function.

Unlike the operational semantics in [30], the compositional semantics allows for a more precise characterization of transaction properties. This is achieved through system-level semantics, which is presented in the next subsection.

We focus on the atomicity and inherent parallelism of transactions. A transaction is an atomic operation. That is, all (complete done) or nothing (zero effect). Therefore, we explicitly distinguish whether a computation is a complete transaction by the subscript t. On the other hand, transactions in different engines are executed in parallel. Each engine operates independently with its own state. The only interaction between engines is through message passing (relay transactions), which does not affect the execution of the current transaction. This parallelism is captured in the system-level semantics.

The rules for transactions are provided in the extended version [31].

3.5 Semantic Rules of the System

We first observe that any rule annotated with the superscript τ can be regarded as a rule annotated with $?(\omega_1, ..., \omega_n, \omega_G)$, by taking each ω_ι to be the empty set.

We define a function $\mu(\Gamma, \Omega, \gamma_G) =_{df} G_1 = G_2 = ... = G_n = G$ that ensures the corresponding components G_i and G in Γ and γ_G are all equal, and another function $\rho(\Gamma_1, \Gamma_2)$ that ensures Γ_1 and Γ_2 are identical except for the components G_i in each of them.

Due to the atomicity of transactions, we only permit the configuration before and after a T-function (a transaction) to constitute the system's configuration. This ensures that at the system level all transactions maintain atomicity.

The execution of a `global` T-function will only modify γ_G with the resulting relay calls reflected in the update of Ω. Before and after execution, the state of each engine remains unchanged, except that the G_i perceived by each engine must be consistent with G.

$$\text{G}\ \frac{\gamma_G \rightarrow_{g,t}^{?(\omega_1,...,\omega_n,\omega_G)} \gamma_G' \qquad \Omega \rightarrow^{!(\omega_1,...,\omega_n,\omega_G)} \Omega' \qquad \rho(\Gamma, \Gamma') \qquad \mu(\Gamma, \Omega, \gamma_G) \qquad \mu(\Gamma', \Omega', \gamma_G')}{(\Gamma, \Omega, \gamma_G) \Rightarrow_g (\Gamma', \Omega', \gamma_G')}$$

The execution of an `address` or `engine` T-function will only modify the configuration of the corresponding engine. The configurations of other engines and the configuration γ_G remain unchanged. According to the execution model, such an execution can only occur at the local phase, that is after all global transactions have been completed. Therefore, we require that $Prog_G = \cdot$.

$$\text{L}\ \frac{\gamma_i \rightarrow_{l,t}^{?(\omega_1,\ldots,\omega_n,\omega_G)} \gamma_i' \quad \Omega \rightarrow^{!(\omega_1,\ldots,\omega_n,\omega_G)} \Omega' \quad \Gamma = (\gamma_1,\ldots,\gamma_i,\ldots,\gamma_n) \quad \Gamma' = (\gamma_1,\ldots,\gamma_i',\ldots,\gamma_n) \quad \gamma_G = (\sigma_G,\cdot) \quad \mu(\Gamma,\Omega,\gamma_G) \quad \mu(\Gamma',\Omega',\gamma_G)}{(\Gamma,\Omega,\gamma_G) \Rightarrow_l (\Gamma',\Omega',\gamma_G)}$$

The rules GA, GS, LA, LS, and GL describe the changes before and after several transactions. We express by $\Rightarrow_l^*$ that there is a chain of local steps, by $\Rightarrow_g^*$ that there is a chain of global steps, and by $\Rightarrow_{gl}^*$ that there is a chain of global steps followed by local steps (See the execution convention). We use GA, GS and GL as examples.

$$\text{GA}\ \frac{\mu(\Gamma,\Omega,\gamma_G)}{(\Gamma,\Omega,\gamma_G) \Rightarrow_g^* (\Gamma,\Omega,\gamma_G)}$$

$$\text{GS}\ \frac{(\Gamma,\Omega,\gamma_G) \Rightarrow_g (\Gamma',\Omega',\gamma_G') \quad (\Gamma',\Omega',\gamma_G') \Rightarrow_g^* (\Gamma'',\Omega'',\gamma_G'')}{(\Gamma,\Omega,\gamma_G) \Rightarrow_g^* (\Gamma'',\Omega'',\gamma_G'')}$$

$$\text{GL}\ \frac{(\Gamma,\Omega,\gamma_G) \Rightarrow_g^* (\Gamma',\Omega',\gamma_G') \quad (\Gamma',\Omega',\gamma_G') \Rightarrow_l^* (\Gamma'',\Omega'',\gamma_G')}{(\Gamma,\Omega,\gamma_G) \Rightarrow_{gl}^* (\Gamma'',\Omega'',\gamma_G')}$$

We present several properties that can be naturally stated and easily proved under the compositional semantics. The proofs are provided in [31].

Theorem 1 (Locality). *For any system-level local step $(\Gamma,\Omega,\gamma_G) \Rightarrow_l (\Gamma',\Omega',\gamma_G')$, there exists a unique $i \in \{1,\ldots,n\}$ such that Γ and Γ' differ only at the i-th component. Moreover, $\gamma_G' = \gamma_G$, and Ω' is obtained from Ω by union with the relay sets produced in the step.*

Theorem 2 (Global isolation). *For any system-level global step $(\Gamma,\Omega,\gamma_G) \Rightarrow_g (\Gamma',\Omega',\gamma_G')$, the engine components may change only in their copies of the global state. And Ω' is obtained from Ω by union with the relay sets produced in the step.*

Theorem 3 (Strong commutativity of independent local steps). *Suppose $C \Rightarrow_l C_i$ and $C \Rightarrow_l C_j$ are two system-level local steps such that the first step updates engine i and the second step updates engine j, where $i \neq j$. Then there exists a unique configuration C' such that $C_i \Rightarrow_l C'$ and $C_j \Rightarrow_l C'$. Equivalently, the two independent local steps commute.*

Theorem 3 is the well-known diamond (commutativity) property. It can be proved easily using the compositional structure together with Theorem 1.

4 Correspondence with the Original Semantics

The compositional semantics introduced in the previous section restructures the execution model of Crystality by separating local and global component. A natural question is whether this new semantics faithfully represents the behavior of the original one. The main result of this section is a *bisimulation theorem* at transaction-level, which proves that the compositional semantics is *semantically equivalent* to the previous one [30]. The proof is organized around two ingredients. First, we define *encoding* and *decoding* functions between the configurations of the two semantics and show that they are mutual inverse. Second, to lift the correspondence from transaction-level to the interior of a transaction, we introduce a code-level correspondence and prove bisimulation theorems for local and global code-level execution. For brevity, we present only the essential definitions and lemmas. Detailed definitions and full proofs are given in [31].

Throughout this section, symbols from the original (non-compositional) semantics are annotated with the superscript $\circ$, while unannotated symbols refer to the compositional semantics. In particular, we write C°, σ_i°, Ω_i°, $Prog_i^\circ$, G° and $\to^\circ$ for the notions in the original semantics.

In the following, we use several auxiliary functions to manipulate transaction sequences and mempools. The functions gprefix and lsuffix extract the global prefix and the local suffix of a program, respectively, reflecting the convention that global transactions precede local ones in Crystality. The functions LTx and GTx extract from a mempool the local and global transactions. Their formal definitions are given in [31].

We first define well-formed configurations for both the original and the compositional semantics, since the correspondence between the two semantics is established only on well-formed configurations.

Definition 1 (Well-formed configurations). *Let*

$$\Gamma = (\gamma_1, \dots, \gamma_n), \qquad \gamma_i = (\sigma_i, Prog_i), \qquad \sigma_i = (\Psi_i, M_i, G_i),$$

$$\gamma_G = (\sigma_G, Prog_G), \qquad \sigma_G = (G, M_G).$$

We define the well-formedness predicate for configurations of the compositional semantics by

$$\mathsf{wf}((\Gamma, \Omega, \gamma_G)) \stackrel{\text{def}}{=} G_1 = G_2 = \cdots = G_n = G.$$

For a configuration of the original semantics

$$C^\circ = (\sigma_1^\circ, \Omega_1^\circ, Prog_1^\circ, \dots, \sigma_n^\circ, \Omega_n^\circ, Prog_n^\circ, G^\circ),$$

we define

$$\mathsf{wf}^\circ(C^\circ) \stackrel{\text{def}}{=} \mathsf{gprefix}(Prog_1^\circ) = \mathsf{gprefix}(Prog_2^\circ) = \cdots = \mathsf{gprefix}(Prog_n^\circ).$$

We then present the definitions of the two key functions, *Enc* and *Dec* .

Definition 2 (Encoding). *Let* $C^\circ = (\sigma_1^\circ, \Omega_1^\circ, Prog_1^\circ, \ldots, \sigma_n^\circ, \Omega_n^\circ, Prog_n^\circ, G^\circ)$ *be a well-formed configuration of the original semantics, where* $\sigma_i^\circ = (\Psi_i^\circ, M_i^\circ)$*.*
Let

$$Prog_G = \mathsf{gprefix}(Prog_i^\circ), \qquad Prog_i = \mathsf{lsuffix}(Prog_i^\circ),$$
$$\Omega_i = \mathsf{LTx}(\Omega_i^\circ), \qquad \Omega_G = \mathsf{GTx}(\Omega_i^\circ).$$

Define

$$M_i = \begin{cases} \emptyset, & Prog_G \neq \cdot, \\ M_i^\circ, & Prog_G = \cdot, \end{cases} \qquad M_G = \begin{cases} M_i^\circ, & Prog_G \neq \cdot, \\ \emptyset, & Prog_G = \cdot. \end{cases}$$

The encoding function $Enc : Conf^\circ \to Conf$ *maps* C° *to the configuration* $(\Gamma, \Omega, \gamma_G)$ *defined by*

$$\Gamma = (\gamma_1, \ldots, \gamma_n), \qquad \gamma_i = ((\Psi_i^\circ, M_i, G^\circ), Prog_i),$$
$$\Omega = (\Omega_1, \ldots, \Omega_n, \Omega_G), \qquad \gamma_G = ((G^\circ, M_G), Prog_G).$$

Definition 3 (Decoding). *Let* $(\Gamma, \Omega, \gamma_G)$ *be a well-formed configuration of the compositional semantics, where*

$$\Gamma = (\gamma_1, \ldots, \gamma_n), \qquad \gamma_i = ((\Psi_i, M_i, G), Prog_i),$$
$$\Omega = (\Omega_1, \ldots, \Omega_n, \Omega_G), \qquad \gamma_G = ((G, M_G), Prog_G).$$

Define

$$M_i^\circ = \begin{cases} M_G, & Prog_G \neq \cdot, \\ M_i, & Prog_G = \cdot. \end{cases}$$

The decoding function $Dec : Conf \to Conf^\circ$ *maps* $(\Gamma, \Omega, \gamma_G)$ *to the configuration* $(\sigma_1^\circ, \Omega_1^\circ, Prog_1^\circ, \ldots, \sigma_n^\circ, \Omega_n^\circ, Prog_n^\circ, G^\circ)$ *defined by*

$$\sigma_i^\circ = (\Psi_i, M_i^\circ), \quad \Omega_i^\circ = \Omega_i \cup \Omega_G, \quad Prog_i^\circ = Prog_G; Prog_i, \quad G^\circ = G.$$

The functions Enc and Dec are structurally dual. Enc decomposes a configuration of the original semantics into the components of the compositional semantics: the global prefix of each program is extracted into the global component, the remaining local suffix stays in each engine, the global transactions in the mempools are separated into Ω_G, and the stacks are distributed between the local and global components depending on whether a global computation is in progress. Conversely, Dec reconstructs a configuration of the original semantics by merging these components: the global program $Prog_G$ is prefixed to each local program, the global mempool Ω_G is merged into each engine mempool, and the stacks are restored according to whether the global program is empty. Enc factorizes a monolithic configuration into compositional components, while Dec assembles these components back into a monolithic configuration.

Lemma 1 (Well-formedness preserved by Enc **and** Dec**).** *If* $\mathsf{wf}^\circ(C^\circ)$ *, then* $\mathsf{wf}(Enc(C^\circ))$*. If* $\mathsf{wf}((\Gamma, \Omega, \gamma_G))$*, then* $\mathsf{wf}^\circ(Dec((\Gamma, \Omega, \gamma_G)))$ *.*

Lemma 2 (Mutual inverse properties of *Enc* and *Dec*). *The functions Enc and Dec are mutually inverse on reachable well-formed configurations.*

(i) For every reachable well-formed configuration C° *of the original semantics,* $Dec(Enc(C^{\circ})) = C^{\circ}$.

(ii) For every reachable well-formed configuration C *of the compositional semantics,* $Enc(Dec(C)) = C$.

The functions *Enc* and *Dec* are defined on all well-formed configurations. We are particularly interested in configurations that occur at *transaction boundaries*, i.e., immediately before a transaction begins or after it completes. Transaction-boundary configurations are formally defined in [31]. Restricting *Enc* and *Dec* to such configurations yields the functions Enc_T and Dec_T.

Using Enc_T and Dec_T, we define a transaction-level correspondence between configurations of the original semantics and the compositional semantics.

Definition 4 (Transaction-level correspondence). *Let* $Conf^{\circ}$ *and* $Conf$ *denote the sets of configurations of the original semantics and the compositional semantics, respectively.*

We define a relation

$$R_T \subseteq Conf^{\circ} \times Conf$$

such that $R_T(C^{\circ}, C)$ *holds iff*

1. C° *is reachable and well formed in the original semantics;*
2. C *is reachable and well formed in the compositional semantics;*
3. *both* C° *and* C *are at transaction boundaries; and*
4. $Enc_T(C^{\circ}) = C$ *(equivalently,* $Dec_T(C) = C^{\circ}$*).*

We now state the main theorem of this section. The proof is available in the extended version of this paper [31].

Theorem 4 (Transaction-level bisimulation). *Let* R_T *be the transaction-level correspondence relation. If* $R_T(C^{\circ}, C)$*, then the following properties hold:*

(i) If $C^{\circ} \to C^{\circ\prime}$ *by a transaction step of the original semantics, then there exists a configuration* C' *such that* $C \Rightarrow C'$ *and* $R_T(C^{\circ\prime}, C')$.

(ii) If $C \Rightarrow C'$ *then there exists a configuration* $C^{\circ\prime}$ *such that* $C^{\circ} \to C^{\circ\prime}$ *by a transaction step of the original semantics, and* $R_T(C^{\circ\prime}, C')$.

Since each transaction is an atomic unit of execution, the correspondence is defined at transaction boundaries, the equivalence between the original semantics and the compositional semantics is naturally stated at transaction boundaries, and the main bisimulation theorem (Theorem 4) relates configurations only at these boundaries.

However, proving this result requires reasoning about the execution inside a transaction. In the compositional semantics, the behavior of the system is defined component-wise: either a local component γ_i executes local code, or the global component γ_G executes global code. To relate these component-level executions with the monolithic execution of the original semantics, we introduce system configurations at the code level.

These configurations should be understood purely as proof artifacts. They do not correspond to observable states in the actual execution, since system-level composition occurs only at transaction boundaries. Instead, they serve as an intermediate bridge in the proof:

$$\gamma \xrightarrow{\text{Wrap}} C \xleftrightarrow{R} C^{\circ},$$

where γ denotes either a local component γ_i or the global component γ_G, C is a system configuration of the compositional semantics, and C° is a configuration of the original semantics. The relation R, defined using the code-level mappings *Enc* and *Dec*, enables us to relate component-level execution with the execution of the entire system in the original semantics.

To establish bisimulation at transaction-level, we first prove two code-level bisimulation theorems, corresponding to local and global execution respectively. In the compositional semantics, code-level rules operate on component configurations γ, whereas in the original semantics they operate on whole-system configurations. Therefore, several auxiliary constructions and definitions are introduced to relate component configurations in the compositional semantics with system configurations in the original semantics. We show that one step of a component in the compositional semantics can be simulated by a corresponding system step in the original semantics, and vice versa.

We directly state the two code-level bisimulation theorems below; the necessary definitions, lemmas, and full proofs are provided in the extended version [31].

Theorem 5 (Local code-level bisimulation). *If $R_l(i, \gamma_i, C^{\circ})$, then the following properties hold:*

(i) If $\gamma_i \rightarrow_l^{?(w_1,\ldots,w_n,w_G)} \gamma_i'$, then there exists a configuration $C^{\circ\prime}$ such that $C^{\circ} \rightarrow C^{\circ\prime}$, $\mathsf{Same}_l^{\circ}(i, C^{\circ}, C^{\circ\prime})$, $\mathsf{MemDiff}^{\circ}(C^{\circ}, C^{\circ\prime}, \Delta\Omega)$, where $\Delta\Omega = (w_1 \cup w_G,\ w_2 \cup w_G,\ \ldots,\ w_n \cup w_G)$, and $R_l(i, \gamma_i', C^{\circ\prime})$.

(ii) If $C^{\circ} \rightarrow C^{\circ\prime}$, $\mathsf{Same}_l^{\circ}(i, C^{\circ}, C^{\circ\prime})$, $\mathsf{MemDiff}^{\circ}(C^{\circ}, C^{\circ\prime}, \Delta\Omega)$, where $\Delta\Omega = (\Delta\Omega_1, \ldots, \Delta\Omega_n)$, then there exists a component γ_i' such that $\gamma_i \rightarrow_l^{?(w_1,\ldots,w_n,w_G)} \gamma_i'$, where $w_j = \mathsf{LTx}(\Delta\Omega_j)$ $(1 \leq j \leq n)$, and $w_G = \mathsf{GTx}(\Delta\Omega_j)$ for any $j \in \{1, \ldots, n\}$, and $R_l(i, \gamma_i', C^{\circ\prime})$.

Theorem 6 (Global code-level bisimulation). *If $R_g(\gamma_G, C^{\circ})$, then the following properties hold:*

(i) If $\gamma_G \rightarrow_g^{?(w_1,\ldots,w_n,w_G)} \gamma_G'$, then there exists a configuration $C^{\circ\prime}$ such that $C^{\circ} \rightarrow C^{\circ\prime}$, $\mathsf{Same}_g^{\circ}(C^{\circ}, C^{\circ\prime})$, $\mathsf{MemDiff}^{\circ}(C^{\circ}, C^{\circ\prime}, \Delta\Omega)$, where $\Delta\Omega = (w_1 \cup w_G,\ w_2 \cup w_G,\ \ldots,\ w_n \cup w_G)$, and $R_g(\gamma_G', C^{\circ\prime})$.

(ii) If $C^{\circ} \rightarrow C^{\circ\prime}$, $\mathsf{Same}_g^{\circ}(C^{\circ}, C^{\circ\prime})$, $\mathsf{MemDiff}^{\circ}(C^{\circ}, C^{\circ\prime}, \Delta\Omega)$, where $\Delta\Omega = (\Delta\Omega_1, \ldots, \Delta\Omega_n)$, then there exists a component γ_G' such that $\gamma_G \rightarrow_g^{?(w_1,\ldots,w_n,w_G)} \gamma_G'$, where $w_i = \mathsf{LTx}(\Delta\Omega_i)$ $(1 \leq i \leq n)$, and $w_G = \mathsf{GTx}(\Delta\Omega_i)$ for any $i \in \{1, \ldots, n\}$, and $R_g(\gamma_G', C^{\circ\prime})$.

5 Related Work

Formal semantics of smart contract languages has been extensively studied, particularly in the context of sequential execution platforms such as Ethereum. Bhargavan [8] formalized a core subset of Solidity [2] in F*, enabling verification of safety properties. Grishchenko [15] developed the KEVM semantics using the K-framework, capturing the EVM bytecode precisely and supporting automated reasoning. Marmsoler [23] introduced a denotational semantics of Solidity. Zakrzewski [33] formalized a big-step semantics for a subset of Solidity. Crosara and Jiao [11,20,21] proposed operational semantics, including executable definitions of Solidity behaviors. Other approaches encode Solidity into intermediate representations: Hajdu [16,17] developed an SMT-based intermediate language to support verification, and Yang [32] presented a formal semantics for a specification language targeting Ethereum contracts in Coq. Luu [22] focused on symbolic analysis of smart contracts to detect common vulnerabilities. These approaches primarily target sequential models and do not address the unique challenges introduced by parallel execution.

Parallel execution in blockchain systems has been proposed to improve scalability. Notable examples include proposals for parallel transaction execution engines [12], and experimental systems such as Chainspace [6]. While these systems provide architectural solutions to concurrency, they rarely define formal operational semantics that explicitly capture cross-engine interactions and asynchronous relay mechanisms at the language level.

Structural operational semantics (SOS) has a long tradition in programming language theory [25]. Modular SOS frameworks, such as MSOS [24], emphasize compositional definitions to enable scalable reasoning about program fragments and language extensions. Our work draws inspiration from these principles but adapts them to the domain of parallel smart contracts, where partitioned state and deferred cross-engine calls require novel semantic treatment. To our knowledge, this paper is the first to define a compositional operational semantics for a smart contract language designed for parallel execution environments.

6 Conclusion

This paper introduces a compositional operational semantics for the smart contract language Crystality. The semantics separates the system into engine components and a global component, making the modular structure of parallel smart contract execution explicit.

The compositional formulation enables clear statements and simple proofs of structural properties that are difficult to express in the original semantics. In particular, we prove locality of local steps, isolation of global execution, and strong commutativity of independent local steps.

We formally establish the correctness of this redesign by proving a transaction-level bisimulation between the compositional semantics and the original monolithic semantics. The proof is based on encoding and decoding functions relating configurations of the two semantics, together with code-level bisimulation results for local and global execution.

These results demonstrate that the compositional semantics provides a cleaner and more modular foundation for reasoning about parallel smart contracts. We believe that this framework can serve as a basis for future verification techniques and formal analyses for languages designed for parallel blockchain.

Acknowledgments. This research was sponsored by National Natural Science Foundation of China Grant No. 92582102, 62572013 and 62172019, and the National Key R&D Program of China under Grant 2022YFB2702200.

References

1. 8 innovations that make solana the first web-scale blockchain (2019). https://solana.com/news/8-innovations-that-make-solana-the-first-web-scale-blockchain
2. Solidity documentation (2021). https://docs.soliditylang.org/en/latest/
3. The aptos blockchain: safe, scalable, and upgradeable web3 infrastructure (2022). https://aptosfoundation.org/whitepaper/aptos-whitepaper_en.pdf
4. The sui smart contracts platform (2023). https://docs.sui.io/paper/sui.pdf
5. Ábrahám, E., de Boer, F.S., de Roever, W.P., Steffen, M.: A compositional operational semantics for java mt. Verification: Theory and Practice: Essays Dedicated to Zohar Manna on the Occasion of His 64th Birthday, pp. 290–303 (2003)
6. Al-Bassam, M., Sonnino, A., Bano, S., Hrycyszyn, D., Danezis, G.: Chainspace: a sharded smart contracts platform. arXiv preprint arXiv:1708.03778 (2017)
7. Anjana, P.S., Kumari, S., Peri, S., Rathor, S., Somani, A.: An efficient framework for optimistic concurrent execution of smart contracts. In: 2019 27th Euromicro International Conference on Parallel, Distributed and Network-Based Processing (PDP), pp. 83–92. IEEE (2019)
8. Bhargavan, K., et al.: Formal verification of smart contracts: short paper. In: Proceedings of the 2016 ACM Workshop on Programming Languages and Analysis for Security, pp. 91–96 (2016)
9. Chen, Y., et al.: Forerunner: constraint-based speculative transaction execution for ethereum. In: Proceedings of the ACM SIGOPS 28th Symposium on Operating Systems Principles, pp. 570–587 (2021)
10. Cheng, M.H., Horspool, R.N., Levy, M.R., Van Emden, M.: Compositional operational semantics for prolog programs. N. Gener. Comput. **10**, 315–328 (1992)
11. Crosara, M., Centurino, G., Arceri, V.: Towards an operational semantics for solidity. VALID, pp. 1–6 (2019)
12. Dickerson, T., Gazzillo, P., Herlihy, M., Koskinen, E.: Adding concurrency to smart contracts. In: Proceedings of the ACM Symposium on Principles of Distributed Computing, pp. 303–312 (2017)
13. Garamvölgyi, P., Liu, Y., Zhou, D., Long, F., Wu, M.: Utilizing parallelism in smart contracts on decentralized blockchains by taming application-inherent conflicts. In: Proceedings of the 44th International Conference on Software Engineering, pp. 2315–2326 (2022)
14. Gelashvili, R., et al.: Block-stm: scaling blockchain execution by turning ordering curse to a performance blessing. In: Proceedings of the 28th ACM SIGPLAN Annual Symposium on Principles and Practice of Parallel Programming, pp. 232–244 (2023)

15. Grishchenko, I., Maffei, M., Schneidewind, C.: A semantic framework for the security analysis of ethereum smart contracts. In: Bauer, L., Küsters, R. (eds.) Principles of Security and Trust. POST 2018. LNCS, vol. 10804, pp. 243–269. Springer, Cham (2018). https://doi.org/10.1007/978-3-319-89722-6_10
16. Hajdu, Á., Jovanovic, D.: SOLC-VERIFY: a modular verifier for solidity smart contracts. In: Chakraborty, S., Navas, J. (eds.) Verified Software. Theories, Tools, and Experiments. VSTTE 2019. LNCS, vol. 12031, pp. 161–179. Springer, Cham (2019). https://doi.org/10.1007/978-3-030-41600-3_11
17. Hajdu, Á., Jovanovic, D.: SMT-Friendly formalization of the solidity memory model. In: Müller, P. (ed.) Programming Languages and Systems. ESOP 2020. LNCS, vol. 12075, pp. 224–250. Springer, Cham (2020). https://doi.org/10.1007/978-3-030-44914-8_9
18. Hoare, C.A.R., He, J.: Unifying Theories of Programming. Prentice Hall, Hoboken (1998)
19. Huet, G., Kahn, G., Paulin-Mohring, C.: The coq proof assistant a tutorial. Rapp. Tech. **178**, 113 (1997)
20. Jiao, J., Kan, S., Lin, S., Sanán, D., Liu, Y., Sun, J.: Executable operational semantics of solidity. CoRR **abs/1804.01295** (2018). http://arxiv.org/abs/1804.01295
21. Jiao, J., Kan, S., Lin, S., Sanán, D., Liu, Y., Sun, J.: Semantic understanding of smart contracts: executable operational semantics of solidity. In: Proceedings of SP 2020, pp. 1695–1712. IEEE (2020)
22. Luu, L., Chu, D.H., Olickel, H., Saxena, P., Hobor, A.: Making smart contracts smarter. In: Proceedings of the 2016 ACM SIGSAC Conference on Computer and Communications Security, pp. 254–269 (2016)
23. Marmsoler, D., Brucker, A.D.: A denotational semantics of solidity in Isabelle/HOL. In: Calinescu, R., Păsăreanu, C.S. (eds.) Software Engineering and Formal Methods. SEFM 2021. LNCS, vol. 13085, pp. 403–422. Springer, Cham (2021). https://doi.org/10.1007/978-3-030-92124-8_23
24. Mosses, P.D.: Modular structural operational semantics. J. Log. Algebraic Program. **60**, 195–228 (2004)
25. Plotkin, G.D.: A structural approach to operational semantics (1981)
26. Qi, X., Jiao, J., Li, Y.: Smart contract parallel execution with fine-grained state accesses. In: 2023 IEEE 43rd International Conference on Distributed Computing Systems (ICDCS), pp. 841–852. IEEE (2023)
27. Sanka, A.I., Cheung, R.C.C.: A systematic review of blockchain scalability: issues, solutions, analysis and future research. J. Netw. Comput. Appl. **195**, 103232 (2021)
28. Wang, H., Pan, M., Wang, J.: Crystality: a programming model for smart contracts on parallel evms. In: Proceedings of the 30th ACM SIGPLAN Annual Symposium on Principles and Practice of Parallel Programming, pp. 412–425. PPoPP '25, Association for Computing Machinery (2025)
29. Winskel, G.: The Formal Semantics of Programming Languages - An Introduction. MIT Press, Cambridge (1993)
30. Xu, Z., Wang, H., Sun, M.: Operational semantics for crystality: a smart contract language for parallel evms. In: Rümmer, P., Wu, Z. (eds.) Theoretical Aspects of Software Engineering. TASE 2025. LNCS, vol. 15841, pp. 303–321. Springer, Cham (2025). https://doi.org/10.1007/978-3-031-98208-8_18
31. Xu, Z., Wang, H., Sun, M.: From monolithic to compositional: a compositional operational semantics for crystality (2026). https://arxiv.org/abs/2604.22210

32. Yang, Z., Lei, H.: Lolisa: formal syntax and semantics for a subset of the solidity programming language. CoRR **abs/1803.09885** (2018). http://arxiv.org/abs/1803.09885
33. Zakrzewski, J.: Towards verification of ethereum smart contracts: a formalization of core of solidity. In: Piskac, R., Rümmer, P. (eds.) VSTTE 2018. LNCS, vol. 11294, pp. 229–247. Springer, Cham (2018). https://doi.org/10.1007/978-3-030-03592-1_13

Timed Games Under Environmental Interference with Real-Time Objectives

Andrea Manini[(✉)], Matteo Rossi, and Pierluigi San Pietro

Politecnico di Milano, Milan, Italy
{andrea.manini,matteo.rossi,pierluigi.sanpietro}@polimi.it

Abstract. Classical Timed Games formulations may be unsuitable, or require substantial modeling effort, to capture complex interaction patterns between a controller and its surrounding environment, in which the non-determinism must be resolved after the controller has chosen which action to perform. This paper introduces Timed CLTLoc Games (TCGs), a novel Timed Game variant designed to facilitate the modeling of such patterns. Unlike classical Timed Games, TCGs partition locations rather than actions, and use Constraint Linear Temporal Logic over clocks formulae to specify the controller's objectives.

We implement algorithms for solving TCGs in our C++20 region-based library TARZAN, leveraging OpenMP for efficient parallelization. We then validate our theoretical results through an empirical evaluation on a Production Cell case study, demonstrating that the region-based implementation is computationally efficient in practice for medium-sized models.

1 Introduction

The interactions between a reactive system [8] and its environment are naturally modeled as game-theoretic problems, in which the system represents a controller acting against an adversarial opponent. Under timing constraints, Timed Games (TGs) over Timed Automata (TA) formalize the controller synthesis problem in real-time settings [10]. However, classical TGs semantics [12], as implemented in state-of-the-art tools such as UPPAAL TIGA [3], may be unsuitable, or require substantial modeling effort, to capture interactions in which the non-determinism over actions and, in some cases, also delays, must be resolved after the controller chooses which action to perform (and possibly also an associated delay).

To facilitate the modeling of such interactions, we propose a novel TG variant, called *Timed CLTLoc Games (TCGs)*, in which the controller always chooses an action to perform, and its objectives (referred to as the *winning condition*) are specified using Constraint Linear Temporal Logic over clocks (CLTLoc) formulae [4,5]. The non-determinism over actions is then resolved by the environment; non-determinism over delays depends on whether a location belongs to the controller or the environment (indeed, TCGs partition locations rather than actions). TCGs are further distinguished by CLTLoc's linear-time nature, which facilitates the specification of constraints over the interaction timeline. Moreover,

G. De Giacomo et al. (Eds.): TASE 2026, LNCS 16697, pp. 343–349, 2027.
https://doi.org/10.1007/978-3-032-30693-7_22

CLTLoc winning conditions can express timing constraints on clocks external to a model, enabling the specification of properties without extending such a model.

Existing tools including UPPAAL TIGA, UPPAAL STRATEGO, PRISM-GAMES, and SYNTHIA target different TG semantics or winning condition logics [3,7,9,14]. Our contribution is two-fold: (i) we introduce TCGs and algorithms for solving them, and (ii) we implement these algorithms in our C++ library TARZAN [11].

2 Theoretical Background

We use the term *action* to refer to the events that a reactive system can exhibit. The timing behavior of such systems is modeled by the formalism of TA [1]:

Definition 1. *A Timed Automaton $\mathcal{A}$ is a tuple $\mathcal{A} = (Act, Q, Q_0, X_{\mathcal{A}}, T, Inv)$, where Act is a finite set of actions, Q is a finite set of locations, $Q_0 \subseteq Q$ is a set of initial locations, $X_{\mathcal{A}}$ is a finite set of clocks, $T \subseteq Q \times Act \times \Gamma(X_{\mathcal{A}}) \times 2^{X_{\mathcal{A}}} \times Q$ is a transition relation, and $Inv : Q \to \Gamma(X_{\mathcal{A}})$ is an invariant-assignment function.*

Let $\mathcal{A}$ be a TA. $\Gamma(X_{\mathcal{A}})$ is a set of clock constraints, defined by the following grammar: $\gamma := x \sim \mathrm{c} \mid \neg\gamma \mid \gamma \wedge \gamma$, where $x \in X_{\mathcal{A}}$, $c \in \mathbb{N}$, and $\sim \in \{\leq, <, =, >, \geq\}$. Notably, we restrict invariants to be convex. The powerset $2^{X_{\mathcal{A}}}$ indicates that a transition may reset a subset of the clocks. A pair (q, v) is a *configuration* of $\mathcal{A}$, where $q \in Q$ and $v : X_{\mathcal{A}} \to \mathbb{R}_{\geq 0}$ is a *clock valuation*; $Eval_{\mathcal{A}}$ denotes the set of all clock valuations of $\mathcal{A}$. Given a subset $Y \subseteq X_{\mathcal{A}}$ of clocks, we denote by $v[Y \leftarrow 0]$ the clock valuation defined as $v[Y \leftarrow 0](x) = 0$ if $x \in Y$ and $v[Y \leftarrow 0](x) = v(x)$ otherwise. Given a constant $\delta \in \mathbb{R}_{\geq 0}$ and a clock $x \in X_{\mathcal{A}}$, the value $(v + \delta)(x)$ is $v(x) + \delta$. The *transition system* $TS(\mathcal{A}) = (S, Act \cup \mathbb{R}_{\geq 0}, I, \hookrightarrow)$ captures the semantics of $\mathcal{A}$, where $S = Q \times Eval_{\mathcal{A}}$, $I = \{(q, v) \mid q \in Q_0 \wedge \forall x \in X_{\mathcal{A}} : v(x) = 0\}$, and $\hookrightarrow$ is a transition relation containing discrete and delay transitions. The Region Transition System (RTS) $\mathcal{R}_{\mathcal{A}} = (\mathcal{S}, Act \cup \{\tau\}, \mathcal{I}, \rightsquigarrow)$ of $\mathcal{A}$ is derived from $TS(\mathcal{A})$ [2], where $\mathcal{S}$ is the set of all state regions (also called states) of $\mathcal{A}$, $\mathcal{I}$ is the set of initial states, and $\rightsquigarrow \subseteq \mathcal{S} \times (Act \cup \{\tau\}) \times \mathcal{S}$ is a transition relation containing discrete and delay transitions (τ is a fictitious action for delay transitions).

Let AP be a finite set of atomic propositions and $X_{\mathcal{W}}$ be a finite set of clocks (which are not necessarily initialized to zero). CLTLoc formulae are defined by the following grammar [5]: $\varphi := p \mid \alpha \sim \beta \mid \neg\varphi \mid \varphi \wedge \varphi \mid \bigcirc\varphi \mid \ominus\varphi \mid \varphi \mathbf{U} \varphi \mid \varphi \mathbf{S} \varphi$, where $p \in AP$, α, β are either a constant in $\mathbb{N}$ or a clock in $X_{\mathcal{W}}$, and $\sim \in \{<, =\}$. We consider the *future-only* fragment of CLTLoc [5]. CLTLoc formulae consisting of Boolean combinations of atomic propositions and clock constraints, without temporal operators, are called *pure*. The CLTLoc semantics is described in [4,5].

3 Timed CLTLoc Games

We focus on *zero-sum, non-Zeno, two-player* games, *i.e.*, games in which exactly two players—the *controller* (**c**) and the *environment* (**e**)—are involved and a win for one player implies a loss for the other. To formalize the adversarial interaction between players, we propose the notions of *Timed Arena (TAr)* and *move*.

Definition 2. *A Timed Arena $\mathcal{A}$ is a TA $\mathcal{A} = (Act, Q, Q_0, X_{\mathcal{A}}, T, Inv)$, where Q is partitioned into controller $Q_{\mathbf{c}} \subseteq Q$ and environment $Q_{\mathbf{e}} \subseteq Q$ locations, such that $Q = Q_{\mathbf{c}} \cup Q_{\mathbf{e}}$ and $Q_{\mathbf{c}} \cap Q_{\mathbf{e}} = \varnothing$. The partition of set Q is reflected on $\mathcal{R}_{\mathcal{A}}$.*

A *winning condition* $\mathcal{W}$ over a TAr $\mathcal{A}$ is a CLTLoc formula such that $AP = Q$, *i.e.*, the atomic propositions of $\mathcal{W}$ predicate over the locations of $\mathcal{A}$. Notice that the set of clocks $X_{\mathcal{W}}$ of $\mathcal{W}$ may overlap with $X_{\mathcal{A}}$, and that a clock in $X_{\mathcal{W}} \backslash X_{\mathcal{A}}$ can still be reset, if needed, to satisfy $\mathcal{W}$. A TCG $\mathcal{T}$ is defined as a pair $\mathcal{T} = (\mathcal{A}, \mathcal{W})$, where $\mathcal{A}$ is a TAr and $\mathcal{W}$ is a winning condition. The way in which $\mathcal{T}$ evolves is defined according to the following notion of move involving both players:

Definition 3. *Let $\mathcal{A}$ be a TAr and (q, v) be a configuration of $\mathcal{A}$. A* move *from (q, v) is a pair (a, δ), where $a \in Act$ is an action always chosen by the controller, and $\delta \in \mathbb{R}_{\geq 0}$ is a delay chosen by the controller if $q \in Q_{\mathbf{c}}$ and by the environment if $q \in Q_{\mathbf{e}}$ (the delay δ must be chosen after action a). Then, from the set of all enabled transitions $(q, a, \gamma, Y, q') \in T$, for which $v + \delta$ satisfies $Inv(q)$ and γ, the environment resolves the non-determinism by choosing a single transition to fire.*

Let $\mathcal{T} = (\mathcal{A}, \mathcal{W})$ be a TCG and $TS(\mathcal{A}) = (S, Act \cup \mathbb{R}_{\geq 0}, I, \hookrightarrow)$. The mapping $step : (S \times (Act \times \mathbb{R}_{\geq 0})) \to \wp(S)$, where $\wp$ denotes the powerset operator, returns all configurations (q', v') reachable from (q, v) with action a and delay δ:

$$step((q,v),(a,\delta)) = \left\{ \aleph = (q', (v+\delta)[Y \leftarrow 0]) \in S \;\middle|\; \begin{array}{l} ((q,v), \delta, (q, v+\delta)) \in \hookrightarrow \\ \wedge\ ((q, v+\delta), a, \aleph) \in \hookrightarrow \end{array} \right\}.$$

Strategies. Let $\mathcal{A}$ be a TAr. A *play* $\rho = (q_0, v_0), (q_1, v_1), \ldots, (q_n, v_n), \ldots$ over $\mathcal{A}$ is an infinite path over $TS(\mathcal{A}) = (S, Act \cup \mathbb{R}_{\geq 0}, I, \hookrightarrow)$ such that: $(q_0, v_0) \in I$ and $\exists a_n \in Act, \exists \delta_n \in \mathbb{R}_{\geq 0} : (q_{n+1}, v_{n+1}) \in step((q_n, v_n), (a_n, \delta_n))$. The set of all finite prefixes of the plays of $\mathcal{A}$ is denoted by *Plays*. Given a play ρ over $\mathcal{A}$, we denote by $\rho_{\leq n}$ its prefix of length $n \geq 0$, reaching a configuration $(q_n, v_n) \in S$.

A *controller strategy* is a mapping $\sigma_{\mathbf{c}} : Plays \to ((Act \times \mathbb{R}_{\geq 0}) \cup Act)$ defined as: $\sigma_{\mathbf{c}}(\rho_{\leq n}) = (a, \delta)$ if $q_n \in Q_{\mathbf{c}}$, while $\sigma_{\mathbf{c}}(\rho_{\leq n}) = a$ if $q_n \in Q_{\mathbf{e}}$, where $a \in Act$ and $\delta \in \mathbb{R}_{\geq 0}$, associating either a move or an action with a finite prefix $\rho_{\leq n} \in Plays$. Next, let $\sigma^1_{\mathbf{e}} : Plays \to \mathbb{R}_{\geq 0}$ be a partial mapping associating a delay in $\mathbb{R}_{\geq 0}$ with a finite prefix in *Plays* if $q_n \in Q_{\mathbf{e}}$; $\sigma^1_{\mathbf{e}}$ is undefined otherwise. We also introduce the mapping $\sigma^2_{\mathbf{e}} : (Plays \times \wp(S)) \to S$, associating a configuration in S with a finite prefix in *Plays* and a subset of configurations of S. Then, an *environment strategy* is a pair $\sigma_{\mathbf{e}} = (\sigma^1_{\mathbf{e}}, \sigma^2_{\mathbf{e}})$. Finally, given a pair of strategies $(\sigma_{\mathbf{c}}, \sigma_{\mathbf{e}})$, their *outcome* $\Theta_{(\sigma_{\mathbf{c}}, \sigma_{\mathbf{e}})} : Plays \to S$ is defined as:

$$\Theta_{(\sigma_{\mathbf{c}},\sigma_{\mathbf{e}})}(\rho_{\leq n}) = \begin{cases} \sigma^2_{\mathbf{e}}(\rho_{\leq n}, step((q_n, v_n), \sigma_{\mathbf{c}}(\rho_{\leq n}))) & \text{if } q_n \in Q_{\mathbf{c}} \\ \sigma^2_{\mathbf{e}}(\rho_{\leq n}, step((q_n, v_n), (\sigma_{\mathbf{c}}(\rho_{\leq n}), \sigma^1_{\mathbf{e}}(\rho_{\leq n})))) & \text{if } q_n \in Q_{\mathbf{e}} \end{cases}.$$

Since TCGs are zero-sum, we will only focus on controller strategies. A play ρ is *consistent* with a controller strategy $\sigma_{\mathbf{c}}$ if there exists an environment strategy $\sigma_{\mathbf{e}}$ such that, for every finite prefix $\rho_{\leq n} \in Plays$, the next configuration reached from (q_n, v_n) in ρ is $(q_{n+1}, v_{n+1}) = \Theta_{(\sigma_{\mathbf{c}}, \sigma_{\mathbf{e}})}(\rho_{\leq n})$.

Table 1. Semantics of CLTLoc formulae over a generic play ρ of a TCG $\mathcal{T} = (\mathcal{A}, \mathcal{W})$.

$$
\begin{aligned}
(\rho,\nu), i \models p &\iff p = q_i, \text{ for } p \in AP \\
(\rho,\nu), i \models \alpha \sim \beta &\iff \nu(i,\alpha) \sim \nu(i,\beta), \text{ for } \sim \in \{<,=\} \\
(\rho,\nu), i \models \neg\varphi &\iff (\rho,\nu), i \not\models \varphi \\
(\rho,\nu), i \models \varphi \wedge \psi &\iff (\rho,\nu), i \models \varphi \text{ and } (\rho,\nu), i \models \psi \\
(\rho,\nu), i \models \bigcirc\varphi &\iff (\rho,\nu), i+1 \models \varphi \\
(\rho,\nu), i \models \varphi \mathbf{U} \psi &\iff \exists j \geq i : (\rho,\nu), j \models \psi \wedge \forall n \in [i,j) : (\rho,\nu), n \models \varphi
\end{aligned}
$$

TCG Semantics. The semantics of a TCG $\mathcal{T} = (\mathcal{A}, \mathcal{W})$ over a given play ρ is defined with respect to a strict linear order $(\mathbb{N}, <)$, which represents positions in time. A position $i \in \mathbb{N}$ denotes the configuration (q_i, v_i) of ρ. A *clock assignment* ν is a mapping $\nu : \mathbb{N} \times (X_\mathcal{A} \cup X_\mathcal{W}) \to \mathbb{R}_{\geq 0}$, defined as: $\nu(i,x) = v_i(x)$ if $x \in X_\mathcal{A}$; $\nu(i,x) \in \mathbb{R}_{\geq 0}$ otherwise, associating a non-negative real value with each clock in $X_\mathcal{A} \cup X_\mathcal{W}$, for every position i. To ensure that time progresses at the same rate for every clock $x \in (X_\mathcal{W} \setminus X_\mathcal{A})$, it must hold that for every position i there exists $\delta_i \in \mathbb{R}_{\geq 0}$ such that: $\nu(i+1,x) = \nu(i,x) + \delta_i$ if time progresses, $\nu(i+1,x) = 0$ if x is reset. An *interpretation* of $\mathcal{W}$ is a pair (ρ,ν). The semantics of $\mathcal{W}$ at position i under (ρ,ν) is defined in Table 1, where $\nu(i,c) = c$ whenever $c \in \mathbb{N}$. We say that $\mathcal{W}$ is *satisfiable* if there exists an interpretation satisfying $\mathcal{W}$ at position $i = 0$. If such an interpretation (ρ,ν) exists, then we say that (ρ,ν) *satisfies* $\mathcal{W}$.

Definition 4 (Winning strategy). *A controller strategy $\sigma_\mathbf{c}$ is* winning *for a given TCG $\mathcal{T} = (\mathcal{A}, \mathcal{W})$ if, for every play ρ consistent with $\sigma_\mathbf{c}$, there exists an interpretation (ρ,ν) that satisfies $\mathcal{W}$. Consequently,* solving $\mathcal{T}$ *requires determining whether there exists a winning controller strategy for $\mathcal{T}$.*

Since plays and strategies are defined over $TS(\mathcal{A})$, and $TS(\mathcal{A})$ is bisimilar to $\mathcal{R}_\mathcal{A}$, no strategy is lost by exploring $\mathcal{R}_\mathcal{A}$ instead of $TS(\mathcal{A})$. Hence, since a RTS is a finite abstraction of $TS(\mathcal{A})$, in the remainder of this work we focus on $\mathcal{R}_\mathcal{A}$.

Computing Predecessors. Let $\mathcal{A}$ be a TAr and $\mathcal{R}_\mathcal{A} = (\mathcal{S}, Act \cup \{\tau\}, \mathcal{I}, \rightsquigarrow)$ be the RTS of $\mathcal{A}$, where $G \subseteq \mathcal{S}$ denotes a subset of states of $\mathcal{R}_\mathcal{A}$. Recall that, by Definition 2, $\mathcal{S} = \mathcal{S}_\mathbf{c} \cup \mathcal{S}_\mathbf{e}$ and $\mathcal{S}_\mathbf{c} \cap \mathcal{S}_\mathbf{e} = \varnothing$ hold. We introduce the *controllable predecessor operator* $\pi : \wp(\mathcal{S}) \to \wp(\mathcal{S})$, used to solve TCGs. We split π into the operators $\pi_\mathbf{c} : \wp(\mathcal{S}) \to \wp(\mathcal{S}_\mathbf{c})$ and $\pi_\mathbf{e} : \wp(\mathcal{S}) \to \wp(\mathcal{S}_\mathbf{e})$, by considering controller and environment states, respectively. Then, $\pi = (\pi_\mathbf{c} \cup \pi_\mathbf{e})$, where:

$$
\pi_\mathbf{c}(G) = \left\{ s \in \mathcal{S}_\mathbf{c} \;\middle|\; \begin{array}{l} \exists a \in Act : \exists s_1 \in \mathcal{S}, \exists s_2 \in G : (s,\tau,s_1), (s_1,a,s_2) \in \rightsquigarrow \\ \wedge\, \neg \exists s_3 \in (\mathcal{S} \setminus G) : (s_1,a,s_3) \in \rightsquigarrow \end{array} \right\}, \tag{1}
$$

$$
\pi_\mathbf{e}(G) = \left\{ s \in \mathcal{S}_\mathbf{e} \;\middle|\; \begin{array}{l} \exists a \in Act : \exists s_1 \in \mathcal{S}, \exists s_2 \in G : (s,\tau,s_1), (s_1,a,s_2) \in \rightsquigarrow \\ \wedge\, \neg(\exists s_3 \in \mathcal{S}, \exists s_4 \in (\mathcal{S} \setminus G) : (s,\tau,s_3), (s_3,a,s_4) \in \rightsquigarrow) \end{array} \right\}. \tag{2}
$$

Algorithm 1: Reachability

```
Data: T = (A, W := φUψ).
Result: G: states the controller
        uses to win in T.
begin
    S_φ ← states satisfying φ;
    G ← states satisfying ψ;
    repeat
        Ḡ ← G;
        G ← G ∪ (π(G) ∩ S_φ);
    until G = Ḡ;
    if (I ∩ G) ≠ ∅ then
        return G;
    return ∅;
```

Algorithm 2: Safety

```
Data: T = (A, W := □φ).
Result: G: states the controller
        uses to win in T.
begin
    G ← states satisfying φ;
    repeat
        Ḡ ← G;
        G ← (π(G) ∩ G);
    until G = Ḡ;
    if (I ∩ G) ≠ ∅ then
        return G;
    return ∅;
```

Fig. 1. Pseudocode of the algorithms used to solve reachability and safety TCG.

Reachability and Safety Winning Conditions. We present two fixed-point backward algorithms to solve a TCG with a *reachability* or *safety* winning condition $\mathcal{W}$. To ensure that π correctly accounts for the resets of clocks that belong exclusively to $\mathcal{W}$, we extend arenas to include such clocks as well, allowing any of them to be reset at each transition of a given arena.

Let φ and ψ be pure CLTLoc formulae. A *reachability* winning condition is $\mathcal{W} := \varphi\mathbf{U}\psi$, where ψ identifies the states of $\mathcal{R}_{\mathcal{A}}$ that the controller must reach to win. If $\varphi \equiv \top$, then $\varphi\mathbf{U}\psi \equiv \Diamond\psi$. A *safety* winning condition is $\mathcal{W} := \Box\varphi$. In this case, the controller is required to always stay within the states identified by φ, regardless of the choices of the environment. The following theorem establishes the correctness of the algorithms for solving reachability and safety TCGs:

Theorem 1. *Algorithm 1 (resp. Algorithm 2) solves a TCG $\mathcal{T} = (\mathcal{A}, \mathcal{W})$, where $\mathcal{W}$ specifies a reachability (resp. safety) winning condition, by computing all and only the states of plays, which are consistent with a winning controller strategy, for which there exists an interpretation that satisfies $\mathcal{W}$ from an initial state.*

4 Implementation and Experimental Evaluation

Tarzan is a C++20 region-based library originally designed for the forward and backward reachability analysis of TA and networks of TA. It has been extended with the algorithms presented in Sect. 3. The implementation is parallelized with OpenMP [13]; together with high-level compiler optimizations, this yields a speedup of nearly 20× over a baseline implementation.

Application to a Production Cell Case Study. We illustrate the modeling capabilities of TCGs through a Production Cell case study [6]. Experiments were conducted on a MacBook Pro with an M3 chip (8 cores) and 24 GB of RAM. The Cell, shown in Fig. 2, models a cyclic production system in which a feed belt, rotary table, press, and depot are serviced by a two-armed robot and a crane. We evaluated different TCGs on the Cell, as summarized in Table 2. Notice that the algorithms have been extended to also handle the $\bigcirc$ operator.

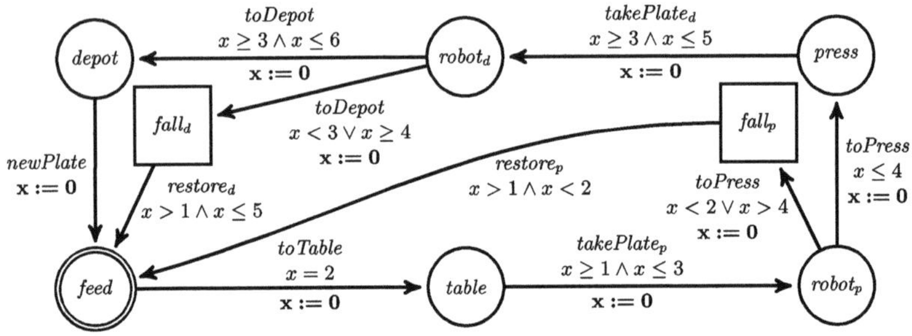

Fig. 2. TAr adaptation of the Production Cell case study. Environment locations, represented as squares, model the uncontrollable time required to restore a fallen plate.

Table 2. Cell experimental results. The table reports time in milliseconds, memory in Megabytes, iteration count (**#Iter**), the number of states in $\mathcal{S}_\varphi$ required by Algorithm 1 (#$\mathcal{S}_\varphi$), the number of states in G before (**#PreG**) and after (**#PostG**) execution, and whether there exists (*i.e.*, WIN; LOSE otherwise) a winning controller strategy (**Sat**).

Optimized		Not Optimized		#Iter	#$\mathcal{S}_\varphi$	#PreG	#PostG	Sat
Time	Mem	Time	Mem					
► $\mathcal{W}_1 := \Diamond(depot \wedge 0 < y \leq 11)$ ◄								
17.543	15.00	299.544	14.00	6	0	440	495	WIN
► $\mathcal{W}_2 := \Box(\neg fall_p \wedge \neg fall_d)$ ◄								
2.066	10.00	22.292	13.00	1	—	180	16	WIN
► $\mathcal{W}_3 := \bigcirc((\neg depot \wedge y > 0)\mathbf{U}(depot \wedge 25 \leq y \leq 30))$ ◄								
93.632	54.00	1818.848	56.00	10	8512	214	572	WIN
► $\mathcal{W}_4 := \bigcirc((\neg depot \wedge y > 0 \wedge 0 \leq x \leq 3)\mathbf{U}(depot \wedge 25 \leq y \leq 30))$ ◄								
37.541	30.00	460.611	32.00	6	4249	214	426	LOSE
► $\mathcal{W}_5 := \bigcirc((\neg depot \wedge y > 0 \wedge (y \geq 15 \Rightarrow 0 \leq x \leq 3))\mathbf{U}(depot \wedge 25 \leq y \leq 30))$ ◄								
68.252	44.00	1064.279	42.00	10	6300	214	535	WIN
► $\mathcal{W}_6 := \begin{matrix}(feed \wedge y = 0) \wedge \bigcirc^5(depot \wedge 10 \leq y \leq 12) \wedge \bigcirc^6(feed \wedge y = 14) \\ \wedge \bigcirc^{11}(depot \wedge 29 \leq y \leq 31) \wedge \bigcirc^{12}(feed \wedge y = 32) \wedge \bigcirc^{17}(depot \wedge y = 43)\end{matrix}$ ◄								
19.149	11.00	239.928	14.00	17	—	14	3	WIN

5 Conclusion and Future Works

This paper introduced Timed CLTLoc Games, a novel variant of Timed Games that facilitates the modeling of reactive systems where a controller always chooses an action, while the non-determinism is resolved after the action has been chosen. After establishing the theoretical foundations and defining algorithms for solving TCGs, we validated the theoretical results on a classical Production Cell case study, which we verified using our library, Tarzan.

Future work will proceed along several directions. We plan to extend Tarzan with strategy synthesis capabilities, generalize TCGs to networks of TCGs, develop and implement in Tarzan more efficient algorithms for solving TCGs, and explore hybrid approaches that complement Tarzan with zone-based techniques, thereby combining the strengths of both abstractions.

References

1. Alur, R., Dill, D.L.: A theory of timed automata. Theoret. Comput. Sci. **126**(2), 183–235 (1994)
2. Baier, C., Katoen, J.P.: Principles of Model Checking (Representation and Mind Series). The MIT Press (2008)
3. Behrmann, G., Cougnard, A., David, A., Fleury, E., Larsen, K.G., Lime, D.: Uppaal-tiga: time for playing games! In: Damm, W., Hermanns, H. (eds.) Computer Aided Verification, pp. 121–125. Springer, Berlin Heidelberg, Berlin, Heidelberg (2007)
4. Bersani, M.M., Rossi, M., San Pietro, P.: A tool for deciding the satisfiability of continuous-time metric temporal logic. Acta Inf. **53**(2), 171–206 (2016)
5. Bersani, M.M., Rossi, M., San Pietro, P.: A logical characterization of timed regular languages. Theor. Comput. Sci. **658**, 46–59 (2017), formal Languages and Automata: Models, Methods and Application In honour of the 70th birthday of Antonio Restivo
6. Burns, A.: How to verify a safe real-time system: The application of model checking and timed automata to the production cell case study. Real-Time Syst. **24**(2), 135–151 (2003)
7. David, A., Jensen, P.G., Larsen, K.G., Mikucionis, M., Taankvist, J.H.: Uppaal stratego. In: International Conference on Tools and Algorithms for Construction and Analysis of Systems (2015)
8. Harel, D., Pnueli, A.: On the development of reactive systems. In: Apt, K.R. (ed.) Logics Models Concurrent Syst., pp. 477–498. Springer, Heidelberg (1985)
9. Kwiatkowska, M., Norman, G., Parker, D., Santos, G.: PRISM-games 3.0: stochastic game verification with concurrency, equilibria and time. In: Lahiri, S.K., Wang, C. (eds.) CAV 2020. LNCS, vol. 12225, pp. 475–487. Springer, Cham (2020). https://doi.org/10.1007/978-3-030-53291-8_25
10. Maler, O., Pnueli, A., Sifakis, J.: On the synthesis of discrete controllers for timed systems. In: Mayr, E.W., Puech, C. (eds.) STACS 1995. LNCS, vol. 900, pp. 229–242. Springer, Heidelberg (1995). https://doi.org/10.1007/3-540-59042-0_76
11. Manini, A., Rossi, M., San Pietro, P.: Tarzan: a region-based library for forward and backward reachability of timed automata (extended version) (2026). https://arxiv.org/abs/2602.15435
12. Markey, N., O.S.: Timed games. In: Fijalkow, N. (ed.) Games on Graphs (2023)
13. OpenMP architecture review board: OpenMP application program interface version 5.0 (2018). https://www.openmp.org/wp-content/uploads/OpenMP-API-Specification-5.0.pdf
14. Peter, H.J., Ehlers, R., Mattmüller, R.: Synthia: verification and synthesis for timed automata. In: Gopalakrishnan, G., Qadeer, S. (eds.) Computer Aided Verification, pp. 649–655. Springer, Heidelberg (2011)

Health-State-Aware Adaptive Bad Block Management for NAND Flash-Based Storage Systems

Tianyang Wang[1], Mingfeng Yang[2(✉)], Jiangjiang Jiang[3], and Hongbiao Liu[3]

[1] School of Computer Science and Technology, Xidian University, Xi'an, China
[2] China Academy of Space Technology, Beijing, China
yangmf@bice.org.cn
[3] Beijing Institute of Control Engineering, Beijing, China

Abstract. As NAND flash-based storage systems operate over time, wear-induced degradation gradually increases page- and block-level faults, threatening system reliability. Existing bad block management (BBM) schemes are typically triggered by hard failure events such as uncorrectable errors or program failures, which fail to capture the gradual evolution of degradation and often lead to reactive management and concentrated reserved block consumption. To address these limitations, this paper proposes a Health-State-Aware Adaptive Bad Block Management method (HABBM). HABBM constructs a lightweight block-level health-state model based on bad-page accumulation and ECC-correctable errors (CE), and incorporates system-wide wear information through an adaptive threshold mechanism to dynamically classify blocks and regulate management decisions. By enabling proactive identification and protection of degraded blocks, HABBM mitigates concentrated replacement behaviors and smooths reserved resource consumption. Experiments using a configurable flash-level simulator with real-world workloads show that HABBM increases the supported cumulative host writes by approximately 1.64–2.04× compared with representative BBM schemes while maintaining low runtime overhead, demonstrating its effectiveness in improving flash storage reliability.

Keywords: Bad block management · Health-state modeling · Adaptive reliability management · Runtime degradation modeling · Storage system reliability

1 Introduction

NAND flash-based storage systems are widely deployed in modern information infrastructures, including server platforms, embedded devices, and high-reliability environments [1]. However, repeated program, erase, and read operations gradually cause physical degradation of flash cells, leading to permanent or

G. De Giacomo et al. (Eds.): TASE 2026, LNCS 16697, pp. 350–367, 2027.
https://doi.org/10.1007/978-3-032-30693-7_23

transient faults at the page or block level [2]. Consequently, Bad Block Management (BBM) has become a fundamental mechanism for ensuring flash storage reliability [3].

During manufacturing, some blocks fail reliability tests and are marked as factory bad blocks during system initialization [4]. In addition, flash cells degrade during runtime due to mechanisms such as tunnel oxide aging, charge trapping, read disturbance, and retention loss, which may lead to newly emerging bad pages or blocks [5,6]. Therefore, storage systems must detect and replace faulty blocks during runtime to maintain reliability [7].

Traditional BBM mechanisms adopt conservative block-level replacement strategies. Once a page within a block encounters a program failure, erase failure, or Uncorrectable Error (UE), the entire block is marked as bad and replaced by a reserved block [8]. Although simple and reliable, this strategy becomes inefficient in modern high-density flash technologies such as MLC, TLC, QLC, and modern 3D NAND architectures, where blocks contain a large number of pages [9]. Discarding an entire block due to a single page failure wastes many functional pages and accelerates reserved block consumption [10].

To improve space utilization, several studies proposed fine-grained BBM mechanisms based on Bad Page Skipping (BPS) [11]. These methods skip faulty pages while continuing to use healthy pages within a block, thereby delaying block retirement and reducing reserved block consumption. However, as bad pages accumulate, intra-block fragmentation increases and may complicate address management and data migration while concentrating program and erase operations on fewer healthy pages [12].

Meanwhile, modern flash systems widely employ Error Correction Code (ECC) mechanisms to mitigate bit errors caused by read disturbance and retention degradation [13]. Within the ECC correction capability, Correctable Errors (CE) are typically treated as transient events [14]. However, frequent CE occurrences may indicate early reliability degradation and strongly correlate with subsequent uncorrectable errors and permanent failures [15]. Ignoring such early signals restricts BBM to reactive responses triggered only after severe failures occur.

Although existing BBM approaches provide basic reliability guarantees, several limitations remain. Most methods trigger management actions only after unrecoverable faults and lack mechanisms to continuously perceive block health states. Moreover, management decisions are often based on fixed thresholds or isolated conditions that cannot adapt to evolving degradation distributions. In addition, wear-leveling considerations are rarely integrated into block replacement or migration decisions, which may aggravate global wear imbalance.

To address these challenges, this paper proposes a Health-State-Aware Adaptive Bad Block Management (HABBM) method. HABBM constructs a block-level health model using bad page distribution and ECC correctable error statistics, while incorporating block wear conditions through an aging-aware adaptive threshold. Adaptive thresholds derived from the global health-state distribution guide block classification and management decisions. In addition, HABBM introduces hierarchical management and a cold data migration strategy to reduce write pressure on degraded blocks, transforming BBM from reactive fault handling into proactive health-aware management.

The main contributions of this work are summarized as follows:

- **Block health-state modeling.** A lightweight block-level health-state model integrating bad page ratio and ECC correctable error statistics to characterize flash block reliability evolution, with wear information further incorporated through adaptive thresholding.
- **Adaptive bad block management.** An adaptive management mechanism based on dynamic thresholds that regulates block handling according to system-wide aging conditions.
- **Cold data migration strategy.** A cold data identification and migration mechanism that reduces write pressure on degraded blocks while considering wear-leveling objectives.
- **Experimental evaluation.** Experiments with real-world workloads demonstrate that HABBM improves lifetime and reserved-resource utilization.

The remainder of this paper is organized as follows. Section 2 presents the background and motivation of bad block management. Section 3 describes the design and mechanisms of HABBM. Section 4 introduces the experimental methodology and evaluation results. Finally, Sect. 5 gives the conclusions and future work.

2 Background and Motivation

2.1 NAND Flash Architecture and Degradation Characteristics

NAND flash memory is organized into pages and blocks, where a page is the smallest unit for read and program operations, while a block is the smallest unit for erase operations. Since flash cells do not support in-place overwrite, updated data must be written to a new free page, and blocks containing invalid pages are later reclaimed through the Garbage Collection (GC) process [16]. These management mechanisms are implemented in the Flash Translation Layer (FTL), making the block the fundamental unit for flash management and reliability control.

During long-term operation, flash cells gradually degrade due to repeated Program/Erase (P/E) cycles as well as read disturbance and retention effects [6]. As degradation accumulates, the probability of bit errors increases and the reliability of different blocks may diverge, resulting in highly non-uniform error distributions across the storage system. Flash degradation typically evolves progressively. In early stages, bit errors may remain within the correction capability of ECC and appear as CE. However, as degradation continues to accumulate, the number of errors may exceed the ECC correction capability and lead to UE [15]. Moreover, failures may initially appear only in a few pages of a block while other pages remain functional.

Therefore, bad pages and bad blocks should be viewed as the outcome of long-term degradation processes rather than isolated failure events. Accurately identifying and managing blocks with different health states during this evolution is therefore essential for improving the reliability of flash-based storage systems.

2.2 Bad Block Management

The primary objective of BBM is to isolate physical degradation in flash storage systems and prevent localized faults from propagating into system-level failures while extending device lifetime. Extensive studies have explored bad block detection, block replacement strategies, bad page utilization, and degradation prediction.

Early BBM approaches mainly adopt block-level replacement strategies. Once a program failure, erase failure, or UE occurs within a block, the entire block is marked as bad and replaced. Chang et al. [17] proposed maintaining runtime error status words and bad block tables to isolate faulty blocks. Ma et al. [18] adopted a similar strategy in embedded flash systems by directly replacing failed blocks with reserved blocks, and practical implementations [19] widely follow this full block replacement mechanism. Although simple and reliable, discarding an entire block due to a single page failure becomes increasingly conservative in modern high-density flash devices.

With the evolution of MLC, TLC, and 3D NAND technologies, the number of pages per block has increased significantly, motivating studies on improving space utilization. Wang et al. [20] distinguished recoverable and unrecoverable failures and allowed healthy pages in partially failed blocks to remain usable. Huh et al. [21] similarly observed that blocks classified as bad may still contain many functional pages and proposed aggregating these healthy pages for continued utilization. These observations indicate that a bad page does not necessarily require retiring the entire block.

Based on this observation, several works proposed page-level BBM schemes based on Bad Page Skipping (BPS). Moon et al. [11] recorded failed page locations and skipped them in subsequent writes, delaying block retirement and reducing reserved block consumption. Maddah et al. [22] similarly proposed reusing healthy pages within partially failed blocks through delayed block retirement. However, the accumulation of bad pages increases intra-block fragmentation and management complexity.

Beyond reactive fault handling, several studies explored predictive approaches using runtime error information. Peleato et al. [23] proposed a degradation-aware method based on Raw Bit Error Rate (RBER) prediction to identify high-risk blocks before ECC failure occurs. Ma et al. [14] further estimated block lifetime by predicting when the error rate approaches the ECC correction limit. Machine learning techniques were later introduced to model degradation trends and improve bad block identification accuracy [15]. However, these approaches often rely on complex prediction models or static thresholds, which may limit their practical deployment.

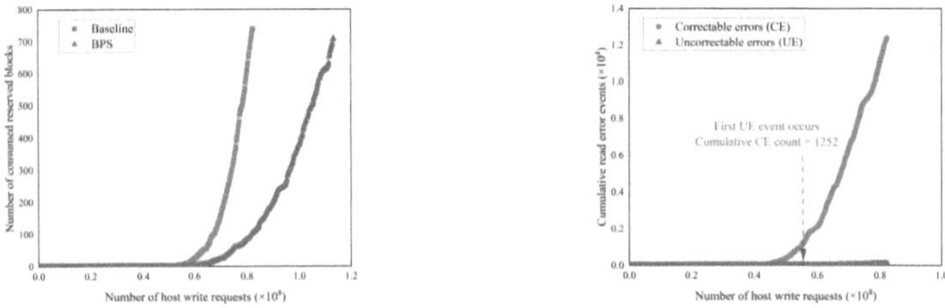

(a) Reserved block consumption (b) Cumulative read errors

Fig. 1. Reserved block consumption and read errors under different BBM methods.

BBM research has also expanded to more complex system scenarios. Maneas et al. [24] analyzed large-scale field data from enterprise SSDs and revealed significant variations in failure behavior across flash technologies and operating environments. Bai et al. [25] proposed a layer-aware BBM strategy for 3D NAND flash to isolate only affected storage layers when page-level faults occur. Yen et al. [26] further exploited spatial correlations among adjacent blocks and proposed a cluster-similarity-based BBM scheme to jointly manage degraded regions. For aerospace applications, Li et al. [27] proposed an SSD reliability analysis model considering both flash degradation and controller hardware faults, while Li et al. [28] designed a high-reliability storage architecture for spaceborne parallel flash systems based on bad block replacement mechanisms. Ma et al. [19] also proposed a real-time bad block detection and replacement strategy for spaceborne solid-state storage systems.

Overall, although existing BBM approaches have improved block replacement, bad page utilization, and degradation prediction, several limitations remain. Most methods lack a unified metric to characterize block health states, and management decisions are often triggered by isolated events or fixed thresholds. Moreover, BBM and wear-leveling mechanisms are usually designed independently without coordinated optimization. These limitations motivate the design of a BBM mechanism that can continuously perceive block-level degradation and adaptively regulate management strategies.

2.3 Motivation

Although existing BBM methods provide basic reliability guarantees for flash-based storage systems, their behavior under long-term degradation still requires further investigation. To analyze the limitations of existing BBM strategies, we conduct a comparative study on representative approaches. The traditional full block replacement strategy [8] is used as the baseline, while Bad Page Skipping (BPS) [11] represents fine-grained BBM schemes. Under identical degradation settings, the system executes the write-intensive workload *prxy_0*. The experiments focus on reserved block consumption and the evolution of read errors. Detailed experimental configurations are provided in Sect. 4.

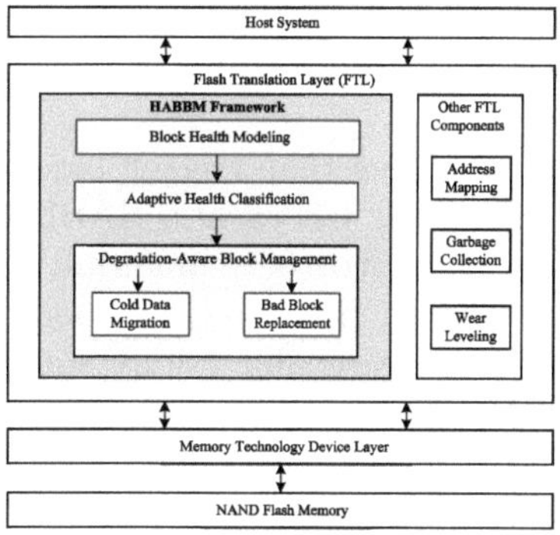

Fig. 2. Overall framework of the HABBM method.

Figure 1(a) shows the reserved block consumption with respect to host write requests. The baseline method exhibits rapid reserved block consumption in the later stage of system operation. Although BPS delays this consumption to some extent, a similar accelerated trend still appears as the system continues to run. This indicates that skipping faulty pages alleviates early space waste but does not fundamentally change the triggering mechanism of BBM decisions.

Figure 1(b) presents the cumulative read error events during system operation, including Correctable Errors (CE) and Uncorrectable Errors (UE). CE events begin to accumulate continuously during the early and middle stages, while UE events rarely occur. When the first UE appears (around 0.556×10^8 write requests), the cumulative CE events have already reached 1252, indicating that substantial degradation information is revealed by CE long before UE occurs.

However, traditional BBM mechanisms usually rely on final failure events such as UE or program/erase failures as triggering conditions. As a result, early degradation signals reflected by CE are largely ignored, delaying management actions and causing concentrated block replacement.

To address this limitation, this paper proposes a Health-State-Aware Adaptive Bad Block Management (HABBM) method. HABBM incorporates CE accumulation into BBM decisions and constructs a block-level health-state model to identify potentially degraded blocks in advance. Through hierarchical block management, HABBM avoids the concentrated replacement behavior of conventional methods and enables smoother reserved block consumption, thereby improving system reliability and lifetime.

3 Health-State-Aware Adaptive Bad Block Management

3.1 Overview

Figure 2 illustrates the overall framework of HABBM, which is integrated within the Flash Translation Layer (FTL). HABBM targets reactive block replacement, concentrated reserved block consumption, and insufficient degradation awareness by extending failure-triggered BBM into proactive health-state-aware management.

Unlike conventional approaches that trigger block replacement only after program failures, erase failures, or UE events, HABBM continuously monitors runtime error behaviors and constructs a quantitative model to characterize the reliability state of each block. Based on this model, early intervention can be applied before blocks enter irreversible failure stages. Specifically, HABBM first establishes a block-level health-state model to evaluate block reliability. Adaptive classification thresholds are then determined according to the global aging condition of the system, enabling blocks to be categorized into different health levels and supporting differentiated management decisions. Based on the classification results, HABBM applies cold-data migration to reduce program and erase pressure on potentially degraded blocks. For blocks that have entered irreversible degradation stages, a progressive detection and replacement strategy is adopted to isolate faulty blocks and maintain system reliability.

Overall, the HABBM framework consists of three major components:

- **Block Health Modeling**: integrates bad page ratio and read error information to construct a lightweight reliability representation.
- **Adaptive Health Classification**: dynamically adjusts health thresholds according to the global degradation state of the system.
- **Degradation-Aware Block Management**: applies differentiated strategies for blocks with different health levels, including *Cold Data Migration* and *Bad Block Replacement*.

3.2 Flash Block Health Modeling and Dynamic Update Mechanism

Traditional BBM schemes typically rely on failure-event-triggered strategies. When program failures, erase failures, or UE events occur, the corresponding block is marked as bad and replaced by a reserved block. Although this mechanism ensures reliability, it is inherently reactive because management actions are triggered only after severe degradation occurs. In practice, flash degradation evolves gradually, and early indicators such as the accumulation of bad pages and CE often appear before irreversible failures. Although CE events can be corrected by ECC, their continuous accumulation may indicate potential reliability degradation.

To capture this degradation evolution, HABBM introduces the concept of the *block health state* to quantitatively evaluate block reliability. The model jointly considers multiple degradation indicators and constructs a unified health score based on the number of bad pages and the cumulative number of CE events in each block. Whenever new bad pages or additional CE events are detected, the health score of the corresponding block is dynamically updated. The model deliberately uses bad-page counts and CE statistics because both can be obtained by the FTL/ECC layer with low overhead. Other physical factors, such as RBER, retention loss, read disturbance, and temperature, may further improve modeling accuracy but usually require lower-level device information; their runtime effects are indirectly reflected through CE accumulation and bad-page evolution.

For an arbitrary flash block i, the health score H_i is defined as follows:

$$H_i = \alpha_1 \left(1 - \frac{BP_i}{P_{blk}}\right) + \alpha_2 \left(1 - \frac{CE_i}{CE_{max}}\right) \tag{1}$$

where the weights are dynamically adjusted according to the global degradation statistics of the system. The initial weights are defined as

$$\alpha_1' = \frac{BP_{avg}}{P_{blk}}, \quad \alpha_2' = \frac{CE_{avg}}{CE_{max}} \tag{2}$$

The final normalized weights are obtained as

$$\alpha_k = \frac{\alpha_k'}{\alpha_1' + \alpha_2'}, \quad k = 1, 2 \tag{3}$$

The parameters in the model are defined as follows: BP_i denotes the number of bad pages in block i, and P_{blk} denotes the total number of pages in a block. CE_i represents the cumulative number of CE events in block i, while CE_{max} is the maximum CE count among all blocks. BP_{avg} and CE_{avg} denote the average bad page count and CE count across all blocks, respectively. α_k represents the weights of bad pages and CE in the health model.

The terms $1 - BP_i/P_{blk}$ and $1 - CE_i/CE_{max}$ represent the remaining health level of a block. As the bad page ratio or CE ratio increases, the corresponding term decreases monotonically, allowing degradation to be directly reflected in the health score. Since each term is normalized to $[0, 1]$ and $\alpha_1 + \alpha_2 = 1$, the health score H_i also lies within $[0, 1]$, where values closer to 1 indicate healthier blocks. The adaptive weighting mechanism improves sensitivity at different degradation stages. In early stages, bad pages are rare while CE events may already accumulate, making α_2 relatively larger. As the system ages and bad pages increase, α_1 gradually becomes larger, allowing the model to focus more on physical damage. By integrating bad page accumulation and CE evolution into a unified health scoring framework, HABBM enables continuous monitoring of flash block degradation and provides the basis for adaptive health classification (Sect. 3.3) and degradation-aware block management (Sect. 3.4).

3.3 Adaptive Health Threshold and Block Classification Mechanism

Although the block health model provides a continuous evaluation of flash block degradation, the health score alone cannot directly determine management actions. In practical systems, management decisions are triggered by discrete conditions, such as identifying potentially degraded blocks and determining whether protection or replacement should be applied. Therefore, the continuous health score must be mapped into discrete health levels. Moreover, fixed thresholds cannot adapt to the evolving degradation characteristics of flash memory

Table 1. Block health classification and corresponding management strategies

Level	Condition	Block State	Management Strategy
Level 0	$H_i \geq T$	Normal block	Normal read/write operations
Level 1	$H_i < T$	Potentially degraded block	Cold data migration protection

during long-term operation. As system wear increases, the management mechanism should gradually become more sensitive to degradation risks. To address this issue, HABBM introduces an adaptive health threshold that adjusts classification sensitivity according to the current aging condition of the system.

The adaptive classification threshold T is defined as

$$T = H_{min} + \gamma(H_{max} - H_{min})\lambda^{\mu} \tag{4}$$

where the aging factor λ is defined as

$$\lambda = \frac{E_{avg}}{E_{max}} \tag{5}$$

E_{avg} denotes the average erase count of all blocks in the system, and E_{max} represents the maximum erase endurance limit of a flash block. The threshold dynamically adapts to both the health score distribution and the global aging condition of the system. The parameters H_{min} and H_{max} denote the current range of block health scores, ensuring that the threshold always lies within this range. The coefficient $\gamma \in (0, 1]$ controls the sensitivity of degradation detection: larger γ values move the threshold closer to the upper bound and enable earlier detection of degraded blocks, while smaller values result in more conservative classification. The aging-driven component λ^{μ} determines how the threshold evolves as the system ages. When the system is in the early stage of operation, λ remains small and the threshold stays closer to H_{min}, avoiding unnecessary management overhead. As erase operations accumulate, λ increases and the threshold gradually shifts toward H_{max}, enabling earlier identification of potentially degraded blocks. The parameter μ controls the growth rate of the threshold with system aging.

Through this mechanism, HABBM dynamically maps continuous health scores to discrete health levels and adapts classification sensitivity according to the system aging condition. This threshold therefore provides the decision basis for the health-level-aware block management strategy described in Sect. 3.4.

3.4 Health-Level–Aware Block Management Strategy

After obtaining the adaptive threshold T, HABBM classifies flash blocks into different health levels according to their health score H_i. Two levels are defined based on the relationship between H_i and T, as summarized in Table 1.

Blocks with $H_i \geq T$ are classified as Level 0 blocks and continue to operate under the standard storage management policy without additional intervention, thereby maintaining high storage utilization and avoiding unnecessary data migration. Blocks with $H_i < T$ are classified as Level 1 blocks, indicating potential degradation. Although these blocks remain functional, the accumulation of bad pages or CE events suggests an increased risk of further degradation. Instead of immediately retiring such blocks, HABBM applies a protection strategy: during GC operations, cold data (i.e., data with low update frequency) are preferentially migrated to these blocks. This placement reduces future write pressure, thereby slowing degradation and extending block lifetime. The detailed cold data identification and migration mechanism is described in Sect. 3.5.

Through this health-level classification, HABBM applies differentiated management strategies based on block degradation conditions. Healthy blocks operate normally, while potentially degraded blocks receive cold-data placement protection, delaying bad block formation and reducing reserved block consumption.

3.5 Cold Data Identification and Migration Mechanism

Blocks classified as Level 1 are considered potentially degraded. To slow further degradation, HABBM applies a cold-data placement mechanism after GC, migrating stable data to these blocks to reduce future write pressure. The mechanism consists of two steps: *cold data identification* and *cold data migration*. By performing lightweight background migration without interfering with the normal write path, HABBM protects degraded blocks while maintaining low runtime overhead.

Cold Data Identification. Cold data identification selects blocks with the lowest update frequency among Level 0 blocks as migration sources. HABBM evaluates data coldness using write interval statistics by maintaining a global write sequence number S_{global} that increases with each page write. For each page p, the most recent write sequence S_p is recorded. The page-level coldness is defined as

$$\Delta S(p) = S_{global} - S_p \tag{6}$$

A larger $\Delta S(p)$ indicates colder data.

Since migration operates at the block level, page coldness is aggregated into block coldness. For block i, the block-level coldness C_i is defined as

$$C_i = \frac{1}{V_i} \sum_{p \in i, valid} \Delta S(p) \tag{7}$$

where V_i denotes the number of valid pages in block i. Blocks with larger C_i are more suitable as migration sources.

After GC, if the reclaimed block is classified as Level 1, the system selects a cold data source block from Level 0 blocks. Candidate blocks are sorted by C_i, and the block with the largest value is chosen as the cold data source B_{cold}. If multiple candidates share the same coldness, the block with the smallest erase count is selected. Once a source block is selected in the current migration round, it is excluded from subsequent source selection to avoid repeatedly migrating data from the same cold block.

Algorithm 1. Cold Data Identification and Migration

Require: Block set $BlockSet$, block level array $Level[blk]$, global write sequence S_{global}, last write sequence S_p of each page
Ensure: Cold data protection for Level 1 blocks
for each block blk_j in $BlockSet$ **do**
  if $Level[blk_j] == Level_1$ **then**
    Select block blk_{cold} with maximum block coldness C_i
    $C_i = Average(\Delta S(p))$ for each Level 0 block
    Break ties using the smallest erase count
    Exclude blk_{cold} from subsequent source selection in the current migration round
    $F_j \leftarrow FreePages(blk_j)$
    Sort valid pages in blk_{cold} by $\Delta S(p)$ (descending)
    Select top F_j pages as $p_{migrate}$
    for each page p in $p_{migrate}$ **do**
      Migrate p to block blk_j
    end for
  end if
end for

Cold Data Migration. After identifying the cold data source block B_{cold}, its valid pages are migrated to the target Level 1 block to reduce future write pressure. Since Level 1 blocks may contain bad pages, their writable capacity is limited. For a Level 1 block j, the number of available pages is

$$F_j = FreePages(j) \tag{8}$$

If the number of valid pages in B_{cold} exceeds F_j, HABBM performs partial migration. Valid pages are sorted by $\Delta S(p)$ in descending order, and the top F_j coldest pages are selected:

$$p_{migrate} = \{p \in B_{cold} \mid \Delta S(p) \text{ ranks among top } F_j\} \tag{9}$$

Migration is triggered after GC completes block reclamation and health evaluation. Since it is executed outside the core GC procedure, it avoids directly increasing foreground GC latency and has limited impact on the normal write path.

Through this strategy, Level 1 blocks mainly store low-update-frequency data, reducing write pressure and slowing wear accumulation. The complete procedure of cold data identification and migration is summarized in Algorithm 1.

3.6 Bad Block Accumulation Detection and Replacement Strategy

During long-term operation, accumulated faults may eventually lead to bad block formation. To balance reliability and lifetime utilization, HABBM adopts a progressive management strategy that combines page-level isolation with block-level replacement.

Factory-marked bad blocks are detected during system initialization and excluded from allocation. During runtime, program failures and UE are handled at the page level: only the affected page is marked as bad while the remaining pages in the block remain usable, avoiding premature block retirement. However, continuous accumulation of bad pages indicates severe degradation. HABBM therefore monitors the bad page ratio of each block during GC. When the ratio exceeds a predefined threshold, i.e., $BP_i/P_{blk} > \theta$, where BP_i is the number of bad pages in block i and P_{blk} is the number of pages per block, the block is considered unreliable and replaced by a reserved block. In contrast, erase failures indicate irreversible degradation. When an erase failure occurs, the block is immediately marked as bad and replaced, and its valid pages are migrated to the replacement block. Through this progressive strategy, HABBM performs page-level isolation in early stages and block-level replacement only when necessary, delaying bad block formation and reducing reserved block consumption.

HABBM is complementary to garbage collection and wear leveling. Garbage collection provides the timing for post-reclamation migration, while HABBM determines whether a reclaimed block should receive cold data according to its health level. Wear leveling balances erase counts, and HABBM reduces write pressure on degraded blocks by placing low-update-frequency data into Level 1 blocks.

4 Evaluation

4.1 Experimental Setup

The effectiveness of HABBM is evaluated through trace-driven simulations on the open-source flash simulation platform SSDsim [29], which models key NAND flash operations including page read/write, block erase, and erase endurance constraints.

In the experiments, the SSD capacity is configured as 4 GB and the erase endurance limit of each block is set to 500 cycles. This configuration emulates embedded flash storage environments with relatively strict endurance constraints and is also used to accelerate degradation so that bad-block events can be observed within a tractable simulation time. The main simulation parameters are summarized in Table 2.

To evaluate the robustness of bad block management strategies under diverse workloads, six real-world I/O traces released by Microsoft Research Cambridge are used [30]. These traces represent different application scenarios with varying access intensities and read/write ratios. Their statistical characteristics are summarized in Table 3.

Table 2. SSDsim simulation platform configuration

Parameter	Value	Parameter	Value
Number of channels	2	Page size	8 KB
Chips per channel	1	Read latency	20 μs
Dies per chip	2	Program latency	200 μs
Planes per die	1	Erase latency	1.5 ms
Blocks per plane	2048	FTL scheme	Page mapping
Pages per block	64	Erase limit	500

Table 3. Workload trace datasets

Trace	Total Requests	Write Ratio (%)	Avg. Write Size (KB)	Avg. Read Size (KB)
prxy_0	12,519,868	96.94	4.65	8.33
rsrch_0	1,433,655	90.68	8.73	10.92
usr_0	2,237,889	59.58	10.28	40.92
ts_0	1,801,734	82.42	8.01	13.68
hm_0	3,993,316	64.50	8.34	7.37
src2_0	1,557,814	88.66	7.09	8.10

Two representative bad block management strategies are used for comparison: **Block Replacement (Baseline)** [8] and **Bad Page Skipping (BPS)** [11]. The Baseline method immediately marks a block as bad and replaces it with a reserved block once a program failure, erase failure, or UE occurs. In contrast, BPS skips failed pages and continues using the remaining healthy pages within a block to improve space utilization, while erase failures and UE still trigger block replacement to maintain consistent fault-handling semantics. These two methods represent the two typical BBM design extremes: conservative block-level retirement and fine-grained page-level salvage, allowing HABBM to be evaluated against representative reactive management strategies.

The key parameters of HABBM are fixed across all workloads rather than tuned for individual traces: the threshold adjustment coefficient $\gamma = 1$, the aging sensitivity exponent $\mu = 1$, and the bad page replacement threshold $\theta = 0.5$. Here, γ controls the aggressiveness of degraded-block identification, μ controls the aging-driven threshold growth rate, and θ determines when a partially failed block should be retired. These unified settings avoid workload-specific overfitting and provide a consistent basis for comparison. The system lifetime is defined as the point when the reserved block pool of any block group is exhausted, and the same termination condition is applied to all compared methods.

4.2 Experimental Results and Analysis

Four metrics are used to evaluate different bad block management strategies, including Total Host Writes, Number of Consumed Reserved Blocks, Host Writes at First Bad Block, and Average Response Time.

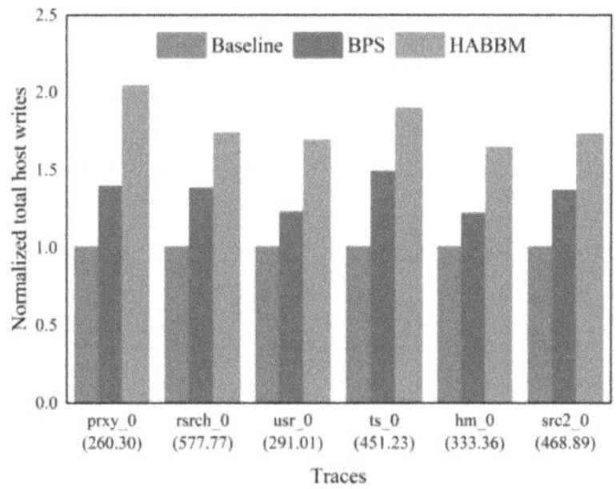

Fig. 3. Normalized total host writes under six workload traces.

Total Host Writes. Total host writes represent the cumulative amount of host write requests that the system can serve before reaching its lifetime limit, reflecting the usable lifetime of the flash storage system. Figure 3 shows the results under six workload traces. All results are normalized with respect to the Baseline method, and the actual host write volume of the Baseline method (in GB) is shown in parentheses on the horizontal axis.

The results show that HABBM consistently achieves the highest total host writes across all workloads. Compared with the Baseline method, HABBM improves the cumulative host write capacity by 1.64×–2.04×, and still achieves improvements of approximately 16%–47% compared with BPS. The Baseline method immediately replaces a block when failures occur, which quickly consumes reserved blocks. Although BPS postpones replacement by skipping failed pages, page fragmentation gradually accumulates and eventually accelerates reserved block consumption. HABBM instead delays premature block replacement through proactive health-aware management.

Number of Consumed Reserved Blocks. The number of consumed reserved blocks reflects the utilization of spare blocks during system operation. Figure 4 illustrates the evolution of reserved block consumption as host writes increase under six workload traces. The horizontal axis represents the number of host write requests (in units of 10^8), and the vertical axis indicates the number of consumed reserved blocks.

As write requests accumulate, all methods gradually consume reserved blocks. The Baseline method starts consuming reserved blocks earlier and exhibits a steeper growth trend. Although BPS postpones the initial consumption by skipping failed pages, reserved block usage still accelerates in later stages due to the accumulation of bad pages and fragmentation. In contrast, HABBM shows smoother and more delayed reserved block consumption across all workloads, indicating more gradual reserved-resource utilization.

Host Writes at First Bad Block. Host writes at the first bad block measure the cumulative host writes when the first irreversible block failure occurs,

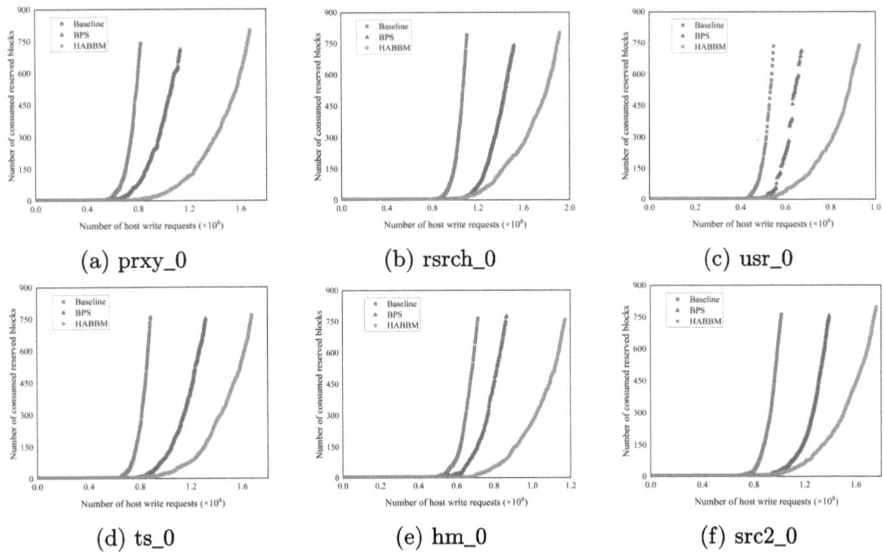

(a) prxy_0 (b) rsrch_0 (c) usr_0

(d) ts_0 (e) hm_0 (f) src2_0

Fig. 4. Reserved block consumption under six workload traces.

reflecting the capability of different methods to suppress early-stage degradation. Figure 5 shows the normalized cumulative host writes at the first bad block under six workload traces. All results are normalized with respect to the Baseline method, and the actual host writes of the Baseline method (in GB) are shown in parentheses on the horizontal axis.

The results show that HABBM consistently postpones the occurrence of the first bad block across all workloads. Compared with the Baseline method, HABBM increases the cumulative host writes at the first bad block by 1.58×, 1.43×, and 1.33× under the write-intensive workloads *prxy_0*, *rsrch_0*, and *ts_0*, respectively. Although BPS delays block replacement by skipping failed pages, its improvement remains smaller than that of HABBM. Under mixed read/write workloads such as *usr_0* and *hm_0*, the improvement becomes less pronounced due to more dispersed write behavior. Nevertheless, HABBM still consistently delays the occurrence of the first bad block, indicating its effectiveness in mitigating early degradation risks.

Average Response Time. Average response time evaluates the runtime overhead introduced by bad block management mechanisms. Figure 6 shows the normalized average response time under six workload traces. All results are normalized with respect to the Baseline method, and the actual response time of the Baseline method (in units of 10^4 ms) is shown in parentheses on the horizontal axis. The results show that response time differences among the three methods remain small across all workloads. Compared with the Baseline method, BPS reduces the average response time by 2.0%–4.8%, while HABBM achieves a

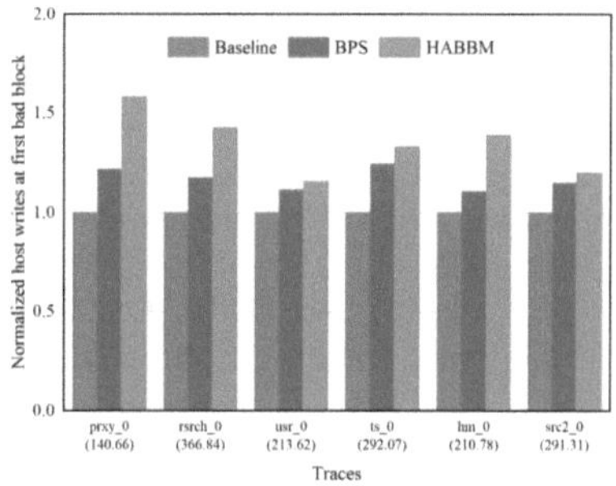

Fig. 5. Normalized cumulative host writes at the first bad block.

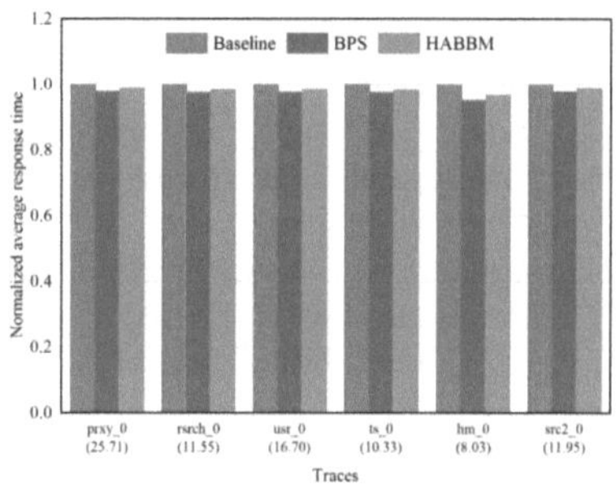

Fig. 6. Normalized average response time under six workload traces.

reduction of 1.0%–3.3%. The slightly higher response time of HABBM is mainly due to additional health monitoring and migration operations.

5 Conclusion

This paper proposes HABBM, a health-state-aware adaptive bad block management method for NAND flash–based storage systems. HABBM uses CE and bad-page evolution to build a lightweight block health model and enables proactive management before irreversible failures occur. Experiments show that HABBM increases cumulative host writes, delays the first bad block, and smooths reserved block consumption with negligible runtime overhead. Future work will extend simulator-based evaluation to broader SSD configurations and real hardware platforms.

Acknowledgments. This work was supported by the National Natural Science Foundation of China (Grant No. 62193273020).

Disclosure of Interests. The authors have no competing interests to declare.

References

1. Boukhobza, J., et al.: A survey on flash-memory storage systems: a host-side perspective. ACM Trans. Storage **21**(3), Article 24 (2025)
2. Gal, E., Toledo, S.: Algorithms and data structures for flash memories. ACM Comput. Surv. **37**(2), 138–163 (2005)
3. Chung, T.-S., Park, D.-J., Park, S., Lee, D.-H., Lee, S.-W., Song, H.-J.: A survey of flash translation layer. J. Syst. Architect. **55**(5–6), 332–343 (2009)
4. Schroeder, B., Merchant, A., Lagisetty, R.: Reliability of NAND-based SSDs: what field studies tell us. Proc. IEEE **105**(9), 1751–1769 (2017)
5. Cai, Y., et al.: Flash correct-and-refresh: retention-aware error management for increased flash memory lifetime. In: IEEE 30th International Conference on Computer Design (ICCD), pp. 94–101. IEEE (2012)
6. Shi, X., Wu, F., Wang, S., Xie, C., Lu, Z.: Program error rate-based wear leveling for NAND flash memory. In: Design, Automation and Test in Europe Conference (DATE), pp. 1241–1246. IEEE (2018)
7. Han, J., Zhu, G., Lee, E., Son, Y.: Design and implementation of an efficient and parallel bad block checker for parallelism of storage devices. Clust. Comput. **26**(5), 2615–2627 (2023)
8. Sreekandath, M., Purkayastha, S.D.: Asynchronous bad block management in NAND flash memory. US Patent **9**, 483395 (2016)
9. Frickey, R., et al.: Comparing the reliability of solid-state drives based on TLC and QLC NAND flash memories. In: IEEE International Reliability Physics Symposium (IRPS), 3A.1-1-3A.1-7. IEEE (2024)
10. Huang, P., Wu, G., He, X., Xiao, W.: An aggressive worn-out flash block management scheme to alleviate SSD performance degradation. In: Proceedings of the Ninth European Conference on Computer Systems (EuroSys), Article 22. ACM (2014)
11. Moon, J., Kang, M., Lee, W., Kim, S.: Salvaging runtime bad blocks by skipping bad pages for improving SSD performance. In: Design, Automation and Test in Europe Conference (DATE), pp. 576–579. IEEE (2022)
12. Jun, Y., Park, S., Kang, J.-U., Kim, S.-H., Seo, E.: We ain't afraid of no file fragmentation: causes and prevention of its performance impact on modern flash SSDs. In: 22nd USENIX Conference on File and Storage Technologies (FAST), pp. 1–16. USENIX Association (2024)
13. Schroeder, B., Lagisetty, R., Merchant, A.: Flash reliability in production: the expected and the unexpected. In: 14th USENIX Conference on File and Storage Technologies (FAST), pp. 67–80. USENIX Association (2016)
14. Ma, R., Wu, F., Zhang, M., Lu, Z., Wan, J., Xie, C.: RBER-aware lifetime prediction scheme for 3D-TLC NAND flash memory. IEEE Access **7**, 44696–44708 (2019)
15. Ma, R., et al.: BlockHammer: improving flash reliability by exploiting process variation aware proactive failure prediction. IEEE Trans. Comput. Aided Des. Integr. Circuits Syst. **39**(12), 4563–4574 (2020)
16. Jiang, J., Yang, M., Qiao, L., Wang, T., Ma, Z., Li, S., Zhu, S.: An adaptive real-time garbage collection method based on file write prediction. In: International Symposium on Theoretical Aspects of Software Engineering (TASE), pp. 224–241. Springer (2024)
17. Chang, Y.-H., Yang, M.-C., Kuo, T.-W., Hwang, R.-H.: A reliability enhancement design under the flash translation layer for MLC-based flash-memory storage systems. ACM Trans. Embed. Comput. Syst. **13**(1), 1–28 (2013)

18. Ma, Y., Du, H., Yang, S.: Independent bad block management for mass storage flash memory arrays. In: IEEE International Conference on Software Engineering and Service Science (ICSESS), pp. 388–391. IEEE (2015)
19. Ma, H., Xiao, J., Zhao, D., He, Y.: Design and application of bad block management strategy for on-board solid-state memory. In: International Conference on Signal and Information Processing, Networking and Computers, pp. 334–340. Springer (2022)
20. Wang, C., Wong, W.-F.: Extending the lifetime of NAND flash memory by salvaging bad blocks. In: Design, Automation and Test in Europe Conference (DATE), pp. 260–263. IEEE (2012)
21. Huh, T., Hussain, F., Jung, S., Song, Y.H.: Lifetime enhancement of NAND flash memory-based storage system by bad block reuse scheme. In: International Conference on Electronics, Information and Communications (ICEIC), pp. 1–2. IEEE (2014)
22. Maddah, R., Cho, S., Melhem, R.: Data dependent sparing to manage better-than-bad blocks. IEEE Comput. Archit. Lett. **12**(2), 43–46 (2013)
23. Peleato, B., Tabrizi, H., Agarwal, R., Ferreira, J.: BER-based wear leveling and bad block management for NAND flash. In: IEEE International Conference on Communications (ICC), pp. 295–300. IEEE (2015)
24. Maneas, S., Mahdaviani, K., Emami, T., Schroeder, B.: A study of SSD reliability in large-scale enterprise storage deployments. In: 18th USENIX Conference on File and Storage Technologies (FAST), pp. 137–149. USENIX Association (2020)
25. Bai, S., Zhou, Y., Wu, F., Xie, C., Kuo, T.-W., Xue, C.J.: LAVA: an effective layer variation aware bad block management for 3D CT NAND flash. In: Design, Automation and Test in Europe Conference (DATE), pp. 1–6. IEEE (2024)
26. Yen, J.-N., et al.: Efficient bad block management with cluster similarity. In: IEEE International Symposium on High-Performance Computer Architecture (HPCA), pp. 503–513. IEEE (2022)
27. Li, P., Dang, W., Qin, T., Zhang, Z., Lv, C.: A competing risk model of reliability analysis for NAND-based SSDs in space application. IEEE Access **7**, 23430–23441 (2019)
28. Li, X., Niu, Y., Yu, J., Zhang, Y.: A bad block management design based on space-borne NAND flash parallel storage system. In: International Conference on Communication Software and Networks (ICCSN), pp. 114–118. IEEE (2022)
29. Hu, Y., Jiang, H., Feng, D., Tian, L., Luo, H., Ren, C.: Exploring and exploiting the multilevel parallelism inside SSDs for improved performance and endurance. IEEE Trans. Comput. **62**(6), 1141–1155 (2013)
30. Traeger, A., Zadok, E., Joukov, N., Wright, C.P.: A nine year study of file system and storage benchmarking. ACM Trans. Storage **4**(2), 1–56 (2008)

First Steps in a Paraconsistent Transition Systems Toolkit

Rodrigo Alves[1], Juliana Cunha[1,2,3](✉), and Alexandre Madeira[1,2]

[1] Department Mathematics, Aveiro University, Aveiro, Portugal
{rodrigoalves,juliana.cunha,madeira}@ua.pt
[2] CIDMA - Center for Research and Development in Mathematics and Applications, Aveiro, Portugal
[3] INESC TEC, Department of Informatics, Minho University, Braga, Portugal

Abstract. Modelling complex information systems (e.g., combinations of heterogeneous data sources, data from hybrid-system sensors, or medical diagnostic exams) often requires managing inconsistencies in which different decisions and instructions may simultaneously align or conflict. Decision and reasoning methods for such scenarios are a focus of paraconsistent logics, which provide a means of handling inconsistencies without collapsing into triviality, treating them as potentially informative rather than anomalous.

Paraconsistent labelled transition systems (PLTS) were introduced as transition structures– parameterised by an underlying lattice– where each transition is characterised by a pair of values: one representing evidence that the transition occurs and the other representing evidence against it. Together with their associated modal logic and process algebra, PLTS provide a formal framework for modelling and reasoning in inconsistent scenarios. In this paper, we present an interactive toolkit that allows users to construct and visualise PLTS, as well as to interpret modal formulae over them. Finally, illustrative examples of the applicability of the framework and the toolkit are explored in fields such as robotics and finance.

Keywords: Paraconsistency · Transition Systems · Inconsistencies

1 Introduction

Modelling complex systems often entails managing inconsistencies, where different decisions or instructions may simultaneously align or conflict. Moreover, the synthesis of transition systems from input data is central to many applications. In such settings, input data is frequently incomplete or even contradictory, especially when collected from multiple, possibly unreliable, sources. For

This work is supported by CIDMA (https://ror.org/05pm2mw36) under the Portuguese Foundation for Science and Technology (https://ror.org/00snfqn58), Grants https://doi.org/10.54499/UID/04106/2025 (UID/04106/2025 and UID/PRR/04106/2025), and with project Banksy COMPETE2030-FEDER-00892000. Cunha is also supported by the FCT PhD Grant 2024.04652.BD.

G. De Giacomo et al. (Eds.): TASE 2026, LNCS 16697, pp. 368–385, 2027.
https://doi.org/10.1007/978-3-032-30693-7_24

example, during a development process, engineering teams often make design decisions based on imprecise and sometimes contradictory requirements elicited from stakeholders with distinct perspectives. Another example arises in robotics, where a robot collecting information through sensors may face inconsistencies, since sensors are sensitive to external conditions. Similar situations also occur in finance, where individuals may rely on different metrics, sometimes contradictory, to assess whether buying or selling a stock is profitable. Consequently, the development of more flexible and robust models for reasoning about systems in environments with potentially conflicting information is becoming increasingly relevant across different contexts.

Motivated by such challenges, paraconsistent labelled transition systems, in short PLTS, together with their associated modal logic, were introduced in [7]. They provide a way to model such situations through paraconsistent reasoning capable of capturing ignorance, truth, falsity, and contradiction.

PLTS and their modal logic follow a parametric approach, in line with works such as [5,18], allowing the framework to support a wider range of application scenarios. Thus, all relevant constructions are parametric over a class of lattices, allowing different instantiations depending on the structure of truth values most suitable for a given problem. More precisely, the framework underlying this paper starts from a complete residuated lattice $\mathbf{A} = (A, \leqslant)$ and constructs the product of $\mathbf{A}$ with its order dual $\mathbf{A}^{\partial}$. The resulting structure, known as a twist structure, a term coined by [17], plays a key role in PLTS research by providing a systematic way to combine pairs of values in A^2. A PLTS is then defined as a transition system whose valuations and transition relations take values in A^2. Informally, a pair $(tt, ff) \in A^2$ can be interpreted such that tt represents the amount of information supporting a statement, while ff represents the amount of information against it. Consequently, this framework accommodates a wide range of epistemic scenarios, since the two values are not required to be complementary. For instance, if the underlying lattice is the Boolean algebra, the four pairs $(1, 0)$, $(0, 1)$, $(1, 1)$, and $(0, 0)$ correspond respectively to truth (only evidence in favor of a statement), falsity (only evidence against a statement), inconsistency (simultaneous evidence both for and against), and vagueness (neither evidence for nor against). Thereby yielding the well-known Belnap-Dunn lattice [4].

Furthermore, in this paper we consider the paraconsistent modal logic introduced in [7], which supports reasoning about PLTS. Paraconsistent logics emerged as a way to reason in the presence of inconsistencies without collapsing into triviality [20]. They have found applications in engineering [2], robotics [1], quantum logic [6], and quantum computing [3]. While the motivations for their use vary, these logics share the fundamental view that inconsistency is not merely an artefact of error or confusion; rather, it may be informative and support meaningful reasoning.

Prior work on PLTS and their corresponding modal logic has been explored from an institution-theoretic perspective in [8,10], following the stepwise implementation methodology outlined by Sannella and Tarlecki. PLTS have also been studied in [9] in the context of reactive graphs, where transitions may affect others and policies are introduced to resolve such conflicts. Finally, potential applications of PLTS in quantum computing have been explored in [3] to model qubit decoherence in quantum circuits that, due to environmental interference, do not behave according to their intended design.

As is well known, a formal method becomes effective in practice only when it is supported by appropriate tools. Moreover, the availability of user-friendly interfaces is essential to broaden the audience of practitioners who can benefit from the formalism. This paper contributes in this direction by introducing a toolkit[1] for the development of PLTS. Namely, by allowing users to:

(i) construct arbitrary finite complete residuated lattices and automatically generate their twist structures;
(ii) build and visualise PLTS parametric over a chosen lattice; and
(iii) interpret modal formulae and check their validity over PLTS using the semantics introduced in [7].

Additionally, this paper explores case studies to illustrate the potential applications of the framework and the proposed toolkit in areas such as robotics and finance. Accordingly, the presented toolkit is expected to play a key role in future applications of the ongoing research agenda on twist structures and PLTS [7–10], aimed at better understanding and reasoning in the presence of inconsistencies. **Structure of the Paper:** Section 2 recalls the necessary background from [7, 10]. Section 3 presents the proposed toolkit, its main features, and illustrative applications. Concluding remarks appear in Sect. 4.

2 Paraconsistent Labelled Transition Systems and Their Modal Logic

This section introduces the parametric framework employed throughout the paper and recalls the necessary background from [7,10].

As in other works [5,18], the approach taken is parametric over a class of lattices, accommodating different instances according to the structure that best suits each concrete application. More precisely, each complete lattice $\mathbf{A} = (A, \leqslant)$ acts over a non-empty set A of finite truth values, bounded by 0 and 1, equipped with binary operations $\sqcap$ (meet) and $\sqcup$ (join) satisfying the usual distributive laws. The adjunction property is stated as $a \sqcap b \leqslant c$ iff $b \leqslant a \rightarrow c$, where $\rightarrow$ denotes the implication operation of $\mathbf{A}$.

Example 1. Well-known examples of complete distributive residuated lattices used throughout this paper include:

- The two element Boolean algebra $\mathbf{2} = (\{0, 1\}, \leqslant_{\mathbf{2}})$ with $0 \leqslant_{\mathbf{2}} 1$, and the meet and join operations are standard Boolean conjunction and disjunction.

[1] Available at https://github.com/juliana-cunha/PLTS_toolkit.git.

– The Łukasiewicz three-valued algebra $\mathbf{3} = (\{0, 1/2, 1\}, \leqslant_{\mathbf{3}})$ with $0 \leqslant_{\mathbf{3}} 1/2 \leqslant_{\mathbf{3}}$ and operations defined as follows:

$\sqcap_{\mathbf{3}}$	0	1/2	1
0	0	0	0
1/2	0	1/2	1/2
1	0	1/2	1

$\sqcup_{\mathbf{3}}$	0	1/2	1
0	0	1/2	1
1/2	1/2	1/2	1
1	1	1	1

$\rightarrow_{\mathbf{3}}$	0	1/2	1
0	1	1	1
1/2	1/2	1	1
1	0	1/2	1

The intermediate truth value 1/2, sometimes denoted by u or #, stands for "possibility", "unknown" or "indeterminacy", respectively c.f. [20].

As stated, this framework is extended by working with pairs $(\mathit{tt}, \mathit{ff}) \in A^2$, parametric over $\mathbf{A}$, where tt captures evidence in favor of a statement, and ff evidence against it. Since these values need not be complementary, this allows the representation of (i) vague information, when the values sum to less than 1; (ii) consistent information, when they are complementary and sum to 1; and (iii) inconsistent information, when they sum to more than 1. Such pairs can be constructed as the product of the lattice $\mathbf{A}$ with its order dual $\mathbf{A}^{\partial}$. The resulting structure forms a twist structure [17], which provides a systematic way to combine pairs of values in A^2. Formally,

Definition 1. *Let $\mathbf{A} = (A, \leqslant)$ be a complete distributive residuated lattice. The $\mathbf{A}$-twist structure is $(A^2, \leqslant_t)$, where for every $x_1, x_2, y_1, y_2 \in A$,*

$$/\!\!/ \, (x_1, y_1) = (y_1, x_1)$$
$$(x_1, y_1) \leqslant_t (x_2, y_2) \text{ iff } x_1 \leqslant x_2 \text{ and } y_1 \geqslant y_2$$
$$(x_1, y_1) \Cap (x_2, y_2) = (x_1 \sqcap x_2, y_1 \sqcup y_2)$$
$$(x_1, y_1) \Cup (x_2, y_2) = (x_1 \sqcup x_2, y_1 \sqcap y_2)$$
$$(x_1, y_1) \odot (x_2, y_2) = (x_1 \sqcap x_2, x_1 \rightarrow y_2 \sqcap x_2 \rightarrow y_1)$$
$$(x_1, y_1) \Rightarrow (x_2, y_2) = (x_1 \rightarrow x_2 \sqcap y_2 \rightarrow y_1, x_1 \sqcap y_2)$$

Therefore, since $(A^2, \leqslant_t)$ is the product of two complete distributive lattices, it is itself a complete distributive lattice. Moreover, operator $\Rightarrow$ is the right adjoint of $\odot$ (cf. [7]), that is, for any $(x_1, y_1), (x_2, y_2), (x_3, y_3) \in A^2$:

$$(x_1, y_1) \odot (x_2, y_2) \leqslant_t (x_3, y_3) \text{ iff } (x_1, y_1) \leqslant_t (x_2, y_2) \Rightarrow (x_3, y_3)$$

Thus, it follows that $(A^2, \leqslant_t)$ is itself a complete distributive residuated lattice.

Informally, a pair in A^2 is said to be more truthful when there is more evidence in favor and less against. Operations $\Cap$ and $\Cup$ correspond respectively to the meet and join under $\leqslant_t$ [13] and $/\!\!/$ is an involutive negation that reverses truth [11], that is, if $(x_1, y_1) \leqslant_t (x_2, y_2)$, then $/\!\!/(x_1, y_1) \geqslant_t /\!\!/(x_2, y_2)$.

The following example illustrates the twist structures induced by the lattices of Example 1.

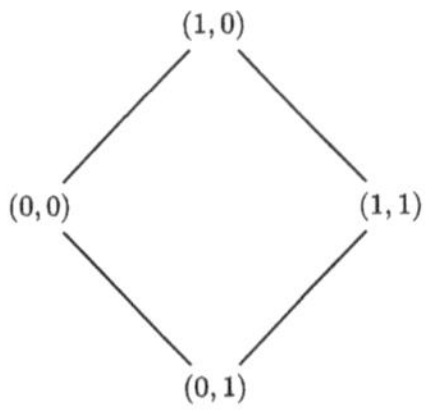

Fig. 1. Lattice $\mathcal{FOUR}$.

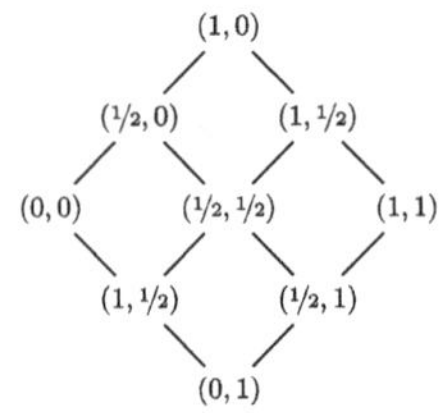

Fig. 2. Lattice $\mathcal{NINE}$.

Example 2. The twist structure over **2** is the lattice $\mathcal{FOUR}$, while that over **3** yields $\mathcal{NINE}$, whose Hasse diagrams are shown in Figs. 1 and 2, respectively.

Following [7,10], transitions and valuations in a paraconsistent transition system take values in A^2, parametrised by an underlying lattice $(A, \leqslant)$. We now recall the formal definition.

Definition 2 ([7]). *An* $(\mathbf{A}, Act, Prop)$*-paraconsistent transition system, in short PLTS, over a complete distributive residuated lattice* $(\mathbf{A}, \leqslant)$*, a set of actions Act and a set of proposition symbols Prop is a structure* (W, R, V) *where:*

- W *is a non-empty set of states;*
- $R : W \times Act \times W \rightarrow A^2$ *is a paraconsistent relation assigning, to each transition, evidence for and against its traversal; and*
- $V : W \times Prop \rightarrow A^2$ *is a valuation assigning, to each state and each proposition, the evidence for and against its holding.*

For readability, transitions weighted by $(0, 1)$, representing only evidence against the transition, are omitted from graphical representations. Additionally, throughout the paper, we assume that the transition function of any PLTS is complete; any undefined transition is assigned the default value $(0, 1)$.

We use the standard set of modal formulae, denoted by $\mathsf{Fm}(\text{Act}, \text{Prop})$, given by the following syntax: $\varphi \coloneqq \bot \,|\, p \,|\, \neg\varphi \,|\, \varphi \wedge \varphi \,|\, \langle a \rangle \varphi$, where $p \in \text{Prop}$ and $a \in \text{Act}$. Additionally, we consider the usual abbreviations from propositional logic: $\top = \neg\bot$, $\varphi \vee \varphi' = \neg(\neg\varphi \wedge \neg\varphi')$, $\varphi \rhd \varphi' = \neg(\varphi \wedge \neg\varphi')$, $\varphi \rhd\!\lhd \varphi' = (\varphi \rhd \varphi') \wedge (\varphi' \rhd \varphi)$ as well as from modal logic $[a]\varphi = \neg\langle a \rangle \neg\varphi$.

Given a PLTS $M = (W, R, V)$ and a formula $\varphi \in \mathsf{Fm}(\text{Act}, \text{Prop})$ the satisfaction relation $\models_M$ assigns to each state $w \in W$ a pair in A^2 capturing evidence for and against φ holding at that state. More precisely,

Definition 3 ([7]). *Let* $M = (W, R, V)$ *be an* $(\mathbf{A}, Act, Prop)$*-PLTS. The satisfaction relation* $\models_M : W \times \mathsf{Fm}(Act, Prop) \longrightarrow A^2$ *is defined recursively as follows:*

$$
\begin{aligned}
(w \models_M \bot) &= (0,1)\\
(w \models_M p) &= V(w,p)\\
(w \models_M \neg\varphi) &= /\!\!/(w \models_M \varphi)\\
(w \models_M \varphi \wedge \varphi') &= (w \models_M \varphi) \Cap (w \models_M \varphi')\\
(w \models_M \langle a\rangle\varphi) &= \bigsqcup_{v\in W} (R_a(w,v) \odot (v \models_M \varphi))
\end{aligned}
$$

for $p \in Prop$ and $a \in Act$.

Note that since $\models_M$ returns a value in A^2, naturally it is defined using the operations of the twist structure in order to compute values in A^2.

One may then naturally extend the local satisfaction relation $\models_M$ to the global satisfaction relation:

$$
(M \models \varphi) = \bigsqcap_{w\in W} (w \models_M \varphi) \tag{1}
$$

Example 3. Let $M = (\{s_0, s_1, s_2\}, R, V)$ be a $(\mathbf{2}, \{a\}, \{p, q\})$-PLTS with transitions in R as depicted in Fig. 3 and the valuation given by $V(s_0, q) = V(s_2, q) = (1,0)$, $V(s_2, p) = (1,1)$ and $V(s_1, p) = V(s_1, q) = V(s_0, p) = (0,1)$.

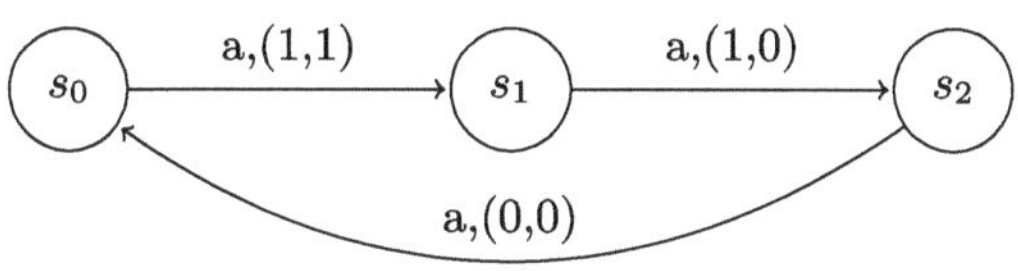

Fig. 3. The $(\mathbf{2}, a, p, q)$-PLTS M.

One may then compute $(s_i \models_M \neg p \vee q) = (1,0)$ for $i \in \{0,1,2\}$, which indicates that there is only evidence in favor of M satisfying the formula. Moreover, $(s_j \models_M [a]p \vee q) = (1,0)$ for $j \in \{0,2\}$ while

$$
\begin{aligned}
(s_1 \models_M [a]p \vee q) &= (s_1 \models_M \neg\langle a\rangle\neg p \vee q)\\
&= (s_1 \models_M \neg\langle a\rangle\neg p) \Cup (s_1 \models_M q)\\
&= /\!\!/ \,(R_a(s_1, s_2) \odot /\!\!/ V(s_2, p)) \Cup V(s_1, q)\\
&= (0,1)
\end{aligned}
$$

which indicates that although s_2 is reachable from s_1, at s_2 the proposition p holds inconsistently; in other words, in this framework classical truth $(1,0)$ does not entail inconsistent truth $(1,1)$.

3 A Toolkit for PLTS and the Associated Modal Logics

This section presents the implementation of the proposed toolkit for constructing and visualising PLTS as well as interpreting formulae over PLTS as defined in Sect. 2. Case studies are also provided to illustrate both the paraconsistent framework and the features of the toolkit.

The proposed toolkit, implemented in Python, is available at https://github.com/juliana-cunha/PLTS_toolkit.git. This open-source tool provides an interactive interface for generating twist structures, visualising PLTS, and interpreting modal formulae. It is built using `PyQt6` [21] graphical interface, with the core logic separating the mathematical definitions from the UI presentation layer. Additionally, model persistence is handled via `JSON`, enabling users to save and reload objects across sessions. Graphical rendering of Hasse diagrams and transition systems is supported through `Matplotlib` [16] and `NetworkX` [14].

The main window, shown in Fig. 4, follows a split-pane layout. The top menus provide the following actions: New, for creating objects; Load, for importing existing ones; Delete for remove objects; See for viewing previously saved JSON files; View, for switching between light and dark mode; and Help which provides mathematical definitions and a legend of the notation used. The left sidebar serves as a project explorer, grouping objects into Lattices, Residuated Lattices, Twist Structures, States, Models, and Propositions; the right panel displays object details, visualisations, and the modal logic interpreter.

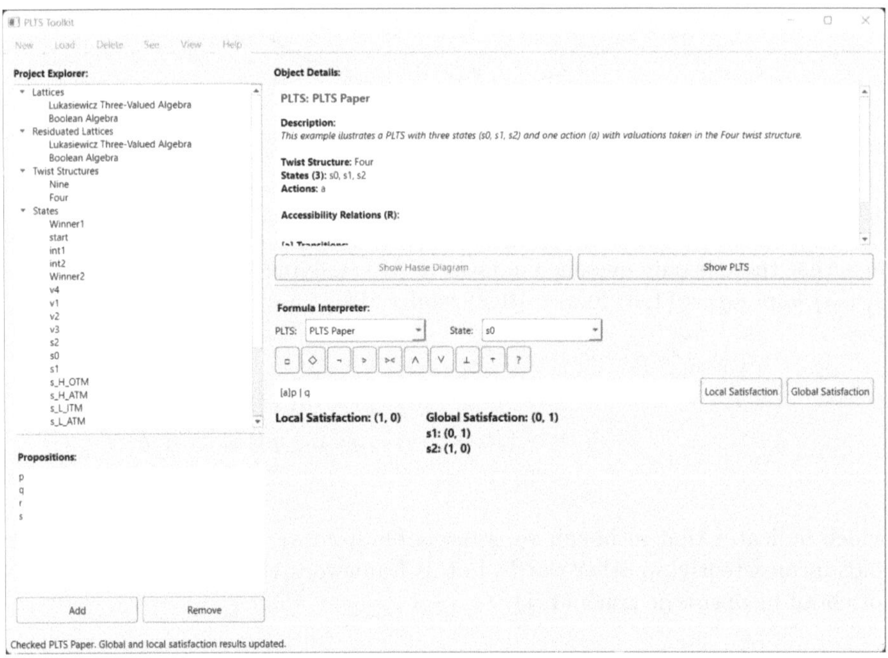

Fig. 4. Screenshot of the PLTS toolkit.

The toolkit provides built-in support for loading preexisting standard lattices, such as **2** and **3** of Example 1, via the Load menu. Custom finite lattices $(A, \leqslant)$ forming complete distributive residuated lattice can also be created via the New menu by specifying the set of truth values A, the partial order $\leqslant$, and optionally the lattice operations.

The toolkit also includes built-in twist structures, allowing users to load $\mathcal{FOUR}$ and $\mathcal{NINE}$ from Example 2. In addition, custom twist structures, defined as the product of a complete lattice with its order dual, can be generated automatically from any existing lattice. As expected, the size of the twist structure grows with the size of the underlying lattice. As noted, the paraconsistent framework is parametric over a class of lattices; this feature is therefore essential, allowing users to select a domain of truth values appropriate to their application and automatically obtain the associated twist structure.

The Hasse diagrams of a lattice and their associated twist structures can be visualised directly in the interface. For example, Fig. 5 shows the rendering of the algebra **3** and its twist structure $\mathcal{NINE}$.

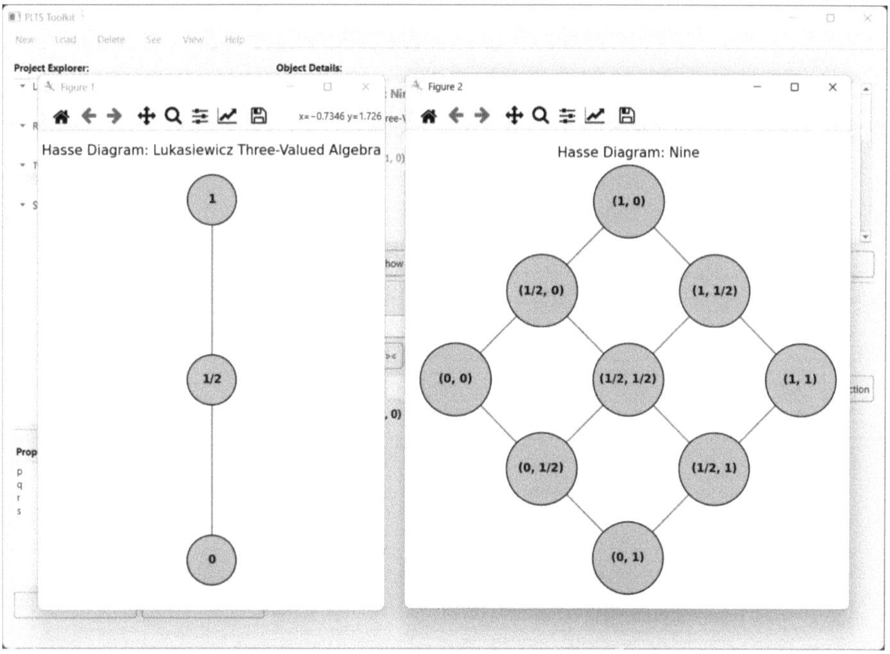

Fig. 5. Screenshot of the PLTS toolkit rendering of the Hasse diagram of **3** and $\mathcal{NINE}$.

At this stage, the toolkit supports complete lattices and their twist structures, enabling the construction of PLTS. More specifically, once a lattice and its twist structure are available, users may create states via the New menu by assigning, for each proposition, a value from the twist structure. Note that multiple states,

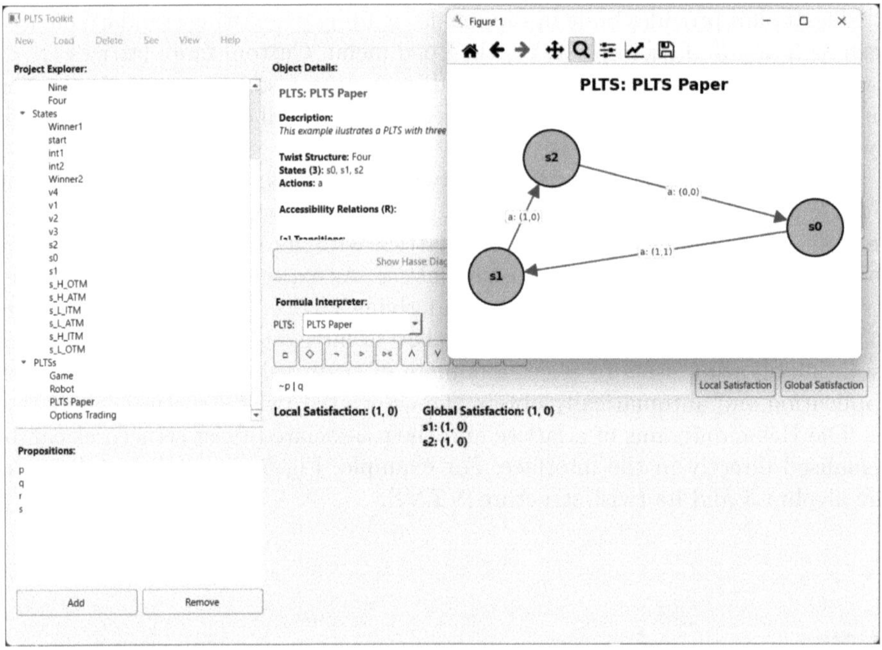

Fig. 6. Screenshot of the PLTS toolkit interpreting a formula for the PLTS in Fig. 3.

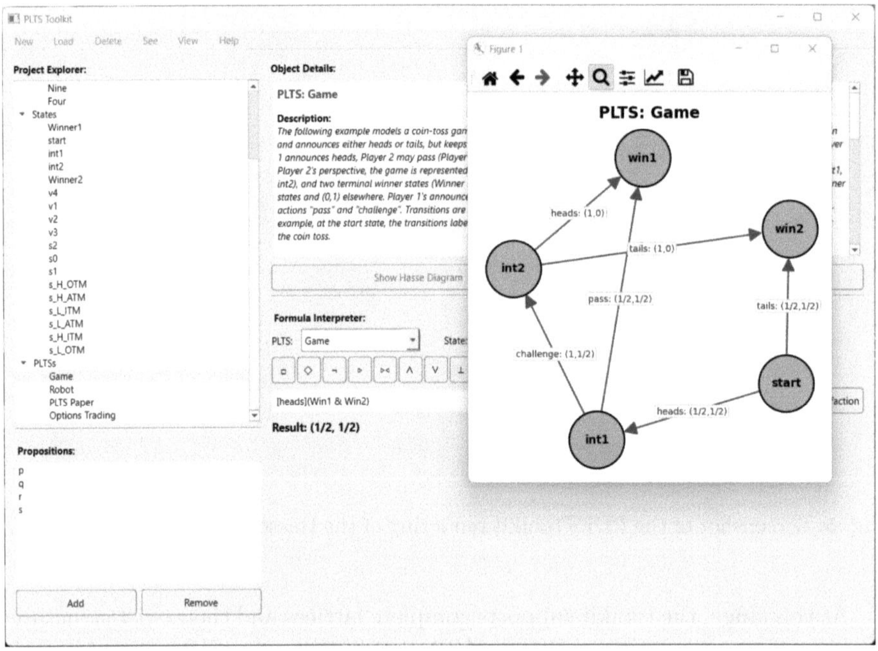

Fig. 7. Screenshot of the PLTS toolkit interpreting a formula for the PLTS in Fig. 9.

whose valuations take values from different twist structures, can be queued and created at once. A PLTS is then defined by selecting a set of states over a chosen twist structure, specifying action labels, and assigning a value in A^2 to each transition. When constructing a PLTS, users may also add a description of the PLTS, which appears alongside the model components in the object-details panel.

Figure 6 illustrates the graphical rendering produced by the toolkit for the PLTS of Fig. 3.

The toolkit also includes a built-in interpreter for the paraconsistent modal logic, recalled in Sect. 2, which validates formula syntax and reports errors. In the interpreter panel on the right, users may select a PLTS and a state, then input a formula using the available connectives. The Local satisfaction button then computes a pair representing evidence for and against the formula holding at the chosen state.

The Global satisfaction feature computes the value given by (1), and reports the value of local satisfaction for each state. Figures 6 illustrates local and global interpretation in the toolkit. Naturally, the cost of validity checking grows with the size of the PLTS.

Example 4. Recall the PLTS of Example 3 its rendering by the toolkit[2] is shown in Fig. 6. Using the interpreter, one can verify that the formula $\neg p \vee q$ is evaluated by the classical truth value $(1, 0)$ in every state. Moreover, the tool confirms that $[a]p \vee q$ evaluates to $(1, 0)$ at every state except s_1, where its value is $(0, 1)$, matching the observations in Example 3.

The remainder of this section presents illustrative case studies of the framework and toolkit on small-scale models. These examples can be loaded via the Load menu. Alongside a description of their components, each includes a brief descriptive summary in the object-details panel.

The following example, adapted from [7] which draws inspiration from [1], describes a robot navigating along a path while receiving possibly inconsistent information about obstacles from multiple sensors.

Example 5. In object detection, different sensors may provide conflicting information due to hardware limitations or environmental conditions. Combining multiple sensor is therefore a common practice to improve reliability and accuracy in obstacle detection and avoidance. We consider two groups of sensors: positive sensors, providing evidence that a path is clear, and negative sensors, providing evidence that it is obstructed.

The robot moves between four checkpoints represented as states of a PLTS. Transitions labelled by the action "move" represent movement between checkpoints and are weighted by values in the twist structure $\mathcal{NINE}$ of Example 2, combining the certainty from positive sensors that the path is clear with the certainty from negative sensors that it is obstructed. Certainty is a central aspect

[2] The corresponding model is available from the Load menu in the toolkit under the name "PLTS Paper".

of object detection, where the system not only identifies objects but also quantifies its confidence in the identification by, e.g. considering limitations in the precision of measurements and disregarding a sensor's output in the presence of environmental conditions that affect measurements.

The proposition Obst indicates whether a checkpoint contains an obstacle: it takes value $(1,0)$ at v_3, the only obstructed checkpoint, and $(0,1)$ at the remaining states. The resulting PLTS is shown in Fig. 8, where the obstructed state v_3 is highlighted[3].

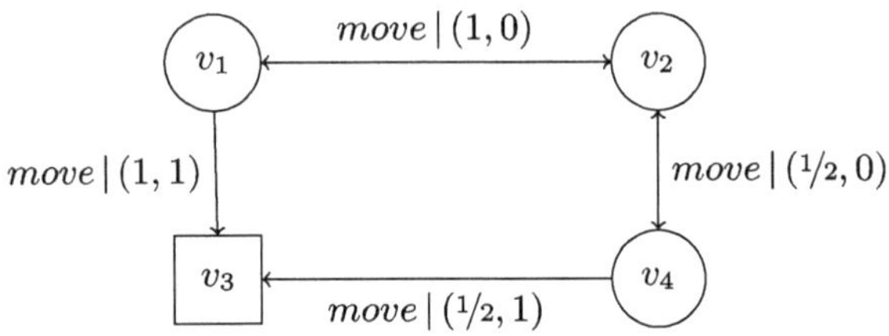

Fig. 8. PLTS representation of a robot navigating along a path with obstacles.

By using the logical interpreter, the formula Obst $\rightarrow$ [move]$\bot$, stating that the robot cannot move from an obstructed state, evaluates to $(1,0)$ at every state. Indeed, the only state satisfying Obst is v_3, and there are no outgoing transitions from v_3, so the formula is evaluated by the classical truth value $(1,0)$ at every state.

Consider also the formula $\langle$move$\rangle$ Obst, indicating that it is possible to move to an obstructed checkpoint. For example, it follows that $(v_2 \models \langle \text{move} \rangle \text{Obst}) = (0,1)$, since there is no transition from v_2 to v_3. Moreover, $(v_4 \models \langle \text{move} \rangle \text{Obst}) = (1/2, 1/2)$, reflecting uncertainty about reaching an obstructed state. This arises because the transition from v_4 to v_3 has the paraconsistent value $(1/2, 1)$, providing non-zero evidence both for and against its transversal.

The following example, adapted from [9], describes a simple coin-toss betting game between two players, a setting often considered in the literature of epistemic logic [19].

Example 6. Games frequently involve bluffing, incomplete information, and conflicting cues, requiring players to reason under uncertainty and possible contradiction. The paraconsistent framework employed in this paper is therefore suited to modelling such scenarios.

The game proceeds as follows. Player 1 always bets on heads, while Player 2 always bets on tails. Player 1 tosses a coin and announces either heads or tails while keeping the true outcome hidden. If Player 1 announces tails, Player 2 immediately wins. If heads is announced, Player 2 may either pass, in which

[3] This model is available via the Load menu in the toolkit under the name "Robot".

case Player 1 wins, or challenge, forcing Player 1 to reveal the true outcome; the player whose bet matches the outcome then wins.

From Player 2's perspective, the game can be represented by a PLTS with a starting state (*start*), intermediate states (*int*1 and *int*2), and winning states (*Winner*1 and *Winner*2). Propositions Win1 and Win2 take value $(1, 0)$ at their respective winner states and $(0, 1)$ elsewhere. Player 1's announcements correspond to actions "heads" and "tails", and Player 2's responses correspond to actions "pass" and "challenge". Transitions are weighted by values in the twist-structure $\mathcal{NINE}$ of Example 2 representing Player 2's evidence for and against each action.

Initially, Player 2 assumes the coin toss is fair, so both announcements "heads" and "tails" from the starting state have value $(1/2, 1/2)$. After a heads announcement, Player 2 evaluates several cues, such as Player 1's past behaviour and personal risk preference, to decide whether to pass or challenge. These considerations may lead to non-complementary degrees of evidence to each action. For instance, Player 2 may reason that:

(1) in the last two rounds Player 1 also announced heads, which seems unlikely;
(2) from prior rounds Player 1 is generally honest;
(3) Player 1 appeared nervous during the announcement;
(4) Player 2 is risk-seeking and inclined to challenge.

Consequently, Player 2 has strong evidence in favor of challenging, supported by arguments (1), (3), and (4), while argument (2) provides evidence against challenging. Hence, the transition labelled "challenge" is assigned the paraconsistent value $(1, 1/2)$.

Conversely, passing is moderately supported by argument (2) but weakened by the considerations in (1) and (3). Accordingly, the transition labelled "pass" receives the consistent value $(1/2, 1/2)$. The resulting PLTS is shown in Fig. 9.

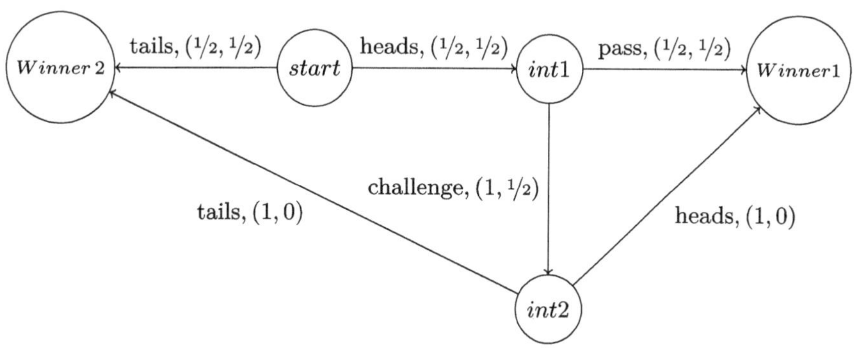

Fig. 9. PLTS representation of a coin-toss betting game.

By using the proposed toolkit[4] it is possible to construct and visualize this model as well as to evaluate specific formulae as depicted in Fig. 7.

One may then verify that the formula [tails]Win2 is evaluated to $(1, 0)$ at any state, i.e., whenever Player 1 announces tails, Player 2 wins. Another such formula is [tails]Win2 $\vee$ [heads]⟨pass⟩Win1 $\vee$ [challenge]⟨heads⟩Win1 indicating that tails guarantees Player 2's win, while heads followed either by passing or by a successful challenge leads to Player 1's win.

Naturally, invalid behaviours evaluate to $(0, 1)$, e.g. ⟨tails⟩⟨challenge⟩$\top$, which would allow Player 2 to challenge after tails, and ⟨pass⟩Win2, stating that Player 2 wins after passing.

Finally,at the starting state the formula [heads](Win1 $\wedge$ Win2) evaluates to $(1/2, 1/2)$, indicating that after a heads announcement the winner is uncertain, since the subsequent choice between pass and challenge remains unresolved.

The following example illustrates the modelling of an options trading scenario using PLTS to reason about conflicting market signals.

Example 7. In the finance industry, an option on a stock is a financial derivative that grants the holder the right, but not the obligation, to buy or sell shares of that stock at a predetermined price, the strike price, within a specific timeframe [15]. American options allow exercise at any time before or on the expiration date, whereas European options can only be exercised on the expiration date.

To model options trading using a PLTS, one could integrate the Black-Scholes-Merton (BSM) model [15] to represent market signals and decision-making under uncertainty. In this framework, the BSM equation provides a theoretical value that serves as a benchmark against which market-defined states $(s_{ITM}, s_{ATM}, s_{OTM})$ are evaluated. Inconsistencies naturally arise when different indicators, such as a sudden volatility spike versus downward price dynamics, provide conflicting signals regarding the option's fair value. By adopting a paraconsistent approach, we can assign degrees of evidence for and against a specific transition, allowing the system to reason through such market contradictions.

The model's state space is defined by two temporal layers based on the time-to-expiration: High (s^H) and Low (s^L). Additionally, within each layer, states are categorised by their moneyness relative to the strike price (K) and current asset price (S), resulting in six possible states:

- s^H_{ITM} and s^L_{ITM} correspond to "In-the-Money" states further from and closer to the expiration date, respectively. In both cases it holds that $S > K$, meaning that the asset price exceeds the strike price and exercising the option would yield profit;
- s^H_{ATM} and s^L_{ATM} correspond to "At-the-Money" states further from and closer to the expiration date, respectively. In these states $S = K$, meaning the asset price equals the strike price and the option essentially breaks even;
- s^H_{OTM} and s^L_{OTM} correspond to "Out-of-the-Money" states further from and closer to the expiration date, respectively. In these states $S < K$, meaning

[4] This model is available via the Load menu in the toolkit under the name "Game".

the asset price is below the strike price and exercising the option would not be profitable.

The proposition profitable represents the evidence for and against an option being profitable at a given state. The valuation of this proposition across the state space may therefore be defined as follows:

- $V(s^H_{ITM}, \text{profitable}) = (1, 0)$, representing clear evidence that the option is profitable when it is in-the-money and still relatively far from expiration.
- $V(s^H_{ATM}, \text{profitable}) = (1/2, 1/2)$, representing balanced evidence when the option is at-the-money.
- $V(s^H_{OTM}, \text{profitable}) = (0, 1)$, representing clear evidence against profitability when the option is out-of-the-money.
- $V(s^L_{ITM}, \text{profitable}) = (1, 1/2)$, since the option is still in-the-money but proximity to expiration adds evidence against profitability, yielding a paraconsistent valuation.
- $V(s^L_{ATM}, \text{profitable}) = (0, 0)$, representing vague or unknown evidence when the option is close to expiration and exactly at the strike price.
- $V(s^L_{OTM}, \text{profitable}) = (0, 1)$, representing confirmed evidence against profitability.

Transitions between the defined states are driven by three categories of dynamics: market price dynamics, representing fluctuations in the underlying asset via price_up and price_down actions; temporal dynamics, using time_pass to model the transition from high to low expiration layers; and volatility dynamics, where vol_spike captures sudden increases in volatility.

For example, if there is a price increase, it becomes possible to transition from an out-of-the-money state to an at-the-money state. Similarly, if the price continues to rise, a transition from at-the-money to in-the-money may occur.

Temporal dynamics also influence the system. When time passes and the option is out-of-the-money, it is likely to remain out-of-the-money, since the remaining time for favourable price movements decreases. However, if time passes while the option is at-the-money, there may be some evidence against remaining in that state, reflecting the increased uncertainty as the expiration date approaches. Naturally, additional transitions could be considered depending on the particular market conditions being modelled.

The resulting PLTS[5] is shown in Fig. 10. By using the toolkit it is possible to construct and visualize this model as well as to evaluate specific formulae as depicted in Fig. 11.

One may then evaluate different formulae over the PLTS by using the built-in logical interpreter. For instance, as illustrated in Fig. 11, at state s^H_{OTM} the formula [price_up][price_up] profitable is evaluated as $(1, 0)$, indicating complete evidence that two successive price increases lead to a profitable state.

Additionally, at state s^H_{ITM} the formula [time_pass]⟨price_down⟩profitable is evaluated as $(0, 0)$, meaning that if the option is currently in-the-money and

[5] This model is available via the Load menu in the toolkit under the name "Options Trading".

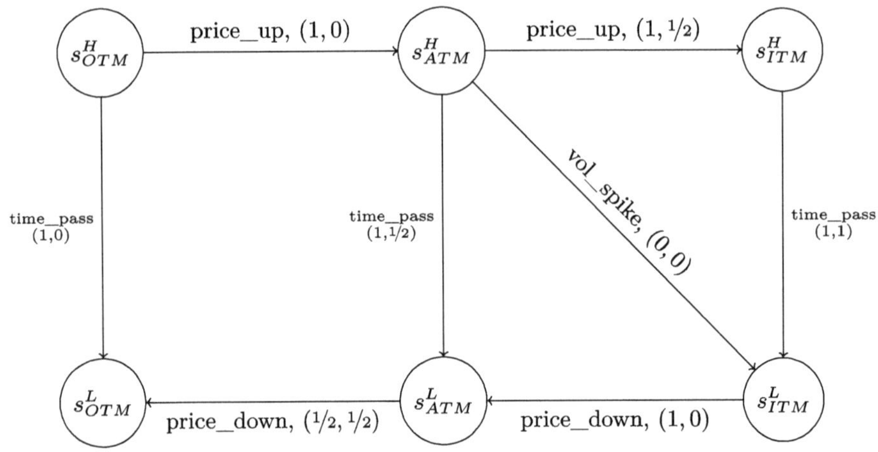

Fig. 10. PLTS representation of an options trading model, illustrating transitions between moneyness states across high and low time-to-expiration layers.

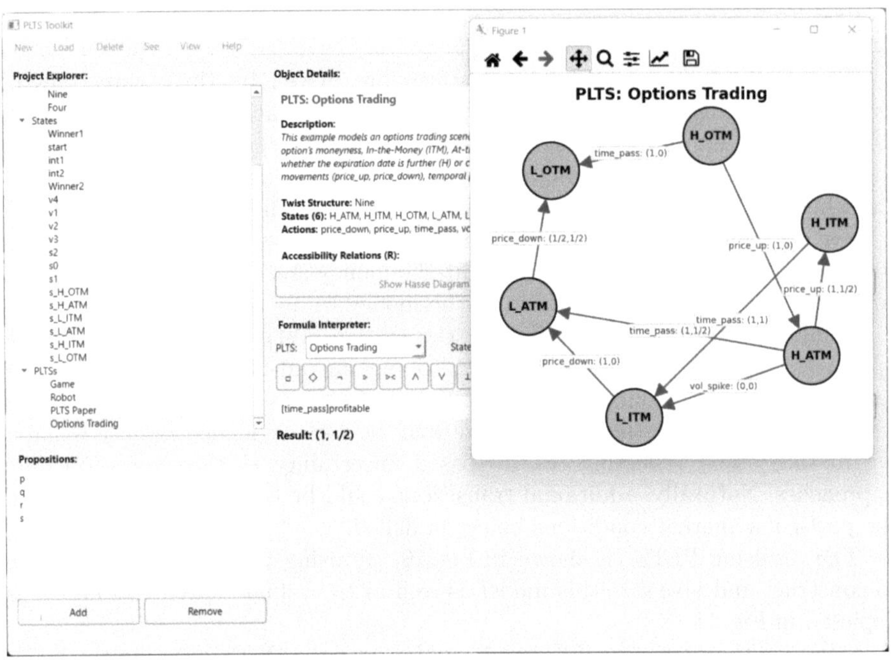

Fig. 11. Screenshot of the PLTS toolkit interpreting and checking the validity of formula for the PLTS in Fig. 10.

time passes, followed by a price decrease, it is uncertain whether the option will remain profitable.

Finally, still at state s^H_{ITM}, the formula $\langle \text{time_pass} \rangle$profitable is evaluated by the inconsistent value $(1, 1/2)$. This indicates that although there is evidence that the option may remain profitable as time passes, there is also some evidence against it. Such inconsistency reflects the fact that the option may approach the strike price as expiration nears, making profitability uncertain.

4 Conclusions

This paper contributes to an ongoing research agenda [7–10] aimed at developing frameworks and tools for representing and reasoning with inconsistent information. Within this line of work, PLTS together with their associated modal logic provide a framework for modelling such scenarios.

In this paper, we present the first steps towards a comprehensive toolkit for PLTS. Its main contribution is an interactive interface that enables users to construct finite arbitrary lattices and automatically generate their associated twist structures; to build and explore PLTS parametric over the chosen lattice; and to evaluate formulae of the paraconsistent modal logic and checks their validity over the resulting systems by using the built-in logical interpreter. Finally, we illustrate the applicability of the toolkit through illustrative case studies.

Several extensions remain for future work. In particular, the current implementation supports only finite lattices, whereas twist structures over infinite lattices also play a significant role in the literature [10,11]. Another promising direction is to allow twist structures to be formed from two possibly distinct lattices $\mathbf{L} = (L, \leqslant_{\mathbf{L}})$ and $\mathbf{R} = (R, \leqslant_{\mathbf{R}})$, yielding what are known as rectangular bilattices [11]. Such structures capture the fact that arguments in favor and against a statement can be evaluated on different scales. In contrast to existing approaches, we plan to directly combine values in $L \times R$ by considering interpretations between lattices, following [12].

Future versions will also implement enrichments of the modal logic with operators from dynamic logic, as introduced in [10], allowing the evaluation of properties such as deadlock avoidance and liveness. Moreover, features discussed in [7], such as checking paraconsistent bisimulations and incorporating a broader range of compositional constructions towards a full process algebra in the style of Nielsen and Winskel [22], are also planned for future versions.

Finally, this toolkit is expected to play a key role in forthcoming applications of this framework. In particular, it is expected to support a recently funded project (COMPETE2030-FEDER-00892000, Bansky – A paraconsistent inference engine for age-related macular degeneration) developed in collaboration with a medical research company. The project aims to model inconsistent datasets in degenerative-disease studies, where paraconsistent reasoning is particularly valuable for handling conflicting or incomplete information in the dataset.

References

1. Abe, J.M., Torres, C.R., Lambert-Torres, G., da Silva Filho, J.I., Martins, H.G.: Paraconsistent autonomous mobile robot emmy III. In: Lambert-Torres, G., Abe, J.M., da Silva Filho, J.I., Martins, H.G. (eds.) Advances in Technological Applications of Logical and Intelligent Systems, Selected Papers from the Sixth Congress on Logic Applied to Technology, LAPTEC 2007, Unisanta, Santa Cecilia University, Santos, Brazil, 21–23 November 2007. Frontiers in Artificial Intelligence and Applications, vol. 186, pp. 236–258. IOS Press (2007). https://doi.org/10.3233/978-1-58603-936-3-236
2. Akama, S. (ed.): Towards Paraconsistent Engineering, Intelligent Systems Reference Library, vol. 110. Springer (2016). https://doi.org/10.1007/978-3-319-40418-9
3. Barbosa, L.S., Madeira, A.: Capturing qubit decoherence through paraconsistent transition systems. In: Chiba, S., Cong, Y., Boix, E.G. (eds.) Companion Proceedings of the 7th International Conference on the Art, Science, and Engineering of Programming, Programming 2023, Tokyo, Japan, 13–17 March 2023, pp. 109–110. ACM (2023). https://doi.org/10.1145/3594671.3594689
4. Belnap, N.D.: A useful four-valued logic, pp. 5–37. Springer Netherlands, Dordrecht (1977). https://doi.org/10.1007/978-94-010-1161-7_2
5. Bou, F., Esteva, F., Godo, L., Rodríguez, R.O.: On the minimum many-valued modal logic over a finite residuated lattice. J. Logic Comput. **21**(5), 739–790 (2009). https://doi.org/10.1093/logcom/exp062
6. Chiara, M.L.D., Giuntini, R.: Paraconsistent ideas in quantum logic. Synth. **125**(1-2), 55–68 (2000). https://doi.org/10.1023/A:1005296018904
7. Cunha, J., Madeira, A., Barbosa, L.S.: Paraconsistent transition structures: compositional principles and a modal logic. Math. Struct. Comput. Sci. **35**, e14 (2025). https://doi.org/10.1017/S0960129525100170
8. Cunha, J., Madeira, A., Barbosa, L.S.: Stepwise development of paraconsistent processes. In: David, C., Sun, M. (eds.) Theoretical Aspects of Software Engineering - 17th International Symposium, TASE 2023, Bristol, UK, 4–6 July 2023, Proceedings. LNCS, vol. 13931, pp. 327–343. Springer (2023). https://doi.org/10.1007/978-3-031-35257-7_20
9. Cunha, J., Madeira, A., Barbosa, L.S.: Paraconsistent reactive graphs. In: Proença, J., Fervari, R., Martins, M.A., Kahle, R., Pluck, G. (eds.) Software Engineering and Formal Methods. SEFM 2024 Collocated Workshops - ReacTS 2024 and CIFMA 2024, Aveiro, Portugal, 4–5 November 2024, Revised Selected Papers. LNCS, vol. 15551, pp. 105–111. Springer (2024). https://doi.org/10.1007/978-3-031-94748-3_9
10. Cunha, J., Madeira, A., Barbosa, L.S.: Specification of paraconsistent transition systems. revisited. Sci. Comput. Program. **240**, 103196 (2025)
11. Deschrijver, G., Arieli, O., Cornelis, C., Kerre, E.E.: A bilattice-based framework for handling graded truth and imprecision. Int. J. Uncertain. Fuzziness Knowl. Based Syst. **15**(1), 13–41 (2007). https://doi.org/10.1142/S0218488507004352
12. Freire, A.R., Martins, M.A.: Modality across different logics. Log. J. IGPL **33**(3) (2025). https://doi.org/10.1093/JIGPAL/JZAE082
13. Ginsberg, M.L.: Multivalued logics: a uniform approach to reasoning in artificial intelligence. Comput. Intell. **4**, 265–316 (1988)
14. Hagberg, A., Swart, P., Chult, D.: Exploring network structure, dynamics, and function using networkx (2008). https://doi.org/10.25080/TCWV9851

15. Hull, J.: Options, Futures, and Other Derivatives. 11 edn., Pearson, Harlow, England (2021)
16. Hunter, J.D.: Matplotlib: a 2d graphics environment. Comput. Sci. Eng. **9**(3), 90–95 (2007). https://doi.org/10.1109/MCSE.2007.55
17. Kracht, M.: On extensions of intermediate logics by strong negation. J. Philos. Log. **27**(1), 49–73 (1998). https://doi.org/10.1023/A:1004222213212
18. Madeira, A., Neves, R., Martins, M.A.: An exercise on the generation of many-valued dynamic logics. J. Logical Algebraic Methods Program. **85**(5, Part 2), 1011–1037 (2016). https://doi.org/10.1016/j.jlamp.2016.03.004, https://www.sciencedirect.com/science/article/pii/S2352220816300256, articles dedicated to Prof. J. N. Oliveira on the occasion of his 60th birthday
19. Mousavi, M.R., Varshosaz, M.: Telling lies in process algebra. In: Pang, J., Zhang, C., He, J., Weng, J. (eds.) 2018 International Symposium on Theoretical Aspects of Software Engineering, TASE 2018, Guangzhou, China, 29–31 August 2018. pp. 116–123. IEEE Computer Society (2018). https://doi.org/10.1109/TASE.2018.00023
20. Priest, G.: Paraconsistency and dialetheism. In: Gabbay, D.M., Woods, J. (eds.) The Many Valued and Nonmonotonic Turn in Logic, Handbook of the History of Logic, vol. 8, pp. 129–204. Elsevier (2007). https://doi.org/10.1016/S1874-5857(07)80006-9
21. Beginning PyQt. Apress, Berkeley, CA (2022). https://doi.org/10.1007/978-1-4842-7999-1
22. Winskel, G., Nielsen, M.: Models for Concurrency, pp. 1–148. Oxford University Press, Inc., USA (1995)

Scenario Matching Problem in Distributed Systems

Puneet Bhateja(✉)

Dhirubhai Ambani University, Gandhinagar, India
puneet_bhateja@dau.ac.in

Abstract. In this paper we address a verification problem called scenario matching problem. The implementation is given in the form of a network of communicating finite-state machines called message-passing automata (MPA). An MPA recognizes a set of scenarios, each formally defined as a message sequence chart (MSC). We can also separately specify an infinite collection of MSCs through a hierarchical structure called high-level message sequence chart (HMSC). The verification problem we address is whether every MSC specified by an HMSC is also recognized by the MPA or not. We show that for a certain class of MPAs and HMSCs, it is algorithmically possible to determine so.

1 Introduction

In the development of telecommunication systems it is important to describe and verify the system design in the early phases of the development process. Message sequence charts (MSCs) are a standardized description language for this purpose. The formal syntax and semantics of this language is defined by the International Telecommunication Union in its document *ITU-T Recommendation Z.120* [12]. Each MSC portrays one possible scenario of the underlying distributed system.

Here we address a verification problem related to MSCs wherein we are given an implementation model and a specification. As an implementation model we consider a network of communicating finite state machines called message passing automata (MPA) [6]. The constituent processes of an MPA communicate with each other by sending messages over FIFO channels. As ordinary finite state automata [11] recognize (or accept) a set of strings, an MPA in comparison recognize a set of MSCs. The specification on the other hand is given to us as a high-level message sequence chart (HMSC) which is a hierarchical structure used to specify a collection of MSCs (or scenarios).

We specifically address the following verification problem. Given an MPA $\mathcal{A}$ and an HMSC $\mathcal{H}$, whether every MSC specified by $\mathcal{H}$ is recognized by $\mathcal{A}$. The problem is important from the decidability point of view, because the number of MSCs specified by an HMSC or accepted by an MPA can each be infinite. The paper contributes by showing that it algorithmically possible to determine so for the case when the given MPA is unreliable (or lossy) and the given HMSC is locally synchronized. Our approach is based on proving that the global reachability problem for lossy MPA is decidable.

G. De Giacomo et al. (Eds.): TASE 2026, LNCS 16697, pp. 386–399, 2027.
https://doi.org/10.1007/978-3-032-30693-7_25

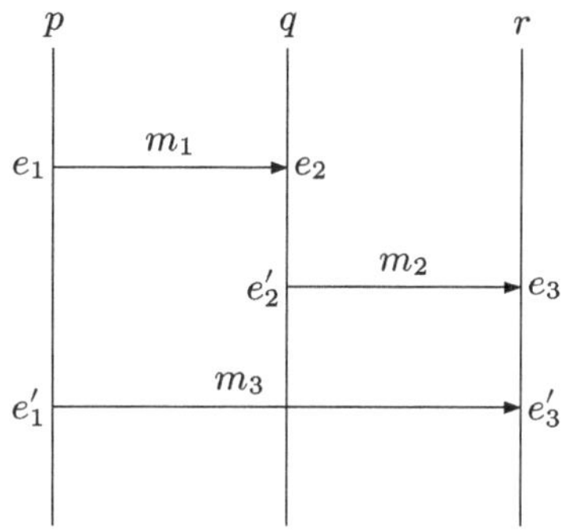

Fig. 1. An MSC over processes $\mathcal{P} = \{p, q, r\}$

The rest of the paper is organised as follows. In Sect. 2, we first explain the formal syntax and semantics of the MSC model. We next show how a set of MSCs can be specified by an HMSC. We also explain what do we mean by locally synchronized HMSCs. In Sect. 3, we formally define the MPA model and describe its operational semantics by an infinite-state labelled transition system (LTS). In Sect. 4, we prove that reachability is a decidable prblem for lossy MPA. In Sect. 5, we state the main verification problem formally as a decision problem, and then show that it is possible to get a conclusive answer to this decision problem for a class of MPAs and HMSCs. Finally, in Sect. 6 we conclude the paper.

2 Message Sequence Charts (MSCs)

2.1 MSCs as a Pictorial Notation

MSCs are a standardized graphical notation for documenting the expected behaviour of a distributed system. Each MSC describes a scenario wherein processes communicate with each other asynchronously by sending messages over channels. The channels are assumed to be reliable and FIFO. Figure 1 shows an MSC over three process p, q, r. Each process is represented by a vertical line, while each message is represented by a horizontal (or downward slopping) arrow from the sending process to the receiving process. An event is either the sending of a message or the receiving of a message. The MSC shown in Fig. 1 has six events, namely $e_1, e'_1, e_2, e'_2, e_3$, and e'_3. The occurrence of two events in an MSC could be ordered or unordered. The following two rules dictate the order. The first rule says that the events of a process occur in the order they are shown on the process line from top to bottom. For example in Fig. 1, the events e_1, e'_1 of process p occur in the said order. This means that the time on process lines flow from top to bottom. The second rule says that a send event occurs before the corresponding receive event. For example in Fig. 1, event e_1 of process p occurs before event e_2 of process q. These two rules together impose a partial order on the set of events in an MSC. This motivates us to define an MSC formally as a labelled poset.

2.2 MSC as a Labelled Poset

Let $\mathcal{P} = \{p, q, r \cdots\}$ be a finite set of processes (or agents) that communicate with each other over channels using a finite set of message types $\mathcal{M}$. For $p \in \mathcal{P}$, let $\Sigma_p = \{p!q(m), p?q(m) \mid p \neq q \in \mathcal{P}, m \in \mathcal{M}\}$ be the set of communication actions in which p participates. The action $p!q(m)$ is read as *p sends the message m to q* and the action $p?q(m)$ is read as *p receives the message m from q*. We denote the set of all actions by $\Sigma = \bigcup_{p \in \mathcal{P}} \Sigma_p$. Each ordered pair of processes (p, q) corresponds to a separate channel. We denote the set of all channels by $\mathcal{C} = \{c_{pq} \mid p \neq q \in \mathcal{P}\}$. These channels are supposed to be reliable and FIFO. We intend to define an MSC formally as a mathematical structure $M = (E, \leq, \lambda)$ where E is a set of events, relation $\leq$ is a partial order, and λ is a labelling function defined as $\lambda : E \rightarrow \Sigma$. Certainly, any arbitrarily labelled poset will not qualify as a valid MSC. We have to formally define conditions for that.

We begin by defining some auxiliary notations. For $e \in E$, let $\downarrow e = \{e' \mid e' \leq e\}$. Likewise for each $X \subseteq E, \downarrow X = \bigcup_{e \in X} \downarrow e$. For $p \in \mathcal{P}$ and $a \in \Sigma$, we set $E_p = \{e \mid \lambda(e) \in \Sigma_p\}$ and $E_a = \{e \mid \lambda(e) = a\}$. Here E_p denotes the set of events that happen at process p, and E_a denotes the set of events that are labelled with action a. Note that both E_p and E_a are subsets of E. Now we define two binary relations over the set E. The first relation $<_{pq}$ is defined corresponding to each pair of processes (p, q), while the second relation $<_{pp}$ is defined corresponding to each process p.

- $e <_{pq} e' \Leftrightarrow \lambda(e) = p!q(m), \lambda(e') = q?p(m)$ and it is the case that $|\downarrow e \cap E_{p!q(m)}| = |\downarrow e' \cap E_{q?p(m)}|$. In simple words, $e <_{pq} e'$ means that the message m read by process q at e' is the one sent by process p at e.

- $e <_{pp} e' \Leftrightarrow e, e' \in E_p \wedge |\downarrow e| < |\downarrow e'|$. In simple words, $e <_{pp} e'$ means that events e and e' both happen at the process p in the said order.

We are now ready to define an MSC formally.

Definition 1. *An MSC over a set of processes $\mathcal{P}$ is a finite labelled poset $M = (E, \leq, \lambda)$ where*

1. *E is a finite set of events.*
2. *$\leq$ is a partial order on the set E, and is equal to the reflexive and transitive closure of the relation $\bigcup_{p,q \in \mathcal{P}} <_{pq}$.*
3. *λ is labelling function $\lambda : E \rightarrow \Sigma$ such that if $p \neq q$ then for each $m \in \mathcal{M}$ it is the case that $|E_{p!q(m)}| = |E_{q?p(m)}|$.*

Note that the third condition in the above definition ensures that no message is lost in the transmission, while the definition of relation $<_{pq}$ above ensures that the messages are received in the order they are sent.

We next show how an MSC M can be represented by a set of finite-length strings $[\![M]\!]$ over the alphabet Σ. If $\pi = e_1 \cdot e_2 \cdots e_n$ is a sequence of events, then we define $\lambda(\pi)$ to be equal to $\lambda(e_1) \cdot \lambda(e_2) \cdots \lambda(e_n)$. For an MSC $M = (E, \leq, \lambda)$, we let $[\![M]\!] = \{\lambda(\pi) \mid \pi$ is a linearization of the poset $(E, \leq)\}$. For instance string $p!q(m_1)\, q?p(m_1)\, q!r(m_2)\, p!r(m_3)\, r?q(m_2)\, r?p(m_3)$ belongs to $[\![M]\!]$ where MSC M is the one shown in Fig. 1. An MSC language is defined as a set of MSCs. This set can even be infinite. In the next section we show how to represent an MSC language.

2.3 High-Level Message Sequence Charts (HMSCs)

A standard way to generate a set of MSCs is by means of an HMSC. Without losing generality, we consider only a subclass of HMSCs here [8,9]. An HMSC basically is a finite-state automaton whose each vertex is labelled by an MSC. Formally, an HMSC is a structure $\mathcal{H} = (Q, \rightarrow, Q_{in}, F, \Phi)$ where Q is a finite set of states, $\rightarrow \subseteq Q \times Q$ is a transition relation, $Q_{in} \subseteq Q$ is a set of initial states, $F \subseteq Q$ is a set of final states, and Φ is a labelling function. At a semantic level the edges of an HMSC represent MSC concatenation. We now define concatenation of two MSCs formally.

Definition 2. *Let $M_1 = (E_1, \leq^1, \lambda_1)$ and $M_2 = (E_2, \leq^2, \lambda_2)$ be two MSCs. The concatenation of M_1 and M_2 is the MSC $M_1 \circ M_2 = (E, \leq, \lambda)$ where*

1. $E = E_1 \cup E_2$
2. *For each $e \in E$, $\lambda(e) = \lambda_i(e)$ if $e \in E_i$ for $i \in \{1, 2\}$*
3. *$\leq$ is the reflexive and transitive closure of the relation $\bigcup_{p,q \in \mathcal{P}} <_{pq}$, where $<_{pp} = <^1_{pp} \cup <^2_{pp} \cup \{(e_1, e_2) \mid e_1 \in E_1, e_2 \in E_2, \lambda(e_1) \in \Sigma_p, \lambda(e_2) \in \Sigma_p\}$ and for each pair of processes (p, q) we have $<_{pq} = <^1_{pq} \cup <^2_{pq}$.*

A path π through an HMSC $\mathcal{H}$ is a sequence $q_0 \rightarrow q_1 \rightarrow \cdots \rightarrow q_n$ such that $(q_{i-1}, q_i) \in \rightarrow$ for $i \in \{1, 2, \cdots, n\}$. The MSC generated by π is $M(\pi) = M_0 \circ M_1 \circ M_2 \circ \cdots \circ M_n$ where $M_i = \Phi(q_i)$. A path $\pi = q_0 \rightarrow q_1 \rightarrow \cdots \rightarrow q_n$ is called run if $q_0 \in Q_{in}$ and $q_n \in F$. The set of MSCs specified by $\mathcal{H}$ is $L(\mathcal{H}) = \{M(\pi) | \pi$ is a run through $\mathcal{H}\}$.

At the end of the last section we showed how an MSC M can be represented by a set of finite-length strings $[\![M]\!]$. Similarly an HMSC $\mathcal{H}$ can be represented by a set of finite-length strings $[\![\mathcal{H}]\!] = \bigcup\limits_{M \in L(\mathcal{H})} [\![M]\!]$

2.4 Locally Synchronized HMSCs

Here we are interested in those HMSCs for which the corresponding string language is regular. However, it is not guaranteed that the string language represented by an arbitrary HMSC is a regular language. Figure 2 shows an HMSC $\mathcal{H}$ with two nodes q_1 and q_2. The node q_1 is mapped to MSC M_1 and the node q_2 is mapped to MSC M_2. Both M_1 and M_2 are also shown in the same figure. We now claim that the language $[\![\mathcal{H}]\!]$ is not regular. We can prove this by contradiction. Suppose the language $[\![\mathcal{H}]\!]$ is regular over the alphabet

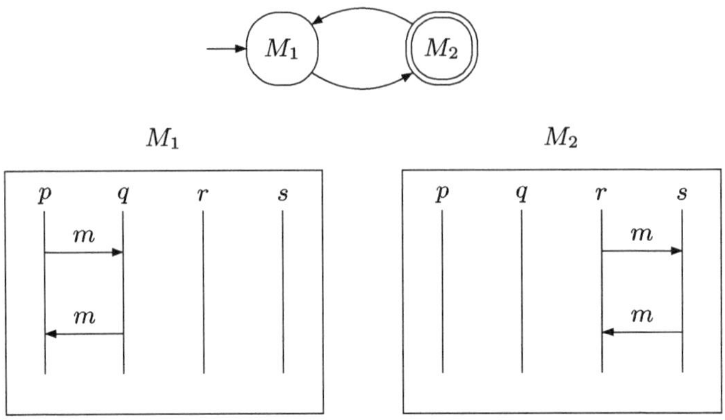

Fig. 2. An HMSC over processes $\mathcal{P} = \{p, q, r, s\}$

$\Sigma = \{p!q(m), q?p(m), q!p(m), p?q(m), r!s(m), s?r(m), s!r(m), r?s(m)\}$. Define a homomorphism $\Psi : \Sigma \to \Sigma^\star$ such that $\Psi(a) = a$, if $a = p!q(m) \vee a = r!s(m)$, and $\Psi(a) = \epsilon$ otherwise. The homomorphic image of the language $[\![\mathcal{H}]\!]$ will be set of all those strings over the alphabet $\{p!q(m), r!s(m)\}$ such that both the symbols in the alphabet appear equal number of times. Since we know that this language is non regular, therefore by contradiction we conclude that $[\![\mathcal{H}]\!]$ is non regular. In general it is undecidable whether an HMSC $\mathcal{H}$ describes a regular string language $[\![\mathcal{H}]\!]$ or not [8]. However, a sufficient condition for $[\![\mathcal{H}]\!]$ to be regular is that $\mathcal{H}$ should be locally synchronized. In the rest of the section we will build up to the concept of locally synchronized HMSCs through a sequence of definitions.

Definition 3. *A communication graph for an MSC $M = (E, \leq, \lambda)$ is a directed graph $CG_M = (\mathcal{P}, \mapsto)$, where*

- *$\mathcal{P}$ is the set of processes of the system.*
- *$(p, q) \in \mapsto$ iff there exists an $e \in E$ with $\lambda(e) = p!q(m)$.*

Definition 4. *An MSC M is said to be com-connected if its communication graph CG_M consists of one non trivial strongly connected component and some isolated vertices.*

Fig. 3. The communication graph $CG_{M_1 \circ M_2}$

Definition 5. *An HMSC* $\mathcal{H} = (Q, \rightarrow, Q_{in}, F, \Phi)$ *is locally synchronized (or bounded) if for every loop* $q_1 \rightarrow q_2 \rightarrow \cdots \rightarrow q_n \rightarrow q_1$ *in the HMSC, the MSC* $\Phi(q_1) \circ \Phi(q_2) \circ \cdots \circ \Phi(q_n)$ *is com-connected.*

The HMSC of Fig. 2 has only one loop, namely $q_1 \rightarrow q_2 \rightarrow q_1$. The communication graph $CG_{M_1 \circ M_2}$ is shown in Fig. 3. It is not difficult to infer that the MSC $M_1 \circ M_2$ is not com-connected.

3 Message-Passing Automata (MPA)

Message passing automata are a distributed computational model which is comprised of a network of finite-state processes. These processes communicate with each other asynchronously by sending messages [6]. Formally an MPA can be defined as follows.

Definition 6. *An MPA over* Σ *is a structure* $\mathcal{A} = (\{\mathcal{A}_p\}_{p \in \mathcal{P}}, s_{in}, \mathcal{F})$ *where*

- *Each component* $\mathcal{A}_p$ *is of the form* $(S_p, \rightarrow_p)$. *Here* S_p *is a finite set of states of process p, and* $\rightarrow_p \subseteq S_p \times \Sigma_p \times S_p$ *is a transition relation of process p.*
- $s_{in} \in \prod_{p \in \mathcal{P}} S_p$ *is the global initial state.*
- $\mathcal{F} \subseteq \prod_{p \in \mathcal{P}} S_p$ *is the set of global final states.*

The local transition relation $\rightarrow_p$ specifies how the process p sends and receives messages. The transition $(s_p, p!q(m), s'_p) \in \rightarrow_p$ says that in state s_p, process p can send the message m to process q and move to state s'_p. Similarly the transition $(s_p, p?q(m), s'_p)$ says that in state s_p, process p can receive the message m from process q and move to state s'_p.

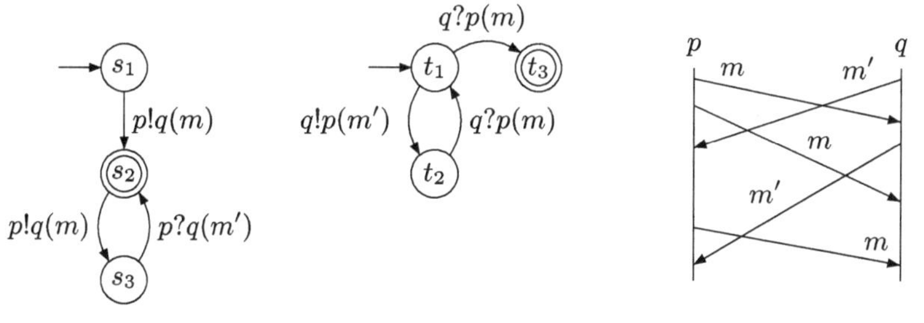

Fig. 4. A message-passing automaton

As ordinary finite-state automata recognize (or accept) a set of strings, MPA on the other hand accept a set of MSCs. An MSC $M = (E, \leq, \lambda)$ is said to be accepted by an MPA $\mathcal{A}$ whenever it finds itself in a global final state, after each constituent process $\mathcal{A}_p$ has finished executing all the events in the set E_p in the order defined by the relation $\leq$.

Figure 4 shows an MPA with two processes p and q. The initial global state of the MPA is (s_1, t_1) and the final global state is (s_2, t_3). An MSC accepted by this MPA is shown in the same figure. An MSC language is a collection (or set) of MSCs. This set could even be infinite. The MSC language accepted by an MPA $\mathcal{A}$ is denoted by $L(\mathcal{A}) = \{M | M \text{ is an MSC accepted by } \mathcal{A}\}$. From the previous section we know that an MSC M can be represented by a set of finite-length strings $[\![M]\!]$. Extending this further, we can associate with each MPA $\mathcal{A}$ a set of finite-length strings $[\![\mathcal{A}]\!] = \bigcup_{M \in L(\mathcal{A})} [\![M]\!]$.

Please recall that the verification problem being addressed in this paper is whether every MSC specified by an HMSC $\mathcal{H}$ is also accepted by the MPA $\mathcal{A}$. The answer to this decision problem boils down to whether $[\![\mathcal{H}]\!] \subseteq [\![\mathcal{A}]\!]$ holds or not.

Each ordered pair of processes correspond to a separate channel in an MPA. For example, the processes p, q in Fig. 4 are separated by two unidirectional channels c_{pq} and c_{qp}. Here channel c_{pq} carries messages from process p to process q, while channel c_{qp} carries messages from process q to process p. It should be further noted that these channels operate on the principle of FIFO, but are unreliable (or lossy) in the sense that a channel can potentially lose a message any time.

The set of global states of an MPA is equal to $\prod_{p \in \mathcal{P}} S_p$. Since S_p is finite for each process p, the number of global states is also finite. For a global state s, we denote the pth component of the global state by s_p. As constituent processes of an MPA exchange messages over channels, the MPA evolves from one configuration to the other. The configuration of an MPA at any point in time is determined by its global state and the contents of the various channels. Formally, a configuration is a pair $\gamma = (s, w)$ where s is a global state and $w : \mathcal{C} \to \mathcal{M}^\star$ is a function that maps each channel to a queue of messages. The initial configuration is (s_{in}, w_ϵ) where $w_\epsilon(c)$ is the empty string ϵ for every channel c. The set of final configurations is $F \times \{w_\epsilon\}$.

We are interested in how the MPA moves from one configuration to other. Formally, we write $\gamma \Rightarrow \gamma'$ if the MPA moves from configuration γ to γ' in one step. Likewise we write $\gamma \overset{\star}{\Rightarrow} \gamma'$ if the MPA moves from configuration γ to γ' in zero or more steps. The global moves of the MPA $\mathcal{A}$ are dictated by the following three rules.

R_1: If there is a local transition $(s_p, p!q(m), s'_p) \in \to_p$ on a process $p \in \mathcal{P}$, then there is a global move $(s, w) \overset{p!q(m)}{\Rightarrow} (s', w')$ where for every $r \neq p$ we have $s_r = s'_r$. Also we have $w'(c_{pq}) = w(c_{pq}) \cdot m$, and for every $c \neq c_{pq}$ we have $w(c) = w'(c)$.

Basically this rule says that if process p of the MPA performs a local action of sending a message m to process q, then we arrive at a new configuration. The global state of the new configuration is same as that of the old configuration, except that local state of the process p changes from s_p to s'_p. Similarly, the contents of each channel in the new configuration is same as the old configuration, except channel c_{pq} where message m gets appended at the rear end.

R_2: If there is a local transition $(s_p, p?q(m), s'_p) \in \rightarrow_p$ on a process $p \in \mathcal{P}$, then there is a global move $(s, w) \stackrel{p?q(m)}{\Rightarrow} (s', w')$ where for every $r \neq p$ we have $s_r = s'_r$. Also we have $w(c_{qp}) = m.w'(c_{qp})$, and for every $c \neq c_{qp}$ we have $w'(c) = w(c)$.

Basically this rule says that if process p of the MPA performs a local action of receiving a message m from the process q, then we arrive at a new configuration. The global state of the new configuration is same as that of the old configuration, except that local state of the process p changes from s_p to s'_p. Similarly, the contents of each channel in the new configuration is same as the old configuration, except channel c_{qp} where message m gets removed from the front end.

R_3: For any channel say c_{pq} we can have the global transition $(s, w) \stackrel{\epsilon}{\Rightarrow} (s, w')$, where $w'(c_{pq}) = x.y$ if $w(c_{pq}) = x.m.y$, and for every $c \neq c_{pq}$ we have $w(c) = w'(c)$. Strings $x, y \in \mathcal{M}^\star$ represent queues of messages here.

Basically this rule says that messages could get lost during communication spontaneous. This rule is different from the first two rules in three respects. One, the global move in this case is not premised on any local condition. Two, the global move in this case is labelled with ϵ. Finally, the global move in this case does not bring about a change in the global state. It should be understood that it is this very rule that categorises the MPA as unreliable. An MPA with only the rules R_1 and R_2 will be categorised as a reliable one.

It should be noted that even though the number of global states in an MPA is finite, the number of configurations is infinite. This is because we don't impose any upper bound on the size of the channels. An MPA in fact induces an infinite-state labelled transition system (LTS) where the set of states is the set of configurations and $\Rightarrow$ is the transition relation. An important observation here is that for a given MPA $\mathcal{A}$, the string language associated with it can equivalently be given by $[\![\mathcal{A}]\!] = \{w \in \Sigma^\star | (s_{in}, w_\epsilon) \stackrel{w}{\Rightarrow} (s_f, w_\epsilon)\}$. In other words, the string language $[\![\mathcal{A}]\!]$ comprises all those strings w which can take the MPA $\mathcal{A}$ from the initial configuration (s_{in}, w_ϵ) to some final configuration (s_f, w_ϵ) by applying only rules R_1 and R_2. This observation will be key to finding an algorithm for the main verification problem of this paper.

For infinite-state LTSs, we say that reachability is decidable if there exists an algorithm to determine whether an arbitrary state is reachable from the initial state or not. In the next section we show that reachability is a decidable problem for unreliable MPA.

4 Reachability Analysis in MPA

In this section we prove that reachability is a decidable problem, provided the MPA is unreliable. It needs mention that if the MPA is assumed to be reliable instead, the reachability problem becomes undecidable [6]. As a matter of fact, a reliable MPA can simulate a Turing Machine and by Rice Theorem reachability property is undecidable [11]. The same problem however is decidable for reliable MPA with bounded channels.

We begin by formally stating the result we want to prove.

Theorem 1. *Given an unreliable MPA $\mathcal{A}$ with the initial configuration $\gamma_0 = (s_{in}, w_\epsilon)$ and an arbitrary global configuration $\gamma = (s, w)$, determine whether $\gamma_0 \overset{\star}{\Rightarrow} \gamma$ holds or not is a decidable problem.*

Our proof of the above theorem is based on the concept of backward reachability. A new transition relation $\rightsquigarrow$ is defined on the set of configurations. The transition relation $\rightsquigarrow$ goes in the opposite direction of the relation $\Rightarrow$, though it is not the exact opposite. Finally we will be able to prove that for configurations γ_0 and γ it is the case that $\gamma_0 \overset{\star}{\Rightarrow} \gamma$ iff $\gamma \overset{\star}{\rightsquigarrow} \gamma_0$. This equivalence reduces the forward reachability to backward reachability.

Please note that this approach is not novel. It was used to prove the same results for lossy channel systems [2]. A lossy channel system is a finite-state process interacting with its environment through a finite set of channels which are assumed to be unreliable, unbounded and FIFO. A lossy channel systems can model many important communication protocols such as Alternating Bit Protocol [4], HDLC [14]. The global behaviour of a lossy channel system differs from our global behaviour in the following way. In a lossy channel system whenever a process p sends a message m to some other process q, the global move is labelled with an invisible action τ. The same hold whenever a process p receives a message m from some other process q. This apart, each process in a lossy channel system can do some local actions which are reflected as visible actions in the global moves of the system. Despite these differences in the labelling of the forward moves, this approach can be incorporated into our setting because forward reachability and backward reachability are equivalent in terms of decidability.

We now define an important notation. For $x_1, x_2 \in \mathcal{M}^\star$, let $x_1 \preceq x_2$ denotes that x_1 is a (not necessarily contiguous) substring of x_2. This notation can now be lifted to multiple channels. If w_1, w_2 are two functions from the set $\mathcal{C}$ to $\mathcal{M}^\star$, then $w_1 \preceq w_2$ denotes that for each channel $c \in \mathcal{C}$ it is the case that $w_1(c) \preceq w_2(c)$. Further, given two configurations (s_1, w_1) and (s_2, w_2), we say that $(s_1, w_1) \preceq (s_2, w_2)$ if it is the case that $(s_1 = s_2) \wedge (w_1 \preceq w_2)$. We say that configuration (s_1, w_1) is simpler than the configuration (s_2, w_2) if $(s_1, w_1) \preceq (s_2, w_2)$ holds. We are now ready to define the relation $\rightsquigarrow$ with the help of following four rules:

R'_1: If $(s,w) \stackrel{p!q(m)}{\Rightarrow} (s',w')$ then we have $(s',w') \stackrel{\mathcal{T}}{\rightsquigarrow} (s,w)$. Here, $w'(c_{pq}) = w(c_{pq}).m$ and for each $c \neq c_{pq}$ it is the case that $w'(c) = w(c)$.

R'_2: If $(s,w) \stackrel{p!q(m)}{\Rightarrow} (s',w')$ such that $w(c_{pq}) \neq \epsilon$ and $last(w(c_{pq})) \neq m$ then we have $(s',w) \stackrel{\mathcal{T}}{\rightsquigarrow} (s,w)$.

R'_3: If $(s,w) \stackrel{p!q(m)}{\Rightarrow} (s',w')$ such that $w(c_{pq}) = \epsilon$ then we have $(s',w) \stackrel{\mathcal{T}}{\rightsquigarrow} (s,w)$.

R'_4: If $(s,w) \stackrel{p?q(m)}{\Rightarrow} (s',w')$ then we have $(s',w') \stackrel{\mathcal{T}}{\rightsquigarrow} (s,w)$. Here, $w(c_{qp}) = m.w'(c_{qp})$ and for each $c \neq c_{qp}$ it is the case that $w'(c) = w(c)$.

Lemma 1. *Given arbitrary configurations γ_1, γ_2 of an MPA, the following implication holds: $\gamma_2 \stackrel{\star}{\rightsquigarrow} \gamma_1$ implies $\gamma_1 \stackrel{\star}{\Rightarrow} \gamma_2$.*

Proof. This can be proved from the above rules by the principle of mathematical induction.

Now we state a result which roughly says that each forward step can be simulated by a backward step.

Lemma 2. *If $\gamma_1 \Rightarrow \gamma_2 \wedge \gamma_3 \preceq \gamma_2$ then $\exists \gamma_4 \preceq \gamma_1$ such that $\gamma_3 \rightsquigarrow \gamma_4$.*

Proof. Let $\gamma_1 = (s_1, w_1)$ and $\gamma_2 = (s_2, w_2)$ and $\gamma_3 = (s_2, w_3)$ where $w_3 \preceq w_2$. There are three cases to check corresponding to the rules R_1, R_2 and R_3. For each case we find w_4 and define γ_4 to be (s_1, w_4). In each case it is easy to check that $\gamma_4 \preceq \gamma_1$ and $\gamma_3 \rightsquigarrow \gamma_4$.

1. If $(s_1,w_1) \stackrel{p!q(m)}{\Rightarrow} (s_2,w_2)$ such that we have $w_2(c_{pq}) = w_1(c_{pq}).m$ and for all $c \neq c_{pq}$ we have $w_2(c) = w_1(c)$, then do the following. If $last(w_3(c_{pq})) = m$, then take w_4 to be same as w_3 except that $w_4(c_{pq}).m = w_3(c_{pq})$. Otherwise if last $w_3(c_{pq}) \neq m$ or $w_3(c_{pq}) = \epsilon$, then $w_4 = w_3$.
2. If $(s_1,w_1) \stackrel{p?q(m)}{\Rightarrow} (s_2,w_2)$ such that $w_1(c_{qp}) = m.w_2(c_{qp})$ and for each $c \neq c_{qp}$ we have $w_1(c) = w_2(c)$, then take w_4 such that $w_4(c_{qp}) = m.w_3(c_{qp})$ and for each $c \neq c_{qp}$ we have $w_4(c) = w_3(c)$.
3. If $(s_1,w_1) \stackrel{\epsilon}{\Rightarrow} (s_2,w_2)$ such that for some $x,y \in \mathcal{M}^\star$ we have $w_1(c) = x.m.y$ and $w_2(c) = x.y$, then take $w_4 = w_3$ which will make $\gamma_4 = \gamma_3$.

We are now ready to state the relation between the forward reachability and backward reachability.

Theorem 2. *If $\gamma_0 = (s_0, \epsilon)$ and $\gamma = (s,w)$, then $\gamma_0 \stackrel{\star}{\Rightarrow} \gamma$ iff $\gamma \stackrel{\star}{\rightsquigarrow} \gamma_0$.*

Proof. From Lemma 2, we can prove the following implication using the principle of mathematical induction: if $\gamma_1 \stackrel{\star}{\Rightarrow} \gamma_2$ then $\gamma_2 \stackrel{\star}{\rightsquigarrow} \gamma_4$ such that $\gamma_4 \preceq \gamma_1$. Now if we replace γ_1 and γ_2 with γ_0 and γ respectively, then the implication becomes as follows. If $\gamma_0 \stackrel{\star}{\Rightarrow} \gamma$, then $\gamma \stackrel{\star}{\rightsquigarrow} \gamma_0$. This is because the only configuration simpler than γ_0 is γ_0 itself. At the same time Lemma 1 will give us the converse of this implication. Hence, the stated theorem is proved.

Input: An MPA $\mathcal{A}$ and a configuration γ.
Output: Is γ reachable from the initial configuration γ_0.
begin
$V = \emptyset$
  while (TRUE) **do**
    do
    if $\gamma = \gamma_0$ **then**
      return(YES)
    else if $\exists \gamma' \in V : \gamma' \preceq \gamma$ **then**
      return(NO)
    else
      $V := \{\gamma\} \cup \{\gamma' | (\gamma' \in V) \wedge (\gamma \not\preceq \gamma')\}$
      $\gamma := \gamma'$ where $\gamma \rightsquigarrow \gamma'$
    end if
  end while
end

Fig. 5. Algorithm for deciding reachability

4.1 Algorithm for Reachability

Let us recap on what we have done so far. In Theorem 1 we stated that our main objective is to determine the decidability of the following problem: Given an unreliable MPA, whether $\gamma_0 \overset{\star}{\Rightarrow} \gamma$ holds or not. Next, we stated in Theorem 2 that determining whether $\gamma_0 \overset{\star}{\Rightarrow} \gamma$ holds or not reduces to determining (through backward search) whether $\gamma \overset{\star}{\rightsquigarrow} \gamma_0$ holds or not. Now the issue here is that this backward search is not a priori bounded. However, in this section we show that it can be made bounded by virtue of the following two results.

1. From Lemma 2 we know that if $\gamma_1 \preceq \gamma_2$ then for each backward path from the configuration γ_2 to the initial configuration γ_0, there is a shorter or equal length backward path from γ_1 to γ_0. This result implies that we do not need to analyse configurations for which simpler configurations have been already analysed.
2. This result is called Higman's Lemma [10]. In our context, it can be stated as follows. If $\mathcal{M}$ is the finite set of messages, then there is no infinite sequence $x_1 x_2 x_3 \cdots$ of elements in $\mathcal{M}^\star$ such that $x_i \not\preceq x_j$ for all $i < j$. The same result can be lifted to configurations as follows. There is no infinite sequence of configurations $\gamma_1 \gamma_2 \gamma_3 \cdots$ such that $\gamma_i \not\preceq \gamma_j$ for all $i < j$.

The reachability algorithm is given in Fig. 5. This non deterministic algorithm takes as input an arbitrary configuration γ, and determines (through backward search) whether the initial configuration γ_0 is reachable from γ or not. The algorithm analyses configurations one by one and maintains a set of configurations V which have been analysed. Initially the set V is empty. When a configuration γ is analysed, three possibilities arise.

1. If γ is equal to the initial configuration γ_0, then return YES.
2. If there exists a configuration γ' in V such that $\gamma' \preceq \gamma$, then return NO.
3. If the above two conditions fail, then perform the following two steps.
   (a) Update V by first moving γ to V and then removing each member γ' from V such that $\gamma \prec \gamma'$.
   (b) Non deterministically choose one of the $\rightsquigarrow$ successor of γ and assign it to γ.

Now the Higman's Lemma will ensure that during the execution of the algorithm, we find the $\rightsquigarrow$ successor only finite number of times. In other words, the algorithm will give a conclusive yes/no answer after finite number of steps. Hence the decision problem stated in Theorem 1 is decidable.

5 Algorithm for Scenario Matching Problem

Let us recall the scenario matching problem. Given an MPA $\mathcal{A}$ and an HMSC $\mathcal{H}$, whether every MSC specified by $\mathcal{H}$ is also recognized by $\mathcal{A}$. Put differently, whether the set of MSCs specified by $\mathcal{H}$ a subset of the set of MSCs recognized by $\mathcal{A}$. We now explain that this problem is decidable, provided the $\mathcal{H}$ is locally synchronized and the $\mathcal{A}$ is unreliable.

Let us assume that $\mathcal{H}$ is locally synchronized. Since $\mathcal{H}$ is locally synchronized, the set of finite-length strings denoted by $[\![\mathcal{H}]\!]$ is a regular language. In [9] there is an effective procedure to obtain a finite-state automaton M from a locally synchronized $\mathcal{H}$ such that the language accepted by M is equal to $[\![\mathcal{H}]\!]$. Let $M = (Loc, \Sigma, \hookrightarrow, I, F)$ be the finite-state automaton accepting the regular language $[\![\mathcal{H}]\!]$. Here Loc is the set of locations, I is the initial location, F is the set of final locations, the set $\Sigma = \{p!q(m), p?q(m) | p, q \in \mathcal{P}, m \in \mathcal{M}\}$ is the alphabet, and $\hookrightarrow$ is the transition relation.

Let $\mathcal{A} = (\{\mathcal{A}_p\}_{p\in\mathcal{P}}, s_{in}, \mathcal{F})$ be an unreliable MPA. We denote the labelled transition system (LTS) corresponding to the MPA $\mathcal{A}$ by $L_{\mathcal{A}} = (Con, \Rightarrow, \gamma_0)$ where Con is the infinite set of configurations, $\Rightarrow$ is the transition relation given by the rules R_1, R_2, and R_3 stated in Sect. 3, and $\gamma_0 = (s_{in}, w_\epsilon)$ is the initial configuration.

Now construct a synchronous product $M \| L_{\mathcal{A}} = (Loc \times Con, \Rightarrow', (I, \gamma_0))$ where the transition relation $\Rightarrow'$ is given by the following rules:

1. If $l_1 \overset{p!q(m)}{\hookrightarrow} l_2$ and $\gamma_1 \overset{p!q(m)}{\Rightarrow} \gamma_2$ then $(l_1, \gamma_1) \overset{p!q(m)}{\Rightarrow'} (l_2, \gamma_2)$.
2. If $l_1 \overset{p?q(m)}{\hookrightarrow} l_2$ and $\gamma_1 \overset{p?q(m)}{\Rightarrow} \gamma_2$ then $(l_1, \gamma_1) \overset{p?q(m)}{\Rightarrow'} (l_2, \gamma_2)$.
3. If $\gamma_1 \overset{\epsilon}{\Rightarrow} \gamma_2$ then $(l, \gamma_1) \overset{\epsilon}{\Rightarrow'} (l, \gamma_2)$.

Note that $M \| L_{\mathcal{A}}$ is an infinite-state LTS which is structurally same as the LTS $L_{\mathcal{A}}$, except the naming of states. For each state (s, w) in $L_{\mathcal{A}}$ there is a corresponding state (l, s, w) in $M \| L_{\mathcal{A}}$. More importantly, this correspondence implies that reachability is decidable for $M \| L_{\mathcal{A}}$.

Finally, the answer to the verification problem is YES iff $\forall l \in F\ \exists s_f \in \mathcal{F}$ such that (l, s_f, w_ϵ) is reachable in $M \| L_{\mathcal{A}}$. Since the size of set $F \times \mathcal{F}$ is finite, it means that the verification problem is decidable.

6 Conclusion

Over the years, scenarios have become popular as part of the requirement specification [1,5]. In the telecommunication domain, these scenarios can be formally defined as message sequence charts (or MSCs). In fact MSC language has been standardized by the International Telecommunication Union [12].

Scenario specifications are typically classified into two categories, positive and negative. Positive scenarios represent desirable behaviour. It is expected that the system should essentially exhibit these scenarios. On the other hand, negative scenarios represent undesirable behaviour and therefore system should avoid these behaviours. This leads to the scenario matching problem: given a distributed implementation and a specification in the form of a set of positive (or negative) scenarios, does the system exhibit (or avoid) these scenarios?

In this paper we have addressed one such scenario matching problem. The implementation is given in the form of an MPA which accepts a set of MSCs, while the specification is an HMSC which can represent a collection of MSCs. The problem is to determine whether the set of MSCs specified by the HMSC a subset of the set of MSCs accepted by the MPA. It is a decision problem whose decidability we want to know. The problem is important from the decidability point of view because each of the two sets of MSCs can be potentially infinite. Here we have proved that it is algorithmically possible to find a conclusive answer to this problem.

Similar problems have been already been discussed in the literature, both in the untimed and timed setting. In the untimed setting, efficient algorithms for the scenario matching problem have been identified in [13]. Further, an automated approach for scenario matching is proposed in [7]. Similar work has also be done in the real-time setting also [3].

References

1. Five reasons for scenario-based design: Interact. Comput. **13**(1), 43–60 (2000)
2. Abdulla, P., Jonsson, B.: Verifying programs with unreliable channels. In: 1993 Proceedings Eighth Annual IEEE Symposium on Logic in Computer Science (1993)
3. Akshay, S., Mukund, M., Kumar, K.N.: Checking coverage for infinite collections of timed scenarios. In: Concurrency Theory, 18th International Conference, Lisbon, Portugal, Proceedings, LNCS, 3–8 September 2007
4. Bartlett, K.A., Scantlebury, R.A., Wilkinson, P.T.: A note on reliable full-duplex transmission over half-duplex links **12**
5. Ben-Abdallah, H., Leue. Mesa, S.: Support for scenario-based design of concurrent systems. In: Tools and Algorithms for the Construction and Analysis of Systems. Springer, Heidelberg (1998)

6. Brand, D., Zafiropulo, P.: On communicating finite-state machines. J. ACM **30**(2), 323–342 (1983)
7. D'Souza, D., Mukund, M.: Checking consistency of SDL+MSC specifications. LNCS
8. Henriksen, J.G., Mukund, M., Kumar, K.N., Sohoni, M.A., Thiagarajan, P.S.: A theory of regular MSC languages. Inf. Comput. **202**(1), 1–38 (2005)
9. Henriksen, J.G., Mukund, M., Kumar, K.N., Thiagarajan, P.S.: On message sequence graphs and finitely generated regular MSC languages. In: 27th International Colloquium on Automata, Languages and Programming, ICALP (2000)
10. Higman, G.: Ordering by divisibility in abstract algebras. In: Proceedings of the London Mathematical Society s3–2 (1952)
11. Hopcroft, J., Ullman, J.: Introduction to Automata Theory, Languages, and Computation. Adison-Wesley Publishing Company, Reading, Massachusets, USA (1979)
12. International Telecommunication Union. Recommendation Z.120: Message sequence chart (MSC) (2011)
13. Muscholl, A., Peled, D., Su, Z.: Deciding properties for message sequence charts. In: Foundations of Software Science and Computation Structures. Springer, Heidelberg (1998)
14. Tanenbaum, A.S., Wetherall, D.J.: Computer Networks, 5th edn. Prentice Hall Press, USA (2010)

Intuitive Verification of Sequential Programs Using Hybrid Reasoning

Shushu Wu, Xiwei Wu, Chengxi Yang, and Qinxiang Cao(✉)

Shanghai Jiao Tong University, Shanghai, China
{Ciel77,yashen,arcadia-y,caoqinxiang}@sjtu.edu.cn

Abstract. Verifying the functional correctness of real-world code with complex algorithms requires reasoning about both implementation correctness and algorithm correctness. Implementation correctness, which relates concrete programs to abstract functional models, is inherently relational, yet is traditionally formalized using standard Hoare logic alone.

This paper proposes a hybrid reasoning approach that combines relational Hoare logic and standard Hoare logic. Our key insight is that verifying implementation correctness naturally calls for relational Hoare logic, while algorithm correctness is well-suited to standard Hoare logic. Compared to traditional verifications that rely exclusively on standard Hoare logic, our approach simplifies proofs and offers more intuitive reasoning patterns. We demonstrate this in a setting where the concrete language is a C-like imperative language and the abstract algorithm is written in a simple nondeterministic functional language. Through case studies on binary search trees and merge sort, we show how our hybrid reasoning approach addresses challenges in verifying complex algorithms, reduces proof complexity, and enhances clarity.

Keywords: Program verification · Relational Hoare logic · Separation logic

1 Introduction

Proving the functional correctness of real-world code that incorporates complex algorithms is challenging [10,11,22,31,40]. A commonly adopted strategy is the two-layer method [3], which separates proofs into two layers. Implementation correctness ensures that the concrete program correctly implements a functional model. Algorithm correctness validates that the functional model meets its specification.

However, proving implementation correctness is often difficult in practice. Most existing work relies on standard Hoare logic, which often leads to verbose proofs or unnatural loop invariants. Consider, for example, verifying a binary search tree (BST) insertion function, as shown in Fig. 1.

G. De Giacomo et al. (Eds.): TASE 2026, LNCS 16697, pp. 400–419, 2027.
https://doi.org/10.1007/978-3-032-30693-7_26

```
void bst_ins(int x, int v,
             struct tree ** p)
{ struct tree *q = *p;
  while (q && x != q->key) {
    if (x < q->key) p = &q->left;
    else p = &q->right;
    q = *p; }
  if (!q) {
    q = malloc(sizeof(struct tree));
    q->key = x; q->value = v;
    q->left = q->right = NULL;
    *p = q; }
  else { q->value = v; }
}
```

```
function insert(x, v, s):
  match s with
  | leaf ⇒ node(leaf, x, v, leaf)
  | node(a, y, w, b) ⇒
     if x < y then
       let a' = insert(x, v, a) in
           node(a', y, w, b)
     else if x > y then
       let b' = insert(x, v, b) in
           node(a, y, w, b')
     else node(a, x, v, b)
  end
```

Fig. 1. BST insertion: concrete C implementation vs. abstract model. leaf denotes the empty tree and node(l, k, v, r) denotes a node with left child l, key k, value v, and right child r.

Its functional correctness requires that after insertion, the resulting tree remains ordered and stores the new key-value pair. To prove this, the two-layer method introduces a functional model insert [2], as shown on the right of Fig. 1, and separates the proof into two parts. Algorithm correctness validates that insert returns a tree whose left subtree keys are smaller than the root and right subtree keys are larger, and that the new key-value pair is correctly stored. Implementation correctness shows the C program faithfully implements insert, and is formalized as:

$$\{\mathsf{storetree}(\mathsf{p}_0, t_0)\}\ \mathtt{bst\_ins}(k, v, \mathsf{p}_0)\ \{\mathsf{storetree}(\mathsf{p}_0, \mathtt{insert}(k, v, t_0))\} \qquad (1)$$

That is, if the memory initially stores a tree t_0 at p_0, then after execution it stores the result of $\mathtt{insert}(k, v, t_0)$. However, proving this triple is tedious. To prove this triple, Cao et al. [10] employ the following loop invariant:

$$\exists t\, P\,.\, P(\mathtt{insert}(k, v, t)) = \mathtt{insert}(k, v, t_0) \wedge \mathsf{storetree}(\mathsf{p}, t) * \mathsf{storezipper}(\mathsf{p}_0, \mathsf{p}, P)$$

This invariant states the storage of a subtree t and its contextual zipper [18] P (a path from the root to t). Importantly, it requires that combining local updates to the currently focused subtree t with the context P is equivalent to global updates to the original tree t_0. Requiring this equivalence is counterintuitive: the concrete program modifies only the local pointer p, yet the proof must consider both local changes of the subtree t and global changes of the entire tree t_0.

This difficulty arises because implementation correctness is inherently relational: it relates a concrete program to an abstract algorithm. Standard Hoare logic, however, can only reason about a single program. The loop invariant cannot directly describe the relationship between the two programs at each intermediate step. Instead, it must encode the abstract program's behavior through value equalities. In the invariant above, $P(\texttt{insert}(k, v, t)) = \texttt{insert}(k, v, t_0)$ serves exactly this purpose: it expresses what the abstract insertion would produce at the current point by relating it to the final result $\texttt{insert}(k, v, t_0)$. This indirection is what makes the invariant unnatural. Relational Hoare logic, which reasons about two programs simultaneously, is a natural fit for such proofs. Besides, relational verification is often simpler than functional verification, particularly when the two programs are similar [6].

```
struct list * mergesort(struct
                         list * x)
{ int l = listlen(x);
  if (l < 8)
    return inssort(x);
  else {
    struct list * p,  * q;
    p = NULL;
    q = NULL;
    split(x, &p, &q);
    p = mergesort(p);
    q = mergesort(q);
    return merge(p, q);
} }
```

```
function extsort_A(x):
  return r such that
       permutation(x, r) ∧ sorted(r)

function mergesort_A(x):
  choose
    extsort_A(x)
  or
    require length(x) ≥ 2;
    let (p1, q1) = split_A(x, nil, nil) in
    let p2 = mergesort_A(p1) in
    let q2 = mergesort_A(q1) in
    merge_A(p2, q2)
  end
```

Fig. 2. Hybrid sorting: concrete C implementation vs. abstract model. The abstract model nondeterministically chooses between an external sorter $\texttt{extsort}_A$ and a recursive merge sort.

However, some refinement proofs naturally reduce to standard functional correctness arguments. Relational proofs can require standard Hoare logic. To illustrate, consider the hybrid sorting algorithm in Fig. 2. The C program uses insertion sort for small inputs (fewer than 8 elements) and merge sort for larger ones. In practice, different implementations may use different thresholds for switching strategies and different algorithms for small inputs. To capture this family of implementations, the abstract model uses a nondeterministic choice between two branches: a recursive merge sort that splits, recursively sorts, and merges, and an external sorter $\texttt{extsort}_A$ that is a black box specifying only that the output is a sorted permutation of the input. Verifying that the concrete program implements this abstract model requires both relational and standard Hoare logic. For the merge sort part, concrete subprograms (e.g., $\texttt{split}(\mathsf{x}, \&\mathsf{p}, \&\mathsf{q})$) align with their abstract counterparts (e.g., $\texttt{split}_A(x, \text{nil}, \text{nil})$), so relational Hoare logic can decompose the proof into small refinement obligations. For the insertion sort part, $\texttt{inssort}(\mathsf{x})$ must refine $\texttt{extsort}_A(x)$. Since $\texttt{extsort}_A$ only requires the output to be a sorted permutation, this reduces to proving the functional correctness of `inssort(x)`, which is naturally handled by standard Hoare logic.

Based on these observations, we propose a hybrid reasoning approach that explicitly combines relational Hoare logic [7,43] and standard Hoare logic [17,32]. We use relational Hoare logic for implementation correctness, enabling more intuitive reasoning patterns and simplifying previously tedious proofs. Relational Hoare logic proofs in turn rely on standard Hoare logic when refinement obligations reduce to functional correctness of individual subprograms. Algorithm correctness continues to rely on standard Hoare logic, and by composing the two layers, the overall functional correctness can be derived.

Our main contributions are as follows:

- We reveal that certain standard Hoare logic proofs for implementation correctness are in essence relational. Formalizing these proofs using relational Hoare logic enables more natural verification and simplifies the previously tedious proofs.
- We propose a hybrid reasoning approach that combines relational Hoare logic and standard Hoare logic. Specifically, we use relational Hoare triples to formalize implementation correctness and standard Hoare triples to formalize algorithm correctness. Furthermore, while proving relational triples, we sometimes employ standard Hoare logic for subprograms.
- We instantiate our approach in a framework where the concrete language is a C-like imperative language and the abstract programs are written in a simple nondeterministic functional language.
- We validate our approach through case studies on BSTs and merge sort. All results are mechanized in Rocq [42].

2 Preliminary: Relational Hoare Logic

Program-as-resource assertions [37] originate from concurrent program verification [15,26,27,33,34,36], where they embed the pending operations of a thread directly into invariants or protocols to reason about inter-thread cooperation. Concretely, a program-as-resource assertion $\mathcal{P}$ is a predicate over the concrete state, the abstract state, and the abstract program itself. The main judgment for refinement is a relational Hoare triple of the form:

$$\{[c^{\mathrm{abs}}] \wedge \mathcal{P}\}\, c^{\mathrm{con}}\, \{r^{\mathrm{con}}.\, \exists r^{\mathrm{abs}}.\, [\mathbf{ret}\ r^{\mathrm{abs}}] \wedge \mathcal{Q}(r^{\mathrm{con}}, r^{\mathrm{abs}})\}$$

where r^{con} and r^{abs} denote the concrete and abstract return values, respectively. Informally, the triple asserts that for any execution of c^{con} from an initial configuration satisfying $\mathcal{P}$, there exists a corresponding execution of c^{abs} such that the return values r^{con} and r^{abs} together satisfy $\mathcal{Q}$. For example, the implementation correctness of BST insertion (Fig. 1) can be expressed as:

$$\begin{array}{l}\{[\mathtt{insert}(k, v, t_0)] \wedge \mathsf{storetree}(\mathsf{p}_0, t_0)\}\\ \quad \mathtt{bst\_ins}(k, v, \mathsf{p}_0)\\ \{\exists r^{\mathrm{abs}}.\, [\mathbf{ret}\ r^{\mathrm{abs}}] \wedge \mathsf{storetree}(\mathsf{p}_0, r^{\mathrm{abs}})\}\end{array} \tag{2}$$

Here $\mathsf{storetree}(\mathsf{p}_0, t_0)$ asserts that the memory stores tree t_0 at address p_0. The precondition embeds $\texttt{insert}(k, v, t_0)$ as the abstract program to be refined, and the postcondition asserts termination with result r^{abs} (via **ret** r^{abs}) now stored at p_0. Since the concrete insertion modifies the tree in place and returns no value, r^{con} is omitted. We prove this triple in Sect. 3.1.

We now formalize the relational Hoare triple in general.

Definition 1 (Relational Hoare Triples). *Triple* $\{\mathcal{P}\}\ c^{\text{con}}\ \{r^{\text{con}}.\ \mathcal{Q}(r^{\text{con}})\}$ *is valid if, given any initial states* σ_1^{con}, σ_1^{abs} *and abstract program* c_1^{abs} *satisfying* $\mathcal{P}$, *for every* $(\sigma_2^{\text{con}}, r^{\text{con}})$ *reachable by executing* c^{con} *from* σ_1^{con}, *there exist* σ_2^{abs} *and* c_2^{abs} *such that*

$$(\sigma_1^{\text{abs}}, c_1^{\text{abs}}) \hookrightarrow (\sigma_2^{\text{abs}}, c_2^{\text{abs}}) \quad \textit{and} \quad (\sigma_2^{\text{con}}, \sigma_2^{\text{abs}}, c_2^{\text{abs}}) \textit{ satisfies } \mathcal{Q}(r^{\text{con}}).$$

Here $(\sigma_1^{\text{abs}}, c_1^{\text{abs}}) \hookrightarrow (\sigma_2^{\text{abs}}, c_2^{\text{abs}})$ *is a reduction relation, which describes how* c_1^{abs} *reduces under state* σ_1^{abs} *to a new program* c_2^{abs} *and (possibly) updated state* σ_2^{abs}.

In this paper, concrete programs are written in a C-like imperative language and abstract programs in a simple nondeterministic functional language (Figs. 1 and 2). Inference rules are introduced as needed in subsequent sections.

3 An Insight: The Relational Nature of Standard Hoare Logic Proofs

In this section, we demonstrate that implementation correctness is relational in nature, and that relational Hoare logic yields more intuitive proofs (Sect. 3.1). We then compose the relational proof with a standard algorithm correctness proof to derive full functional correctness (Sect. 3.2).

3.1 Implementation Correctness as Relational Hoare Triples

As shown in Sect. 2, the implementation correctness of BST insertion can be expressed as the relational triple (2), which states that the concrete program $\texttt{bst\_ins}(k, v, \mathsf{p}_0)$ (pointer manipulation in loops) and the abstract program $\texttt{insert}(k, v, t_0)$ (recursive tree operations) produce consistent results. We now show how relational Hoare logic yields a more intuitive proof.

Figure 3 presents the relational inference rules used in this proof. Rel-Wh[1] handles while loops with a relational invariant $\mathcal{P}$. Rel-Seq decomposes a sequential concrete program $c_1^{\text{con}}; c_2^{\text{con}}$ into two relational subgoals, connected by an intermediate assertion $\mathcal{R}$. Con-Store handles memory stores, updating the heap while preserving the rest of the assertion via separating conjunction. Abs-Pure rewrites the abstract program via a pure reduction $\rightarrow_p$ (function unfolding, let-in reassociation, etc.).

[1] The Rel-Wh rule assumes the loop body contains no return or break statements; that is, every execution of the body either continues to the next iteration or exits via the loop condition.

$$\textsc{Rel-Wh}\quad \frac{\{\mathcal{P} \wedge b^{\text{con}}\}\ c^{\text{con}}\ \{\mathcal{P}\}}{\{\mathcal{P}\}\ \text{while}\ b^{\text{con}}\ \text{do}\ c^{\text{con}}\ \{\mathcal{P} \wedge \neg b^{\text{con}}\}}$$

$$\textsc{Abs-Pure}\quad \frac{c_1^{\text{abs}} \to_p c_2^{\text{abs}} \qquad \{[c_2^{\text{abs}}] \wedge \mathcal{P}\}\ c^{\text{con}}\ \{r^{\text{con}}.\ \mathcal{Q}(r^{\text{con}})\}}{\{[c_1^{\text{abs}}] \wedge \mathcal{P}\}\ c^{\text{con}}\ \{r^{\text{con}}.\ \mathcal{Q}(r^{\text{con}})\}}$$

$$\textsc{Rel-Seq}\quad \frac{\{\mathcal{P}\}\ c_1^{\text{con}}\ \{\mathcal{R}\} \qquad \{\mathcal{R}\}\ c_2^{\text{con}}\ \{r^{\text{con}}.\ \mathcal{Q}(r^{\text{con}})\}}{\{\mathcal{P}\}\ c_1^{\text{con}}; c_2^{\text{con}}\ \{r^{\text{con}}.\ \mathcal{Q}(r^{\text{con}})\}}
\qquad
\textsc{Con-Store}\quad \frac{}{\{\mathsf{p} \mapsto _ * \mathcal{F}\}\ \mathsf{store}(\mathsf{p}, e)\ \{\mathsf{p} \mapsto e * \mathcal{F}\}}$$

Fig. 3. An excerpt of relational inference rules.

Since the concrete program primarily consists of a while loop, we apply Rel-Wh to reduce the proof to finding a loop invariant. Because the invariant is a program-as-resource assertion, it must describe both the current concrete memory and the remaining abstract computation at each iteration. The concrete memory can be partitioned into two disjoint segments: the subtree t rooted at the current focus p, which corresponds to the tree manipulated by the abstract program's recursive calls, and a zipper context P [18] that records the path from the root p_0 to p. Intuitively, P is a tree with a hole: the hole marks where the focused subtree belongs. At each iteration, the remaining abstract computation is: first perform the recursive insertion on t, then fill the hole in P with the result. Consider the example in Fig. 4, where each node stores a key-value pair (we write w_0 for the value at y_0, and w_1 for the value at y_1). After the first iteration ($k < y_0$), $P = \mathtt{node}(\Box, y_0, w_0, b_0)$, where $\Box$ denotes the hole. After the second ($k > y_1$), P grows to $\mathtt{node}(\mathtt{node}(a_1, y_1, w_1, \Box), y_0, w_0, b_0)$. In general, P is the composition of such one-hole contexts along the entire path from the root to the current focus. Using the separating conjunction '$*$' [32] to assert disjointness, we obtain the following loop invariant:

$$\exists t, P.\ [\textbf{let}\ x = \mathtt{insert}(k, v, t)\ \textbf{in}\ P(x)] \wedge \mathsf{storetree}(\mathsf{p}, t) * \mathsf{storezipper}(\mathsf{p}_0, \mathsf{p}, P)$$

Next, we need to prove that the loop body preserves this invariant. Consider the case when k is greater than the key y_1 of the root of the focused subtree t, such as in Fig. 4. Suppose $t = \mathtt{node}(a_1, y_1, w_1, b)$, where a_1 and b are the left and right subtrees. With rule Abs-Pure , we can transform the abstract program:

Proposition 1. *When $k > y_1$ and $t = \mathtt{node}(a_1, y_1, w_1, b)$:*

$$\begin{aligned}
&\textbf{let}\ x = \mathtt{insert}(k, v, t)\ \textbf{in}\ P(x)\\
\to_p\ &\textbf{let}\ x = (\textbf{let}\ r = \mathtt{insert}(k, v, b)\ \textbf{in}\ \mathtt{node}(a_1, y_1, w_1, r))\ \textbf{in}\ P(x)\\
\to_p\ &\textbf{let}\ r = \mathtt{insert}(k, v, b)\ \textbf{in}\ \textbf{let}\ x = \mathtt{node}(a_1, y_1, w_1, r)\ \textbf{in}\ P(x)\\
\to_p\ &\textbf{let}\ r = \mathtt{insert}(k, v, b)\ \textbf{in}\ P(\mathtt{node}(a_1, y_1, w_1, r))
\end{aligned}$$

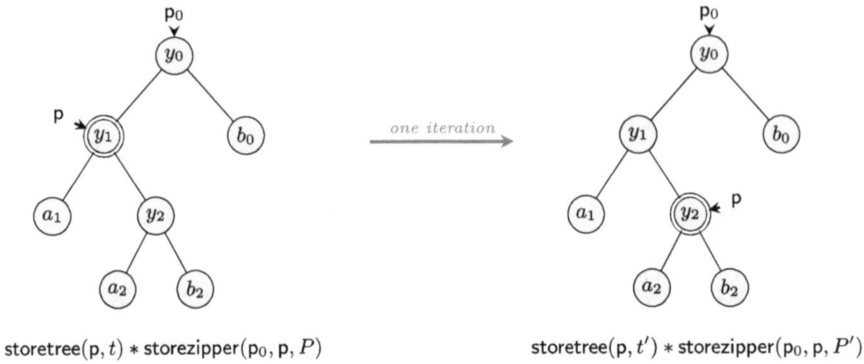

Fig. 4. Zipper decomposition during BST insertion ($k < y_0$ and $k > y_1$). The double-circled node is the focus pointed to by p. One iteration advances p from y_1 to y_2: the focused subtree shrinks and the zipper context grows.

After this reduction, the abstract program becomes:

$$\mathbf{let}\ r = \mathtt{insert}(k, v, b)\ \mathbf{in}\ P(\mathrm{node}(a_1,\ y_1,\ w_1,\ r))$$

For the concrete side, we apply REL-SEQ and CON-STORE to evaluate the loop body, which advances pointer p from y_1 to y_2 in Fig. 4. It remains to show that combining the root node (y_1, w_1), the subtree a_1, and the old context P yields the updated zipper context, which is straightforward.

In contrast, the traditional two-layer method formalizes implementation correctness as the standard Hoare triple (1), whose loop invariant is:

$$\exists t\, P\, .\, P(\mathtt{insert}(k, v, t)) = \mathtt{insert}(k, v, t_0) \land \mathsf{storetree}(\mathsf{p}, t) * \mathsf{storezipper}(\mathsf{p}_0, \mathsf{p}, P)$$

Both invariants require the consistent representation of the subtree and zipper context. However, in the relational proof, there is no need to explicitly reason that combining the context P with the updated subtree $\mathtt{insert}(k, v, t)$ yields the overall result $\mathtt{insert}(k, v, t_0)$. Instead, this equivalence is implicitly decomposed by the abstract program transformations in the relational Hoare triple.

This observation simplifies a key part of the reasoning: the loop invariant. In program verification, identifying appropriate invariants is often the most difficult step. Our relational formulation suggests invariants that align naturally with the structure of the implementation and its abstract specification, reducing the proof burden. Thus, we argue that implementation correctness is best understood as a relational property, and that employing relational Hoare triples brings more intuitive loop invariants and less complex proofs.

3.2 Composing Program Refinement with Algorithm Correctness

Since the relational triple shows that the concrete program refines the abstract model, correctness properties proven for the abstract program (e.g., preservation of the BST property) transfer directly to the concrete implementation.

Concretely, for the BST insertion example, we use the following standard Hoare triple to formalize the correctness of the abstract program:

$$\{\mathsf{ordered}(t_0) \wedge t_0 \sim m\}\ \texttt{insert}(k, v, t_0)\ \{r^{\text{abs}}.\,\mathsf{ordered}(r^{\text{abs}}) \wedge r^{\text{abs}} \sim m[k \mapsto v]\}$$

Here $\mathsf{ordered}(t)$ asserts that t is an ordered tree: every node's key is greater than all keys in its left subtree and smaller than all keys in its right subtree. $t \sim m$ asserts that the key-value pairs stored in t correspond to the finite map m. This triple states that inserting (k, v) into a valid BST t_0 yields a valid BST r^{abs} that corresponds to the updated map $m[k \mapsto v]$.

We can then compose this triple with the relational triple (2) to derive the functional correctness of the concrete program. Here $\mathsf{storemap}(\mathsf{p}_0, m)$ denotes that there exists a valid BST t_0 stored at p_0 with key-value pairs corresponding to a mapping m:

$$\{\mathsf{storemap}(\mathsf{p}_0, m)\}\ \texttt{bst\_ins}(k, v, \mathsf{p}_0)\ \{\mathsf{storemap}(\mathsf{p}_0, m[k \mapsto v])\} \tag{3}$$

In this paper, we refer to this composition as *vertical composition*. Our relational Hoare logic provides the following vertical composition rule:

$$\frac{\{[c^{\text{abs}}] \wedge \mathcal{P}\}\ c^{\text{con}}\ \{r^{\text{con}}.\,\exists\, r^{\text{abs}}.\,[\textbf{ret}\ r^{\text{abs}}] \wedge \mathcal{Q}(r^{\text{con}}, r^{\text{abs}})\} \qquad \{P\}\ c^{\text{abs}}\ \{r^{\text{abs}}.\,Q(r^{\text{abs}})\}}{\{\mathcal{P} \odot P\}\ c^{\text{con}}\ \{r^{\text{con}}.\,\exists\, r^{\text{abs}}.\,\mathcal{Q}(r^{\text{con}}, r^{\text{abs}}) \odot Q(r^{\text{abs}})\}}$$

Here $\mathcal{P}$, $\mathcal{Q}$ are program-as-resource assertions and P, Q are assertions over the abstract state. The operator $\odot$ projects to a concrete-state predicate: $\mathcal{P} \odot P$ holds for σ^{con} when there exists an abstract state σ^{abs} such that $\mathcal{P}$ holds for $(\sigma^{\text{con}}, \sigma^{\text{abs}})$ and P holds for σ^{abs}. In the BST example, $\mathcal{P}$ is $\mathsf{storetree}(\mathsf{p}_0, t_0)$ and P is $\mathsf{ordered}(t_0) \wedge t_0 \sim m$, so $\mathcal{P} \odot P$ is equivalent to $\mathsf{storemap}(\mathsf{p}_0, m)$, i.e., $\exists t_0.\,\mathsf{storetree}(\mathsf{p}_0, t_0) \wedge \mathsf{ordered}(t_0) \wedge t_0 \sim m$. Composing the relational triple (2) with the above algorithm correctness triple yields (3).

4 Hybrid Reasoning with Relational and Standard Hoare Logics

In this section, we present our hybrid reasoning approach that combines relational and standard Hoare logic to verify programs with function calls. We give a high-level overview in Sect. 4.1 and formalize the language and logic in Sect. 4.2.

4.1 The Hybrid Reasoning Approach

As illustrated in Sect. 1, the hybrid sorting example (Fig. 2) involves concrete function calls that require different proof strategies. Some calls, such as `split` and `merge`, align with abstract counterparts and are best verified relationally. Others, such as `inssort`, reduce to standalone functional correctness and are best handled by standard Hoare logic. In particular, the relational proof of `mergesort` invokes the standard Hoare logic proof of `inssort`. Conversely, using the two-layer method to prove functional correctness requires implementation correctness, which relies on relational Hoare logic. To support this interplay, we augment both standard and relational Hoare triples with proof contexts that record verified function specifications, allowing each proof to reuse results established by either approach. Concretely, a standard proof context $S_\forall$ collects function specifications

$$(f : \Pi\,(\overrightarrow{a} : A).\,\{P(\overrightarrow{a})\}\,\{r^{\text{con}}.\,Q(\overrightarrow{a}, r^{\text{con}})\})$$

Here $\Pi\,(\overrightarrow{a} : A)$ binds a vector $\overrightarrow{a}$ of typed parameters, which may include the function's arguments as well as logical variables that relate the precondition P and the postcondition Q. The specification thus states that, for any such $\overrightarrow{a}$, calling f from a state satisfying $P(\overrightarrow{a})$ yields a return value and state satisfying $Q(\overrightarrow{a}, r^{\text{con}})$. A relational proof context $S_{\forall\exists}$ collects relational specifications

$$(f : \Pi\,(\overrightarrow{a} : A).\,\{[c^{\text{abs}}] \wedge \mathcal{P}(\overrightarrow{a})\}\,\{r^{\text{con}}.\,\exists r^{\text{abs}}.\,[\textbf{ret}\ r^{\text{abs}}] \wedge \mathcal{Q}(\overrightarrow{a}, r^{\text{con}}, r^{\text{abs}})\})$$

stating that calling f refines an abstract program c^{abs}. The two primary contextual judgments are:

$$S_\forall, S_{\forall\exists} \vdash \{P\}\ c^{\text{con}}\ \{r^{\text{con}}.\,Q(r^{\text{con}})\} \qquad S_\forall, S_{\forall\exists} \vdash \{\mathcal{P}\}\ c^{\text{con}}\ \{r^{\text{con}}.\,\mathcal{Q}(r^{\text{con}})\}$$

Both are natural extensions of their context-free counterparts: the triple holds for any environment that validates both $S_\forall$ and $S_{\forall\exists}$. Formal definitions are given in Sect. 4.2.

Using these judgments, we prove the functional correctness of a concrete program c^{con} that refines an abstract algorithm c^{abs}. The interplay between the two logics works in both directions:

Relational Hoare logic for standard Hoare logic Decompose the proof into implementation correctness and algorithm correctness.

- *Implementation correctness via relational Hoare logic*: We formalize that the concrete program c^{con} refines the abstract algorithm c^{abs} using a relational Hoare triple

$$\{[c^{\text{abs}}] \wedge \mathcal{P}\}\ c^{\text{con}}\ \{r^{\text{con}}.\,\exists r^{\text{abs}}.\,[\textbf{ret}\ r^{\text{abs}}] \wedge \mathcal{Q}(r^{\text{con}}, r^{\text{abs}})\}.$$

- *Algorithm correctness via standard Hoare logic*: We prove that c^{abs} satisfies its specification via a standard Hoare triple

$$\{P\}\ c^{\text{abs}}\ \{r^{\text{abs}}.\,Q(r^{\text{abs}})\}$$

where P and Q are predicates over abstract states.

- *Composition*: Applying the vertical composition rule to compose the implementation correctness and algorithm correctness, we obtain a correctness triple for the concrete program c^{con}.

VERTICAL-COMP

$$\frac{S_\forall, S_{\forall\exists} \vdash \{[c^{\text{abs}}] \wedge \mathcal{P}\}\ c^{\text{con}}\ \{r^{\text{con}}.\ \exists\, r^{\text{abs}}.\ [\textbf{ret}\ r^{\text{abs}}] \wedge \mathcal{Q}(r^{\text{con}}, r^{\text{abs}})\} \qquad \{P\}\ c^{\text{abs}}\ \{r^{\text{abs}}.\ Q(r^{\text{abs}})\}}{S_\forall \vdash \{\mathcal{P} \odot P\}\ c^{\text{con}}\ \{r^{\text{con}}.\ \exists\, r^{\text{abs}}.\ \mathcal{Q}(r^{\text{con}}, r^{\text{abs}}) \odot Q(r^{\text{abs}})\}}$$

Standard Hoare logic for relational Hoare logic Conversely, relational proofs may reduce to standard Hoare logic proofs when part of the concrete program does not interact with the abstract side. The CON-FOCUS rule supports this by decomposing $c_1^{\text{con}}; c_2^{\text{con}}$ and verifying c_1^{con} via a contextual standard Hoare triple, so that function specifications from the proof contexts can be used:

CON-FOCUS

$$\frac{S_\forall, S_{\forall\exists} \vdash \{P^{\text{con}}\}\ c_1^{\text{con}}\ \{R^{\text{con}}\} \qquad S_\forall, S_{\forall\exists} \vdash \{\mathcal{F} \wedge R^{\text{con}}\}\ c_2^{\text{con}}\ \{r^{\text{con}}.\ \mathcal{Q}(r^{\text{con}})\}}{S_\forall, S_{\forall\exists} \vdash \{\mathcal{F} \wedge P^{\text{con}}\}\ c_1^{\text{con}}; c_2^{\text{con}}\ \{r^{\text{con}}.\ \mathcal{Q}(r^{\text{con}})\}}$$

Here $\mathcal{F}$ is any assertion independent of the concrete state, so that it is preserved by the execution of c_1^{con}. In Sect. 3, individual concrete statements (e.g., memory stores) are handled by basic relational rules such as CON-STORE. These rules suffice when the concrete side involves primitive operations. For function calls with a clear abstract counterpart, the proof reduces to a sub-refinement goal. However, in the merge sort example, the call to `inssort` reduces to proving its standalone functional correctness, which is naturally expressed as a standard Hoare triple. The CON-FOCUS rule enables this by delegating c_1^{con} to standard Hoare logic with access to the proof contexts. Note that the rules in Fig. 3 remain valid when augmented with proof contexts.

4.2 Formalization

Concrete language. Concrete programs are written in a C-like imperative language Imp with standard constructs (assignment, sequencing, conditionals, loops, and function calls). The behavior of a program $c^{\text{con}} \in \text{Imp}$ is captured by a ternary relation: $(\sigma_1^{\text{con}}, r^{\text{con}}, \sigma_2^{\text{con}})$ means that executing c^{con} from state σ_1^{con} may terminate at state σ_2^{con} with return status $r^{\text{con}} \in \text{Val}_\perp$. Here $\text{Val}_\perp$ is the lifted value type: $r^{\text{con}} = \perp$ when execution encounters no return statement, and $r^{\text{con}} = v$ when a return statement yields value v.

To reason about function calls, we parameterize the semantics with an environment $\chi : \texttt{Fn} \to \mathscr{P}(\Sigma^{\text{con}} \times \text{Val} \times \Sigma^{\text{con}})$, mapping each function name to its input-output behavior. We write $[\![c^{\text{con}}]\!]^\chi$ for the denotation of c^{con} under environment χ. For a sequencing composition $c_1^{\text{con}}; c_2^{\text{con}}$, when c_1^{con} encounters no return ($r^{\text{con}} = \perp$), execution continues with c_2^{con}; when c_1^{con} returns a value, the result propagates directly and c_2^{con} is skipped.

$(\sigma_1^{\text{con}}, r^{\text{con}}, \sigma_2^{\text{con}}) \in [\![c_1^{\text{con}};; c_2^{\text{con}}]\!]^\chi$ if

$$\begin{cases} (\sigma_1^{\text{con}}, \bot, \sigma_0^{\text{con}}) \in [\![c_1^{\text{con}}]\!]^\chi \text{ and } (\sigma_0^{\text{con}}, r^{\text{con}}, \sigma_2^{\text{con}}) \in [\![c_2^{\text{con}}]\!]^\chi \\ (\sigma_1^{\text{con}}, r^{\text{con}}, \sigma_2^{\text{con}}) \in [\![c_1^{\text{con}}]\!]^\chi \text{ and } r^{\text{con}} \neq \bot \end{cases}$$

For function calls, we distinguish two forms:

$$(\sigma_1^{\text{con}}, \bot, \sigma_2^{\text{con}}) \in [\![\mathsf{call}\ f]\!]^\chi \qquad \text{if } (\sigma_1^{\text{con}}, v, \sigma_2^{\text{con}}) \in \chi(f)$$

$$(\sigma_1^{\text{con}}, \bot, \sigma_2^{\text{con}}[x \mapsto v]) \in [\![x := \mathsf{call}\ f]\!]^\chi \qquad \text{if } (\sigma_1^{\text{con}}, v, \sigma_2^{\text{con}}) \in \chi(f)$$

A bare call $\mathsf{call}\ f$ discards the return value, while $x := \mathsf{call}\ f$ stores it in x. Neither form triggers a return in the caller.

Abstract language. Abstract programs are nondeterministic specifications written in a simple functional language (Figs. 1 and 2). An abstract program c^{abs} of return type A over state space Σ^{abs} is given a denotational semantics $[\![c^{\text{abs}}]\!] \subseteq \Sigma^{\text{abs}} \times A \times \Sigma^{\text{abs}}$, where $(\sigma_1^{\text{abs}}, a, \sigma_2^{\text{abs}}) \in [\![c^{\text{abs}}]\!]$ means that from state σ_1^{abs}, the program may return a and transition to σ_2^{abs}. For example, $[\![\mathbf{ret}\ a]\!] = \{(\sigma^{\text{abs}}, a, \sigma^{\text{abs}}) \mid \sigma^{\text{abs}} \in \Sigma^{\text{abs}}\}$. We define the reduction relation $(\sigma_1^{\text{abs}}, c_1^{\text{abs}}) \hookrightarrow (\sigma_2^{\text{abs}}, c_2^{\text{abs}})$ as follows:

$(\sigma_1^{\text{abs}}, c_1^{\text{abs}}) \hookrightarrow (\sigma_2^{\text{abs}}, c_2^{\text{abs}})$ holds if,
for any a and σ_3^{abs}, $(\sigma_2^{\text{abs}}, a, \sigma_3^{\text{abs}}) \in [\![c_2^{\text{abs}}]\!]$ implies $(\sigma_1^{\text{abs}}, a, \sigma_3^{\text{abs}}) \in [\![c_1^{\text{abs}}]\!]$.

Proposition 2. $(\sigma_1^{\text{abs}}, c^{\text{abs}}) \hookrightarrow (\sigma_2^{\text{abs}}, \mathbf{ret}\ a)$ *iff.* $(\sigma_1^{\text{abs}}, a, \sigma_2^{\text{abs}}) \in [\![c^{\text{abs}}]\!]$.

Contextual Triples. The proof contexts $S_\forall$ and $S_{\forall\exists}$ collect standard and relational function specifications, respectively. An environment χ is *valid* with respect to $S_\forall$, written $\text{Valid}(\chi, S_\forall)$, if for every specification in $S_\forall$, any $\overrightarrow{a}$, any σ_1^{con} satisfying $P(\overrightarrow{a})$, and any $(r^{\text{con}}, \sigma_2^{\text{con}})$ such that $(\sigma_1^{\text{con}}, r^{\text{con}}, \sigma_2^{\text{con}}) \in \chi(f)$, σ_2^{con} satisfies $Q(\overrightarrow{a}, r^{\text{con}})$.

We write $\text{RelValid}(\chi, S_{\forall\exists})$ when χ is *relationally valid* with respect to $S_{\forall\exists}$: for every relational specification in $S_{\forall\exists}$, any $\overrightarrow{a}$, any σ_1^{con} and σ_1^{abs} satisfying $\mathcal{P}(\overrightarrow{a})$, and any $(\sigma_1^{\text{con}}, r^{\text{con}}, \sigma_2^{\text{con}}) \in \chi(f)$, there exist r^{abs} and σ_2^{abs} such that $(\sigma_1^{\text{abs}}, r^{\text{abs}}, \sigma_2^{\text{abs}}) \in [\![c^{\text{abs}}]\!]$ and $(\sigma_2^{\text{con}}, \sigma_2^{\text{abs}})$ satisfies $\mathcal{Q}(\overrightarrow{a}, r^{\text{con}}, r^{\text{abs}})$.

Definition 2 (Contextual Hoare Triple). *For proof contexts $S_\forall$, $S_{\forall\exists}$ and a program $c^{\text{con}} \in \text{Imp}$,*

$$S_\forall, S_{\forall\exists} \vdash \{P\}\ c^{\text{con}}\ \{r^{\text{con}}.\, Q(r^{\text{con}})\}$$

holds if, for any χ with $\text{Valid}(\chi, S_\forall)$ and $\text{RelValid}(\chi, S_{\forall\exists})$, any σ_1^{con} satisfying P, and any $(\sigma_2^{\text{con}}, r^{\text{con}})$ such that $(\sigma_1^{\text{con}}, r^{\text{con}}, \sigma_2^{\text{con}}) \in [\![c^{\text{con}}]\!]^\chi$, we have that σ_2^{con} satisfies $Q(r^{\text{con}})$.

Definition 3 (Relational Contextual Hoare Triple). *For proof contexts* $S_\forall$*,* $S_{\forall\exists}$ *and a program* $c^{\mathrm{con}} \in \mathrm{Imp}$*,*

$$S_\forall, S_{\forall\exists} \vdash \{\mathcal{P}\}\ c^{\mathrm{con}}\ \{r^{\mathrm{con}}.\, \mathcal{Q}(r^{\mathrm{con}})\}$$

holds if, for any χ *with* $\mathit{Valid}(\chi, S_\forall)$ *and* $\mathit{RelValid}(\chi, S_{\forall\exists})$*, any* σ_1^{con}*,* σ_1^{abs}*,* c^{abs} *satisfying* $\mathcal{P}$*, and any* $(\sigma_1^{\mathrm{con}}, r^{\mathrm{con}}, \sigma_2^{\mathrm{con}}) \in [\![c^{\mathrm{con}}]\!]^\chi$*, there exist* c_2^{abs} *and* σ_2^{abs} *such that* $(\sigma_1^{\mathrm{abs}}, c^{\mathrm{abs}}) \hookrightarrow (\sigma_2^{\mathrm{abs}}, c_2^{\mathrm{abs}})$ *and* $(\sigma_2^{\mathrm{con}}, \sigma_2^{\mathrm{abs}}, c_2^{\mathrm{abs}})$ *satisfies* $\mathcal{Q}(r^{\mathrm{con}})$*.*

Inference rules. Figure 5 presents additional inference rules for hybrid reasoning. The SIM-BIND rule supports symmetric reasoning by aligning the concrete sequential composition $c_1^{\mathrm{con}}; c_2^{\mathrm{con}}$ with the abstract let-binding let $r = c^{\mathrm{abs}}$ in $K(r)$. The first judgment connects c_1^{con} to the abstract computation c^{abs} that produces a result r; the second relates c_2^{con} to the abstract continuation $K(r)$. The REL-CALL rule allows relational proofs for functions to be reused. This rule can be used for symmetric reasoning for concrete functions by assigning different abstract programs to different function calls through rule SIM-BIND. The HOARE-CALL rule looks up a function's standard specification from $S_\forall$ and produces the corresponding standard Hoare triple. Combined with the CON-FOCUS rule, it enables independent evaluation of function calls within the concrete program. The ABS-CHOICE rules handle nondeterministic abstract programs: to refine **choice**(c_1^{abs}, c_2^{abs}), it suffices to refine either branch.

SIM-BIND

$$\frac{\begin{array}{c} S_\forall, S_{\forall\exists} \vdash \{[c^{\mathrm{abs}}] \wedge \mathcal{P}\}\ c_1^{\mathrm{con}}\ \{\exists r^{\mathrm{abs}}.\, [\mathbf{ret}\ r^{\mathrm{abs}}] \wedge \mathcal{R}(r^{\mathrm{abs}})\} \\ S_\forall, S_{\forall\exists} \vdash \forall r^{\mathrm{abs}}.\, \{[K(r^{\mathrm{abs}})] \wedge \mathcal{R}(r^{\mathrm{abs}})\}\ c_2^{\mathrm{con}}\ \{r^{\mathrm{con}}.\, \mathcal{Q}(r^{\mathrm{con}})\} \end{array}}{S_\forall, S_{\forall\exists} \vdash \{[\mathbf{let}\ r^{\mathrm{abs}} = c^{\mathrm{abs}}\ \mathbf{in}\ K(r^{\mathrm{abs}})] \wedge \mathcal{P}\}\ c_1^{\mathrm{con}}; c_2^{\mathrm{con}}\ \{r^{\mathrm{con}}.\, \mathcal{Q}(r^{\mathrm{con}})\}}$$

REL-CALL

$$\frac{(f : \Pi(\overrightarrow{a} : A).\{[c^{\mathrm{abs}}] \wedge \mathcal{P}(\overrightarrow{a})\}\ \{r^{\mathrm{con}}.\, \exists r^{\mathrm{abs}}.\, [\mathbf{ret}\ r^{\mathrm{abs}}] \wedge \mathcal{Q}(\overrightarrow{a}, r^{\mathrm{con}}, r^{\mathrm{abs}})\}) \in S_{\forall\exists}}{S_\forall, S_{\forall\exists} \vdash \{[c^{\mathrm{abs}}] \wedge \mathcal{P}(\overrightarrow{a})\}\ \mathsf{call}\ f\ \{r^{\mathrm{con}}.\, \exists r^{\mathrm{abs}}.\, [\mathbf{ret}\ r^{\mathrm{abs}}] \wedge \mathcal{Q}(\overrightarrow{a}, r^{\mathrm{con}}, r^{\mathrm{abs}})\}}$$

HOARE-CALL

$$\frac{f : \Pi(\overrightarrow{a} : A).\{P(\overrightarrow{a})\}\{r^{\mathrm{con}}.\, Q(\overrightarrow{a}, r^{\mathrm{con}})\} \in S_\forall}{S_\forall, S_{\forall\exists} \vdash \{P(\overrightarrow{a})\}\ \mathsf{call}\ f\ \{r^{\mathrm{con}}.\, Q(\overrightarrow{a}, r^{\mathrm{con}})\}}$$

ABS-CHOICE-L

$$\frac{\{[c_1^{\mathrm{abs}}] \wedge \mathcal{P}\}\ c^{\mathrm{con}}\ \{r^{\mathrm{con}}.\, \mathcal{Q}(r^{\mathrm{con}})\}}{\{[\mathbf{choice}(c_1^{\mathrm{abs}},\ c_2^{\mathrm{abs}})] \wedge \mathcal{P}\}\ c^{\mathrm{con}}\ \{r^{\mathrm{con}}.\, \mathcal{Q}(r^{\mathrm{con}})\}}$$

ABS-CHOICE-R

$$\frac{\{[c_2^{\mathrm{abs}}] \wedge \mathcal{P}\}\ c^{\mathrm{con}}\ \{r^{\mathrm{con}}.\, \mathcal{Q}(r^{\mathrm{con}})\}}{\{[\mathbf{choice}(c_1^{\mathrm{abs}},\ c_2^{\mathrm{abs}})] \wedge \mathcal{P}\}\ c^{\mathrm{con}}\ \{r^{\mathrm{con}}.\, \mathcal{Q}(r^{\mathrm{con}})\}}$$

Fig. 5. More Inference Rules for Hybrid Reasoning

5 Case Study: Hybrid Sorting

In this section, we apply our approach to a recursive implementation of a hybrid sorting algorithm depicted in Fig. 2. We explain the overall proof strategy and demonstrate how relational and standard Hoare logics can be combined to efficiently verify implementation correctness.

The concrete program takes a singly linked list, and if the list contains fewer than 8 elements, it employs an insertion sort. For input lists with 8 or more elements, this program proceeds with a merge sort approach. In contrast, the abstract program nondeterministically selects an external sorting, which is agnostic regarding the specific sorting mechanics applied, and merge sort. Following our approach, we formalize the implementation correctness using the following relational Hoare triple:

$$\begin{array}{l}\{[\texttt{mergesort}_A(l_x)] \land \mathsf{storesll}(\mathsf{x}, l_x)\} \\ \quad \texttt{mergesort}(\mathsf{x}) \\ \{r^{\mathrm{con}}.\, \exists l_r.\, [\mathbf{ret}\ l_r] \land \mathsf{storesll}(r^{\mathrm{con}}, l_r)\}\end{array} \tag{4}$$

Here, $\mathsf{storesll}(\mathsf{x}, l_x)$ asserts that variable x stores a singly linked list l_x. This triple states that if the abstract program is about to sort the same list l_x stored at x, then once the concrete program terminates with return value r^{con}, there exists a list l_r stored at r^{con} such that the abstract program can produce exactly l_r.

To prove this relational Hoare triple, we first exploit a clear alignment between the concrete and abstract programs. In particular, the abstract program is structured as a nondeterministic choice. We must angelically select the branch in the abstract program that aligns with the if-branching of the concrete program. Specifically, when the input list l_x has a length of at least 8, we can apply rule ABS-CHOICE-R to let the abstract program angelically choose the merge sort branch to mirror the concrete merge sort steps. More concretely, when the concrete statement $\texttt{split}(\mathsf{x}, \&\mathsf{p}, \&\mathsf{q})$ splits the input list, the abstract program $\texttt{split}_A(l_x, l_p, l_q)$ can likewise simulate this splitting. When the concrete statement $\texttt{mergesort}(\mathsf{p})$ performs a merge sort on the split sublist, the abstract program $\texttt{mergesort}_A(l_p)$ can simulate the merge sort. Finally, when the concrete statement $\texttt{merge}(\mathsf{p}, \mathsf{q})$ merges the respective sub-results, the abstract program $\texttt{merge}_A(l_p, l_q)$ can simulate this same merge operation. Then, we can apply rules SIM-BIND and REL-CALL to decompose the proof into several small refinements, such as proving that $\texttt{split}(\mathsf{x}, \&\mathsf{p}, \&\mathsf{q})$ refines $\texttt{split}_A(l_x, l_p, l_q)$:

$$\begin{array}{l}\{[\texttt{split}_A(l_x, l_p, l_q)] \land \mathsf{storesll}(\mathsf{x}, l_x) * \mathsf{storesll}(\mathsf{p}, l_p) * \mathsf{storesll}(\mathsf{q}, l_q)\} \\ \quad \texttt{split}(\mathsf{x}, \&\mathsf{p}, \&\mathsf{q}) \\ \{\exists l'_x, l'_p, l'_q.\, [\mathbf{ret}\ (l'_x, l'_p, l'_q)] \land \mathsf{storesll}(\mathsf{x}, l'_x) * \mathsf{storesll}(\mathsf{p}, l'_p) * \mathsf{storesll}(\mathsf{q}, l'_q)\}\end{array}$$

Next, we consider the scenario when the input list l_x is shorter than eight elements, in which case the concrete program selects insertion sort. For this case, we apply rule ABS-CHOICE-L to guide the abstract program to employ the external sort. Because this external sort behaves as a black box (any sorted result is valid), we independently evaluate the abstract program and the concrete program. For the abstract program, we apply rule ABS-PURE to reduce $\texttt{extsort}_A(l_x)$ to **ret** l_r where l_r is a sorted permutation of l_x. For the concrete program, we apply rules CON-FOCUS and HOARE-CALL to evaluate the call statement $\texttt{inssort}(\mathsf{x})$. This reduces to proving the insertion sort's functional correctness as described by the following Hoare triple:

$$\{\mathsf{storesll}(\mathsf{x}, l_x)\}\ \texttt{inssort}(\mathsf{x})\ \{r^{\text{con}}.\mathsf{permutation}(l_x, l_r) \wedge \mathsf{sorted}(l_r) \wedge \mathsf{storesll}(r^{\text{con}}, l_r)\}$$

This demonstrates how the hybrid approach delegates part of the relational proof to standard Hoare logic when the concrete program has no abstract counterpart.

Having verified the implementation, we must now establish the algorithm correctness of the abstract program and then compose the two proofs. The specification for the abstract program is:

$$\{\mathsf{True}\}\ \texttt{mergesort}_A(l_x)\ \{l_r.\,\mathsf{permutation}(l_x, l_r) \wedge \mathsf{sorted}(l_r)\}$$

Composing this with implementation correctness via rule VERTICAL-COMP , we derive the functional correctness of the concrete program:

$$\begin{array}{l}\{\mathsf{storesll}(\mathsf{x}, l_x)\} \\ \quad \texttt{mergesort}(\mathsf{x}) \\ \{r^{\text{con}}.\,\exists l_r.\,\mathsf{permutation}(l_x, l_r) \wedge \mathsf{sorted}(l_r) \wedge \mathsf{storesll}(r^{\text{con}}, l_r)\}\end{array}$$

In summary, this example illustrates how our hybrid reasoning approach can flexibly employ relational Hoare logic and standard Hoare logic to prove that the concrete program implements the abstract specification for complex algorithms.

6 Related Work

Here, we discuss related work, including approaches for verifying functional correctness and frameworks for relational Hoare logic.

Functional Correctness for Complex Programs. Wang et al. [40] developed a graph library in Rocq. Subsequently, Mohan et al. [31] extended this library to support undirected graphs. Their line of work directly proves the functional correctness of C programs that manipulate graph data structures using standard Hoare logic. In contrast, this paper proves the functional correctness of imperative programs through implementation correctness and algorithm correctness. Precisely, our approach proves that a recursive DFS implementation refines an iterative abstract description, and the algorithm correctness proof can be reused for different concrete implementations. During the verification, our work builds upon their fundamental definitions of graphs, enabling the algorithm correctness proof to leverage existing theorems in graph theory. Cao et al. [10] proved the functional correctness of an imperative insertion function for BSTs with the two-layer method [3]. Meanwhile, LAProof [22] offers a specialized library for verifying linear algebra programs, featuring case studies such as matrix multiplication. However, they both employ standard (separation) Hoare logic to establish the implementation correctness. In this paper, we emphasize that such an implementation correctness proof is essentially relational since it connects the abstract specification of tree insertion with its concrete imperative counterpart. We thus prove correctness via relational Hoare logic, offering a more intuitive reasoning pattern.

Building on the Isabelle Refinement Framework [25], Lammich and Neumann [24] proposed a layered method to prove the functional correctness of DFS-based abstract functional algorithms. With Imperative HOL [9], this framework enables one to first verify the correctness of algorithm descriptions, which are purely functional, and then refine that abstract description step by step. The final result is an executable imperative program. While we both rely on refinement to prove implementation correctness, we employ relational Hoare triples and support abstract programs with nondeterminism and state.

Relational Hoare Logic Frameworks. Relational Hoare logic, introduced by Benton [7], extends traditional Hoare logic to relate two programs. Many relational verification frameworks have been proposed to verify relational properties, including equivalence [4,23,30,41,43] and refinement [5,12]. This paper focuses on verifying program refinement, which can be formally captured via simulation relations. For concurrent program verification, Liang and Feng [26] and Turon et al. [37] proposed program-as-resource assertions and relational Hoare triples based on powerful ghost states [39]. Follow-up research includes a series of works [27–29] and another series [14,33,34] based on the Iris framework [20,21]. Among existing relational logics, ReLoC [15] is especially closely related to our work in its support for refinement reasoning. Although program-as-resource assertions were originally designed for concurrent settings, we adopt them for verifying sequential programs. This specialization enables several advantages. First, it allows us to use denotational semantics for sequential programs, avoiding the complexity of step-indexed models. Second, program-as-resource assertions allow us to leverage powerful reasoning principles, such as the REL-WH rule, to address nontrivial refinements between structurally dissimilar programs. At the same time, general frameworks like Iris provide benefits that are orthogonal to our goals. For example, Timany et al. [35] proposed a well-bracketed Hoare logic based on Iris, for reasoning about well-bracketed sequential programs, where each function call must return before its caller can resume execution.

Aguirre et al. proposed a unary higher-order logic (UHOL) and a relational High-order logic (RHOL) [1] for reasoning about relational properties of a simply typed λ-calculus. RHOL provides inference rule [UHOL-L] to allow RHOL proofs to fall back to UHOL reasoning. This rule serves a role similar to the focusing rule CON-FOCUS in this paper, enabling independent evaluation on one side. While RHOL inherits the type-directed structure of relational refinement type systems and aims to support more automation, this paper emphasizes focusing and alignment rules (e.g., Con-Focus, Sim-Bind) that allow provers to flexibly switch between relational and standard Hoare reasoning within a single proof.

The work of Gladshtein et al. [16] focuses on verifying the correctness of operations where identical or sparse data are stored in arrays through compression or other space-efficient representations. Such implementations often involve multiple loops with intricate invariants. The authors argue that relational program logics are well-suited to address these verification tasks, an assessment that aligns with our own perspective. Relational Hoare logic can offer an intuitive and convenient framework for proving implementation correctness. However, they introduce the framework LGTM (Logic for Graceful Tensor Manipulation), which dynamically determines the number k of traces to compare, allowing k to depend on program variables, while we rely on relational Hoare triples.

Dickerson et al. [13] propose RHLE, a logic dedicated to verifying $\forall\exists$ relational properties. A central feature of their framework is the proof context $S_\exists$ which leverages function specifications and ghost variables to ensure that abstract programs achieve some existential behaviors. By combining $S_\exists$ with the standard proof context $S_\forall$ for concrete programs, they can derive $\forall\exists$ Hoare judgments. In contrast, our work does not define a $\exists$ proof context for abstract programs. We employ the relational proof context $S_{\forall\exists}$ that relates the concrete program's functions to abstract programs.

Several works have proposed automated approaches for relational verification. Unno et al. [38] present a constraint-based approach to relational verification that supports a variety of relational properties, including refinement. Beutner and Finkbeiner [8] propose an automated method for verifying $\forall^*\exists^*$ hyperproperties, and Itzhaky et al. [19] reduce hyperproperty verification to the satisfiability of constrained Horn clauses (CHCs). In this paper, we concentrate on interactive verification of refinement properties. Nonetheless, techniques developed in those works may complement our method in future integration efforts.

7 Conclusion and Future Work

In this paper, we propose a hybrid reasoning method that combines relational and standard Hoare logic for verifying sequential programs. We show that employing relational Hoare logic for implementation correctness is advantageous: it enables more intuitive loop invariants and allows us to leverage algorithm correctness to reduce proof complexity during implementation verification. A key feature of our approach is the Vertical-Comp rule, which supports modular verification by cleanly separating verification. Implementation correctness is established relationally, while algorithm correctness is proven once using standard Hoare logic. This compositional structure significantly reduces proof duplication and facilitates reuse across implementations.

In this work, we focus on partial correctness; that is, we do not address reasoning about nontermination. One possible indirect approach to handling total correctness is to enrich the abstract program state with time credits and prove that the program must terminate within the given bounds. If the time budget reaches zero, the program produces an error. While this technique can be encoded in our framework, a more principled and general treatment of nontermination remains an important direction for future work. Another promising direction is to automate the verification of implementation correctness, for instance, through novel tactics and symbolic execution. Such automation can reduce the proof burden and make our approach more accessible for large-scale verification projects. Besides, we aim to support richer program features, such as function pointers, to further demonstrate both the flexibility and scalability of the method. Ultimately, we hope that our hybrid approach will serve as a robust foundation for broadly applicable verification frameworks.

References

1. Aguirre, A., Barthe, G., Gaboardi, M., Garg, D., Strub, P.: A relational logic for higher-order programs. Proc. ACM Program. Lang. **1**(ICFP), 1–29 (2017). https://doi.org/10.1145/3110265
2. Appel, A.W.: Verified functional algorithms, vol. 3 (2020). https://softwarefoundations.cis.upenn.edu/vfa-current/index.html
3. Appel, A.W.: Coq's vibrant ecosystem for verification engineering (invited talk). In: Popescu, A., Zdancewic, S. (eds.) CPP '22: 11th ACM SIGPLAN International Conference on Certified Programs and Proofs, Philadelphia, PA, USA, 17–18 January 2022, pp. 2–11. ACM (2022).https://doi.org/10.1145/3497775.3503951
4. Banerjee, A., Nagasamudram, R., Naumann, D.A., Nikouei, M.: A relational program logic with data abstraction and dynamic framing. ACM Trans. Program. Lang. Syst. **44**(4), 1–136 (2022). https://doi.org/10.1145/3551497
5. Barthe, G., Crespo, J.M., Kunz, C.: Beyond 2-safety: asymmetric product programs for relational program verification. In: Artëmov, S.N., Nerode, A. (eds.) Logical Foundations of Computer Science, International Symposium, LFCS 2013, San Diego, CA, USA, 6–8 January 2013, Proceedings, Lecture Notes in Computer Science, vol. 7734, pp. 29–43. Springer (2013).https://doi.org/10.1007/978-3-642-35722-0_3
6. Beckert, B., Ulbrich, M.: Trends in relational program verification. In: Müller, P., Schaefer, I. (eds.) Principled Software Development - Essays Dedicated to Arnd Poetzsch-Heffter on the Occasion of his 60th Birthday, pp. 41–58. Springer (2018). https://doi.org/10.1007/978-3-319-98047-8_3
7. Benton, N.: Simple relational correctness proofs for static analyses and program transformations. In: Jones, N.D., Leroy, X. (eds.) Proceedings of the 31st ACM SIGPLAN-SIGACT Symposium on Principles of Programming Languages, POPL 2004, Venice, Italy, 14–16 January 2004, pp. 14–25. ACM (2004). https://doi.org/10.1145/964001.964003
8. Beutner, R., Finkbeiner, B.: Software verification of hyperproperties beyond k-safety. In: Shoham, S., Vizel, Y. (eds.) Computer Aided Verification - 34th International Conference, CAV 2022, Haifa, Israel, August 7-10, 2022, Proceedings, Part I. Lecture Notes in Computer Science, vol. 13371, pp. 341–362. Springer (2022). https://doi.org/10.1007/978-3-031-13185-1_17
9. Bulwahn, L., Krauss, A., Haftmann, F., Erkök, L., Matthews, J.: Imperative functional programming with Isabelle/HOL. In: Mohamed, O.A., Muñoz, C., Tahar, S. (eds.) TPHOLs 2008. LNCS, vol. 5170, pp. 134–149. Springer, Heidelberg (2008). https://doi.org/10.1007/978-3-540-71067-7_14

10. Cao, Q., Wang, S., Hobor, A., Appel, A.W.: Proof pearl: magic wand as frame. arXiv preprint: arXiv:1909.08789 (2019)
11. Chen, R., Cohen, C., Levy, J.J., Merz, S., Thery, L.: Formal proofs of Tarjan's algorithm in why3. coq, and Isabelle (2018)
12. Clochard, M., Marché, C., Paskevich, A.: Deductive verification with ghost monitors. Proc. ACM Program. Lang. **4**(POPL), 1–26 (2020). https://doi.org/10.1145/3371070
13. Dickerson, R., Ye, Q., Zhang, M.K., Delaware, B.: RHLE: modular deductive verification of relational ∀ ∃ properties. In: Sergey, I. (ed.) Programming Languages and Systems - 20th Asian Symposium, APLAS 2022, Auckland, New Zealand, 5 December 2022, Proceedings. Lecture Notes in Computer Science, vol. 13658, pp. 67–87. Springer (2022). https://doi.org/10.1007/978-3-031-21037-2_4
14. Frumin, D., Krebbers, R., Birkedal, L.: ReLoC: a mechanised relational logic for fine-grained concurrency. In: Dawar, A., Grädel, E. (eds.) Proceedings of the 33rd Annual ACM/IEEE Symposium on Logic in Computer Science, LICS 2018, Oxford, UK, 09–12 July 2018, pp. 442–451. ACM (2018). https://doi.org/10.1145/3209108.3209174
15. Frumin, D., Krebbers, R., Birkedal, L.: ReLoC reloaded: a mechanized relational logic for fine-grained concurrency and logical atomicity. CoRR abs/2006.13635 (2020). https://arxiv.org/abs/2006.13635
16. Gladshtein, V., Zhao, Q., Ahrens, W., Amarasinghe, S.P., Sergey, I.: Mechanised hypersafety proofs about structured data. Proc. ACM Program. Lang. **8**, 647–670 (2024). https://doi.org/10.1145/3656403 PLDI
17. Hoare, C.A.R.: An axiomatic basis for computer programming. Commun. ACM **12**(10), 576–580 (1969). https://doi.org/10.1145/363235.363259
18. Huet, G.: The zipper. J. Funct. Program. **7**(5), 549–554 (1997). https://doi.org/10.1017/S0956796897002864
19. Itzhaky, S., Shoham, S., Vizel, Y.: Hyperproperty verification as CHC satisfiability. In: Weirich, S. (ed.) Programming Languages and Systems - 33rd European Symposium on Programming, ESOP 2024, Held as Part of the European Joint Conferences on Theory and Practice of Software, ETAPS 2024, Luxembourg City, Luxembourg, 6–11 April 2024, Proceedings, Part II. Lecture Notes in Computer Science, vol. 14577, pp. 212–241. Springer (2024). https://doi.org/10.1007/978-3-031-57267-8_9
20. Jung, R., Krebbers, R., Jourdan, J., Bizjak, A., Birkedal, L., Dreyer, D.: Iris from the ground up: a modular foundation for higher-order concurrent separation logic. J. Funct. Program. **28**, e20 (2018). https://doi.org/10.1017/S0956796818000151
21. Jung, R., et al.: Iris: monoids and invariants as an orthogonal basis for concurrent reasoning. In: Rajamani, S.K., Walker, D. (eds.) Proceedings of the 42nd Annual ACM SIGPLAN-SIGACT Symposium on Principles of Programming Languages, POPL 2015, Mumbai, India, 15–17 January 2015, pp. 637–650. ACM (2015). https://doi.org/10.1145/2676726.2676980
22. Kellison, A.E., Appel, A.W., Tekriwal, M., Bindel, D.: LAProof: a library of formal proofs of accuracy and correctness for linear algebra programs. In: 2023 IEEE 30th Symposium on Computer Arithmetic (ARITH), pp. 36–43 (2023). https://doi.org/10.1109/ARITH58626.2023.00021
23. Kundu, S., Tatlock, Z., Lerner, S.: Proving optimizations correct using parameterized program equivalence. In: Hind, M., Diwan, A. (eds.) Proceedings of the 2009 ACM SIGPLAN Conference on Programming Language Design and Implementation, PLDI 2009, Dublin, Ireland, 15–21 June 2009, pp. 327–337. ACM (2009). https://doi.org/10.1145/1542476.1542513

24. Lammich, P., Neumann, R.: A framework for verifying depth-first search algorithms. In: Proceedings of the 2015 Conference on Certified Programs and Proofs, pp. 137–146 (2015)
25. Lammich, P., Tuerk, T.: Applying data refinement for monadic programs to Hopcroft's algorithm. In: International Conference on Interactive Theorem Proving, pp. 166–182. Springer (2012)
26. Liang, H., Feng, X.: Modular verification of linearizability with non-fixed linearization points. In: Boehm, H., Flanagan, C. (eds.) ACM SIGPLAN Conference on Programming Language Design and Implementation, PLDI '13, Seattle, WA, USA, 16–19 June 2013, pp. 459–470. ACM (2013). https://doi.org/10.1145/2491956.2462189
27. Liang, H., Feng, X.: A program logic for concurrent objects under fair scheduling. In: Bodík, R., Majumdar, R. (eds.) Proceedings of the 43rd Annual ACM SIGPLAN-SIGACT Symposium on Principles of Programming Languages, POPL 2016, St. Petersburg, FL, USA, 20–22 January 2016, pp. 385–399. ACM (2016). https://doi.org/10.1145/2837614.2837635
28. Liang, H., Feng, X.: Progress of concurrent objects with partial methods. Proc. ACM Program. Lang. **2**(POPL), 1–31 (2018). https://doi.org/10.1145/3158108
29. Liang, H., Feng, X., Shao, Z.: Compositional verification of termination-preserving refinement of concurrent programs. In: Henzinger, T.A., Miller, D. (eds.) Joint Meeting of the Twenty-Third EACSL Annual Conference on Computer Science Logic (CSL) and the Twenty-Ninth Annual ACM/IEEE Symposium on Logic in Computer Science (LICS), CSL-LICS '14, Vienna, Austria, 14–18 July 2014, pp. 1–10. ACM (2014). https://doi.org/10.1145/2603088.2603123
30. Maillard, K., Hritcu, C., Rivas, E., Muylder, A.V.: The next 700 relational program logics. Proc. ACM Program. Lang. **4**(POPL), 1–33 (2020). https://doi.org/10.1145/3371072
31. Mohan, A., Leow, W.X., Hobor, A.: Functional correctness of C implementations of Dijkstra's, Kruskal's, and prim's algorithms. In: Silva, A., Leino, K.R.M. (eds.) Computer Aided Verification - 33rd International Conference, CAV 2021, Virtual Event, 20–23 July 2021, Proceedings, Part II. Lecture Notes in Computer Science, vol. 12760, pp. 801–826. Springer (2021). https://doi.org/10.1007/978-3-030-81688-9_37
32. Reynolds, J.C.: Separation logic: a logic for shared mutable data structures. In: 17th IEEE Symposium on Logic in Computer Science (LICS 2002), 22–25 July 2002, Copenhagen, Denmark, Proceedings, pp. 55–74. IEEE Computer Society (2002). https://doi.org/10.1109/LICS.2002.1029817
33. Spies, S., et al.: Transfinite iris: resolving an existential dilemma of step-indexed separation logic. In: Proceedings of the 42nd ACM SIGPLAN International Conference on Programming Language Design and Implementation, PLDI 2021, pp. 80–95. Association for Computing Machinery, New York (2021). https://doi.org/10.1145/3453483.3454031
34. Tassarotti, J., Jung, R., Harper, R.: A higher-order logic for concurrent termination-preserving refinement. In: Yang, H. (ed.) Programming Languages and Systems - 26th European Symposium on Programming, ESOP 2017, Held as Part of the European Joint Conferences on Theory and Practice of Software, ETAPS 2017, Uppsala, Sweden, 22–29 April 2017, Proceedings. Lecture Notes in Computer Science, vol. 10201, pp. 909–936. Springer (2017). https://doi.org/10.1007/978-3-662-54434-1_34
35. Timany, A., Guéneau, A., Birkedal, L.: The logical essence of well-bracketed control flow. Proc. ACM Program. Lang. **8**(POPL), 575–603 (2024). https://doi.org/10.1145/3632862

36. Turon, A., Dreyer, D., Birkedal, L.: Unifying refinement and Hoare-style reasoning in a logic for higher-order concurrency. In: Proceedings of the 18th ACM SIGPLAN International Conference on Functional Programming, ICFP '13, pp. 377–390. Association for Computing Machinery, New York (2013). https://doi.org/10.1145/2500365.2500600
37. Turon, A.J., Thamsborg, J., Ahmed, A., Birkedal, L., Dreyer, D.: Logical relations for fine-grained concurrency. In: Giacobazzi, R., Cousot, R. (eds.) The 40th Annual ACM SIGPLAN-SIGACT Symposium on Principles of Programming Languages, POPL '13, Rome, Italy - 23–25 January 2013, pp. 343–356. ACM (2013). https://doi.org/10.1145/2429069.2429111
38. Unno, H., Terauchi, T., Koskinen, E.: Constraint-based relational verification. In: Silva, A., Leino, K.R.M. (eds.) CAV 2021. LNCS, vol. 12759, pp. 742–766. Springer, Cham (2021). https://doi.org/10.1007/978-3-030-81685-8_35
39. Vafeiadis, V.: Modular fine-grained concurrency verification. Ph.D. thesis, University of Cambridge, UK (2008). https://ethos.bl.uk/OrderDetails.do?uin=uk.bl.ethos.612221
40. Wang, S., Cao, Q., Mohan, A., Hobor, A.: Certifying graph-manipulating C programs via localizations within data structures. Proc. ACM Program. Lang. **3**(OOPSLA), 1–30 (2019). https://doi.org/10.1145/3360597
41. Wang, Y., Dillig, I., Lahiri, S.K., Cook, W.R.: Verifying equivalence of database-driven applications. Proc. ACM Program. Lang. **2**(POPL), 1–29 (2018). https://doi.org/10.1145/3158144
42. Wu, S., Wu, X., Yang, C., Cao, Q.: Intuitive verification of sequential programs using hybrid reasoning: case studies (2026). https://doi.org/10.5281/zenodo.19787359
43. Yang, H.: Relational separation logic. Theor. Comput. Sci. **375**(1–3), 308–334 (2007). https://doi.org/10.1016/J.TCS.2006.12.036

Incremental Reinforcement Learning with Temporally Dependent Goals

Yi Yang[1], Shufang Zhu[2], Giuseppe De Giacomo[3,4], Qin Zhao[1], Xinchao Li[1], and Dongdong An[1(✉)]

[1] Shanghai Normal University, Shanghai, China
{1000468002,1000590412}@smail.shnu.edu.cn,
{q_zhao,andongdong}@shnu.edu.cn
[2] University of Liverpool, Liverpool, UK
shufang.zhu@liverpool.ac.uk
[3] University of Oxford, Oxford, UK
giuseppe.degiacomo@cs.ox.ac.uk
[4] Sapienza University of Rome, Rome, Italy

Abstract. Reinforcement Learning (RL) has shown significant success in sequential decision making for single (reachability) goals, but many practical tasks require pursing a series of goals with temporal dependencies among them. We introduce an *incremental RL* framework that leverages Linear Temporal Logic on finite traces (LTL_f) specifications to express such goals. Our framework is formalized through Clocked Goal-Augmented Markov Decision Process (MDP), in which each goal corresponds to an atomic proposition, and the objective is to learn an optimal policy that satisfies LTL_f formulas constructed from these propositions. We propose solution techniques by training a Gated Recurrent Unit (GRU)-based RL network to learn policies for a set of single goals and employ DFA-based reward machines to guide their composition toward temporally-dependent goals. This technique enables incremental RL, allowing further temporally dependent goals and potential safety constraints (between ongoing and newly introduced ones) to arrive during execution without retraining the base network. Empirical evaluation on benchmark environments shows that under our approach, the success rate stablizes and converges empirically on incrementally specified temporally dependent goals, demonstrating stable and efficient learning.

Keywords: Reinforcement Learning · Incremental RL · Temporally Dependent Goals

1 Introduction

Reinforcement Learning (RL) has achieved remarkable advances in sequential decision making [1], with methods successfully applied to a wide range of complex tasks in domains such as games [25,29], robotics [16], and autonomous driving [15]. These successes highlight the strength of RL in producing optimal policies for well-defined single (reachability) goals. However, in contrast

G. De Giacomo et al. (Eds.): TASE 2026, LNCS 16697, pp. 420–438, 2027.
https://doi.org/10.1007/978-3-032-30693-7_27

to human intelligence, which develops skills for achieving individual goals and flexibly reuses them across more complex tasks, standard RL methods remain largely limited to single objectives. Humans typically solve complex problems by composing previously learned skills, often involving multiple goals with temporal dependencies, such as "deliver mail *after* getting it", which classical RL frameworks do not naturally support.

Research directions that have been explored to address this gap are goal-conditioned RL [18] and multi-task RL [23,27], with the idea to train a single policy network that is able to handle multiple goals by conditioning its input on a representation of the desired goal. In this way, the same network can generate behaviors toward different targets, improving flexibility compared to standard RL [20]. However, goal-conditioned RL typically treats goals as independent and static such that the network is trained to reach any of the goals it is conditioned on, but it does not reason about temporal dependencies or logical relations among them.

Another line of work studies RL with goals expressed as logic specifications [2,23], such as Linear Temporal Logic (LTL) [21], to capture logical relations along a state trajectory [10,13,23,30]. For example, [12] compile LTL into reward machines to structure the learning process, while [11] use automata-based shaping to improve sample efficiency. More recently, [22] proposed combining goal-conditioned RL with temporal logic objectives by augmenting the conditioning signal with LTL specifications.

While these approaches show that RL can be guided to satisfy logical formulas, they typically focus on producing a state trajectory that satisfies a given specification. Consequently, policy learning is often tightly related to the logical specification itself: policies are trained to satisfy a specific temporal logic formula, or a fixed set of formulas [14,26,28,33]. As a result, when a new, previously unseen formula arrives, the agent usually requires retraining or fine-tuning to adapt to the new trajectory-level constraints.

In this paper, we focus on a different perspective aimed at enabling *incremental* RL [19,32]. Rather than enforcing LTL satisfaction at the trajectory level, we distinguish between high-level goal progression and low-level action execution along the trajectory. For instance, the LTL formula $\mathsf{X}^!(\texttt{mail})$ is interpreted as *make mail pickup the next goal to pursue*, rather than as *pickup mail at the next timestep*. Our framework is formalized through Clocked Goal-Augmented Markov Decision Process (MDP), an extension of the goal-augmented MDP that introduces a clock mechanism to separate high-level goal progression from low-level action execution. In the clocked goal-augmented MDP, each single goal corresponds to an atomic proposition, and temporally dependent goals are expressed as LTL_f formulas over these propositions. The objective is to learn an optimal policy such that the low-level action execution corresponds to a high-level goal progression trace satisfying the LTL_f formula. This enables the framework to handle incremental goal arrivals: new temporally dependent goals may arrive during execution, requiring the policy to continue making progress on ongoing goals while incorporating the new ones.

Building on this framework, we develop a solution technique that combines model-based and learning-based components. First, we train a Gated Recurrent Unit (GRU)-based RL network once to learn policies for a set of single goals. The resulting policies, represented within a single network, are reusable building blocks for composing to achieve complex temporally dependent goals. Training such multi-goal networks is a common approach in multi-task RL and is also used to improve the generalization ability of RL [7,9,24]. At execution, temporally dependent goals in LTL_f are compiled into Deterministic Finite Automata (DFAs) and encoded as reward machines, which guides the composition of single-goal policies toward temporally dependent objectives. This separation of temporal progress from single-goal policy learning enables incremental RL [19,32]. Reward machines naturally store goal progress, allowing completion of remaining goals while incorporating new arrived temporally dependent goals. To address conflicts between ongoing and newly introduced ones, we further employ DFA-based monitors that are built from LTL_f safety constraints. In our approach, training over single goals is performed only once, while incremental RL is realized through compositional execution that handles new temporally dependent goals on the fly.

Our empirical evaluation was conducted in GridWorld and Zone benchmark environment to assess the effectiveness of the proposed incremental RL framework. First, we compared GRU-based RL networks with non-GRU baselines. The results showed that the GRU-based model achieved significantly higher success rates and reached nearly 100% success on temporally dependent goals, demonstrating the effectiveness in handling temporally dependencies. We then evaluated the framework in scenarios where new goals with safety constraints were introduced during the execution of ongoing goals. In these settings, the framework again achieved nearly 100% success in completing both ongoing and newly introduced goals without violating safety constraints. Evaluations on accumulative rewards for both scenarios further confirm stable convergence.

2 Preliminaries

LTL_f, or Linear Temporal Logic on finite traces, is a specification language to express temporal properties for finite and non-empty traces [6]. LTL_f shares the syntax with LTL [21], but is interpreted over finite non-empty traces. Given a set of atoms AP, the LTL_f formulas over AP are generated as follows:

$$\varphi ::= p \mid \neg\varphi \mid \varphi_1 \wedge \varphi_2 \mid \mathsf{X}^!\varphi \mid \varphi_1 \,\mathsf{U}\, \varphi_2.$$

$p \in AP$ is an *atom*, $\mathsf{X}^!$ (*Next*), and U (*Until*) are temporal operators. We use standard Boolean abbreviations such as $\vee$ (or) and $\supset$ (implies), *tt* (true) and *ff* (false). Moreover, we define the following abbreviations *Weak Next* $\mathsf{X}\varphi \equiv \neg\mathsf{X}^!\neg\varphi$, *Eventually* $\mathsf{F}\varphi \equiv tt \,\mathsf{U}\, \varphi$, *Always* $\mathsf{G}\varphi \equiv \neg\mathsf{F}\neg\varphi$, and *Release* $\varphi_1 \,\mathsf{R}\, \varphi_2 \equiv (\varphi_2 \,\mathsf{U}\, (\varphi_1 \wedge \varphi_2)) \vee \mathsf{G}\varphi_2$. $\text{LTL}_f(AP)$ denotes the set of formulas produced by the above grammar over AP.

LTL$_f$ formulas are interpreted over finite non-empty traces π over the alphabet $\Sigma = 2^{AP}$, i.e., the alphabet consisting of the propositional interpretations of the atoms. Thus, for $i \leq \texttt{lst}(\pi)$, we have that $\pi[i] \in 2^{AP}$ is the i-th interpretation of π and $\pi[i:j]$ $(j \geq i)$ is the fragment of π from instant i up to instant j. We also denote by $\pi[i:-]$ the suffix of π starting from i. An LTL$_f$ formula φ *holds* at instant i of a trace π is defined inductively on the structure of φ as:

- $\pi, i \models p$ iff $p \in \pi_i$;
- $\pi, i \models \neg\varphi$ iff $\pi, i \not\models \varphi$;
- $\pi, i \models \varphi_1 \wedge \varphi_2$ iff $\pi, i \models \varphi_1$ and $\pi, i \models \varphi_2$;
- $\pi, i \models \mathsf{X}^!\varphi$ iff $i < \texttt{lst}(\pi)$ and $\pi, i+1 \models \varphi$;
- $\pi, i \models \varphi_1 \mathsf{U} \varphi_2$ iff $\exists j$ such that $i \leq j \leq \texttt{lst}(\pi)$ and $\pi, j \models \varphi_2$, and $\forall k, i \leq k < j$ we have that $\pi, k \models \varphi_1$.

We say that π *satisfies* φ, written as $\pi \models \varphi$, if $\pi, 0 \models \varphi$. It is also shown in [6], for every LTL$_f$ formula φ, one can construct a Deterministic Finite Automaton (DFA) $Aut_\varphi = (2^{AP}, \mathcal{Q}, q_0, \delta, acc)$, where 2^{AP} is a finite alphabet, $\mathcal{Q}$ is a finite set of states, $q_0 \in \mathcal{Q}$ is the initial state, $\delta : \mathcal{Q} \times 2^{AP} \to \mathcal{Q}$ is the transition function, and $acc \subset \mathcal{Q}$ is the set of accepting states, such that for every trace π we have $\pi \models \varphi$ iff π is accepted by Aut_φ.

LTL$_f$ formulas can be used to express safety properties using the all-prefix semantics. Specifically, one can specify all possible safety conditions expressible in LTL, i.e., all first-order (logic) safety properties [17], using LTL$_f$ with all-prefix semantics [4,5].

Definition 1. *LTL$_f$ under all-prefix semantics expresses LTL safety properties: a trace is safe if all of its non-empty finite prefixes satisfies φ, i.e., $\pi \models_\forall \varphi$.*

A **goal-augmented MDP** [18] is a tuple $M = (S, A, \mathcal{G}, L, Tr, R, \gamma)$, where S is a finite set of states, and A is a finite set of actions. $\mathcal{G}$ denotes the space of single goals, each of which corresponds to a unique reachability objective (e.g., go to the mail room or visit the administration desk). The labeling function is $L : S \to 2^{\mathcal{G}}$, which maps each state $s \in S$ to a set of single goals $L(s) \subseteq \mathcal{G}$, indicating goals that are achieved at that state (note that it is also possible that $L(s) = \emptyset$). Tr is the transition function $Tr : S \times \mathcal{G} \times A \to \Delta(S)$, which returns a distribution over the next state for each state s with the current desired goal $g \in \mathcal{G}$ and action $a \in A$. The reward function $R : S \times \mathcal{G} \times A \times S \to \mathbb{R}$ specifies the reward (a real value) an agent receives when taking action a to transition from state s to s' for a specific goal g. $\gamma \in [0, 1)$ is a discount factor that controls the relative importance of immediate versus future rewards.

In a goal-augmented MDP, the solution is a function known as a goal-oriented policy, denoted as $\rho : S \times \mathcal{G} \times A \to [0, 1]$. The value of policy ρ at state s when the goal is g, denoted as $v_\rho(s, g)$, represents the expected sum of rewards obtained by starting from state s and following policy ρ for the goal g, i.e., $v_\rho(s, g) = \mathbb{E}\Big[\sum_{t=0}^{\infty} \gamma^t \cdot R(s_t, g, a_t, s_{t+1}) + \mathbb{1}[g \in L(s_t)]\Big]$. It is typically assumed that the goal-augmented MDP starts from an initial state s_0, so the optimality of the policy is evaluated relative to $v_\rho(s_0, g)$. An optimal policy ρ^* always exists for every goal-augmented MDP.

The task of Reinforcement Learning (RL) is to learn a potentially optimal policy that can achieve every goal in $\mathcal{G}$ within such a goal-augmented MDP, starting from the initial state s_0. In this process, the only known elements are the set of states S, the set of actions A, the set of single goals $\mathcal{G}$, and the labeling function L, while the transition function Tr and the reward function R are unknown (see, for example, [18,22,31]).

A **Gated Recurrent Unit (GRU)** [3] is an efficient variant of Recurrent Neural Networks (RNNs) that maintains a hidden state summarizing recent history, which the policy uses together with the current state to decide the next action. This representation enables a single shared network to learn policies for multiple goals.

3 RL with Temporally Dependent Goals

We introduce the foundational model of our incremental RL framework, the Clocked Goal-Augmented Markov Decision Process (MDP) with temporally dependent goals, which extends the goal-augmented MDP with a clock function to track the sequence of achieved goals, ensuring consistency with the temporal dependency expressed in LTL_f.

3.1 Problem Formalization

A Clocked Goal-Augmented MDP is a tuple $M = (S, A, \mathcal{G}, L, Tr, R, \gamma, f)$, which extends the goal-augmented MDP with a clock function $f : S \times \mathcal{G} \to \{0, 1\}$ mapping a state-goal pair to a binary value. Since our focus is on the temporal dependency of goals in $\mathcal{G}$, we use f to track whether a desired goal g is achieved at state s. Specifically, $f(s, g) = 1$ indicates that goal g is reached at state s, $f(s, g) = 0$ otherwise. Formally, $f(s, g) = 1$ if $g \in L(s)$, and $f(s, g) = 0$ otherwise.

Temporally dependent goals are written in LTL_f over the alphabet $AP_\mathcal{G} = \{p_g \mid g \in \mathcal{G}\}$. Since every goal is unique, we use one-hot encoding semantics such that exactly one proposition from $AP_\mathcal{G}$ is true. Formally let $I_g = p_g \wedge \bigwedge_{g' \in \mathcal{G} \setminus \{g\}} \neg p_{g'}$[1], and we only allow goals in $\mathcal{G}$ by adding $\mathsf{G}(\bigvee_{g \in \mathcal{G}} I_g)$ (G is temporal operator *Always*) to every temporally dependent goal. For simplicity, it is clear from the context so we don't explicitly mention this constraint henceforth. For instance, the goal of first picking up mail (*mail*) and then delivering it to the administration desk (*admin*) is written as $\varphi = \mathsf{F}((p_{mail} \wedge \neg p_{admin}) \wedge (\mathsf{X}^!(\mathsf{F}(\neg p_{mail} \wedge p_{admin}))))$. We write $\text{LTL}_f(\mathcal{G})$ for the set of LTL_f formulas over $AP_\mathcal{G}$ under the one-hot semantics just described.

A policy for a temporally dependent goal φ is denoted by $\rho(\varphi) : S \times \mathcal{G} \times A \to [0, 1]$, which induces trajectories of the form $\tau = (s_0, g_0, a_0, r_0), (s_1, g_1, a_1, r_1), \ldots$

[1] One could also use binary encoding for uniqueness interpretation. Here we just use one-hot encoding as an example to enforce distinction between single goals.

where g_i is the desired goal at step i. Recall that in goal-augmented MDP, the desired goal remains fixed along the trajectory. Here in order to satisfy a temporally dependent goal φ, the policy $\rho(\varphi)$ may switch between different single goals in $\mathcal{G}$ during execution. Each trajectory corresponds to a clocked-trace through the clock function f, we have that $\tau|_f = \ell_0, \ell_1, \ell_2 \dots$ such that $\ell_i = I_{g_i}$ if $f(s_i, g_i) = 1$, and $\ell_i = \emptyset$ otherwise.

We would like to construct a policy ρ^* such that for every temporally dependent goal $\varphi \in \text{LTL}_f(\mathcal{G})$, the induced policy $\rho^*(\varphi)$ maximizes the accumulated reward while ensuring that φ is satisfied as quickly as possible. To formalize this, for each time step t with trajectory prefix $\tau[0:t]$, we write $\tau[0:t]|_f \models^k \varphi$ to denote that the prefix $\tau[0:t]$, when projected through the clock function f, requires at least k further individual goal achievements to satisfy φ. Formally, k is defined as the length of the shortest extension $h \in (2^{AP_{\mathcal{G}}})^*$ such that $\tau[0:t]|_f \cdot h \models \varphi$. Ultimately, we have that

$$\begin{aligned} \rho^*(\varphi) &= \arg\max_{\rho} \mathbb{E}_{\tau\sim\rho} \sum_{t=0}^{\infty} \left[r(\tau, t) + \gamma^t \cdot R(s_t, g_t, a_t, s_{t+1}) \right] \\ r(\tau, t) &= e^{(1-k)} \cdot \mathbb{1}[\tau[0:t]|_f \models^k \varphi] \end{aligned} \tag{1}$$

Here, the objective is to maximize $\gamma^t \cdot R(s_t, g_t, a_t, s_{t+1})$ while minimizing k, which indicates consistent progress toward completing the temporal goal.

3.2 Solution Technique

To address the problem described in Sect. 3.1, we propose an LTL_f-guided solution technique with two components. We first train a GRU-based RL on the underlying goal-augmented MDP to obtain policies for any goals in $\mathcal{G}$. Specifically, since temporally dependent goals in our framework require switching between individual goals during execution, GRU provides a natural support for such goal switching within one unified policy. The temporally dependent goal φ is converted to a deterministic finite automaton (DFA), based on which we build a reward machine. This reward machine projects state trajectories into traces of achieved goals through the clock function, therefore tracking progress in the DFA and determines the next goal for the RL to execute.

GRU-Based RL. We propose a GRU-based RL method utilizing the actor–critic RL framework to learn policies for goals in $\mathcal{G}$. As shown in Fig. 2 (Step 1), this method consists of three parts: a *GRU-based context encoder*, which at every time step t summarizes the interaction history until the current state s_t into a hidden state z_t, i.e., the context, a *context-conditioned actor* that uses (s_t, z_t, g_t) to produce the action a_t, and a *context-conditioned critic*, which evaluates the state-action pair (s_t, a_t) in the context of z_t.

GRU-Based Context Encoder. Note that the hidden state z_t is designed to capture all goal-relevant information required for action selection and evaluation. Therefore, we represent such information as an interaction history, which includes not only recent states, actions, and rewards but also the current goal being pursued. Formally, at time step t, the interaction history is defined as the sequence of the past k interactions:

$$H_t = \{(s_{t-k}, g_{t-k}, a_{t-k}, r_{t-k}), \ldots, (s_{t-1}, g_{t-1}, a_{t-1}, r_{t-1})\}.$$

Here, $k \geq 1$ is a fixed window size specifying how many steps of history are considered, and g_i for $t-k \leq i \leq t-1$ is the goal pursed at step i. At each step, the GRU processes H_t and updates the hidden state as $z_t = \text{GRU}(H_t)$.

Context-Conditioned Actor. Our actor is a policy network $\hat{\rho}$ that outputs an action distribution conditioned on the current state s_t, the hidden state (context) z_t from the GRU current goal g_t:

$$a_t \sim \hat{\rho}(\cdot|s_t, z_t, g_t).$$

In practice, the actor receives the concatenated input $[s_t, z_t, g_t]$, i.e., current state, the context and current goal, enabling the policy to adapt its behavior at s_t according to the goal-relevant information encoded in z_t and g_t.

Context-Conditioned Critic. The critic is a value network Q (the Q-function) that estimates the expected return of a state-action pair under the context:

$$Q(s_t, a_t, z_t) = \mathbb{E}\left[\sum_{i=0}^{\infty} \gamma^i \cdot R(s_{t+i}, a_{t+i}, z_{t+i})\right].$$

By conditioning on z_t, the critic provides goal-sensitive value estimates, so the same pair (s_t, a_t) may have substantially different values under different contexts. This leads to more accurate gradient signals for optimizing the policy.

During training, all goals in $\mathcal{G}$ are included and the policy $\hat{\rho}(s, z)$ is optimized within the actor–critic framework. The actor outputs actions, while the critic evaluates them through Q and provides gradients for policy updates. This optimization leads the policy to select actions that maximize long-term returns, i.e., to maximize Q. As a result, the learned policy converges asymptotically to the optimal policy $\hat{\rho}^*$. During evaluation, $\hat{\rho}^*$ produces the action a_t at each step given (s_t, z_t, g_t). Since the GRU-based representation incorporates the current goal, $\hat{\rho}^*$ produces policies for the underlying goal-augmented MDP in our problem described in Sect. 3.1 and allows for goal (g) switching at any time.

RM-Guided Goal Switching. In this section, we show how to employ the GRU-based RL method to obtain policies for temporally dependent goals in the clocked goal-augmented MDP, thereby addressing the problem defined in Sect. 3.1. Specifically, given a temporally dependent goal $\varphi \in \text{LTL}_f(\mathcal{G})$, we build a reward machine from the DFA Aut_φ by assigning rewards to DFA transitions that correspond to progress toward goal satisfaction. In this way, the reward machine guides goal switching during execution and ensures that the resulting policy achieves the temporal specification as quickly as possible.

Constructing Reward Machine. Recall that an optimal policy for a temporally dependent goal should not only maximize accumulated reward but also satisfy φ as quickly as possible (cf. Eq. (1)). Therefore, we represent φ as a DFA Aut_φ. In particular, we require Aut_φ to be minimal, thus the shortest path from the initial state to an accepting state captures the minimal number of individual goal completions required to satisfy φ. Based on this, we construct a reward machine by assigning rewards to transitions along the shortest path, thereby aligning the reward signal with progress toward satisfying φ. Formally, given a DFA $Aut_\varphi = (2^{AP_\mathcal{G}}, \mathcal{Q}, q_0, \delta, acc)$, we construct the corresponding reward machine as follows:

$$RM_\varphi = (2^{AP_\mathcal{G}}, \mathcal{Q}, q_0, \delta, acc, \alpha)$$

where $\alpha : \mathcal{Q} \times 2^{AP_\mathcal{G}} \times \mathcal{Q} \to \mathbb{R}$ assigns a real-valued reward to each transition, while other elements are the same as in Aut_φ.

Generating Policy. The reward machine works together with the optimal policy $\hat{\rho}^*$, obtained from the GRU-based RL method described in Sect. 3.2, to generate policies for temporally dependent goals expressed in LTL$_f$. Specifically, at the beginning of the execution, the MDP starts from its initial state s_0 and the reward machine is initialized at its start state q_0. At every time step t, given the current state of the reward machine q_t, the current goal g_t is determined from outgoing transitions of q_t, prioritizing the one with the highest reward. The pair (s_t, g_t) is then passed to the policy $\hat{\rho}^*$, which returns an action a_t. After executing a_t and moving to the next state s_{t+1}, we check whether the goal g_t has been satisfied, i.e., check whether $g_t \in L(s_{t+1})$. If it is satisfied, the reward machine performs the corresponding transition to its next state q_{t+1}, from which the next goal g_{t+1} is determined. Note that g_{t+1} may either differ from or the same as g_t, depending on the outgoing transitions of q_{t+1}. If the goal is not satisfied, the reward machine remains at the same state and such that $q_{t+1} = q_t$ and the goal remains unchanged, i.e., $g_{t+1} = g_t$.

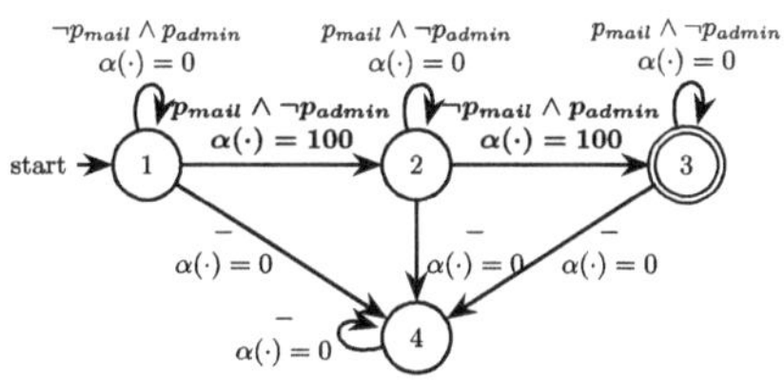

Fig. 1. Reward machine for φ.

By construction, the policy generated through the composition of the reward machine and the policy $\hat{\rho}^*$ satisfies two properties. First, since the reward machine makes transitions only when a goal is completed, in which case $f(s, g) = 1$, the projected trace of achieved goals $\tau|_f$ corresponds exactly to an accepting run of the DFA Aut_φ, hence satisfying the temporally dependent goal φ. Moreover, since rewards are assigned along shortest accepting paths of the DFA, the resulting policy also achieves φ as quickly as possible following the optimality criterion of Eq. (1). Hence, the composed policy is an optimal policy for the temporally dependent goal.

Example. We use the mail delivery example, where the temporally dependent goal is the LTL$_f$ formula $\varphi = \mathsf{F}((p_{mail} \wedge \neg p_{admin}) \wedge (\mathsf{X}^!(\mathsf{F}(\neg p_{mail} \wedge p_{admin}))))$, which requires the robot to pickup a mail at the mail station and deliver it to the administration desk. The corresponding reward machine is shown in Fig. 1, each edge is labeled by its condition (interpretations over $AP_{\mathcal{G}}$) and its reward $\alpha(\cdot)$. For brevity, we use '–' on the edge to denote the missing conditions (any interpretations over $AP_{\mathcal{G}}$ not already covered by other outgoing edges), since the reward machine is constructed from DFA Aut_{φ}. Initially, the reward machine is at state 1, so the current goal is '*mail*' (go to the mail room), since the outgoing edge $1 \rightarrow 2$ with $p_{mail} \wedge \neg p_{admin}$ has the highest reward $\alpha(\cdot) = 100$. Executing policy $\hat{\rho}*(s_0, z_0|g_0 = mail)$ achieves '*mail*', enabling the transition to state 2, where the current goal becomes '*admin*' (suppose at time step t). Then $\hat{\rho}*(s_t, z_t|g_t = admin)$ is executed to achieve '*admin*', after which the reward machine transits to accepting state 3. The corresponding trajectory is $\tau = (s_0, mail, a_0, r_0), \cdots, (s_t, admin, a_t, r_t), \cdots$ and the projected trace is $\tau|_f = (p_{mail} \wedge \neg p_{admin}), (\neg p_{mail} \wedge p_{admin})$, which indeed satisfies φ and as quickly as possible.

4 Incremental RL with Temporally Dependent Goals

In most RL settings, the agent is given a single goal to accomplish and terminate once it is satisfied. In practice, however, additional goals can arrive while the original one is being pursued. For instance, a hospital delivery robot begins with a pickup at the mail station, and during execution, receives a delivery request for the lab. A strict "finish-then-restart" policy is often suboptimal or even infeasible. Sometimes deferring a new goal may get it unachievable due to the temporal structure, and the agent may miss low cost policies to satisfy it while already passing through useful states. Moreover, newly arriving goals can conflict with the ongoing one or activate safety constraints among single goals. In the delivery example, a hospital safety rule may require completing all clean-zone tasks (such as picking up sample from the sample room) before performing normal-zone operations (such as delivering to the lab, collecting mail, or delivering to the administration desk), so the delivery to administration desk must be deferred until the sample has been collected.

In this section, we go beyond the basic framework and consider an advanced RL setting that allows both newly arriving goals and the enforcement of possible safety constraints, enabling incremental RL. When a new goal arrives, we compose it with the ongoing goal through reward machines, and continue acting online while integrating objectives without violating safety constraints.

4.1 Problem Formalization

Note that there is a crucial difference between ongoing and newly arriving temporally dependent goals. An ongoing goal must be realized from the start of execution, while a new goal must be achieved only after a finite history, that is, from the moment it is assigned to the agent. Newly arriving temporally dependent goals always come with an arrival time along the trajectory. We represent such an arrival, including safety constraints, as $(\hat{\varphi}, \hat{\psi}, m)$. Both $\hat{\varphi}$ and $\hat{\psi}$ are LTL_f formulas over $\mathcal{G}$ such that $\hat{\varphi}, \hat{\psi} \in \text{LTL}_f(\mathcal{G})$. $m \geq 0$ is the arrival time step along τ. The completion of $\hat{\varphi}$ is considered on the suffix of τ after m such that $\tau[m+1:-]|_f \models \hat{\varphi}$. The safety constraint is interpreted under all-prefix semantics (cf. Sect. 2) from m such that every prefix of the trajectory starting after m must satisfy $\hat{\psi}$, i.e., $\tau[m+1:-]|_f \models_\forall \psi$.

Given a clocked goal-augmented MDP $M = (S, A, \mathcal{G}, L, Tr, R, \gamma, f)$, we would like to construct a policy $\rho^* : S \times \mathcal{G} \times A \to [0,1]$ such that for any ongoing goal $\varphi \in \text{LTL}_f(\mathcal{G})$ and newly arriving goal with safety constraint $(\hat{\varphi}, \hat{\psi}, m) \in \text{LTL}_f(\mathcal{G}) \times \text{LTL}_f(\mathcal{G}) \times \mathbb{N}$ at arbitrary time step m, the induced trajectory τ satisfies

$$\tau \;|_f\!\models \varphi \text{ and } \tau[m+1:-] \;|_f\!\models \hat{\varphi} \text{ and } \tau[m+1:-] \;|_f\!\models_\forall \hat{\psi},$$

as well as maximizes the cumulative reward while ensuring that φ and $\hat{\varphi}$ are satisfied as quickly as possible while not violating the safety constraint $\hat{\psi}$.

Specifically, before the arrival of $(\hat{\varphi}, \hat{\psi}, m)$, that is for all time steps $t \leq m$, the policy ρ^* focuses on satisfying φ as quickly as possible. After m, for all $t > m$, ρ^* aims to satisfy the remaining part of φ and the entire $\hat{\varphi}$ as quickly as possible while aligning with the safety constraint $\hat{\psi}$. We capture "quick completion" through progress reward r (pre new goal arrival)

$$r(\tau, t) = e^{(1-k)} \cdot \mathbb{1}\left[\tau[0:t] \;|_f\!\models^k \varphi\right]$$

and r' (post new goal arrival):

$$\begin{aligned} r'(\tau, t) = {} & e^{(1-k)} \cdot \mathbb{1}\left[\tau[0:t]|_f \models^k \varphi \wedge \tau[m+1:t]|_f \models_\forall \hat{\psi}\right] \\ & + e^{(1-k')} \cdot \mathbb{1}\left[\tau[m+1:t]|_f \models^{k'} \hat{\varphi} \wedge \tau[m+1:t]|_f \models_\forall \hat{\psi}\right] \end{aligned}$$

where $\models^k$ recalls that the projected prefix requires at most k further single-goal completions to satisfy the formula.

Ultimately, we have that:

$$\rho^* = \arg\max_{\rho} \mathbb{E}_{\tau \sim \rho}\left[\sum_{t=0}^{m} r(\tau, t) + \sum_{t=m+1}^{\infty} \left[r'(\tau, t) + \gamma^t \cdot R(s_t, g_t, a_t, s_{t+1})\right]\right] \tag{2}$$

Note that although we expect smaller k at every time step along the trajectory to maximize $\gamma^t \cdot R(s_t, g_t, a_t, s_{t+1})$. For $0 \leq t \leq m$, maximizing $\gamma^t \cdot R(s_t, g_t, a_t, s_{t+1})$ concerns completing φ only, for $t > m$, it concerns the remaining of φ together with $\hat{\varphi}$ while respecting $\hat{\psi}$.

4.2 Solution Technique

To address further temporally dependent goals with safety constraints described in Sect. 4.1, we extend our solution technique from Sect. 3.2. Recall that the approach in Sect. 3.2 consists of two components: a GRU-base RL network that learns policies for single goals, and a RM-guided goal switching mechanism to obtain policies for temporally dependent goals in LTL_f. In particular, the reward machine tracks progress of the ongoing temporally dependent goal by following the DFA state of the LTL_f specification through the clock function and outputs the next single goal to pursue. This tracking naturally records what has been completed and what remains, which we now leverage to incorporate newly arriving goals and to enforce safety constraints.

Incremental RM-Guided Goal Switching. For simplicity, we first set the safety constraint to $\hat{\psi} = true$ (no safety constraints) when the new temporally dependent goal $\hat{\varphi}$ arrives at time step m. The general case $\hat{\psi} \in \mathrm{LTL}_f(\mathcal{G})$ is handled in the next section. An optimal policy ρ^* as formalized in Sect. 4.1 works in two phases: (i) for all time steps $t \leq m$, ρ^* focuses on completing φ as quickly as possible, using the approach in 3.2, (ii) for all $t > m$, ρ^* aims to complete, as quickly as possible, the remaining part of φ together with the entire $\hat{\varphi}$. We now elaborate on how to achieve phase (ii).

Constructing Post-arrival Reward Machine. We first build a reward machine $RM_{\hat{\varphi}} = (2^{AP_{\mathcal{G}}}, \hat{\mathcal{Q}}, \hat{q}_0, \hat{\delta}, \hat{acc}, \hat{\alpha})$ for the new goal $\hat{\varphi}$. Then we track the current state of the reward machine $RM_{\varphi} = (2^{AP_{\mathcal{G}}}, \mathcal{Q}, q_0, \delta, acc, \alpha)$ for the ongoing goal φ using the clocked prefix up to m, so we have $q_0^m = \delta(q_0, \tau[0:m]|_f)$. We set q_0^m as the new initial state and obtain $RM_{\varphi}^m = (2^{AP_{\mathcal{G}}}, \mathcal{Q}, q_0^m, \delta, acc, \alpha)$. Finally we build the product reward machine (cf. Step 2 in Fig. 2)

$$RM_{\otimes} = RM_{\varphi}^m \otimes RM_{\hat{\varphi}} = (2^{AP_{\mathcal{G}}}, \mathcal{Q} \times \hat{\mathcal{Q}}, (q_0^m, \hat{q_0}), \delta_{\otimes}, acc_{\otimes}, \alpha_{\otimes})$$

where we have $\delta_{\otimes}((q, \hat{q}), \ell) = (\delta(q, \ell), \hat{\delta}(\hat{q}, \ell))$, $acc_{\otimes} = acc \times \hat{acc}$, and $\alpha_{\otimes}((q, \hat{q}), \ell, (q', \hat{q'})) = \alpha(q, \ell, q') + \hat{\alpha}(\hat{q}, \ell, \hat{q'})$.

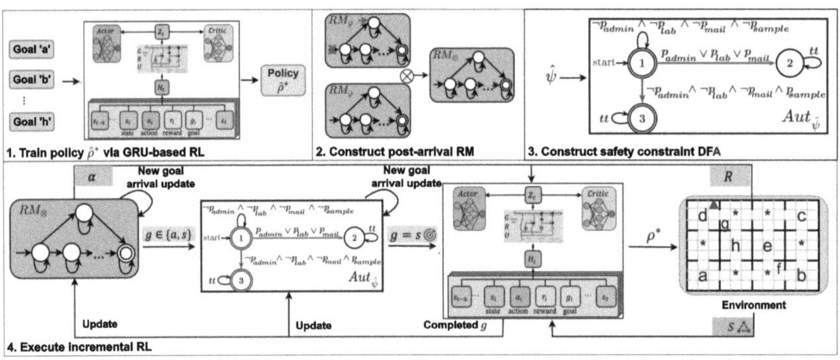

Fig. 2. Incremental RL with Temporally Dependent Goals

Generating Post-arrival Policy. Note that it is possible that $\hat{\varphi}$ is incompatible with the remaining of φ, such that $RM_{\otimes}$ has no accepting run that can achieve both $\hat{\varphi}$ and the remaining of φ. This can be checked by performing a standard reachability test on $RM_{\otimes}$. In this case, we move back a single-RM machine case by considering the one that has a shorter shortest accepting path ($d_{\varphi} = dist_{RM_{\varphi}}(q_0^m \rightarrow acc)$ and $d_{\hat{\varphi}} = dist_{RM_{\hat{\varphi}}}(\hat{q_0} \rightarrow \hat{acc})$). This reduction still preserves "as quickly as possible" optimality and combining two phases remains overall optimality.

If $\hat{\varphi}$ is compatible with the remaining of φ, we proceed with composing the product reward machine with the single policy $\hat{\rho}^*$ (from GRU-based RL). In fact, the policy is generated exactly as in the single-RM case (but with the product reward machine). By construction, the policy generated through the composition of the product reward machine and the policy $\hat{\rho}^*$ advances $RM_{\otimes}$ only on single-goal completions that lead to the progress of at least one of $\{\varphi, \hat{\varphi}\}$. Consequently, the projected trace $\tau[m+1 : -]|_f$ leads to an accepting run of the product reward machine $RM_{\otimes}$, hence satisfying the remaining of φ, i.e., $\tau|_f \models \varphi$, and the entire $\hat{\varphi}$, i.e., $\tau[m+1 : -]|_f \models \hat{\varphi}$. With $\alpha_{\otimes} = \alpha + \hat{\alpha}$ and the post-arrival reward r', expected return increases only when a goal's remaining-steps counter k decreases, therefore any policy that delays such decreases is suboptimal. Hence, the composed policy finishes each goal as quickly as possible and is optimal for the post-arrival case.

Handling Safety Constraints. In the previous section, we described how newly arriving goals can be combined with ongoing temporally dependent goals through reward machines, allowing the agent to continue acting online while integrating the goal. We now focus on ensuring that the combined execution remains safe, i.e., that all trajectories after m satisfy the activated safety constraints such that $\tau[m+1 : -]|_f \models_{\forall} \hat{\psi}$.

Safety constraints are expressed as a set of LTL$_f$ formulas $\Psi \subseteq \text{LTL}_f(\mathcal{G})$. Each formula in Ψ specifies certain temporal relationships among single goals. Continuing with the hospital delivery example, a safety rule might require that all clean-zone operations (e.g., pickups from the sample room) must be completed before normal-zone activities (e.g., deliveries to the lab or to the administration desk and mail handling), ensuring contamination-free operation. To ensure such rules are enforced during execution, we activate only those safety constraints that are relevant to the single goals that are necessary to complete $\hat{\varphi}$ and the remaining of φ. When $\hat{\varphi}$ arrives, we identify all safety formulas in Ψ that involve single goals along the shortest paths on RM_{φ}^m and $RM_{\hat{\varphi}}$. These active constraints are then combined into a single conjunctive formula $\hat{\psi} = \bigwedge_{\psi_i \in \Psi_{active}} \psi_i$. This formula $\hat{\psi}$ captures all safety conditions that are applicable from m.

To efficiently monitor and enforce these conditions during execution, we translate $\hat{\psi}$ into a DFA $Aut_{\hat{\psi}} = (2^{AP_{\mathcal{G}}}, \mathcal{Q}_{\hat{\psi}}, q_0^{\hat{\psi}}, \delta_{\hat{\psi}}, acc_{\hat{\psi}})$. Accepting state $q \in acc_{\hat{\psi}}$ indicates that the current trajectory prefix satisfies the safety constraint $\hat{\psi}$; otherwise, a bad prefix has been reached and $\hat{\psi}$ is permanently violated. This automaton provides a structured way to track the satisfaction or violation of safety rules as the agent executes single goals over time, enabling online pruning of unsafe actions before they occur.

Figure 2 illustrates the complete workflow of our incremental RL framework. At execution time, $Aut_{\hat{\psi}}$ runs in parallel with $RM_{\otimes}$. At each time step t, the policy network ρ^* has: (*i*) a current reward-machine state q_t, (*ii*) a current safety-machine state $q_{\hat{\psi}_t}$, and (*iii*) a set of possible next single goals determined by the outgoing transitions of $RM_{\otimes}$. Before executing a single goal g_t, the agent checks, using $\delta_{\hat{\psi}}$, whether transitioning under g_t from $q_{\hat{\psi}_t}$ would lead to a non-accepting state. If so, g_t is removed. The agent thus only selects goals that keep the safety constraint DFA $Aut_{\hat{\psi}}$ within accepting states, ensuring that the trajectory from m satisfies $\tau[m+1:-]|_f \models_{\forall} \hat{\psi}$.

Furthermore, since the product reward machine is constructed on the fly by running both reward machines in parallel, without performing an explicit product. In this case, when a temporally dependent goal is completed, its corresponding reward machine can simply be removed from the product, and the set of active safety constraints Ψ_{active}, together with the corresponding constraint DFA, is updated accordingly. This ensures that both the product reward machine and the constraint DFA grow only with currently being pursued goals and active safety constraints, rather than with the total number that have arrived over time, therefore preventing unbounded growth of the state space.

The policy ρ^* is guided by both the reward machine and the safety constraint DFA, ensuring that all active safety rules are satisfied while pursuing temporally dependent goals. Consequently, the resulting policy remains optimal with respect to the safety compliant trajectories, guaranteeing maximal cumulative reward under the active safety constraints.

Example. We use the same delivery robot example. As shown in Step 4 of Fig. 2, the current temporally dependent goal is $\varphi = \mathsf{F}((p_{mail} \wedge \neg p_{admin}) \wedge (\mathsf{X}^!(\mathsf{F}(\neg p_{mail} \wedge p_{admin}))))$ representing the task of picking up a mail at the mail station and delivering it to the administration desk. After the robot has already picked up the mail (i.e., p_{mail} has been achieved but p_{admin} has not yet), a new temporally dependent goal arrives: $\varphi = \mathsf{F}((p_{sample} \wedge \neg p_{lab}) \wedge (\mathsf{X}^!(\mathsf{F}(\neg p_{sample} \wedge p_{lab}))))$ corresponding to picking up a sample from the sample room and delivering it to the lab. The active safety constraint is $\hat{\psi} = (((p_{sample} \wedge \neg \cdots) \mathsf{R} \neg(p_{admin} \wedge \neg \cdots)) \wedge ((p_{sample} \wedge \neg \cdots) \mathsf{R} \neg(p_{lab} \wedge \neg \cdots)))$ which enforces that lab delivery and administration desk delivery tasks must not occur before completing operations in the clean sample room. Note that not all normal-zone operations are considered here, such as mail pickups, since it is not relevant to the completion of $\hat{\varphi}$ and the remaining of φ. At this point, the reward machine is in state $(q_2, \hat{q}_1)$, where the candidate single goals are $G = \{admin, sample\}$. According to the safety constraint $\hat{\psi}$, selecting *admin* in the current state would lead to a non-accepting state, as it violates the clean-zone-before-normal-zone rule. Therefore, the agent selects *sample* (picking up sample from sample room) ensuring that the resulting trajectory remains safe and compliant with hospital hygiene constraints.

5 Empirical Evaluation

The implementation is built in Python 3.10. The core RL component is based on the Twin Delayed Deep Deterministic policy gradient (TD3) from [8], which provides stable actor–critic optimization. Our evaluation focuses on two main aspects: (*i*) the effectiveness of GRU-based RL in handling temporally dependent goals, and (*ii*) the adaptability of the incremental RL framework when new goals and safety constraints are introduced during execution.

5.1 Experiment Design

The experiments are conducted in two simulated environments: a 9×12 GridWorld and a Zone environment, as illustrated in Fig. 3.

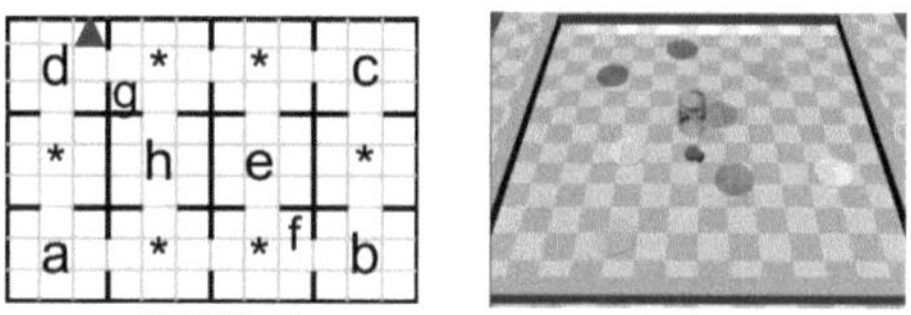

a. GridWorld b. Zone

Fig. 3. Visualisations of environments.

- **GridWorld Environment:** The environment consists of discrete cells, where specific locations are designated as goals $\mathcal{G} = \{a, b, \ldots, h\}$. Walls (solid lines) divide the map into regions that cannot be crossed, while obstacles (stars) impose a penalty when the agent collides with or attempts to move through them. The agent, initialized at the blue triangle position, can move using discrete actions {up, down, left, right, stay}.
- **Zone Environment:** The environment, adopted from [31], is defined over a continuous 2D space, containing multiple circular regions as goal zones $\mathcal{G} = \{JetBlack, White, \ldots, Magenta\}$. The agent, initialized at the red dot position, can move using two continuous actions {linear-velocity, angular-velocity}.

Each successful goal completion leads to a positive reward, whereas every movement step incurs a small negative cost to promote efficient behavior. This setup enables the evaluation of the agent's capability to pursue temporally dependent goals constructed from $\mathcal{G}$ and adapt to new goals and safety constraints within a dynamic environment.

For evaluation, we compare the performance of our GRU-based TD3 approach with the standard (non GRU-based) TD3 baseline, as well as the adaptability of the proposed incremental RL framework when new goals and safety constraints are introduced during execution. The evaluations use two performance metrics: the *success rate* and the *normalized average validation return*.

The success rate is computed as $1 - \frac{\text{remaining single goals to complete the overall goal}}{\text{total length of the shortest path}}$, capturing how efficiently the agent progresses toward completing temporally dependent goals. The normalized average validation return reflects both goal achievement and path efficiency.

Table 1 shows the LTL_f formulas used in the GridWorld and Zone environment. For simplicity, we use every goal $g \in \mathcal{G}$ instead of its encoding I_g in every LTL_f formula. The results in Figs. 4 and 5 use φ_2 as the initial goal and φ_4 as new tasks. These formulas are adapted from [13]. The first five rows, φ_1–φ_5, represent individual tasks, while the last three rows correspond to newly arriving tasks $\hat{\varphi}$. When new tasks arrive, they may introduce safety constraints Ψ. The selection of Ψ is based on the relevant goals along the shortest paths from the current state to the accepting states in the reward machines RM_{φ} and $RM_{\hat{\varphi}}$.

Table 1. LTLf formulas and safety constraints in GridWorld and Zone environment

Domain	Task	LTL_f Formula
GridWorld	φ_1	$\mathsf{F}(a) \wedge (\neg a \,\mathsf{U}\, (b \wedge c))$
	φ_2	$\mathsf{F}(b \wedge (\neg c \,\mathsf{U}\, d)) \wedge \mathsf{F}(c)$
	φ_3	$\mathsf{F}(c \wedge \mathsf{F}(d)) \wedge \mathsf{F}(e)$
	φ_4	$\neg d \,\mathsf{U}\, (e \wedge (\neg f \,\mathsf{U}\, h)) \wedge \mathsf{F}(d) \wedge \mathsf{F}(f)$
	φ_5	$\mathsf{F}(f) \wedge \mathsf{F}(g) \wedge \mathsf{F}(h) \wedge (\neg f \,\mathsf{U}\, h)$
	Ψ	$a\, R\, \neg d$
		$c\, R\, \neg f$
		$c\, R\, \neg h$
Zone	φ_1	$\mathsf{F}(\text{JetBlack}) \wedge (\neg\text{JetBlack} \,\mathsf{U}\, (\text{White} \wedge \text{Blue}))$
	φ_2	$\mathsf{F}(\text{White} \wedge (\neg\text{Blue} \,\mathsf{U}\, \text{Green})) \wedge \mathsf{F}(\text{Blue})$
	φ_3	$\mathsf{F}(\text{Blue} \wedge \mathsf{F}(\text{Green})) \wedge \mathsf{F}(\text{Red})$
	φ_4	$\neg\text{Green} \,\mathsf{U}\, (\text{Red} \wedge (\neg\text{Yellow} \,\mathsf{U}\, \text{Magenta})) \wedge \mathsf{F}(\text{Green}) \wedge \mathsf{F}(\text{Yellow})$
	φ_5	$\mathsf{F}(\text{Yellow}) \wedge \mathsf{F}(\text{Cyan}) \wedge \mathsf{F}(\text{Magenta}) \wedge (\neg\text{Yellow} \,\mathsf{U}\, \text{Magenta})$
	Ψ	$\text{JetBlack}\, R\, \neg\text{Green}$
		$\text{Blue}\, R\, \neg\text{Yellow}$
		$\text{Blue}\, R\, \neg\text{Magenta}$

5.2 Results

Our experiments act as a proof of concept of the practical feasibility of our approach, We utilized the GridWorld and Zone to clearly isolate and demonstrate the logical compositionality and safety constraints handling. Figures 4 and 5 show the experimental results in terms of success rate and normalized average validation return as the number of training timesteps increases. Each plot consists three curves: (*i*) the standard TD3 baseline without GRU for temporally dependent goals, (*ii*) the GRU-based TD3 model for temporally dependent goals, and (*iii*) the GRU-based TD3 model with additional goals and safety constraints. We can see that the standard TD3 has a very low success rate. In contrast, in the GridWorld environment, the GRU-based TD3 shows a clear performance improvement after around 130,000 timesteps of training, and in the Zone environment this improvement occurs after about 5,000 training timesteps.

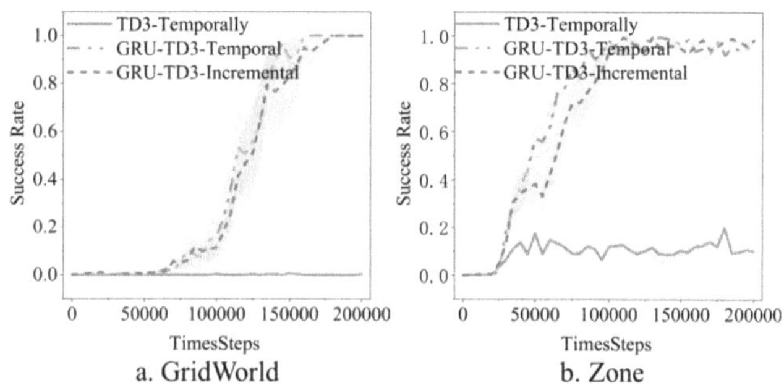

Fig. 4. Changes in success rate as the number of training timesteps increases.

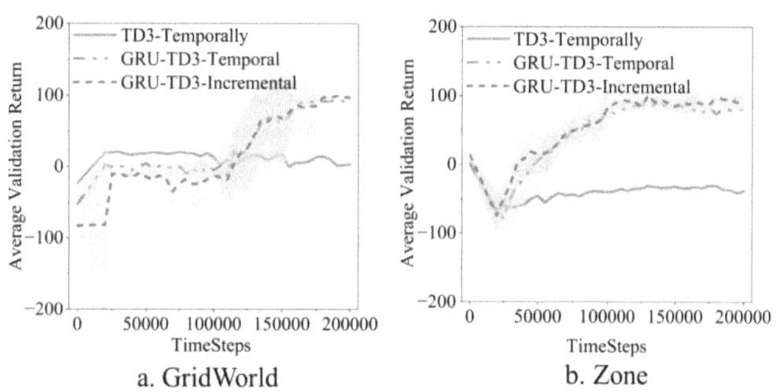

Fig. 5. Changes in normalized average validation return as the number of training timesteps increases.

Eventually, the success rate reaches nearly 100% in both environments. Moreover, even when additional goals and safety constraints are introduced, our approach maintains efficient learning and stable performance, demonstrating that the proposed incremental RL framework shows strong convergence and robustness in handling incrementally specified temporally dependent goals and potential safety constraints.

6 Conclusion and Future Work

We presented an incremental RL framework that supports temporally dependent goals that arrive incrementally, while accounting potential safety constraints. This framework extends goal-augmented MDPs with a clock mechanism and leverages GRU-based RL policies together with reward machines to achieve compositional goal execution. By constructing the product reward machine and safety constraint DFA on the fly, the agent can integrate newly arriving goals and constraints at any time, ensuring safety while maintaining optimality over feasible trajectories. This enables scalable and online adaptation without retraining, as both DFAs grow only with currently pursued goals and active constraints. In the future, we plan to generalize the framework to support goal preferences and soft safety constraints through probabilistic or weighted temporal logic specifications. This extension will allow the policy to balance between satisfying multiple goals and safety constraints rather than enforcing all of them strictly, enabling adaptive policies in more complex, real-world scenarios with conflicting objectives.

Acknowledgments. This work was supported in part by the National Natural Science Foundation of China under Grant 62302308, and in part by the UKRI Erlangen AI Hub on Mathematical and Computational Foundations of AI (No. EP/Y028872/1).

References

1. Connell, J.H., Mahadevan, S. (eds.): Robot learning. Kluwer, Boston (1993/1997). Robotica **17**(2), 229–235 (1999)
2. Camacho, A., Icarte, R.T., Klassen, T.Q., Valenzano, R.A., McIlraith, S.A.: LTL and beyond: formal languages for reward function specification in reinforcement learning. In: IJCAI, pp. 6065–6073 (2019)
3. Cho, K., et al.: Learning phrase representations using RNN encoder–decoder for statistical machine translation. In: Proceedings of the 2014 Conference on Empirical Methods in Natural Language Processing (EMNLP), pp. 1724–1734 (2014)
4. De Giacomo, G., Di Stasio, A., Tabajara, L.M., Vardi, M.Y., Zhu, S.: Finite-trace and generalized-reactivity specifications in temporal synthesis. In: IJCAI, pp. 1852–1858 (2021)
5. De Giacomo, G., Di Stasio, A., Tabajara, L.M., Vardi, M.Y., Zhu, S.: Finite-trace and generalized-reactivity specifications in temporal synthesis. Formal Methods Syst. Des. **61**(2), 139–163 (2022)
6. De Giacomo, G., Vardi, M.Y.: Linear temporal logic and linear dynamic logic on finite traces. In: IJCAI, pp. 854–860 (2013)
7. Fakoor, R., Chaudhari, P., Soatto, S., Smola, A.J.: Meta-q-learning. CoRR abs/1910.00125 (2019)

8. Fujimoto, S., van Hoof, H., Meger, D.: Addressing function approximation error in actor-critic methods. In: ICML, pp. 1587–1596 (2018)
9. Grigsby, J., Sasek, J., Parajuli, S., Adebi, D., Zhang, A., Zhu, Y.: AMAGO-2: breaking the multi-task barrier in meta-reinforcement learning with transformers. In: NeurIPS, pp. 87473–87508 (2024)
10. Hasanbeig, H., Kroening, D., Abate, A.: Certified reinforcement learning with logic guidance. Artif. Intell. **322**, 103949 (2023)
11. Hasanbeig, M., Abate, A., Kroening, D.: Logically-constrained reinforcement learning (2019)
12. Icarte, R.T., Klassen, T.Q., Valenzano, R.A., McIlraith, S.A.: Teaching multiple tasks to an RL agent using LTL. In: AAMAS, pp. 452–461 (2018)
13. Jackermeier, M., Abate, A.: DeepLTL: learning to efficiently satisfy complex LTL specifications for multi-task RL. In: ICLR (2025)
14. Jothimurugan, K., Bansal, S., Bastani, O., Alur, R.: Specification-guided reinforcement learning. In: Neural and Symbolic Learning and Reasoning (NeuS), pp. 316–330 (2025)
15. Kiran, B.R., et al.: Deep reinforcement learning for autonomous driving: a survey. IEEE Trans. Intell. Transp. Syst. **23**(6), 4909–4926 (2022)
16. Kober, J., Bagnell, J.A., Peters, J.: Reinforcement learning in robotics: a survey. Int. J. Robot. Res. **32**(11), 1238–1274 (2013)
17. Lichtenstein, O., Pnueli, A., Zuck, L.D.: The glory of the past. In: Logic of Programs, pp. 196–218 (1985)
18. Liu, M., Zhu, M., Zhang, W.: Goal-conditioned reinforcement learning: problems and solutions. In: IJCAI-22, pp. 5502–5511 (2022). survey Track
19. Pan, C., et al.: A survey of continual reinforcement learning. CoRR abs/2506.21872 (2025)
20. Plappert, M., et al.: Multi-goal reinforcement learning: challenging robotics environments and request for research. arXiv preprint: arXiv:1802.09464 (2018)
21. Pnueli, A.: The temporal logic of programs. In: FOCS, pp. 46–57 (1977)
22. Qiu, W., Mao, W., Zhu, H.: Instructing goal-conditioned reinforcement learning agents with temporal logic objectives. NeurIPS **36**, 39147–39175 (2023)
23. Sadigh, D., Kim, E.S., Coogan, S., Sastry, S.S., Seshia, S.A.: A learning based approach to control synthesis of Markov decision processes for linear temporal logic specifications. In: CDC, pp. 1091–1096 (2014)
24. Shala, G., Biedenkapp, A., Grabocka, J.: Hierarchical transformers are efficient meta-reinforcement learners (2024)
25. Shao, K., Tang, Z., Zhu, Y., Li, N., Zhao, D.: A survey of deep reinforcement learning in video games (2019)
26. Shukla, Y., Burman, T., Kulkarni, A., Wright, R., Velasquez, A., Sinapov, J.: Logical specifications-guided dynamic task sampling for reinforcement learning agents. In: ICAPS, pp. 532–540 (2024)
27. Sodhani, S., Zhang, A., Pineau, J.: Multi-task reinforcement learning with context-based representations (2021)
28. Svoboda, J., Bansal, S., Chatterjee, K.: Reinforcement learning from reachability specifications: PAC guarantees with expected conditional distance. In: ICML (2024)
29. Szita, I.: Reinforcement Learning in Games, pp. 539–577. Springer Berlin Heidelberg, Berlin, Heidelberg (2012)
30. Toro Icarte, R., Klassen, T.Q., Valenzano, R., McIlraith, S.A.: Teaching multiple tasks to an RL agent using LTL. In: AAMAS, pp. 452–461 (2018)

31. Vaezipoor, P., Li, A.C., Icarte, R.A.T., Mcilraith, S.A.: LTL2Action: generalizing LTL instructions for multi-task RL. In: International Conference on Machine Learning, pp. 10497–10508. PMLR (2021)
32. Wang, Z., Chen, C., Li, H.X., Dong, D., Tarn, T.J.: Incremental reinforcement learning with prioritized sweeping for dynamic environments. IEEE/ASME Trans. Mechatron. **24**(2), 621–632 (2019)
33. Yalcinkaya, B., Lauffer, N., Vazquez-Chanlatte, M., Seshia, S.A.: Compositional automata embeddings for goal-conditioned reinforcement learning. In: NeurIPS (2024)

Symbolic Model Checking for Linear Temporal Dynamic Logic via Compositional Testers

Xiangyu Luo[1(✉)], Li Li[2], Lijun Wu[3], Kaile Su[4], Zuxi Chen[1], and Lixiao Zheng[1]

[1] College of Computer Science and Technology, Huaqiao University, Xiamen, China
luoxy@hqu.edu.cn

[2] School of Information Science and Technology, Xiamen University Tan Kah Kee College, Zhangzhou, China

[3] School of Computer Science and Engineering, University of Electronic Science and Technology of China, Chengdu, China

[4] School of Computer and Control Engineering, Yantai University, Yantai, China

Abstract. We propose a symbolic model checking framework for Linear Temporal Dynamic Logic (LTDL) via compositional testers, extending Linear Dynamic Logic (LDL) with bidirectional LTL operators. This enables past-time specifications (unattainable in pure LDL) while preserving LTL's conciseness and verification efficiency, without increasing theoretical expressiveness. We make four contributions: (1) algorithms for constructing and optimizing regular grammars for LTDL path expressions to eliminate redundant variables and productions; (2) an algorithm for eliminating zero-delay cycles in regular grammars to avoid algebraic loops; (3) a method for generating compositional testers from LTDL; and (4) *LTDLTester*, an open-source tool for producing SMV-compatible LTDL testers. This reduces verification to checking the initial states of a system-tester synchronous parallel composition against output assertions, allowing direct application of standard symbolic checkers (e.g., NuSMV). Experiments show our approach significantly outperforms MCMAS_{LDLK}, the first native LDL model checker.

Keywords: Temporal Tester · Symbolic Model Checking · Regular Grammar · Linear Dynamic Logic · Linear Temporal Logic

1 Introduction

Linear Temporal Logic (LTL) [5] is a foundational standard for specifying system behaviors, yet it lacks the expressiveness required for complex industrial applications. This gap spurred the development of powerful but theoretically complex logics like ForSpec [2], PSL [1], and SVA [16]. Linear Dynamic Logic (LDL) [15] emerged as a canonical alternative, blending LTL's intuitive syntax with the ability to express all ω-regular properties [10,15]. LDL provides robust expressive

G. De Giacomo et al. (Eds.): TASE 2026, LNCS 16697, pp. 439–457, 2027.
https://doi.org/10.1007/978-3-032-30693-7_28

power (integrating regular expressions and dynamic operators like $\langle\rho\rangle\varphi$) while preserving LTL's PSPACE-complete model checking complexity [10] via shared automata-based foundations. Theoretically, Faymonville and Zimmermann proposed an automata-based PLDL model checking algorithm without implementation [10]. Later, Kong and Lomuscio developed MCMAS_{LDLK} [12], extending MCMAS [13] as the first implemented LDL checker. Though the industrial logic PSL [1] subsumes LDL, it lacks LDL's ability to natively embed tests within regular expressions. While temporal testers were proposed for LTL, MITL and PSL [14] (and tools like Spot handle LTL/PSL [9]), LDL fundamentally lacks past-oriented modalities.

To address the limitations above, we propose *Linear Temporal Dynamic Logic (LTDL)*, extending LDL with bidirectional LTL operators. This temporal symmetry enables concise specifications referencing historical states without increasing theoretical complexity, while inherently yielding smaller testers. Temporal testers [11] are compositional transducers perfectly suited for LTDL's nested modalities. We introduce an LTDL model checking framework, optimizing and extending the PSL method [14], featuring three key advantages: (1) *Full Compositionality:* Modular construction elegantly handles subformula tests via direct transition relation wiring, avoiding cumbersome automata embeddings; (2) *Symbolic Efficiency:* Purely symbolic representations bypass exponential explicit-state conversions, enabling direct BDD (Binary Decision Diagram)/SAT (Satisfiability) integration; (3) *Unified Framework:* A single tester supports model checking, run-time monitoring [6], and correct-by-construction policy synthesis [6,8].

This paper is organized as follows: Sect. 2 introduces LTDL. Sections 3 and 4 detail regular grammar and LTDL tester construction. Section 5 presents the verification approach and evaluates it against MCMAS_{LDLK}. Section 6 concludes.

2 Linear Temporal Dynamic Logic

LTDL provides a unified formalism that integrates future and past LTL temporal operators with LDL's tested regular path expressions. These tests can reference both past and future states, enabling the expression of sophisticated property patterns that interleave historical conditions with anticipatory constraints.

2.1 Syntax of Linear Temporal Dynamic Logic

Formally, LTDL formulas φ are defined by the following grammar:

$$\varphi ::= a \mid \neg\varphi \mid \varphi_1 \wedge \varphi_2 \mid \varphi_1 \vee \varphi_2 \mid \langle\rho\rangle\varphi \mid [\rho]\varphi \mid X\varphi \mid Y\varphi \mid \varphi_1 U \varphi_2 \mid \varphi_1 S \varphi_2$$
$$\rho ::= \psi \mid \varphi? \mid \rho_1 + \rho_2 \mid \rho_1 ; \rho_2 \mid \rho^*$$

where a is an atomic formula over a set of typed variables $\mathcal{V}$ over finite domains, ρ is a path expression, and ψ is an assertion over $\mathcal{V}$. *Atomic formulas* are either Boolean variables in $\mathcal{V}$ or the application of different predicates to the expressions over $\mathcal{V}$, and *assertions* are first-order formulas constructed from atomic formulas using Boolean connectives or quantification of variables [6].

LTDL formulas φ are built up from atomic formulas, Boolean connectives, the existential/universal dynamic modality $\langle\cdot\rangle/[\cdot]$, the future LTL operators X (next) and U (until), and the past LTL operators Y (Previous) and S (Since). We define the Boolean abbreviations $\top = a \vee \neg a$ and $\bot = a \wedge \neg a$ for some atomic formula a, and use the usual abbreviations of the Boolean connectives $\rightarrow$ and $\leftrightarrow$. We refer to an LTDL formula whose main operator is a temporal operator ($X, Y, U, S, \langle\cdot\rangle$ and $[\cdot]$) as a *principally temporal formula*, which is called *basic* if all its subformulas are assertions. The dual dynamic modalities satisfy $[\rho]\varphi = \neg\langle\rho\rangle\neg\varphi$.

Path expressions ρ comprise assertions ψ, tests $\varphi?$ (embedding LTDL formulas within paths), and standard regular operations ($+$, ;, *). ρ is *test-only* if its atoms are exclusively tests. Intuitively, $\langle\rho\rangle\varphi$ (resp., $[\rho]\varphi$) holds over a path iff there exists some (resp., for every) finite prefix matching ρ such that φ holds on the remaining suffix.

Given a set of typed variables $\mathcal{V}$ over finite domain, we denote by $dom(v)$ the finite domain of $v \in \mathcal{V}$, and denote by $dom(\mathcal{V})$ the Cartesian product of the domains of all variables in $\mathcal{V}$. We write $s \models \psi$, if a variable valuation $s \in dom(\mathcal{V})$ satisfies an assertion ψ. We denote by $\mathcal{V}(\varphi)$ the set of variables that occur in φ. We define the *length* of an LTDL formula φ, denoted by $|\varphi|$, as the number of nodes in the syntax tree of φ.

2.2 Semantics of Linear Temporal Dynamic Logic

We define the semantics of LTDL with respect to both finite and infinite traces (words) over the alphabet $dom(\mathcal{V})$. To characterize both finite and infinite traces with unified terminology, we denote a trace over the alphabet $dom(\mathcal{V})$ as $w = w_0 w_1 \cdots w_{last}$, where $last \in \mathbb{N} \cup \{\infty\}$. We assume that the symbol ∞ is greater than any natural number; thus, w is infinite if $last = \infty$, and finite if $last \in \mathbb{N}$. The length $|w|$ of w is defined as the number of letters in w. Given two instants $j \geq i \geq 0$, we denote the infinite suffix $w_i w_{i+1} \cdots$ as $w^{i..}$, and the finite segment $w_i w_{i+1} \cdots w_j$ as $w^{i..j}$. The length of w is denoted by $|w|$: $|w| = 0$ if w is the empty word ϵ; if w is infinite, then $|w| = \infty$ and $|w^{i..j}| = j - i + 1$; If w is a finite trace $w_0 w_1 \ldots w_{last}$ with $last \in \mathbb{N}$, then $|w| = last + 1$, and: $|w^{i..j}| = |w^{i..last}|$ if $i \leq last < j$, $|w^{i..j}| = 0$ if $last < i$.

Given an LTDL formula φ, a finite/infinite trace $w = w_0 w_1 w_2 \cdots$ over the alphabet $dom(\mathcal{V})$, and an instant $i \in \mathbb{N}$ ($i \in [0, last]$ if w is finite), the doubly-inductive semantics [7] of φ being true at instant i of w, denoted $(w, i) \models \varphi$, is defined inductively as follows:

- $(w, i) \models a$ where a is an atomic formula $\iff w_i \models a$
- $(w, i) \models \neg\varphi \iff (w, i) \not\models \varphi$
- $(w, i) \models \varphi_1 \wedge \varphi_2 \iff (w, i) \models \varphi_1$ and $(w, i) \models \varphi_2$
- $(w, i) \models \varphi_1 \vee \varphi_2 \iff (w, i) \models \varphi_1$ or $(w, i) \models \varphi_2$
- $(w, i) \models \langle\psi\rangle\varphi$ where ψ is an assertion $\iff i < last$ and $(w, i) \models \psi$ and $(w, i+1) \models \varphi$

- $(w, i) \models \langle \varphi_1? \rangle \varphi_2 \iff (w, i) \models \varphi_1$ and $(w, i) \models \varphi_2$
- $(w, i) \models \langle \rho_1 + \rho_2 \rangle \varphi \iff (w, i) \models \langle \rho_1 \rangle \varphi \vee \langle \rho_2 \rangle \varphi$
- $(w, i) \models \langle \rho_1; \rho_2 \rangle \varphi \iff (w, i) \models \langle \rho_1 \rangle \langle \rho_2 \rangle \varphi$
- $(w, i) \models \langle \rho^* \rangle \varphi \iff (w, i) \models \varphi$, or ρ is not test-only and $i < last$ and $(w, i) \models \langle \rho \rangle \langle \rho^* \rangle \varphi$
- $(w, i) \models [\psi] \varphi$ where ψ is an assertion $\iff i \geq last$ or $(w, i) \not\models \psi$ or $(w, i+1) \models \varphi$
- $(w, i) \models [\varphi_1?] \varphi_2 \iff (w, i) \not\models \varphi_1$ or $(w, i) \models \varphi_2$
- $(w, i) \models [\rho_1 + \rho_2] \varphi \iff (w, i) \models [\rho_1] \varphi \wedge [\rho_2] \varphi$
- $(w, i) \models [\rho_1; \rho_2] \varphi \iff (w, i) \models [\rho_1][\rho_2] \varphi$
- $(w, i) \models [\rho^*] \varphi \iff (w, i) \models \varphi$, and ρ is test-only or $i \geq last$ or $(w, i) \models [\rho][\rho^*] \varphi$
- $(w, i) \models X \varphi \iff i < last$ and $(w, i+1) \models \varphi$
- $(w, i) \models Y \varphi \iff i > 0$ and $(w, i-1) \models \varphi$
- $(w, i) \models \varphi_1 U \varphi_2 \iff (w, i') \models \varphi_2$ for some $i' \in [i, last]$, and $(w, i'') \models \varphi_1$ for all $i'' \in [i, i'-1]$
- $(w, i) \models \varphi_1 S \varphi_2 \iff (w, i') \models \varphi_2$ for some $i' \in [0, i]$, and $(w, i'') \models \varphi_1$ for all $i'' \in [i'+1, i]$

We write $w \models \varphi$ for $(w, 0) \models \varphi$ and say that w satisfies φ.

2.3 LTDL Temporal Testers

We take Just Discrete Systems (JDS) as our computational models. A JDS $\mathcal{D} = (\mathcal{V}, \Theta, \mathcal{R}, \mathcal{J})$ consists of the following components: (1) $\mathcal{V}$ is a finite set of typed variables over finite domain $dom(\mathcal{V})$; (2) Θ is the initial condition, which is an assertion over $\mathcal{V}$ characterizing the set of initial states; (3) $\mathcal{R}(\mathcal{V}, \mathcal{V}')$ is the transition relation, which is an assertion over $\mathcal{V} \cup \mathcal{V}'$, where $\mathcal{V}'$ is the set of primed variables v' for each $v \in \mathcal{V}$; (4) $\mathcal{J}$ is a set of justice constraints. Each constraint is an assertion over $\mathcal{V}$.

A *state* of $\mathcal{D}$ is a type-consistent variable interpretation in $dom(\mathcal{V})$. For a state s and a variable $v \in \mathcal{V}$, we denote by $s[v]$ the value assigned to v by the state s. A state is initial if Θ is true under the variable interpretation of the state. We say that state s' is a successor of state s, if and only if $s \cup s' \models \mathcal{R}(\mathcal{V}, \mathcal{V}')$.

A *path* π is an infinite sequence of states created by exhaustively unwinding the transition relation from a state of $\mathcal{D}$. We denote by $\pi(i)$ the state located at the position i of path π, and denote by π^i the suffix of path π starting from position i. A path π is *fair* if it contains infinitely many J-states, i.e., the states satisfying J, for all $J \in \mathcal{J}$. A path π is also called a *run* if the first state $\pi(0)$ is an initial state of $\mathcal{D}$. A run π is called a *computation* if it is fair. We denote by $\Pi(\mathcal{D})$ the set of all computations of $\mathcal{D}$. Fair states are all states of fair paths, while *feasible states* are states of computations. In other words, the set of feasible states of $\mathcal{D}$ is exactly the set of fair states reachable from initial states of $\mathcal{D}$. Given two JDSs $\mathcal{D}_1 = (\mathcal{V}_1, \Theta_1, \mathcal{R}_1, \mathcal{J}_1)$ and $\mathcal{D}_2 = (\mathcal{V}_2, \Theta_2, \mathcal{R}_2, \mathcal{J}_2)$, their synchronous parallel composition, denoted by $\mathcal{D}_1 \parallel \mathcal{D}_2$, is defined as the JDS $(\mathcal{V}_1 \cup \mathcal{V}_2, \Theta_1 \wedge \Theta_2, \mathcal{R}_1 \wedge \mathcal{R}_2, \mathcal{J}_1 \cup \mathcal{J}_2)$.

Definition 1. *A temporal tester for an LTDL formula φ is a JDS $\mathcal{T}(\varphi)$, which has an output assertion $\chi(\varphi)$, such that:*

- *Soundness: For every computation* $\pi : s_0, s_1, s_2, \cdots$ *of* $\mathcal{T}(\varphi)$, $s_i \models \chi(\varphi)$ *iff* $\pi^i \models \varphi$.
- *Completeness: For every sequence of states* $\pi' : s'_0, s'_1, s'_2, \cdots$, *there is a computation* $\pi : s_0, s_1, s_2, \cdots$ *of* $\mathcal{T}(\varphi)$ *s.t. for each* i, s_i *and* s'_i *agree on the interpretation of* $\mathcal{V}(\varphi)$, *the variables that occur in* φ.

We define the temporal tester for LTDL as in Definition 1. Note that our tester is an optimization of the one introduced in [14]. The tester from [14] creates a new Boolean output variable for every subformula, resulting in a number of output variables that is proportional to the length of the formula.

In contrast, our tester only introduces new Boolean output variables for principally temporal subformulas and does not create output variables for Boolean connectives. Given an LTDL formula φ, the formula obtained by replacing all principally temporal subformulas in φ with their corresponding Boolean output variables is referred to as the *output assertion* $\chi(\varphi)$. In practice, since most temporal formulas contain numerous Boolean connectives, the testers we define over output assertions are typically smaller and more efficient.

We say that a JDS $\mathcal{D}$ satisfies an LTDL formula φ if and only if $\pi(0) \models \chi(\varphi)$ for all computations $\pi \in \Pi(\mathcal{D} \parallel \mathcal{T}(\varphi))$.

3 Regular Grammar for Path Expressions

The tester construction for LTDL follows the same principle as for PSL in [14]: compositionality and symbolic representation via a distinguished output variable. The key challenge stems from the need to construct regular grammars and testers capable of handling LTDL's unique features. Specifically, its regular path expressions can contain tests of LTDL subformulas that must hold immediately and without consuming input—a critical requirement not supported by PSL.

3.1 A Regular Grammar Construction Method for Path Expressions

The regular grammar $G = (V, T, P, S)$ for a path expression ρ comprises four components: (1) V: a finite set of variables; (2) T: a finite set of terminals including the empty word ϵ, tests $\varphi?$, and assertions over V (assuming $V \cap T = \emptyset$); (3) P: a finite set of productions restricted to six right-linear forms ($v \to \epsilon$, $v \to \varphi?$, $v \to a$, $v \to w$, $v \to \varphi?w$, and $v \to aw$, where $a \in T$ is an assertion, and $v, w \in V$); and (4) $S \in V$: the start symbol.

A production $p \in P$ mapping variable v to an expression containing variable w is *for* v (which *has* p) and *references* w. The right-hand side of p specifies an action triggered when v is satisfied. The set of all productions for v forms its *variable definition*, enumerating the actions non-deterministically selected upon satisfying v. This definition is *deterministic* if v has exactly one production. Similarly, a reference to v is *deterministic* if exactly one production references v. Productions of the forms $v \to a$ and $v \to aw$ are termed *consuming* because they take one time step, whereas all other forms are considered *instantaneous* as they take no time. Productions that do not reference any variables are called *terminal.*

A regular grammar G is *associated* with a path expression ρ if they define the same language. Assuming sub-grammars $G_1 = (V_1, T_1, P_1, S_1)$ and $G_2 = (V_2, T_2, P_2, S_2)$ for ρ_1 and ρ_2 are already constructed, the grammar $G(\rho) = (V, T, P, S)$ for ρ is built inductively according to Table 1. Specifically, base cases ($\varphi?$, ψ) and union operations ($\rho_1 + \rho_2$) introduce a new start variable v to derive terminals or branch to S_1 and S_2. For concatenation ($\rho_1; \rho_2$) and Kleene star (ρ_1^*), S_1 remains the start symbol. In $\rho_1; \rho_2$, S_2 is appended to P_1's terminal-deriving productions (explicitly handling ϵ-transitions via $w \rightarrow \epsilon \in P_1$) to strictly chain the languages. For ρ_1^*, the production $S_1 \rightarrow \epsilon$ is added to model zero repetitions; to model arbitrary repetitions, any P_1 production capable of terminating a sequence is duplicated and appended with S_1 to enable recursive loop-backs.

Table 1. The regular grammar $G(\rho) = (V, T, P, S)$

ρ	Grammar $G(\rho) = (V, T, P, S)$
$\varphi?$	$V = \{v\}, T = \{\varphi?\}, S = v, P = \{v \rightarrow \varphi?\}$
ψ	$V = \{v\}, T = \{\psi\}, S = v, P = \{v \rightarrow \psi\}$
$\rho_1 + \rho_2$	$V = \{v\} \cup V_1 \cup V_2, T = T_1 \cup T_2, S = v, P = \{v \rightarrow S_1\} \cup \{v \rightarrow S_2\} \cup P_1 \cup P_2$
$\rho_1; \rho_2$	$V = V_1 \cup V_2, T = T_1 \cup T_2, S = S_1,$ $P = \{v \rightarrow S_2 \mid v \rightarrow \epsilon \in P_1\} \cup \{v \rightarrow \varphi?S_2 \mid v \rightarrow \varphi? \in P_1\} \cup \{v \rightarrow aS_2 \mid v \rightarrow a \in P_1\} \cup \{v \rightarrow w \mid v \rightarrow w \in P_1\}$ $\cup \{v \rightarrow \varphi?w \mid v \rightarrow \varphi?w \in P_1\} \cup \{v \rightarrow aw \mid v \rightarrow aw \in P_1\} \cup \{v \rightarrow S_2 \mid v \rightarrow w \in P_1, w \rightarrow \epsilon \in P_1\}$ $\cup \{v \rightarrow \varphi?S_2 \mid v \rightarrow \varphi?w \in P_1, w \rightarrow \epsilon \in P_1\} \cup \{v \rightarrow aS_2 \mid v \rightarrow aw \in P_1, w \rightarrow \epsilon \in P_1\} \cup P_2$
ρ_1^*	$V = V_1, T = T_1, S = S_1,$ $P = \{S_1 \rightarrow \epsilon\} \cup \{v \rightarrow \epsilon, v \rightarrow S_1 \mid v \rightarrow \epsilon \in P_1, v \neq S_1\} \cup \{v \rightarrow \varphi?, v \rightarrow \varphi?S_1 \mid v \rightarrow \varphi? \in P_1\}$ $\cup \{v \rightarrow a, v \rightarrow aS_1 \mid v \rightarrow a \in P_1\} \cup \{v \rightarrow w \mid v \rightarrow w \in P_1\} \cup \{v \rightarrow \varphi?w \mid v \rightarrow \varphi?w \in P_1\}$ $\cup \{v \rightarrow aw \mid v \rightarrow aw \in P_1\} \cup \{v \rightarrow \epsilon, v \rightarrow S_1 \mid v \rightarrow w \in P_1, v \neq S_1, w \rightarrow \epsilon \in P_1\}$ $\cup \{v \rightarrow \epsilon \mid v \rightarrow w \in P_1, v = S_1, w \rightarrow \epsilon \in P_1\} \cup \{v \rightarrow \varphi?, v \rightarrow \varphi?S_1 \mid v \rightarrow \varphi?w \in P_1, v \neq S_1, w \rightarrow \epsilon \in P_1\}$ $\cup \{v \rightarrow \varphi? \mid v \rightarrow \varphi?w \in P_1, v = S_1, w \rightarrow \epsilon \in P_1\} \cup \{v \rightarrow a, v \rightarrow aS_1 \mid v \rightarrow aw \in P_1, w \rightarrow \epsilon \in P_1\}$

Lemma 1. *For any path expression ρ, the regular grammar $G(\rho)$ constructed via Table 1 correctly recognizes the language defined by ρ, i.e., $L(G(\rho)) = L(\rho)$.*

Proof. By structural induction on ρ. Base cases $\rho = \varphi?$ and $\rho = \psi$ trivially hold via productions $v \rightarrow \varphi?$ and $v \rightarrow \psi$. Inductively assume G_1 and G_2 perfectly recognize $L(\rho_1)$ and $L(\rho_2)$ respectively. For $\rho_1 + \rho_2$, introducing $v \rightarrow S_1$ and $v \rightarrow S_2$ natively captures the language union. For $\rho_1; \rho_2$, appending S_2 to the terminal-producing derivations of P_1 ensures strings from $L(\rho_2)$ strictly follow those from $L(\rho_1)$, specifically maintaining correctness when ϵ-transitions ($w \rightarrow \epsilon \in P_1$) are involved. For ρ_1^*, the production $S_1 \rightarrow \epsilon$ handles zero occurrences, while appending S_1 to terminal derivations in P_1 mathematically models a recursive loop, allowing finite arbitrary repetitions of $L(\rho_1)$, satisfying Kleene star semantics.

Lemma 2. *The number of variables and productions in the regular grammar $G(\rho)$ constructed via Table 1 is linear in the length of ρ.*

Proof. By Table 1, forms $\varphi?$, ψ, and $\rho_1 + \rho_2$ introduce exactly one variable, while $\rho_1; \rho_2$ and ρ^* introduce none, ensuring $\mathcal{O}(|\rho|)$ variables. For productions, base cases $\varphi?$ and ψ yield exactly one. Inductively, $\rho_1 + \rho_2$ adds two new productions to $P_1 \cup P_2$. For $\rho_1; \rho_2$ (resp., ρ_1^*), P_2 is preserved, and each production in P_1 is replaced by at most two (resp., three) new productions depending on whether $w \to \epsilon \in P_1$, alongside one additional $S_1 \to \epsilon$ for ρ_1^*. Consequently, each structural operation increases the production count by at most a constant factor, guaranteeing total productions are linear in $|\rho|$.

3.2 Grammar Preprocessing: Elimination of Zero-Delay Cycles

A *zero-delay cycle* (ϵ-cycle) in a regular grammar occurs when a sequence of instantaneous transitions—such as ϵ-transitions ($u \to w$) or test transitions ($u \to \psi?w$)—forms a directed loop (e.g., $v \to \psi_1?w$ and $w \to \psi_2?v$) without consuming any input letter (i.e., without advancing the temporal step). Eliminating these cycles prior to symbolic tester construction is mandatory for two primary reasons:

(1) Avoiding Algebraic Loops: In symbolic transition relations, variables dynamically depend on their right-hand derivations. A zero-delay cycle creates an immediate circular dependency at the exact same temporal instant (e.g., defining $v \leftrightarrow \psi \wedge v$), leading to unresolvable algebraic loops in BDD/SAT environments.

(2) Preventing Infinite Divergence: Naive closure computations using Abstract Syntax Trees (AST) or string concatenations fail on such cycles (e.g., recursively expanding $\langle(a? + b?)^*\rangle c$ diverges infinitely) due to their inability to natively enforce boolean absorption (e.g., $a \vee (a \wedge b) \equiv a$).

To circumvent state explosion and guarantee convergence, we introduce an exact elimination procedure (Algorithm 1) relying on algebraically canonical logical operations (specifically via Reduced Ordered Binary Decision Diagrams, ROBDDs [3]) combined with a simple-path Depth-First Search (DFS). By formally representing and manipulating all boolean conditions (e.g., *ReachCond* and ϕ) as ROBDDs [3], logical equivalence and absorption laws (e.g., $A \vee (A \wedge B) \equiv A$) are automatically enforced during standard BDD operations. Algorithm 1 operates in three phases:

(1) **Unconditional ϵ-SCC Merging:** ϵ-SCCs, the Strongly Connected Components (SCCs) of unconditional instantaneous transitions ($u \to v$), are merged into a single representative variable, as they are unconditionally equivalent.

(2) **Conditional ϵ-Cycle Bypassing:** For ϵ-cycles involving conditional tests ($u \to \varphi?v$), equivalence depends dynamically on the output assertion $\chi(\varphi)$. A DFS from the target of a ϵ-cycle-inducing back-edge explores strictly zero-delay cycle-free simple paths. Accumulated conditions are logically aggregated using canonical boolean BDD `Apply` operations (denoted by $\wedge$ and $\vee$), ensuring redundancy absorption. The optimal logical result is used to bypass the original back-edge, shifting consuming or terminal productions directly to the source node.

(3) **Dead Production Elimination:** A final Breadth-First Search (BFS) reachability analysis from the start variable removes unreachable productions.

Algorithm 1: *eliminateZeroDelayCycles*(G)

Input : the regular grammar $G = (V, T, P, S)$
Output: the zero-delay cycle-free regular grammar G
`// Phase 1: Unconditional ϵ-SCC Merging`
foreach *SCC* $\mathcal{C}$ $(|\mathcal{C}| > 1)$ *of unconditional edges* $(x \to y) \in P$ **do**
  Merge nodes in $\mathcal{C}$ into representative $r \in \mathcal{C}$ (preferring S); Remove self-loops;
`// Phase 2: Conditional ϵ-Cycle Bypassing via Canonical DFS`
foreach *back-edge* $e = (v \to \varphi_{back}?u) \in P$ **do** `// treat` $v \to u$ `as` $v \to \mathsf{True}?u$
  $\mathit{ReachCond}(w) \leftarrow \mathsf{False}$ for all $w \in V$; $\mathit{visited} \leftarrow \emptyset$;
  $\mathsf{DFS}(u, \mathsf{True}, e)$; `// Accumulate simple-path Boolean reachability`
  foreach *node* $w \in V$ *where* $\mathit{ReachCond}(w) \neq \mathsf{False}$ **do**
    $\psi_{bp} \leftarrow \chi(\varphi_{back}) \wedge \mathit{ReachCond}(w)$; `// Logical AND canonicalization`
    foreach $(w \to ax) \in P$ *where* x *can be empty* **do**
      if $(\psi_{bp} \wedge a) \neq \mathsf{False}$ **then** Add $v \to (\psi_{bp} \wedge a)x$ to P;
    if $\psi_{bp} \neq \mathsf{False}$ *and* $(w \to \epsilon) \in P$ **then** Add $v \to \psi_{bp}?$ to P;
    foreach $(w \to \varphi?) \in P$ **do**
      if $(\psi_{bp} \wedge \chi(\varphi)) \neq \mathsf{False}$ **then** Add $v \to (\psi_{bp} \wedge \chi(\varphi))?$ to P;
  Remove back-edge e from P;
`// Phase 3: Dead Production Elimination`
Remove unreachable nodes (variables) and productions via BFS from S;
return the zero-delay cycle-free regular grammar G;

Function DFS(*node* n, *condition* ϕ, *back-edge* e)
  $\mathit{ReachCond}(n) \leftarrow \mathit{ReachCond}(n) \vee \phi$; `// OR absorbs redundancies`
  $\mathit{visited} \leftarrow \mathit{visited} \cup \{n\}$;
  foreach $(n \xrightarrow{\varphi?} x) \in P \setminus \{e\}$ *and* $x \notin \mathit{visited}$ **do** `// treat` $n \to x$ `as` $n \to \mathsf{True}?x$
    $\mathsf{DFS}(x, \phi \wedge \chi(\varphi), e)$;
  $\mathit{visited} \leftarrow \mathit{visited} \setminus \{n\}$; `// Backtrack`

Lemma 3. *Algorithm 1 correctly eliminates all zero-delay cycles in a regular grammar $G = (V, T, P, S)$ while preserving its semantics.*

Proof. Exploring exclusively simple paths during DFS is logically complete because canonical boolean absorption ($A \vee (A \wedge B) \equiv A$) natively covers logic accumulated by any cyclic paths. Specifically, since *ReachCond* is strictly maintained as an ROBDD [3], any redundant path condition explored by the DFS is structurally absorbed during the logical OR step via a BDD `Apply` operation, guaranteeing semantic equivalence with exhaustive cyclic search. Bypassing preemptively shifts consuming or terminal productions to the source v under the exact aggregated conditions, preserving the grammar language while breaking zero-delay cyclic dependencies.

Lemma 4. *Algorithm 1 terminates in $\mathcal{O}(|V| \cdot |P| + K \cdot 2^{|V|} \cdot B)$ time, where K is the number of back-edges, and B is the boolean aggregation time (taking*

$\mathcal{O}(|G_1| \cdot |G_2|)$ time and space for a BDD **Apply** *operation over operand BDD graphs G_1 and G_2).*

Proof. Phase 1 takes $\mathcal{O}(|V| \cdot |P|)$. In Phase 2, the DFS explores up to $\mathcal{O}(2^{|V|})$ simple paths for each of the K back-edges. Since each canonical boolean aggregation costs $\mathcal{O}(B)$, this phase strictly bounds to $\mathcal{O}(K \cdot 2^{|V|} \cdot B)$. In this context, B remains tractable because the variables within these operand BDDs are strictly bounded by the finite set of atomic tests present in the specific ϵ-cycle being bypassed. Phase 3 requires $\mathcal{O}(|V| + |P|)$ via BFS. Summing these phases yields the overall complexity, with termination natively ensured by the acyclic DFS tracking.

3.3 Optimizing Regular Grammars

To minimize the exponential state space induced by Boolean variables in a tester, Algorithm 2 iteratively eliminates redundant variables and productions from $G(\rho)$ across three phases—production merging, deterministic variable definition reduction, and deterministic variable reference reduction—until no more changes occur.

Algorithm 2: *optimizeGrammar*(G)

Input : a regular grammar $G = (V, T, P, S)$
Output: the optimized regular grammar G

repeat
    repeat `// Phase 1: production merging`
        foreach *variable* $v \in V$ *and form* $f \in \{\varphi?, a, \varphi?w, aw\}$ **do**
            if *v has $m \geq 2$ productions $p_1, \ldots, p_m$ of form f* **then**
                Merge $p_1, \ldots, p_m$ into a production by disjoining their terminals;
    until *No production is modified*;
    repeat `// Phase 2: deterministic variable definition reduction`
        foreach *variable $w \neq S$ defined by a single production p_r* **do**
            if *combine(p_l, p_r) is valid for all $p_l \in P$ referencing w* **then**
                Replace all such p_l with *combine*(p_l, p_r); Remove w and p_r;
    until *No production is modified*;
    repeat `// Phase 3: deterministic variable reference reduction`
        foreach *variable $w \neq S$ referenced by a single production p_l* **do**
            if *combine(p_l, p_r) is valid for all $p_r \in P$ defining w* **then**
                Replace all such p_r with *combine*(p_l, p_r); Remove w and p_l;
    until *No production is modified*;
until *No production is modified in this loop*;
Apply BFS from S to renumber (starting from 1) all visited variables;

Phase 1 (Production Merging): This phase iteratively merges productions sharing the same left-hand variable and right-linear form by disjoining their terminals. It terminates when each $v \in V$ has at most one production for forms $v \to \epsilon$, $v \to \varphi?$, and $v \to a$, and at most one for forms $v \to w$, $v \to \varphi?w$, and

$v \to aw$ per pair (v, w) (where v and w may be identical). This rapid formation of deterministic definitions and references significantly accelerates subsequent reduction phases.

Phase 2 (Deterministic Variable Definition Reduction): This step eliminates redundant deterministic variable definitions. A variable defined by multiple productions necessitates non-deterministic action selection and cannot be removed. Conversely, a variable $w \neq S$ defined by a single production p_r operates deterministically. Such a variable and its definition p_r are deemed *redundant* and systematically removed if *all* productions p_l referencing w can be validly replaced by $combine(p_l, p_r)$ (defined in Table 2) without altering the overall semantics.

Table 2. Grammar combination function $combine(p_l, p_r)$, where $v \neq w$ and $w \neq w'$

$p_l \in P$ / $p_r \in P$	$v \to w$	$v \to \varphi_1?w$	$v \to aw$
$w \to \epsilon$	$v \to \epsilon$	$v \to \varphi_1?$	$v \to a$
$w \to \varphi_2?$	$v \to \varphi_2?$	$v \to (\varphi_1 \wedge \varphi_2)?$	-
$w \to b$	$v \to b$	$v \to (\varphi_1 \wedge b)$ if φ_1 is an assertion	-
$w \to w'$	$v \to w'$	$v \to \varphi_1?w'$	$v \to aw'$
$w \to \varphi_2?w'$	$v \to \varphi_2?w'$	$v \to (\varphi_1 \wedge \varphi_2)?w'$	-
$w \to bw'$	$v \to bw'$	$v \to (\varphi_1 \wedge b)w'$ if φ_1 is an assertion	-

Assume that $p_l = v \to t_1w$ and $p_r = w \to t_2w'$, where the terminals t_1 and t_2 may be empty. By replacing the referenced variable w in p_l with the right-hand side t_2w' of the production p_r for w, we obtain a new "production" $v \to t_1t_2w'$. If t_1t_2 can be transformed in a semantically equivalent way into a valid terminal t', then p_l and p_r can be combined into a new valid production $v \to t'w'$.

Phase 3 (Deterministic Variable Reference Reduction): This phase eliminates variables with deterministic references. A reference to $w \neq S$ is deterministic if exactly one production p_l (e.g., $v \to t_1w$) references w. Being the unique entry point, w can be bypassed by forwarding t_1 to w's subsequent actions. For every production p_r defining w (e.g., $w \to t_2w'$), we replace it with the semantically equivalent $combine(p_l, p_r)$ (yielding $v \to t'w'$ where $t' \equiv t_1t_2$). If this substitution is valid for all definitions of w, both w and p_l are eliminated. Algorithm 2 iterates these three phases until a fixed point is reached.

Finally, by viewing the optimized grammar as a directed graph (variables as nodes and productions as edges) a breadth-first search from the start symbol renumbers all variables starting from 1. Moreover, this optimization significantly reduces the variables and productions compared to the initial linear bounds from Lemma 2, as the left-hand variables of all eliminated productions are also completely removed.

Lemma 5. *Algorithm 2 correctly reduces the regular grammar $G(\rho)$ while strictly preserving its recognized language $L(G(\rho))$.*

Proof. Production merging applies valid disjunctive semantics to structurally identical non-deterministic choices. Deterministic definition and reference reductions perform sound inline substitutions (per Table 2), safely bypassing intermediate states without altering the accepted terminal sequences. BFS renumbering is an isomorphic transformation. Thus, semantic equivalence is maintained throughout.

Lemma 6. *Algorithm 2 terminates in* $\mathcal{O}((|V| + |P|)^2)$ *worst-case time.*

Proof. Each full iteration of the outer loop strictly reduces the total number of variables or productions, guaranteeing at most $\mathcal{O}(|V| + |P|)$ iterations. Within each iteration, scanning variables, merging, and substituting productions (via *combine*) takes $\mathcal{O}(|V|+|P|)$ time, as degree per node is practically bounded. The final BFS takes $\mathcal{O}(|V| + |P|)$. The total worst-case time is therefore quadratic.

To further optimize performance in engineering, applying grammar optimization using Algorithm 2 before executing Algorithm 1 often significantly reduce the workload of Algorithm 1. Therefore an optimized zero-delay cycle-free regular grammar $G(\rho)$ can be constructed via the processing sequence of Table 1, Algorithms 2, 1 and 2.

Theorem 1. *The construction of the optimized zero-delay cycle-free regular grammar* $G(\rho)$ *is correct, i.e.,* $L(G(\rho)) = L(\rho)$.

Proof. The proof follows from the transitivity of semantic equivalence. Lemma 1 ensures the initial grammar is correct. Lemmas 3 and 5 establish that Algorithms 1 and 2 strictly preserve the recognized language. Thus, the final optimized grammar recognizes $L(\rho)$.

Theorem 2. *The optimized zero-delay cycle-free regular grammar* $G(\rho)$ *is constructed in* $\mathcal{O}(|\rho| + (|V| + |P|)^2 + K \cdot 2^{|V|} \cdot B)$ *time.*

Proof. Construction via Table 1 is $\mathcal{O}(|\rho|)$ (Lemma 2). Algorithm 2 adds $\mathcal{O}((|V|+|P|)^2)$ (Lemma 6), and Algorithm 1 adds $\mathcal{O}(|V| \cdot |P| + K \cdot 2^{|V|} \cdot B)$ (Lemma 4). The total complexity is the sum of these steps.

4 LTDL Tester Construction

By definition, a temporal tester's output assertion holds iff the formula itself holds. Composite LTDL formulas with nested temporal operators are systematically simplified via a bottom-up post-order syntactic tree traversal. Each principally temporal subformula is recursively replaced by its output assertion after its tester is constructed. This ensures that when visiting a temporal operator, its subformulas are already basic output assertions, yielding the complete temporal testers and assertions upon traversal completion.

4.1 Testers for Future and Past LTL Temporal Operators

Given an LTL principally temporal formula φ, Table 3 defines the tester $\mathcal{T}(\varphi) = (V_\varphi, \Theta_\varphi, R_\varphi, \mathcal{J}_\varphi) \parallel \mathcal{T}(\varphi_1) \parallel \mathcal{T}(\varphi_2)$ and output assertion $\chi(\varphi) = x$, where x is the fresh Boolean output variable introduced for φ. Future formula $\varphi_1 U \varphi_2$ requires non-empty justice constraint $\mathcal{J}_\varphi = \{\neg x \vee \chi(\varphi_2)\}$ to ensure eventual fulfillment. Past operators Y and S evaluate finite historical states. Since history strictly extends backward to the initial state, no justice constraints are needed ($\mathcal{J}_\varphi = \emptyset$). We properly constrain the initial states Θ_φ at $i = 0$: For $Y\varphi_1$, $i > 0$ is required, making $\Theta_\varphi = \neg x$; for $\varphi_1 S \varphi_2$, the backward interval $[i' + 1, i]$ is empty at $i = 0$, yielding $\Theta_\varphi = x \leftrightarrow \chi(\varphi_2)$.

Table 3. The tester $\mathcal{T}(\varphi) = (V_\varphi, \Theta_\varphi, R_\varphi, \mathcal{J}_\varphi) \parallel \mathcal{T}(\varphi_1) \parallel \mathcal{T}(\varphi_2)$

φ	$\mathcal{V}_\varphi$	Θ_φ	$\mathcal{R}_\varphi$	$\mathcal{J}_\varphi$
$X\varphi_1$	$\{x\} \cup \mathcal{V}(\chi(\varphi_1))$	$\top$	$x \leftrightarrow \chi'(\varphi_1)$	$\emptyset$
$Y\varphi_1$	$\{x\} \cup \mathcal{V}(\chi(\varphi_1))$	$\neg x$	$x' \leftrightarrow \chi(\varphi_1)$	$\emptyset$
$\varphi_1 U \varphi_2$	$\{x\} \cup \mathcal{V}(\chi(\varphi_1)) \cup \mathcal{V}(\chi(\varphi_2))$	$\top$	$x \leftrightarrow (\chi(\varphi_2) \vee (\chi(\varphi_1) \wedge x'))$	$\{\neg x \vee \chi(\varphi_2)\}$
$\varphi_1 S \varphi_2$	$\{x\} \cup \mathcal{V}(\chi(\varphi_1)) \cup \mathcal{V}(\chi(\varphi_2))$	$x \leftrightarrow \chi(\varphi_2)$	$x' \leftrightarrow (\chi'(\varphi_2) \vee (\chi'(\varphi_1) \wedge x))$	$\emptyset$

4.2 Tester for Existential Dynamic Modality

Since $[\rho]\varphi = \neg\langle\rho\rangle\neg\varphi$, we focus on $\langle\rho\rangle\varphi$. After the optimized zero-delay cycle-free regular grammar $G(\rho)$ is constructed, Algorithm 3 translates $\langle\rho\rangle\varphi$ into its output assertion and tester, whose transition relation $\mathcal{R}$ is over Boolean variables X, Y and primes X', Y', where $|X| = |Y| = |V|$. Productions $v_i \rightarrow \epsilon, v_i \rightarrow \varphi_j?, v_i \rightarrow v_j, v_i \rightarrow \phi_j?v_j$ consume no transition steps, while $v_i \rightarrow a_j, v_i \rightarrow b_j v_j$ consume one step (modeled via primed assertions, e.g., $a_j \wedge \chi'(\varphi)$). Semantically, $s_j \ldots s_k \models \langle\rho\rangle\varphi$ iff a variable sequence matches the consumed assertions. To enforce finite-length paths, we adopt a double-variable representation [14] introducing x_i, y_i for each $v_i \in V$. Justice constraints ensure X is eventually copied to Y ($\bigwedge(x_i \leftrightarrow y_i)$) and all Y eventually become false ($\neg\bigvee y_i$), preventing infinite generation. Unlike PSL, LTDL allows empty finite traces, explicitly handled by zero-step productions.

4.3 Tester Construction for Arbitrary LTDL Formulas

Given any LTDL formula φ, Algorithm 4 outlines post-order recursive construction of $\mathcal{T}(\varphi)$ and $\chi(\varphi)$. A caching mechanism ("*cache*": a map from LTDL formulas to their testers and output assertions) is introduced to avoid duplicate tester generation for identical subformulas. Upon encountering a principally temporal subformula φ', the cache is queried for φ'; if absent, the sub-tester $\mathcal{T}(\varphi')$ and the output assertion $\chi(\varphi')$ are built, cached, and $\chi(\varphi')$ replaces occurrences. Each cached sub-tester $(\mathcal{V}, \Theta, \mathcal{R}, \mathcal{J})$ is then mechanically translated into SMV code.

Algorithm 3: *testerDiamond*($\langle\rho\rangle\varphi$)

Input : an LTDL formula $\langle\rho\rangle\varphi$
Output: the tester $\mathcal{T}(\langle\rho\rangle\varphi)$; the output assertion $\chi(\langle\rho\rangle\varphi)$

Build initial $G(\rho)$ by Table 1, apply Algorithms 2, 1 and 2 sequentially, yielding optimized zero-delay cycle-free grammar $G(\rho) = (V, T, P, S)$ where $V = \{v_1, \ldots, v_n\}$;
Create $X \leftarrow \{x_1, \ldots, x_n\}$ and $Y \leftarrow \{y_1, \ldots, y_n\}$ of V and the prime versions X' and Y';
$\chi(\langle\rho\rangle\varphi) \leftarrow x_1$; $\Theta \leftarrow \top$; $\mathcal{R} \leftarrow \top$; $\mathcal{T}' \leftarrow (\emptyset, \top, \top, \emptyset)$;
foreach $v_i \in V$ **do**
  $d \leftarrow \bot$;
  if $v_i \to \epsilon \in P$ **then** $d \leftarrow d \vee \chi(\varphi)$;
  foreach $v_i \to \varphi_j? \in P$ *and* $j \in [1, m]$ **do** $d \leftarrow d \vee (\chi(\varphi_j) \wedge \chi(\varphi))$; $\mathcal{T}' \leftarrow \mathcal{T}' \parallel \mathcal{T}(\varphi_j)$;
  foreach $v_i \to a_j \in P$ *and* $j \in [1, k]$ **do** $d \leftarrow d \vee (a_j \wedge \chi'(\varphi))$;
  foreach $v_i \to v_j \in P$ *and* $v_j \in V$ **do** $d \leftarrow d \vee x_j$;
  foreach $v_i \to \phi_j?v_j \in P$ *and* $v_j \in V$ **do** $d \leftarrow d \vee (\chi(\phi_j) \wedge x_j)$; $\mathcal{T}' \leftarrow \mathcal{T}' \parallel \mathcal{T}(\phi_j)$;
  foreach $v_i \to b_j v_j \in P$ *and* $v_j \in V$ **do** $d \leftarrow d \vee (b_j \wedge x'_j)$;
  $\mathcal{R} \leftarrow \mathcal{R} \wedge (x_i \leftrightarrow d) \wedge (y_i \to d)$;
$\mathcal{J} \leftarrow \{(x_1 \leftrightarrow y_1) \wedge \cdots \wedge (x_n \leftrightarrow y_n), \neg(y_1 \vee \cdots \vee y_n)\}$;
return $\mathcal{T}(\langle\rho\rangle\varphi) = (\mathcal{V}(\mathcal{R}), \Theta, \mathcal{R}, \mathcal{J}) \parallel \mathcal{T}'$ and $\chi(\langle\rho\rangle\varphi)$;

Algorithm 4: *tester*(φ)

Input : an LTDL formula φ without redundant negation symbol and $[\cdot]$ operator
Output: the output assertion $\chi(\varphi)$; the tester $\mathcal{T}(\varphi)$ is stored in *cache*;

if *φ is an assertion* **then** $\chi(\varphi) \leftarrow \varphi$;
else if $\varphi = \neg\varphi_1$ **then** $\chi(\varphi_1) \leftarrow$ *tester*(φ_1); $\chi(\varphi) \leftarrow \neg\chi(\varphi_1)$;
else if $\varphi = \varphi_1 \oplus \varphi_2$ *where* $\oplus \in \{\wedge, \vee, \to, \leftrightarrow\}$ **then** $\chi(\varphi_1) \leftarrow$ *tester*(φ_1); $\chi(\varphi_2) \leftarrow$ *tester*(φ_2); $\chi(\varphi) \leftarrow \chi(\varphi_1) \oplus \chi(\varphi_2)$;
else `// φ is of the form ⊕φ1 or φ1 ⊕ φ2 where ⊕ ∈ {⟨ρ⟩, X, Y, U, S}`
  $\chi(\varphi_1) \leftarrow$ *tester*(φ_1); **if** $\varphi = \varphi_1 \oplus \varphi_2$ **then** $\chi(\varphi_2) \leftarrow$ *tester*(φ_2);
  if *No tester and output assertion for φ in cache* **then**
    if $\oplus = \langle\rho\rangle$ **then** $\varphi' \leftarrow \oplus\chi(\varphi_1)$; Build $\mathcal{T}(\varphi')$, $\chi(\varphi')$ by *testerDiamond*(φ') ;
    else if $\oplus \in \{X, Y\}$ **then** $\varphi' \leftarrow \oplus\chi(\varphi_1)$; Build $\mathcal{T}(\varphi')$, $\chi(\varphi')$ by Table 3 ;
    else $\varphi' \leftarrow \chi(\varphi_1) \oplus \chi(\varphi_2)$; Build $\mathcal{T}(\varphi')$, $\chi(\varphi')$ by Table 3 ;
    Push $\mathcal{T}(\varphi')$, $\chi(\varphi')$ into *cache*, as the tester and output assertion of φ;
  else Fetch $\mathcal{T}(\varphi), \chi(\varphi)$ from *cache* ;
return $\chi(\varphi)$;

4.4 Correctness and Complexity of the LTDL Tester

To establish the formal validity and scalability of our framework, we formulate the correctness and complexity theorems for the composite temporal testers.

Theorem 3. *For any LTDL formula φ, the tester $\mathcal{T}(\varphi)$ constructed via Algorithm 4 correctly satisfies the soundness and completeness conditions of Definition 1.*

Proof. We proceed by structural induction on φ. For base cases (assertions) and Boolean connectives, correctness follows directly from the definition of output assertions and the synchronous parallel composition of JDSs. Inductively, assume the testers for all principally temporal subformulas of φ are sound and complete.

For LTL operators (X, Y, U, S), the transition relations and initial conditions defined in Table 3 natively encode their exact semantic unwinding (e.g., $\varphi_1 U \varphi_2 \equiv \varphi_2 \vee (\varphi_1 \wedge X(\varphi_1 U \varphi_2)))$. The single-step evaluation via output variables maintains exact behavioral equivalence with standard LTL temporal testers [14], and the justice constraint for U strictly enforces eventual fulfillment.

For $\varphi = \langle \rho \rangle \varphi_1$, Algorithm 3 translates the optimized zero-delay cycle-free regular grammar $G(\rho)$ (correct by Theorem 1) into a double-variable transition relation over X and Y. The state variables x_i dynamically trace the non-deterministic valid executions along the path expression. The variables y_i serve as explicit termination monitors. The instantaneous epsilon and test transitions natively synchronize with their sub-testers $\mathcal{T}(\varphi_j)$ without advancing the temporal step. Crucially, the justice constraints $\bigwedge(x_i \leftrightarrow y_i)$ and $\neg \bigvee y_i$ strictly ensure that any accepted execution sequence must reach a valid terminal derivation within a finite number of steps, thereby correctly mapping the finite-trace semantic requirement of $\langle \rho \rangle \varphi_1$. Therefore, $\mathcal{T}(\varphi)$ strictly accepts paths satisfying φ (soundness) and seamlessly interleaves with any valid environmental computation (completeness).

Theorem 4. *Given an LTDL formula φ, the construction of $\mathcal{T}(\varphi)$ via Algorithm 4 terminates in $\mathcal{O}\left(|\varphi| + \sum_{\langle \rho \rangle \in \varphi} (|\rho| + (|V_\rho| + |P_\rho|)^2 + K_\rho \cdot 2^{|V_\rho|} \cdot B)\right)$ time, introducing exactly $\mathcal{O}(|\varphi| + \sum_{\langle \rho \rangle \in \varphi} |V_\rho|)$ new symbolic variables.*

Proof. Algorithm 4 utilizes a bottom-up *cache* mechanism, structurally guaranteeing that each unique principally temporal subformula is evaluated and constructed exactly once. Thus, the recursive traversal takes exactly $\mathcal{O}(|\varphi|)$ composition steps.

For individual LTL operators and boolean connectives, Table 3 introduces exactly one new Boolean output variable and a constant number of symbolic transition relations per operation, processing in $\mathcal{O}(1)$ time per operator and contributing a total of $\mathcal{O}(|\varphi|)$ time.

For each $\varphi = \langle \rho \rangle \varphi_1$, Algorithm 3 is invoked. By Theorem 2, constructing, optimizing, and eliminating zero-delay cycles for $G(\rho)$ strictly takes $\mathcal{O}(|\rho| + (|V_\rho| + |P_\rho|)^2 + K_\rho \cdot 2^{|V_\rho|} \cdot B)$ time. Because the symbolic tester avoids explicitly computing state-space cross-products, wiring the boolean equivalence gates for the transition relations and justice constraints requires time linearly proportional to the size of the optimized grammar, which is bounded by the grammar construction time. Summing the structural traversal overhead and the localized regular grammar processing for each nested path expression yields the exact total execution time. Furthermore, the construction natively introduces exactly one output variable per temporal subformula and $2|V_\rho|$ state tracking variables (X and Y tracking sets) alongside their primed counterparts per path expression, guaranteeing the space complexity.

4.5 An Example of LTDL Tester Construction

Consider a network program executing Srv (Serve) upon request req, or performing $diag$ (instantaneous diagnosis) when idle. If an err (error) occurs post-service, it runs Rec (Recover); otherwise, it continues. The LTDL property $[\rho_{ex}]\neg err$ captures this seamlessly, where

$$\rho_{ex} \equiv ((req?; wrk; Srv; \neg wrk; (((\neg(\neg err\ S\ wrk))?; Rec) + (\neg err\ S\ wrk)?)) + (\neg req?; diag?))^*. \quad (1)$$

The past-time test $(\neg err\ S\ wrk)?$ verifies no errors occurred since wrk (working) started. Notably, the sub-expression $(\neg req?; diag?)$ within the Kleene star consumes no time steps, thereby inducing a zero-delay cycle.

Figure 1(a) shows the unoptimized $G(\rho)$ via Table 1. Figure 1(b) illustrates the grammar after applying the preliminary optimization via Algorithm 2. Figure 1(c) shows the zero-delay cycle-free grammar after applying Algorithm 1 to the optimized grammar. Specifically, during Phase 2 of Algorithm 1, production (4) in Fig. 1(b) acts as the zero-delay back-edge. The conjunction of the test `!req & diag` in production (4) and the assertion `req & wrk` in the uniquely consuming production (2) for variable 11 evaluates to False. Consequently, in Fig. 1(c), no bypassed production is generated, and the instantaneous back-edge production (4) is simply deleted.

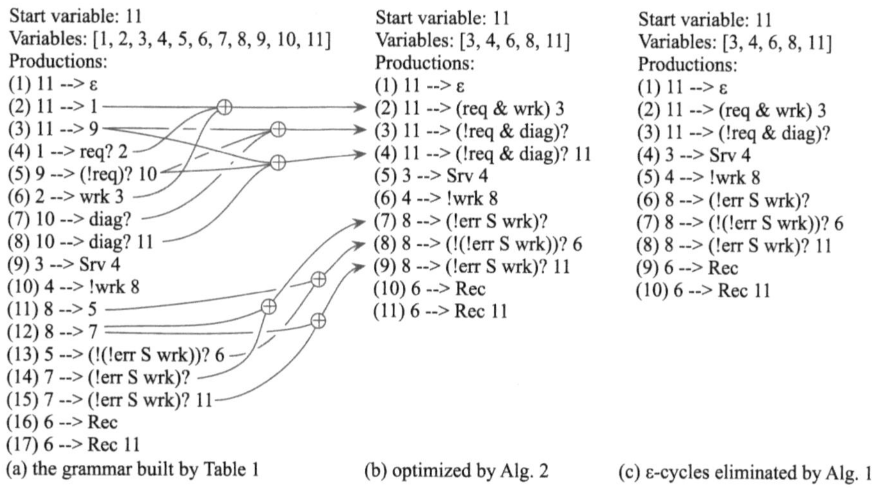

Fig. 1. The grammar construction process for the path expression in Eq. (1).

Figure 2 presents the SMV code generated by Algorithm 4: only two sub-testers are cached for $\neg err\ S\ wrk$ (output $W1$) and $\langle\rho_{ex}\rangle err$ (output $X1$), making the final output assertion $\neg X1$. Note that $[X1, \ldots, X5]$ corresponds to the variable sequence $[11, 3, 4, 8, 6]$, representing the variables visited by BFS starting from the start variable 11 in Fig. 1(c).

```
--The tester for ¬err S wrk
VAR W1:boolean;
--output variable
INIT W1 <-> wrk;
TRANS next(W1) <->
      (next(wrk) | (next(!err) & W1));
--The tester for ⟨ρex⟩err
VAR X1,...,X5,Y1,...,Y5:boolean;
--X1 is the output variable
TRANS X1 <->
      ((!err | ((!req & diag) & !err))
      | ((req & wrk) & next(X2)));
TRANS X2 <-> (Srv & next(X3));
TRANS X3 <-> (!wrk & next(X4));
TRANS X4 <-> (((W1 &
      !err) | (!W1 & X5)) | (W1 & X1));
TRANS X5 <-> ((Rec &
      next(!err)) | (Rec & next(X1)));
TRANS Y1 ->
      ((!err | ((!req & diag) & !err))
      | ((req & wrk) & next(Y2)));
TRANS Y2 -> (Srv & next(Y3));
TRANS Y3 -> (!wrk & next(Y4));
TRANS Y4 -> (((W1 &
      !err) | (!W1 & Y5)) | (W1 & Y1));
TRANS Y5 -> ((Rec &
      next(!err)) | (Rec & next(Y1)));
JUSTICE (((X1=Y1 &
      X2=Y2) & X3=Y3) & X4=Y4) & X5=Y5;
JUSTICE (((!Y1
      & !Y2) & !Y3) & !Y4) & !Y5;
```

Fig. 2. The SMV code generated by LTDLTester for $[\rho_{ex}]\neg err$.

5 LTDL Tester-Based Model Checking and Experiments

5.1 LTDL Model Checking Framework

We developed **LTDLTester**, an open-source Java-based tool available on GitHub (https://github.com/lxy-cn/LTDLTester). LTDLTester implements the proposed algorithms by employing ANTLR 4 to parse LTDL syntax and utilizing the `JavaBDD` package for symbolic Boolean operations, subsequently generating the SMV code for the tester and the output assertion of a specified LTDL formula. Given an LTDL formula φ and an SMV model M, the LTDL model checking framework via LTDLTester and NuSMV [4] is presented as follows:

(1) **LTDL Tester Construction:** Generate the SMV code for the tester $\mathcal{T}(\varphi)$ and the output assertion $\chi(\varphi)$ using LTDLTester.
(2) **Model Composition:** Embed $\mathcal{T}(\varphi)$ into the main module of M to construct the synchronous parallel composition $M \parallel \mathcal{T}(\varphi)$.
(3) **LTDL Verification:** Evaluate $\chi(\varphi)$ over $M \parallel \mathcal{T}(\varphi)$ using NuSMV. If the verification fails, NuSMV generates a counterexample to trace the violation; otherwise, the formula φ is satisfied by M.

5.2 Experiments

To compare the performance of our method with MCMAS_{LDLK}, we selected two experimental cases from the MCMAS_{LDLK} package: the Bit Transmission Protocol (`bit_transmission_protocol_ldl.ispl`) and the Go-Back-N ARQ Protocol (`go_back_n_4bits.ispl`). We constructed equivalent models of the two cases using the SMV input language, based on the provided ISPL files. These SMV files are available in the LTDLTester package. The experiments for both cases were conducted on a laptop equipped with a 3.30GHz CPU, 32GB of RAM, and the Ubuntu 24.04.2 LTS operating system. In these experiments, we employed NuSMV 2.7.0 as the model checker for our method.

Because MCMAS_{LDLK} omits counterexample generation by default, we applied the -dcx flag to NuSMV to disable this feature, thereby ensuring parity. No further parameters were introduced during the execution of either tool. It is worth noting that while both approaches could potentially benefit from

OBDD dynamic variable reordering, exploring this optimization is orthogonal to our current study. Thus, to preserve the relative fairness of the experimental evaluations, all tests were conducted without parameter-based performance tuning.

Case 1: Bit Transmission Protocol. A sender transmits bits over a lossy channel, stopping upon receiving an acknowledgment (*ack*). We verify the frequently-used LTDL formula $\varphi_{btp} = bit0 \rightarrow \langle (bit0^n)^* \rangle recack$ under justice constraint $\{envworks\}$ (indicating the channel works properly), where $bit0$ indicates that the transmitted bit is 0, $recack$ indicates that the sender has received the acknowledgment, and $bit0^n$ denotes the concatenation of n instances of $bit0$. The property evaluates to TRUE for all n. Table 4 shows MCMAS_{LDLK} computation time and memory explode with formula length n, whereas our symbolic method requires significantly less resources and remains highly stable. The notations such as "> 9605" in Tables 4 and 5 denote experiments forced to stop at 9,605 s due to excessive runtime.

Case 2: Go-Back-N ARQ Protocol. A sender transmits M packets over an unreliable channel, sending up to a window of N unacknowledged packets. Duplicate ACKs or window limits trigger retransmission from the first unacknowledged packet. Setting $M = 4, N = 2$, we verify the LTDL formula $\varphi_{arq} = ([(((envworks; envbroken) + (envbroken; envworks))^n)^*]\top) \rightarrow \langle \top^* \rangle senderDone$, where $envbroken$ indicates that both the sending and receiving channels are broken, and $senderDone$ indicates that the sender has already sent all packets. To achieve better performance, we optimize the subformula $\langle \top^* \rangle senderDone$ to $\top\ U\ senderDone$. Verification yields FALSE under justice constraint $\{envworks\}$. Table 5 identically demonstrates that our method substantially outperforms MCMAS_{LDLK} in both execution time and memory consumption, where "-" indicates that it is unnecessary to conduct the experiment corresponding to this unit, as similar experiments with smaller parameters have already consumed excessive time.

Table 4. Experimental results for Case 1

	Time(s)		Memory(MB)	
n	MCMAS_{LDLK}	Ours	MCMAS_{LDLK}	Ours
6	0.06	0.01	19.54	15.5
8	0.66	0.01	45.63	15.6
10	10.74	0.01	71.01	16.14
12	1020.11	0.01	218.52	16.78
40	> 9605	0.15	15236.89	44.67

Table 5. Experimental results for Case 2

	Time(s)		Memory(MB)	
n	MCMAS_{LDLK}	Ours	MCMAS_{LDLK}	Ours
2	0.45	0.09	40.07	24.08
4	0.94	0.08	61.98	26.01
6	171.56	0.1	295.66	27
8	> 3906	0.09	1247.9	43.06
10	> 2737	0.1	2361.52	43.05
100	-	0.5	-	117.4

6 Conclusions

We introduced a symbolic model checking framework for Linear Temporal Dynamic Logic (LTDL), combining bidirectional LTL and LDL's dynamic regular expressions to concisely specify past-dependent reactive systems. Our open-source tool, LTDLTester, generates purely symbolic compositional testers that significantly outperform MCMAS_{LDLK} via NuSMV. Future work integrates LTDL with reinforcement learning to train agents for complex, temporally-extended tasks in uncertain environments (e.g., autonomous driving). Leveraging these testers for run-time monitoring and policy synthesis will ensure provably correct behaviors under strict timing and safety constraints, utilizing tester compositionality to gracefully decompose learnable sub-tasks.

Acknowledgments. We thank the reviewers for their detailed and insightful feedback. This study was funded by the Natural Science Foundation of Fujian Province, China, under Grant 2023J01137, the Natural Science Foundation of Xiamen, China, under Grant 3502Z20227191, and Yantai's "Double Hundreds Plan" for Highend Talent Cultivation.

References

1. IEEE standard for property specification language (PSL). IEEE Std 1850-2010 (Revision of IEEE Std 1850-2005), pp. 1–182 (2010). https://doi.org/10.1109/IEEESTD.2010.5446004
2. Armoni, R., et al.: The ForSpec temporal logic: a new temporal property-specification language. In: Katoen, J.P., Stevens, P. (eds.) Tools and Algorithms for the Construction and Analysis of Systems, pp. 296–311. Springer, Berlin Heidelberg, Berlin, Heidelberg (2002)
3. Bryant, R.E.: Graph-based algorithms for Boolean function manipulation. IEEE Trans. Comput. **35**(8), 677–691 (1986)
4. Cimatti, A., et al.: NuSMV 2: an OpenSource tool for symbolic model checking. In: Brinksma, E., Larsen, K.G. (eds.) CAV 2002. LNCS, vol. 2404, pp. 359–364. Springer, Heidelberg (2002). https://doi.org/10.1007/3-540-45657-0_29
5. Clarke, E.M., Grumberg, J.O., Kroening, D., Peled, D., Veith, H.: Model Checking, 2nd edn. The MIT Press, Cambridge (2018)
6. Clarke, E.M., Henzinger, T.A., Veith, H., Bloem, R.: Handbook of Model Checking. Springer, Cham (2018). https://doi.org/10.1007/978-3-319-10575-8

7. De Giacomo, G., Vardi, M.Y.: Linear temporal logic and linear dynamic logic on finite traces. In: Proceedings of the Twenty-Third International Joint Conference on Artificial Intelligence, IJCAI '13, pp. 854–860. AAAI Press (2013)
8. De Giacomo, G., Vardi, M.Y.: Synthesis for LTL and LDL on finite traces. In: Proceedings of the 24th International Conference on Artificial Intelligence, IJCAI'15, pp. 1558–1564. AAAI DPress (2015)
9. Duret-Lutz, A., Lewkowicz, A., Fauchille, A., Michaud, T., Renault, É., Xu, L.: Spot 2.0 — a framework for LTL and ω-automata manipulation. In: Artho, C., Legay, A., Peled, D. (eds.) Automated Technology for Verification and Analysis, pp. 122–129. Springer International Publishing, Cham (2016)
10. Faymonville, P., Zimmermann, M.: Parametric linear dynamic logic. Inf. Comput. **253**, 237–256 (2017). https://doi.org/10.1016/j.ic.2016.07.009
11. Kesten, Y., Pnueli, A., Raviv, L.o.: Algorithmic verification of linear temporal logic specifications. In: Larsen, K.G., Skyum, S., Winskel, G. (eds.) Automata, Languages and Programming, pp. 1–16. Springer Berlin Heidelberg, Berlin (1998)
12. Kong, J., Lomuscio, A.: Model checking multi-agent systems against LDLK specifications. In: Proceedings of the Twenty-Sixth International Joint Conference on Artificial Intelligence, IJCAI-17, pp. 1138–1144 (2017). https://doi.org/10.24963/ijcai.2017/158
13. Lomuscio, A., Qu, H., Raimondi, F.: MCMAS: an open-source model checker for the verification of multi-agent systems. Int. J. Softw. Tools Technol. Transfer **19**(1), 9–30 (2015). https://doi.org/10.1007/s10009-015-0378-x
14. Pnueli, A., Zaks, A.: On the merits of temporal testers. In: Grumberg, O., Veith, H. (eds.) 25 Years of Model Checking. LNCS, vol. 5000, pp. 172–195. Springer, Heidelberg (2008). https://doi.org/10.1007/978-3-540-69850-0_11
15. Vardi, M.Y.: The rise and fall of LTL. In: Proceedings of Second International Symposium on Games, Automata, Logics and Formal Verification, Minori, Italy (2011)
16. Vijayaraghavan, S., Ramanathan, M.: A Practical Guide for SystemVerilog Assertions. Springer, Cham (2005)

Author Index

G. De Giacomo et al. (Eds.): TASE 2026, LNCS 16697, pp. 459–460, 2027.
https://doi.org/10.1007/978-3-032-30693-7